SOVIET POLITICS: STRUGGLING WITH CHANGE

SOVIET POLITICS

STRUGGLING
WITH
CHANGE

Second Edition

GORDON B. SMITH
University of South Carolina

St. Martin's Press   New York

For Brooke

Senior editor: Don Reisman
Managing editor: Patricia Mansfield
Project editor: Elise Bauman
Production supervisor: Alan Fischer
Graphics: G&H Soho
Cover design: Judy Forster
Cover photo: Wide World

For information, write:
St. Martin's Press, Inc.
175 Fifth Avenue
New York, NY 10010

ISBN: 0-312-03655-8 (paper)
      0-312-06614-7 (cloth)

Library of Congress Cataloging-in-Publication Data

Smith, Gordon B.
    Soviet politics : struggling with change / Gordon B. Smith.—2nd
ed.
        p.   cm.
    ISBN 0-312-06614-7—ISBN 0-312-03655-8 (pbk.)
    1. Soviet Union—Politics and government—20th century. 2. Soviet
Union—Social conditions—1917– I. Title.
JN6511.S564 1992
947.084—dc20   89-63934
                                                        CIP

Published and distributed outside North America by:

THE MACMILLAN PRESS LTD.

Houndsmills, Basingstoke, Hampshire RG21 2XS and London

Companies and representatives throughout the world.

ISBN: 0-333-53576-6

Acknowledgments and copyrights appear on page 396, which constitutes an extension of the
copyright page.

 The text of this book has been printed on recycled paper.

Preface

Since coming to office in March 1985, Mikhail Gorbachev has revolutionized the Soviet political system. His policies of *glasnost'*, *perestroika*, democratization, and "new thinking" have severely undermined the foundations of the Stalinist political and economic system and opened the political process to new groups and interests. The pace of political change in the Soviet Union has increased dramatically since the August 1991 attempted coup against Gorbachev's government. In the wake of the coup, the activities of the Communist Party have been suspended and the Party's assets have been seized. The KGB and the armed forces have been purged of their most conservative figures and the organizations have been made more accountable to elected officials and bodies. The failed coup also has accelerated the breakup of the USSR into its constituent national republics. The struggle for change in the USSR has assumed a momentum that now threatens Gorbachev's political career and the very existence of the Soviet Union as we have known it for the past 74 years.

Soviet Politics was written with the goal of explaining the forces that are reshaping the Soviet political system today. Much has changed since 1988, when the first edition was published, and the present edition reflects those changes through the end of August 1991. The events surrounding the attempted overthrow of Gorbachev appear at the end of the Introduction and in the Afterword, where I assess the impact of the coup on the system. Other revisions chart the evolution of the Soviet Union's leading policy-making bodies. For example, the chapter on the Communist Party now discusses the Party's loss of support and the rise of opposition parties. Chapter 6, "Democratization and the State," documents the shift of power from the CPSU to newly created governmental bodies and offices, most notably the Supreme Soviet and the Presidency, as well as explaining the new electoral system.

Many of Gorbachev's reforms were initiated in order to restructure the outmoded Stalinist system that had dominated the Soviet political and economic scene for more than fifty years. I have added a chapter that examines Stalin, his role in creating Soviet political and economic institutions, and how his legacy continues to influence his successors.

The nationality problem, more than any other issue, is likely to influence the future of the Soviet system. Chapter 7 explores the rise of national, regional, and local movements that have forced the redistribution of power from the center to republic and local institutions. Chapters have also been added to this edition exploring Gorbachev's major policy initiatives—*glasnost'*, *perestroika*, and "new thinking."

Through case studies and the use of my personal experiences in the USSR, I have attempted to go beyond the formal depiction of political institutions and their powers in order to illustrate how the political system works in practice. I hope that this approach will enable students to see behind the formal facade of the Soviet political system and appreciate it in a wider, comparative perspective.

The central theme of the book is the Soviet struggle with change. The Soviet political system is very much in flux and that fact has made writing this book both exciting and frustrating. Perhaps the most difficult decision I confronted was the choice of a verb tense—whether to use the present or past. Old political institutions, practices, and characteristics persist, although they are gradually dying out, while new institutions, practices, and characteristics are emerging. It is an instructive reminder for all students of politics that political systems are not static, but dynamic, evolving organisms. The frustration from the author's viewpoint is that change has been occurring more rapidly than I could write about it. Several of the chapters in this edition had to be revised several times to keep up with new developments. As one friend put it, "It's like changing a tire on a car while it's moving."

Beneath the changes that are capturing our attention, I hope the readers also see continuities in Russian and Soviet political culture and the ebb and flow of reform and reaction across history. Despite all the changes in the party structure, governmental institutions, and policies, elements of Russian and Soviet political culture endure.

This book was written with the support of many individuals, and it is a pleasure to record my gratitude and indebtedness to them. I wish to thank the University of South Carolina, especially the Department of Government and International Studies, for supporting my work over the years. I am grateful to my colleagues for their encouragement, criticism, and friendship.

A number of individual scholars assisted me in the preparation of this book. Their comments and criticisms were invaluable and greatly appreciated. It goes without saying that they bear no responsibility for errors in the text. Specifically, I wish to acknowledge the contributions of professors Barbara A. Chotiner, William Clark, Tsyoshi Hasegawa, Andrzej Korbonski, Jean-Claude Lanne, Ronald H. Linden, Linda Lubrano, S. Neil MacFarlane, R. Judson Mitchell, Donald C. Rawson, Daniel R. Sabia, Jr., Robert Sharlet, Edward Taborsky, John E. Turner, Vincent Wright, and William Zimmerman, who shared their ideas on the manuscript in whole or in part.

I am especially indebted to my graduate assistant Roger Moore for assisting me throughout the process of completing the book. I also wish to thank Don Reisman, Margie Mahrdt, Elise Bauman, and Frances Jones at St. Martin's Press for their skillful assistance in bringing this project to fruition.

Finally, I would like to express my boundless appreciation to Brooke, Hillarie, and Doak for putting up with me during the writing of this book. Their love and encouragement make it all worthwhile.

Gordon B. Smith

Contents

Introduction

June 12, 1991, Leningrad

Today, approximately four million Leningraders go to the polls to decide the future of their city. Voters at the Kuybyshev district polling station No. 29 are handed three ballots. The first is for the Presidency of the Russian Republic, which is the largest of the USSR's fifteen republics, stretching from the Pacific to the western borders with the Ukraine and Belorussia. The second ballot is for the "mayor" of Leningrad, a post currently occupied by progressive reformer Anatolii Sobchak. The third ballot asks voters in Leningrad whether they want to change the name of their city to its original name, St. Petersburg. For weeks the evening television shows have been devoted to the campaign. Central Moscow television aired an hour-long interview with each of the six candidates for the Russian presidency—one each evening for a week. The last session was a roundtable free-for-all with all candidates except the favorite, Boris Yeltsin, who was busy doing last-minute campaigning in the provinces.

The campaign is a landmark event: the first-ever direct election of a Soviet leader. The range of opinions among the six candidates reflects the breadth of opinion in this suddenly hyperpoliticized country. Yeltsin, the front-runner and current President of the Russian Republic, is expected to walk away with some 60 percent of the vote. His support lies primarily in the big cities, Moscow and Leningrad; with the intelligentsia; and with voters under 35. His success depends, in large measure, on his ability to broaden his political appeal to other regions and groups. He must carry the medium-sized cities in the heart of Russia, cities such as Smolensk, Saratov, Kursk, and Voronezh. He is expected to sweep his hometown of Sverdlovsk—the gigantic Urals engineering center. His popularity in the Urals is likely to carry over to neighboring urban centers—Tiumen, Omsk, and Tomsk. In order to win, Yeltsin also needs the support of the non-Russian minorities residing in the republic. The day before the election, he signed an accord with leaders of the Komi Autonomous Republic, granting them substantial control over their own economic resources. The signing ceremony, also prominently displayed on the newly established television station of the Russian republic and broadcast nationwide, clearly set a precedent for the other 100 national groups living within the Russian republic.

For many voters, a vote for Yeltsin represents a vote against the past, against the Communist Party, even a vote against Mikhail Gorbachev, whose reforms are widely seen as having become bogged down in bureaucratic red tape and parliamentary wrangling. For others, a vote for Yeltsin represents a vote for a rapid transition to a market economy, for economic "shock therapy," and for more decentralization of power to regions and republics.

Yeltsin's chief challenger is Nikolai Ryzhkov, Gorbachev's longtime Premier, who has consistently pushed for a moderate (some would say minimalist) approach to economic reform, fearing the consequent social unrest. Ryzhkov's support rests primarily with the older generation, who feel severely pressed by the recent price increases and decry the resultant breakdown in social order and control. Ryzhkov's go-slow approach also appeals to those who favor keeping the country firmly united. Ryzhkov must overcome two weaknesses. He had a mild heart attack in December 1990, soon after he was released as Premier by Gorbachev. Commentators have made his health an issue. Even more of a liability is his record as Premier for six years—years in which many citizens feel reforms dragged along much too slowly.

Vadim Bakatin, until recently the Minister of Internal Affairs and now Gorbachev's chief domestic policy adviser, is widely seen as "Gorbachev's man" for the Russian presidency. His "tough cop" approach appeals to those who seek a restoration of law and order, continued dominance of the CPSU, and the use of force, if necessary, against recalcitrant republics.

General Al'bert Makashov, an even more conservative alternative, based his appeal on traditional symbols: the Party as the "leading and guiding force" in Soviet society, patriotism, and the armed forces and police as guarantors of social control. He is expected to garner widespread support among the five million members of the armed forces.

On the reactionary extreme is V. V. Zhirinovsky, a Russophile, whose nationalistic appeals have strong anti-Semitic and anti-Moslem overtones. He challenges the very foundations of Gorbachev's policies of *perestroika*, privatization of the economy, and democratization as a violation of the Soviet Constitution and, therefore, illegal.

The final candidate, Aman-Gel'dy Tuleev, a Moslem from Kazakhstan, is a moderate. Tuleev is pinning his hopes on appealing to non-Russian minorities.

With characteristic aplomb, the creative intelligentsia of this once thriving intellectual and artistic hot spot in Europe cannot resist flirting with anarchy. Radical students outside the major downtown department store brandish loudspeakers urging voters to stay away from the polls. The satiric writer Mikhail Mishin announced his intention of voting for all six candidates:

> In terms of power over our heads, we long ago surpassed all the countries of the world combined. And as a result, nowhere else in the world are there so many empty-headed, senseless, extreme people. How can we choose? By our logic we *still* don't have enough bosses. It is a shame to have to select one from among these six. I would rather vote for all of them.[1]

A well-educated, highly respected official who characterizes herself as a "political moderate" said she nevertheless voted for the reactionary Zhirinovsky. "People say he is not well mentally and is expected to come in last. I felt sorry for him, so I gave gim my vote," she explains.[2]

Voters in the Kuybyshev district polling station No. 29 do not have to wait long to cast their ballots. This particular polling station is set up in a dirty, grey stone middle school. Voters receive their ballots from a stern-looking woman at the registration table and then step into a booth to cross out the names of those for whom they do not wish to vote. It is somehow appropriate that the electoral system is structured as a "negative" voting process. Many voters seem to feel that Yeltsin represents the least objectionable of the six candidates, although they still have reservations about him. He is accused by some as being a bullheaded, uncompromising egotist. Others are worried that he is on a collision course with Gorbachev that could, at the best, result in paralysis of the governmental system, or at the worst, civil war. Gorbachev's moderate turn in the spring of 1991 and his success in negotiating a new Union Treaty with nine of the republics (including Yeltsin's Russian republic) lessened fears of a direct Gorbachev-Yeltsin clash and may have helped swing more support in Yeltsin's direction.

The race for the "mayor" of Leningrad is also capturing substantial attention here. The election—the first-ever free, contested election of the chairman of the Leningrad city council (Lensovet)—pits the moderate reformer and incumbent, Anatolii Sobchak, against Yuri Sevenard and Oleg Karataev. Sevenard, the director of a construction company, is running as a "businessman" with firsthand experience in reforming the economy. Nevertheless, his platform is firmly grounded in the CPSU.

Karataev is the assistant director of an institute that trains public prosecutors and criminal investigators. He is a member of the Party and based his appeal on the conservative *troika*: patriotism, orthodoxy, and order. A few days prior to the election, he withdrew his name from the ballot.

Sobchak is immensely popular here. Like Yeltsin, he dropped out of the Communist Party after the Twenty-Eighth Party Congress in 1990. He was a prominent member of the Inter-regional group, elected first to the Congress of People's Deputies and then the USSR Supreme Soviet in 1989. In the local elections of March 1990, liberal reformers, including Sobchak, captured more than 65 percent of the seats in the Lensovet, ousting a well-entrenched party machine headed by Boris Gidyaspov.

Sobchak widened his support in 1990 when he asked the Metropol of the city to reconsecrate Saint Isaac's Cathedral and hold services there on Easter and other holy days. Sobchak also drew support from among the several thousand employees of the Leningrad city government. Since he is the front-runner, some city employees are not inclined to vote against Sobchak, even if they do not agree with his policies. For some of the remaining old guard, voting seems to be more of a reflex than a conscious personal preference. As one elderly official of the Lensovet notes, "I'm on Sobchak's team. He's my boss, so of course I voted for him."[3] But when the conversation turns to *glasnost'*, privatization, price increases, and democratization, it is apparent that this old Brezhnevite is not sympathetic to Sobchak's program.

The vote that has aroused the strongest emotions is the referendum on changing the name of the city from Leningrad to St. Petersburg. Support for reverting to the original name is strongest among students, white-collar employees, and those under 30. Yeltsin supporters are much more likely to favor changing the name to St. Petersburg than supporters of other candidates.[4]

Arguments against the name change include concerns of denigrating Lenin and the defense of the city during the 900-day seige during the Second World War. Others argue that changing the name of the city would cost as much as 40 million rubles. Still others point out that with all the problems confronting the city—overcrowded and inadequate transportation systems, poor-quality municipal services (including water too contaminated to drink without first being boiled), chronic deficits and shortages of essential foodstuffs, a ten-year waiting list for housing, and environmental pollution problems—the Lensovet should attack these problems first and worry about the name of the city later.

The turnout today at the Kuybyshev district polling station No. 29 is heavy. Despite their cynicism and the allure of spending the day off in the countryside, voters are lining up to receive their ballots. As one man observes, "I'd rather be drinking or out working on my garden plot, but I'm here because I want to send 'them' a message." When asked who "they" are, he simply smiles, shrugs his shoulders, and points to the black-and-white portrait of Lenin hanging on the wall. "Them."

June 21, 1991, Leningrad

Today the official election results were published. For the most part, they confirmed what people had expected. Yeltsin captured 57.3 percent of the vote. His nearest challenger, Nikolai Ryzhkov, received 16.85 percent. Sobchak was a big winner in Leningrad with some 65 percent of the vote. The nonbinding referendum on the name of the city indicated that 56.8 percent of the public favored the name St. Petersburg.[5]

The election victory for Yeltsin confers on him popular legitimacy surpassing that of any other Soviet leader, including Gorbachev. In the United States, a candidate winning more than 57 percent of the votes in a race with only one opponent is usually credited with having won a "landslide" victory. That Yeltsin was able to amass such a strong following against five opponents

Table 1. June 12, 1991 Election Results for the Russian Presidency*

Candidate	Votes for	%	Votes against	%
Yeltsin	45,552,041	57.30	32,229,442	40.54
Ryzhkov	13,395,335	16.85	64,386,148	80.99
Zhirinovsky	6,211,007	7.81	71,570,476	90.03
Tuleev	5,417,464	6.81	72,364,019	91.03
Makashov	2,969,511	3.74	74,811,972	94.10
Bakatin	2,719,757	3.42	75,061,726	94.42

*Figures do not add up to 100 percent due to invalidated ballots.
Source: Trud, June 21, 1991, p. 1.

without the need for a runoff election is truly impressive. Certainly, the election strengthens Yeltsin's position vis-à-vis Gorbachev, who has never run for
any office in a popular election.

The election not only casts a shadow over Gorbachev, but over the future
role of the Presidency, the Congress of People's Deputies, and the USSR
Supreme Soviet. Clearly the public prefers to elect its leaders directly, including the President. Pressures are likely to mount on Gorbachev to face the
voters prior to March 1995, when his term expires. His chances of surviving
such an election depend on how the office of the President evolves in the next
several months and years. With power flowing to the republics, many Soviet
scholars and political commentators envision the Soviet Presidency becoming
like the Presidency of Germany, a largely ceremonial, figurehead post granted
to a widely respected senior statesman. Negotiations on the Union Treaty
reveal just such a tendency toward a much weaker Presidency and all-union
institutions. Under the Treaty, national political bodies will be responsible
only for defense and national security matters, foreign policy, currency matters, transportation, and communications. All other powers will reside with
the republics.

The Congress of People's Deputies, an unwieldy and conservative body
of 2,250 representatives, has not proven to be either an effective parliament,
nor is it representative of public opinion. It is likely that the Congress will be
eliminated, leaving the USSR Supreme Soviet as the parliament at the national
level. There is also widespread criticism of the Supreme Soviet, since its 572
members are selected from among the 2,250 deputies in the Congress of
People's Deputies. The problem is the *method* for selecting who serves in the
smaller body. Charges have been frequently aired that Gorbachev, in cooperation with the Party and other conservative institutions, packed the Supreme
Soviet with conservatives and moderates. The overwhelming election victories of liberal and radical reformers challenge the representativeness and,
therefore, the legitimacy of the Supreme Soviet.

While the election of June 12 has important ramifications for the future
course of several political institutions, it can also be seen as a protest against
the system that has led Soviet society into its current crisis. People are clearly
frustrated with the slow, halting pace of Gorbachev's reforms. The symbolic
nature of the vote was most evident here in Leningrad, where citizens confronted the question of renaming their city. For many citizens, the vote to
revert to the name St. Petersburg was a protest vote against the Party, against
Lenin and three-quarters of a century of socialist mismanagement and authoritarian rule. It was a protest vote against a system that has not been able to
keep pace with the West or even with its own citizens' expectations for decent
transportation, municipal services, clean water, ample food supply, adequate
housing, and a healthy environment.

There is a sense that by reverting to St. Petersburg, the city can go back to
a crucial juncture when the country was faced with a painful choice—
whether to proceed through a perilous process of industrialization and modernization following the capitalist West or launch an experiment in building a
socialist workers' state. There is a desire to turn back the clock, to contem-

plate how these past seventy-four years might have been different had another direction been taken. This city, like the rest of the USSR today, is struggling with its past as much as it is struggling with its future. It is a society profoundly embroiled in a struggle with change.

August 19, 1991

The morning news reports are grim. A group of eight conservative Kremlin leaders have seized control of the Soviet government. Mikhail Gorbachev, on vacation at his dacha on the Black Sea coast, has been put under house arrest. The new leaders, who have formed something called the Committee for the State of Emergency, have issued decrees shutting down all independent newspapers, banning strikes and public demonstrations, imposing new censorship rules on radio and television, and declaring a state of emergency. Tanks are rolling into Moscow, occupying all major streets and encircling the building housing the parliament of the Russian Republic.

The timing of the coup is not accidental—it occurred on the eve of the signing of the Union Treaty between Gorbachev and the leaders of nine of the republics. The treaty would have transferred substantial powers from the center to the republics, seriously undermining the traditional bastions of conservatism—the armed forces, the KGB, the police, and the CPSU apparat. These are precisely the groups behind the coup.

The ostensible leader of the coup is Gennadi Yanaev, a party hack whom Gorbachev nominated to the largely meaningless post of Vice-President last year in an effort to placate the conservatives. The real powers behind Yanaev, however, are Vladimir Kryuchkov, the Chairman of the KGB; Dmitri Yazov, Minister of Defense; Boris Pugo, Minister of Internal Affairs; and Premier Valentin Pavlov. The three lesser-known members of the group are Oleg Baklanov, first deputy Chairman of the Defense Council; Vasily Starodubtsev, Chairman of the Farmer's Union; and A. I. Tizyakov, President of the Association of State Enterprises and Industrial Construction. Respectively, they represent the defense industry, agricultural interests, and heavy industrial sectors that have been adversely affected by privatization and other of Gorbachev's economic reforms. All eight are Gorbachev's own appointees, but their loyalties are clearly to the conservative vested interests they represent rather than to their political patron.

The new Union Treaty would likely have accelerated the pace of economic and political reforms in the country by transferring power to republic leaders who are much more reform-minded than Gorbachev. By decentralizing policy-making, the Union Treaty also would have weakened the ability of the armed forces, the KGB, and the Party to resist and subvert those reforms.

Other recent developments also appear to explain the high-risk strategy adopted by the leaders of the coup. Just last week, Boris Yeltsin issued a decree banning Communist Party cells in all offices and enterprises within the Russian republic, including military units and the secret police. Another decree mandated the widespread conversion of defense plants to produce consumer goods. Furthermore, Gorbachev's dramatic loss of popular support has left him a weakened leader. The coup organizers are banking on public disaffection with his leadership and the state of economic and social crisis in the country to dampen public outrage. Finally, the stunning victories of liberal reformers at the polls in the elections of June 12 clearly indicated that the conservatives could not win by constitutional means, so they have opted to seize power through unconstitutional means, through the use of force.

Whether the coup succeeds depends on two factors: the response of the Soviet public and the degree of cohesion within the new leadership. After six and one-half years of *glasnost'* and the opportunity to express themselves freely in public, in print, and at the polls, it is likely that the citizens of the USSR will not permit a self-appointed group of generals to seize power illegally without widespread resistance. Yeltsin mounted a tank in front of the Russian parliament building and urged his followers to resist the illegal seizure of power. Already reports are coming in of Muscovites taking to the streets to halt columns of tanks from rolling through the capital. Makeshift barricades are being constructed around the Russian parliament building, where Yeltsin and the Russian Supreme Soviet leaders are engaged in desperate efforts to protect their fledgling democracy. Popular resistance will raise the ante for the leaders of the coup, forcing them to resort to violence against unarmed protesters in order to restore calm.

The success of the coup also depends on continued cohesion and support among the interests behind the coup. While many in the top echelons of the armed forces and the KGB are known to have opposed *glasnost'*, *perestroika*, and democratization, the reforms have been widely accepted and supported among junior officers as well as rank and file soldiers. It is estimated that as many as three million members of the armed forces voted for Yeltsin in the June 12 elections. Yeltsin also commands some following within the KGB. A critical question is whether the leaders of the coup can count on their military forces and secret police special forces to follow orders, especially orders to shoot unarmed citizens. As of tonight, the answers to these questions remain unclear.

August 20, 1991

There are some signs today that the coup that has ousted President Gorbachev is breaking up. Crowds in front of the Russian parliament building have swelled to several thousand. At least one tank unit has been persuaded to defend Yeltsin's democratically elected government. An airborne batallion from Ryazan also arrived in front of the parliament building with six armored personnel carriers, and has offered to provide protection.

Meanwhile, there are reports that three of the members of the Committee for the State of the Emergency have defected. Premier Pavlov was reported to be suffering from a heart attack, while Defense Minister Yazov and KGB chief Kryuchkov apparently have resigned from the emergency committee.

In Leningrad and Kishinev, the capital of Moldavia, hundreds of thousands of citizens rallied today to protest the takeover of power. Calls have been issued for a general strike.

Tonight, tanks deployed around the Russian parliament building attempt to clear away buses, cars, and barricades blocking access to Yeltsin's head-quarters. Yeltsin, in an emergency telephone call to Britain's prime minister, John Major, indicates that he and his government may not have long to survive. Outside, crowds of angry citizens bombard encroaching tanks with homemade firebombs. Scattered shooting is heard. Three young men are reported crushed to death by tanks. It is clear that the Russian people are willing to stand up and resist this coup. What is not clear is how willing the coup's leaders are to resort to brutality to subdue them. The image of Tienanmen Square is all too clear in everyone's minds.

August 21, 1991

The tide has turned. The crowds protecting the Russian parliament build-ing have succeeded in dissuading an all-out attack. Several of the members of the Committee for the State of Emergency are reported to have fled Moscow and are headed to Central Asia. Tanks have been seen leaving the capital. The Soviet legislature met in an emergency session today and nullified Yanaev's emergency decrees. Restrictions on the press and broadcasting have been lifted. President Gorbachev spoke with President Bush by telephone and in-formed him that the coup was over. The leaders of the takeover have been arrested, except for Boris Pugo, who has reportedly committed suicide.

Sixty-three hours after it began, the coup has collapsed. The immediate threat is over. Gorbachev has been returned to office and is reported to be flying back to Moscow. But the future of Gorbachev's presidency is very much in doubt. How will power be shared with the republics now that Yeltsin and the Russian parliament have rescued Gorbachev? What measures will follow to bring the military, the secret police, and the Party under control? What changes will the people of the USSR demand now that they have, for the first time in the history of their country, stood up to their leaders and won?

Gorbachev is returning to a capital that has been transformed by the events of the past three days. He is returning to face even larger challenges than he has confronted since coming to office six and one-half years ago. The democratic revolution in Russia began today. Where it will lead, and why it has taken seventy-four years to occur is the subject of this text.

Notes

1. *Chas pik,* 10 June 1991, p. 1.
2. From a conversation with the author, Leningrad, 12 June 1991.
3. From a conversation with the author, Leningrad, 25 June 1991.
4. *Nevskoe vremya,* 8 June 1991, p. 1.
5. *Nevskoe vremya,* 14 June 1991, p. 1.

1

Russian Political Culture

Russia is a land of contradictions. It is a modern superpower, capable of challenging the military might of the United States. Yet it is also a country where citizens routinely stand in long lines to buy milk, meat, and potatoes, and where items such as fresh fruit, toilet paper, and typewriters are chronically in short supply. Soviet youth today wear Levis purchased on the black market and listen to the latest Western rock music, yet their attitudes and values are not entirely Western. There is a mysticism, a fatalism, an attachment to the Russian soil that transcends simple patriotism. As one citizen remarked, "My parents and grandparents—like me—were born out of this black Russian soil. And when they died, they returned to the soil. This is my place, this is where I belong."[1]

Soviet society produces talented musicians and writers, distinguished scientists, and superb dancers. Yet, until recently, it also has imprisoned those who have pushed the boundaries of creative thought too far. For years, the Soviet political system appeared to be a grey monolith in which the Party eliminated all controversy and conflict. Beneath the seeming uniformity of Soviet politics, however, Western specialists saw glimpses of innumerable political conflicts pitting bureaucracies, regions, ethnic groups, and personalities against one another. With the advent of Mikhail Gorbachev and his policies of *glasnost'* and *perestroika,* these conflicts and controversies are no longer played out behind closed doors. Politics is abundantly evident today, and it touches virtually every aspect of Soviet society.

Russia is indeed a land of contradictions. It is best understood not as a uniform mass, but as a patchwork quilt of geographic, ethnic, religious, economic, and political diversity. Our exploration of the Soviet Union and its political system begins with an examination of some of the contradictions that define and shape political attitudes and values in the USSR.

RICH LAND/POOR LAND

Although the Soviet Union is immense in area and rich in natural resources, it is inherently poor in the elements needed to sustain existence. The USSR, which occupies roughly one-sixth of the earth's land surface, is by far the largest nation in the world; it is twice the size of the United States, larger than all of South America, and only slightly smaller than the entire continent of Africa. By sheer size and expanse, the Soviet Union is both a major European power and a major Asian power. From its Pacific shores to the western frontier with Poland, the USSR stretches over 6800 miles, spanning eleven time zones. From the northernmost reaches above the Arctic Circle to the desert borders with Turkey, Iran, and Afghanistan, it covers more than 3500 miles. Yet vast areas of the USSR are uninhabitable, and the bulk of the population resides in only a fraction of its territory.

The Soviet Union is so large that it is easy to lose sight of its immensity. For instance, the Caspian Sea is larger in area than the entire United Kingdom. Lake Baikal, which on the map of the USSR appears modest in comparison to the surrounding reaches of Siberia, contains one-fifth of the world's fresh water—more than all the water of the Great Lakes combined.

While the immensity of Russia has afforded it some degree of isolation throughout history, it has also caused problems. Efficient transportation and communication, necessary ingredients to any modern state, were virtually nonexistent before the 1860s, when railway and telegraph communications were established in European Russia. Even today, there are obvious difficulties in coordination: at the same time that Muscovites are going to bed at night, the people in Vladivostok are having breakfast the next morning.

The Soviet Union has more than 26,000 miles of coastline—more than any nation in the world. Yet most of its coasts are to the north, on the Barents, Kara, Laptev, East Siberian, and Chukchi Seas. Few ports are navigable during the long winters, when massive ice floes clog the Arctic Ocean. Ships leaving the warmwater ports of the Soviet Union in the Baltic Sea, the Black Sea, and the Sea of Japan must pass through narrow straits to reach open waters. Over the years, much has been made of the quest for warmwater ports as a primary motivating force in Russian and Soviet territorial expansion in the Balkans and the Far East.

The northerly position of the Soviet Union on the Eurasian continent, compounded by the effect of the large continental landmass, results in a notoriously harsh climate. With no major bodies of water to moderate temperatures, the massive continental expanse allows rapid warming of the land in summer and rapid cooling in winter. The northernmost 15 percent of the Soviet Union lies above the Arctic Circle and consists mostly of treeless tundra. The permafrost zone, in which the subsoil is permanently frozen, covers more than 40 percent of the country. In the tundra and permafrost regions, only moss and low shrubs will grow. At Verkhoyansk in northeastern Siberia, a world-record low temperature of −90° F was reported. During the winter, the sun does not shine, whereas in the summer, temperatures reach above 80° F and the sun never sets.

To the south of the tundra is a wide belt of taiga, or woodlands, extending across Russia's middle latitudes. The taiga accounts for more than one-third of all the forests in the world. In the European part of Russia, the forests have largely been cleared; this region provides the Soviet Union with much of its arable land, known as the "non–black-earth zone." In the taiga, winter turns to summer with such suddenness that spring is almost nonexistent. In April and early May, the rapidly melting snow floods the streams, the soil thaws, and "all Russia is an epic of mud."[2] (See Figure 1–1.)

Further south, stretching from Hungary to Mongolia, is the steppe, vast grasslands and semiarid plains that are suitable for grazing livestock. For

Figure 1-1. Regions of the Union of Soviet Socialist Republics

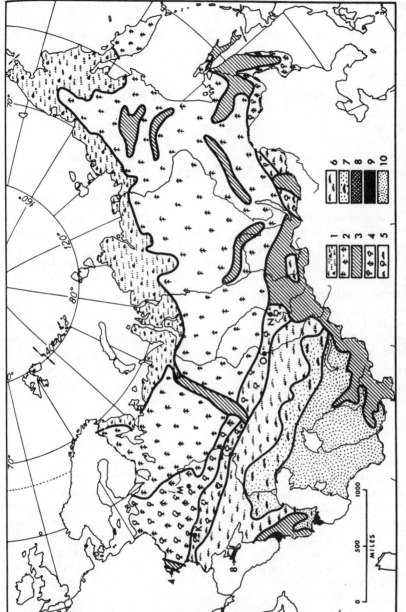

1 = tundra, 2 = tayga, 3 = mountain (vertical zoning), 4 = mixed forest, 5 = wooded steppe, 6 = steppe, 7 = semi-desert, 8 = Mediterranean, 9 = wet sub-tropical, 10 = desert

Source: David J. M. Hooson, *The Soviet Union* (London: University of London Press, 1966), p. 43.

centuries, the steppe was controlled by fierce, nomadic Mongol tribes who drove the pastoral Slavs into the forests to seek protection. The climate in the steppe is typical of continental regions; in the winter, temperatures frequently hit −40° F, and in the summer, highs in the eighties and nineties are normal. During winter, the days are only 4 to 5 hours long. It is in these regions of European Russia that the vast majority of the Soviet population resides. For point of reference, Moscow is located approximately as far north as Hudson Bay and Juneau, Alaska, and Leningrad is as far north as Anchorage. The southernmost border of the Soviet Union is on a parallel with Philadelphia and San Francisco.

Finally, in the southernmost regions of the country, to the east of the Caspian Sea, there are deserts in which the average summer temperature is likely to soar to 110° to 120° F.

Russia is blessed with an abundance of natural resources, including massive deposits of coal, iron ore, gold, bauxite, other nonferrous metals, oil, and gas. Its rivers offer boundless potential for developing hydroelectric power, and its forests afford a virtually endless supply of lumber and pulp. In recent years, the Soviet leadership has undertaken ambitious plans to develop these vast resources.

Much of this wealth of natural resources, however, exists in the northern tundra far above the Arctic Circle. The brutal cold in this region halts all construction and makes it extremely difficult to harvest timber, to mine ore, and to drill for oil and gas. Under these severe climatic conditions, equipment breaks down and rubber boots shatter like glass. In the summer, the top few feet of the tundra thaw and become a soggy marsh, making transportation even more difficult than it is in the winter. Sometimes, pieces of earthmoving equipment being used at oil and gas construction sites in northwest Siberia simply disappear into the mud. As a result, they have had to be fitted with ejector seats for their drivers.

The harsh climate of the Soviet Union seriously affects the food supply. The northerly climate shortens the growing season to four or five months. Moreover, limited and erratic rainfall in much of the country results in chronic agricultural crop failures. Many regions with black soil, such as parts of Kazakhstan, receive inadequate rainfall, while regions with ample rain have sandy or loamy soil. The major portion of the precipitation usually comes in the second half of the summer when it is least needed. Historically, these factors have resulted in one bad harvest out of three in Russia.[3]

·   The sheer difficulty of survival in such conditions resulted in the development of a communal peasant culture. The single-family farms that dotted the countryside in the rural United States and fostered a sense of individualism were ill-suited for Russia. Long before the Revolution and Stalin's collectivization of agriculture, Russian peasants found it necessary to assist one another with planting, tilling, and harvesting. The collective character of farming and the need for ample labor favored an extended family structure. Thus, for centuries, Russian peasants lived in communal settlements called the *dvorishche*. In some of the most northerly regions, peasants conserved energy by living in communal housing rather than in the traditional cottage, or *izba*. Because of the short growing season, farm work was concentrated in a few months; cottage industries and alcohol consumed the long winters.

The harshness of the climate inevitably helped to shape the Russian mind-set. Russians often think of the world as cold and inhospitable. For centuries, Russian peasants had to cope with epidemics, endless toil, famine, and political and economic repression, but these ills were largely accepted as "God's will." This fatalism was reinforced by the Russian Orthodox church, which taught that life is fraught with toil and trials and which made a virtue of asceticism and suffering.

DOGMATISM AND INTOLERANCE

The physical boundlessness of Russia initially found expression in a primitive natural paganism that later merged with Orthodoxy to mold Russian spiritual values. In pre-Christian Russian society, the illiterate peasants attributed supernatural powers to forces in their environment that they could not understand or control. For instance, the wolf, which preyed on the peasants and their flocks, became an object of worship. Fire also was ascribed a mystical power, being a necessity for life in the harsh winters, but also the cause of the destruction of whole villages and frequently of death.

With the conversion of Russia to Christianity, this paganism was not completely eradicated; rather, the primitive natural beliefs of the Russian people were absorbed into Orthodoxy. On the exterior of some of the oldest surviving Christian churches in the Soviet Union, one can still find pagan gargoyles and figures whose purpose was to keep away evil spirits. Remnants of these early beliefs can also be seen today in Russian *skazki*, or fairy tales, which depict Father Frost, fire, wolves, and other animals and natural forces.

The Christianization of Russia during the ninth and tenth centuries was the result of a conscious decision by Grand Prince Vladimir of Kiev to modernize the country and forge stronger political ties with the Byzantine Empire centered in Constantinople. According to ancient chronicles, Vladimir was visited by religious delegations of various faiths: Roman Catholics from Germany, Khazars professing Judaism, Bulgar Moslems, and Orthodox Christians from Byzantium. Legend has it that Vladimir spurned Islam because it forbade alcohol; as the prince noted, "Drink is the joy of the Russian."[4] Likewise, he decided against Judaism because he believed it was the faith of a defeated and homeless people. His choice of Eastern Orthodoxy for Russia determined the direction not only of the country's religious development, but also its political and cultural evolution. By choosing Orthodoxy, Vladimir opened Russia to influence from the highly developed Byzantine culture, and Kievan literature, art, architecture, law, and customs reflected this. The decision also meant that Russia would remain outside the influence of the Roman Catholic church, thus contributing to the country's isolation from the rest of Europe and from such important intellectual movements as the scholastic tradition and the Renaissance.

The Eastern Orthodox church constructed an authoritarian hierarchy, which intertwined with and strengthened an equally authoritarian political structure. The values stressed by the Church were those of asceticism, self-denial, suffering, piety, and dogmatism. It was a religion that ensured the maintenance of power in the hands of a few and that discouraged the peasants from seeking power or change. The doctrines of the Church corresponded to the life experience of the Russian peasant. The Orthodox church taught that life is to be endured, not enjoyed. Not only were the peasants instructed to suffer the harshness of the climate and the authoritarian, often corrupt rule of the tsar and his provincial governors, they were also to learn piety from suffering; there was something noble about "bearing one's cross." As a result, in a few isolated Siberian villages, some sects took to the extremes of self-flagellation, extended fasts, isolation, and other acts of self-denial. Rather than focusing on this world, Russian Orthodoxy displayed a strong mystical and transcendental element that stressed the hereafter.

Orthodoxy helped to develop in the Russian peasant a mystical attachment to the soil, to Mother Russia. Some scholars believe that the origins of the word *Russia* (*Rus'*) are tied to those of *rodina* ("motherland").[5] It is significant that such concepts are usually of the feminine gender. The rich, black soil of Russia is likened to the womb, the source of all life. The Russian serfs of the seventeenth century through the first half of the nineteenth century were not only legally bound to the land, they were religiously and mystically attached to it. In small villages that could not afford to pay for a priest, peasants would go out into the fields and confess their sins not to the heavens, but to the soil, to Mother Russia.

Many of the attributes of Russian Orthodoxy spilled over into the social realm as well. When Russians adopted a belief system, they often did so dogmatically, totally and without reservation. This dogmatism, whether on religious issues or on political issues, has led to numerous apocalyptic events throughout Russian history.[6] For instance, in the seventeenth century, a schism occurred within the Russian Orthodox church over the introduction of certain liturgical reforms. A group that came to be called the Old Believers split from the Orthodox church because they opposed the triple "Hallelujah"—repeating the Hallelujah chant three times—and persisted in making the sign of the cross with two fingers rather than three.

Russians, whether orthodox, heretics, or schismatics, have tended to be apocalyptic and nihilistic and to be willing, even eager, to suffer for their beliefs. All belief systems are held and defended with equal fervor. Religious dogmatism has often translated into intolerance for those who stray from the true belief. Whether among the Old Believers in the seventeenth century, the Russian revolutionaries, anarchists, and nihilists of the nineteenth century, the Marxist-Leninists of the twentieth century, or the nationalistic and anti-Semitic members of the Pamyat Society today, dogmatism and intolerance have gone hand in hand. These qualities transcend religious issues and have permeated social and political values as well.

A MESSIANIC STATE WITH AN INFERIORITY COMPLEX

Russian Orthodoxy also transcended the Russian Empire, upholding itself not only as the defender of the Slavic people (even those residing beyond the borders of the empire) but also as the defender of the true Christianity. After the fall of the Byzantine Empire—the Second Rome—the doctrine of the Third Rome emerged in the Muscovite state. In 1510, the monk Filofei wrote to Tsar Vasily III:

> Of all kingdoms in the world, it is in thy royal domain that the holy Apostolic Church shines more brightly than the sun. And let thy Majesty take note, O religious and gracious Tsar, that all kingdoms of the Orthodox Christian Faith are merged into thy kingdom. Thou alone, in all that is under heaven, art a Christian Tsar. And take note, O religious and gracious Tsar, that all Christian kingdoms are merged into thine alone, that two Romes have fallen, but the third stands, and there will be no fourth. Thy Christian kingdom shall not fall to the lot of another.[7]

Thus, the Russian state was infused with a messianic zeal that justified territorial expansion. Nationalism and Orthodoxy were effectively merged into one powerful ethic.

The expansion of the Russian Empire continued from the sixteenth through the nineteenth century, beginning with the consolidation of the empire in the territories west of the Urals, including the Baltic, the Don region, and the North Caucasus, and then expanding into contiguous territories to the east and south. Territorial expansion in Russia was itself a contradictory process, vacillating between compulsion and voluntary assimilation. At times, the authorities dammed back the influx of new peoples into the empire; at other times, they pressed control over neighboring peoples by force.

The conquest of Siberia began in earnest in the late sixteenth century, and by the mid-eighteenth century, Russian outposts extended all the way to the Pacific. As a result of the Napoleonic Wars (1805–1814), the Caucasus was added to the empire. The consolidation of Russian influence in the Far East and Alaska was formalized from 1858 to 1860. In contrast, Russian occupation and control of Central Asia was a gradual and lengthy process spanning the period from 1868 through 1885.

The causes of Russian territorial expansion were many. First, the empire was surrounded by sparsely settled territories that invited incorporation. Second, lacking any natural borders, the empire tended to expand in search of security. Third, empires of the nineteenth century often measured their power and influence in terms of the extent of territory controlled and the size of their populations. Fourth, because much of the arable land in Russia was of poor quality and traditional farming techniques tended to deplete the soil quickly, the peasants were constantly seeking more fertile farming areas. Finally, because England, France, and other European powers could no longer expand their territories on the European continent without precipitating war, they turned toward the acquisition of extensive colonial holdings that would provide sources of raw materials for their industry and markets for their newly acquired industrial capability. The Russian Empire, anxious to compete and be recognized as a major European power, was afforded the opportunity to expand into contiguous territories that presented many of the advantages of a colonial empire, but without some of the risks and costs.

Eventually, the territorial expansion of the Russian empire brought the tsarist state into conflict with other empires: there were wars with the Napoleonic Empire in Europe, the Ottoman Empire in the South, the British Empire in the Crimea, the Japanese in the Far East and Manchuria (1904–1905), and the Austro-Hungarian and German empires in Eastern Europe (1914–1917). These wars had important implications. They brought Russians into increased contact with Western nations and cultures. They also reinforced existing tendencies toward the centralization of power that was needed to mount an army and to support military ventures. In addition, they brought to the attention of the tsarist regime the necessity of promoting industrialization to free Russia from its dependence on imported steel and other products necessary for manufacturing military hardware.

The expansion of Russia, especially in Asia, the Caucasus, and the Baltic, inevitably introduced non-Slavic peoples into the empire. By the time of the Revolution, Russia was a multiethnic state consisting of peoples speaking more than 150 distinct dialects or languages. Religiously, they ranged from Catholics and Protestants in the western regions of the Ukraine, Belorussia, and the Baltic, to Orthodox believers in European Russia, to Shiite Moslems in Central Asia, Buddhists in the Far East, and shamanists in isolated villages throughout eastern Siberia.

Non-Russian influences were also introduced during centuries of invasion and occupation by foreign powers. The list of invaders of Russia includes the Scythians, Mongols, Sarmatians, Goths, Huns, Avars, Khazars, Tatars, Swedes, Poles, Lithuanians, Turks, French, Japanese, and Germans. During the twentieth century alone, six major wars or foreign interventions have occurred on Russian soil. With no bodies of water or major mountain ranges to impede their assault, invaders have repeatedly occupied Russia and subjugated its people. The longest occupation came at the hands of the Mongol-Tatar invaders and lasted more than 250 years—from the thirteenth through the first half of the fifteenth century. The Mongol influence was such that the Marquis de Custine wrote: "Scratch a Russian and he bleeds Mongol blood!" The repeated foreign incursions have ingrained in the Russian people a sense of vulnerability and a feeling of being exposed.

RUSSIFICATION VERSUS NATIONAL SELF-DETERMINATION

The Bolsheviks inherited from the tsars a diverse multiethnic empire comprising more than one hundred distinct nationalities. In 1903, the Bolshevik party program proclaimed the right of self-determination and national autonomy for the nationality groups that lived within the Russian Empire, but this was largely a political ploy to win greater support among disgruntled ethnic groups. The Bolsheviks considered any concession granted to nationality groups to be minor since they believed the nationality problem was a short-term one. In the long run, with the triumph of socialism, national boundaries and differences would wither away; under communism nationalities would merge into a homogeneous culture.

The downfall of the tsarist regime, and the ensuing political chaos during the Revolution and the Civil War, permitted several nationality groups to establish independent governments. At the time of the Revolution in 1917 and the conclusion of a separate peace treaty with Germany, the Baltic nations—Latvia, Lithuania, and Estonia—were under German occupation. The peoples in these areas expressed strong anti-Russian sentiments; consequently, they were not incorporated into the Bolshevik state. Finland, which had been a largely autonomous province of the Russian Empire until the Revolution, fought for and won its national independence in 1920.

Despite its earlier pledges to honor national self-determination and autonomy, the Bolshevik regime forcibly incorporated into the Soviet Republic various nationality groups that tried to assert their national independence. In 1917, for example, the Ukrainian nationalist assembly (Rada) established a Ukrainian People's Republic and supported the Whites during the Civil War. Less than one month later, however, the Red Army seized control of the entire Ukraine, and the region was incorporated into the Soviet Republic. Numerous national governments also arose in the Caucasus, in some cases with the support of Britain, Germany, and Turkey. Soviet forces intervened in Azerbaidzhan and Armenia, however, and these regions became Soviet republics in 1920. The Georgian Menshevik government was toppled the following year.

The 1924 Constitution established the federal structure for the USSR, and each republic was granted (in theory, if not in fact) the right to conduct diplomatic relations and the right to secede. The present version of the Constitution retains these rights, but it remains to be seen how a republic could actually secede.

The fifteen most populous ethnic groups, occupying territory on the perimeter of the USSR, are accorded the status of union-republics. In each union-republic, the official language is that of the indigenous ethnic group (i.e., Ukrainian in the Ukraine, Uzbek in Uzbekistan, and so forth). Each union-republic has its own constitution; its own legislative, executive, and judicial institutions; and its own party structures. Smaller ethnic groups are also accorded a limited degree of national autonomy as autonomous republics, autonomous regions, and national districts. Unlike the United States, which prides itself on being a melting pot in which diverse nationalities merge to become "American," the Soviet Union has an official policy of fostering and preserving diverse national cultures and languages. This policy, however, inevitably produces dilemmas: how can ethnic minorities be encouraged to maintain their unique languages and cultures but still be assimilated into Soviet society in order to enjoy upward mobility? How can national self-determination be promoted without allowing parochial, ethnic tendencies to supersede loyalty to the USSR? How can investments be allocated to benefit the least-developed areas but at the same time maximize the benefits to the general economy? In short, how can the centrifugal forces of nationalism be reconciled with the centripetal forces of Russification and the Soviet state?

EAST VERSUS WEST

Until the nineteenth century, Russia was largely isolated from the events and developments that influenced the course of Western Europe. As a result, Russia was shaped by profoundly different political, economic, religious, and cultural forces than those that molded Western Europe. In Russia, there was no Renaissance or Reformation. The concept of separation of church and state, each with its own independent realm of authority, was totally foreign to Russian thinking. The Industrial Revolution came late to Russia; when industry developed, it was not due to the rise of a middle class of entrepreneurs but to state decree. Russia entered the twentieth century never having experienced elections or legalized political parties and never having had a constitution to limit the powers of the tsar. In short, the idea of government as a social contract between the rulers and the ruled was foreign to Russian society. Civil liberties were unknown as legal or political concepts. Democracy was unheard of among the peasants and denounced by rulers too frightened to conceive of sharing power with the common people. Thus, Russia entered the twentieth century as an authoritarian state with a largely backward, agrarian economy and a deeply divided social class system.

Russia was neither wholly Eastern nor wholly Western, and the clash of Eastern and Western cultural traditions and values within the country has been the subject of repeated controversy. When the young Peter the Great assumed the throne in 1692, he immediately began a series of wrenching reforms designed to modernize and strengthen the Russian state. As a young man, Peter studied carpentry, shipbuilding, and navigation, because he recognized that Russia needed to have a modern navy to compete with its adversaries. From 1697 to 1698, he led a delegation of his advisors and craftsmen on an extensive tour of Europe to acquire Western technological "know-how."

Peter believed in enlightened despotism. He envisioned a modern Russian state, freed from the superstitions and corruption of the Church and from the conservatism of the Muscovite establishment and all that it represented. He strove to raise the Russian people from their ignorance and backwardness, but in so doing, he was quite willing to resort to ruthless tactics. Peter promulgated a revolution from above. At great human expense, he built a new capital, St. Petersburg, which was intended to be Russia's "window on the West." He ordered all military officers to shave their beards "for the glory and comeliness of the State and the military profession," and levied a tax on those citizens who persisted in growing beards.[8] He established the Academy of Sciences and encouraged members of the nobility to study abroad.

Peter was especially severe in his policies toward the Russian Orthodox church, which he believed had retarded the development of the Russian state. Copying the relationship between church and state in Lutheran countries of northern Europe, he replaced the patriarch with the Holy Synod. When his policies encountered opposition, he dealt with his critics mercilessly; he imprisoned his wife and sister and executed his own son for opposing his reforms.

Much of Peter the Great's reign was occupied with the Great Northern War (1700–1721). In fact, only one year during his entire reign was without war. Many of his reforms were motivated by the desire to strengthen the State in order to enhance Russia's military capability. For example, Peter instituted general conscription and reorganized the army into more effective fighting units. He also helped to build the first Russian navy and aspired to turn

*Slavophiles: Russian peasantry (muzhik)
peasant commune (MIR)
Orthodoxy
rural life*

Russia into a naval power that would rival the great navies of Britain, France, and Holland.

Peter reorganized the haphazard, unwieldy governmental bureaucracy into nine *collegia*, or ministries. In addition, he is credited with establishing the first treasury and a universal system of coinage to replace the previous system of barter. This facilitated the collection of taxes to support his military campaigns. In short, Peter's reforms both strengthened the Russian state and forced Western enlightenment on a segment of the population. The changes, however, also served to widen the gulf between the peasants, who were largely unaffected by them, and the upper classes.

Another outcome of Peter's reforms was the gradual emergence in Russia of an intelligentsia—a class of well-educated persons, primarily from the nobility, who were profoundly influenced by Western ideas. The influx of Western culture, however, also generated a reactionary backlash among those who rejected these ideas and chose instead to preserve the uniqueness of Russian culture. By the nineteenth century, the conflict between the Western ideas introduced since the time of Peter and the indigenous Slavic mores was manifested in two opposing schools of thought—the Westernizers and the Slavophiles. The Westernizers held that Russia must follow the Western model of development. The Slavophiles, on the other hand, glorified the superior achievements and historical mission of Orthodoxy and of Russia. While the Westernizers promoted industrialization, secularization, and the rise of a middle class, the Slavophiles stressed the simple idealistic virtues of the Russian peasant (*muzhik*), the peasant commune (*mir*), Orthodoxy, and rural life.

The Westernizer–Slavophile debate continued throughout the nineteenth century, and analogies can be found even during the Soviet period. For instance, today a debate is raging in the press pitting advocates of market-oriented economic reform and democratic, Western-style political and legal systems against right-wing Russian nationalists. The Moscow-based Russian Patriotic Society "*Otchestvo*" [Fatherland] was organized in March 1989 to "unite all who are concerned about the native land and about Russia."[9] The leader of *Otchestvo*, Apollon Kuz'min, writing in the conservative journal *Literaturnaya Rossiya* (Literary Russia), noted, "the now fashionable little word 'pluralism' should not conceal a rejection of the search for truth."[10] That truth is the return to traditional Russian values.

Even more extreme nationalistic, anti-Western values are articulated by Dmitri Vasil'ev, head of Pamyat [Memory] Society. Asked by a Western scholar to list the basic points of Pamyat, Vasil'ev harked back to Count Serge Uvarov's three principles of official nationality[11]: (1) Autocracy: Vasil'ev advocates the restoration of the Russian monarchy. (2) Orthodoxy: Vasil'ev not only wants the Russian Orthodox church to once again become the official church of Russia, he also wants the church to assume primary responsibility for the moral education of the Russian people. The patriarch of the church should serve "as the right hand of the tsar." (3) Nationality (*narodnost'*): according to Vasil'ev, the people would only have the right to advise the tsar through institutions such as the Senate and the Duma, but neither institution could in any way restrict the power of the monarch.

Pamyat claims a following of some 20,000 in Moscow alone, while in Leningrad it reports more than 5000 members and 10,000 "sympathizers."[12]

The clash between Western and Slavophile views even extended to Gorbachev's Presidential Council, where the conservative, nationalist author Valentin Rasputin and the anti-Western conservative mine worker organizer Veniamin Iarin contended with several prominent reformers and Western-oriented intellectuals such as Stanislov Shatalin, Albert Kauls, and Chingis Aitmatov.

FROM ANARCHY TO AUTOCRACY

Another dominant contradiction within Russian political culture is a tendency to seek anarchy and the absence of order and control on the one hand, and autocracy on the other. A noted authority on imperial Russian history observed, "The *muzhiki* (peasants) preferred absolutism to any other form of government except anarchy."[13] The immensity of the Russian landmass and the absence of boundaries is reflected in the inclination toward anarchy. While in the West geographic, social, and political boundaries were clearly established, in Russia organization, limits, and order did not come naturally. In a sense, the Russian political system fell victim to the size of the nation; it was incapable of establishing stability and order over such an extensive, diverse, and socially divided empire. V. O. Kliuchevsky, a distinguished Russian historian of the nineteenth century, remarked, "The state expands, the people grow sickly."[14]

Some Russian historians explain the despotic character of Russian government as necessary for creating order and setting limits for a country and a people for whom no limits existed. Traditionally, Russians have turned to the State to create order out of the chaos of their society. In doing so, they have often sacrificed their own interests to those of the State.

The concept of the State in Russia was originally derived from the role of the head of the extended family in early peasant society. The father was sovereign of the household, an autocrat in the broadest sense of the word. He literally owned all the property of the clan and its members as well; they could be sold as one might sell a cow. He alone was responsible for punishing members of the family; whipping a son to death was not uncommon. In parts of Siberia, as late as the mid-nineteenth century, a father who killed a family member was liable only to a penance issued by the Church.

Until the middle of the seventeenth century, Russians had no concept of the State as Westerners know it. The State, insofar as they thought of it at all, meant the sovereign (*gosudar'*)—that is, the tsar—his private staff, and his family. Like the father of an extended family, the prince or tsar emerged as the sole proprietor in public right of all the subjects and all the territory in his principality.

It was under Peter the Great that there first emerged a notion of the State as a power distinct from and superior to the tsar. Yet the idea that legal norms were binding on the sovereign and could restrict his powers gained only shallow acceptance and was overshadowed by the traditional stress on the patrimonial state. Thus, the concept of the State in Russian political culture is synonymous with a fusion of power and proprietorship, with unchallenged authority. There were no recognized formal limits on the tsar's political authority and no rule of law, and individual liberties existed only insofar as they were granted by the tsar.

The preeminent role of the State was officially recognized by Tsar Nicholas I (1825–1855) and promulgated by means of the doctrine referred to as "official nationality." Formally proclaimed in 1833 by Count Serge Uvarov, the tsar's Minister of Education, the decree contained three principles: Orthodoxy, autocracy, and nationality. *Orthodoxy* referred to the official church and its role as the ultimate source of ethics and ideals that gave meaning to human life and society. *Autocracy* meant the absolute power of the sovereign, which was considered the indispensable foundation of the Russian state. *Nationality (narodnost')* referred to Russian nationality, which was preeminent over all other Slavic and non-Slavic groups within the rapidly expanding empire.

The Russian Orthodox church was fragmented, decentralized, and made subservient to the State's messianic interests and goals. It was unable to challenge the power or authority of the State and stood by silently while an Ivan the Terrible or a Stalin slaughtered thousands. Ultimately, the inability or unwillingness of the Church to speak out on issues of social and political injustice created a spiritual vacuum that was filled with secular ideologies.

THE RULERS AND THE RULED

In Western societies, the notion is that ultimate political power and authority derive from the people and that the State exists as the manifested will of the governed. In the Soviet Union, as in prerevolutionary Russia, the State and political power, while considered necessary elements of Russian life, were seen to derive from forces external to the people themselves. Political decisionmakers were so far removed from the average Russian peasant that policies and laws appeared to come "from above," "from outside." This we–they schism characterizing the Russian view of the State is symbolized by the tale of the earliest Russian ruler, Rurik (862 A.D.). According to the *Primary Chronicle*, a series of annals recorded by monks during the Kievan era, the Russians—a pastoral people residing in the region of Novgorod—were suffering from a lack of order and state discipline, so they sought leadership from abroad:

> The [Russians] set out to govern themselves. There was no law among them, but tribe rose against tribe. Discord thus ensued among them, and they began to war one against another. They said to themselves, "Let us seek a prince who may rule over us, and judge us according to the law." They accordingly went overseas to the Varangian Rus' (Scandinavia): these particular Varangians were known as Rus', just as some are called Swedes, and other Normans, Angles, and Goths, for they were thus named. The Chuds, the Slavs, and the Kirvichians then said to the people of Rus', "Our whole land is great and rich, but there is no order in it. Come to rule and reign over us." They thus selected three brothers, with their kinfolk, who took

with them all the Rus', and migrated. The oldest, Rurik, located himself in Novgorod; the second, Sineus, in Beloozero; and the third, Truvor, in Izborsk. On account of these Varangians, the district of Novgorod became known as Russian (Rus') land. The present inhabitants of Novgorod are descended from the Varangian race, but aforetime they were Slavs. After two years, Sineus and his brother Truvor died, and Rurik assumed the sole authority.[15]

Thus, the Slavs, recognizing their own lack of ability to govern themselves, had to send out for government.

Serfdom developed in Russia, as in the feudal West, with peasants entering contractual arrangements with lords. During the latter sixteenth and early seventeenth centuries, serfdom spread as the tsar granted lands to his gentry class as a reward for loyal service. Serfdom in Russia appeared simultaneously with the emergence of a centralized monarchy, not with feudal dispersal of power, as in Western Europe. As the tsar consolidated more political authority in Moscow, he gained more power to award new lands to his supporters; thus, serfdom spread. It was accompanied by a growing economic dependence of the peasant on the landlord, and by active Muscovite government support of the gentry class. Initially, the peasants were bound to the land and became the property of the gentry when the lands they worked were granted by the tsar. Most peasants considered serfdom an injustice, but they laid the blame primarily on the local nobility, rather than on the tsar himself. An old Russian expression captures their sentiments: "God is high in heaven and the tsar is far away." The peasants saw the tsar as endowed by God, as a benevolent father figure and shepherd of his flock. On the other hand, they often saw the tsar's local governors and nobility as greedy and corrupt. It is said that the Russian peasant came into contact with the government through two officials—the tax collector, who took away as much as 60 percent of the peasant's harvest, and the conscription officer, who drafted young men to fight in wars. Nevertheless, the notion developed that the good and merciful tsar cared about his flock and would right these injustices if only he were aware of them. But like God, who is high in heaven, the tsar was far away.

The peasants, having a legal, economic, and spiritual attachment to the Russian soil, found it wrong that nobles should possess vast tracts of land. The soil was God's, and all who toiled and labored on it should be able to enjoy its use. Concepts of private property in early Russian law did not extend to the land; rather, most of the peasants' land was held in a primitive agrarian communal institution, the *mir*. (The word *mir* means both "peace" and "world," which conveys a great deal about how the Russian peasant viewed the peasant commune. It represented a harmonious and peaceful world, and the borders of the commune were almost literally the borders of the peasant's world.)

After the emancipation of the serfs in 1861, much as in the aftermath of the Emancipation Proclamation two years later in the United States, the serfs did not gain the financial means to exist as free persons. Many continued in a quasi-serf status, dependent upon local landlords, who had fewer obligations to their tenant farmers than they had had toward their serfs prior to emancipation. Other peasants migrated to the cities in search of employment in the newly emerging industries. There, they contributed to the rise of a working class, a class of uprooted and disaffected people who lived in squalor in makeshift hovels. Once these people were isolated from the supportive social structures of Russian village life, their individual woes became merged into the widespread and sometimes violent political demands of an incipient working class.

At the time of the Revolution in 1917, the nobility constituted less than 5 percent of the total population. For the last 100 years of the tsarist regime, many nobles traveled frequently to European capitals to acquire Western fashions and education. French, German, Italian, and English tutors, architects, chefs, and artisans were imported by the gentry and nobility to raise the level of Russian culture. Many of the gentry and nobility intermarried with other European aristocracies. Western culture affected only those at the top of Russian society, however, and served to further alienate them from the masses of the population.[16] Unlike the nobility in England that opposed the monarchy and succeeded in limiting the power of the throne, the Russian aristocracy had no rights independent of those granted by the tsar. Consequently, it became an arm of the tsarist autocracy, which also inhibited social and political change in Russia.

In contrast to the nobility, the Russian peasants, who constituted more than 80 percent of the population in 1900, were largely illiterate, conservative, superstitious, and above all devoutly religious. They looked with suspicion upon the Western ways adopted by the nobility, some of whom were not Orthodox and a few of whom spoke only French and German. As the rift between the Russian peasants and the nobility widened, the tsarist regime responded with coercion and repression in a futile attempt to replace its eroding credibility and diminishing popular support with political control. It was this cycle of repression and revolution that culminated in the Bolshevik seizure of power in 1917.

Notes

1. From a conversation with the author in Leningrad, November 1975.

2. G. Melvyn Howe, *The Soviet Union: A Geographical Survey* (Plymouth, Devonshire, England: Macdonald & Evans, 1983), 33.

3. Richard Pipes, *Russia under the Old Regime* (London: Weidenfeld and Nicolson, 1974), 5.

4. Quoted in Nicolas Berdyaev, *The Origin of Russian Communism* (London: Geoffrey Bles, 1937), 10.

5. The origin of the word *Rus'* is much debated. For the peasant attachment to the soil, see Georgi P. Fedotov, *The Russian Religious Mind* (Cambridge: Harvard University Press, 1966).

6. This theory was first developed by Nicolas Berdyaev in *The Origin of Russian Communism*.

7. From the *Primary Chronicle*, available in English in Serge A. Zenkovsky, ed., *Medieval Russia's Epics, Chronicles, and Tales* (New York: E. P. Dutton, 1963).

8. B. H. Summer, *Peter the Great and the Emergence of Russia* (New York: Collier, 1962).

9. Cited in Douglas Smith, "Moscow's 'Otchestvo': A Link Between Russian National-ism and Conservative Opposition to Reform," *Radio Liberty Report on the USSR* 1, no. 30 (28 July 1989): 6.

10. *Literaturnaya Rossiya*, 23 June 1989, p. 1.

11. John B. Dunlop, "A Conversation with Dmitri Vasil'ev, the leader of 'Pamyat,' " *Radio Liberty Report on the USSR* 1, no. 50 (15 December 1989): 13–14.

12. Ibid., p. 13.

13. Pipes, *Russia under the Old Regime*, 250.

14. V. O. Kliuchevsky, *A Course of Russian History*, trans. C. J. Hogarth (London: J.M. Dent, 1911).

15. From the *Primary Chronicle*, in Zenkovsky, *Medieval Russia's Epics, Chronicles, and Tales*, 50.

16. Wladimir Weidle, *Russia: Absent and Present* (New York: Vintage, 1961).

Selected Bibliography

Benet, Sula, ed. and trans. *The Village of Viriatino*. Garden City, NY: Doubleday, 1970.

Berdyaev, Nicolas. *The Origin of Russian Communism*. London: Geoffrey Bles, 1937.

Billington, James. *The Icon and the Axe*. New York: Alfred A. Knopf, 1966.

Clarkson, Jesse D. *A History of Russia*. 2d ed. New York: Random House, 1969.

Custine, Marquis de. *Journey for Our Time: The Russian Journals of the Marquis De Custine*. Trans. and ed. Phyllis Penn Kohler. Chicago: Henry Regnery Company, 1951.

Fedotov, Georgi P. *The Russian Religious Mind*. Cambridge: Harvard University Press, 1966.

Harcave, Sidney. *Russia: A History*. Chicago: Lippincott, 1953.

Hingley, Ronald. *The Tsars, 1533–1917*. New York: Macmillan, 1968.

Howe, G. Melvyn. *The Soviet Union: A Geographical Survey*. 2d ed. Plymouth, Devonshire, England: Macdonald & Evans, 1983.

Mellor, Roy E. H. *The Soviet Union and Its Geographical Problems*. London: Macmillan Press, 1982.

Pipes, Richard. *Russia under the Old Regime*. London: Weidenfeld and Nicolson, 1974.

Pokrovsky, M. N. *History of Russia*. New York: Russell & Russell, 1966.

Riasanovsky, Nicholas V. *A History of Russia*. 2d ed. New York: Oxford University Press, 1969.

Schapiro, Leonard. *The Origin of Communist Autocracy*. Cambridge: Harvard University Press, 1955.

Sumner, B. H. *Peter the Great and the Emergence of Russia*. New York: Collier, 1962.

Vernadsky, George. *A History of Russia*. 6th ed. New Haven: Yale University Press, 1969.

Zenkovsky, Serge A., ed. *Medieval Russia's Epics, Chronicles, and Tales*. New York: E. P. Dutton, 1963.

2

Russia's Revolutionary Heritage

In Russia, there is a legacy of repression and revolution. Throughout the nineteenth and into the twentieth century, an increasingly anachronistic regime, immobilized by fear and inertia, confronted rapidly changing social forces. Those who criticized the regime or spoke out for reforms were imprisoned or exiled. A self-perpetuating cycle developed: calls for reform resulted in police harassment, which further radicalized the dissidents and hardened their demands. With every repetition of the cycle, the political demands grew more strident, the protests more violent, and the responses of the authorities more repressive and brutal.

THE FIRST RUMBLINGS OF DISSENT

Opposition to the tsarist regime began with the rise of the intelligentsia in the early eighteenth century. As the intelligentsia—the educated and enlightened class—emerged as a social force, its members began to call for change. Their modest petitions brought them only sacrifice, suffering, and imprisonment, however. One of the first critics of the regime was Alexander Radishchev. A member of the gentry and a government official, Radishchev was educated at the University of Leipzig, where he acquired a thorough knowledge of eighteenth-century European thought; he was especially influenced by the works of Rousseau. Radishchev returned to Russia, and in 1790, he wrote his famous book *Journey from Petersburg to Moscow*. In the book, written in the form of a travelogue, Radishchev described the lives of the Russian serfs he had seen during his journey: the auction of members of a peasant family to different buyers; serfs working their fields on Sunday, the only day they could work their own land; arranged marriages; and the poverty of peasant existence. The book shattered the facade of the "progressive and enlightened" character of the reign of Catherine the Great (1762–1796). Frightened by the events of the French Revolution and fearing similar occurrences in Russia, Catherine condemned Radishchev to death. The sentence was later commuted to banishment to Siberia. Such was the reward for criticizing the injustices of Russian society or advocating even modest political and social reforms.

Change was bound to come to Russia, however. During the reign of

Alexander I (1801–1825), Russia experienced a cultural renaissance that resulted in, among other things, the golden age of Russian poetry. Freemasonry gained a wide following and was responsible for spreading education, thus opening Russian society to new ideas and social movements. The Napoleonic Wars brought Russia into direct contact with the West and Western ideas. Alexander himself was a man of enlightenment. On a visit to England, he met with Robert Owen, the English utopian socialist, and worshiped with Quakers. Alexander relaxed restrictions on travel abroad and on the entry of foreigners into Russia. He granted an amnesty to many political prisoners incarcerated during Catherine's reign. Torture and forced confessions were abolished, and censorship was eased. An 1801 law provided for the voluntary emancipation of serfs by their masters.

Although the first half of Alexander's reign was enlightened and progressive, it was followed by a period of reaction during which Alexander grew impatient and increasingly intolerant of his critics. The change in his policies can be attributed to several factors. The Napoleonic Wars and subsequent alliances with foreign powers preoccupied the Tsar for much of this period (1805–1812), distracting him from internal matters. From 1807 to 1812, the Tsar's chief assistant and adviser was Michael Speransky, who came not from the gentry, but from the poor village clergy. In 1809, Speransky proposed that the Tsar enact a constitution, recognize civil rights, and observe strict norms of legality, including the election of judges. Although these reforms were not acted upon, they indicate the liberal influence Speransky exerted on the Tsar. However, Speransky was removed from his influential role in 1812 and replaced with the reactionary General Alexis Arakcheev. Arakcheev's most notable innovation was the establishment of "military settlements." Villages were declared to be military property, and the peasants were forced to farm under military order. The coerciveness of the "military settlements" is illustrated by Arakcheev's regulations ordering that every married woman bear a child every year.

Another factor in the hardening of policies during the second half of Alexander's reign was the rise of a political and religious backlash to the Enlightenment ideas that had gradually filtered into Russia over the previous decades. Prince Alexander Golitsyn, president of the Bible Society in Russia, became Alexander's Minister of Education and imposed his extremist ideas on the universities. Golitsyn believed that all knowledge was contained in the Bible and that all other sources of learning were suspect. The faculties of the universities were purged, libraries were ransacked, and students were encouraged to inform on one another.

THE FIRST RUSSIAN REVOLUTION

The reactionary turn of Alexander's reign gave impetus to the first revolutionary movement in Russian history, the Decembrist uprising of 1825. The Decembrists, a group of army officers from aristocratic families, well-educated and influenced by the ideas of the Enlightenment and the French Revolution, called for the establishment of a constitutional regime in Russia and the abolition of serfdom. On December 26, 1825, using the death of Tsar Alexander as an opportunity to take power, regiments in St. Petersburg mutinied and marched to Senate Square, where they confronted troops loyal to the government. Artillery was brought in, and after several volleys, sixty to seventy of the Decembrists were dead and the others were arrested.[1] Nicholas I, who succeeded his brother, condemned several of the leaders to death and exiled more than three hundred to Siberia.

The reign of Nicholas I (1825–1855) represented another downward turn in the cycle of reform and reaction that characterized Russia in the nineteenth century. Nicholas had been brought up during the Napoleonic Wars and the last years of Alexander's rule. He possessed a love and admiration for military life and engineering. As Tsar, he displayed cunning, decisiveness, and an iron will. The Decembrist uprising merely reconfirmed his determination to preserve autocracy and eliminate any vestiges of dissent.

During the time of Nicholas I, the Russian intelligentsia was crushed between a reactionary autocratic monarchy on one side and an unenlightened mass of peasantry on the other. It was perhaps inevitable that the attempts of Catherine, Alexander I, and Nicholas I to suppress even moderate proposals for reform would engender more radical demands in the future.

In the 1840s, the ideas of the utopian socialists Claude-Henri Saint-Simon, Charles Fourier, and Pierre-Joseph Proudhon and the German Romanticists Georg Hegel and Friedrich Schelling were especially influential among the intelligentsia of Moscow and St. Petersburg. Utopian socialism helped to promote the Western philosophies espoused by Peter Chaadaev, among others. In 1836, Chaadaev, an influential member of Moscow society, published a letter in an intellectual journal denouncing Russia for being neither Eastern nor Western. He accused Russia of lacking the dynamic social principles of Catholicism that were the foundation of Western culture. Chaadaev was declared a madman and imprisoned in an insane asylum. After his release, he partially recanted in his *Apology of a Madman*. Nevertheless, Chaadaev had raised the question that troubled many of the intelligentsia: Did Russia's destiny lie with the West or with the East? Clearly, he and others favored the adoption of Western values.

Of the many salon groups formed during the mid-nineteenth century, one of the most famous was the Petrashevsky circle. Heavily influenced by ideas of utopian socialism, these intellectuals, many of whom were of aristocratic origin, met regularly to discuss the ideas and philosophies that were popular in Europe. Far removed from the diversity and pluralism of intellectual discourse that prevailed in Western Europe, however, the Russian intelligentsia tended to take the tentative ideas of Western thinkers and promote them as absolutist doctrines. Fyodor Dostoyevsky, a prominent member of the Petrashevsky circle, depicted the salon society and its rather naive calls for social reform in *The Possessed*. Although the Petrashevsky circle merely discussed ideas and did not undertake actions to subvert the regime, Nicholas I ordered his secret police to round up and arrest its members. Dostoyevsky was condemned to death and received a reprieve only at the last minute, when he was standing before the firing squad. Twenty-one of his associates from the Petrashevsky group were not so fortunate. Dostoyevsky's near death represented a turning point in his life. He renounced his earlier liberal views, and his subsequent books reflect more conservative sentiments.

Most of the intelligentsia were members of the gentry. Well-schooled and knowledgeable about European affairs and philosophies, many were troubled by a nagging sense of guilt over owning serfs and enjoying special privileges. Their idealization of the simple, illiterate, God-fearing Russian peasant—the *muzhik*—was an admiration from afar (often from the salons of Paris, London, and Vienna). Their humanitarian concern was for an abstract class of the downtrodden, not for the individual peasants with whom they had contact. In a sense, they were parlor liberals; they seldom attempted to translate their ideas into political action. Above all, they were painfully aware of the gulf separating them from the Russian masses whom they proposed to liberate "for their own best interest."

(1812-1870) Alexander Herzen, who had witnessed the revolutions in Western Europe and had been disillusioned by their outcomes, was the first to advocate a uniquely Russian form of socialism. Herzen, in exile in Western Europe, began an underground newspaper, *The Bell*, which voiced his socialist ideals; he was consequently harassed repeatedly by the Tsar's secret police. Nevertheless, each month, the latest issue of *The Bell* made its way to Nicholas's desk, a source of endless annoyance to the Tsar. Despite repeated investigations and interrogations, the newly created political police (the Third Section) were never able to ascertain who was responsible for smuggling the newspaper into the Tsar's chambers.

According to Herzen, Russia possessed the latent power to transform society, to fashion a new and more just social order. That power lay with the *muzhik*. Reacting to the dislocations of Western capitalism and the traumas of the Industrial Revolution, Herzen and the other *narodnik* socialists charted a special course for Russia.* They advocated a form of agrarian or populist socialism. *Narodnik* socialism believed, first, in the character of the Russian people to redeem society, and second, in the principle of communal socialist organization. *Narodnik* socialism repudiated Western philosophies and experience, but without accepting the Slavophile attachment to autocracy and Orthodoxy. Instead, *narodnik* socialism hailed the peasant commune—the *mir*—as a progressive socialist institution that would allow Russia to advance to socialism more quickly than the capitalist West. Herzen and the other *narodniki* also noted that the concept of private property was alien to the Russian people. In this sense, *narodnik* socialism was the intellectual antecedent of Marxist communism; unlike Marxism, however, it viewed the development of industry as an evil because it destroyed peasant life.[2]

THE REFORMS OF ALEXANDER II

In the mid-nineteenth century, Russia was alive with new ideas and social movements. Under the relatively enlightened and progressive rule of Alexander II (1855–1881), society was opened to change. Alexander concluded the

* *Narodnik* is derived from *narod*, meaning "people."

manifesto announcing the end of the Crimean War with a promise of reform. Inexorable pressures—both economic and moral—were building for the abolition of serfdom. As agriculture grew more competitive, many landlords could no longer afford to care for their serfs. In addition, serfdom began to engender political unrest. While the Pugachev peasant rebellion of 1773 to 1775 was the most famous, peasant insurrections occurred more frequently and became more violent in the first half of the nineteenth century. Official records of the tsarist government report more than five hundred peasant uprisings in the nineteenth century prior to the emancipation of the serfs in 1861.[3] Furthermore, the intelligentsia of all philosophical orientations opposed the institution of serfdom as morally wrong. Ivan Turgenev, for example, indirectly condemned serfdom in his work *A Sportsman's Sketches*, which contained realistic descriptions of the plight of the serfs. Publication of the book led to Turgenev's forced exile to his estate in 1852.

Emancipation finally came on March 3, 1861. At the time, approximately 20 million peasants owned 115 million dessiatins of land; a mere 30,000 of the gentry class owned more than 95 million dessiatins.[4] Except in the Ukraine, land was sold not to individual peasants but to the peasant commune, which divided the land among its members and was responsible for taxes and the provision of recruits for the army. Because few peasants could afford to buy land from the gentry, the government acquired the land for them and was reimbursed through heavy redemption payments, which rapidly created a class of impoverished peasants. Thus, for many serfs, the so-called emancipation altered only slightly their everyday existence.

The emancipation was not the only reform undertaken by Alexander II. He also created district and city *zemstva*, or assemblies, which granted limited self-rule to the local units of government and representation for the peasants. The *zemstvo* system provided free health care and education and unintentionally fostered increased support for socialist policies among the peasant class.

Alexander II introduced a widespread reform of the judicial system in 1864. Under the new provisions, the judiciary became an independent branch of government. Trials had to be conducted in public. Judicial procedure was streamlined and codified, and the courts were reorganized into a single, unified system under the Senate. Other reforms of the 1860s included the creation of the State Bank, establishment of a single state treasury, publication of the state budget, liberalized rules in education, and relaxed censorship.

FROM THE SALON TO THE STREET

The reforms instituted by Alexander II, instead of placating those calling for change, invited increasingly strident political demands and sharpened the reactionary policies of the conservative aristocracy. Unrest swept the universities. At St. Petersburg University, students occupied the administrative offices and closed the university with strikes. Male students grew their hair long, while female students cut their hair short and wore rose-tinted glasses. Students boasted of breaking social norms and experimented with new institutions, such as coed communes. The parallels between the student radicalism in Russia in the 1860s and in the United States in the 1960s are striking.

A decisive change in Alexander II's policies came in 1866, in reaction to a deranged student's attempt to assassinate the Tsar. Count Dmitrii Tolstoy was named Minister of Education and ordered to restore discipline and control over the universities. Press censorship was stiffened, and political cases were exempted from regular judicial procedures.

The intelligentsia of Russia during the 1860s and 1870s was experiencing a generation gap. The "fathers" of the 1840s generation were isolated and bewildered by the "sons" of the 1860s and 1870s.[5] Whereas the older generation emphasized humanistic, metaphysical, and aesthetic approaches to Russia's salvation, the younger generation, led by radicals such as Nicholas Chernyshevsky, Mikhail Bakunin, Dmitri Pisarev, Sergei Nechaev, and Felix Dzerzhinsky, supported nihilism, anarchy, and violent revolution.

The rebels of the 1860s were political activists who took their philosophies to the streets. Earlier generations of Russian intellectuals had been social philosophers who criticized the regime on philosophical grounds while enjoying brandy and cigars in the salons; their defiance extended only to publishing their ideas in underground newspapers and pamphlets. In contrast, the younger generation advocated a more violent and direct course of action.

Many of the younger generation advocated nihilism as the spiritual liberation of the individual, a necessary first step toward political liberation. Nihilism (from the Latin *nihil*, or "nothing") was the negation of all value and order. A characteristically Russian phenomenon, nihilism sought absolute liberation for the individual in a quasi-religious, apocalyptic fashion. The nihilists wanted to break every established social norm and convention, to destroy all traditional institutions that they claimed enslaved humanity. True liberation could come, they maintained, only through the total destruction of the old regime. Nihilists demanded liberation from all concepts (soul, God, art, standards) as well as institutions (law, the state, marriage, the family). For instance, they argued that marriage, by its very nature, enslaved women; the full emancipation of women would come only with the total destruction of the institution of marriage.

Nihilism embodied a strong religious element, a sense of seeking purification and spiritual rejuvenation through the total rejection and negation of conventional society and values. The ideas of nihilism were especially popular among seminarians and the children of priests, who were alienated by the intellectual corruption and decadence of the Russian Orthodox church. Chernyshevsky's utopian novel, *What Is to Be Done?*, is a virtual textbook of nihilism. The hero, Rakhmetov, sleeps on a bed of nails as a trial of will and self-sacrifice, while the heroine, Vera Pavlova, dreams of utopian cooperative workshops and free love. Karl Marx reportedly learned Russian just so that he could read Chernyshevsky's book.

While the nihilists rejected the decadence and moral decay of Russian society and sought the liberation of the individual, the *narodniki* of the 1860s, strongly influenced by Bakunin and Herzen, offered a program of political action aimed at the eventual overthrow of the tsarist regime. The anarchistic ideas of Bakunin, and Herzen's stress on populism, grew in popularity after their deaths and animated a movement that came to be called "To the People." Eventually the movement evolved into the Socialist Revolutionary party. Responding to Herzen's admonition to "go to the people," more than 2500 students and intellectuals went into the countryside, some to teach and provide health care, others to radicalize the peasants. Much like the handful of American student activists of the 1960s and early 1970s who determined that they must radicalize the "hard hats" and "rednecks" in order to successfully challenge the Establishment, these Russian radicals were received in the villages with suspicion and sometimes violence. Bakunin had predicted that, if properly inspired, the peasants would rise spontaneously in revolt, but the populist campaign failed. The Tsar's secret police made mass arrests, and more than 200 members of the movement were tried and exiled in 1877.

The failure of the peasants to rebel spontaneously prompted some of the radicals to reexamine the course of revolution in Russia. They concluded that what was needed was an effective organization to mobilize the populace for revolution. In 1876, Peter Tkachev published a tract, *Revolution and the State*, in which he argued that the seizure of power must precede the transformation of society. The revolution would not come about as the result of an uprising of the masses, but as a coup engineered by a small, conspiratorial group acting on behalf of the masses. Peter Lavrov and Sergei Nechaev felt that the masses would play a supporting role in the revolution, but that they must be led by a tightly organized band of professional revolutionaries. In *Catechism of a Revolutionary*, Nechaev advocated a revolutionary party organization consisting of highly centralized cells designed to force the masses to revolt. Lavrov predicted that, after a successful revolution, a transitional period of dictatorship would ensue, during which the illiterate, conservative, and deeply religious Russian peasant would be transformed through propaganda and education. The ideas of Lavrov and Nechaev were later adopted and perfected by Lenin and the Bolsheviks.

Others used the failure of the "To the People" experiment to rationalize the use of still more coercive measures. Felix Dzerzhinsky, a dedicated revolutionary who would later become the first chief of the Cheka, Lenin's secret police, advocated creating suffering among the peasants to stimulate them to rise in revolution. Dzerzhinsky and his followers engaged in activities designed to inflict hardship on the peasants, such as setting fire to their fields to induce starvation in the countryside.

Many of the instances of violence in the early 1870s were spontaneous countermeasures against increasingly brutal tactics of the police. By the late 1870s, however, a well-organized conspiratorial anarchist society, the People's Will, had emerged. Members of the People's Will hoped that a few well-chosen terrorist acts would seriously disrupt the excessively centralized tsarist regime and inspire the peasants to rebellion. The People's Will called for Alexander II's death and made numerous bold attempts on his life. In one incident, the Tsar's dining room in the Winter Palace was totally destroyed by explosives, but the Tsar escaped unharmed. In 1878, Vera Zasulich, a member of the People's Will, shot and wounded the military governor of St. Petersburg, who had ordered the flogging of a political prisoner.

Alexander II, besieged by the activities of the anarchists and receiving little sympathy from the public, decided that a more moderate policy might lead to a rapprochement. He appointed Count Mikhail Loris-Melikov Minister of the Interior, instructing him to develop a plan to counteract terrorism. Melikov's proposals called for sweeping reforms to broaden public participation in policy-making. Alexander approved the proposals and was to have signed them into law on the afternoon of March 1, 1881, but he was assassinated on his way to a ceremonial review of the troops that morning. The People's Will had carefully plotted the murder, placing members along all of the routes from the Winter Palace to the parade ground. Each terrorist carried a recently invented device—a nitroglycerin bomb. The two anarchists who lobbed their bombs at Alexander's carriage died instantly in the explosion. The Tsar's legs were blown off by the force of the explosion; he died in the arms of his son and heir, Alexander III, who swore to avenge his father's death by initiating a reign of terror against the anarchists.

FROM REFORM TO REACTION

Alexander III, a dedicated reactionary, was determined to suppress revolution and maintain autocracy at all costs. He instituted counterreforms giving the authorities sweeping powers to deal with the press and political critics of the regime. Summary search, arrest, imprisonment, exile, and secret trials by courts-martial became common. A new university statute of 1884 outlawed student unions and placed the universities under the strict supervision of the Ministry of Education. Alexander II's liberal advisors and ministers resigned in protest and were replaced by well-known conservatives and reactionaries, such as Constantine Pobedonostsev and Dmitrii Tolstoy. Pobedonostsev, tutor to Alexander III and to his successor, Nicholas II, feared Westernization, urbanization, and industrialization because they threatened to bring change. In fact, he once expressed the desire "to keep people from inventing things."[6]

In order to strengthen its hold on the increasingly restive peasants, the regime established the office of *zemskii nachal'nik* (land captain), whose responsibilities included exercising direct control over the peasants throughout the empire. The land captains, who were appointed by the minister of the interior, had the power to approve or disapprove peasants elected to local offices, to override the decisions of the communes, and to fine, arrest, and imprison peasants.

The reactionary character of Alexander III's regime manifested itself in the treatment of non-Orthodox denominations. Roman Catholics and Lutherans, who comprised a majority in some of the western regions, were discriminated against, and campaigns to convert Moslems and Buddhists in Central Asia and the Far East were organized. The most coercive tactics were reserved for the Old Believers, Baptists, and Jews. The Jewish Pale, the area of western Russia in which all Jews had to live, was reduced in size, forcing many families to relocate. Jews were prohibited from farming, thus forcing them into the trades and professions. In 1887, the government imposed quotas on

Jewish enrollment in institutions of higher learning, further restricting their ability to enter various professions. Throughout the late 1800s and early 1900s, violent popular outbreaks against the Jews swept Russia, resulting in the destruction of Jewish property and the deaths of many Jews. These pogroms occurred with the silent consent, if not the active encouragement, of the government. Pobedonostsev, the Tsar's most trusted advisor, once remarked that "the Jewish problem" in Russia would be solved by the conversion to Orthodoxy of a third of the Jews, emigration of another third, and the deaths of the remaining third.[7]

The counterreforms of Alexander III did not come without opposition, however. Despite the stepped-up measures of the secret police, remnants of the People's Will continued their underground activities. In 1887, a group that included Alexander Ulyanov, Lenin's older brother, was arrested and executed for plotting to assassinate the Tsar.

The execution of his brother had a deep, lasting effect on the seventeen-year-old Lenin. Born Vladimir Ilich Ulyanov in Simbirsk in 1870, Lenin was the son of a provincial school inspector.[8] Radicalized by the death of his brother, he began to read the works of the German socialist Karl Marx. After finishing law school at St. Petersburg University, he devoted his time to revolutionary activity. In 1895, he was arrested and exiled to Siberia. In exile, he wrote his first major work, *The Development of Capitalism in Russia*, an attack on the populist ideas of the Socialist Revolutionaries. Lenin held no great admiration for the Russian peasants; his socialism was a product of the rapid industrialization that was transforming Russia into a more modern, capitalist state.

The reigns of the last two Romanov tsars, Alexander III and Nicholas II, were marked by reaction, repression, and a pathological fear of change. Support for the regimes lay almost exclusively with the gentry, whose political and economic power was waning. The provincial governors who controlled the countryside on the Tsar's behalf were a backward group who sought only to preserve their own interests. They were the subject of derision in the satirical writings of noted nineteenth-century Russian authors, including Mikhail Saltykov-Shchedrin and Nikolai Gogol. Saltykov-Shchedrin had himself been deputy governor of Tver and the Ryazan provinces under Alexander II. In *Provincial Sketches*, he portrayed one provincial governor as having a soup bowl in place of a head. Inevitably, the governor stumbled in a rutted street, shattered his "head," and was thereafter condemned to go through life headless—with no perceptible impairment of his mental faculties. Another of Saltykov-Shchedrin's fictional provincial governors, widely hailed as a progressive and forward-thinking man, was found dead one morning, devoured by his own fleas.

Graft and corruption were rampant among the provincial bureaucrats. Saltykov-Shchedrin wrote that it was more prudent to invest in bribes than in bank deposits, because bribes spared one harassment by the authorities, which could be even more costly.[9] Nikolai Gogol's story "The Nose" is a caricature of a provincial bureaucrat so concerned with advancing his own career and elevating his rank that he was transformed into nothing but an uplifted nose.

In 1894, Alexander III died unexpectedly at the relatively young age of 49, leaving his 26-year-old son, Nicholas II, ill-prepared to assume power. Unlike his father, Nicholas lacked the drive, authority, and determination to tackle difficult problems. He proved to be narrow-minded, weak, and—most important—unusually dependent upon the advice of his ministers and aides. Toward the end of Nicholas's reign (1894–1917), the power behind the throne was his wife, the German-born tsarina Alexandra.

The one area of intelligent and farsighted policy under Nicholas II was in the Ministry of Finance, headed by Count Sergei Witte. Witte recognized that in order to remain a strong empire, Russia had to develop its industry and build railroads. Under his direction, heavy industry was developed, and the railroad network doubled in mileage, including the completion of the Trans-Siberian line. Thus, industrialization did not come about spontaneously from the investment of private entrepreneurs, but as the result of government policies and decrees and foreign investment.

The completion of the Trans-Siberian Railroad enabled Russia to engage in more aggressive and adventurous policies in the Far East. These policies culminated in the outbreak of the Russo-Japanese War (1904–1905). The Tsar initially welcomed the onset of the war to distract the public from problems at home, but the war also extracted a heavy price on the already strained economy. In a surprise attack, the Japanese sank the entire Russian Pacific fleet in the harbor of Port Arthur in 1904. The Tsar then dispatched his Baltic fleet to the Pacific. After making the long journey from the Baltic, through the Atlantic, around the Cape of Good Hope, through the Indian Ocean, to the Sea of Japan, the antiquated fleet was destroyed in a single battle. The peace treaty ending the hostilities ceded Korea and the southern half of Sakhalin Island to Japan.

THE REVOLUTION OF 1905

The humiliating loss to the Japanese compounded problems in Russia and resulted in the first popular revolt against the tsarist government—the Revolution of 1905. Opposition to the Tsar's regime had become more hostile and organized toward the turn of the century. A devastating famine in 1891 and 1892 had driven many peasants to the cities in search of employment and food. A formative labor movement began to develop as industrialization took place. By 1900, more than two million industrial workers were concentrated in a few major cities of European Russia.[10] Strikes spread throughout the country, and student protests became more frequent. Sporadic peasant disturbances disrupted rural life and gave added support to the Socialist Revolutionary party, which favored populist and agrarian elements. Some factions of the Party resumed terrorist activities, assassinating several prominent government officials, including Nicholas II's second cousin. In 1902 and 1903, doctors, teachers, and other professional groups began to demand social and political reforms and a voice in the policy-making process.

The labor movement was instrumental in the introduction into Russia of Marxist ideas, advocated by the Social Democratic party. In 1898, Georgii

Plekhanov founded the Social Democratic party, the first Marxist party in Russia. A historic split occurred in the Social Democratic party at the second congress of the Russian Social Democratic Labor Party, held in Brussels and London in 1903. Lenin and his faction, who came to be called the *Bolsheviks* (from *bol'shinstvo*, meaning "majority"), argued that the Party should be tightly organized and composed solely of professional revolutionaries. Lenin strongly opposed incorporating "mere trade unionists," liberals, and others who might blunt the Party's revolutionary objectives. The Mensheviks (from *men'shinstvo*, meaning "minority") preferred a broader, looser party structure, incorporating a wide spectrum of liberal and socialist elements. Lenin's faction carried the argument and thereafter adopted the name Bolshevik.

The Bolsheviks and Mensheviks also clashed over issues of Marxist doctrine. While the Mensheviks maintained that Russia must first proceed through the stage of capitalism before advancing to socialism, the Bolsheviks advocated skipping the capitalist stage of development and proceeding directly to socialism by harnessing and guiding the revolutionary potential of the Russian peasantry.

Russia was on the brink of an explosion on January 22, 1905, when a priest, Father Gapon, led thousands of workers on a march to the Winter Palace to petition Tsar Nicholas II for bread and land. Many of the marchers carried icons and portraits of the Tsar; they were his faithful subjects petitioning him for redress and assistance. The palace guards were ordered to fire on the peaceful, unarmed demonstrators, and they killed 130 people and wounded several hundred others.[11] This incident, known as "Bloody Sunday," forever eradicated the view that the Tsar was a good and honest man who was simply out of touch with the suffering of the Russian people. His government lost all credibility.

The massacre sparked spontaneous strikes and violence throughout the country. For the first time, millions of ordinary Russian citizens took part in a mass movement in opposition to the regime, thus giving support to the more radical parties. Facing increased pressure, Nicholas II declared his intention to convoke a Duma, or Constituent Assembly. He also repealed some of the more coercive legislation relating to non-Orthodox religious groups and ethnic minorities. However, it was a case of too little, too late. Strikes and peasant uprisings continued throughout 1905. The Duma had no real powers and did not satisfy the masses clamoring for the end of autocracy. In the fall, a general strike was called throughout Russia. In the cities, electricity and water were cut off, and railroad service came to a halt. Leadership of the strike was organized by a council (*soviet*) comprised of the heads of the various socialist parties and representatives of the workers. The leader of the strike movement was Lev Bronstein, later known as Leon Trotsky.

Due to the initiative of Count Witte, a manifesto was issued on October 30, 1905, which amounted to a capitulation by the government to the demands of the populace. The manifesto recognized civil liberties, legalized the formation of political parties, and created a Duma with full powers. The manifesto was a tentative step toward transforming the tsarist regime into a constitutional monarchy. In practice, however, these innovations did not significantly impinge on the powers of the Tsar.

Elections were held for the first time in Russian history, and the results were not encouraging to the regime. Of the 497 representatives elected to the Duma, only 10 percent came from the parties of the Right. Both the Socialist Revolutionaries and the Social Democrats boycotted the election, giving the largest bloc of votes to the Constitutional Democrats (Kadets). The First Duma, which convened in May 1906, was dissolved by the Tsar after only seventy-three days of futile bickering and factionalism.

Another round of elections was called; this time, the Socialist Revolutionaries and the Social Democrats participated. Leftist parties increased their representation to approximately 43 percent of the elected representatives. The Second Duma lasted for little more than three months before reaching an impasse with the government over granting immunity to sixteen Social Democratic deputies arrested for treason. On the same day that Nicholas II dissolved the Second Duma, he arbitrarily and unconstitutionally changed the electoral law, justifying his action on the principle that he had the right to abrogate what he had granted. The electoral law was rewritten to reduce drastically peasant and worker representation, while increasing the representation of the gentry.

Having emasculated the Duma, the government initiated its own legislative program. The chief architect of the program was Pyotr Stolypin, Minister of the Interior. Stolypin placed much of the country under martial law. Thousands were imprisoned or executed, and many leading revolutionaries (including Lenin) were forced to flee abroad. Once relative calm had been restored, Stolypin introduced land-reform legislation aimed at counteracting revolutionary influences by granting the peasantry private plots of land. Stolypin hoped that a class of well-to-do peasants would have a stabilizing influence in the countryside. The reform was a partial success, but it did not lead to the calm that Stolypin had anticipated. In 1911, less than one year after the enactment of his agrarian reform, Stolypin was assassinated in the presence of the Tsar by a revolutionary.

THE TWO REVOLUTIONS OF 1917

The domestic difficulties that troubled the tsarist regime at the turn of the century were compounded by the outbreak of World War I in 1914. In the initial days of the war, there was a rapprochement between the government and the public. This soon broke down, however, due to the Tsar's stubborn intransigence in refusing to cooperate with the Duma. Against the advice of his aides and ministers, the Tsar went to the front to command the Russian forces, leaving the capital and the government in the hands of the tsarina, Alexandra, and the infamous monk Grigorii Rasputin. Initially, the war effort went well for the Russians; they advanced through Poland and were pressing toward Hungary when the Germans and Austrians mounted a counteroffensive in May 1915. The Russians were then forced to retreat, surrendering control of the newly won regions as well as of much of the western portion of the empire. There were staggering casualties—two million in 1915 alone.

More than three million civilian refugees retreated with the Russian army, placing an additional burden on the already overcrowded cities and towns.[12]

Famine and disease were widespread throughout the winter of 1916–1917. From March 8 through March 11, 1917, shortages of coal and bread sparked riots and demonstrations in the capital, whose name had been changed from the Germanic "St. Petersburg" to the Slavic version, "Petrograd." Troops sent to quell the disturbances joined forces with the protesters, and all authority collapsed. On March 12, in an effort to restore order, the Duma created a Provisional Government headed first by Prince Lvov and later by Alexander Kerensky, a Socialist Revolutionary. Three days later, on March 15, the Tsar bowed to the inevitable and abdicated his throne. The tsarist regime fell without a single shot being fired.

In Petrograd and in numerous other cities and regions throughout the country, dual sets of political institutions arose: councils created by the Provisional Government, and the workers' councils (soviets), which were formed more or less spontaneously and were dominated by the Mensheviks and Socialist Revolutionaries. Order No. 1 of the executive committee of the Petrograd soviet provided that the military orders of the Provisional Government should be obeyed only if they did not conflict with those of the soviets. Throughout much of 1917, nevertheless, the soviets did not openly oppose the Provisional Government—but neither did they allow it to consolidate power.

Word of the Tsar's abdication reached Lenin, who was in exile in Zurich. He had spent most of the war years there, having been declared persona non grata by the Tsar's secret police. Ironically, Lenin had confessed in a lecture just two months earlier: "We of the older generation may not live to see the decisive battles of this coming revolution."[13] Upon hearing the news of the collapse of the Tsar's government, Lenin set out for Russia with the assistance of the Germans, who were more than happy to provide a special train to transport him through the war zone. Lenin arrived at the Finland Station in Petrograd on April 16 and was met by a huge throng. On the train platform, he made a speech demanding that the Bolsheviks and their followers oppose the Provisional Government. In his April Theses, Lenin reiterated his call for opposition to the Provisional Government and declared, "All Power to the Soviets!" That is, he recognized the legitimacy of the soviets and hoped to transform them into revolutionary institutions dominated by the Bolsheviks.

Throughout 1917, the population was demanding "peace, bread, and land"—but the Provisional Government was reluctant to withdraw from the war and to redistribute land without first obtaining a mandate from the people. Chaos and the collapse of all civilian authority, however, made holding elections extremely difficult. In July 1917, Kerensky's vacillation and inaction led to an attempt by the Bolsheviks to overthrow the Provisional Government.

During the July Days affair, soldiers and sailors, together with the Bolsheviks, tried to seize power in Petrograd. However, the Petrograd soviet, which was then dominated by Mensheviks, remained loyal to the Provisional Government. Kerensky used the police to root out his opponents, forcing Lenin to flee to Finland, where he continued to direct the Bolsheviks. The Provisional Government moved its base of operations to the former Winter Palace—a decision of immense symbolic importance. The July Days episode left Lenin more convinced than ever that a successful revolution in Russia could not occur as a spontaneous popular uprising; it must be the work of a tightly organized, conspiratorial band of professional revolutionaries. His efforts from July through the autumn of 1917 were devoted to creating such an organization.

Meanwhile the Provisional Government continued to promote the war effort and refused to recognize the redistribution of land going on in the countryside. Finally, on the night of October 25 (November 7 on the new calendar), the battleship *Aurora*, moored in the Neva River across from the Winter Palace, fired a signal.* Bolshevik-led troops from the Petrograd garrison and sailors from Kronstadt stormed the palace. A handful of people were killed in the unsuccessful attempts of the Provisional Government to resist what was in essence a palace coup. Two days later, the Bolsheviks formed the Council of People's Commissars, headed by Lenin, who had returned to Petrograd.[14]

The new regime acted quickly to redistribute land and secure peace—the two pressing needs that the Provisional Government had been unwilling or unable to fulfill. A decree of November 8 transferred all private and church lands to the state and granted peasants as much land as they could till. This decree merely ratified what was already occurring in the countryside, where peasants were ransacking the large estates of the gentry and confiscating the land and personal property for their own use. On December 5, a preliminary armistice agreement with the Germans was reached at Brest-Litovsk.

A number of social reforms were quickly instituted, destroying any vestiges of the old regime. The marriage and divorce laws were repealed, and only civil marriages were recognized; the Gregorian calendar was adopted; and the Cyrillic alphabet was simplified. The government proclaimed the separation of church and state, and placed all former parochial schools under secular control. Banks were nationalized, and large factories were placed under the direction of workers' committees. Revolutionary tribunals replaced the tsarist judicial system and were instructed to decide cases based on "revolutionary conscience and the revolutionary concept of justice."[15]

The Constituent Assembly, in which the Socialist Revolutionaries held an absolute majority, was disbanded. The Bolsheviks solidified their control of the soviets, which sprang up in most cities, towns, villages, and rural districts. The Cheka (Extraordinary Commission to Combat Counterrevolution), a secret police organization under the direction of Felix Dzerzhinsky, was authorized to hunt down Constitutional Democrats, Socialist Revolutionaries, Mensheviks, and other "counterrevolutionaries." Lavrov's prediction of a transitional dictatorship was rapidly becoming a reality.

---

*At the time of the Revolution, Russia still used the Julian calendar. In 1918, the Gregorian calendar was adopted, and today the Great October Revolution is actually celebrated on November 7.

THE CIVIL WAR: 1918–1921

The Russian Revolution arrived in the countryside not through the popular uprising of the peasants, but by telegraph. After the collapse of the tsarist regime, most areas of the empire were not in the firm hands of the Bolsheviks, but were experiencing the breakdown of all civil authority. Many of the ethnic nationalities seized this opportunity to assert their national independence.

Counterrevolutionaries, frequently referred to as the White forces, resisted Bolshevik attempts to consolidate their hold on the country. The Whites consisted of army officers, members of the bourgeois class of merchants, and a wide array of political groups, including reactionary monarchists on the extreme right and Socialist Revolutionaries on the left. The struggle of these White forces with the Reds culminated in a civil war that ravaged Russia from 1918 to 1921.

The Civil War was complicated by foreign interventions and a war with Poland. In 1918, troops from fourteen countries (primarily Japan, Great Britain, France, and the United States) landed at various ports in Russia. The intervention was supposedly intended to prevent war materiel from falling into the hands of the Germans, with whom the Western powers were still fighting. However, there is little question that the primary aim of the intervention was to lend assistance to the White forces trying to topple the Bolsheviks. The Allied intervention, an episode that every Soviet student learns about at an early age, reinforced the Bolsheviks' fears of capitalist encirclement—that the capitalist powers would go to any length to reverse socialist successes.

The defeat of Kolchak's army in the East in late 1919 led to the withdrawal of all Allied forces from Siberia, with the exception of the Japanese, who maintained troops in the far eastern region until October 1922. In the Ukraine, the Caucasus, and the north, Allied armies began to withdraw in late 1919 and by 1920 the Bolsheviks were in control of virtually the entire country, except for isolated pockets of White resistance. By 1921, the Bolshevik victory was complete.

In the first heady days of the Russian Revolution, the Bolsheviks believed that it would be a catalyst, inspiring the workers of Germany, Great Britain, France, and the United States to rise up and overthrow their governments. Trotsky, who assumed the title of Foreign Commissar, glibly pronounced that his job would be exceedingly easy: all he would have to do was issue a few revolutionary proclamations and then close up shop. Once the worldwide socialist revolution came, there would be no need for diplomats or foreign commissariats. Revolutionary activity was strong elsewhere. In Germany, the Social Democratic Party and the Spartakus League commanded a large following, especially among the industrial laborers. In late 1918, a coalition of leftist parties staged an attempted revolution in Berlin. Two of the movement's leaders, Karl Liebknecht and Rosa Luxemburg, were assassinated, however, and the police crushed the abortive revolution. The failure of the German revolution shocked Lenin and the other Bolshevik leaders, who gradually came to realize that they might remain the only socialist state in a world dominated by capitalist powers.

In 1919, the Third Communist International (Comintern) was convened in Moscow. Marxist parties from many countries sent representatives to be "officially recognized" by the Comintern leadership. Headed by Lenin's associate Grigorii Zinoviev, the Comintern proclaimed its intention to foster international revolution.

THE NEW ECONOMIC POLICY (NEP): 1921–1928

The end of the Civil War brought a much-needed period of reconstruction. World War I, the revolutions of 1917, and the Civil War wreaked havoc on Russian society and on the economy. Industrial production had fallen to only 14 percent of pre-World War I levels; steel production fell to just 5 percent of prewar levels.[16] The fields lay untended, and what little agricultural production the peasants were able to carry out was done for their own consumption. Few agricultural commodities made their way to the cities.

Lenin recognized that a new direction was required. Resurrecting an earlier doctrine, he advocated "taking one step forward, two steps back." In other words, the Bolsheviks had achieved a major step forward with the Revolution, but now they needed to retreat from socialist revolutionary goals, at least temporarily, in order to gain the support of the peasants. Lenin introduced the New Economic Policy (NEP) to restore order, consolidate Bolshevik political gains, and reconstruct the devastated economy. The New Economic Policy represented a partial restoration of capitalism. Peasants were granted the right to farm their own plots, and small- and medium-sized industries were allowed to function much as they had prior to the Revolution. The commanding heights of the economy, however, remained in the hands of the State.

The agricultural problem was exacerbated by drought and famine in 1921 and 1922. Lenin appealed to the League of Nations for humanitarian relief for his fledgling government, but aid was denied. The United States, under the leadership of President Herbert Hoover, provided some aid for victims of the famine. American businessman Armand Hammer (later chief of Occidental Petroleum) also organized a relief mission to deliver food and medical supplies to Russia. Hammer met Lenin in Russia, and continued to maintain close personal contacts with Soviet leaders until his death in 1990.

NEP also entailed a relaxation in social policies. Censorship was lifted, and the arts flourished. After a long period of suppression and turmoil, the creative energies of Russian society were released. There was a heady sense of being part of a new social experiment, of creating a just and equitable social order. Aleksandra Kollontai, the outspoken Bolshevik authority on the "women's question," advocated the abolition of marriage and the communal rearing of children. In her view, children were "the common possession of all the workers."[17] During the NEP period, women achieved their first real prominence in the arts and other professions.

NEP also spawned the futurist and the constructivist schools of art and literature. The former depicted the glorious future society that would be created by the new socialist order. The latter group applied their artistic talents and abilities in the service of the Revolution by constructing futuristic buildings and designing factories that incorporated revolutionary concepts of architecture.

The regime was continually troubled by internal political dissension. In March 1921, the sailors at Kronstadt mutinied and had to be put down by garrisons of the Red Guards. Within the Party, opposition to NEP emerged. To many, NEP represented an unacceptable retreat from the gains the Bolsheviks had achieved in the Revolution. Others, called the Workers' Opposition, who were closely aligned with Trotsky, criticized the increasing centralization of power and favored turning power over to the trade unions. All of these divergent views erupted at the Tenth Party Congress in March 1921. In an attempt to silence his critics, Lenin hammered through the Decree on Party Unity, which prohibited the formation of political factions to oppose party policies. In sum, the decree supported relatively open discussion of policies before they were ratified by the Party, but outlawed any criticism of policies once they were enacted. The decree, however, prohibited the existence of factions with their own organizations and policy goals. Furthermore, the Central Committee was given the power to expel party members who violated this rule. The decree was used to silence Lenin's critics, and it succeeded for a short time.

In 1922, with the New Economic Policy scarcely underway, Lenin suffered a debilitating stroke. Joseph Stalin at that time occupied the post of General Secretary of the Central Committee, a largely bureaucratic position responsible for the management of internal party affairs. Nevertheless, Stalin used his powers to recruit and dismiss party members, thereby strengthening his position among the ruling elite. In fact, Stalin's tactics were so ruthless that Lenin wrote a letter from his deathbed to his comrades on the Central Committee, warning them of Stalin's dangerous ambitions. On January 21, 1924, Lenin died, and the regime confronted its first succession crisis.

FROM AUTOCRACY TO AUTOCRACY

The cycle of rebellion and repression, and of revolution and counterrevolution, that had characterized Russia throughout the nineteenth century continued into the twentieth. It is ironic that the Bolsheviks, who succeeded in overthrowing the tsarist autocracy, should witness the methodical and relentless reinstitution of autocratic dictatorship under Stalin.

Stalin moved quickly to divide Lenin's successors. First, he split with Trotsky over the issue of supporting international revolution. Whereas Trotsky saw the main hope for socialism in worldwide revolution, Stalin reflected more nationalistic sentiments and favored "socialism in one country." The left and right also disagreed in their stances toward NEP. Trotsky, Grigorii Zinoviev, and Lev Kamenev denounced the NEP as a retreat from the gains of the Revolution, while Nikolai Bukharin, Mikhail Tomsky, and Aleksei Rykov allied themselves with Stalin in support of NEP. Stalin launched an attack first on Trotsky, then on Zinoviev, then on Kamenev on the left. In 1926, Trotsky was forced to resign as War Commissar, and the next year he and Zinoviev were removed from the Party. In 1928, Trotsky fled into exile. (Still troublesome even in exile, he was assassinated in Mexico City in 1940.) Having defeated his adversaries on the left, Stalin then turned on his former allies on the right.

At the Fifteenth Party Congress in December 1927, Stalin declared that the economy had been restored to prewar levels and that the next task was to undertake bold new directions. He advocated the amalgamation of small peasant farms into large-scale agricultural enterprises and the vigorous construction of new industry. Stalin's departure from NEP alarmed Bukharin and other members of the right, who supported the construction of socialism, but "at a snail's pace."

During the 1920s, Stalin demonstrated remarkable flexibility in manipulating policies and forming alliances with various factions in order to isolate and defeat his adversaries. He also used his position as General Secretary of the Party to promote loyal followers into influential positions. Stalin was a preeminent organizational infighter, and it was exactly this cunning and ruthless drive for power that had prompted Lenin to advise his comrades to find a way to remove him.

Having eliminated all major opposition, Stalin emerged in the 1930s as a bold and forceful leader committed to expanding the Soviet Union's industrial might as rapidly as possible. Although he was fond of comparing himself to Peter the Great and Ivan the Terrible, his autocratic rule was not a simple return to tsarist autocracy. Stalin's regime was a twentieth-century form of dictatorship. Technological advances in mass communications, the development of more effective social and governmental organizations, and the emergence of a modern industrial economy allowed him to extend dictatorial control over the country more completely than any previous ruler had. Furthermore, his power was strengthened by the development of an elaborate ideology that eventually became transformed into a personality cult. The utopian goals of the Bolshevik Revolution were crushed under the weight of Stalin's authoritarian regime. What emerged formed the foundation of the political system of the Soviet Union that would endure for more than three decades after his death—until the rise of Mikhail Gorbachev.

Notes

1. Nicholas V. Riasanovsky, *A History of Russia*, 2d ed. (New York: Oxford University Press, 1969), 357.

2. It is noteworthy that Lenin came into contact with the ideas of the *narodniki* before he was exposed to the works of Marx.

3. The figures are those of Vasilii Ivanovich Senaevsky, cited in Riasanovsky, *A History of Russia*, 410.

4. One dessiatin equals 2.7 acres. The statistics are those of Petr Ivanovich Liashchenko, cited in Riasanovsky, *A History of Russia*, 414.

5. See Ivan Turgenev, *Fathers and Sons* (Moscow: Progress Publishers, 1977).

6. Cited in Riasanovsky, *A History of Russia*, 434.

7. Ibid., 437.

8. Pseudonyms were commonly employed by Russian revolutionary leaders to protect them from persecution by the police. The name "Lenin" comes from the Lena River in Siberia.

9. Mikhail Saltykov-Shchedrin cited in Richard Pipes, *Russia under the Old Regime* (London: Weidenfeld and Nicolson, 1974), 284–285.

10. Riasanovsky, *A History of Russia*, 474.

11. Ibid., 451.

12. Donald W. Treadgold, *Twentieth-Century Russia*, 2d ed. (Chicago: Rand McNally, 1964), 116.

13. Cited in Edmund Wilson, *To the Finland Station* (New York: Farrar, Straus, and Giroux, 1972), 533.

14. The term "people's commissar" was chosen rather than the more traditional "minister" because of the latter's association with the tsarist regime.

15. Decree of D. S. Kurskii, cited in Peter H. Juviler, *Revolutionary Law and Order* (New York: Free Press, 1976), 21.

16. Treadgold, *Twentieth-Century Russia*, 200.

17. Cited in Theodore H. Von Laue, *Why Lenin? Why Stalin?* (Philadelphia: Lippincott, 1971), 159.

Selected Bibliography

Berdyaev, Nicolas. *The Origin of Russian Communism*. London: Geoffrey Bles, 1937.

Brinton, Crane. *The Anatomy of Revolution*. New York: Vintage, 1952.

Carr, E. H. *A History of Soviet Russia*. London: Macmillan, 1950–1953.

Conquest, Robert. *The Harvest of Sorrow*. New York: Oxford University Press, 1986.

Fainsod, Merle. *How Russia Is Ruled*. Cambridge: Harvard University Press, 1953.

Herzen, Alexander. *My Past and Thoughts*. New York: Alfred S. Knopf, 1973.

Pipes, Richard. *Russia under the Old Regime*. London: Weidenfeld and Nicolson, 1974.

Pipes, Richard. *The Russian Revolution*. New York: Alfred A. Knopf, 1990.

Rabinowitch, Alexander. *Prelude to Revolution*. Bloomington: Indiana University Press, 1968.

Reed, John. *Ten Days That Shook the World*. New York: International Publishers, 1919.

Riasanovsky, Nicholas V. *A History of Russia*. 2d ed. New York: Oxford University Press, 1969.

Schapiro, Leonard. *The Origin of Communist Autocracy*. Cambridge: Harvard University Press, 1955.

Solzhenitsyn, Alexander. *Lenin in Zurich*. New York: Farrar, Straus, and Giroux, 1976.

Treadgold, Donald W. *Twentieth-Century Russia*. 2d ed. Chicago: Rand McNally, 1964.

Ulam, Adam. *The Bolsheviks*. New York: Macmillan, 1965.

Von Laue, Theodore H. *Why Lenin? Why Stalin?* 2d ed. Philadelphia: Lippincott, 1971.

Wilson, Edmund. *To the Finland Station*. New York: Farrar, Straus, and Giroux, 1972.

Wolfe, Bertram D. *Three Who Made a Revolution*. New York: Dell Publishing, 1948.

3

Stalinism, Stagnation, and the Mandate for Reform

More than any other figure, Stalin was the architect of the Soviet political system. He shaped the massive bureaucratic apparatus to bring the economy under his command. He transformed the Party from a diverse array of more-or-less free-thinking leftist intellectuals into a tightly controlled and monolithic force, subservient to his will. He destroyed the "rural mentality" of the Russian peasant through collectivization. He harnessed virtually every resource in his headlong drive to develop and modernize the Soviet Union. He led the people through the traumas of the Great Patriotic War and supervised the postwar reconstruction. If Stalin is immortalized as larger than life, it is because he *seems* larger than life—a man of excesses, given to both brutality and gentleness, resolute yet paranoid. Stalin was as contradictory as the society over which he ruled.

STALIN, THE *VOZHD'*

Between 1928 and 1953 Stalin revolutionized Soviet society. Yet in many ways his policies marked a retreat from the revolutionary goals of Bolshevik socialism. He rejected the idealism of the early revolutionary period, with its emphasis on world revolution, and instead favored the development of "socialism in one country." Not only did this policy represent a radical departure from Lenin's support of a worldwide proletarian revolution; it also meant that the Soviet state had to develop its own economic base without relying on external support. Such a task called for the creation of a massive organizational infrastructure to harness the energies of the nation. Stalin was a master of organization and mobilization. Drawing on his experience as Commissar of Nationalities and then as General Secretary of the Communist Party of the Soviet Union (CPSU), responsible for managing party affairs, he built a command structure that centralized power in his hands.

By 1928, NEP had fulfilled its purpose of restoring the country to prewar levels of production in most sectors of the economy. But NEP was also plagued by many problems: unemployment, income inequalities, and peasant resistance to central authority. The leadership recognized its tenuous hold on power, especially in rural areas. In 1927 and 1928, peasants became unwilling to sell grain to the government at the officially set prices. Chronic shortages of consumer goods meant that there was little for the peasants to buy. Instead of selling their produce, they hoarded their grain, waiting for higher prices, or fed it to their own livestock. The result was a serious shortage of food in the cities, which resulted in rationing.

Stalin blamed the unraveling economic situation on the wealthy peasants or *kulakhs* and launched a series of "extraordinary measures" of grain procurement. He traveled to the Urals and Siberia in January 1928 and personally supervised the forced seizure of grain in what came to be called the "Urals-Siberian" method of grain requisitioning.

In industry, the introduction of the First Five-Year Plan in 1928 facilitated the transfer of materials, equipment, and labor to high-priority factories and construction sites. Consumer production all but ceased as every available resource was pressed into the program of rapid industrial expansion in capital-intensive heavy industries (e.g., steel, coal, and machinery).

In April 1929 Stalin proclaimed the goal of "catching up and then overtaking the level of industrial development of the advanced capitalist countries in a relatively short period."[1] Under the First Five-Year Plan, industrial output was slated to increase by 180 percent, investment by 228 percent, consumption by 70 percent, and agricultural output by 55 percent.[2] Those who warned that such targets were unrealistic were branded "right-deviationists" and subject to arrest for treason.

Virtually all the resources of Soviet society were mobilized to support Stalin's development program. With such slogans as "There are no fortresses Bolsheviks cannot storm!" workers constructed mammoth hydroelectric dams, forged steel, and dug irrigation canals. Artists and writers were directed to portray "the glories of labor" and forsake the artistic experimentation that had characterized the NEP period. Some Soviet citizens became so imbued with the spirit of industrialization in the 1920s and 1930s that they gave their children such unlikely names as Elektrosila (Electric Power), Dynamo, Traktor, or MEL (in honor of Marx, Engels, and Lenin).

The First Five-Year Plan was declared fulfilled by the end of 1932—a full year ahead of schedule. Productivity was low, resources were wasted, and sound economic principles were disregarded; nevertheless, the First Five-Year Plan had achieved notable successes. Stalin hailed these achievements and unveiled the Second Five-Year Plan, an even more ambitious program for industrial growth.

In many respects, Stalin's policies of rapid growth and economic development were successful. From 1928 through the mid-1930s, the average annual increase in the Soviet national income was estimated at 14 to 18 percent. In contrast, during the most intensive period of industrialization in the United States, from 1865 to 1914, the economy grew at a rate of only 5 percent per year. GNP growth rates in Germany and Japan since 1960—8 and 9 percent, respectively—come closest to matching Soviet performance.[3]

The Stalinist economic policies favored extensive growth—that is, growth by increasing inputs: labor, raw materials, factories and plants, and investment capital. With a large pool of unemployed or underemployed workers, seemingly endless supplies of oil, gas, coal, and other raw materials, ample land for cultivation, and capital squeezed from the rural sector through collectivization, Soviet planners during the 1930s and 1940s treated inputs as virtually infinite and inexhaustible.

Exhortations were made to workers to throw themselves into their work for the sake of "building socialism." One Ukrainian coal miner, Alexei Stakhanov, supposedly overfulfilled his work norm fourteen-fold in a single work shift and consequently became a folk hero. Other workers were urged to become "Stakhanovites" of labor, but such campaigns and "storming" led to the widespread waste of resources, publicity-seeking, and falsification of labor records.

The extension of planning to every sector of the economy necessitated the creation of a massive administrative apparatus. Gosplan, the state planning agency, which had been established in 1921 to oversee economic performance and to issue general "control" figures for the most prominent sectors, grew rapidly in size and influence. Ministries were created with responsibilities for supervising every branch of industry, as well as for the allocation of housing and other social benefits to workers. Production directives flowed from the center downward through a strict hierarchy that left little leeway for discretion or initiative to plant managers. In essence, Stalin placed the Soviet economy on a wartime footing, reminiscent of war communism. The private sector that had flourished under NEP was systematically eliminated, and resources were diverted to heavy industry.

The only sector of the Soviet economy capable of financing this industrialization drive was agriculture. In 1928 more than 97 percent of the farmland was in the hands of individual peasant farmers.[4] The experience with peasant hoarding convinced Stalin that more coercive measures of forced requisitioning were necessary. Compulsory collectivization was his answer for extending party–state control over the peasants. To redirect the predictable hostile response of the peasants to collectivization, Stalin proclaimed war on the wealthier peasants, the *kulakhs*. The *kulakhs*, who constituted only some 3 to 4 percent of all farmers, employed no one and owned, at most, three cows and three mules or horses. Nevertheless, on December 27, 1929, Stalin issued a decree calling for the "liquidation of the *kulakhs* as a class."[5] The result was a virtual civil war in the countryside, as the land, cattle, and equipment of the *kulakhs* were redistributed to the poorer peasants only to be taken over by collectives. Peasant resistance was widespread. Many peasants burned their crops and slaughtered their cattle rather than hand them over to the collectives. Some twelve million people who resisted collectivization were deported to Siberia, and another one million were sent to labor camps.[6] Robert Conquest estimates that in the famine that followed collectivization an additional seven million people died from hunger in 1932 and 1933 alone.[7]

The crisis in the countryside prompted many able-bodied young men to leave and move to the cities, where they could find work in the rapidly developing industrial economy. In 1926, prior to Stalin's introduction of collectivization, 86.7 percent of the Soviet population lived in towns and villages of fewer than 15,000. By 1953, the rural population had decreased to only 58.1 percent.[8] In 1931 alone some four million peasants moved to the cities.[9]

Despite the resistance, Stalin's brutal methods achieved results. During the period from 1928 to 1931, 25 million peasant farms—some 60 percent of all peasant households—were forcibly combined into 250,000 collective farms (*kolkhozy*)—one or two per village.[10] Agricultural machinery, formerly the property of individual peasants, was pooled in state-directed machine-tractor stations (MTS); land and cattle were held in common ownership by the collective. Collective farms were required to deliver a large portion of their produce to the State at centrally set low prices. Crops were requisitioned to feed the rapidly growing urban labor force or exported for hard currency to buy Western equipment. At the same time, by organizing the peasants into state-controlled collectives, Stalin destroyed any vestiges of economic and political resistance to his regime that remained in the rural areas.

In late 1930 Stalin slowed the pace of collectivization. In his article entitled "Dizzy with Success" published in *Pravda*, Stalin criticized those who carried out his policies with excessive zeal. Peasants took advantage of this temporary lull in pressure and left the collectives by the millions. The percentage of peasant households in collectives quickly fell to 23 percent.[11] But presssure was soon reasserted, and by 1936, 90 percent of all farms had been collectivized.[12]

Stalin's drive to modernize the Soviet economy must be viewed in the light of international conditions. In the late 1920s and early 1930s the Western capitalist nations were in the throes of the Depression, faced with mass unemployment, industrial decline, and financial collapse. Whatever faults may have been found in Stalin's ambitious economic programs must have seemed minor by comparison. As the 1930s progressed, the Soviet Union became increasingly isolated and threatened by hostile capitalist powers. One of Stalin's few ideological contributions to Marxist-Leninist theory held that the class struggle would intensify as society approached socialism. This doctrine alerted the regime to the increasing threat of enemies both internal and external. In his famous 1931 speech entitled "The Jungle Law of Capitalism" Stalin noted that the USSR lagged behind Germany and the United States by some 50 to 100 years. Furthermore, he predicted that if the USSR did not catch up in just ten years, the Soviet Union would not survive. In 1933 Hitler came to power in Germany, and ten years after the "Jungle Law" speech, Nazi forces invaded the USSR.

Not only did collectivization and forced industrialization revolutionize the rural areas, they unleashed a cultural revolution on Soviet society. The peasants, the young communists, and the rapidly growing urban industrial labor class waged open warfare on the old intelligentsia. Old Bolsheviks, those who had joined the Party prior to 1917, were purged from the Party and many were deported to Siberia.

The whole society began to work on a command basis. Internal passports were issued in 1932 to cut down on workers moving from one job to another, and labor books were introduced to record an individual's work record. Collective farmers were not issued internal passports and were, thus, not able to leave their farms. Criminal penalties were imposed for labor violations. The death penalty was extended to various economic offenses such as hoarding of silver coins, "wrecking" (sabotage), negligence resulting in damage of state property, and theft of public property. Absenteeism or chronic tardiness in appearing for work was interpreted as an act against the state and punished by up to five years in prison. Persons over the age of twelve could be tried as adults in criminal cases. In line with Stalin's conservative family policies, abortions were outlawed except in cases of medical necessity, and laws on divorce were made much more restrictive.

The introduction of centralized economic planning and the drive for rapid industrialization and collectivization of agriculture destroyed the relative diversity and eclecticism of the arts in the Soviet Union. Signs of a monolithic official cultural doctrine were already evident by 1932, when a party decree "On the Reconstruction of Literary and Artistic Organizations" established exclusive unions for artists, writers, musicians, and architects. All privately or cooperatively owned printing presses were brought under the centralized control of the Association of State Publishing Houses, thus facilitating the work of the censors. Two years later, at a congress of the Union of Soviet Writers, Stalin imposed the concept of "socialist realism." A resolution adopted at the congress affirmed: "We must depict reality in its revolutionary development and create works with a high level of craftsmanship, with high ideological and artistic content."[13] The content of socialist realism, whether in the graphic arts or literature, centered around the glorification of the workers and the peasants, on the one hand, and the glorification of Lenin and Stalin on the other. An anonymous observer defined socialist realism more caustically as "a method of portraying our leaders in a way they will understand."[14] However defined, socialist realism was the sole official cultural policy for at least the next twenty years.

Socialist realist novels such as Nikolai Ostrovsky's *How the Steel Was Tempered* and F. V. Gladkov's *Cement* played on the themes of heroism and selfless striving for the goals of the society. Artists produced murals, posters, and other public art that depicted men with bulging muscles working in steel mills and women (also with bulging muscles) working in the fields or milking cows. Perhaps the closest equivalent in the United States to socialist realist art are the WPA murals painted in many public buildings during the Depression.

A new official class was promoted into positions of authority in party and state institutions, owing their careers to Stalin and his top advisors. In contrast to the early years of the Soviet regime, when men and women of insight and intellect engaged in lively debates over political, economic, and social policies, Stalin introduced a climate of intellectual chill. Gone were the days of debate and experimentation. In virtually every sphere of life there evolved one organization, one doctrine, one correct position. The people who rose in this system were not the most intelligent, nor the most competent. Rather they were elevated primarily due to their loyalty to the *Vozhd'*, or leader. For their loyalty, they were rewarded with appointments to powerful posts, nice apartments, summer cottages, and access to "closed stores" that sold goods unavailable on the open market.

By the mid-1930s the pressure on Soviet society had taken a heavy toll. The country was impoverished and exhausted. In the cities there were lines for food, rationing, rapidly rising prices, and a chronic housing shortage. It was quite common for three or four families to be housed in a single room. In the midst of these conditions, Stalin delivered a speech in which he asserted,

"It is clear that the workers' living standards are rising all the time. Anyone who denies this is an enemy of Soviet power."[15] Not only did the citizens have to endure the hardships that Stalin's policies inflicted, but they had to deny the very existence of those hardships.

At the Seventeenth Party Congress in early 1934, dubbed the "Congress of Victors," Stalin was hailed as the "architect of our victories." Former opponents, such as Tomsky and Preobrazhensky, admitted their errors and Stalin appeared to be in complete control. Sergei Kirov, the popular party chief of Leningrad, delivered a major address to the Congress in which he hailed the success of Stalin's policies and implied that now the pressures could be relaxed. In the subsequent election of a new Central Committee, Kirov received more votes than Stalin, but Lazar Kaganovich, Stalin's trusted lieutenant, falsified the results. Nevertheless, Stalin feared Kirov's rising popularity. In December 1934 Kirov was assassinated in his Leningrad office under mysterious circumstances. Stalin rushed to Leningrad to supervise the investigation into the murder—a murder which many historians believe he had ordered. Summary executions and mass arrests and deportations followed. Stalin used the incident as an excuse to launch a violent campaign against his opponents. Grigorii Zinoviev and Lev Kamenev, Stalin's chief opponents in the Politburo, were arrested, and local and regional party organizations were ordered to expel former members of the Trotsky and Zinoviev oppositions. Those eliminated from the party ranks tended to be Old Bolsheviks (those who had joined the Party prior to 1917) and middle-ranking party and state officials. During the wave of purges, the Party declined by about half a million members.[16] Many of those expelled from the Party were subsequently accused of crimes against the State and disappeared into the Gulag (prison-camp system), never to emerge. The camps swelled to the millions and became a major resource in the economy. Most of the showplaces of Moscow—the subway stations, Moscow University, and ironically, even the new KGB offices (Lubianka) were built with convict labor.

Under Stalin's lead, the secret police were authorized to shoot their victims without trial, most frequently for supposedly sabotaging Stalin's economic campaigns. Among those secretly tried and executed and those executed without trial were bacteriologists charged with causing an epidemic among horses; officials of the food industry charged with sabotaging food supplies; and several agricultural experts, state farm officials, and academics accused of mismanagement and "wrecking." Higher-level officials charged with sabotage were treated to elaborate show trials at which most confessed after long periods of interrogation and torture by the secret police.

In April 1935 a new provision was introduced into the law that extended criminal penalties including execution, to children as young as twelve. The purpose of the law was to allow police interrogators to threaten those under investigation with the prosecution of their children.

The terror culminated in three major show trials of Stalin's political rivals during the period from 1936 to 1938. The first trial began on August 19, 1936. Sixteen persons, including Zinoviev and Kamenev, were charged with being members of a Trotskyite terrorist circle. The trial was held in the October Hall of the House of Trade Unions and heard by the Military Collegium of the Supreme Court. The audience consisted of a group of carefully selected, well-rehearsed employees of the secret police (NKVD) and approximately thirty foreign journalists and diplomats.[17] With only two exceptions, the accused pleaded guilty to a long list of charges, including organizing the murder of Kirov and plotting the murder of Stalin and several other members of the Presidium. No evidence was offered in the trials other than the confessions wrested from the accused while they were held by the secret police. All were convicted and executed within 24 hours. No appeals were permitted.

With Zinoviev eliminated, Stalin turned his attention to two remaining adversaries, Bukharin and Rykov. Before plotting their elaborate show trials, however, he first dismissed Henry Yagoda as head of the NKVD and replaced him with Nikolai Ezhov. Six months after his dismissal, Yagoda was arrested, and he was later tried and executed. He thus carried to his grave extensive knowledge of Stalin's involvement in Kirov's murder and countless other atrocities.

The second major show trial took place in Moscow in January 1937. Among the seventeen persons arraigned were Gregori Pyatakov, Deputy Commissar for Heavy Industry, and the publicist Karl Radek. In a new twist, many of the defendants were accused of economic sabotage (wrecking trains, introducing gas into coal mines, and so on). All were found guilty, and most were shot.

Throughout 1937, Ezhov rounded up and liquidated Yagoda's former senior subordinates in the NKVD. More than 3000 NKVD officers were executed in 1937 alone.[18] Many others committed suicide, some by leaping from the windows of their Lubianka offices in full view of the Moscow populace. The purge, known as the *Ezhovshchina* after the newly appointed secret police chief, reached a climax in May through September 1937. Arrests, exile, imprisonment, and execution affected all sections of the population, but focused especially on the elite.

The purge did not spare foreign residents in the USSR. Polish and German Communists who had sought refuge in the Soviet Union because their parties were illegal in their home countries were arrested and imprisoned or shot. Conversely, the *Ezhovshchina* liquidated Soviet citizens who had become contaminated by contact with the West. Diplomatic officials and NKVD spies abroad were ordered or lured back to Moscow for arrest; those who refused to return to the USSR were marked for assassination.

One estimate places the number of arrests in 1937 and 1938 at seven million, and at least five million people had been arrested prior to the *Ezhovshchina*. Some two million persons probably perished in forced labor camps during 1937 and 1938.[19]

Ezhov's demise came in late 1938, but the facts surrounding his disappearance and death are still unclear. The Georgian deputy chief of the NKVD, Laventri Beria, assumed the post vacated by Ezhov in December 1938. Following Ezhov's precedent, Beria eliminated most of the high-ranking officials in the NKVD and replaced them with his own trusted clients from the Caucasus.

The German invasion of the Soviet Union in 1941 caught Stalin by surprise, despite the numerous reports and warnings of diplomats and NKVD agents in Germany and Japan. During the first year of fighting, the Soviet forces were in steady retreat. More than one-quarter of the European portion of the USSR fell to the Germans, including major agricultural and industrial regions. Leningrad, a city of some four million people, was encircled by Nazi troops; supplies were almost completely cut off, and Hitler ordered his forces to starve the city into submission. More than 750,000 people died during the three-year siege of Leningrad, most of them civilian casualties.[20] One survivor reported that his family endured the siege only because his father worked in a post office and they were able to eat the glue used to seal packages. Pets were eaten, and there were even reports of isolated cases of cannibalism, as the city endured the brutal winter of 1943.

As the tide of war turned after the battle of Stalingrad, the NKVD faced a new responsibility—the execution and imprisonment of Red Army soldiers who had fallen into German hands. Many Soviet soldiers were liberated from German concentration camps only to be charged with collaboration and thrown into similar facilities in the USSR.

Some inmates of the Gulag were offered the opportunity to earn their freedom by fighting in the so-called *shtrafnoi* battalions (i.e., penal battalions), which were often used to spearhead military offensives. Only a fraction of the members of the battalions survived these charges; they were then reconstituted into new battalions, and so on, until the end of the war.

The impact of World War II was profound not only on the wartime generations, but also on Soviet citizens born long after the conflict. The extent of the devastation was staggering: 20 to 25 million casualties, one-quarter of all housing destroyed, 25 million homeless, half of the USSR's railway network demolished, and a large portion of its industries destroyed.[21]

The postwar reconstruction brought the reimposition of strict controls. A resolution of the CPSU Central Committee in August 1946 initiated a campaign against Mikhail Zoshchenko, Anna Akhmatova, and other writers. New norms of socialist realism required literary and other artistic works to reflect official optimism, nationalism, patriotism, and glorification of Stalin. A. A. Zhdanov, Stalin's commissar for culture, also purged such respected musicians as Dmitri Shostakovich and Sergei Prokofiev, accusing them of "formalism" and lacking party spirit.

Another decree of September 19, 1946 tightened discipline on collective farms and cut down on private economic activities of all kinds. The systematic use of terror was resumed. In 1948 most of the party leaders of Leningrad, who had led the city through the siege, were arrested and shot.

The dictatorial nature of the postwar Stalinist regime was also reflected in scholarly and scientific fields. Stalin considered himself an authority in many scientific fields, including biology, evolution, linguistics, philosophy, and the social sciences, and he did not hesitate to impose his theories. Furthermore, he extended his own authoritarian style of leadership to every branch of science. "Scientific leaders" in each research field were charged not only with administering their respective research projects, but also with developing the "correct" theoretical line to be followed by all researchers. Such policies enabled T. D. Lysenko to rise to prominence in the fields of biology and agriculture. Lysenko advocated a dubious theory (later proved erroneous) based on the inheritance of acquired characteristics. He offered false hopes to

Stalin that by subordinating pure science to practice (*praktikat*), science would dramatically and immediately enhance industrial and agricultural performance. Under Lysenko, the field of genetics was set back two or three decades, and it has yet to recover fully.

Stalin's harsh policies at home were mirrored in Eastern Europe, where the Soviets sought to consolidate their power. As compensation for the wartime losses incurred during the liberation of Eastern Europe from Nazi occupation, the Soviets confiscated many assets. Whole factories were dismantled, shipped to the USSR, and reassembled. The total value of confiscated assets from Eastern Europe has been estimated at $14 billion.[22] By 1949, communist parties subservient to Moscow were firmly entrenched throughout Eastern Europe. They dutifully voiced fraternal support for the USSR and hailed Stalin as the "visionary leader" of the socialist movement.

In January 1953, *Pravda* announced the arrest of a group of Kremlin physicians who had supposedly confessed to the murder and attempted murder of various leading Soviet figures. Stalin was apparently planning to use the alleged "Doctors' Plot" as an excuse to launch a new wave of purges. Both Beria and Malenkov appeared to be targets of the impending purge. However, on March 4, before the purge could begin, it was announced that Stalin had suffered a stroke two days earlier. He died on the evening of March 5, 1953. The circumstances surrounding Stalin's death remain obscure. Suspicions that he was murdered or that his death was hastened were reinforced by the sudden disappearance of several of his closest associates. At Stalin's funeral on March 9, Molotov alone displayed genuine grief. Malenkov's and Beria's eulogies were dispassionate. They urged the Soviet public to avoid "confusion and panic." The succession was under way.

STALIN'S LEGACY

Stalin dominated the Soviet political system for more than a quarter of a century, and his influence was felt long after his death. He molded Soviet society and the political institutions to his whim. Successive leaders have struggled to reform the system Stalin left behind. What was Stalin's legacy? We now enumerate some of the most important elements of the Stalinist system.

• Stalin created and perfected the use of mass terror to insure his primacy in the system and the blind obedience of his advisors and the citizens. While state-sponsored coercion had been very much in evidence under Lenin during the Revolution and the civil war, Stalin carried the use of police terror to new levels. Western estimates, now corroborated by Soviet authorities, indicate that as many as twenty million Soviet citizens may have perished as a direct consequence of Stalin's brutal policies.[23]

• Under Stalin's leadership the Party ceased being a social and political movement and was transformed into a bureaucratized institution. The Party grew from approximately 1.3 million members in 1927 to 7 million at the time of Stalin's death.[24] The criteria for admission were altered to pack the party with people loyal to Stalin. At the same time, Old Bolsheviks and others who favored Lenin's notion of the Party as a loose coalition of radical forces were systematically purged. Collective decision-making gave way to commands being issued from the top. This same system of command was duplicated at regional and local levels, where Stalin's appointees functioned as absolute dictators in their respective areas.

● During his last several years in office, Stalin had ruled primarily through the state apparatus, rather than through the Party. Stalin preferred the title of Premier or Marshal to that of General Secretary. From early 1939 until his death in 1953, only one party congress was convened. He also enlarged the Politburo to twenty-five members and changed its name to the Presidium of the Central Committee. Many of the new members held powerful posts in the state apparatus, rather than in the Party. It appeared in 1953 that Stalin's "counterrevolution" represented not a victory of the Party, but a victory of the State over the Party.

● Under the influence of centralized planning, the economy also became heavily bureaucratized. Ministries were established for each branch of industry and production orders were passed down from these ministries to each factory and farm. While this system facilitated command and control, it stifled initiative and wasted scarce human and material resources in bureaucratic red tape.

● Stalin's emphasis on heavy industries (Sector A) continued to hamper Soviet economic performance for decades after his death. Throughout the 1930s and 1940s, steel output was seen as a barometer of the general growth in the economy. Because the Soviet economy was confronting shortages virtually everywhere, the problem of satisfying demand for particular types and grades of steel was of secondary concern; whatever was produced would find a ready buyer. Consequently, planning and shortages resulted in an emphasis on quantity, rather than on quality or assortment.

● In agriculture, Stalin's legacy of collectivization extended the command and control system to the villages. Not only did this ensure a food supply for the cities, but it also resulted in a massive migration of able-bodied workers from agriculture into industry, thus creating a proletarian class.

● Stalin was a master at mobilizing the people in support of his economic and political goals. The drive to industrialize, collectivization, the war effort, and postwar reconstruction were all accomplished by mobilizing resources on a massive scale. The mobilizational nature of Stalin's rule has led Robert Tucker to label Stalin's system a "movement-regime."[25]

● In order to mobilize the population effectively, Stalin relied on traditional goals and symbols. He adopted conservative, nationalistic views. He played upon the traditional Russian xenophobia by portraying the outside world as hostile and threatening. He unified the country in pursuit of an overarching goal—catching up with the West economically.

● In order to facilitate these goals and his mobilizational approach, Stalin demanded cultural conformity, conservatism, and obedience. He eschewed the notions of the creative role of the intelligentsia, social equality, and personal freedom, which had been popular during the NEP years. Instead, he favored a strict and unified policy on culture, science, and intellectual endeavors, and differentiated economic and social rewards to stimulate productivity.

Stalin was a man of great accomplishments. He galvanized the nation in defeating Nazi Germany. He is credited with the incorporation of the East European states into the Soviet bloc, ending the USSR's isolation in the world community. As he promised in his 1931 "Jungle Law of Capitalism Speech," he modernized the Soviet economy at an unprecedented rate. It has been said that Stalin inherited a country symbolized by the wooden plow and left it a country with a nuclear arsenal, surpassed only by that of the United States.

• Finally, Stalin's dictatorship was enhanced by the development of a personality cult. Beginning with his fiftieth birthday in 1929 and accelerating thereafter, Stalin was portrayed as a "genius," a "visionary," and the "great leader of the world socialist movement." Stalin was, and in some quarters still is, revered for his dynamic and forceful leadership. He often likened himself to Peter the Great and Ivan the Terrible, tsars who were known for their achievements on behalf of the Russian people, but also for their brutal destruction of anyone who stood in their way. Stalin, the *Vozhd'*, was respected as well as feared. As his pseudonym, the man of steel, implied, he was a strong leader, galvanizing Soviet society in the pursuit of a compelling goal. When he died, thousands of mourners lined up to file past his bier. A former inmate in one of Stalin's labor camps in Siberia remembers that when news of Stalin's death reached the camp, even the prisoners wept for the fallen leader.[26]

ENTER KHRUSHCHEV

Stalin guarded his power jealously, and consequently did not name an heir apparent. To do so would have invested one of his subordinates with power and authority that could be used against him. Instead, Stalin was careful to keep power divided among many subordinates and competing institutions. His principal successors included Lavrenti Beria, the head of the secret police; Georgii Malenkov, Premier; Vyacheslav Molotov, Minister of Foreign Affairs; and Nikita Khrushchev, party secretary. Of these, Beria was the most universally mistrusted and posed the most immediate threat to all the other potential successors. Therefore, it was in everyone's collective interest to see that Beria and the secret police power be brought under control. Two days after the death of Stalin, *Pravda* announced sweeping changes in the Party and State. The secret police and the regular militia were being fused into a single ministry—the MVD (Ministry of Internal Affairs), with Beria as minister. Stalin's successors moved quickly to reduce the level of purge hysteria. Regular judicial procedure was restored. The accused Kremlin doctors were released, and within three months Beria himself was apprehended and executed.

After Beria, the most powerful potential successor to Stalin was Georgii Malenkov. Malenkov rose through the ranks of the CPSU, supervising personnel appointments during the height of the purges. After World War II he was named Deputy Chairman of the Council of Ministers and promoted onto the Politburo. In 1950, Malenkov's responsibilities in supervising party appointments were shifted to Khrushchev and he concentrated on questions of economic policy and, to a lesser extent, foreign policy. For the last several years of Stalin's life, Malenkov functioned as Stalin's chief policy advisor. Upon Stalin's death, Malenkov assumed the title of Premier, or Chairman of the USSR Council of Ministers. Thus, Malenkov, occupying the pivotal post of Premier, was well-positioned to succeed Stalin.

Molotov, while having extensive experience in the important area of foreign policy, did not have the institutional support outside of the Ministry of Foreign Affairs necessary for a contender to power. In addition, Molotov had been more closely associated with Stalin for a longer period of time than many of the other potential successors and was the most conservative.

Khrushchev was the only one of the potential successors whose career had been built entirely within the ranks of the Party. Khrushchev was raised in the coal-mining region of the Donets basin in the Ukraine. He joined the CPSU in 1918, and after studying at Kharkov University engaged in propaganda work in the Ukraine, where he attracted the attention of Lazar Kaganovich, then First Secretary of the Ukraine. In 1931 Kaganovich was transferred to Moscow as chief of the Moscow party organization and he brought Khrushchev with him. Khrushchev served initially as secretary of the Bauman district party organization in Moscow, and then rose to second secretary and eventually, in 1935, to first secretary of the Moscow party organization. Thus, Khrushchev was in Moscow during the height of the purges of the regional party apparatuses, which may explain his survival. Furthermore, his unassuming, uncouth and peasantlike personality may have made him appear less threatening to Stalin.

In 1938, Khrushchev was elevated to the Politburo and transferred to the Ukraine to serve as First Secretary, replacing Pavel Postyshev, who had been arrested and would later be executed. In the Ukraine, Khrushchev oversaw a ruthless purge of the Ukrainian party organization. During World War II, Khrushchev took part in the three major battles: Stalingrad, Kursk, and the liberation of Kiev. After the war, he returned to the Ukraine to serve first as Chairman of the Ukrainian Council of Ministers and then as First Secretary. Khrushchev's background in both industry and agriculture made him an ideal candidate to supervise the reconstruction in this vital region. In 1949 he returned to Moscow as First Secretary of the Moscow city party committee and also as a member of the Central Committee Secretariat responsible for supervising party affairs in the various republics.

At the time of Stalin's death, Khrushchev and Malenkov were the only full members of the Party's Presidium who also held posts in the Central Committee Secretariat. Malenkov, however, was urged by his colleagues to drop his party post in favor of the premiership because they feared the concentration of too much power in the hands of one man. This crucial decision left Khrushchev as *de facto* First Secretary of the Party. Khrushchev immediately began to use his connections within the Party and his position as Secretary for national party affairs to build a substantial power base among regional and local party organizations.

With Stalin's death, the Soviet political system went through a major transition. Whereas Lenin had ruled by force of personality and charisma, and Stalin by terror and mass mobilization, the challenge confronting Khrushchev was how to develop legitimacy in the post-Stalinist system.

Khrushchev was hardly the sort of political figure to inspire followers by charismatic leadership; neither could he consolidate power and instill terror as Stalin had. Instead, Khrushchev sought to build authority by a threefold strategy. First, he set to work to rebuild the status and might of the CPSU. Second, he appointed his supporters to positions of influence throughout the party organization. Third, he articulated policies that would win broad popular support. Thus, the legitimacy that Khrushchev sought was a legitimacy based on results, on effectively solving the problems confronting Soviet society.

By 1953 the Soviet public was clearly ready for relief from Stalin's police terror. At the time of Stalin's death there were an estimated 8 million people in forced-labor camps—approximately 15 percent of the entire adult male population.[27] Within days of Stalin's death, Khrushchev moved to curtail the powers of the police, in general, and Beria, in particular. He was instrumental in the removal of Beria from the Presidium and the release of many political prisoners from forced-labor camps. Khrushchev engineered these policies to eliminate a potential opponent, but in so doing he also hoped to win support among a broad cross section of the population.

In 1953 Malenkov proposed a "New Course" in economic policy that would have shifted resources to consumer goods industries. He also advocated cutting defense spending and exploring peaceful coexistence with the West. Khrushchev countered by emphasizing agriculture. At the September 1953 plenum of the Central Committee, Khrushchev pushed through a program for raising payments for agricultural products to stimulate output and called for more capital investment in agriculture and better training for agricultural specialists.

When agricultural production continued to decline in 1953, Khrushchev unveiled a grandiose scheme—his Virgin Lands program. He advocated plowing up virgin prairielands in Kazakhstan, Siberia, the North Caucasus, and the Volga basin, and planting corn to use as feedgrain in order to expand beef production. Using a mobilizational style reminiscent of the Stalin years, he called for university students, Komsomol organizations, and other groups to go to the Virgin Lands and contribute to this great campaign that promised to solve the grain problem "in a few years." Unfortunately, the lands in these regions are semiarid. Once the prairie grass was removed, the topsoil blew away, creating massive dust storms. The growing season in these regions is also quite short; consequently, the crops were not able to mature sufficiently. Since Khrushchev put forth the idea of the Virgin Lands program as his own solution to the USSR's agricultural problems, and because he had raised the citizens' expectations by promising miraculous results, the failure of the program was a blow to Khrushchev's prestige and popularity.

In order to rebuild his lagging popularity, Khrushchev launched an attack on Stalin. In February 1956, Khrushchev delivered a concluding speech to the Twentieth Party Congress in which he denounced Stalin for abusing his power, breaching the Leninist principle of collective leadership, establishing a personality cult, and orchestrating the purges that terrorized innocent people for more than twenty years. Furthermore, Khrushchev criticized Stalin for his purges of the military command and his disregard of intelligence reports of the impending German attack, which had left the country woefully unprepared for war. Finally, Khrushchev attacked Stalin for undermining the role of the Party and for the purging of rank-and-file party members. The assembled delegates sat in stunned disbelief during Khrushchev's four-hour tirade. Some wept; others acknowledged the truth in Khrushchev's charges with applause or shouts of "Da!" Most were in a state of silent shock. Never before had they heard such frank and brutal charges leveled against the man who for almost thirty years had been portrayed as almost a god.

Khrushchev cleverly manipulated the de-Stalinization program to bolster his own popularity. The faults of the Stalinist system were all laid at the feet of Stalin, the man, not Stalinism, the system. The fact that Khrushchev and all the other members of the Politburo had been among Stalin's closest subordinates and had dutifully carried out his policies was conveniently overlooked. Khrushchev did not criticize collectivization or forced industrialization, nor did he rehabilitate any of Stalin's most notorious opponents, Trotsky, Zinoviev, Kamenev, Bukharin, and Rykov.

At the same time, the de-Stalinization campaign enhanced the role of law in Soviet society. Khrushchev advocated strengthening "socialist legality," and lawyers took advantage of the more open atmosphere to push through major revisions in criminal and civil law. It was during this period of legal reform that Mikhail Gorbachev was studying at Moscow University law school.

Khrushchev's de-Stalinization opened the floodgates of long-suppressed artistic grievances and sparked a flurry of creativity in the arts. The metaphor most often used to describe the post-Stalin revival in the arts is *ottepel'* (the thaw), taken from a novel of that title by Ilya Ehrenburg. The thaw was, however, selective. Not all of the Stalinist strictures were lifted, just those whose removal suited Khrushchev's purposes. The central theme of the period echoed the new party line denouncing Stalin's cult of the personality and abuses of socialist legality. Representative was Aleksandr Solzhenitsyn's *One Day in the Life of Ivan Denisovich*, a semiautobiographical account of a political prisoner's day in one of Stalin's labor camps. This was, however, the only one of Solzhenitsyn's novels to be officially published in the USSR; *The First Circle, Cancer Ward,* and *The Gulag Archipelago* appeared only in the West until recently. Boris Pasternak's epic novel *Doctor Zhivago* came close to being approved for publication in the liberal literary journal *Novy Mir*, but a new crackdown was under way before final authorization could be obtained. The novel was relegated to the growing category of unofficial *samizdat* (self- published) literature, which circulated relatively freely in typewritten copies.

De-Stalinization had a destabilizing effect in Eastern Europe, where Stalinist leaders continued to rule over their respective communist parties that had been imposed after World War II. Khrushchev's denunciation of Stalin was taken as a signal for the people of the region to demand leadership changes. Strikes broke out in Poland, precipitating a confrontation between hard-liners and reformers. In Hungary the reformist faction, led by Imre Nagy, stirred up expectations among Hungarians for democratic elections, freedom of speech, the elimination of censorship, and independence from

Moscow. In October 1956, Soviet tanks had to be called in to quell public disturbances and topple the Nagy government.

Khrushchev's consolidation of power and the destabilizing effect of his policies combined to spark dissension among the party leadership. In June 1957 Malenkov, Molotov, Shepilov, and Kaganovich led a faction within the Presidium that demanded Khrushchev's resignation. Khrushchev refused to comply and convened an emergency meeting of the Central Committee. Marshal Zhukov, a Khrushchev supporter, mobilized the air force to fly Central Committee members to Moscow for the hastily convened plenum. Local and regional party secretaries loyal to Khrushchev were heavily represented in the Central Committee, and more than 200 members took the floor to speak in defense of the First Secretary.[28] After a stormy eight-day session, the Central Committee issued a resolution condemning the attempted ouster and labeling the opponents "the Anti-Party Group." The four leaders of the abortive coup were dismissed from all their government and party posts. Malenkov was sent to manage a power station in Siberia. Molotov was appointed ambassador to Mongolia. It was, nevertheless, a testimony to Khrushchev's reforms that the four were not arrested and executed, as they surely would have been under Stalin.

Having disarmed his opponents, Khrushchev moved to introduce further reforms in the economy. During the Stalin years, the industrial ministries had become powerful and conservative bureaucracies that opposed innovation and stifled efficient management. The Stalinist model of economic growth, which stressed quantity over quality and treated inputs as if they were abundant and essentially cost-free, was no longer able to sustain rapidly rising economic growth rates. In 1957 the economy was performing so poorly that Khrushchev scrapped the Sixth Five-Year Plan and drafted a new, more ambitious seven-year plan. GNP growth rates declined from 9.9 percent in 1958 to 3.9 percent in 1959. Productivity dropped from 5 percent to 3.3 percent and the capital-to-output ratio rose steadily.[29]

Khrushchev attacked the problem with organizational methods. He abolished the economic ministries and transferred their functions to 105 regional economic councils, which were in turn subordinated to the union republics. The economic councils (*sovnarkhozy*) were intended to supervise plans made by Gosplan and enhance coordination among all enterprises in the region. Prior to the reform, Khrushchev had severely criticized economic ministries for lack of coordination, duplication of effort, and "empire-building." He cited cases in which ministries sent parts and components all over the USSR to "their" enterprises, rather than use items produced by local enterprises reporting to another ministry. The *sovnarkhoz* reform, however, simply replaced ministerial empire-building with regional empire-building. *Mestnichestvo*, or localism, hindered coordination between and among enterprises in different regions.

Economic indicators moved upward somewhat in the early 1960s, only to fall again in 1962. GNP growth was 5.0 percent in 1960, 6.5 percent in 1961, but fell to 2.2 percent in 1962.[30] The Soviet economy in the 1960s exhibited very low and declining rates of consumption as an ever-larger portion of the productive resources was devoted to producers' goods and defense, rather than to consumer items. In 1962, the Soviet national income was approximately half that of the United States, yet per capita consumption was only one-quarter that of the United States.[31] The problems in the Soviet economy were clearly systemic.

For years, the Stalinist model of economic growth had been predicated on the scarcity of goods. Soviet citizens were poorly clothed and fed, so increases in production of clothing and food, regardless of quality, would be consumed. By the 1960s, however, the Soviet economy had succeeded in satisfying the basic needs of the population. Per capita consumption and housing standards had risen substantially. The number of people moving into new apartments each year more than doubled from 1950 to 1960, while the average consumption of meat and shoes increased by 53 and 64 percent, respectively, over the same period.[32] Economic plans continued to stress quantity over quality, however, resulting in the production of ever-increasing amounts of low-quality goods, which the public simply refused to buy.

Responding to this situation, Evsei Liberman, an economist from Khar'kov, published an article in *Pravda* in September 1962 in which he called for greater autonomy for factory managers in deciding what style, assortment, quality, and quantity of goods to produce. Liberman also proposed that factories be evaluated not on the basis of gross output, but on the basis of profitability. Records would be kept by stores to indicate which merchandise sold and which did not. Producers of high-quality, desirable goods would be rewarded, while those who continued to turn out unattractive, low-quality items would suffer. Profitability was also intended to ensure the efficient use of inputs.

Liberman's proposals in *Pravda* had undoubtedly been cleared by Khrushchev and the Politburo and were presented as a trial balloon to see how the public, industrial managers, economic planners, and party officials would react. A vigorous public debate ensued for three years, with economists, factory managers, consumers, party officials, and central planners voicing their views. In time, two diametrically opposed schools emerged, referred to here as the conservatives, or neo-Stalinists, and the liberals. The conservatives favored central determination of the level of investment, size of the labor force, wages, and production, while the liberals preferred to give decision-making power to local officials and factory managers. On the questions of "success indicators," or how performance would be assessed, the conservatives favored gross output and labor productivity as the major criteria, while the liberals proposed a single measure: profitability. Conservatives and liberals also disagreed over investment priorities. The former favored heavy industry and defense, while the latter put more emphasis on consumer goods and agriculture.

The conservatives were led by a group of Soviet computer specialists who maintained that the USSR could retain its heavily centralized planning apparatus but implement a more rational and efficient planning process through the use of computers. Chief among these scientists were A. M. Birman, L. V. Kantorovich, and V. S. Nemchinov—all mathematical modelers and proponents of cybernetics. They envisioned the day when the entire Soviet Union, every farm and every factory, would be linked by a massive computer network through which would flow commands coordinating all economic units to ensure optimal utilization of resources.

Given the size and complexity of the Soviet economy, however, computer simulation or modeling of economic interactions would be virtually impossible. A group of mathematicians in Kiev calculated that in order to draft an accurate and fully integrated plan of material-technical supply for one year for the Ukrainian Republic alone would require the labor of the entire world population for ten million years.[33] Undoubtedly, this estimate overstated the problem, but the general point was well taken: Soviet planning efforts almost inevitably fell short of the optimum. In time, the Soviets came to hold more modest and practical hopes for the application of computers in the economy.

Debate over the Liberman reforms continued until late 1965, when a compromise position was introduced that included profitability as one of several indicators by which factories and enterprises were evaluated. Factory managers were also afforded a slightly greater degree of discretion over production decisions. Nevertheless, the economy remained heavily centralized and bureaucratic.

The story of the Liberman proposals provides several useful insights into the ways in which Soviet leaders approached policy innovation in the post-Stalin years. They would occasionally float a reform proposal in order to stimulate discussion by a wide spectrum of the public. After a lengthy period of debate, a moderate (or even minimal) compromise solution would be implemented. Reforms themselves seemed to be assessed in the light of three considerations:

1. Will the proposed reform alter the power structure (i.e., the position of the CPSU in the political system)?
2. Is the proposal ideologically acceptable?
3. Will the reform result in substantial economic, social, or military improvements?

It is likely that Liberman's proposals, if adopted, would have significantly improved the quality of production in the USSR, but they would have given a great deal of independent authority to factory managers and might have resulted in problems in coordinating interrelated industries. The proposals also risked creating unemployment or inflation as industries sought to lower production costs and respond to pent-up consumer demands for high-quality products. Finally, the incentives to meet consumer demands might ultimately have raised the portion of Soviet economic resources allocated to consumer goods, thereby reducing allocations for defense and heavy industry. These factors explain why Liberman's proposals were never fully implemented.

Khrushchev also instituted important changes in foreign policy, designed to reduce the USSR's isolation in the world and to facilitate a shift of resources from defense to agriculture and consumer goods industries. In 1955 Khrushchev compromised on the conclusion of a peace treaty with Austria, attempted to reconcile differences with Tito in Yugoslavia, and participated in a summit meeting with President Eisenhower in Geneva. He revised Lenin's doctrine on the inevitability of war between socialist and capitalist states and cut back on defense allocations. From 1955 to 1958, the Soviet army was reduced by more than two million men.[34] After the events in Eastern Europe in 1956 he acknowledged "polycentrism" and differing roads to socialism.

Khrushchev's policy of peaceful coexistence with the West culminated in 1959 in the first visit of a Soviet leader to the United States. He met with President Eisenhower at Camp David, traveled to Iowa to learn about hybrid corn, and toured IBM facilities and Disneyland in California. The foundations of peaceful coexistence proved to be fragile, however. On May 1, 1960 an American U-2 reconaissance plane was shot down over Sverdlovsk and the pilot was captured. The U-2 episode badly embarrassed Khrushchev, who had been attempting to placate his disgruntled military commanders with assurances that diplomacy could lessen the Western threat to the USSR, thereby justifying budget cuts. The U.S.-sponsored invasion of Cuba at the Bay of Pigs in April 1961 further exacerbated relations and reinforced the hard-liners.

In an attempt to revive his flagging popularity, Khrushchev renewed his de-Stalinization campaign at the Twenty-Second Party Congress in October 1961. Stalin's body was removed from the mausoleum in Red Square, where it had lain in state beside Lenin's body, and was buried next to the Kremlin, marked only by a simple plaque. Stalin's name was removed from thousands of factories and streets, and Stalingrad reverted to the name Volgograd.

Khrushchev used the occasion of the Twenty-Second Party Congress to unveil a new party program to replace the one passed in 1919. The new program was ludicrously overoptimistic. It called for the Soviet Union to overtake and surpass the United States economically by 1970 and predicted that by 1980 the USSR would be a communist society. Reflecting the achievement of "advanced socialism," Khrushchev declared that the state was no longer a dictatorship of the proletariat, but a "state of all the people." He expanded the bounds of popular participation by strengthening the powers of the soviets and the trade unions. Voluntary citizens' militias (*druzhiny*) were organized to patrol streets, parks, and residential areas to maintain public order. Comrades' courts were set up to handle minor disputes and infractions in housing complexes, factories, and collective farms. While such populist policies did expand participation, they also threatened the well-established bureaucracies that balked at Khrushchev's other reforms.

Khrushchev's authority was also undermined by the Cuban missile crisis in 1962. Against the advice of his leading military strategists, Khrushchev took the risky action of deploying medium- and long-range missiles in Cuba. Khrushchev's strategy was to bring about instant parity with the United States by threatening it close to its own borders, just as the U.S. had deployed missiles in Turkey. The plan was a classic Khrushchev maneuver—a sudden, bold initiative taken with a minimum of consultation and reflection. If it had succeeded, it would have eliminated American strategic superiority over the USSR. It was also much cheaper than engaging in a massive research, development, and deployment program of new intercontinental ballistic missile systems. However, the failure of his policy and the humiliation of being forced to remove the missiles led to profound dissatisfaction with Khrushchev among Kremlin hard-liners and the military.

Finally, Khrushchev launched a series of reforms that eroded his support in his traditional power base, the CPSU. In 1960 and 1961 Khrushchev mounted an extensive purge of regional and local party secretaries. More than half of all party secretaries at these levels were removed and new people loyal to Khrushchev were appointed.[35]

At the Twenty-Second Party Congress he called for the principle of rotation of offices within the Party. Maximum terms of office were set for the Presidium, the Central Committee, and regional and local party committees, effectively abolishing job security in the Party. In 1962 he also sought to pack the Party with supporters by dividing the party apparatus into industrial and agricultural branches. Rather than resulting in greater economic integration and efficiency, the bifurcation of the CPSU led to an expansion of bureaucracy, confused lines of command, and rivalries between the two branches of the Party in every region of the country.

Khrushchev's attempts to reform the Stalinist system and develop his own legitimacy based on effective leadership and successful policies failed utterly. On October 12, 1964, Khrushchev was called to a meeting of the Presidium and informed that by a unanimous vote he was being relieved of all responsibilities. His attempt to take the decision to the Central Committee, as he had in 1957, was foiled by the lack of cooperation of the armed forces, who refused to fly Central Committee members to Moscow for an emergency meeting. Khrushchev was stripped of all his titles and permitted to retire in comfort and isolation, far from the corridors of power. The leaders in the ouster were, not surprisingly, the people selected to succeed Khrushchev: Leonid Ilych Brezhnev became General Secretary; Aleksei Kosygin, Chairman of the Council of Ministers, and Nikolai Podgorny, Chairman of the Presidium of the Supreme Soviet.

BREZHNEV'S CONSOLIDATION OF POWER

After the tumultuous Khrushchev years, Brezhnev sought to consolidate his power and enhance his authority by promising to restore stability in Soviet politics. Brezhnev criticized Khrushchev for, among other things, "the unjustified transferring and replacing of personnel," and pledged to restore "respect for cadres" (party personnel).[36] Consequently, relatively few personnel changes were immediately forthcoming. In his first ten months in office, Brezhnev replaced only 9 percent of the regional party secretaries and only two of the fourteen republic first secretaries.[37] More extensive organizational and personnel changes were undertaken in the state apparatus, however. Brezhnev abolished the regional economic councils that Khrushchev had created and reestablished the industrial ministries along pre-1957 lines, necessitating the promotion of numerous people to ministerial posts. Yet approximately two-thirds of the ministers appointed in 1965 had been ministers or deputy ministers in 1957.[38] Continuity and stability, rather than the infusion of new blood, appear to have been the principal motivating factors in the appointments and personnel changes of the early Brezhnev period.

In time, however, Brezhnev was able to bring into the Politburo and other leading bodies long-time friends and associates, especially those from his home region in Dnepropetrovsk, from the Eighteenth Army during the war, and from his tenure as first secretary of Moldavia and Kazakhstan.

A prime example of a Brezhnev protégé was Konstantin Chernenko. He became associated with Brezhnev in 1950, when the latter was named first secretary for the newly acquired Moldavian republic. Chernenko was Chief of the Propaganda and Agitation Department in Moldavia at the time. When Brezhnev was promoted to candidate member of the Politburo and Party Secretary for heavy industry in 1956, Chernenko followed him to Moscow. Shortly after Khrushchev's ouster and the election of Brezhnev to General Secretary, Chernenko was named Chief of the CPSU General Department and made candidate member of the Central Committee. At the Twenty-Fourth Party Congress in 1971, he was elevated to full member of the Central Committee. Vacancies in the Politburo brought about by the advancing age of the Brezhnev cohort, together with the declining vigor of the General Secretary and his increasing reliance on Chernenko, combined to catapult Chernenko into the Politburo as a full member in 1978.

Of the thirteen full members of the Politburo in February 1981 (excluding Brezhnev), eight could be classified as Brezhnev protégés. Half of those dated their association with Brezhnev back to the 1940s, when he was a secretary in the Dnepropetrovsk *obkom* and then first party secretary of the Zaporozh'e *obkom* in the Ukraine.

The emphasis on restoring stability in the Soviet political system was also evident in Brezhnev's policies. Brezhnev denounced Khrushchev's "harebrained" schemes, which were often undertaken without proper consultation with experts. Under Brezhnev, the stress shifted from mass participation in politics, which Khrushchev had championed, to expanded involvement of specialists in decision-making. Scientific councils and collegia were established within ministries and research institutes to broaden the range of expertise and opinions on which policymakers relied. In contrast to Khrushchev, Brezhnev promised stability, professionalism, and conservatism.

Brezhnev's conservatism and reliance on going through bureaucratic channels ensured that policy change would be incremental and minimal. Bureaucratic interest groups utilized their newly acquired powers to foster self-serving policies, especially on budget questions. Defense spending absorbed an estimated 15 to 17 percent of the total Soviet GNP, compared to approximately 7 percent in the United States.[39] Meanwhile, investment in social services and consumer goods sectors, which were not represented by such powerful bureaucratic interests, fell precipitously. For example, expenditures on health care accounted for 6.5 percent of the state budget in 1965, but declined to 5.2 percent in 1975 and 5.0 percent in 1980.[40] Investment in housing dropped from 23.2 percent of all capital investment in the Sixth Five-Year Plan (1956–1960) to just 13.3 percent in the Eleventh Five-Year Plan (1981–1985).[41]

By the mid–1970s the Brezhnev leadership had lost its dynamism. The average age of members of the Politburo rose from 58 years in 1960 to 68 years in 1978. Vacancies created by the death or retirement of Brezhnev's old guard tended to be filled by others from the same age cohort. For example, when Defense Minister Marshal Grechko died at the age of 70, he was replaced by 68-year-old Dmitri Ustinov. Similarly, Brezhnev named 75-year-old Nikolai Tikhonov Chairman of the USSR Council of Ministers after the death of Aleksei Kosygin, age 76. This lack of turnover and the ossification of the Brezhnev leadership was mirrored in the Central Committee and the Council of Ministers.

At the Twenty-Fifth Party Congress in 1976, Brezhnev's speech was slurred and at times unintelligible. References to "socialist legality" (*sotsialisticheskaya zakonnost'*) sounded instead like "sausage legality" (*sosiskaya zakonnost'*). Reports circulated that Brezhnev was suffering from cancer of the jaw. Some observers speculated that he might use the occasion of the Party Congress to step down voluntarily, retiring with all the pomp and circumstance befitting a leader who had guided the USSR for more than a decade, raising the country from a position of military inferiority to the status of a superpower. But the General Secretary held onto the reins of power and the next year ratified a new Constitution—widely referred to as "the Brezhnev Constitution"—and also assumed the title of President of the USSR, forcing Podgorny into retirement.

By the late 1970s, however, the "stability of cadres" promised by Brezhnev had become tantamount to stagnation. Many of the party secretaries and ministers who had been named to their posts in 1965 were still in office when Brezhnev died seventeen years later. In the early 1980s, the economic growth rate fell to its lowest level since World War II, resulting in chronic shortages of meat, dairy products, vegetables, and other staples. (See Table 3-1.) Lagging economic performance gave rise to a burgeoning "second economy" and to widespread theft and other economic crimes. Labor productivity declined as a result of chronic absenteeism, alcoholism, and the lack of incentives. Workers routinely left their jobs early to shop for groceries, a task that could require two to three hours every day. While average Soviet citizens confronted these difficulties, the elite enjoyed more and more privileges. Special stores were opened, carrying difficult-to-find items ranging from meat and caviar to imported shoes and cameras. Usually, Soviet citizens are either cynical about such privileges or accept them grudgingly as a fact of life, but the ostentatious-

Table 3-1. Economic Stagnation under Brezhnev (by percentages)

	7th FYP	8th FYP	9th FYP	10thFYP	11th FYP
	1961–65	1966–70	1971–75	1976–80	1981–85
GNP	4.7	5.0	3.0	2.3	2.0
Industrial production	8.8	8.3	7.4	4.5	3.7
Agricultural production	2.4	4.3	0.6	1.5	2.1
Labor production	5.5	6.8	4.6	3.3	3.1
Total investment	6.3	7.5	7.0	3.3	3.5
Per capita income	3.9	5.9	4.4	3.3	2.1

Source: Ed A. Hewett, *Reforming the Soviet Economy* (Washington, DC: Brookings Institution, 1988), 52.

ness, the flaunting of wealth and position by the elite under Brezhnev, sparked increasing resentment among the populace.[42]

In foreign affairs, policy problems accumulated with the demise of détente, the increasing defense deployments by the United States in Western Europe, the failure of arms negotiations to reach any concrete reductions, the continued tense relations with China, and the protracted involvement of Soviet forces in Afghanistan. The need for change—both in policy and personnel—was the chief agenda item confronting Brezhnev's successors.

Reflecting the growing incapacity of the General Secretary, the Soviet political system appeared to lose its momentum and sense of direction in the late 1970s and early 1980s. As in past leadership transitions in the USSR, most party and state bodies adopted a cautious and conservative approach. With the future of Brezhnev's leadership in doubt, state and party administrators, not wishing to undertake any long-term plans or policy commitments, muddled through with short-term, interim decisions until the new leader had clearly established his policy orientation. Meanwhile, unresolved problems continued to mount.

The extent to which elite politics penetrates into even low levels of administration is not often appreciated outside the USSR. For example, in 1978 a researcher in the Institute of State and Law of the USSR Academy of Sciences complained privately that in the absence of decisive and dynamic leadership "from the top," the Institute could not plan its long-range research agenda. "Everyone is just waiting for Brezhnev to die," he said.[43]

As if to compensate for Brezhnev's declining health and vigor, a cult of Brezhnev began to arise. Brezhnev awarded himself the rank of Marshal, the first civilian since Stalin to hold such rank. Cities, factories, and new housing districts were named after him. In Leningrad an art show was staged featuring only portraits of Brezhnev—Brezhnev as a young boy, Brezhnev as a student, Brezhnev and the heroic defense of the Motherland, Brezhnev the world leader.

By the time of the Twenty-Sixth Party Congress in 1981, Brezhnev's subordinates were jockeying for position to succeed him. Konstantin Chernenko, Brezhnev's trusted right-hand man, rose to the third-ranking position within the Politburo behind Brezhnev and the senior party "second secretary" and chief ideologist Mikhail Suslov. Suslov's death on January 25, 1982 precipitated a rapid series of shifts within the ruling elite. Yuri Andropov, the former KGB chief, gradually assumed Suslov's former responsibilities within the CPSU Secretariat and presented himself as a clear alternative to Chernenko.[44]

Without Suslov to protect him, Brezhnev was increasingly vulnerable politically. Evidence of widespread corruption began to surface, in some cases involving his own family. Brezhnev's daughter Galina was reportedly having an affair with "Boris the Gypsy," a performer in the Moscow Circus. Boris had risen to an administrative post, controlling which acts would travel with the circus when it toured abroad. In the spring of 1982, Boris was arrested for accepting bribes—mostly in the form of gold and diamonds for Galina.[45]

Meanwhile, Galina's husband, Yuri Churbanov, the Deputy Minister of Internal Affairs, was at the center of a bribery and racketeering ring. He would later be convicted of accepting more than $145,000 in bribes and would be sentenced to twelve years in prison. These scandals not only embarrassed Brezhnev personally, they also illustrated his inability to exert control over his own family, not to mention the entire political system. Most telling of all, the disclosure of these scandals indicated that Brezhnev no longer wielded sufficient power to order these episodes hushed up.

➔ Death finally came to Leonid Ilich Brezhnev on November 10, 1982. Just three days earlier, looking frailer than usual, the man whom the press had come to refer to in the most grandiose terms as General Secretary of the CPSU, President of the USSR, Chairman of the USSR Defense Council, Marshal of the Armed Forces, and farsighted leader of socialism, had stood atop Lenin's mausoleum in an icy drizzle. From there, he had reviewed the seemingly endless procession of troops, gymnasts, and workers marching through Red Square in honor of the sixty-fifth anniversary of the Bolshevik Revolution. Following the parade, Brezhnev was carried to his limousine and driven to his estate outside the city. It was there that he suffered a heart attack and died.

Muscovites first suspected that Brezhnev had succumbed to failing health on November 11 when Radio Moscow and the central television channels interrupted their scheduled programming and switched to solemn music. Within hours, the public announcement was made. Portraits of the fallen leader, which had become increasingly prominent and numerous on public buildings during the latter half of his rule, were draped in black crepe. Lines formed at the Hall of the Trade Unions, where the body lay in state. Yuri Andropov was named to head the funeral commission, signaling his selection as the next General Secretary. The succession was confirmed by an extraordinary plenum of the CPSU Central Committee on November 12. Thus, by the time Brezhnev was buried beside Lenin's mausoleum on November 15, the succession had been largely resolved.

THE REVOLVING DOOR

Brezhnev's death resulted in a transfer of power at the pinnacle of the CPSU, but it also symbolized a generational transfer of power, which had begun in the mid-1970s and would continue into the mid-1980s. In 1981, at the time of the Twenty-Sixth Party Congress, the average age of Politburo members was seventy years. The remarkable continuity and stability of the Brezhnev generation, "the Class of '38," which had been propelled into positions of power by Stalin's purges, had resulted in long tenures in office, as well as in the aging, not only of the top officials, but of officials throughout the party and state apparatuses.

Andropov moved quickly to rejuvenate the party and state apparatuses and to set a new tone of leadership style. During his fifteen months in office, Andropov replaced one-fifth of all regional party secretaries, one-fifth of all ministers, and one-third of the department heads of the Central Committee Secretariat.[46] The chief targets of Andropov's firings were corrupt party and state officials. The consumer and transportation industries were particularly hard hit by the firings. However, after only eight months in office, the General Secretary dropped from public view, reportedly suffering from "a cold." He died in February 1984. Andropov's prolonged illness and short term in office, however, precluded further, more sweeping personnel changes.

In his policies and style of leadership, Andropov represented a sharp contrast to his predecessor. The tough-minded former KGB chief shed many of the luxurious trappings that Brezhnev had enjoyed. Andropov's limousine drove at normal speeds down Moscow's streets, rather than racing along the specially designated center lane that had been reserved for Brezhnev's motorcades. Andropov visited factories and government offices to appear to be more in touch with average citizens. He also clamped down on the special privileges of the elite.

In order to reverse the negative economic trends plaguing the USSR, Andropov adopted a two-part strategy stressing discipline and reform. He mobilized the KGB, police, and trade unions for a massive crackdown on absenteeism, alcoholism, shoddy work, and black-market activities. In some cases, police went to movie theatres and public bathhouses to check the work documents of the people they found there. If they were supposed to be on the job, they were fined and sent back to work.

Andropov also advocated economic reforms. In particular, Andropov called for greater independence for factories, enterprises, and state and collective farms; he pointed to the successes of economic experiments in East Germany and Hungary as meriting closer scrutiny. Ultimately, however, Andropov's policy agenda remained unfulfilled because of his declining health and long absence from power.

At the time of Andropov's death, there were two principal rivals for the office of General Secretary: Konstantin Chernenko and Mikhail Gorbachev. Chernenko, whose power and influence in the Politburo had waned during the early months of Andropov's rule, was able to stage a political comeback during the General Secretary's long absence. Chernenko stood in for the ailing Andropov at the parade marking the anniversary of the October Revolution and reportedly chaired the weekly meetings of the Politburo. At the same time, the Gorbachev faction was also solidifying its position. In late 1983, several pro-Gorbachev officials were named to the Central Committee Secretariat and Politburo, as well as to the influential regional party posts.

The choice of Chernenko to succeed Andropov appears to have been supported by a coalition of former Brezhnev associates and conservative party secretaries within the ruling Politburo. It is not known how strongly Gorbachev contested Chernenko's selection. It is likely that in return for acquiescing in the succession of Chernenko, he was rewarded with expanded responsibilities and powers and, most importantly, was recognized as the heir apparent.

Konstantin Chernenko, succeeding Andropov, built his power base on a return to the stability of the Brezhnev era, particularly the policy of "stability of cadres." The sudden personnel and policy changes that had occurred under Andropov, the widely publicized shake-up of several regional party organizations, and the disclosure of official corruption had aroused considerable trepidation within the ranks of the CPSU. In contrast to the extensive personnel changes under Andropov, only four new ministers were appointed during Chernenko's thirteen-month tenure, and no changes were forthcoming in the composition of the Politburo and the Central Secretariat.[47] At regional and local levels of the Party, only a few new appointments were made.

Chernenko's status quo orientation was also evident in his lack of a coherent policy program. The new General Secretary inherited from his predecessor the discipline campaign and the economic experiments in several ministries, but he pursued both with less vigor. One of the few policy initiatives linked to the Chernenko regime was a campaign to improve education and "upbringing."[48] Curiously, this campaign undermined the drive to improve labor discipline by implying that the declining performance of Soviet workers was the fault of improper socialization and indoctrination, rather than the fault of the workers themselves.

During Chernenko's brief thirteen months in office, Gorbachev played an increasingly visible role. In addition to his responsibilities within the Secretariat in supervising cadre policy and economic policy, he added foreign policy, ideological affairs, and cultural policy to his portfolio. When Chernenko's health began to fail in the fall of 1984, Gorbachev assumed the leading role in the Politburo and became much more active and visible in foreign affairs. The fact that Gorbachev's election to General Secretary occurred on March 11, 1985, the same day that Chernenko's death was made public, also suggests that the succession had been agreed to in advance.[49]

GORBACHEV THE REFORMER

Gorbachev's statements both prior to and after becoming General Secretary indicated his willingness to consider moderate economic and political reforms. In a speech on February 20, 1985, he blamed the Soviet economic slowdown in part on the failure of economic officials to undertake necessary changes.[50] On many occasions, he advocated granting greater decision-making authority to factory, state-farm, and collective-farm managers, which would free central planners and ministerial officials to concentrate on larger problems, such as investment priorities, regional development, living standards, and foreign economic policy.

Gorbachev advocated consolidating the more than sixty industrial ministries and state committees into five to seven "superministries," thus reducing the fragmentation of the economy that impedes the development of advanced technology and undermines coordination among sectors. In his first year in office, he succeeded in creating three such "superministries"—in agriculture, machine-building, and energy.[51]

Gorbachev's reformist orientation was also confirmed by his support for the reform-oriented Institute of Economics and Organization of Industrial Production of the Siberian division of the USSR Academy of Sciences. Abel Aganbegyan, the former director of the Institute and a widely recognized advocate of fundamental economic reforms, was brought from Novosibirsk to Moscow to be Gorbachev's chief economic advisor. Many proposals for reforming the economy were openly discussed after Gorbachev took office.

These proposals included greater self-financing of R&D (research and development) and capital expansion projects; reduction in the number of output indicators, placing greater emphasis on labor productivity, profitability, and contract fulfillment; and greater stability in plan inputs and targets. In agriculture, Aganbegyan noted that a land rent was being considered to stimulate agricultural units to use land more efficiently.[52]

In order to undertake fundamental economic reforms, however, Gorbachev would have to overcome the opposition of the status-quo-oriented interests. The ministries and mid-level economic administrators in industrial associations represent the single most consistent obstacle to the introduction of economic reforms in the USSR. They are the most conservative segments in the economy and are also the groups criticized by Aganbegyan and Gorbachev.[53] Past reforms, such as those introduced in 1973 and 1979 and the "economic experiments" launched in five ministries in 1984, encountered foot-dragging and outright opposition; ministers refused to delegate power to enterprise managers and fought to preserve their powers to shift inputs and adjust enterprise production plans in order to ensure overall plan fulfillment by the ministry. Gorbachev's ability to overcome this opposition depended on his success in expanding his authority and extending his power through patronage.

Under Gorbachev, changes occurred rapidly in the makeup of the ruling elite. In fact, Gorbachev's record in making personnel changes early in his tenure eclipsed that of any previous leader of the USSR. In his first year in office, Gorbachev removed 47 of 121 regional party secretaries and replaced more than one-half of the CPSU Central Committee.[54] Sweeping changes occurred at the city and local levels, with younger, better-educated party apparatchiki, many with experience in agriculture and industry, assuming influential party posts. Gorbachev's purge was not restricted to the ranks of the Party. The number of newly appointed ministers rose to forty-two—more than one-half of the Council of Ministers, compared to only twelve under Andropov and four under Chernenko.[55] The average age of Gorbachev's new ministerial appointees was 56, while the ministers who were dismissed averaged 69 years of age and had held their posts for an average of twelve years.[56]

Gorbachev's ministerial changes did not hit each sector of the economy equally; rather, they were concentrated in the agricultural, construction, energy, and basic-industries sectors. It is notable that the defense industries were not subject to Gorbachev's initial ministerial personnel changes. The defense sector may have been spared because it operates on a fundamentally different basis than civilian industries and is more efficient and technologically progressive.

In his ministerial appointments, Gorbachev promoted capable specialists from within various ministries. However, in a few crucial ministries (e.g., Foreign Affairs, Internal Affairs, and Agriculture), he relied on the appointment of trusted party secretaries.

The career backgrounds of Gorbachev's ministerial appointees also provided a signal as to his goals and motivations. Several of the newly appointed officials had distinguished themselves in the most productive and technologically advanced industrial enterprises in the USSR—such "show-case factories" as the gigantic Uralmash machine-building complex in Sverdlovsk, whose former director, Nikolai Ryzhkov, became Premier of the USSR. Such appointments indicated that Gorbachev acknowledged the successes of these prestigious factories and eneterprises and wanted to see them more widely emulated. In effect, he may well have been saying, "These industries and enterprises have succeeded in operating within the existing economic structure, and they are efficient and technologically advanced. Why can't others do the same?"

Gorbachev's personnel changes in the party apparatus reflected similar trends and priorities in reshaping the state apparatus. After coming to power, Gorbachev replaced more than half of the heads of Central Committee departments charged with overseeing various economic sectors. The party secretaries of many of the principal industrial regions and cities were also changed during the first year of Gorbachev's rule, including the secretaries of Ivanovo, Kemerovo, Leningrad, Moscow, Orel, Sverdlovsk, Minsk, and Gorky. Many of the new secretaries had had some previous training and experience in industry or agriculture as well as extensive experience in party work. Approximately half had served as inspector (*inspektor*) in the CPSU Central Committee, a position that entails conducting investigations of local and regional party organizations to ferret out graft, corruption, and inefficient management.[57] These positions are few in number and are held by rapidly rising party *apparatchiki* for a period of two to three years. The Gorbachev regime, manifesting both the ability and the will to introduce economic reforms, was clearly placing new personnel in key industrial ministries and regional party apparatuses in order to impose "reforms from above" on reluctant ministries, managers, and economic administrators.

Yet there were also grounds for questioning how extensive Gorbachev's reforms would be. The stresses and strains between the need to enact reforms and the stubborn resistance to change were visible within the Gorbachev regime, even in the speeches of the General Secretary. In his public statements, Gorbachev assiduously avoided using the word *reform*, preferring instead the phrase "improving the economic mechanism." Aganbegyan's positions also became more moderate and accommodating after he came to Moscow. He too avoided using *reform* and instead talked of a "major structural rebuilding" of the economy.[58] Gorbachev's appointments of industrial ministers also reflected his recognition that efficient, high-technology production was possible within the existing organization and incentive structures of the Soviet economy. Had his appointees come from enterprises that were models of experimentation or reform (e.g., the Shchekino Chemical Combine), there would have been more grounds for concluding that Gorbachev favored basic reform of the economic system. The fact that the majority of the newly appointed ministers were promoted from within cast some doubt upon the likelihood of fundamental or radical changes in the economy.

During his first year in power, Gorbachev confronted the problem of revitalizing the economy and instilling a greater sense of urgency and purpose in political organs without shedding the fundamentals of the Soviet political and economic system, without abandoning central planning, without introducing market mechanisms, and without threatening the leading role of the Party. In sum, Gorbachev tried to define a course that would rejuvenate the economy and the political system, but one that would not deviate from the essential nature of the political and economic system established by Stalin in the 1920s and 1930s. This proved to be an impossible task, and in time, the momentum of events pushed Gorbachev to consider fundamental reform.

TWENTY-SEVENTH PARTY CONGRESS

The Twenty-Seventh Party Congress convened in late February and early March 1986, just one year after Gorbachev had risen to power. Having consolidated his leadership, Gorbachev used the congress to demonstrate his command of the political system, to set a constructive tone, and to announce new policy directions. Prior to the congress, several major personnel questions had already been resolved. In July, Gorbachev had succeeded in removing his principal rival in the Politburo, Georgii Romanov, the former chief of the Leningrad party organization; just a few weeks before the congress, a second adversary, Viktor Grishin, head of the Moscow party apparatus, was dropped from the Politburo. Similarly, major personnel changes in regional and local party organs as well as in state ministries had occurred prior to the congress and were ratified after the fact by the 5000 delegates in attendance.

While Gorbachev acted quickly and decisively in making personnel changes in the party and state apparatuses, many observers anticipated more extensive changes in the Politburo than actually occurred. In this sense, the congress was an exercise in caution and confidence. Only one new member was named to the Politburo at the Twenty-Seventh Party Congress—Lev Zaikov, the new party leader from Leningrad. That appointment brought the membership to twelve. (During most of the Brezhnev era, the Politburo had consisted of fifteen to sixteen members.) Furthermore, Gorbachev retained the Ukrainian party secretary, V. V. Shcherbitskii, and the Kazakh first secretary, D. A. Kunaev, despite their advanced ages (75 and 68, respectively) and despite the fact that they had been strong supporters of Brezhnev and were thus out of step with Gorbachev's policies. Whether the leadership continuity in the Politburo reflected Gorbachev's attempt to follow a low-key course to avoid alienating key figures or whether it was a sign of his lack of strength in the Politburo is much debated.

More substantial changes occurred in the Central Committee Secretariat, indicating that it has become more important in policy-making. Nine of eleven members of the CPSU Secretariat (excluding Gorbachev) were newly elected or reassigned to new positions within the body. Experienced officials, such as long-time ambassador to the United States Anatolii Dobrynin, were brought in to supervise foreign affairs; dynamic party *apparatchiki*, such as G. P. Razumovsky, were assigned to spearhead efforts to seek out careerists and corrupt party officials. Aleksandra Biryukova, the first woman to hold a top leadership post since the Khrushchev regime, was named to the Secretariat to supervise light industry, consumer services, and the food industry. In a departure from past practice and reflecting Gorbachev's faith in the ability of high technology to revitalize the Soviet economy, V. A. Medvedev, the head of the Central Committee Department of Science and Education, was elevated to secretary status.

An important aspect of authority building is manipulating diffuse appeals in order to project the image of a confident and dynamic leader. The Twenty-Seventh Party Congress was most significant in this respect. After coming to office, Gorbachev had striven to project the image of a vigorous, candid, confident, pragmatic, and demanding leader. A general consensus seems to have existed since the late 1970s that these characteristics were lacking in Soviet politics. As Brezhnev grew more feeble and less involved in policy matters, the cult of Brezhnev increased appreciably. The General Secretary accumulated more and more titles and awards, his books were reviewed in glowing terms in all newspapers, art exhibits depicting his life were organized, and the media heaped praise on his accomplishments at home and abroad. In contrast, Gorbachev deliberately tried to project a self-assured, modest, and less regal image. In fact, he initiated a "cult of modesty." At the Twenty-Seventh Party Congress, he chided one speaker for making too many references to his name during an address.[59]

In another departure from past practice, Gorbachev called for more openness (*glasnost'*) and candor in discussing the problems confronting the USSR. In a country in which information about airplane crashes, earthquakes, and crime was strictly censored, such frankness was startling. A *Pravda* editorial on the new policy stated: "Timely and frank release of information is evidence of trust in the people, respect for their intelligence, and feeling for their ability to assess events."[60]

The first big test of Gorbachev's *glasnost'* policy was the accident at the Chernobyl nuclear reactor in the Ukraine in April 1986. Initially, the leadership maintained tight secrecy on news coverage of the near-disaster and even denied that there was a problem. In the weeks following the accident, however, press reports, television coverage, and news conferences gradually reconstructed the events surrounding the accident. While the Soviet handling of the Chernobyl episode represented a departure from previous practice, it clearly fell short of what some Western observers had expected.

The stress on *glasnost'* was also used to apply public pressure to ministers, factory managers, and economic officials. For example, ministers and factory officials were asked to appear on television and radio programs to answer consumer complaints. Unlike Brezhnev and Chernenko, who promised the bureaucrats stability, Gorbachev expected results. As Gorbachev boldly stated in a 1985 address in Leningrad: "Those who do not intend to adjust and who are an obstacle to the solution of these new tasks simply must get out of the way, get out of the way and not be a hindrance."[61]

In terms of setting a new policy agenda, the Twenty-Seventh Party Congress offered few departures from the past. The overriding concern of the Gorbachev leadership was revitalizing the stagnating economy in the face of serious shortages of labor, investment capital, and hard (foreign) currency. Gorbachev's solution was fourfold. First, Gorbachev and Premier Ryzhkov called for a "radical restructuring of the economy," consolidating numerous cumbersome ministries into a handful of "superministries" and giving greater autonomy to factory and farm managers. Second, the Twelfth Five-Year Plan, which was ratified by the congress, redirected economic resources to favor the development and application of high technology and the renovation of existing factories. No new grandiose projects were envisaged in the plan, and the bulk of investment funds were slated for the European portion of the country, rather than for Siberia. Third, Gorbachev renewed the campaign, begun under Andropov, to improve work discipline and cut down on alcoholism, one of the chief causes of absenteeism and low labor productivity. Finally, the new leadership noted that the revitalization of the economy required the revitalization of the society in general, and the CPSU in particular. Party officials were urged to be more vigilant with regard to economic performance, holding factory managers and workers strictly accountable for fulfilling their production plans. At the same time, Gorbachev cautioned party members to limit their involvement to supervision and not to intrude in administrative matters. The distinction between party supervision and party interference, however, remained fuzzy. The fact that many of the newly appointed regional party secretaries had distinguished records in agricultural and industrial management indicated both the rising level of expertise within the Party and a greater degree of sensitivity by party secretaries to the problems confronting the productive sector.

On the political front, the Twenty-Seventh Party Congress was particularly noteworthy in two respects. First, the delegates ratified a new Party Program, substantially revising the previous program, which had been enacted under Khrushchev in 1961. Work on the new Party Program was begun under Brezhnev and continued under the direction of his successors. Both Brezhnev and Andropov noted that some provisions of the 1961 document "had not stood the test of time," particularly the promises that, by 1970, the Soviet economy would overtake that of the United States in per capita production and that, by 1980, communism, complete with an abundance of housing, consumer goods, and social services, would be largely realized.[62]

During the drafting phase of the new program, a heated debate occurred over the wording of a clause referring to "socialist self-administration." There were disagreements as to whether workers should be allowed to have a direct say in the appointment of managers and in managerial decisions. The Party Program, as enacted by the congress, called for increased participation of workers in administration and also reflected Gorbachev's stress on *glasnost'* in calling for greater openness in the press and increased attention to public opinion.

In contrast to Khrushchev's utopian predictions, the new document acknowledged that the advance of humanity toward communism is "uneven, complex, and controversial."[63] The program does, however, propose that national income and industrial output be doubled by the year 2000. These goals are to be achieved by granting greater independence to enterprises, abandoning wage equalization among workers, introducing the brigade method of labor organization more widely, using material incentives to encourage the population to work harder, and applying advanced technology in production.

A second dominant political feature of the Twnety-Seventh Party Congress was the tendency to blame the Brezhnev leadership for the economic, social, and political problems confronting the country. While not mentioning the former General Secretary by name, Gorbachev criticized the "inertness" of the Brezhnev years and noted that the Kremlin leaders had tried "to improve things without changing anything."[64]

Blaming one's predecessors has become routine in the USSR since Khrushchev's famed denunciations of Stalin at the Twentieth and Twenty-Second Party Congresses. But the criticisms of Brezhnev marked the first time that he was singled out for public reproof at a party gathering. On the third anniversary of Brezhnev's death, *Pravda* published an article entitled "Flattery and Obsequiousness" that attacked the idolatry that had characterized the Brezhnev era.[65] Delegates to the Twenty-Seventh Party Congress were urged to develop a new "cult of modesty" and to shy away from the "self-congratulatory ways of the past."[66]

Gorbachev's policy agenda began to emerge more clearly in his second year in office. In 1986, he began to speak more forcefully in favor of decentralizing economic planning, granting greater power to factory managers to make decisions.[67] Serious efforts were undertaken to revamp wages and prices in order to create greater incentives for workers to work diligently, while pensions were modified to prevent price increases from impoverishing the Soviet Union's large retired population.

In a major address to the January 1987 plenum of the CPSU Central Committee, Gorbachev described the problems confronting the USSR with brutal honesty, even using the word *crisis* to describe the USSR's social and economic predicament.[68] He noted that the political leaders had grown "deaf to social issues." Housing, health care, education, and consumer needs had been neglected. Furthermore, he observed that this "social corrosion" profoundly affected public morale, resulting in cynicism, consumerism, alcoholism, corruption, and infringements of labor discipline.

Gorbachev placed the blame for these conditions at the top: "Comrades, it is the leading bodies of the Party and the State that bear responsibility for all this."[69] Gorbachev's proposed remedies were nothing short of revolutionary: He proposed "democratizing" the political system by instituting multiple-candidate elections for local soviets and party posts, involving more nonparty members in the government and the economy, allowing workers to select their factory directors, and expanding the sphere of private economic activity.

In the arts, Gorbachev encouraged a thaw unparalleled in the past thirty years. Long-suppressed works such as Boris Pasternak's *Doctor Zhivago* and Anatolii Rybakov's *Children of the Arbat* were approved for publication. The latter was just one of several works published that reexamined the trauma of the Stalin years. A shake-up of Goskino, the Soviet film agency, resulted in the release of several previously banned movies. Among them was the widely acclaimed movie *Repentance,* a chilling examination of Stalin's purges.

Famous émigrés, such as ballet stars Mikhail Baryshnikov and Natalia Makarova, and Yuri Lyubimov, former director of the Taganka Theater, were invited to return to the USSR. At the same time, repression of dissidents was reduced appreciably, and barriers to emigration were relaxed.

The *glasnost'* campaign continued to gather momentum during 1986 and 1987, with unprecedented coverage of misconduct by KGB officials in arresting a Soviet reporter who had uncovered corruption in a coal-mining region of the Ukraine, and with press reporting of anti-Russian rioting in the Central Asian city of Alma-Ata.[70] Television coverage of the West was also less polemical. Favorable reports were broadcast on a variety of subjects including Western fashion, rock music, and fast-food restaurants.

All of these developments did not come without stiff opposition, however. Gorbachev's speeches were replete with references to stagnation (*zastoi*), inertia, bureaucratic opposition, and foot-dragging.[71] In a 1986 address to a conference of social scientists, Gorbachev indicated that an acute, uncompromising struggle of ideas was under way between "the old ways" and "profound and revolutionary changes in Soviet society."[72] Sergei Zalygin, editor of the literary journal *Novy Mir,* characterized Soviet society as split between "progressives and conservatives."[73] The press also reported numerous cases of efforts to "sabotage" Gorbachev's ambitious economic and political reforms.[74]

Gorbachev responded to these challenges by vigorously implementing a policy of "exchange of cadres" in order to break up local patronage networks. He made sweeping personnel changes throughout the party and state apparatus, in most cases appointing officials from Moscow to local posts. At the January 1987 Central Committee plenum, he succeeded in securing the promotion of three allies (one to candidate of the Politburo and two to the Party Secretariat) and the removal of Kazakh Party First Secretary D. A. Kunaev from the Politburo. However, none of Gorbachev's protégés were elevated to full, voting status on the Politburo, indicating that the Central Committee members still had reservations about the scope and pace of Gorbachev's proposed reforms.

During his first two years in office, Gorbachev dramatically altered the makeup of the Council of Ministers, Gosplan, and most of the important industrial ministries, as well as the party apparatus charged with overseeing economic performance. With his own personnel in place, Gorbachev was well-positioned to use his extensive powers to impose reforms from above and to use political pressure to hold local party and state officials strictly accountable for implementing his policies. No one doubted his abilities, vigor, and resolve. During his speech nominating Gorbachev to office, former Foreign Minister Andrei Gromyko observed, "This man has a nice smile, but he has iron teeth."[75] A former classmate characterized Gorbachev as "a reformer who considers politics as a means to an end, with its objective being to meet the needs of people."[76] These two sides of Gorbachev's character—the reform-oriented, flexible, pragmatic politician and the tough-minded disciplinarian—emerged in his speeches and in his policies. Gorbachev recognized that discipline alone would not solve the country's nagging economic, social, and political problems; he also recognized that reform without firm discipline and controls could be politically dangerous. Both approaches are necessary if a leader is to be successful in resolving the challenges that confront the Soviet Union today.

Notes

1. Stalin, Plenum of the CPSU Central Committee, April 1929.

2. Alec Nove, *Stalinism and After,* 3d ed. (Boston: Unwin and Hyman, 1989), 37.

3. Alexander Gerschenkron, "The Rate of Industrial Growth in Russia Since 1885," *The Journal of Economic History* 7, supplement (1947): 167. In the USSR, economists refer to national income rather than GNP.

4. Richard Sakwa, *Soviet Politics: An Introduction* (London: Routledge, 1989), 45.

5. Moshe Lewin, *Russian Peasants and Soviet Power* (London: George Allen and Unwin, 1968), 446–481.

6. *Literaturnaya gazeta,* 3 August 1988.

7. Robert Conquest, *The Harvest of Sorrow: Soviet Collectivization and the Terror-Famine* (New York: Oxford University Press, 1986), 303.

8. Robert A. Lewis and Richard H. Rowland, *Population Redistribution in the USSR* (New York: Praeger, 1979), 166.

9. Sakwa, *Soviet Politics,* 48.

10. A. A. Baikov, *The Development of the Soviet Economy* (Moscow: Statistika, 1946), 347.

11. Calculated from data in Donald W. Treadgold, *Twentieth Century Russia,* 2d ed. (Chicago: Rand McNally, 1959), 269.

12. Ibid., 293.

13. Cited in *The Cambridge Encyclopedia of Russia and the Soviet Union* (Cambridge: Cambridge University Press, 1982), 1976.

14. Ibid.

15. Nove, *Stalinism and After,* 47.

16. T. H. Rigby, *Communist Party Membership in the USSR, 1917–1967* (Princeton: Princeton University Press, 1968), 209.

17. Ronald Hingley, *The Russian Secret Police* (London: Hutchinson, 1970), 161.

18. Ibid., 166–167.

19. Robert Conquest, *The Great Terror* (London: Macmillan, 1969), 532.

20. Alexander Werth, *Russia at War, 1941–1945* (New York: Carroll and Graf Publishers, 1964), 324.

21. M. F. Parkins, *City Planning in Soviet Russia* (Chicago: University of Chicago Press, 1953), 56.

22. Cited in Charles Gati, *The Bloc that Failed* (Bloomington: Indiana University Press, 1990), 123. Paul Marer also estimates the value of confiscated property at $14 billion. See Paul Marer, "The Economies and Trade of Eastern Europe," in William E. Griffith, ed., *Central and Eastern Europe: The Opening Curtain?* (Boulder, CO: Westview, 1989), 53.

23. Conquest, *The Great Terror,* 533. More recent estimates by Conquest place the death toll due to collectivization and famine at 14.5 million; see Conquest, *The Harvest of Sorrow,* p. 306. These estimates, along with his previous figure of 13 million killed during the period 1936–1950, indicate that as many as 27.5 million people may have perished as a result of Stalin's policies.

24. Calculated from data cited in Rigby, *Communist Party Membership in the USSR,* 300.

25. Robert Tucker, "Towards a Comparative Politics of Movement-Regimes," *The American Political Science Review* 55, no. 1 (June 1961): 281–289.

26. From PBS television documentary, "Stalin," 4 June 1990.

27. Ger P. Van Den Berg, *The Soviet System of Justice: Figures and Policies* (Dordrecht, the Netherlands: Martinus Nijhoff, 1985), ch. 6.

28. Jerry F. Hough and Merle Fainsod, *How the Soviet Union Is Governed* (Cambridge: Harvard University Press, 1979), 218.

29. For Soviet national income data, see *Narodnoe khozyastvo v SSSR, 1974* (Moscow: Statistika, 1975), 5.

30. Ibid.

31. Ibid.

32. *Strana Sovetov za 50 let: Sbornik statisticheskikh materialov* (Moscow: Statistika, 1969), 251, 253–254.

33. O. K. Antonov, *Dlya vsekh i dlya sebia: o sovershenstvovanii pokazatelei planirovaniya sotsialisticheskogo promyshlennogo proizvodstva* (Moscow: Ekonomika, 1965), 23.

34. Hough and Fainsod, *How the Soviet Union Is Governed,* 229,

35. Ibid., 232.

36. *Pravda,* 17 November 1964, p. 1. Also, *Pravda,* 7 November 1964; p. 1. 27 March 1965 p. 1; and 28 September 1965 p. 3.

37. Hough and Fainsod, *How the Soviet Union Is Governed,* 253.

38. Ibid., 254.

39. U.S. Congress, Joint Economic Committee, *Allocation of Resources in the Soviet Union and China, 1983* (Washington, DC: U.S. Government Printing Office, 1984), 230.

40. *Zarya Vostoka,* 15 July 1984.

41. Henry W. Morton, "What Have Soviet Leaders Done about the Housing Crisis?," in Henry W. Morton and Rudolf L. Tokes, eds., *Soviet Politics and Society in the 1970's* (New York: The Free Press, 1974), 168; *Narodnoe khozyastvo v SSSR v 1983* (Moscow: Finansy i statistika, 1984); and "Stroiteli v startovom godu pyatletki," *Ekonomika stroitel'stva* 1 (1986): 3–11.

42. The low point for public respect for Brezhnev may well have been at his funeral. Leading Brezhnev's funeral procession through Red Square, Brezhnev's daughter scandalized the public by wearing knee-high Italian leather boots and a full-length fox fur coat, in sharp contrast to the customary dark wool coat.

43. From a conversation with the author in Moscow in 1978.

44. See Archie Brown, "Andropov: Discipline and Reform," *Problems of Communism* (January–February, 1983): 18–31.

45. *Wall Street Journal,* 12 September 1987, p. 3.

46. Based on biographical data from Borys Lewytzkyj, ed., *Who's Who in the Soviet Union* (Munich: K. G. Saur, 1984).

47. Ibid.

48. For example, see *Pravda,* 11 April 1984, pp. 1–2; *Pravda,* 29 May 1984, pp. 1–2; and *Pravda,* 6 November 1984, p. 1.

49. Archie Brown, "Gorbachev: New Man in the Kremlin," *Problems of Communism* (May–June, 1985): 1–23.

50. *Pravda,* 21 February 1985, p. 2.

51. In the case of agriculture, all of the former agriculturally related ministries were abolished and placed under the direction of the State Committee for the Agro-Industrial Complex. In the other two sectors, however, the ministries were retained, but were subordinated to an "umbrella" coordinating body within the Presidium of the USSR Council of Ministers.

52. Cited in Elizabeth Teague, "Aganbegian Outlines Gorbachev's Economic Policy," *Radio Liberty Research Bulletin,* 338 (1985): 356, 362.

53. For example, see "The Novosibirsk Report," *Survey* (Spring 1984): 88–108; and Abel Aganbegyan, "Na novom etape ekonomicheskogo stroitel'stva," *EKO* 8 (1985): 3–24.

54. Based on a survey of TASS announcements published in the Soviet press in 1985 and 1986. Figures for party secretaries are based on data compiled by Professor Nobuo Shimotomai of Seikei University and presented to a conference on Soviet studies held at the Slavic Research Center, Hokkaido University, Sapporo, Japan, January 31–February 1, 1986.

55. Ibid.

56. Ibid.

57. Ibid.

58. Aganbegyan, "Na novom etape ekonomicheskogo stroitel'stva"; and Abel Aganbegyan, "Strategiya uskoreniya sotsial'no-ekonomicheskogo razvitiya," *Problemy mira i sotsializma* 9 (1985): 13–18.

59. *Pravda*, 7 March 1986, p. 1.

60. *Pravda*, 27 March 1985, p. 1.

61. *Leningradskaya pravda*, 18 May 1985, pp. 1–2.

62. For example, see Yuri Andropov, "Ucheniie Karla Marksa i nekotorye voprosy sotsialisticheskogo stroitel'stva v SSSR," *Kommunist* 3 (1983): 9–23.

63. "Programma Kommunisticheskoi Partii Sovetskogo Soyuza," *Pravda*, 7 March 1986, pp. 3–10.

64. *Pravda*, 26 February 1986, p. 1.

65. *Pravda*, 10 November 1985, p. 1.

66. *Pravda*, 26 February 1986, p. 1.

67. For example, see *Pravda*, 29 August 1986, p. 1.

68. TASS, 27 January 1987, reported in Elizabeth Teague, "Gorbachev Discusses Personnel Policy," *Radio Liberty Research Bulletin* 5 (3418) (28 January 1987): 1.

69. *New York Times*, 28 January 1987, p. 4.

70. See *Pravda*, 4 January 1987, p. 3; and *Literaturnaya gazeta*, 1 January 1987, p. 10.

71. For example, see *Pravda*, 2 August 1986, pp. 1–2.

72. Moscow Television, 1 October 1986, reported in Elizabeth Teague, "Charges of Resistance to Restructuring Intensify," *Radio Liberty Research Bulletin* (26 January 1987): 1.

73. Ibid.

74. *Izvestiya*, 17 January 1987, p. 1.

75. Cited in Dusko Doder, "A Nice Smile but Iron Teeth: Gorbachev's Smooth Rise," *Washington Post*, 17 March 1985, A1.

76. Zdenek Mlynar, "My Fellow Student Mikhail Gorbachev," *L'Unita* (Rome), 9 April 1985, p. 9.

Selected Bibliography

Barghoorn, Frederick. "Problems of Policy and Political Behavior." *Slavic Review* (June 1978): 211–215.

Bialar, Seweryn. *Stalin's Successors: Leadership, Stability, and Change in the Soviet Union.* Cambridge: Cambridge University Press, 1980.

Bialer, Seweryn, and Thane Gustafson, eds. *Russia at the Crossroads: The 26th Congress of the CPSU.* London: George Allen and Unwin, 1982.

Breslauer, George. *Khrushchev and Brezhnev as Leaders: Building Authority in Soviet Politics.* London: George Allen and Unwin, 1982.

Breslauer, George. "Reformism and Conservatism." *Slavic Review* (June 1978): 216–19.

Brown, Archie. "Andropov: Discipline and Reform." *Problems of Communism* (January–February, 1983): 18–31.

Brown, Archie. "Gorbachev: New Man in the Kremlin." *Problems of Communism* (May–June, 1985): 1–23.

Cohen, Stephen F. "The Friends and Foes of Change: Reformism and Conservatism in the Soviet Union." *Slavic Review* (June 1979): 187–202.

Colton, Timothy J. *The Dilemma of Reform in the Soviet Union.* New York: Council on Foreign Relations, 1984.

Hough, Jerry. *Soviet Leadership in Transition.* Washington, DC: Brookings Institution Press, 1980.

Hough, Jerry, and Merle Fainsod. *How the Soviet Union Is Governed.* Cambridge: Harvard University Press, 1979.

Linden, Carl. *Khrushchev and the Soviet Leadership, 1957–1964.* Baltimore: The Johns Hopkins Press, 1966.

McCauley, Martin, ed. *Khrushchev and Khrushchevism*. Bloomington: Indiana University Press, 1987.

Meissner, Boris. "Transition in the Kremlin." *Problems of Communism* (January–February, 1983): 8–17.

Nogee, Joseph L. *Soviet Politics: Russia after Brezhnev*. New York: Praeger, 1985.

Nove, Alec. *Stalinism and After: The Road to Gorbachev*. 3d ed. Boston: Unwin and Hyman, 1989.

Rigby, T. H. "Forward from Who Gets What, When, How." *Slavic Review* (June 1978): 203–207.

Rigby, T. H., Archie Brown, and Peter Reddaway, eds. *Authority, Power, and Policy in the USSR*. London: Macmillan, 1980.

Rush, Myron. "Succeeding Brezhnev." *Problems of Communism* (January–February, 1983): 2–7.

Starr, S. Frederick. "Unity, Duality, or Fragmentation?" *Slavic Review* (June 1978): 208–210.

Tucker, Robert, ed. *Stalinism: Essays in Historical Interpretation*. New York: W. W. Norton, 1977.

Urban, G. R. *Stalinism: Its Impact on Russia and the World*. London: Maurice Temple Smith, 1982.

Von Laue, Theodore. *Why Lenin? Why Stalin?*. Philadelphia: J.B. Lippincott, 1971.

Zlotnik, Marc D. "Chernenko Succeeds," *Problems of Communism* (March–April, 1984): 17–31.

4

Ideology
and Political Socialization

The Soviet state was born out of a revolutionary ideology, and for more than seventy years that ideology dominated its political life. The past few years have witnessed the startling collapse of the socialist regimes in Eastern Europe and the wholesale rejection of Marxist-Leninist ideology not only there, but among some sectors of Soviet society as well. Western commentators have rushed to declare the demise of communism as an ideology. Francis Fukuyama, in a widely read and influential article, goes so far as to assert that the total exhaustion of communism marks "the end point of man's ideological evolution" and the triumph of Western liberal democracy "as the final form of human government."[1] But is it possible for a political system to alter its fundamental values so rapidly and completely?

Ideology may be defined as a set of values and beliefs held in common and used to guide political action.[2] In this sense, ideologies exist in all societies and perform a variety of functions. Ideology explains the nature of reality, defining the individual's place in the social universe and providing a framework of values and identity for its adherents. By validating a particular distribution of power, ideology legitimizes the political regime. Finally, it orders the goals of political action and mobilizes adherents in support of the regime.[3]

Soviet society is not unique in manifesting an ideology. On the contrary, all societies espouse values and beliefs that undergird their systems. In the United States, for example, elements of a democratic ideology include individualism, laissez-faire, freedom of travel, freedom of speech, freedom of religion, resolution of conflicts by majority rule, and competitive two-party elections.[4] What distinguishes the ideology of the USSR from that of most other societies? The answer is the degree to which it has been formalized into an "official ideology"—a doctrine that is defined, interpreted, and defended by the state and the Communist party. Hereafter, the term ideology will refer to this body of official doctrine, rather than to the popular ideology or political culture of the Soviet people.

The official ideology of the USSR is Marxism-Leninism. Grounded in the ideas of Karl Marx and Friedrich Engels and adapted by Lenin, it has undergone a continuous process of evolution and revision since 1917. In order to assess the impact of Marxism-Leninism on the USSR today, it is essential to understand the origin and development of Marxist thought.

MARXISM

Karl Marx was born in Germany in 1818. Educated at the University of Bonn and the University of Berlin, he was heavily influenced by the German philosophers Georg Hegel and Ludwig Feuerbach, by radical French thinkers and historiographers, and by such English economic philosophers as David Ricardo and Adam Smith. The trauma of the Industrial Revolution—child labor, long work days in dangerous and unhealthy conditions, urban overcrowding, and virtually nonexistent public education and health care—provided the background for Marx's thought and writing.

During his career, which spanned more than thirty-five years, Marx produced voluminous scholarly works and political tracts.[5] Ironically, it is for one of his least scholarly works, *The Manifesto of the Communist Party*, published in 1848, that Marx is most frequently remembered.

Marx posited that there are identifiable laws governing human historical development and that these laws are determined by the mode of material production.[6] The economic character of a society (i.e., its base or *infrastructure*) determines, or at least strongly affects, everything else about the society (i.e., its *superstructure*). In other words, the economic system of a society shapes its social classes, political institutions, laws, and social norms. As a result, changes in the economic system inevitably lead to changes in social and political institutions.

Marxist philosophy fuses two essential elements: dialectical materialism and historical materialism. Drawing on the work of Hegel and Feuerbach, Marx argued that contradictions in the physical, material world result in constant change. Using historical materialism, Marx attempted to explain the historical development of societies. Combining the two philosophical arguments, Marx described the evolution of all human societies based upon a dialectical process of the clash of economic forces or classes.[7] A change in economic systems, argued Marx, would bring about economic contradictions and economic conflict that, in turn, would give rise to social and class conflict. The opening lines of *The Communist Manifesto* proclaim: "The history of all hitherto existing society is the history of class struggles."[8]

Marx noted that the most primitive tribal societies were founded on a communal economy. The sheer difficulty of sustaining life forced primitive people to hunt together and to share equally in the reward. In time, however, hunting-and-gathering tribes developed more efficient methods of farming. Tribes became consolidated into city-states, accompanied by sharp class distinctions between citizens and slaves. In addition to communal ownership, the concept of private property gradually developed.

In contrast to city-states with slave-based economies, feudalism developed in the sparsely populated countryside. Feudal society was divided between the landlords, who owned the land, and the peasants or serfs, who farmed it. As in all societies, Marx argued, one's economic status defined one's class. Feudalism, like primitive communal society, manifested contradictions. As Marx phrased it, each society "contains the seeds of its own destruction."[9] In time, a middle class of artisans and industrial entrepreneurs emerged to challenge the two existing classes.[10] Capitalism is the resulting economic system. Under capitalism, there are also two dominant social classes, which Marx defined in terms of ownership of the means of production.[11] He called the two classes the *bourgeoisie* and the *proletariat*. The bourgeoisie consists of those people who own the means of production—the land, the housing, and the factories. The proletariat is the working class that works in the factories and rents the land and the housing. Its members do not own the means of production; rather, they own only their labor, which they must sell on the labor market.

Not only does the bourgeoisie own the means of production, it also controls the political institutions, utilizing them to preserve and promote its own economic interests. In Marx's view, law, courts, police, legislatures, and other governmental institutions serve primarily to protect the economic interests of the dominant class and to suppress other classes.

Like earlier societies, however, capitalism contains the seeds of its own destruction. Marx maintained that the number of people in the bourgeois class would diminish as capital accumulated in fewer and fewer hands. Monopolies would replace competing economic interests, thus concentrating more power in the hands of a minority. The proportion of powerless, disenfranchised, and alienated workers would increase until they constituted the vast majority of the population. Their alienation would eventually explode in a socialist revolution in which the workers would take over the means of production and hold them in common, public ownership.

Marx devoted most of his writings to analyzing existing capitalist society. His descriptions of socialism and communism are both sketchy and vague. In his "Critique of the Gotha Programme," he suggested that socialism may be defined by the principle "From each according to his ability, to each according to his work."[12] That is, each citizen will contribute his or her talents and creative energies to the society and will be paid on the basis of how much he or she works. Socialism was, for Marx, merely a transitory stage in the progression toward the final development of a classless, communist society.

In the same tract, Marx defined communism by the principle "From each according to his ability, to each according to his needs."[13] In other words, every citizen under communism will work for the benefit of the society and will be paid in accordance with how much he or she needs. It is recognized that the disabled, the sick, the elderly, and the young, who are able to contribute less to society, also have greater needs for social services than do healthy, able-bodied workers. Communism presupposes an abundant society in which goods and services are more than adequate to satisfy citizens' demands, as well as to provide for necessary capital investment. Communism also assumes that citizens will have a new outlook; they will be ready and willing to work diligently for the society and not hoard or take more than they need. Most Western critics view Marx's vague references to communism as utopian. The absence in his writings of a concrete, detailed analysis of how communist society would work has resulted in numerous interpretations, many of which are markedly simplistic. For instance, Nikita Khrushchev once declared that communism will be achieved when workers can go into the bread stores and take as much bread as they need without paying.[14]

Under communism, all the means of production will be held in common ownership. Consequently, Marx predicted, there will be no basis for making class distinctions; everyone will be equal. There will also be no internal class tensions. Communism is, in short, the highest stage of economic, social, and political development. Because there is no longer a ruling class with privileges to protect, all institutions of the state will "wither away." There will be no courts, no law, and no police, because these are merely tools used by one class to subjugate other classes. Communist society will be free of exploitation and coercion; it will be a society of true equality for men and women of all ethnic groups, regions, occupations, and levels of education. In short, communism will allow its citizens the maximum freedom to express their creative abilities.

Marx considered this evolution of societies based on economic character not a theory, not a hypothesis, not even a policy to be followed. He argued that the evolution of societies toward communism is a proven scientific fact; it is inevitable. The evolution of all societies toward communism may suffer temporary setbacks, he maintained, but the internal contradictions in capitalist society ordain that a socialist revolution will occur eventually. From this perspective, the Soviets feel that their social system is more advanced than that of the capitalist West and that time is on their side.

Given the logic of Marx's theories, one would have expected (and Marx did expect) that socialist revolutions would appear first in the most-developed capitalist states, such as Germany or Great Britain.[15] During most of the nineteenth century, Russia was still a feudal society, far from having a well-developed and well-organized class of industrial workers. Despite the country's economic backwardness, however, Russian revolutionaries of the 1880s and 1890s were attracted to Marxism because it espoused the revolutionary transformation of society. The early Russian Marxists differed from the Socialist Revolutionaries in that they favored industrialization and considered the peasants the least likely class to support revolution. They also split from terrorist groups such as the People's Will because they believed the transformation of Russian society would come about only through a broad-based social revolution, not through sporadic terrorist acts.

Georgii Plekhanov, founder of the Social Democratic Workers' party, spoke of a double yoke of oppression: the Russian people were oppressed both by the tsarist autocracy and by capitalism. Thus, he maintained, the revolution must come in two phases. In the first, the bonds of the tsarist regime would be cast off; in the second, the capitalist economy would be replaced by socialism. But he cautioned that a genuine socialist revolution would not come about soon in the backward Russian state.[16]

Some Marxists even argued for cooperating with liberals in speeding the development of capitalism in Russia.[17] But such a position, while consistent with Marxist philosophy, was unacceptable to such impatient revolutionaries as Lenin and Trotsky, who were seeking to overthrow the tsarist government. Plekhanov warned that an attempt to skip the capitalist stage of development and pursue a socialist revolution prematurely might result in a dictatorship by a small revolutionary minority.[18] By 1917, however, the leadership of the Social Democratic Workers' Party in Russia had shifted from theoreticians to political activists. Although Lenin and his comrades continued to use Marxist references in their speeches and writings, they introduced an ideology that diverged significantly from Marxism.

LENINISM

Lenin's chief talent was as a political organizer and charismatic leader, not as a philosopher. He had devoted his life to overthrowing the tsarist regime. Succeeding in this, however, he then had to begin the difficult job of building the new socialist order. Marxist ideology offered little guidance in this task. Most of Marx's writings, including his greatest work, *Das Kapital*, contain only vague descriptions of socialist society. Should the new Soviet state create a new police force or abolish the police altogether? How should crime and other antisocial behavior be handled? Should incomes be set by the State, and if so, should they be made equal and uniform? Should banks be allowed to make loans, and if so, should they charge interest? These were just a few of the many mundane questions confronting Lenin, questions to which Marx provided no clear answers.

Lenin's most notable contributions to Marxist theory consisted of defining the nature of the Party and the State in socialist society. Lenin conceived of the Party as a tightly knit, centralized organization comprised of dedicated professional revolutionaries. He advocated the formation of party cells in every factory, village, and military unit. The functions of the party cells were twofold: (1) to mobilize the rank-and-file workers, peasants, and soldiers in favor of the Bolshevik cause, and (2) to relay information from the grass-roots level to the Party's top leadership. Rather than a mass party of the working class, Lenin's party was an elitist party, open only to a small portion of the workers, whom it purported to represent. Reflecting the earlier ideas of Peter Tkachev and Peter Lavrov, Lenin argued that a broadly based party could accomplish nothing. Instead, the Party was described as the "vanguard of the working class," made up of a relatively select group of revolutionaries who could see the plight of the workers more clearly than the workers themselves and who would help raise the class consciousness of the workers and peasants.[19] The inherent dangers in this concept of the vanguard party were soon apparent. Lenin proclaimed that because the Party represented the working class, the workers were obliged to accept the Party's leadership.[20]

The potential for authoritarian rule was evident not only in Lenin's concept of the vanguard party, but also in his theory of the State and the "dictatorship of the proletariat."[21] As Lavrov had argued thirty years earlier, the Party must first seize power and then use the power of the State to transform society. Lenin had no qualms about promoting dictatorship because, as a Marxist, he considered all forms of government to be coercive and dictatorial. He justified the "dictatorship of the proletariat" on the grounds that, unlike capitalist dictatorships in which a minority rules over a majority of the people, Russia would need a period in which the majority would rule over the minority. The coercive power of the State would be required to strip the former privileged class of its ill-gained wealth and power. Lenin anticipated that this transitional stage of proletarian dictatorship would continue for quite a long time. In the end, as Georgii Plekhanov had predicted, it was not so much a dictatorship of the proletariat as a dictatorship of the Communist party.

Unlike Marx, who placed hopes for revolution solely on the working class, Lenin proposed forging an alliance of all the social classes that had suffered under the tsarist regime. In short, he advocated an alliance of peasants (who constituted a majority in Russia) and workers, under the leadership of the Communist party.

Although Lenin was instrumental in laying the ideological foundations of the Party and the socialist state and in defining the tactics of revolution, he died before he was able to complete the socialist transformation of Russian society. The nature and the structure of the Soviet regime bear the imprint of Lenin's successors more than that of Lenin himself.

TROTSKYISM

Of the early revolutionary leaders, Leon Trotsky was clearly the most distinguished for his ideological and philosophical insights. He justified socialist revolution in Russia by noting that the communal heritage of the people, the weakly ingrained notions of private property, and the willingness of a well-organized revolutionary group to seize power might enable the country to skip "bourgeois democracy" and proceed directly to socialism.[22] Although capitalism was only in a rudimentary stage of development in Russia, Trotsky argued that a socialist revolution was both possible and desirable. He noted that the capitalist powers comprised a huge international imperialist system; to destroy the system, it was necessary to attack its weakest link, its least developed member—namely, Russia.[23]

Recognizing Russia's backwardness, Trotsky maintained that the success of the revolution was dependent upon revolutions elsewhere. As long as capitalism existed, it would perceive socialism in Russia as a threat and would seek to overthrow it. He predicted, "Without the direct State support of the European proletariat, the working class of Russia cannot remain in power."[24] The Bolsheviks were confident that a successful socialist revolution in Russia would inflame the workers of Great Britain, France, and the United States and thus usher in a worldwide socialist revolution.[25]

It was over the issue of supporting international revolution that Trotsky first clashed with Joseph Stalin. A dedicated revolutionary, Trotsky despised nationalism. He declared more allegiance to a British worker or a German worker than he did to a member of the Russian gentry. Stalin, in contrast, advocated building "socialism in one country." The failure of socialist revolutions in Germany and elsewhere isolated the Soviet Union and reinforced Stalin's position.

Despite—or perhaps because of—Trotsky's ideological brilliance, he was perceived as a threat to Stalin, removed from power, and forced to emigrate. Later, he was brutally murdered in Mexico City, allegedly at Stalin's command. For many years Trotsky was considered a nonperson in the USSR. His published works were removed from libraries, and his name was excised from official histories and textbooks. Stalin even had Trotsky "removed" from a group portrait of early Bolshevik leaders that hangs above the main staircase of the Lenin Library in Moscow; where Trotsky once stood, there now appears a potted plant. In 1987 and 1988, however, Gorbachev's policy of *glasnost'* forced a reexamination of Soviet history. Long-suppressed figures, including Bukharin and Trotsky, reemerged. Bukharin, along with Zinoviev, Kamenev, and Rykov, was rehabilitated in 1988. Bukharin's outspoken support of NEP and the role of the private sector, especially in agriculture, have found favor with Gorbachev and have obviously influenced his full restoration. The case of Trotsky, however, will serve as a real test of historical *glasnost'*. Unlike Bukharin, Trotsky opposed the NEP and favored forced industrialization and a harsh line toward the peasants. In short, Trotsky's policies are at odds with Gorbachev's current reforms. Any effort to restore him to his rightful place in Soviet history will be based solely on the desire for historical accuracy, not because his policies legitimize Gorbachev's policy initiatives.

STALINISM

Stalin's proclamation of "socialism in one country" was a major turning point in Soviet ideology. As initially set forth in 1924, this doctrine asserted that the Bolsheviks had to push on to socialism whether or not the world revolution came about, or else the regime was doomed to continue the policies of the New Economic Policy. Stalin argued that, drawing on its vast resources and protected by its physical isolation, Russia could achieve socialism and was not dependent upon the success of a worldwide revolution. The right wing of the Politburo supported Stalin's theory, but they were in no hurry to leave NEP. Nikolai Bukharin, a leader of the Right, noted: "We shall creep at a snail's pace, but we are building socialism and we shall complete the building of it."[26]

Stalin's aims, however, were hardly those of Bukharin. Having defeated his principal opponents on the Left and Right and secured control over the secret police, the trade unions, and the army, Stalin launched his famed "Second Revolution" in 1928. Although the introduction of the First Five-Year Plan is widely remembered for its goal of rapidly expanding capital goods, it was foremost a plan for radically transforming the economy and the society along socialist lines. Similarly, the collectivization of agriculture was not designed primarily to improve agricultural performance, but to break down the peasants' attachment to their private farms and to enable the regime to squeeze revenues out of the agricultural sector in order to finance rapid industrialization.

Stalin also manipulated Marxist-Leninist ideology to bolster his legitimacy as Lenin's faithful associate and heir. Stalin initiated the "cult of Lenin," which glorified the founder of the Soviet state.[27] He changed the name of Petrograd to *Leningrad* ("city of Lenin") and renamed the small town of Lenin's birth *Ulyanovsk*, derived from *Ulyanov*, Lenin's family name. The Order of Lenin was established as the highest civilian honor, and portraits of Lenin began to appear throughout Soviet cities and in most offices and factories.

Consistent with Stalin's determined efforts to develop the Soviet Union and rapidly expand its economic and military might, the size and the complexity of the state apparatus grew at a phenomenal rate. Gone were the days when scholars and theoreticians could refer to "the withering away of the state." In his report to the Sixteenth Party Congress in 1930, Stalin clumsily attempted to justify the mushrooming bureaucracy:

> We stand for the strengthening of the dictatorship of the proletariat, which represents the mightiest and most powerful authority of all forms of State that have ever existed. The highest development of the State power for the withering away of the State power—this is the Marxian formula. Is this "contradictory"? Yes, it is "contradictory." But this contradiction springs from life itself and reflects completely the Marxian dialectic.[28]

Abandoning the notion of the "withering away of the state" was just one of Stalin's "deviations" from Marxism.[29] In the 1930s, there was an evident return to traditional Russian values of nationalism, order, isolation, and xenophobia. Stalin formulated the concept of "capitalist encirclement" and the "two camp" theory of world affairs, both of which stressed the Soviet Union's isolation in a world dominated by capitalist powers. Stalin used this fear of a hostile capitalist world to legitimize his policies and his personal dictatorship. He sought to inculcate in Soviet citizens a strong link between himself and order. He employed propaganda and political repression on an unprecedented scale to persuade people that the survival of Soviet society was at stake and that, without the *Vozhd'* (Leader), the whole society would crumble.

Stalin deviated from Marx in arguing that "subjective factors" were instrumental in achieving successful policies in the USSR. He criticized his opponents for a lack of faith in party policies. It was not enough for the Party to enact effective policies. Rather, the public and the leaders themselves must also believe wholeheartedly in the correctness of those policies. This fanaticism, this demand for unswerving support and total belief in the correctness of Stalin's path, raised the use of terror to unprecedented levels. In Stalin's view, those who failed to believe absolutely in his programs were just as dangerous as those who sabotaged his policies. Stalin's preoccupation with power culminated in the development of an elaborate "cult of personality." He was depicted as the *Vozhd'*, the visionary leader of socialism, and the modern counterpart to Peter the Great and Ivan the Terrible. Stalinism represented a synthesis derived from the clash of the revolutionary organizational principles of Leninism with the traditionally Russian autocratic and nationalistic values of the tsarist regime.

IDEOLOGY SINCE STALIN

After Stalin's death in 1953, his political heirs moved quickly to dismantle many elements of his autocratic system. Lavrenti Beria, head of the Ministry of Internal Affairs, was arrested, convicted, and executed for treason, and the secret police were brought under party and state control. At the Twentieth Party Congress in 1956, Nikita Khrushchev stunned the delegates with an unprecedented denunciation of "Stalin's crimes." Khrushchev's "Secret Speech" accused Stalin of abuses of authority and of surrounding himself with a "cult of personality." Khrushchev also noted that Marxism-Leninism was conceived as a flexible guide to policy-making, not the inflexible dogma it had become under Stalin.

The de-Stalinization period under Khrushchev witnessed not only a reduction in the use of terror, but also a reversal on several ideological points. At the Twenty-First Party Congress in 1959, Khrushchev announced "the final and complete victory of socialism in the USSR" and the end of capitalist encirclement. No longer could the threat of external pressures be used to justify the extensive party and state controls over the populace. Progress in diminishing class and ethnic divisions in the USSR and in socializing Soviet youth toward socialist values also meant that state coercion was no longer as necessary as it had been under Stalin.

The Twenty-Second Party Congress in October 1961 represented a landmark in Khrushchev's ideological program. At the congress, Khrushchev renewed his attack on Stalin and used the occasion to announce several doctrinal innovations. He declared that the transitory period of the "dictatorship of the proletariat" had been superseded by "the state of the whole people."[30] Khrushchev maintained that all Soviet citizens, not just party members, were actively engaged in constructing communism. Khrushchev's populist notions called into question the need for elitist decision-making that persisted throughout the party and state apparatuses. The new party program ratified by the congress repudiated Stalin's notion of "revolution from above," stressing popular mass participation instead. The work of various state agencies was turned over to public organizations.

All of these changes amounted to an assault on the bureaucratic prerogatives of state officials. As a result, they engendered considerable opposition—but Khrushchev was undeterred. He was, in fact, using the party congress as a forum for playing on the adversarial relationship between the officials and the masses. His doctrinal innovations appear to have been designed primarily to bolster his legitimacy.

The new party program also reflected Khrushchev's naively optimistic view that socialism was achieving rapid gains in the USSR. This document maintained that the Soviet Union had entered "the period of full-scale construction of communism," with communism to be achieved by 1980. Indeed, Khrushchev boasted that the USSR would soon surpass the United States, not only in heavy industrial production, but also in per capita production of meat, milk, and butter.[31] He also called for the housing shortages to be resolved within ten to twelve years, and proposed a major shift of resources from heavy industry to consumer goods. While the material conditions of Soviet citizens did show marked improvements during the Khrushchev years, his grandiose proclamations ultimately remained largely unfulfilled, and the predictions of 1961 became an embarrassment to his successors.

In the 1950s and early 1960s, the growing schism between the USSR and other socialist states (most notably Yugoslavia and China) and the rise of numerous national liberation movements in the Third World mandated other doctrinal revisions. Khrushchev recognized that the CPSU was no longer the sole authority on ideological matters and that there were "differing roads to socialism," including parliamentary election. He also reversed the doctrine that war between capitalist and socialist systems is inevitable, setting the stage for pursuing peaceful coexistence with the capitalist West. This doctrinal maneuver also legitimized Khrushchev's attempt to redirect resources from military industries to consumer goods industries.

Soviet ideology continued to evolve and develop after Khrushchev's ouster in 1964. The doctrinal innovations of his successor, Leonid Brezhnev, had important implications for policies. While playing down the mass participation and "campaignism" that had been prominent under Khrushchev, the Brezhnev regime expanded the role of specialists in decision-making. The Party was no longer seen as a "vanguard" that exclusively possessed the knowledge necessary to transform Soviet society.

In 1971, Brezhnev introduced the concept of "developed socialism," and noted that the scientific-technical revolution that was sweeping Western capitalist societies was also transforming the USSR; science had become a direct productive force in the economy.

The Soviet economy began to falter in the mid-1970s, forcing some modifications in Brezhnev's emphasis and ideological focus. Party ideologists and the *agitprop* (agitation-propaganda) apparatus curtailed their glowing representations of "developed socialism" and the scientific-technical revolution because both tended to inflate the public's expectations, especially for consumer goods. Instead, the ideologists attacked "consumerism," avarice, alcoholism, loafing, parasitism, and hooliganism. Greater stress was placed on the labor collective, not only as an economic unit, but also as a social unit for reaffirming the political and moral standards of Soviet society. The increased East–West contact afforded by détente made the leaders, and to a lesser extent the general population, aware of the widening gap between Soviet and Western living standards. The ideologists responded by asserting "the *qualitative* superiority of the socialist way of life."[32]

CENTRAL TENETS OF MARXISM-LENINISM

Although the official ideology of the USSR is quite diverse and has evolved over the years in response to changing political, social, and economic conditions, certain features of Marxism-Leninism remained consistent from 1917 until recently. For instance, the official doctrine recognized the absolute primacy of the Communist Party of the Soviet Union. Article 6 of the 1977 constitution proclaimed:

> The leading and guiding force of Soviet society and the nucleus of its political system, of all state and public organizations, is the Communist Party of the Soviet Union. The CPSU exists for the people and serves the people.
>
> The Communist Party, armed with Marxism-Leninism, determines the general perspectives of the development of society and the line of domestic and foreign policy of the USSR, directs the great constructive work of the Soviet

people, and imparts a planned, systematic, and theoretically substantiated character to their struggle for the victory of communism.[33]

Article 6 came under attack at the December 1989 Congress of People's Deputies. A sizable faction of the deputies favored abolition of Article 6, but an impassioned speech by Gorbachev convinced the majority to retain this provision. However, on February 7, 1990, Article 6 again became the focus of debate. Support for the repeal of Article 6 had grown rapidly, and Gorbachev, bowing to the inevitable, finally spoke out for eliminating the Communist Party's exclusive control of the political system. The decision effectively permitted the establishment of opposition political parties. Even with the elimination of Article 6, however, the CPSU still wields considerable power. It will take many years for other parties to build the financial resources, power bases, and personnel networks to challenge the position of the CPSU.

Also essential to Marxism-Leninism was centralized state control of the economy. Although the centralized planned economy proved to be inefficient, it gave the political leaders direct and powerful control over the rank-and-file citizens and economic enterprises. They also claimed that it enabled them to make investment decisions that would have the greatest potential benefit for the society as a whole. More fundamentally, private economic and social activity were discouraged because, until recently, they were thought to promote individualism and selfishness and to widen class differences in society; they were seen as retarding rather than promoting the development of the collective consciousness necessary for the achievement of communism.

Private enterprise has enjoyed a substantial comeback under Gorbachev, but not without extensive efforts to justify it ideologically. Gorbachev has drawn on the NEP period and the views of Bukharin and Lenin to legitimize his program of privatization of agriculture and some service and light industries. However, even if Gorbachev's economic reforms succeed, he does not envision privatizing heavy industry or public services and transportation. The State will continue to play a dominant role in controlling and directing economic activity in the USSR.

Under Marxism-Leninism, the individual citizen is an important member of a larger social-political group, rather than an independent possessor of rights. Thus, the concept of rights is inextricably tied to the citizens' duties and obligations to the society. For instance, although the Constitution of the USSR guarantees freedom of speech, its exercise must be in accordance with the general interests of Soviet society. The interests of the State supersede those of the individual. Thus, the penalties for destroying public property are more severe than those for destroying private property.

Under Stalin and his successors, traditional Russian nationalism was merged with Marxism-Leninism. The success of communism is considered synonymous with the success of the Soviet Union. While Marxism-Leninism is no longer the ideology of a cohesive international movement, Soviet ideology does tend to view the world in terms of "progressive" and "regressive" forces. Soviet ideologists speak of "the correlation of forces" that has shifted in favor of socialism. By this, they mean that many of the countries of the Third World now favor a socialist rather than a capitalist path of development.

Finally, Marxism-Leninism professed atheism. Religion, which emphasizes values and allegiances that differ from those of Marxism-Leninism, has been viewed as contradictory to the interests of the Soviet regime. After the Revolution, extensive efforts were undertaken to restrict religious practice in the USSR. The most prestigious cathedrals, synagogues, and mosques were closed in the 1920s, and children below the age of eighteen were prohibited from participating in religious ceremonies or receiving religious instruction outside of the home.

In some respects, Marxism-Leninism became a secular religion. It provided to its adherents an explanation of the course of human development. It projected a glorious future society, free of exploitation, injustice, and poverty, and asked its adherents to make sacrifices for the attainment of this future society. Even in symbolic ways, Marxist-Leninist ideology attempted to displace Russian Orthodoxy. Just as some Christians wear crucifixes, those who professed their belief in Marxism-Leninism often wore lapel pins (*znachki*) depicting Lenin or other revolutionary themes. Revolutionary leaders were deified; they became figures larger than life. Lenin's embalmed body lies enshrined in a glass coffin in a mausoleum in Red Square. Even today, people stand in line for hours in the dead of winter just to file past his bier. For workers, collective farmers, students, and soldiers rewarded with a trip to the capital, Lenin's tomb is an obligatory stop.

The names and pictures of Lenin and Marx appear everywhere. Almost every book published in the Soviet Union begins with a quote from or reference to Lenin or Marx. (Lenin's collected works total fifty-five volumes, so there is no shortage of material to choose from.) Streets and cities have been renamed to honor revolutionary heroes of the past. On the November 7 celebration of the October Revolution and again on May 1, huge parades in Red Square march past four-story-tall portraits of Marx, Engels, and Lenin. On one extended visit to the USSR, the author met a French exchange student who was the great-great-granddaughter of Karl Marx. She said that Soviet officials simply did not know how to deal with her. "It is as if I were the great-great-granddaughter of God!" she exclaimed.

While some of the key elements of the Marxist-Leninist ideology have been eliminated or revised in recent years, new elements have been added. Gorbachev's programs of *glasnost'*, *perestroika*, and democratization have been introduced with a degree of central orchestration and rhetoric not unlike Stalin's introduction of ideological innovations in the 1920s and 1930s. Armies of party *agitprop* workers churn out books and commentaries, and deliver speeches, in praise of *perestroika*. *Glasnost'* has permitted a much wider range of issues and views that can be expressed. Ironically, one of the views that cannot be openly aired is that *glasnost'* itself is a bad idea. In other words, everyone is now expected at least to pay lip service to *glasnost'*, *perestroika*, and democratization. As in the past, historians are employed to establish the ideological roots for these new policies. The long-suppressed works of Nikolai Bukharin have been republished because his gradual approach to the revolution and tolerance for private ownership help to legitimize the policies currently in vogue under Gorbachev.

IDEOLOGY AND POLITICAL SOCIALIZATION

Marx recognized that the ultimate realization of communism depended upon restructuring the values and behavior of individuals, and the Soviet regime went to considerable lengths to inculcate the values of Marxism-Leninism in the people. Under Stalin, writers devoted much attention to the concept of the "new Soviet man." This idealized citizen of socialism was an enthusiastic worker, selfless in devoting time to civic activities. He or she was self-disciplined, dependable, and imbued with a sense of collective spirit, rather than of individualism. This citizen possessed a firm grasp of party policies and stood vigilant against enemies of the Party and the nation. In the 1960s the concept of the "new Soviet man" withered into obscurity. By the 1970s people were no longer willing to make sacrifices on behalf of the ideology when they saw Brezhnev and his cronies enriching themselves at the public's expense. Futhermore, attempts to rally public support by invoking the image of hostile foreign powers lost their cogency during the period of détente.

The system for instilling Communist values is extensive. It begins virtually at birth and envelopes the Soviet citizen throughout every stage of life. As in all societies, the family is the most important institution of socialization for children. Because approximately 80 percent of all Soviet women work, however, much of the responsibility for the socialization of children falls to people other than their mothers. Half of all Soviet schoolchildren attend nursery school or kindergarten; the rest receive their early training at home.[34]

Traditionally, Russian families incorporated the grandparents, with the grandmother (*babushka*) assuming the household chores as well as child-rearing responsibilities. As the Soviet population has become increasingly mobile and urbanized, however, grandparents have often been left behind in the villages. This has placed a heavy demand on child-care programs in the major cities. It is also common for young working couples to send their children to the country to be raised by the *babushka* until they are of school age. The *babushka* plays a role in the socialization not only of children, but even of adults. Wearing traditional head scarves, *babushki* have been known to scold strangers for not wearing hats or dressing warmly enough on cold days. They often launch into verbal attacks against public drunkards or chide young women for wearing too much makeup or skirts that are too short. In a sense, the *babushki* are the self-appointed guardians of public morality in Soviet society.

In addition to the home and family, early socialization frequently occurs in child-care centers (*yasli*) for children from six weeks to four years old. These centers are usually clean, well-staffed, and affordably priced. Some are operated by factories or other large enterprises for the children of their employees. Kindergartens for children ages four to six are also readily available and inexpensive. In the kindergartens, the children not only begin to acquire basic skills, but they also are instructed about the Soviet flag, Lenin, and other political topics. They are taught to be orderly, conforming, obedient, and cooperative. Heavy emphasis is placed on the group (*kollektiv*) as opposed to the individual.

In primary schools, the stress on the *kollektiv* is even more pronounced. Although there is competition, it is not individual competition. One row may compete with another row, a class may compete with another class, or the boys may compete against the girls. Within the group, students are encouraged to assist one another. Their efforts are not for their own recognition, but for the group's, and rewards and punishments are handed out not to individuals, but to groups. The students learn both cooperation and competition, but always in the context of the *kollektiv*.

Several political institutions in the USSR are directly charged with socializing Soviet children and youth. Most children of ages 7 to 10 join the Young Octobrists. Members of this organization wear red kerchiefs with their mandatory school uniforms, making it easy to identify any child who does not join. A similar organization for youngsters aged 10 through 14 is the Young Pioneers, in which membership is almost universal. Like the Young Octobrists, the Pioneers wear red scarfs and engage in social, civic, and recreational activities similar to those of the Boy Scouts or Girl Scouts. Most cities have Pioneer Palaces where afterschool programs are organized.[35] In the summer, Pioneers attend camps in the countryside or at the beach. The rules of membership in the Pioneers reflect the values the regime wishes Soviet youth to acquire:

> The Pioneer loves his motherland and the Communist Party of the Soviet Union. He prepares himself for membership in the Komsomol [Young Communist League].
> The Pioneer reveres the memory of those who have given their lives in the struggle for the freedom and the well-being of the Soviet Motherland.
> The Pioneer is friendly with the children of all the countries of the world.
> The Pioneer studies diligently and is disciplined and courteous.
> The Pioneer loves to work and to conserve the national wealth.
> The Pioneer is a good comrade, who is solicitous of younger children and who helps older people.
> The Pioneer grows up to be bold and does not fear difficulties.
> The Pioneer tells the truth and guards the honor of his detachment.
> The Pioneer strengthens himself and does physical exercises every day.
> The Pioneer loves nature; he is a defender of planted areas, of useful birds and animals.
> The Pioneer is an example for all children.[36]

At the age of 14 or 15, most Soviet children enter the Komsomol, a more advanced organization for young men and women up to the age of 28. Membership in the Komsomol is not as universal as it is in the Pioneers or Young Octobrists, although for years it was expected that any student who wished to be admitted to a university be a Komsomol member. Interviews with émigrés indicate that most Soviet youth joined the Komsomol for political and social reasons, rather than opportunistic ones. Many reported a "sense of pride" at having been accepted into the Komsomol. One émigré observed, "I joined the Komsomol for purely ideological reasons when I was fourteen or fifteen years old and when I truly believed in the cause of the Party and the general cause of Soviet power."[37] Others indicate that they joined the Komsomol with their entire class; to refuse membership was to isolate oneself. "The road that leads from cradle to Komsomol is a straight one. I did not think about it. . . . What matters is not to separate oneself from the collective. . . . I wanted to be like everyone else."[38] Another émigré observed, "It was more difficult not to join than to join."[39]

Interest in the Komsomol typically tapers off as the student grows older, however. In 1974, for instance, approximately 63 percent of 15- to 17-year-olds were members, but only 20 to 25 percent of 26-year-olds and 27-year-olds were.[40] One émigré who had succeeded in avoiding membership in the Komsomol was confronted by her supervisor and told: "In your work you cannot be a nonmember. When you get to be 28 you can do as you like."[41] A former graduate student at Sverdlovsk University observed, "Those who categorically refuse to enter the Komsomol and the Party place themselves outside the frame of the society and close all doors to themselves."[42]

The Komsomol is more overtly political than the organizations for younger children. It is considered the training ground for aspiring party members. In fact, of all new members of the CPSU, almost three-fourths enter through their Komsomol affiliations.[43] The organization of the Komsomol is virtually identical to that of the CPSU, and Komsomol secretaries gain valuable leadership experience, preparing them for future assignments in the Party. To ensure effective control over the Komsomol, its highest offices are exempted from the 28-year-old age ceiling. As a result, many of the Komsomol leaders are in their thirties and even early forties.

The Komsomol directs the energies of Soviet youth in constructive ways and provides a channel to the leaders for information about the attitudes of the young. The organization also mobilizes young men and women in support of the regime. During the summer, Komsomol brigades are sent to work on construction projects in Siberia or to assist in the harvest. In the mid-1950s, Komsomol laborers were used in Khrushchev's Virgin Lands program, in which previously untilled regions of Kazakhstan were plowed and planted in an attempt to solve the Soviet Union's chronic agricultural problems.

With the introduction of social and political reforms under Gorbachev, the popularity of the Komsomol has been greatly diminished. By 1988 membership had fallen to 38 million, down approximately 4 million from 1985.[44] The proportion of all 14- and 15-year-olds entering the Komsomol has dropped by some 25 percent.[45] Even the head of the Komsomol, Viktor Mironenko, is reported to be having difficulty convincing his own son to join.[46] Attrition within the ranks of the Komsomol is even more dramatic in the non-Slavic republics. In Georgia, for example, the Komsomol has been disbanded entirely and its massive headquarters in downtown Tbilisi is being used to provide office space for the numerous opposition parties that have sprung up in recent years.

The efforts of the Soviet regime to instill socialist values in its citizens do not stop when citizens reach the age of 28. In virtually every village and every city neighborhood, there are agitation-propaganda (agitprop) centers. These Soviet equivalents to community centers in the United States organize public lectures on topics ranging from "The Soviet Peace Program in the Middle East" to "Perestroika and the Need for Better Work Discipline." Propagandists for the agitprop centers are trained at the Academy of Social Sciences in Moscow and are invariably party members.

Most cities and towns also have Houses of Culture that offer an array of public lectures and social events. Public interest in such meetings is notoriously low, however; most of the youth attend only if coerced by their Komsomol leaders or if it is necessary in order to gain admission to a dance or rock concert.

For the adult population, public propaganda and agitation work is also carried out in factories, enterprises, housing units, and offices. Members of the CPSU are expected to devote a minimum of one day per week to "party work." A distinguished professor at the Leningrad University law school confessed that she would probably not have joined the Party if her husband had not been killed in World War II and her children had not grown up and moved far away. She simply would not have had enough time for party work—which in her case meant speaking to workers in factories on such legal topics as the rights of workers under Soviet law, legal problems in divorce, and legal protections of pregnant workers.

FUNCTIONS OF IDEOLOGY
IN THE USSR

Ideology in the USSR has performed several significant functions. It has been used over the years to mobilize the public in support of the goals of the regime. Millions of citizens have participated in parades, demonstrations, party meetings, and public lectures, all designed to instill in them a sense of involvement, civic responsibility, support for the CPSU, and the willingness to endure hardship in the struggle to "build communism."

Marxist-Leninist ideology was also used to legitimize the regime and its policies. Lacking the legitimacy of a popularly elected democratic regime, the Soviet leadership had to base its legitimacy on the notion that the policies of the vanguard party would benefit the whole society and that they therefore merited the support of the populace. Political leaders went to great lengths to find appropriate quotations from Lenin to justify their policies. When no quotation was available, as once happened in 1962, one was conveniently "discovered."[47] While two diametrically opposed policies may both be justified ideologically, it is significant that the Soviet leadership feels obliged to legitimize each policy initiative and each new decision in ideological terms.

Ideology served as a shared language of political discourse. Policy disputes and the conflicting ambitions of aspiring political leaders were often expressed in ideological terms. As noted earlier, the contest between Stalin and Trotsky to succeed Lenin focused not on their respective personal traits and abilities, but on the issue of "socialism in one country" versus "international revolution."

Historically, Marxist-Leninist ideology has also fulfilled an integrating function. For years it unified peoples of diverse ethnic origins, classes, regions, and levels of education in a common cause. Social integration and cohesion is especially important in the USSR, where wide ethnic, cultural, regional, and economic differences exist. In recent years the integrative capacity of Soviet ideology has diminished and ethnic and regional conflicts have become much more prominent.

Finally, as noted previously, Marxist-Leninist ideology fulfilled a symbolic function. It provided Soviet citizens with something to believe in, instilling in them patriotism, national pride, and support for the regime. For succeeding generations of Soviet citizens, however, the ideological appeal of Marxism-Leninism has waned. Increasingly, the legitimacy of the Soviet regime rests not on its ideological foundations, but on its ability to enact effective policies that improve standards of living and maintain the security of Soviet citizens.

The economic and social stagnation of the Brezhnev years precipitated an ideological dilemma by the 1980s. The more enfeebled the leadership, and the more society degenerated into corruption and sloth, the more the leadership heralded the glories of "advanced socialism." Brezhnev, like Stalin, attempted to create a cult around himself. Factories and cities were named after him. Art exhibits were devoted to portraits of Brezhnev. The widening gap between reality and the triumphant claims of the official ideology resulted in massive cynicism and popular rejection of Marxism-Leninism, especially among the intelligentsia and youth.

THE DECLINE OF IDEOLOGY

How successful are these efforts to inculcate political values in the Soviet people? Surveys indicate that despite the government's extensive *agitprop* efforts, the majority of the populace ignores official propaganda.[48]

There appear to be few "true believers" in the USSR. While some citizens feel obliged to defend Soviet policies and offer frequent references to Marxist-Leninist principles, few realistically anticipate the dawn of communism, the withering away of the State, or the sudden eradication of social classes.

The decline in virtually all spheres of Soviet life which has characterized the last two decades has had a significant impact on the mentality of the Soviet people and on their attitudes toward the official ideology. Support for the doctrine has evaporated quickly in recent years. A 1990 poll showed that only one in five Soviet citizens support the ideals of socialism.[49] When Soviet citizens were asked what the main tasks facing the country are, only 9.4 percent responded "to return to the road of building genuine socialism."[50] Demonstrators in the streets of Moscow carry placards reading "Down with communism," "Down with the cult of Lenin!" and have called for Gorbachev and other leaders to resign. The largely empty slogans that once adorned the tops of public buildings have all been removed because they became embarrassing reminders of the gaps between reality and the grandiose claims of the the ideology. Statues of Lenin and other revolutionary leaders have been removed in many towns and cities, and the names of the cities, districts, streets, and squares dedicated to the Bolshevik past have reverted to their historic, prerevolutionary names. Many Soviet citizens are too cynical even to try to change things. A Soviet shopper reflected: "Maybe I am to blame, after all. I am not out there demonstrating and demanding change the way the people did in Prague. But after seventy years of Communism, we have been robbed of our belief that we can bring about change."[51]

THE POPULAR IDEOLOGY
OF THE SOVIET PEOPLE

That intelligent Soviet citizens are increasingly rejecting the tenets of the official ideology does not mean that all efforts at political socialization are a failure. Many elements of the Soviet popular ideology, or political culture, reflect (and are reinforced by) Marxist-Leninist principles. For instance, Soviet citizens place a heavy stress on collectivism, rather than individualism. Graffiti and vandalism are not as common in the USSR as in the West, because there is a sense that public property belongs to everyone and should be guarded. One former Leningrad University student remarked, "I don't like to drink in public—it doesn't present the best picture of our society."[52] This is not to imply that public intoxication does not occur in the USSR; in fact, it is nearing epidemic proportions.[53] But among many Soviet citizens, there is a greater tendency than in the West to consider the consequences of one's behavior for the society as a whole.

A strong sense of egalitarianism characterizes Soviet political culture.[54] A survey conducted in October 1989 found that 49 percent of those polled agreed that "the government should not permit too large a difference between high and low incomes."[55] Almost 60 percent did not favor permitting private citizens to own large factories, and 36.2 percent noted that the expansion of private ownership will increase the divisions between "the wealthy" and "the poor."[56]

Soviet citizens are accustomed to turning to the State to guarantee their quality of life. The State functions in loco parentis, providing jobs, housing, health care, education, and pensions for its citizens. Many Soviet citizens who have emigrated to the West are so accustomed to the paternalism of their government that they are bewildered by the responsibilities they must assume for themselves. They must find their own jobs, locate their own housing, purchase their own health insurance, and save for their children's educations. Some émigrés bitterly criticize Western governments for "luring" them to the West without guaranteeing them jobs and housing. Most émigrés do not appear to be seeking political or religious freedom so much as the opportunity to share in the material abundance that the capitalist West offers. In fact, they are often perplexed and offended by the wide diversity of viewpoints allowed to be expressed in a free, open society. One émigré watching a march by a group of neo-Nazis in Chicago exclaimed, "There should be a law against this!"[57]

While Soviet citizens turn to the State to guarantee their livelihood, they continue to view the political leaders as detached from the masses. In the popular conception, power does not "bubble up" from the people, but "trickles down" from above. Only 32.5 percent of citizens surveyed recently felt that the State exists to serve the interests of the citizens. (See Table 4-1.) It is a classic we–they dichotomy: we the people, they the leaders. "There is nobody

Table 4-1. The State of the Nation

Question: With which of the following statements about the relationship between the state and its citizens do you most agree?[a]

Our state has given us everything, no one has the right to demand anything more from it	4.4
The state has given us quite a lot, but we can demand even more	11.3
The state has given us so little that we are not obligated to it in any way	8.4
Our state is now in such a bad condition that we must help it, even if we have to make sacrifices	33.2
We should become free people and demand that the state serve our interests	32.5
No opinion	10.3

[a]2,687 Soviet citizens responded to this question.
Source: New Outlook, 1, no. 3 (Summer 1990): 22.

in this country, nobody, who has ever experienced true democracy," says
Zinaidu Zaslavsky, a bakery worker from Moscow. "This country has always
been ruled by a dictator of some sort, and now the dictator is telling us there
will be democracy."[58]

Nationalism runs deep in the Soviet people, who possess a strong sense
of attachment to Russia, to the soil. While Soviet youth, especially in the
cities, are attracted to Western styles and popular culture, they remain patriotic, ardent supporters of their country.

The greater freedom to express views afforded by *glasnost'* has combined
with deteriorating economic conditions to turn nationalism into intolerance.
National chauvinism has fueled ethnic conflicts in Georgia, Armenia,
Azerbaidzhan, Kazakhstan, Moldavia, and numerous other areas. In general,
there has been a breakdown in social trust and a hardening of views on social
deviance. In a 1990 public opinion poll, a significant portion of the respondents favored "eliminating" (executing) the following classes of "social devi-
ants": murderers (71.9 percent), homosexuals (33.7 percent), prostitutes
(28.4 percent), drug addicts (28.0 percent), persons born with birth defects
(22.7 percent), "rockers" and "skinheads" (21.2 percent). Some nationalistic
movements, such as Pamyat, have attempted to exploit such intolerance for
their own political gain.

Western visitors to the USSR are constantly bombarded with questions:
"How many rooms are there in your apartment?" (Single-family houses are
virtually unheard of in the USSR.) "How many years' salary does it take to
buy a car?" "How much do blue jeans cost in the United States?" In one such
session with an official in an institute of the Academy of Sciences, the ques-
tioner apparently felt uncomfortable that the USSR was not measuring up
favorably. He thought a second and then blurted out, "Well, at least in the
Soviet Union we don't lynch blacks!" The steadfast loyalty to Russia and
pride in being Russian transcends politics. As one student remarked, "We
have lived under autocratic governments for centuries, but this is still Russia;
this is our country. We will endure!"

Finally, despite their revolutionary origins and revolutionary rhetoric,
the Soviet people are preoccupied with order and stability (*poryadok*). The
Brezhnev generation of leaders who rose to prominence as a result of Stalin's

bloody purges in the 1930s were the products of bureaucracy, not of revolution. They placed a premium on caution, going through channels, and not challenging the status quo. They bore a closer resemblance to corporate boards of directors in the capitalist West than to the fiery Russian intellectuals and revolutionaries of the late 1800s and early 1900s.

The conservatism of Soviet officials is aptly illustrated by an incident recounted by an American professor. In 1968, the professor was asked to lead a visiting delegation of Soviet politicians on a tour of New York City. At one point, the American offered to take the visitors to see Columbia University, where, he explained, a group of leftist students had taken over the administration building. A large portrait of Marx was draped from the president's office window, and a student strike had halted classes. The Soviet officials, all distinguished members of the Party, were visibly shaken at the prospect of witnessing such a "disturbance." They remarked, "You should have all those hooligans arrested!"

Notes

1. Francis Fukuyama, "The End of History?" *National Interest* (Summer 1989): 4.

2. For a discussion of ideology, see Lyman Tower Sargent, *Contemporary Political Ideologies*, 4th ed. (Homewood, IL: Dorsey Press, 1978), 3–6.

3. Peter C. Sederberg, *The Politics of Meaning* (Tucson: University of Arizona Press, 1984), 168–169.

4. It is common for ideologies to incorporate idealized concepts and values. That the American economic system bears little resemblance today to a laissez-faire economy is not as important as the fact that laissez-faire is still a widely held value in the American popular culture. See Murray Edelman, *The Symbolic Uses of Politics* (Urbana, IL: The University of Illinois Press, 1967).

5. Tom Bottomore, Laurence Harris, V. G. Kieman, and Ralph Milliband, eds., *A Dictionary of Marxist Thought* (Cambridge: Harvard University Press, 1983). According to these authors, Marx's work is fraught with ambiguities and contradictions that contemporary readers often overlook.

6. For example, see Karl Marx, "Wage Labor and Capital," in Robert C. Tucker, ed., *The Marx-Engels Reader*, 2d ed. (New York: W. W. Norton, 1978), 207–208.

7. This view of class conflict leading to social evolution was also expressed by Friedrich Engels. See "Socialism: Utopian and Scientific," in Tucker, *Marx-Engels Reader*, 699.

8. Karl Marx and Friedrich Engels, "Manifesto of the Communist Party," in Tucker, *Marx-Engels Reader*, 473.

9. Ibid., 478, 483.

10. This evolutionary process is gradual, according to Marx. One stage of development is not necessarily clearly distinguished from the next, so that, in advanced feudalism, there are not only peasants and landlords but also a growing capitalist class that in time becomes dominant.

11. Karl Marx and Friedrich Engels, "The German Ideology," in David McLellan, ed., *Karl Marx: Selected Writings* (Oxford: Oxford University Press, 1977), 161.

12. Karl Marx, "Critique of the Gotha Program," in *Karl Marx: Selected Writings*, 569.

13. Ibid.

14. *Pravda*, 28 January 1959, 1.

15. Marx suggested that revolutions may be nonviolent in Britain, the United States, or Holland because of the well-established democratic institutions in these countries.

16. Georgii V. Plekhanov, *Sochineniya*, 3d ed., vol. 2 (Moscow: 1923), 329.

17. This view is usually associated with the Mensheviks; however, few Marxists in Russia were prepared to admit the possibility that any major stage might be skipped altogether. Even some of Lenin's early writings support this view.

18. Plekhanov, *Sochineniya*, 329.

19. V. I. Lenin, "What Is to Be Done?," in *Lenin: Selected Works* (New York: International Publishers, 1967), 189–202.

20. V. I. Lenin, "One Step Forward, Two Steps Backward," in *Lenin: Selected Works*, 257–449.

21. V. I. Lenin, "Two Tactics of Social-Democracy in the Democratic Revolution," in *Lenin: Selected Works* (New York: International Publishers, 1971), 105.

22. Leon Trotsky, *The Permanent Revolution* (New York: Pathfinder Press, 1970), 194.

23. Ibid.

24. Ibid. This statement was later used by Stalin to engineer Trotsky's demise.

25. In the early twentieth century, rudimentary communist parties and rapidly growing labor union movements existed in all three societies. See Christopher Lasch, *The American Liberals and the Russian Revolution* (New York: McGraw-Hill, 1962).

26. Cited in Donald W. Treadgold, *Twentieth-Century Russia* (Chicago: Rand McNally, 1964), 223.

27. Lenin was modest and believed in collective leadership. He indicated before he died that he did not wish to become immortalized. Stalin, nevertheless, chose to glorify Lenin in order to strengthen his own political position among Lenin's heirs.

28. Joseph Stalin, Political Report of the Central Committee to the Sixteenth Congress of the Communist Party, June 27, 1930.

29. See Nicholas S. Timasheff, *The Great Retreat* (New York: Dutton, 1946). For instance, under Stalin, ranks were reintroduced into the Red Army, "people's commissariats" reverted to the traditional designation as "ministries," and the Party was eclipsed by the state apparatus.

30. *KPSS v rez.* 8 (1961): 273.

31. Jerry F. Hough and Merle Fainsod, *How the Soviet Union Is Governed* (Cambridge: Harvard University Press, 1979), 225.

32. For a discussion of ideological developments after Khrushchev, see Alfred Evans, Jr., "The Decline of Developed Socialism?," *Soviet Studies* (January 1986): 1–23.

33. Constitution of the USSR (1977), Article 6.

34. Nigel Grant, *Soviet Education* (New York: Penguin Books, 1964), 88.

35. Soviet juvenile-affairs officials occasionally note that Pioneer Palaces and Komsomol groups need to expand afterschool activities. Because both parents work, youths are often unsupervised in the late afternoon. Soviet studies indicate that this is the prime time for delinquent acts to be committed by juveniles.

36. Cited in Allen Kassof, *The Soviet Youth Program* (Cambridge: Harvard University Press, 1965), 79.

37. Cited in Aryeh L. Unger, "Political Participation in the USSR: YCL and CPSU," *Soviet Studies* 33 (January 1981): 107–124.

38. Ibid.

39. Ibid.

40. Ibid.

41. Ibid.

42. Ibid.

43. *Pravda*, 26 September 1983, p. 2.

44. Ben Eklov, *Soviet Briefing: Gorbachev and the Reform Period* (Boulder, CO: Westview, 1989), 46.

45. Ibid.

46. Ibid.

47. The 1962 controversy surrounded Khrushchev's position that economic matters should take precedence over political matters. Khrushchev was accused of violating the tenets of Leninism on this point. However, a "rediscovered" unpublished chapter of Lenin's 1918 article "Immediate Tasks of Soviet Power" conveniently supported Khrushchev's position. See Carl Linden, *Khrushchev and the Soviet Leadership* (Baltimore: Johns Hopkins University Press, 1966), 149.

48. Ellen Mickiewicz, "Policy Issues in the Soviet Media System," in Erik P. Hoffman, ed., *The Soviet Union in the 1980s* (New York: Academy of Political Science, 1984), 114.

49. Cited on "All Things Considered," NPR, 6 November 1990.

50. Opinion poll conducted by the All-Union Center for the Study of Public Opinion Institute Fall 1989 and Spring 1990, cited in *New Outlook* 1, no. 3 (Summer 1990): 23.

51. *New York Times*, 8 February 1990, p. A9.

52. From a conversation with the author in 1976.

53. See Nick Eberstadt, "The Health Crisis in the USSR," *New York Review of Books*, 19 Febuary 1981.

54. Cited in *New York Times Magazine* 28 October 1990, p. 71.

55. *Ibid.*, p. 10.

56. *Ibid.*, pp. 18, 20.

57. *New York Times*, 10 July 1978, p. 14.

58. *New York Times*, 8 February 1990, p. A9.

Selected Bibliography

Berdyaev, Nicolas. *The Origins of Russian Communism*. London: Geoffrey Bles, 1955.

Berlin, Isaiah. *Karl Marx*. New York: Time, 1963.

Brzezinski, Zbigniew. *Ideology and Power in Soviet Politics*. New York: Praeger, 1967.

Deutscher, Isaac. *The Prophet Armed*. New York: Vintage, 1959.

———. *The Prophet Unarmed*. New York: Vintage, 1959.

———. *The Prophet Outcast*. New York: Vintage, 1959.

———. *Stalin: A Political Biography*. New York: Vintage, 1949.

Kassof, Allen. *The Soviet Youth Program*. Cambridge: Harvard University Press, 1965.

Lane, Christel. *The Rites of Rulers: Ritual in Industrial Society—The Soviet Case*. Cambridge: Cambridge University Press, 1981.

Lenin, V. I. *Lenin: Selected Works*. New York: International Publishers, 1967.

———. *Lenin: Selected Works*. New York: International Publishers, 1971.

Meyer, Alfred. *Communism*. New York: Random House, 1960.

———. *Leninism*. Cambridge: Harvard University Press, 1957.

Miliband, Ralph. *Marxism and Politics*. Oxford: Oxford University Press, 1977.

Trotsky, Leon. *The Permanent Revolution*. New York: Pathfinder Press, 1970.

Tucker, Robert C. *The Marx-Engels Reader*. New York: W. W. Norton, 1978.

———. *Stalin as Revolutionary, 1879–1929*. New York: W. W. Norton, 1973.

Tucker, Robert C., ed. *Stalinism*. New York: W. W. Norton, 1977.

Ulam, Adam. *The Bolsheviks*. New York: Collier, 1965.

Venturi, Franco. *Roots of Revolution*. New York: Grosset & Dunlap, 1960.

Wolfe, Bertram D. *Three Who Made a Revolution*. New York: Dell, 1948.

5

The CPSU
and the Emerging
Multiparty System

From 1917 until 1990 the Communist Party of the Soviet Union (CPSU) was the nucleus of all political activity in the USSR. It proclaimed itself the "leading and guiding force of Soviet society."[1] At all levels of government, it was charged with making policy and supervising the prompt, efficient execution of policy decisions. Then in mid-March 1990, the Congress of People's Deputies amended the Soviet Constitution to legalize the existence of other parties in the USSR. In a matter of months, the Soviet Union has evolved from a single-party system in which policies were determined by a limited number of powerful bureaucrats and party officials to a fledgling multiparty democratic system. Yet the CPSU, given its size, degree of organization, control of newspapers, and recruitment network, still predominates.

CPSU GROWTH

Since its founding in 1898, the CPSU has grown at a phenomenal rate. The first Marxist party in Russia and forerunner of the Communist Party, the Russian Social Democratic Worker's Party, was founded in 1898. In January 1917, just prior to the overthrow of the tsarist regime, the Party numbered only 23,600 members.[2] The personal danger associated with membership in revolutionary parties and the secrecy with which the early Party had to operate combined to limit membership to a relatively small number. Party membership was also restricted by Lenin's belief that party members should be an elite band of dedicated revolutionaries.

The legalization of the Party after the Tsar's abdication led to an influx of 50,000 new members by April 1917. Another massive enrollment occurred after the October Revolution. T. H. Rigby notes that this growth was still highly spontaneous and subject to little guidance by party leaders.[3] Party membership had swelled to approximately 350,000 by the Eighth Party Congress in March 1919, which ordered the reregistration of party members to sift out political opportunists—in most cases those who had joined the Party after the October Revolution. The Civil War temporarily diminished party ranks as members were subject to mobilization for the front, and membership fell to less than 150,000 by August 1919.

Following the successful conclusion of the Civil War, a renewed effort was made to strengthen the Party, especially among peasants and workers. By the time of the Tenth Congress in 1921, the Party totaled three-quarters of a million members. Membership was especially attractive to peasants, who could expect rapid upward mobility. However, this also led to an increase in corruption and careerism.

With the normalization of domestic affairs under the New Economic Policy begun in 1921, Lenin instructed the Party to purge from its ranks members guilty of "passivity, careerism, and failure to carry out instructions."[4] Between August 1921 and early 1922, the Party lost almost one-fourth of its membership.

Mass recruitment into the Party has been a feature of every period of crisis in the history of the Soviet regime, and the succession crisis following Lenin's death was no exception. In an effort to pack the CPSU with his supporters, Stalin launched the "Lenin enrollment" in 1924. In three months, the Party expanded by more than 40 percent, and by 1927, the CPSU totaled 1.3 million members. The major expulsions during this period were Trotsky-ists and other opponents of Stalin.

The beginning of Stalin's drive for collectivization of agriculture and rapid industrialization in 1928 necessitated better party representation in the countryside and on the factory floor. Between 1928 and 1931, more than 900,000 new party members were recruited—a 70 percent increase.

Having consolidated his position and enforced a strict planning regime in the economy, Stalin launched the purges, which totally reshaped the Party from top to bottom. The purges (*chistki*) lasted from 1933 through 1938 and occurred in three waves, each more far-reaching and violent than the preceding one. In January 1933, a joint resolution of the CPSU Central Committee and the Central Control Commission ordered the verification of party documents of all party members, resulting in the expulsion of 16 percent of the party membership. The "paper purge" took its toll mainly among workers and peasants who had entered the Party in 1929 during the mass recruitment drive that accompanied collectivization and forced industrialization. Older party members were largely untouched by this purge.

In response to the assassination of Leningrad party chief, Sergei Kirov, in December 1934, Stalin ordered a purge resulting in the removal of thousands of Old Bolsheviks from the ranks of the Party. By 1936 and 1937, the purges had expanded to middle-ranking party and state officials. During this second wave of purges, party membership declined by about half a million members.

The last and most violent wave of purges began in late 1936, with the show trials of Zinoviev, Kamenev, and fourteen other "enemies of the people." All confessed and were promptly executed. The trials did not end the reign of terror, which came to be called the *Ezhovshchina*, after N. I. Ezhov, Stalin's newly appointed head of the secret police. The *Ezhovshchina* wiped out the elite of virtually all institutions of Soviet society. The military was especially hard hit; an estimated one-fifth to one-half of all officers were purged.[5] In aggregate figures, the CPSU membership dropped from 3.5 million in 1933 to 1.9 million in 1938. More than 100,000 party members were purged in 1937 alone, and the purge appears to have focused on the most prominent members of the Party.

The Central Committee plenum of January 1938 marked the end of the purges. Having eliminated virtually all opposition and eradicated a whole generation of Soviet party and administrative officials, Stalin began rapidly to promote white-collar specialists to fill the posts vacated during the purges. This group, which enjoyed unprecedented upward mobility in the Soviet system, came to be known as the "Class of '38." It counted among its numbers Leonid Brezhnev, Alexei Kosygin, Andrei Kirilenko, and Mikhail Suslov, all of whom received their first major appointments within the Party in 1938 or 1939.

One of the Party's first responses to the German invasion in 1941 was to instruct local party committees to broaden their recruitment efforts, especially among production workers. The Party's entrance requirements were significantly relaxed. Although the wartime loss of 20 million Soviet citizens included more than 3.5 million party members, an active recruitment campaign more than compensated for the casualties. The Party grew by almost two million members during the period 1941–1945. By 1946, in fact, many local party organizations were experiencing difficulty in assimilating, training, and deploying newly recruited party members, a problem that was exacerbated by the discharge from the armed forces of large numbers of party members. During the immediate postwar years, the Party first achieved a significant representation in the collective farms because the overload of members enabled the leadership to assign extra party personnel to rural areas. Admission standards were toughened again after the war, and expulsions increased to 100,000 per year.

The longest, most sustained increase in the Party's ranks came during the Khrushchev era (1953–1964). Stalin's death in 1953 began a protracted succession struggle, a crisis that was never fully resolved throughout the decade in which Khrushchev served as First Secretary. Although the annual intake of new party members was only a fraction of what it had been during earlier periods of heavy recruitment, the fact that the influx lasted for a full decade resulted in a 70 percent increase in party membership after Stalin's death.

Soon after Khrushchev's ouster in October 1964, the Central Committee's journal *Partiinaya zhizn'* published a decree that signaled renewed restrictive policies on recruitment into the Party. Three changes were introduced into the party rules to tighten admission procedures: the vote of the primary party organization needed to nominate someone for party membership was raised from a majority to two-thirds of the members; sponsors had to have been party members for a minimum of five years instead of three; and the age for admissions through the Young Communist League (Komsomol) was raised from 18–20 to 18–23. The annual rate of party growth steadily diminished from 6.7 percent in 1965 to 1.3 percent in 1973. From the mid-1970s to the mid-1980s, the rate of growth stabilized at between 1.5 to 2.5 percent per year.[6] In recent years, however, the Party has experienced rapid attrition.

In 1987 and 1988 the Party's popularity began to wane. Numerous independent groups began to emerge, coalescing around ethnic, ideological, and policy issues. By 1989 several of these groups were acting as quasi-parties, developing policy platforms and endorsing candidates for the newly created Congress of People's Deputies. The "destroika" of the CPSU was signaled by Gorbachev's decision in February 1990 to revise Article 6 of the Constitution, which granted the Party a monopoly on power. In the local elections of March 1990, candidates associated with the CPSU did not fare well, while those affiliated with various independent groups won impressive victories.

The rapidly declining popularity of the CPSU is reflected in membership and recruitment statistics. In 1989 alone the CPSU declined by 260,000 members.[7] During the first six months of 1990, party membership in the Soviet Far East declined by 3.5 percent.[8] In Sverdlovsk, Boris Yeltsin's hometown, the Party declined by 3.2 percent over the same period.[9] In Sakhalin the decline was 4.5 percent, and it was 5.8 percent in the Magadan region.[10] In Alma-Ata, the capital of the Kazakh republic, officials expected more than a 10 percent decline in party membership in 1990.[11] At the same time, admissions to the CPSU have fallen to the lowest levels in history.

PARTY COMPOSITION AND SATURATION

As the Party has grown over the years, major changes have occurred in its composition. The social-class profile of the Party in 1917 reflected its proletarian outlook: 60 percent of the membership came from the working class, 32 percent were members of the intelligentsia, and only 8 percent were peasants.[12] During the New Economic Policy, Soviet power was gradually extended to the countryside, and this resulted in the gradual increase of peasant representation to 27 percent by 1927.

Stalin's introduction of rapid industrialization in 1928 signaled a shift to the "proletarianization" of the Party, an effort to enhance worker representation. The percentage of new recruits into the CPSU from the working class jumped from 57 percent in the period from July 1924 to July 1928 to 78 percent in 1929.[13] Despite the tendency for working-class party members to move into supervisory white-collar jobs, 43.8 percent of all party members were actually employed in manual labor by 1932.[14]

In the aftermath of the purges and World War II, the CPSU stabilized its ranks with ever-increasing numbers of white-collar specialists. As Table 5-1 shows, white-collar representation rose to 48.3 percent in 1947, making the intelligentsia the single largest component of the Party. A decade later, Khrushchev allowed the percentage of white-collar experts to slip above the 50-percent mark, a truly startling development in a Party billing itself as the "party of the workers and peasants." Khrushchev justified this trend toward the deproletarianization of the Party by declaring that the concept of the vanguard party was no longer applicable; he introduced instead the concept of "the Party of the whole people."[15]

The changes in the social composition of the Party reflect ongoing

Table 5-1. CPSU Composition by Social Class, 1917–1989 (in percent)

Year	Workers	Peasants	White Collar
1917	60.2	7.5	32.2
1927	55.1	27.3	32.2
1947	33.7	18.0	48.3
1957	32.0	17.3	50.7
1967	38.1	16.0	45.9
1977	42.0	13.6	44.4
1983	44.1	12.4	43.5
1989	43.2	11.4	45.4

Sources: T. H. Rigby, *Communist Party Membership in the USSR, 1917–1967* (Princeton: Princeton University Press, 1967), 85; "KPSS v tsifrakh," *Partiinaya zhizn'* 1, 21 (1977): 20–43; *Pravda*, 26 September 1983; and *Izvestiya Ts. K. KPSS* 1, no. 2 (1989).

changes in the nature of Soviet society. With the mechanization of agriculture, fewer peasants were needed in the countryside. The cities offered improved housing, running water, central heat, better-quality consumer goods, and access to cultural amenities. Consequently, the 1930s and 1940s witnessed a migration from rural areas to the cities, especially by the young.

During the postwar years, there was also a growing realization that effective decision-making in the CPSU required the participation of the best minds, the most experienced experts, and the most able administrators in policy-making. The proliferation of state administrative agencies also created new white-collar positions to be filled by party members.

Since 1957, there has been a small but consistent reduction in both white-collar and peasant representation, while the percentage of workers has risen steadily. However, many of those today classified as workers are engaged in technical fields such as petrochemicals, instrument-making, electronics, and engineering, not in traditional "smokestack" industries. These are the workers most likely to rise out of the ranks of the working class and into white-collar professions.

The percentage of women in the ranks of the Party has increased gradually from only 7.5 percent in 1920 to 33 percent in 1990.[16] Nevertheless, women, who constitute 53.5 percent of the total Soviet population, are still drastically underrepresented. There are several reasons for the small proportion of women in the Party. Party membership entails the commitment of a substantial amount of time to party work, usually one day per week. Approximately 80 percent of all Soviet women work outside the home; in addition, they bear the full responsibility for running the household, shopping, cooking, and cleaning. In reality, most Soviet women today are engaged in dual employment and have little time or energy to devote to party affairs.

Those women who are party members tend to be relegated to lower levels in the party apparatus and are placed within traditional women's specializations: cultural affairs, education, the Komsomol, consumer affairs, and light industry. The only women to attain full member status on the Politburo represented "women's fields." Ekaterina Furtseeva served as a party secretary and then as Minister of Culture under Khrushchev and Brezhnev and Galina

Semyonova supervises "women's issues" on the Politburo. Among the 307 full members elected to the CPSU Central Committee at the Twenty-Eighth Party Congress in 1990, there were 31 women.[17] In fact, female representation on the Central Committee has declined from 9.7 percent in July 1917 to only 7.5 percent today.[18] In recent years, women have accounted for approximately one-third of all the secretaries of primary party organizations; 20 percent of district party organizations; few, if any, first secretaries of *oblast'* party committees; and only 3.2 percent of all *obkom* bureau members.[19]

Women have achieved some limited gains under Mikhail Gorbachev. The number of women elected to the CPSU Central Committee at the Twenty-Seventh Party Congress in 1986 increased to fifteen, compared to only eight at the Twenty-Sixth Party Congress in 1981, and the number at the Twenty-Eighth Congress rose to thirty-one.* Gorbachev also promoted Aleksandra Biryukova to the Secretariat, where she is responsible for supervising light industry, the food industry, and consumer services. In October of 1988 she was also elevated to candidate member of the Politburo. In July 1990, however, Gorbachev restructured the top party organs and Biryukova lost her seat on the Politburo. Instead, Galina Semyonova, the editor of the popular magazine *Krestyanka*, was added to the Politburo and placed in charge of "women's issues."

In terms of nationality, the Party has always granted a disproportionate share of its membership to Russians and other Slavs, while non-Slavs have been underrepresented. As Table 5-2 shows, Russians are overrepresented by 9.7 percent, while the Central Asian nationalities (especially the Tadzhiks, Uzbeks, and Turkmen) and the Moldavians are seriously underrepresented.

Some progress toward achieving parity has been made over the years. In 1922, Russians were overrepresented in the ranks of the Party by 19 percent.[20] However, recent demographic trends among the Central Asian nationalities will make it difficult for them to achieve full representation in the Party's ranks. The birthrate among the Moslems of Central Asia is four times the national average. By the year 2000, it is estimated, the Islamic peoples will constitute the largest ethnic group in the USSR. These nationality groups have historically been the least likely to assimilate into Soviet society and also the least inclined to join the Party. Since 1987, however, the proportion of Russians, Ukranians, Belorussians, Latvians, Lithuanians, and Estonians has declined, while the proportion of members from the least-developed areas—Central Asia, Transcaucasus, and Moldavia—has risen. Thus, the ethnic composition of the CPSU is changing; the Party is becoming less European and more Asian.[21]

In contrast, Georgians and Belorussians have proven very able to assimilate and seek advancement through the Party and are slightly overrepresented. The most disproportionate representation in the Party is for Jews, who have more than twice their share of the adult population in the Party.[22] Given the

---

* However, the majority of the women elected at both the Twenty-Seventh and Twenty-Eighth Congresses were "token" representatives. See Elizabeth Teague, "Fall in Representation of Party Apparatus in CPSU Central Committee," *Radio Liberty Report on the USSR* 1, no. 19 (12 May 1989): 5.

Table 5-2. Party Membership by Nationality and Percentage of Overrepresentation or Underrepresentation, January 1, 1989

Nationality	Percent of Population	Percent of CPSU	Overrepresentation or Underrepresentation[a]
Russian	52.4	57.5	+9.7
Ukrainian	16.0	15.9	−0.6
Uzbek	4.7	2.5	−46.8
Belorussian	3.6	3.8	+5.5
Kazakh	2.5	2.1	−16.0
Azerbaidzani	2.0	1.8	−10.0
Armenian	1.6	1.5	−6.3
Georgian	1.4	1.7	+21.4
Lithuanian	1.0	0.8	−20.0
Moldavian	1.1	0.6	−45.4
Tadzhik	1.1	0.5	−54.5
Turkmen	0.8	0.5	−37.5
Kirghiz	0.7	0.4	−42.9
Latvian	0.6	0.4	−33.3
Estonian	0.4	0.3	−25.0
Other	10.1	9.7	−4.0

[a]The data in this column were calculated by taking the difference and dividing it by the percentage of the population to arrive at the percentage overrepresented or underrepresented in the CPSU.

Sources: Population figures from the 1979 USSR census; CPSU figures from Pravda, 26 September 1983, p. 1; Izvestiya Ts. K. KPSS 1, nos. 1 and 2 (1989).

strong correlation between level of education and party membership, much of the apparent variation in party membership by nationality actually reflects the variation in education.[23] The educational profile of the CPSU indicates that there is still room for improvement. In 1983, a total of 29.5 percent of the Party had a higher (university-level) education, 2.2 percent had an incomplete higher education, 43 percent had a secondary education, 15.7 percent had an incomplete secondary education, and 9.6 percent had only a primary-school education.[24] However, virtually all party secretaries have higher educations. As Table 5-3 shows, this represents a substantial improvement since World War II.

The stability of cadres promised under Brezhnev resulted in a marked decline in CPSU turnover. Fewer members were expelled or forced to retire, and recruitment dropped to a fraction of the level it had been under Khrushchev. The consequence was the aging of the Party, as indicated in Table 5-4. The percentage of party members over 51 years of age increased by 5 percentage points, while the percentage of party members between 31 and 51 decreased by 6 percentage points.

The massive influx of the Class of '38, which enjoyed rapid upward mobility at a relatively early age (most of those promoted after the purges were in their early to mid-thirties), filled the party nomenklatura positions for the next thirty to forty years before they retired or died. For the succeeding

Table 5-3. Educational Level of Party Secretaries, 1946–1983 (in percent)

Level	1946	1952	1956	1969	1983
Higher	50.2	77.8	92.6	99.0	99.9
Secondary	39.0	21.5	6.3	1.0	0.1
Primary	10.8	0.7	0.0	0.0	0.0

Sources: Pravda, 26 September 1983, p. 2; and "KPSS v tsifrakh," Partiinaya zhizn', no. 21 (1977): 20–43.

generation of aspiring party members—those entering the CPSU after World War II—few opportunities for advancement existed until the late 1970s and early 1980s, when the Class of '38 began to pass from the scene.

The Leninist conception of the Party held that membership should be reserved for a relatively small, elite group of professional revolutionaries who would act as the "vanguard of the proletariat." The CPSU is not a mass party; it comprises only 6 percent of the population of the Soviet Union. Yet this figure is misleading. It obscures the extent to which membership in the CPSU affords Soviet citizens a chance to participate in the political process. When one considers factors such as level of education, the Party has a high level of representation among the secondary elite.

The party rules state that the minimum age for joining the Party is 18. Nevertheless, few citizens are permitted to join that early; the average age of admission was 27 years in 1975 (down from 31 years in 1965).[25] At the other end of the age spectrum, the retirement age is 65 for most men and 62 for women. When the young and the retired segments of the population are excluded, the percentage of citizens between the ages of 30 and 65 who are party members is 12.5.[26]

For reasons cited earlier, female representation in the Party is small. Hough found that 21 percent of all Soviet men between the ages of 31 and 60 were in the CPSU, and more than 50 percent of the male college graduates in that age group were party members.[27] This group corresponds to that segment of the population that is upwardly mobile, career-oriented, and most attentive to political issues. Since party membership represents a substantial commitment of time and energy, participation is not casual; it affords a great potential for this segment of Soviet population to affect policies.

Some interesting trends in party membership are revealed by examining the degree of party membership among various occupation groups (see Table

Table 5-4. Age Profile of the CPSU, 1977–1983 (in percent)

Age	1977	1978	1983
25 or younger	5.8	6.0	6.4
26–30	10.8	11.2	11.2
31–40	25.8	24.5	20.8
41–50	26.4	26.1	25.4
51–60	18.1	19.0	21.1
61 or older	13.0	13.2	15.1

Sources: 1977 data from Partiinaya zhizn', no. 21 (November 1977): 31; 1978 data from Kommunist (1978): 203; and 1983 data from Pravda, 26 September 1983, p. 2.

Table 5-5. Party Saturation by Occupation Group

Occupation	Percent in CPSU
Party officials	100
Komsomol officials	100
Ministers (e.g., Minister of Defense)	100
Judges	90
Public prosecutors	82
Journalists	75
Writers	50
Scientists	50
Composers	33
Engineers	25
Schoolteachers	25
Agronomists, livestock specialists	20–25
Artists	20
Physicians	16.6

Sources: Pravda, 26 September 1983, p. 2. The figures for judges and public prosecutors were reported in Gordon B. Smith, The Soviet Procuracy and the Supervision of Administration (Leiden, The Netherlands: Sijthoff & Noordhoff, 1978), 25.

5-5). Rigby classifies occupations in the USSR into three types: party-restricted, high-saturation, and low-saturation occupations.[28] Party-restricted occupations are those in which virtually every person is a party member, and membership appears to be a requirement or highly desired for appointment. Examples would include party, Komsomol, ministerial, and high-ranking state administrative officials; judges, public prosecutors, police and military officers, editors and journalists; and directors of major state farms, factories, plants, and enterprises.

High-saturation occupations are those in which 20 to 50 percent of the category are party members. Examples include scientists, scholars and academics, writers, composers, principals and other school administrators, and defense attorneys. Low-saturation occupations encompass the majority of the working class, that is, workers who are without professional qualifications or who do not perform managerial or administrative functions. High levels of party saturation help to extend the Party's control over virtually every institution in Soviet society.

Recent defections from the ranks of the CPSU have diminished somewhat its saturation of the leading positions in Soviet society. Nevertheless, the Party continues to occupy a commanding force in virtually every institution.

PARTY RECRUITMENT

Joining the Party represents a commitment to the Soviet system and a pledge to support party policy, uphold the values of the society, and abide by party rules. To those who enter its ranks, CPSU membership affords many privileges; but it also entails many obligations. Under Gorbachev, many of the special privileges enjoyed by party members have been abolished.

In most cases, aspiring party members do not apply for admission; they are invited to join by their Komsomol organization or the primary party organization (PPO) at work. The Komsomol is the major conduit for admission into the Party's ranks. In recent years, three-fourths of all new recruits have come from Komsomol organizations.[29] The admission procedure is long and arduous and designed to ensure that the applicant is, as the Soviets put it, "worthy of the lofty title of communist." The Party prides itself on selecting only the best and the brightest.

Aspiring entrants into the Party must receive letters of nomination from three persons who have been party members for at least five years. For those seeking admission via the Komsomol, references must be provided by the district or city Komsomol committee.

Applicants then fill out formal application forms, which detail their educational background, awards and honors, job experience, military record, and personal information such as age and date of birth. Also included in the application are a brief autobiography and a personal statement.

The application is then presented to the PPO bureau in the factory, office, or institution in which the applicant is employed. The PPO committee or bureau makes an informal recommendation to the full meeting of the PPO; in practice, this recommendation is usually decisive. Soviet authors have stressed that the PPO considerations should be open to nonmembers as well, because it is important to know how the applicant is viewed by his or her peers.[30] The applicant is present at the full meeting of the PPO and may be asked to clarify points of information or to ascertain his or her knowledge of party affairs and sincerity in seeking admission. A vote is held; a two-thirds majority is required for admission. The PPO's decision, if affirmative, must then be confirmed by the district or city party committee superior to the PPO.

After payment of a modest entrance fee and monthly membership dues, the newly elected member begins one year of candidate or probationary membership (*kandidatskii stazh*). At the end of this period, the candidate's application is again brought before the PPO for a final vote. This decision is far from pro forma. One Soviet source reported that between 1966 and 1971, almost 112,000 candidates were denied full membership after their probationary years.[31] Nevertheless, this represents only 3.5 to 4 percent of all candidates.

THE OBLIGATIONS AND PRIVILEGES OF PARTY MEMBERSHIP

CPSU members are obliged to be model workers and to take an active part in public life. They are expected to devote much of their leisure time to party meetings, public discussions and lectures, election work, and organizing party affairs. In their personal lives, party members are supposed to be above reproach. Alcoholism or scandal can prompt an investigation by the party committee and can result in a member's reprimand or even expulsion from the Party.

While a CPSU member is expected to be well-versed in Marxist-Leninist ideology and to undertake advanced ideological training at the Higher Party School, being ardent and doctrinaire does not guarantee admission into the Party. The CPSU is intent on admitting only persons who are loyal, capable, and bright, not dogmatic and inflexible.

Although party membership carries many burdens, it also confers some privileges and benefits. Clearly, the greatest benefit is the elite status it conveys. Membership in the CPSU opens the doors to advanced training at the prestigious universities and institutes. It makes possible appointments to influential, well-paid positions in industry and state administration, as well as within the Party. Party membership also affords citizens the opportunity to become politically involved and to influence policy.

Although it is impermissible for party members to abuse their privileges in pursuit of personal aims or gains, such cases did occur in the past, especially during the Brezhnev years, and are not unheard of today.

ORGANIZATION OF THE CPSU

The CPSU derives much of its power and influence not only from its size and its hold on the major positions in the society, but also from its highly bureaucratized organizational structure. The CPSU constitutes a pseudo-government parallel to the official organs of the State. Power is invested in its highest offices and is effectively transmitted to every factory and farm in the USSR via a highly centralized and authoritative structure.

The Primary Party Organization.   From its inception in Russia, the Party has adopted a cellular structure. That is, in every factory, every collective farm, every enterprise, every hospital in which there are three or more party members, a primary party organization (PPO) is formed. The adoption of the cellular structure was initially necessary to facilitate secrecy and minimize the danger to political revolutionaries, whose activities were closely watched by the tsar's secret police. Clandestine workers' meetings were less conspicuous in the workplace than they were after work hours in the homes of fellow revolutionaries.

The cellular structure of the CPSU, as a form of grass-roots organization, has persisted in part due to tradition. Lenin's conception of the Party also retains a powerful ideological appeal. In addition, the Party has been able to use its link to the workplace effectively to mobilize workers in support of party policies. The Party relies on the PPOs in every factory, enterprise, and collective to be its "eyes and ears" at the grass-roots level, reporting on problems, inefficiency, and mismanagement.

Without exception, every member of the CPSU must be a member of a primary party organization. As of January 1, 1983, there were 425,897 PPOs in the USSR.[32] The number of members in the PPOs varies from three in small shops or rural collectives to several hundred in large industrial complexes. The average size of a PPO in industrial enterprises is 103 members; on state farms, 68 members; on collective farms, 60 members; and in construction organizations, 39 members.[33]

In small collectives, shops, offices, and restaurants, the PPOs have a simple structure; party members simply meet periodically to elect a secretary, who maintains party records, collects dues, and reports to higher party officials. In such organizations, the PPO secretary's job is not a full-time occupation for which the secretary is paid, but rather a voluntary, civic duty. Approximately 40 percent of all PPOs are of this type, although the trend is clearly away from such simple organizations.[34]

In large industrial plants employing thousands of people, PPOs may consist of several hundred members. Such enterprises are frequently divided into subsections, scattered throughout a city or region. In such instances, the simple model of a PPO described previously is clearly inadequate to fulfill the Party's functions. In large enterprises, PPOs are divided into production-unit party organizations, each headed by a bureau (or executive committee) and a secretary. These production-unit party organizations report to a party committee for the entire industrial plant, which also is chaired by a secretary. In large PPOs such as this, the secretary is a powerful figure who is a full-time party functionary, often serving as deputy director of the enterprise. He or she is assisted by a staff that is responsible for keeping records and organizing political education programs.

Regardless of its size or degree of complexity, the PPO is governed by the general meeting of its members, usually held on a monthly basis. The general meeting formally elects the committee and secretary for a one-year term in small PPOs, and for two or three years in larger PPOs. The general meeting also admits and expels members. In 1979, only 88 of the 400,000 PPO secretaries were elected by ballot; the rest were nominated by higher party organs and ratified by the general meeting.[35] The general meeting of the PPO also elects delegates to the party conference of the district or town in which the PPO is located.

One of the principal functions of the PPO is investigating shortcomings in the administration of the institution with which it is associated. This is referred to as *pravo kontrolya* ("the right of control"). Soviet sources define *pravo kontrolya* as the "systematic verification of the execution of laws, directives of the Party, and decrees of the government."[36] Until 1971, *pravo kontrolya* was granted only to PPOs in economic enterprises, factories, and farms. PPOs within the state bureaucracy did not enjoy the right of control because the State was considered to be under the "control" of the Party's central organs. This changed, however, at the Twenty-Fourth Party Congress in 1971. Under the new party rules, PPOs in state administrative agencies, local soviets, ministries, and scientific and other institutions are authorized to exercise "control."

In the early years of the Soviet regime, *pravo kontrolya* of the PPOs often brought party secretaries into direct conflict with industrial managers; this came to be called the "red/expert" dilemma. Facing the need to stimulate production in a given factory, the "red" (secretary of the PPO) would halt production for agitation-propaganda sessions to inspire the workers to achieve more. The factory manager, on the other hand, would advocate longer shifts and oppose stopping the assembly lines so that the workers could listen to a political harangue. During the 1920s, the "reds" often controlled the factory manager, but in recent years the two have tended to work in tandem, and as the prestige of the CPSU has fallen, more and more power rests with the factory manager and less with the PPO secretary.

Recent analysis of career patterns suggests that PPO secretaries are less pivotal in policy-making than are chief administrators and enterprise directors. However, when matters of principle (*prinstipyal'nye voprosy*) arise, PPO secretaries participate in discussions. For example, the decision within a machine-tool plant to adopt the brigade form of labor organization and to reward workers not for their individual performance but according to the brigade's performance would involve the PPO secretary. While secretaries cannot veto actions of administrators, they can and do refer matters to higher party organizations. The relatively subordinate role of PPO secretaries is also evidenced by the fact that the office of the secretary is in most cases a part-time (*neosvobozhdennyi*) position.

Complicating this relationship is the fact that most managers and heads of state agencies are themselves party members, and most of them serve on party committees at the district, city, or regional level. As such, they are regarded as "persons trusted by the Party and the State."[37] In most cases, the PPO secretary and the administrative chief occupy *nomenklatura* positions; thus they enjoy the confidence of higher party committees, and each has distinct political resources upon which to draw in case of a conflict.

Many Western specialists have viewed party *kontrol'* primarily as a conflictual relationship between local party officials and state agencies and enterprises. However, Hough indicates that, in practice, the relationship is often a cooperative one, incorporating a degree of division of authority on the basis of expertise.[38] In fact, the principal significance of the PPO in state administrative agencies may not be in controlling administrative activities, but rather in expanding participation in decision-making to a wider circle of persons with practical expertise.

Finally, the PPO is crucial in the recruitment of new party members from the work force. Party cells also identify competent, aggressive party members suitable for promotion into positions of responsibility within the ranks of the CPSU.

LOCAL PARTY ORGANS

Above the PPO level, the CPSU is geographically organized. The lowest level of territorial party organization is the district (*raion*) in rural areas and the city party organization in urban areas. Every two years, PPOs within a district select delegates to the *raion* party conference. To be named a delegate to the party conference is an honor accorded to exemplary workers and powerful PPO secretaries. The *raion* party conference normally reaffirms the party line, under the watchful eyes of a representative of higher authority.[39] In addition, delegates to the conference ratify a slate of predetermined candidates to serve as members of the district party committee, including the first secretary, for a term of two years.

At the district level, the real political power rests with the *raikom* (*raion party committee*), which convenes approximately six times per year in plenary sessions to discuss edicts from central party organs, to monitor plan fulfillment in industry and agriculture within the district, and to issue directives to subordinate PPOs. The *raikom* is composed of up to one hundred members, the majority of whom are full, voting members. Candidate or nonvoting members normally constitute 25 to 30 percent of the total and may be consulted on policy matters. These individuals constitute a reserve from which new members may be selected. The membership of the *raikom* typically includes party and state officials of the district; trade union and Komsomol leaders; the directors of major industrial enterprises, collectives, or state farms; a few representatives of the scientific-technical, educational, and cultural establishments; and a few rank-and-file workers and peasants.

Given its large size and its infrequent sessions, the *raikom* delegates much of its day-to-day authority to an executive body, a political bureau (*politburo*) comprising approximately twelve powerful local party and government officials and representatives of major industrial enterprises. The *raikom* bureau meets several times a month to discuss major political and economic issues confronting the district. Frequently, specialists and party functionaries are invited to *raikom* bureau sessions to give reports and to discuss particular problems.

The first secretary presides over the *raikom* and the bureau. The first secretary is often the most powerful political figure in the district, the direct link between the district party organization and higher party bodies. The first secretary is ultimately responsible for supervising the efficient implementation of party policies in the district. Success or failure in this major political assignment will determine the first secretary's ultimate career prospects. Should the district prosper, should major industrial concerns fulfill their plan targets, should no major scandals cast a cloud on the administration's performance, the secretary will most likely be promoted, perhaps to a larger, more prominent district or city. Thus, the first secretary functions somewhat as did the boss of a political machine in an American city during the late 1800s and early 1900s.

The first secretary's job also requires the mediation of disputes that invariably arise between various interests within the district. Under the pressure of striving to fulfill their production quotas, various industrial enterprises may come to the first secretary to request extra personnel or resources. Local police and social workers may present the official with varying solutions to juvenile delinquency. State farms in the district may complain that they should be granted special allocations to raise the quality of rural housing to the same level as in the cities. Thus, the first secretary is not only a "boss," but also a "broker," allocating resources and setting priorities for the district as a whole.

At the Nineteenth Party Conference in July 1988, Gorbachev proposed fusing the functions of local and regional first secretaries with those of the chairmen of local and regional soviets. This was a controversial proposal that would in effect merge party and state positions, strengthening even more the local and regional party secretaries, at the expense of state governmental bodies. The proposal encountered so much opposition from both local party and state officials that it was tabled indefinitely.

Attached to the *raikom* is the party *apparat*, the bureaucracy responsible for the day-to-day management of party affairs. The *apparat* is organized into several departments. Among the most important are the propaganda and agitation department (*agitprop*), and the organizational department, which handles local party records and the approval of nominees to PPO secretaryships. District party committees also have departments of agriculture and of industry and transportation, which supervise the economic activities of their respective sectors within the district. While the party secretaries specializing in production matters are not supposed to interfere in or substitute for industrial management, they are concerned with minute details affecting economic performance. The general department handles the internal affairs of the *raikom*, setting the agenda and scheduling meetings of the *raikom* and the bureau, handling correspondence, and duplicating and circulating documents and texts of decisions. The typical structure of a *raion* party committee is presented in Figure 5-1.

The outlines of the Party's structure at the district level remain essentially the same at higher levels—in large cities, regions, and republics, as well as at the All-Union level. For instance, the next territorial level above the district is the region (*oblast'*). As of January 1, 1983, there were 151 *oblasti* in the USSR, ranging from 544,000 square miles to 1740 square miles. Thus, an *oblast'* is somewhat larger than a county in the United States, but smaller than most states. It is the modern equivalent of the prerevolutionary province. The regional party committee (*obkom*) is elected by a party conference that convenes every three years. Delegates to the *oblast'* party conference are selected at the district (*raion*) party conferences. Like the *raikom*, the *obkom* meets infrequently, delegating much of its day-to-day decision-making responsibility to the *obkom* bureau, an executive body of approximately ten to fifteen powerful officials that is headed by the regional first party secretary.

The larger territory and more diverse responsibilities of the regional party organization are reflected in a greater number of departments. Attached to the *obkom* is a secretariat—a body comprised of approximately twelve party secretaries, each of whom heads a department. The typical *obkom* secretariat has the following departments: administrative organs, agriculture, construction, culture, general, information, industrial-transportation, light industry and food industry, organizational party work, propaganda and agitation, science and education, trade, and financial and planning organs. In a region where a particular sector of the economy dominates, there may be a separate department devoted to it (for example, the coal deparment in the Donets region of the Ukraine, or the oil department in the Tiumen region in western Siberia).

In the fifteen republics that form the USSR, party organizations are structured much like those at the district and regional levels. Every five years, the republic party congress is held to elect a republic central committee,

Figure 5-1. Structure of a District Party Committee

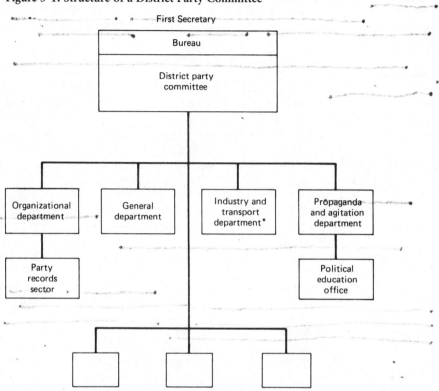

Ad hoc departments and commissions

*May be replaced by an agricultural department in a rural *raikom*.
Source: Adapted from *KPSS—naglyadnoe posobie* (1973): 63, and Ronald J. Hill and Peter Frank, *The Soviet Communist Party* (London: George Allen and Unwin, 1981), 59.

comprising the leading party, state, educational, industrial, and cultural officials of the republic as well as a few token workers and farmers. Like their
counterparts at lower levels, the republic central committees delegate authority to a political bureau (*politburo*), while day-to-day administration of party
affairs is handled by the republic secretariat.

CENTRAL ORGANS OF THE CPSU

The CPSU is organized according to the principle of *democratic centralism*. Article 19 of the party rules defines *democratic centralism* in terms of
four criteria: (1) all leading party bodies are elected from below, but elections
in the Party are indirect; (2) party organs are expected to make periodic
reports of their activities to the general meeting (conference or congress) of its
members and to higher-ranking party organs; (3) strict party discipline is
observed, and the will of the minority is subordinated to that of the majority;
and (4) the decisions of higher party organs are binding on lower-ranking

party bodies. The strong centralizing elements in the organization of the Party ensure that supreme power resides in its central organs—the CPSU Congress, the CPSU Central Committee, the Politburo, and the CPSU Secretariat. (See Figures 5-2 and 5-3.)

Recently the doctrine of democratic centralism has come under attack. Speaking to a plenum of the CPSU Central Committee in February 1990, Gorbachev declared: "The renewal of the Party presupposes its profound, all-embracing democratization and a rethinking of the principle of democratic centralism with an accent on democratization and the power of the Party masses."[40] However, the bureaucratic apparatus of the CPSU has succeeded so far in protecting its power and influence. While Gorbachev and others have called for opening the Party to greater influence by the masses, little has changed in the actual process of decision-making within the Party.

Party Congress. Every five years, more than five thousand delegates gather in the Palace of Congresses in the Kremlin for the CPSU Congress. According to party rules, the body, which convenes for approximately ten days, wields ultimate political authority over party affairs.[41]

Congress sessions are devoted to formal speeches by the party leadership on domestic and foreign-policy issues confronting the USSR. In recent years, the congresses have featured the presentation of two major reports: one by the General Secretary of the Party dealing with the domestic and foreign-policy concerns of the Central Committee, and one by the Chairman of the Cabinet of Ministers on the new Five-Year Plan.

The congresses also afford local and regional party officials the opportunity to report on the achievements of their regions and to criticize the Ministry of Economics and Forecasting or central ministries. Heads of foreign communist parties are also invited to attend and usually address the gathering. The Party Congress serves as a forum for the leadership to articulate new policy directions and reaffirm past decisions. Since the Twentieth Party Congress in 1956, when Khrushchev stunned the delegates with his "Secret Speech," an unprecedented denunciation of Stalin and his "crimes," the congresses have tended to be, at least on the surface, rather dull, formal, and

Figure 5-2. Central Organs of the CPSU

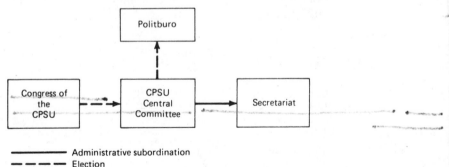

———————— Administrative subordination
— — — — Election

Source: Based on CPSU statutes.

Figure 5-3. The Territorial Structure of the CPSU

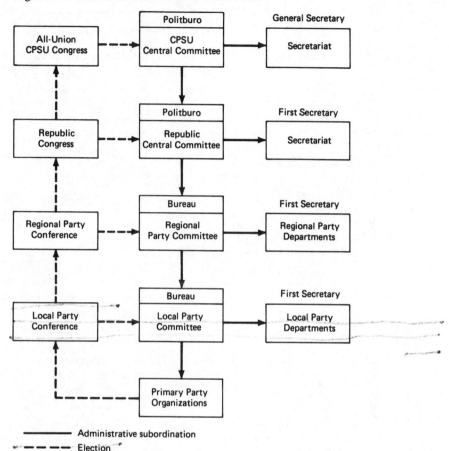

Source: Based on CPSU statutes. The figure omits the levels of territory (*krai*) and national area (*okrug*). Also, some cities are directly subordinated to republic party committees rather than to regional party committees. Within large cities, there may be district (*raion*) committees between the PPOs and the city party committee.

above all, predictable. Behind the scenes, however, there is a great deal of informal politicking.

One of the most important tasks of the Party Congress is to ratify a slate of candidates for membership in the CPSU Central Committee. The list of persons nominated for Central Committee membership is determined in advance of the congress, probably by the Politburo. The congress also elects members of the Central Auditing Commission, which supervises party finances, and selects the chairman of the Party Control Committee, which is responsible for ruling on the expulsion of party members.

CPSU Central Committee. Between Party Congress sessions, the CPSU Central Committee wields the supreme authority in the Party. This collective body, which in 1990 consisted of 412 full members, represents a diverse array of powerful individuals and institutions. The largest group within the Central Committee, accounting for 35 to 40 percent of the membership, is the local, regional, and national party secretaries. The second most prominent bloc is composed of writers, artists, cultural officials, and scientists (11.4 percent); followed by ministers and chairs of state committees (7.7 percent); high-ranking military officials (4.1 percent); and a few factory managers, trade-union officials, and diplomats. In addition, the Central Committee awards membership as an honor to outstanding workers and peasants, who in 1990 constituted roughly 30 percent of the Central Committee membership.[42]

Only 8 percent of the Central Committee members are women, and 75 percent of the members have completed college.[43] The Central Committee includes members of thirty-four nationalities; non-Russians constitute forty-seven percent of the total.[44] More than half (52 percent) of the members are 50 years of age or less.[45]

The composition of the CPSU Central Committee elected at the Twenty-Eighth Party Congress in July 1990 differs dramatically from previous Central Committees. For example, the percentage of rank-and-file workers and peasants almost doubled from 15 percent to 29.8 percent. The portion of women also doubled, from four to eight percent; while non-Russians increased from 38 percent to 47 percent of the members. The most startling change occurred in the age profile of the Central Committee. Previously, only 5.3 percent of the members were under the age of 50, compared to 52 percent today.

On the one hand, it would appear that the Party is attempting to reach out to groups who have traditionally been underrepresented. On the other hand, the incorporation of more workers and peasants, women, non-Russians and younger officials may reflect the loss of power of the body. The latter view is corroborated by the decline in the number of Central Committee members being elected to seats in parliamentary bodies. In 1988, 76 percent of the Central Committee members were also deputies to the Supreme Soviet. Today only 25 percent of the members hold seats in the Congress of People's Deputies.[46]

The Central Committee is mandated to convene in plenary sessions at least twice a year, usually for only three to five days per session. Central Committee meetings are devoted to hearing reports on party matters, including the promotion, demotion, and expulsion of members; ratifying Central Committee decrees, which are binding on all party members; and discussing pressing national and international issues. Plenums are normally convened prior to and after major state and party events—Supreme Soviet sessions, Party Congresses, introduction of new Five-Year Plans, and the ratification of a new constitution. Plenums have also been convened to discuss international crises and major new policy initiatives. For instance, plenums were called to consider the Middle East crisis in 1967, the invasion of Czechoslovakia in 1968, the opening of détente with the West in 1971 and 1972, and the invasion of Afghanistan in 1979 and 1980. The purpose of the plenum on these occasions appears not to have been the airing of differing viewpoints, but the demonstration of support for the policies of the ruling Politburo.

Central Committee plenums are a mixture of largely ceremonial functions and meaningful deliberations on policy problems. However, the infrequency and short duration of the committee sessions restrict participation considerably. Thus, on an average, only about one-third of the full members speak at Central Committee plenums.[47] Officials of large or especially important regions are apparently given precedence in speaking to the body. The first secretaries of the largest republics (Ukraine, Kazakhstan, Belorussia, and Uzbekistan) routinely take the rostrum, as do the party leaders of Moscow and Leningrad. Similarly, ministers of prominent ministries and chairmen of influential state committees (e.g., Ministry of Defense and KGB) frequently address the Central Committee on economic and political matters.

On occasion, the Central Committee may be called upon to resolve matters over which the Politburo is deeply divided. The most notable case of this occurred in 1957, when Khrushchev convened an emergency plenum of the Central Committee after a faction within the Politburo attempted to oust him.

Little is known about the process for selecting Central Committee members. One Soviet source indicates that a list of candidates is drawn up before the Party Congress and is discussed by party leaders of the various regional, territorial, and republic delegations before being presented to the congress for a vote.[48]

Candidates to the Central Committee are chosen on the basis of a combination of personal merit and position. Robert Daniels has noted that the Central Committee is merely a collection of individuals selected to represent various functional groups and regional interests.[49] Certain positions and titles appear to confer automatic Central Committee membership; in fact, as much as 90 percent of the body may be determined in this manner.[50] Thus, the Central Committee contains a broad spectrum of policy expertise, experience, skill, and preferences upon which the top leadership may draw. For those Central Committee members whose selection is not explained by position, other factors—personality, ties to the General Secretary, region, nationality, or gender—may weigh heavily in the decision. For example, the well-known film actor Mikhail Ulyanov is a member of the Central Committee.

Since Khrushchev's time, turnover of Central Committee membership has remained very low. Brezhnev rose to power, in part, by promising to bring "stability of cadres." Nowhere is this stability as evident as in the lack of change in the Central Committee. Of the members elected to the body in 1971, 90 percent were reelected in 1976, and 90 percent of the 1976 members were returned to the Central Committee in 1981. The token worker and peasant delegates rotate somewhat more frequently; only five of the twelve worker and peasant Central Committee members elected at the Twenty-Fifth Party Congress were reelected at the next congress. Although individual worker and peasant representatives change over time, the general profile of representation does not vary substantially.

Recent developments indicate that Gorbachev is attempting to shift the locus of decision-making from the Central Committee to the Supreme Soviet, that is, from the Party to the State. At the April 1989 Central Committee plenum, 110 members of the Central Committee and the Central Auditing

Commission were forced to resign. Among those ousted were several regional party first secretaries, "dead souls" who had suffered defeat in the March 1989 elections to the Congress of People's Deputies. As a result of these resignations, the representation of party officials in the body fell from 44.5 percent in 1986 to 33.9 percent in 1989, the lowest proportion of seats since the Stalin period. Military representation decreased from twenty-three to eleven seats (from 7.5 percent to 4.4 percent).

At the same time, twenty-four candidate members were elevated to full membership. Of these, nine (almost 40 percent) are workers or peasants. Their promotion raised the level of representation of "tokens" to thirty-six, or approximately 15 percent of the Central Committee membership. The elevation of rank-and-file workers may have been motivated by Gorbachev's desire to reach out to the masses to enhance his popularity, and at the same time bring in nonprofessional politicians who will likely support the General Secretary on crucial votes.

At the Twenty-Eighth Party Congress in 1990, the Central Committee was enlarged to 412 members, but the position of candidate (nonvoting) member was abolished. Only fifty-nine of the members elected at the Congress were members of the previous Central Committee, the highest turnover rate in the history of the body.

The Politburo.   For more than seventy years the real power over day-to-day decisions in the USSR resided in the Politburo. Gorbachev, however, has succeeded in significantly limiting the Politburo's dominance over policy-making. In recent years the body has varied in size between eleven and fifteen full members and roughly six to eight nonvoting candidate members. Like the Central Committee, the Politburo has increased in size over the years. In 1919, it consisted of only five full members and three candidate members. The institution has historically been dominated by Russian males; only two women have ever served on the Politburo as full members: Ekaterina Furtseeva, Khrushchev's Minister of Culture, and Galina Semyonova, whom Gorbachev appointed to supervise "women's issues."

The workings of the Politburo remain shrouded in secrecy. Western specialists learned only in 1973 from an interview with Leonid Brezhnev in the *New York Times* that the Politburo met once a week, on Thursday mornings, with the General Secretary presiding.[51] Yuri Andropov, who was General Secretary from November 1982 to February 1984, lifted the curtain of secrecy somewhat further by permitting the agendas of Politburo meetings to be reported in *Pravda*. Although sketchy, the reports give Soviet citizens an idea of the wide range of issues considered by the political leaders.

Until the Twenty-Eighth Party Congress in 1990, the Politburo included among its members the leading political, economic, and foreign policy figures in the country. Table 5-6 shows the Politburo prior to the Congress. Reflecting its role as the principal policy-making institution, the Politburo represented a broad mix of regional, economic, and political interests. Decisions in the Politburo were reached by a process of coalition-building.

As a result of the Twenty-Eighth Congress, the Politburo was substantially reconfigured. (See Table 5-7 on page 116.) The changes enlarge Politburo size to twenty-four members. The largest portion of the new body

Table 5-6. CPSU Politburo Prior to the Twenty-Eighth Party Congress

Full Members of Politburo

Mikhail Gorbachev	General Secretary; Chairman, USSR Supreme Soviet
Yegor Ligachev	Party Secretary; Chairman, Agrarian Policy Commission
Vadim Medvedev	Party Secretary; Chairman, Ideological Commission
Nikolai Ryzhkov	Chairman, USSR Council of Ministers
Eduard Shevardnadze	Minister of Foreign Affairs
Nikolai Slyun'kov	Party Secretary, Chairman, Socioeconomic Policy Commission
Vitalii Vorotnikov	Chairman, Russian Republic, Supreme Soviet Presidium
Aleksandr Yakovlev	Party Secretary; Chairman, International Policy Commission
Lev Zaikov	Party Secretary; First Secretary Moscow City Party Committee
Vladimir Kryuchkov	Chairman, Committee for State Security (KGB)
Yurii Maslyukov	First Deputy Premier; Chairman Gosplan

Candidate Members of Politburo

Aleksandra Biryukova	Deputy Premier, Light Industry Consumer and Social Affairs
Anatolii Luk'yanov	First Deputy Chairman, USSR Supreme Soviet
Georgii Razumovsky	Party Secretary; Chairman, Party Building and Cadre Policy Commission
Aleksandr Vlasov	Chairman, Russian Republic Council of Ministers
Dmitrii Yazov	Minister of Defense
Evgenii Primakov	Chairman, Council of the Union, USSR Supreme Soviet
Boris Pugo	Chairman, Party Control Committee

are the first secretaries of the fifteen union-republics. In addition, the Politburo includes the heads of several party departments and the editor of the CPSU's newspaper, *Pravda*. Gone are the influential policy-makers holding governmental positions—Premier, Minister of Foreign Affairs, Minister of Defense, Chairman of the KGB, and Chairman of Gosplan.

The new Politburo is substantially weaker than its predecessor. Not only does it no longer include leading government officials, but its unwieldy size and built-in regional antagonisms (for example, Armenia versus Azerbaidzhan, the Baltic republics versus Russia) have reduced its ability to reach consensus. Furthermore, Politburo meetings have been cut back from once a week to once a month. These changes signify that the Politburo is no longer the single most powerful decision-making body in the USSR. Power has shifted from the Party to the Presidency, the Security Council, and the Council of the Federation. (These bodies will be discussed in more detail in Chapter 6.)

The General Secretary.   There is little doubt that the most prominent and influential figure in the Politburo is the General Secretary. Nevertheless, the party statutes and Soviet textbooks do not mention his power, nor do they

Table 5-7. CPSU Politburo Elected at the Twenty-Eighth Congress[a]

Mikhail Gorbachev	General Secretary; Chairman, Presidium, USSR Supreme Soviet
Vladimir A. Ivashko	Deputy General Secretary
Aleksandr S. Dzasokhov	Ideology Commission chief
Gennadii Yanaev	International Commission chief
Yegor Stroiev	Agricultural Commission chief
Yurii A. Prokofiev	Head of Moscow party organization
Galina Semyonova	Responsible for women's issues
Oleg Shelnin	Responsible for organizational issues
Ivan T. Frolov	Editor in chief, *Pravda*

Party Leaders of the Republics

Ivan K. Polozkov	Russia
Stanislav I. Gurenko	Ukraine
Yefrem Y. Sokolov	Beelorussia
Enn Arno Sillari	Estonia
Mikolas Burakeviclus	Lithuania
Givi G. Gumbaridze	Georgia
Islam A. Karimov	Uzbekistan
Pyotr K. Luchinsky	Moldavia
Absomat M. Masaliiev	Kirghizia
Kakhar M. Makhkamov	Tadzhikistan
Vladimir M. Movsisyan	Armenia
Ayaz N. Mutalibov	Azerbaidzhan
Nursuitan Nazarbaiev	Kazakhstan
Sapar A. Niyazov	Turkmenia
Alfreds A. Rubiks	Latvia

[a]As of July 9, 1990.

define his role. Westerners may find this oversight odd, because the General Secretary dominates the Soviet political scene to an extent unimagined in the West. Huge portraits of the General Secretary adorn many public buildings, and in the past factories and cities were named in honor of the General Secretary.

Despite the honors and accolades heaped on the General Secretary, the emphasis within the Party is on collective decision-making. Lenin established the principle of collective rule by the Politburo, and as is so often the case in the USSR, what Lenin enshrined in 1917 cannot be easily undone today.[52] Even during Stalin's autocratic reign, orders for the execution of high-ranking officials were signed by the entire Politburo.[53]

On many occasions, Nikita Khrushchev violated the principle of collective decision-making. In the process, he lost the support of his most powerful constituency—the local and regional party secretaries. Khrushchev's ill-conceived and often impulsive reforms, including the Virgin Lands program, the bifurcation of the party apparatus, and the decision to place missiles in Cuba, proved to be embarrassing failures that resulted in his ouster in 1964.

Leonid Brezhnev, who was selected to succeed Khrushchev, promised to adhere to the norm of collective decision-making. Brezhnev's leadership style stressed gradualism, going through channels, and consultation with all interested institutions. Greater effort was made under Brezhnev to involve experts in policy-making in order to avoid the problems that had plagued Khrushchev.

One unanticipated consequence of Brezhnev's shift to consultation and collective decision-making, however, was a dramatic dampening of reform and dynamism in decision-making. Problems festered while committees drafted reports, institutions lobbied, and experts were consulted. The stagnation of the latter half of the Brezhnev administration can be attributed to the General Secretary's failing health and lack of dynamic leadership. An energetic Brezhnev had been able to enlist the support of Premier Alexei Kosygin and Andrei Gromyko, Minister of Foreign Affairs, in favor of détente to overcome the opposition of conservative military officers and party ideologues. In the late 1970s, however, he was incapable of coping with steadily declining production rates and seriously eroding labor discipline.

Clearly, the General Secretary sets the overall tone and policy agenda of the regime. Yuri Andropov came to power for a brief fifteen-month period in 1982 and 1983, offering dynamic leadership, long-hoped-for reforms and innovations, stricter work discipline, and above all, a renewed sense of purpose and vigor. As one Soviet citizen confided, "When Andropov died, everyone cried. He was exactly what we needed. He would have ruled with an iron fist."[54]

The General Secretary's powers in the Politburo depend upon his ability to build a ruling coalition. Politburo decisions usually involve mediating conflicting institutional and regional interests, interests that are often represented by fellow Politburo members. Decision-making in such circumstances entails striking compromises, brokering differences, and bargaining. If the General Secretary is astute in these matters, he is likely to succeed on policy issues of vital importance to him. The limits upon his power appear to be those imposed by the Politburo members' internalized sense of what is proper and improper for him to do, and the collective power of his colleagues in the Politburo to constrain his actions.

No one has proven as adept at coalition building and bargaining within the Politburo as Mikhail Gorbachev. Gorbachev moved quickly after coming to office in March 1985 to consolidate his power within the Politburo. After just one year in office, Gorbachev had succeeded in replacing five of the twelve members of the Politburo, and, on most issues, could count on support from several of the other members. By the summer of 1987, Gorbachev had appointed three more Politburo members, replacing the corrupt former First Secretary of Azerbaidzhan, Geydar Aliev, and Mikhail Solomentsev, the Chief of the Party's Control Commission that is charged with ferreting out corruption. By this time Gorbachev could rely on the support of approximately three-fourths of the Politburo. In September 1989 Gorbachev succeeded in removing the last Brezhnevite from the Politburo, Vladimir Shcherbitsky, First Secretary of the Ukraine.

It is ironic that at the point that Gorbachev had thoroughly consolidated his hold on the Politburo, the Party itself began to lose public support and legitimacy. Responding to this development in 1989 and 1990, Gorbachev began to shift his focus from the Politburo to creating a new power base outside the CPSU—the Presidency.

The Party Control Committee. The Party Control Committee is the disciplinary arm of the CPSU, overseeing the investigation of violations of party rules and the expulsion of members. The committee also hears appeals of members who have been reprimanded or expelled by lower party organs. The composition of the Control Committee is not made public; only the chairman's name is known. Under Brezhnev, the Control Committee acted more as the passive "supreme court" of the Party, rather than as an aggressive investigatory body.[55] However, Gorbachev's vigorous campaign against corruption has expanded the scope of the Party Control Committee's activities. The Central Committee's journal, *Partiinaya zhizn'*, regularly publishes the decisions of the Control Committee, often in conjunction with an exposé condemning official misconduct or corruption by lower officials.

The Secretariat. Of paramount importance among the top party institutions is the Central Committee Secretariat. This organ, headed by the General Secretary, currently consists of twelve secretaries. Some of the secretaries are also members of the Politburo, and many of them are powerful heads of commissions in the Central Committee apparatus. The Central Committee secretaries and officials of their departments act on behalf of the Central Committee. Party secretaries are elected by the Central Committee, while their subordinate officials in the various Central Committee departments (*otdely*) are appointed. The latter are frequently referred to collectively as the *apparat*—the full-time party bureaucrats. The Secretariat meets weekly to discuss the work of the staff.

In 1990, there were twenty-five Central Committee departments, each with responsibility for supervising specific ministries, state committees, and other public organizations. Within each department are sectors (*sektory*) that further focus party attention on specialized problems, especially in economic matters. Within the Agriculture Department, for example, there are sectors for land cultivation, mechanization, procurement, reclamation and water conservation, forestry, and agricultural science, as well as sectors dealing with each of the major agricultural regions of the USSR.

One of the chief functions of the Central Committee Secretariat is the supervision of the exact and full execution of party policy by all ministries, state committees, and public organizations. The parallel structure of the Central Committee departments and the numerous state agencies enables the Secretariat to carry out this supervision effectively. Western experts even refer to the party secretaries as "shadow ministers." The principal function of this specialized party apparatus is to supervise and direct the work of the state bureaucracy. Thus, there is a close correspondence and frequent contact between the staff members of Central Committee departments and their counterparts in the ministries. Occasionally, a minister who dies or retires will be replaced by the party secretary who supervised his ministry. More than 20 percent of Gorbachev's ministerial appointments have come from the ranks of the Central Committee Secretariat.[56]

The Central Committee Secretariat is also charged with drafting decisions and policy memoranda for the Politburo and the Central Committee. Although this may appear to be a mundane, clerical task, in reality it provides the Secretariat with a critical role in policy-making. The Soviet decision-making system is structured so that most power resides in the center. Consequently, the political leaders in the Politburo are constantly flooded with requests, complaints, and appeals from institutions and individuals. Because there is so little delegated decision-making authority at lower levels, the Politburo is the final arbiter. Compounding the overload of decision-making authority in the Politburo is the tendency, originating under Brezhnev and continued by his successors, to allow for widespread consultation on policy decisions by all interested (*zainteresovannye*) institutions. Brezhnev once plaintively observed that so many vested interest groups were included in decision-making that it often delayed the implementation of party policies.[57] The Central Committee departments are frequently called upon to sort out a myriad of conflicting demands and positions and to draft policy statements for Politburo consideration.

The drafting of party proposals is often facilitated by the creation of temporary commissions within Central Committee departments. These bodies, which are under the direction of Central Committee staff but also incorporate experts, scholars, and state officials, have opened the policy-making process to a wider spectrum of the Soviet elite. At the same time, the commissions have enhanced the role of the Central Committee departments vis-à-vis the Politburo.

Finally, the Secretariat and its subordinate secretarial counterparts at the republic, regional, and local levels are responsible for personnel recruitment and selection. Numerous Soviet writers have acknowledged the critical role of the selection of cadres. According to one, "Cadre policy was and remains the key link of party leadership and the powerful lever through which the Party influences all affairs in society."[58] Another has written, "The most important component of the political leadership of the soviets is the active influence of the Party on the selection and placement of cadres in the soviets."[59] A third observer noted, "It is precisely in the realm of cadre policy that the commanding function (*vlastnaya funktsiya*) of the Communist Party as a leading force of socialist society manifests itself."[60]

One of the chief instruments by which the Party controls Soviet society is by approving appointments to key positions. Referred to as the power of *nomenklatura*, the Party's appointment responsibilities extend not only to influential party and government officials, but also to regional and local administrators, judges, police chiefs, school principals, hospital administrators, factory managers, and directors of state farms.

Party committees from the district to the CPSU Central Committee compile two lists, one of political and administrative posts for which the party committee is responsible, and one of the names of responsible citizens deemed suitable for filling those posts. A person need not be a party member in order to be considered for a position under the *nomenklatura* system. For example, prior to 1961 those who served as presidents of the USSR Academy of Sciences had not been party members. Nevertheless, the CPSU considered them sufficiently reliable and competent to be appointed to such an important post.

The *nomenklatura* exercised by the CPSU Central Committee encompasses more than 300,000 positions.[61] The *nomenklatura* systems of the fifteen republic party committees add another 260,000 positions, while *nomenklatura* positions at the regional level are estimated at 76,000 nationwide.[62] Most Soviet cities have several hundred *nomenklatura* positions, and even large factories and enterprises may have as many as four hundred such positions.[63] One observer estimates that the entire *nomenklatura* system in the USSR extends to more than three million positions.[64]

From fragmentary references by Soviet officials, Western specialists have concluded that Central Committee *nomenklatura* extends to most directors and some chief engineers of major plants and factories in the Soviet Union. High-ranking police and military officers; judges and public prosecutors; rectors of major educational institutions; editors of newspapers and magazines; and influential officials in social organizations such as the trade unions, the Komsomol, and cultural societies also come under the *nomenklatura* of the Central Committee. Collective-farm managers are appointed through the *nomenklatura* of the regional (*oblast'*) party committees, although it is expected that local and district party committees play an active role in the selection process.

In recent years, the *nomenklatura* system has come under criticism for promoting persons lacking proper credentials. Connections (*blat*), family ties, regional and ethnic loyalties, and corruption occasionally determine the suitability of candidates more than do experience and ability. Furthermore, the *nomenklatura* system has been criticized for inhibiting the influx of young, dynamic, highly qualified personnel into influential posts.

The future role of the *nomenklatura* in the Soviet political system is very much in doubt. Changes in Soviet election procedures and the legalization of opposition parties have limited the ability of the CPSU to control who is elected as deputies to local, regional, republic, and even all-union soviets. Many factories have also introduced "democracy in the workplace" by empowering the workers to elect factory managers.

In practice, however, the CPSU continues to dominate political life in the USSR and has jealously held on to its powers, including the power to influence appointments to major positions. Until the CPSU divests itself of the instrument of *nomenklatura*, the Soviet Union cannot develop a truly pluralistic, democratic political system.

CAREER ADVANCEMENT AND THE CPSU

Western scholars have only recently become aware of the widely varying career specializations associated with various party cadres. If one traces the careers of *obkom* bureau members, both prior and subsequent to *obkom* tenure, five clear patterns or types emerge: agricultural specialists, industrial specialists, ideological specialists, cadre specialists, and generalists.[65]

During their careers, upwardly mobile party members are commonly appointed to positions in both the state and the party apparatuses, while remaining in their fields of specialization. For example, a party member with an advanced degree in agronomy may serve as the deputy director of a regional agricultural administration prior to being named to the agriculture department of the *oblast'* party committee. From this position, he or she may move up to state deputy chairman of a rural district or perhaps director of the state agricultural administration in the region. From this state post, he or she may be promoted to first party secretary in a predominantly agricultural region.

Similar mixed party-state career paths are also typical of party members with specializations in industry, and to a lesser extent in ideological affairs and education. Industrial specialists in the Party may serve interchangeably as *obkom* secretary of industry, first party secretary of an industrial region or city, or chairman of the regional trade union council.[66] Ideological specialists tend to be assigned as *obkom* ideological secretaries in charge of agitation and propaganda activities, editors of regional newspapers, first secretaries of regional Komsomol organizations, or directors of state cultural or educational administrations affiliated with regional governments (soviets).

The mixed career path for the aspiring party leaders provides them with valuable experience not only in the Party, where policy decisions are made, but also in the state administration, where those decisions are implemented. This period of apprenticeship and relatively rapid promotion from position to position gives the party member valuable practical experience in both realms of the Party and State and in virtually every stage of the policy-making process. The appointment of party members to state administrative positions also enhances party control over state administrative bodies, ensuring that they effectively carry out the will of the party leadership.

One unintended consequence of the rapid rotation of party members is that, in a relatively short time, they become acquainted with a large number of upwardly mobile, young party members, all seeking to advance through the system. Informal power networks form, based upon shared experience in a given region or personal affiliations with a powerful figure. Traditionally, the best path to success in the Soviet political system has been to become the trusted associate, or client, of a powerful and rapidly rising patron. For example, most party members who rose to positions of prominence on Brezhnev's coattails were his long-time associates from his home region in Dnepropetrovsk, from the Eighteenth Army during the war, or from his tenure as First Secretary of Moldavia and Kazakhstan.

Gorbachev has brought along several of his past associates from his home region of Stavropol', including Vsevold Murakhovsky, Chairman of Gosagroprom, I. S. Boldyrev, First Secretary of Stavrapol' Kraikom, and V. G. Afonin, First Secretary of Kuibyshev. Anatolii Lukyanov was a fellow law student with Gorbachev at Moscow State University in the 1950s. Other officials, such as A. P. Lushchikov, N. E. Kruchina, V. I. Boldin, and A. S. Chernaev, were closely associated with Gorbachev during his early years in the Party Secretariat.

As the preceding discussion indicates, regional groupings and power bases play a crucial role in the determination of a person's political advancement in the Soviet Union. Lenin warned about the dangers of "family circles"—that is, powerful local and regional bonds between party officials and state administrators. Repeated efforts have been made to break up these local and regional constellations of power by rapidly circulating cadres. Yet they persist today. Some of the major power centers and people associated with them include:

Leningrad:	V. A. Medvedev, D. T. Yazov, L. N. Zaikov, A. Sobchak
Chelyabinsk:	V. G. Afanas'ev, Yu. Solov'ev, G. G. Vedernikov
Stavropol':	V. G. Afonin, M. S. Gorbachev, V. S. Murakhovsky, I. S. Boldyrev, V. I. Kalashnikov, B. M. Volodin
Kemerovo:	V. V. Bakatin
Moscow:	A. P. Biryukova, V. A. Grigor'ev, Ye. M. Primakov, N. V. Talyziev, V. V. Zagladin, G. Popov
Dnepropetrovsk:	V. M. Chebrikov
Kiev:	S. V. Chernonenko, A. S. Kapto, V. I. Mironenko, I. I. Skiba
Sverdlovsk:	B. N. Yeltsin, N. I. Ryzhkov, G. V. Kolbin, Yu. V. Petrov, Ya. P. Riabov, L. A. Voronin
Saratov:	V. K. Gusev
Krasnodar:	A. A. Khomyakov, G. P. Razumovsky, I. K. Polozkov
Novosibirsk:	E. K. Ligachev
Minsk:	N. N. Slyunkov, E. E. Sokolov, N. A. Stashenkov

These regional affiliations may on occasion reinforce personalistic patron–client ties, and on other occasions and on other policy issues may cut across those relationships. As might be expected, regional power centers are especially active in lobbying on issues of allocation of resources, capital investment, economic development, housing and consumer affairs, and nationality rights (especially those affecting language).

Clientalism is not unknown in other political systems, of course. Many of Ronald Reagan's cabinet members and White House staff had worked for him when he was governor of California. Jimmy Carter brought many of his Georgia associates to Washington when he assumed the presidency in 1976. In the Soviet political system, however, the tendency toward clientalism is especially pronounced. Several characteristics of the Soviet political system account for this marked tendency toward the development of patron–client relations. First, promotion within the various bureaucratic hierarchies dominating the Soviet political scene is the only path to power. Second, the decisive criteria for promotion are a mix of objective standards, achievements, and qualifications on the one hand, and loyalty and trust on the other. Third, the rivalries that exist among competing bureaucratic interests are especially evident within the highest political institutions in the USSR—the CPSU Central Committee and the Politburo. Finally, policy-making in such an environment forces officials to conspire and even to resort to quasi-legal or illegal means to achieve prescribed goals.[67] In short, the General Secretary is confronted with the task of forging a coalition within his Politburo on virtually every major issue. The Politburo represents in its members a wide variety of institutional, regional, and, in some cases, clientele interests. Consequently, there are enormous pressures to promote those individuals whom the General Secretary has long known and trusted and, most importantly, who are obligated to the General Secretary for their career advancement.

The salience of patron–client relationships and regional power centers may be waning in the light of the fundamental changes occurring in the Soviet political system. When the CPSU held an absolute monopoly on the reins of power in Soviet society, the focus of political activity, naturally enough, was on intra-Party conflict. Thus, political conflict between personal rivals, competing regions and institutions, and factions representing opposing positions on issues was manifested within the bounds of the Communist Party.

Now that the political process is gradually opening up to opposition parties, and interest groups have been able to organize and lobby publicly, political conflict has transcended the CPSU. Regional conflicts between Moscow and Leningrad, Slavic areas and non-Slavic areas are out in the open. So too, the personal rivalries between Gorbachev and Boris Yeltsin are openly and directly expressed rather than sublimated through patronage conflicts. That is not to say, however, that candidates do not employ patron–client relations to further their careers. But today the realm of the Soviet political system has expanded far beyond the narrow confines that once characterized party politics in the USSR.

THE EMERGENCE OF OPPOSITION PARTIES

On March 13, 1990, the Congress of People's Deputies amended Article 6 of the USSR Constitution, removing the Communist Party's monopoly on political power. For two or three years prior to this momentous decision, various factions and groups had organized and were beginning to function as alternative parties. In July 1989 a group of liberal, reform-minded deputies to the newly elected Congress of People's Deputies began to refer to themselves as the Inter-regional Group. This faction, led by progressive, reformist deputies Yuri Afanas'ev, Gavriil Popov, Nikolai Shmelev, Boris Yeltsin, and the late Andrei Sakharov, pushed for faster, more comprehensive political and economic reforms. The majority of the Inter-regional Group (83 percent) are members of the CPSU, but they formed to oppose a conservative faction represented by Ligachev and much of the Party's *apparat*. As the name implies, the Inter-regional Group includes deputies from various areas besides Moscow—from Leningrad, the Baltic republics, and the Ukraine. Of the Congress of People's Deputies' 2,250 members, 393 attended the founding meeting of the group and 260, or 11 percent of the Congress's membership, officially chose to affiliate with the group. While this would indicate that the Inter-regional Group is a fairly small minority, their influence appears larger than their numbers. Members of the Inter-regional Group claim the support of some 388 deputies, or 17 percent of the entire body.

In anticipation of local and regional elections in March 1990, the Inter-regional Group supported the formation of a larger, more broadly based organization known as the "Democratic Platform of the CPSU." Founded in January 1990, the organization hopes, in time, to develop into a full-fledged Social Democratic party. The group calls for the establishment of a multiparty system, transformation of the CPSU into a "normal" parliamentary party, and recognition of civil liberties.

The new faction claimed stunning victories in local races in Moscow, Leningrad, and numerous other cities. In Moscow, progressives affiliated with "Democratic Russia" claimed more than 60 percent of the seats in the Moscow City Soviet. Gavriil Popov, one of the founding fathers of the Inter-regional Group, was elected chairman of the Moscow Soviet, a post tantamount to mayor. In contrast, the "mainstream" party faction supported by Gorbachev polled only 20 percent.

The success of progressive forces at the polls has alarmed those from the center and the right, who are now forming their own political party organizations. In early August 1989 the Christian Democratic Union of Russia was founded as a center-right political party which favors parliamentary democracy; a multiparty system; separation of legislative, executive, and judicial branches; and free elections. In addition, the party advocates freedom of speech, press, assembly, religious practice, emigration, and choice of place of residence. In the economic sphere, the party calls for the creation of a "multi-tiered market economy," in which private, cooperative, collective, and state property will coexist on an equal footing.

There are also Christian Democratic-affiliated groups in several of the republics, including Georgia, Armenia, Belorussia, and the Baltic republics. The leader of the Christian Democratic Union, Aleksandr Ogorodnikov, was a former political prisoner under Brezhnev and editor of a *samizdat* journal. He claims that his party attracted more than 1000 members in the first month of its existence.[68]

In less than one year after the legalization of opposition parties, numerous groups have sprung up, many promoting very particularistic demands. There is a budding Green party, focusing on environmental issues; there are regionally based parties; and there are parties representing every conceivable position on the ideological spectrum, from anarchists and Maoists on the left to monarchists and neofascists on the right.

This diversity is mirrored outside the capital as well. For example, in 1990 there were more than 160 registered parties in the Georgian republic alone. Such fragmentation could further strengthen the CPSU, by keeping the opposition divided. However, in the Fall 1990 elections in Georgia, a coalition of twenty-three parties, called the Roundtable, succeeded in capturing the majority of the seats in the Georgian parliament. The Communist Party succeeded in garnering only 29 percent of the vote.

Clearly, the future emergence of a multiparty democracy in the USSR depends on the forging of strong coalitions among the numerous parties and factions that currently vie for influence. Despite recent losses, the CPSU still claims 19 million members, an extensive bureaucratic structure extending into every factory, shop and farm in the country, and fixed assets (such as buildings, automobiles, resorts, and housing complexes) valued at 4.9 billion rubles.[69] It will take several years for opposition parties to amass the numbers and resources necessary to challenge the CPSU's institutional might. On the other hand, the sudden drop in the Party's popularity in 1989 and 1990, its embarrassing failures at the polls, and internal squabbling have seriously eroded the authority of the once-dominant institution. It is likely that the CPSU will grow increasingly obsolete and fragmented under the pressures unleashed by *glasnost'*, *perestroika*, and democratization. But the transition to multiparty democracy in the USSR is likely to be fraught with dangers and difficulties.

Notes

1. Preamble to the rules of the Communist Party of the Soviet Union.
2. T. H. Rigby, *Communist Party Membership in the USSR, 1917–1967* (Princeton: Princeton University Press, 1968), 59.
3. Ibid., 65.
4. Ibid., 97.
5. Ibid., 248–250.
6. Darrell P. Hammer, "The Dilemma of Party Growth," *Problems of Communism*, 20. no. 4 (July–August 1971), 17; and Ronald J. Hill and Peter Frank, *The Soviet Communist Party*, 3rd ed. (Boston: Unwin & Hyman, 1986) 32.
7. *Izvestiya TsK*, no. 4 (1990), p. 113.
8. *Moscow News*, no. 32, 19–26 August 1990, p. 6.
9. Ibid.
10. Ibid.
11. Ibid.
12. Rigby, *Communist Party Membership*, 63.
13. I. N. Yudin, *Sotsialn'naya baza rosta KPSS* (Moscow: Politizdat, 1973), 117, 162. Cited in Jerry Hough and Merle Fainsod, *How the Soviet Union Is Governed* (Cambridge: Harvard University Press, 1979), 327.
14. Rigby, *Communist Party Membership*, 184.
15. For an analysis of the evolution of this concept, see Ronald J. Hill, "The All-People-State and Developed Socialism," in Neil Harding, ed., *The State in Socialist Society* (London: Macmillan, 1984), 104–128.
16. The figure for female membership in the CPSU in 1920 was cited in Hough and Fainsod, *How the Soviet Union Is Governed*, 342. The figure for 1983 comes from *Pravda*, 26 September 1983, p. 2.
17. Herwig Kraus, ed., "The Composition of Leading Organs of the CPSU, 1952–1982" (Munich: *Radio Liberty Research Bulletin Supplement*, 30 May 1982).
18. Ibid.
19. For a discussion of the status of women in the Party, see Gail Warshofsky Lapidus, "Political Mobilization, Participation, and Leadership," *Comparative Politics* (October 1975): 90–118; and Joel C. Moses, "Women in Political Roles," in Dorothy Atkinson, Alexander Dallin, and Gail Warshofsky Lapidus, eds., *Women in Russia* (Stanford: Stanford University Press, 1977), 333–353.

20. Rigby, *Communist Party Membership*, 365–369.

21. Bohdan Harasymin, "Changes in the Party's Composition: The 'Destroika' of the CPSU," presented to the IV World Congress for Soviet and East European Studies, Harrogate, England, 21–26 July 1990, p. 21.

22. Ibid., 386.

23. Hough and Fainsod, *How the Soviet Union Is Governed*, 351.

24. *Partiinaya zhizn'*, no. 15 (August 1984): 14–32.

25. *Voprosy istorii KPSS*, 8 (August 1976): 27, cited in Jerry Hough, *The Soviet Union and Social Science Theory* (Cambridge: Harvard University Press, 1977), 126.

26. Jerry Hough, *The Soviet Union and Social Science Theory*, 125.

27. Ibid., 129–131.

28. Rigby, *Communist Party Membership*, 449–453.

29. *Pravda*, 26 September 1983, p. 2.

30. M. I. Khaldeev et al., *Pervichnaya partiinaya organizatsiya: opyt, formy i metody raboty* (Moscow: Politizdat, 1975), 273.

31. A. V. Shumakov and V. V. Zudin, eds., *Knizhka partiinogo aktivista 1974* (Moscow: Politizdat, 1973), 143.

32. *Partiinaya zhizn'*, no. 8 (April 1983): 20–21.

33. Ibid.

34. Ronald J. Hill and Peter Frank, *The Soviet Communist Party* (London: George Allen & Unwin, 1981), 49.

35. Ibid., 53.

36. *Yuridicheskii slovar'*, vol. 1 (Moscow: Yuridicheskaya literatura, 1956): 512.

37. Yu. V. Derbinov et al., eds., *Pervichnaya partiinaya organizatsiya—avangard trudovogo kollektiva* (Moscow: Mysl', 1975), 97.

38. Hough and Fainsod, *How the Soviet Union Is Governed*, 505.

39. Hill and Frank, *Soviet Communist Party*, 139.

40. *Pravda*, 6 February 1990, p. 1.

41. Leonard Schapiro, *The Communist Party of the Soviet Union* (New York: Vintage, 1960), 173. Originally, party congresses were held much more frequently and involved a smaller number of members. From 1917 through 1927, congresses were held every year with the exception of 1926, while the number of delegates gradually increased from 267 to 1669.

42. *Izvestiya Ts. K. KPSS*, 8 (1990), 3–5.

43. Ibid.

44. Compiled by William Clark from data in *Izvestiya Ts. K. KPSS* (1990), 10–12.

45. *Izvestiya Ts. K. KPSS*, 8 (1990), 3–5.

46. Ibid.

47. Hough and Fainsod, *How the Soviet Union Is Governed*, 462–463.

48. L. A. Apollonov, *Verkhovnyi organ leninskoi partii* (Moscow: Politizdat, 1876), 185–186.

49. Robert V. Daniels, "Office Holding and Elite Status: The Central Committee of the CPSU," in Paul Cocks, Robert V. Daniels, and Nancy Heer, eds., *The Dynamics of Soviet Politics* (Cambridge: Harvard University Press, 1976), 77–95.

50. Ibid.

51. *New York Times*, 15 June 1973, p. 3.

52. It is frequently noted with approval by Soviet scholars that Lenin often deferred to a majority in the Politburo with whom he disagreed. For example, see L. A. Slepov, "Osnovnye cherty leninskogo stilya partiinogo i gosudarstvennogo rukovodstva," in I. I. Pronin and S. A. Smirnov, eds., *Zhiznennaya sila leninskikh printsipov partiinogo stoitel'stva* (Moscow: Politizdat, 1970), 222–223.

53. The official name of the Politburo under Stalin had been changed to the Presidium of the CPSU Central Committee.

54. From a conversation with the author, June 1984.

55. Hough and Fainsod, *How the Soviet Union Is Governed*, 418.

56. Gordon B. Smith, "Gorbachev and the Council of Ministers: Leadership Consolidation and Its Policy Implications," *Soviet Union/Union Soviétique*, 14, no. 3 (1987), 358.

57. L. I. Brezhnev, *Ob aktual'nykh problemakh partiinogo stroitel'stva*, 2d ed. (Moscow: Politizdat, 1976), 274.

58. I. Kapitonov, "Rukovodyashchaya napravlyayushchaya sila sovetskogo obshchestva," *Partiinaya zhizn'*, no. 23 (1977): 25–27.

59. N. Vikulin and A. Davydov, "Partiya i sovety," *Partiinaya zhizn'*, no. 4 (1978): 32.

60. P. P. Ukrainets, *Partiinoe rukovodstvo i gosudarstvennoe upravlenie* (Minsk: Belorus', 1976), 65.

61. Rolf H. W. Theen, "Party and Bureaucracy," in Gordon B. Smith, ed., *Public Policy and Administration in the Soviet Union* (New York: Praeger, 1980), 42.

62. Bohdan Harasymiw, "Die sowjetische Nomenklatur: I. Organisatien und Mechanismen," *Osteuropa* 27 (1977): 585.

63. Theen, "Party and Bureaucracy," 44.

64. Bohdan Harasymiw, "Nomenklatura: The Soviet Communist Party's Leadership Recruitment System," *Canadian Journal of Political Science* 2 (1969): 511.

65. See Joel C. Moses, "Functional Career Specialization in Soviet Regional Elite Recruitment," in T. H. Rigby and Bohdan Harasymiw, eds., *Leadership Selection and Patron–Client Relations in the USSR and Yugoslavia* (Boston: George Allen & Unwin, 1983), 17–21.

66. Rigby and Harasymiw, *Leadership Selection and Patron–Client Relations*, 18.

67. These characteristics were first developed by T. H. Rigby in "The Soviet Leadership: Toward a Self-Stabilizing Oligarchy?" *Soviet Studies* 22, no. 2 (1970): 177.

68. John B. Dunlop, "Christian Democratic Party Founded in Moscow," *Radio Liberty Report on the USSR* 1, no. 41, 13 October, 1989, 2.

69. *Moscow News*, no. 43, 4–11 November 1990, p. 14.

Selected Bibliography

Bialer, Seweryn. *Stalin's Successors: Leadership, Stability and Change in the Soviet Union*. Cambridge: Cambridge University Press, 1980.

Breslauer, George W. *Khrushchev and Brezhnev as Leaders: Building Authority in Soviet Politics*. London: George Allen & Unwin, 1982.

Harasymiw, Bohdan. "Nomenklatura: The Soviet Communist Party's Leadership Recruitment System." *Canadian Journal of Political Science* 2, no. 4 (December 1969): 505–512.

Hill, Ronald J., and Peter Frank. *The Soviet Communist Party*. London: George Allen & Unwin, 1981.

Hough, Jerry F. *Soviet Leadership in Transition*. Washington, DC: The Brookings Institution Press, 1980.

Hough, Jerry F., and Merle Fainsod. *How the Soviet Union Is Governed*. Cambridge: Harvard University Press, 1979.

Linden, Carl A. *Khrushchev and the Soviet Leadership, 1957–1964*. Baltimore: The Johns Hopkins University Press, 1966.

Moses, Joel C. "Regional Cohorts and Political Mobility in the USSR: The Case of Dnepropetrovsk." *Soviet Union/Union Soviétique* 3, pt. 1 (1976): 63–89.

———. *Regional Party Leadership and Policy-Making in the USSR*. New York: Holt, Rinehart & Winston, 1974.

Rigby, T. H. *Communist Party Membership In the USSR, 1917–1967*. Princeton: Princeton University Press, 1968.

Rigby, T. H., and Bohdan Harasymiw, eds. *Leadership Selection and Patron–Client Relations in the USSR and Yugoslavia*. London: George Allen & Unwin, 1983.

Ryavec, Karl W., ed. *Soviet Society and the Communist Party*. Amherst: The University of Massachusetts Press, 1978.

Schapiro, Leonard. *The Communist Party of the Soviet Union*. New York: Random House, 1960.

Tatu, Michel. *Power in the Kremlin: From Khrushchev to Kosygin*. New York: Viking, 1968.

Theen, Rolf H. W. "Party and Bureaucracy." In Gordon B. Smith, ed. *Public Policy and Administration in the Soviet Union*. New York: Praeger, 1980, 18–52.

6

Democratization and the State

Until Gorbachev's reforms changed the face of the Soviet political system, the Government, or state apparatus, in the USSR did not make major decisions affecting the domestic or foreign policies of the country. Rather, the principal function of the state apparatus was to implement policies articulated by the party leadership. In recent years, however, newly created legislative and executive bodies have assumed real power. As the influence of the CPSU has declined, power has shifted to the Supreme Soviet, the Presidency and the republic soviets. This shift signifies the gradual emergence of a genuine parliamentary system, one that seeks to balance the need for the representation of diverse interests in Soviet society with the need for strong leadership while maintaining checks on the exercise of executive authority. These are hopeful signs. But the development of a pluralistic, parliamentary democracy in the USSR will take a long time and must overcome a number of serious impediments, including the absence of historical experience with parliamentary democracy, an entrenched party and state bureaucracy reluctant to relinquish power, rising popular expectations, and threats of economic collapse and ethnic fragmentation.

FEDERAL STRUCTURE OF THE USSR

Occupying such a vast and varied territory, the USSR is divided into a variety of subordinate territorial-political units to facilitate governance and administration (see Figure 6–1). The name of the nation—the Union of Soviet Socialist Republics—implies the existence of a federal state. The territorial-administrative structure of the USSR is organized along two different and sometimes conflicting principles. There are divisions and subdivisions that recognize nationality or ethnic groups, and there are divisions and subdivisions that are purely geographic or territorial. In fact, however, the USSR is not a genuine federal system because each level of government (republic, region, city, and so on) does not have independent powers within its jurisdiction. Rather, most decisions affecting cities and regions are still made in the center (i.e., Moscow).

The fifteen most-populous ethnic groups, occupying territory on the perimeter of the USSR, are accorded the status of *union-republics*. They are:

Figure 6-1. The Union of Soviet Socialist Republics

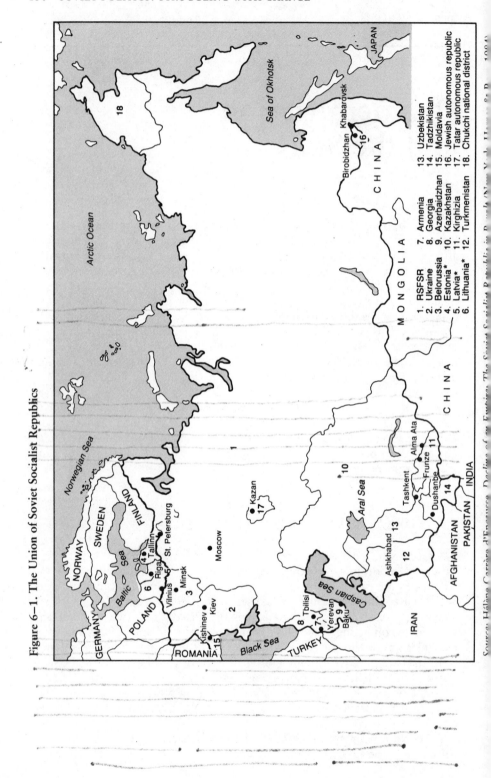

1. RSFSR
2. Ukraine
3. Belorussia*
4. Estonia*
5. Latvia*
6. Lithuania*
7. Armenia
8. Georgia
9. Azerbaidzhan
10. Kazakhstan
11. Kirghizia
12. Turkmenistan
13. Uzbekistan
14. Tadzhikistan
15. Moldavia
16. Jewish autonomous republic
17. Tatar autonomous republic
18. Chukchi national district

Source: Hélène Carrère d'Encausse, *Decline of an Empire: The Soviet Socialist Republics in Revolt* (New York: Harper & Row, 1994).

Armenia, Azerbaidzhan, Belorussia, Estonia, Georgia, Kazakhstan, Kirghizia, Latvia, Lithuania, Moldavia, Russia, Tadzhikistan, Turkmenistan, the Ukraine, and Uzbekistan. In each union-republic, the official language is that of the major ethnic group (i.e., Ukrainian in the Ukraine, Uzbek in Uzbekistan, and so forth). Each union-republic has its own constitution; its own legislative, executive, and judicial institutions; and its own party structure. Until recently the Russian republic did not have such institutions; however, in 1990 a movement began to create separate legislative and executive institutions for the Russian republic. This movement emerged in reaction to demands for secession or increased autonomy from Moscow by various ethnic groups, most notably the three Baltic nationalities—the Lithuanians, Latvians, and Estonians. Boris Yeltsin seized upon Russian nationalistic sentiments to pursue his own political comeback by being elected Chairman of the Presidium of the RSFSR Supreme Soviet.

Article 72 of the Constitution states that each union-republic "shall retain the right freely to secede from the USSR."[1] However, as has been demonstrated in the cases of the Baltic republics, central authorities are reluctant to permit union-republics to secede.

Large nationality groups not located on the perimeter of the USSR are accorded the status of *autonomous republics*. There are twenty autonomous republics, sixteen located within the Russian Soviet Federated Socialist Republic (RSFSR), two in Georgia, and one each in the Uzbek and Azerbaidzhan republics. Although autonomous republics have their own party and state institutions, they do not have the right to secede. The official language of the autonomous republic is that of the majority indigenous nationality.

For smaller nationality groups there are autonomous regions (*avtonomnye oblasti*), of which there are eight today. Most of them are located in remote and underdeveloped areas. Autonomous regions elect their own deputies to the regional soviet, as well as local party officials. Like union-republics, autonomous regions enjoy the right to their own language and culture. One of the more curious twists of Soviet history involves the Jewish autonomous region in the desolate, remote region of Birobidzhan on the Chinese border, more than 4000 miles from Moscow. The Jewish autonomous region was created in 1934 to provide Soviet Jews with their own territory and a limited degree of ethnic self-determination, but few Jews opted to leave the cities of European Russia. Today, Jews constitute less than 10 percent of the population of the Jewish autonomous region.

The smallest nationality-based division is the national district (*natsional'nyi okrug*). There are ten such districts, all located in the RSFSR. Although the districts may be very large, the populations are tiny and primitive. For instance, the Chukchi national district provides some self-determination for the 14,000 Chukchi, or Soviet Eskimos, who inhabit the peninsula directly across the Bering Strait from Alaska.

In the geographic or territorial division of the USSR, there are also units subordinate to the union-republics. The largest republics are divided into regions, or *oblasti*. There are 151 *oblasti* in the USSR, ranging in size from 1740 square miles to 544,000 square miles.[2] Thus, *oblasti* are roughly equivalent in size to states in the United States. Regions have their own administrative, judicial, and party institutions, but they are also strictly accountable to union-republic and to all-union party and state organs.

Another administrative-territorial unit is the *krai*, or territory. There are eight *kraia* in the USSR today. *Kraia* differ from *oblasti* primarily in that the former are very large but sparsely populated.

At the local level are the cities and rural districts (*raiony*). Each *raion* has its own legislative, administrative, judicial, and party bodies. Large cities are divided into boroughs or urban districts (*gorodskie raiony*), whereas rural districts are comprised of villages and settlements (*sela*).

THE SOVIETS: THE LEGISLATIVE APPARATUS

The soviets (*sovety*) are representative legislative bodies elected on a periodic basis. They date back to the 1905 revolution and came to be dominated by the Bolsheviks in 1917. Until the first competitive multicandidate elections in the USSR in March 1989, the soviets had little independent power to make policy. However, in recent years they have emerged as freely elected bodies that debate policies, pass legislation, and serve to restrict the powers of local as well as national leaders. (See Figure 6–2).

The March 1989 elections selected 2250 deputies to a newly formed body, the Congress of People's Deputies. A total of 750 of the members were elected from single-member districts, 750 were elected from nationality areas, and 750 were elected by various social organizations (e.g., the CPSU, Komsomol, trade unions, the Academy of Sciences). All deputies are elected to serve a five-year term. This election scheme, however, has been criticized as being undemocratic. Most of the 275 delegates elected in 1989 from the CPSU, the Komsomol, and trade unions ran unopposed.[3] In 1990 the laws affecting election to the Congress of People's Deputies were changed. When the next elections are held, in 1994, all deputies will be elected in competitive elections based on either single-member districts or nationality areas.

While 87.6 percent of the deputies elected in 1989 were members of the CPSU, top party officials did not fare well. Only 93 of the 301 members of the CPSU Central Committee were elected to the Congress. The largest portion of the deputies come from the upper and middle ranks of administration. The Congress also includes occupational groups never before represented in any

Table 6–1 Occupational Makeup of Congress of People's Deputies (in percent)

Top political leadership	0.7
Upper and middle echelons of administration	39.8
Lower echelons of administration	24.7
Workers, farmers, service employees	23.1
Intelligentsia, specialists	9.7
Clergy	0.2
Pensioners	1.8
Total	100.0

Source: *Izvestiya*, 6 May 1989, p. 3.

Figure 6–2. Governmental Structure of the USSR

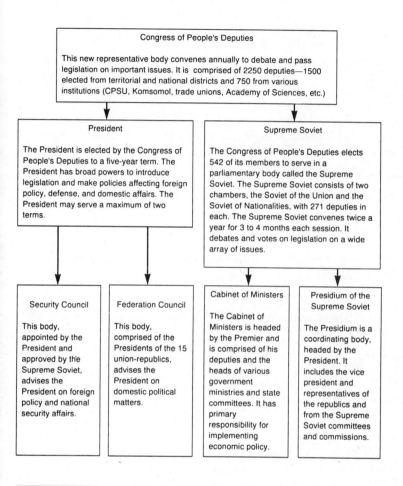

Congress of People's Deputies

This new representative body convenes annually to debate and pass legislation on important issues. It is comprised of 2250 deputies—1500 elected from territorial and national districts and 750 from various institutions (CPSU, Komsomol, trade unions, Academy of Sciences, etc.)

President

The President is elected by the Congress of People's Deputies to a five-year term. The President has broad powers to introduce legislation and make policies affecting foreign policy, defense, and domestic affairs. The President may serve a maximum of two terms.

Supreme Soviet

The Congress of People's Deputies elects 542 of its members to serve in a parliamentary body called the Supreme Soviet. The Supreme Soviet consists of two chambers, the Soviet of the Union and the Soviet of Nationalities, with 271 deputies in each. The Supreme Soviet convenes twice a year for 3 to 4 months each session. It debates and votes on legislation on a wide array of issues.

Security Council

This body, appointed by the President and approved by the Supreme Soviet, advises the President on foreign policy and national security affairs.

Federation Council

This body, comprised of the Presidents of the 15 union-republics, advises the President on domestic political matters.

Cabinet of Ministers

The Cabinet of Ministers is headed by the Premier and is comprised of his deputies and the heads of various government ministries and state committees. It has primary responsibility for implementing economic policy.

Presidium of the Supreme Soviet

The Presidium is a coordinating body, headed by the President. It includes the vice president and representatives of the republics and from the Supreme Soviet committees and commissions.

leading governmental body—clergymen (five), private cooperative owners (six), private farmers (thirteen), and pensioners (thirty-seven).[4] Women constituted only 17 percent of the elected deputies. (See Table 6–1).

The Congress, which meets at least once a year, constitutes the official parliament of the USSR. Its sessions, televised nationally, are devoted to debating the most important problems confronting the Soviet Union. Debates in the Congress are often heated and include criticisms of Gorbachev and other leaders. With 2250 members, the Congress is proving to be an unwieldy body. Many of its members are too busy with other careers to dedicate themselves to full-time legislative work. It is likely that the Congress will evolve into a formalistic body and transfer its legislative functions, including the power to amend the Constitution, to the Supreme Soviet.

Figure 6–3 Commissions of the USSR Supreme Soviet

Commissions of the Council of the Union

- Industry, Energy, Machinery, and Technology Development

- Labor, Prices, and Social Policy
    Subcommissions:
        Labor, Rate of Employment, and Demography
        Problems of Price Setting
        Social Priorities
        Standard of Living and Social Guarantees
        Taxation Issues

- Planning, Budget, and Finance

- Transportation, Communications, and Information Technology

Commissions of the Council of Nationalities

- Consumer Goods, Trade, and Municipal, Consumer, and Other Services

- Culture, Language, National and International Traditions, and Protection of Historical Heritage

- Nationalities Policy and Interethnic Relations

- Social and Economic Development of Union and Autonomous Republics, Oblasts, and Okrugs

Joint Committees of the USSR Supreme Soviet*

- Agrarian and Food

- Construction and Architecture

- Defense and State Security
    Subcommittees:
        Armed Services
        Defense Industry
        State Security

✳ The Congress elects from its members 542 deputies to constitute the Supreme Soviet. *The Supreme Soviet* is the bicameral legislature consisting of the Soviet of the Union and the Soviet of Nationalities, each with 271 members who serve a five-year term. The Supreme Soviet meets in spring and autumn sessions, each lasting three or four months. The Soviet of the Union, or lower chamber, consists of deputies representing regions throughout the USSR.

In advanced political systems, the upper chambers of legislatures often provide representation for special groups or interests. Fearing a tyranny of the large, populous states over the smaller states, the founders of the United States gave equal representation in the Senate to all the states. So too in the USSR, the upper chamber—the Soviet of Nationalities—gives special representation to 53 of the 109 legally recognized nationality groups that constitute Soviet society. Each of the fifteen constituent republics representing the

- Ecology and the Rational Use of Natural Resources
    Subcommittee:
        Nuclear Ecology

- Economic Reform

- *Glasnost'* and Citizens' Rights and Appeals

- Health

- International Affairs
    Subcommittees:
        Foreign Economic, Scientific and Technical, and Trade Relations
        Foreign Policy and Legal Questions
        Humanitarian and Cultural Relations

- Legislation, Legality, and Law and Order
    Subcommittees:
        Constitutional Legislation and Political Reform
        Court Reform and Criminal Legislation
        Economic Legislation

- Science, Education, Culture, and Upbringing

- Soviets of People's Deputies and Management and Self-Management
  Development

- Veteran and Invalid Affairs

- Women's Affairs and Family, Mother, and Child Protection

- Youth Affairs

Source: Central Intelligence Agency, Directorate of Intelligence, *Directory of Soviet Officials*
(Washington, DC: U.S. Government Printing Office, 14 September 1989), pp. 157–166.
*Fifty percent of the members of these committees are deputies to the People's Congress who
currently do not serve in the Supreme Soviet.

fifteen most-populous ethnic groups elects eleven deputies to the body; each
autonomous republic elects four deputies; each autonomous region elects two
deputies; and each autonomous area elects one deputy.[5]

Whereas the former Supreme Soviet was largely a rubber-stamp body,
the newly elected Supreme Soviet is rapidly becoming a meaningful parliament. Soon after convening in May 1989, the Supreme Soviet set up 25
committees to study subjects ranging from agriculture to military affairs. But
the committees, being new, have been hampered by lack of office space, staff,
and institutionalized authority. "This is a new frontier," said a Soviet official.[6] (See Figure 6–3, Commissions of USSR Supreme Soviet.) The deputy
chairman of the Defense and State Security Committee acknowledged a conscious effort to pattern Supreme Soviet committees after those of the U.S.
Congress. To that end, several delegations of U.S. Congressional representatives have traveled to Moscow to advise their Soviet counterparts.

In addition to its powers to debate issues in public and pass laws, the Supreme Soviet is charged with confirming appointees to the Cabinet of Ministers. In June 1989 the body considered 71 names of ministers proposed by then-Premier Nikolai Ryzhkov. After lengthy and heated committee hearings, Ryzhov withdrew the names of six ministerial nominees—including those in charge of culture, the state bank, the state price committee, and the petroleum industry. Two other nominees asked to have their names withdrawn rather than face likely defeat. One of these, Vladimir I. Kalashnikov, who had been appointed to head up the troubled food production sector, was a protégé of Gorbachev and former first party secretary from Gorbachev's home region, Stavropol'. The Supreme Soviet also rejected three nominees to the Supreme Court in 1989 on the grounds that they were not well versed in the law.

Supreme Soviet sessions are lively and occasionally even raucous. For example, when the late Andrei Sakharov took the podium in June 1989 to denounce Soviet military operations in Afghanistan, Aleksandra Biryukova, the only woman on the Politburo, cupped her hands to her mouth and shouted "Shame!" Other conservative deputies tried to drown out Sakharov by clapping, whistling, and stomping their feet in protest. Televised sessions have proven so popular with Soviet viewers that they have had to be curtailed. During the first few weeks of televised debate, production declined by more than 20 percent as workers took time out from their jobs to watch television.[7] Now portions of Supreme Soviet sessions are taped for broadcast in the evenings.

THE PRESIDENT AND THE EXECUTIVE APPARATUS

The Presidency.   The President of the USSR is elected by a secret ballot of the Congress of People's Deputies. Service is limited to two five-year terms. The President has broad powers to initiate legislation, conduct military and foreign policy, and appoint ministers. The amendments to the Soviet Constitution creating the presidency which were approved by the Congress of People's Deputies on March 13, 1990, give the President the power to declare martial law in cases of civil emergencies. The President also has the power to veto legislation, but the Supreme Soviet can override a presidential veto with a two-thirds vote.

New emergency legislation also empowers the President to ban disturbances of the public order, including strikes, demonstrations, publications, movements, and organizations that pursue "militant and anticonstitutional goals." The President can also impose "temporary presidential rule" over particular regions or republics, suspending the authority of their governments, revoking their legislation, and dissolving their parliaments. These emergency powers have been harshly criticized by numerous Soviet officials. For example, Sergei Stankevich, a liberal deputy to the Congress and Supreme Soviet and deputy mayor of Moscow, refered to the new powers as creating an "imperial presidency." Anatolii Sobchak, the mayor of Leningrad, calls the presidency an "all-union gendarme."[8]

Despite the expanded powers of the office, the Presidency lacks the legitimacy that would obtain were it directly elected by the people. Gorbachev has supported the notion of a popularly elected President and has indicated that when his present term runs out in March 1995, the nation will probably move to direct election to the office. The most significant feature of the newly established Presidency is that it creates a power base for the Soviet leader outside the Party, a power base that guarantees its occupant a set tenure in office. Not only does this represent a transference of power from the CPSU to the State, but it also insulates the President from the crosscutting pressures and interests represented in the Politburo.

The Vice Presidency. The post of Vice President was created in December 1990. The duties of the Vice President are to assist the President in his various responsibilities and to take his place when he is absent or unable to carry out his duties. The Vice President is nominated by the President and, like the President, is elected by the Congress of People's Deputies to a five-year term. Should the President die, the Vice President would assume the position for up to 60 days, at which time new elections would be held.

The first Vice President of the USSR is Gennadii Yanaev, the former chairman of the Congress of Trade Unions and a close Gorbachev aide. Since assuming the Vice Presidency, Yanaev has played an active role in organizing the work of the Council of the Federation.

The Security Council. Gorbachev has assembled two advisory bodies to assist him in making policy and to broaden his appeal and enhance his legitimacy. The Security Council was created in December 1990 to replace the former Presidential Council. The Security Council, which was patterned after the National Security Council in the United States, is charged with briefing the President on questions of defense, security, and interethnic relations. Current members include: Foreign Minister Aleksandr Bessmertnykh; KGB chief Vladimir Kryuchkov; Defense Minister Dmitrii Yazov; Premier Valentin Pavlov; Interior Minister Boris Pugo; former Interior Minister Vadim Bakatin; and diplomat Evgenii Primakov. Bakatin, the only moderate reformer in the group, is responsible for coordinating domestic security affairs, while Primakov concentrates on economic security and foreign policy.

The Security Council is centrist in its orientation. Aleksandr Yakovlev, Gorbachev's former liberal foreign policy adviser was not included; neither was Stanislav Shatalin, the liberal economist and author of the 500-day economic program for the transition of the Soviet economy to a market system. Both men had been members of the President Council until it was abolished in late 1990. All members of the Security Council, with the exception of Pugo, are Russian; whereas the Presidential Council included one Georgian, one Latvian, one Kirgiz, one Ukrainian, and one Armenian.

Members of the Security Council are appointed by the President, but those appointments must be confirmed by the Supreme Soviet. Gorbachev's personal adviser, Valerii Boldin, failed to garner sufficient votes to be approved, but Gorbachev has nevertheless entrusted him with responsibility for organizing the work of the Security Council.

The Council of the Federation. A second presidential advisory body is the Council of the Federation, which is comprised of the heads of each of the

Figure 6–4 The Security Council

Mikhail S. Gorbachev: *President of the USSR; General Secretary, CC CPSU; Chairman, USSR Defense Council*

. Russian. Born on March 2, 1931. Gorbachev joined the Komsomol and began work as a workhand at a machine-tractor station in Stavropol' in 1946. He joined the Party in 1952 and was the All-Union Komsomol organizer of the Law Faculty at Moscow State University from 1952 to 1954. He worked his way up through the party apparatus in Stavropol', becoming a full member of the Central Committeee in 1971. He was CC Secretary of Agriculture from 1978 to 1985. He was named candidate member of the Politburo in 1979, and a full member in 1980. He became General Secretary of the CPSU and Chairman of the USSR Defense Council in March 1985, and was elected President of the USSR in 1990.

Vadim V. Bakatin: *Security Council Member*

Russian. Born on November 6, 1937. Bakatin began his career in the construction industry in Kemerovo in Central Siberia. He joined the Party in 1964 and gradually rose within the Kemerovo city and district party organization, supervising the construction industry. He was transfered to Moscow in 1983 where he served as an Inspector with the CPSU Central Committee until 1985. From 1985 until 1988 he served as First Secretary of party organizations, first in Kirov and then in Kemerovo. In 1988 he was named Minister of Internal Affairs, a post he held until 1990, when he was replaced with Boris Pugo. Bakatin's dismissal came amid criticisms aired in the Supreme Soviet that he failed to take aggressive action to control street demonstrations and to stem the rising incidence of crime.

Aleksandr Bessmertnykh: *Minister of Foreign Affairs*

Russian. Born on November 10, 1933. Bessmertnykh graduated from the Moscow State Institute of International Relations and spent his entire career in the diplomatic corps. He specialized in policies toward the United States and the United Nations. In 1989 he was named Ambassador to the United States. He was appointed Minister of Foreign Affairs following the resignation of Eduard Zhervardnadze in late 1990.

Vladimir A. Kryuchkov: *Chairman, KGB*

. Russian. Born on February 29, 1924. Kryuchkov rose within the party organization of Volgograd, where he specialized in legal affairs from 1944 to 1954. In 1954 he was assigned to a diplomatic post in the Soviet embassy in Hungary, where he became associated with the Ambassador Yurii Andropov. He entered the KGB in 1967 and rose to be Chief of the First Main Administration in 1974 and in 1988 he was promoted to the post of Chairman. He became a member of the Politburo in 1989.

fifteen union-republics. The Council is supposed to advise the President on interethnic disputes and related issues. Leaders of the autonomous republics have also been granted membership on the Council, while top officials from autonomous regions and districts are entitled to participate in Council sessions. The Council acts as a collective decisionmaking body; a two-thirds vote

Valentin Pavlov: *Premier*

Russian. Born in 1937. Pavlov graduated from the Moscow Institute of Finance with a degree in economics and began his career working as an inspector with a district finance department. He transferred to the Ministry of Finance, where he rose from economist to First Deputy Minister. He served as a member of the collegium of the State Planning Committee (Gosplan) and then in 1986 he was named Chairman of the USSR State Committee on Prices. In 1989 he became Minister of Finance.

Evgenii M. Primakov: *Security Council and Director, Institute for World Economy and International Relations*

Russian. Born on October 29, 1929. Primakov, a specialist on the Middle East, graduated from the Moscow Institute for Oriental Studies and worked as a commentator and editor of several publications from 1956 until 1970. In 1970 he was named Deputy Director of the Institute for World Economics and International Relations (IMEMO). In 1977 he became Director of the Institute for Oriental Studies; and in 1985 he assumed the directorship of IMEMO. He was elected to the Congress of People's Deputies and the Supreme Soviet, serving as Chairman of the Council of the Union in 1989 and 1990. He is a full member of the USSR Academy of Sciences.

Boris K. Pugo: *Minister of Internal Affairs*

Latvian. Born on February 19, 1937. Pugo graduated from the Riga Polytechnic Institute in 1960 and rose through the Latvian party organization, specializing in industrial production. He was named First Secretary of the Riga city party committee in 1975 and then in 1976 he shifted to working for the KGB under the leadership of Yuri Andropov. In 1984 through 1988 he served as First Secretary of the Latvian communist party organization. In 1988 he was appointed Chairman of the Party Control Committee, an organization charged with investigating corruption within the CPSU. In this post, he earned the reputation for being a hardliner. His appointment as Minister of Internal Affairs in late 1990 was a move by Gorbachev to placate his conservative critics.

Gennadii I. Yanaev: *Vice President*

Russian. Born in 1937. Pavlov jointed the CPSU in 1962 and held several posts in youth affairs and cultural relations with foreign countries until 1986, when he was named Vice-Chairman of the All-Union Central Council of Trade Unions. In 1990 he became Chairman of the trade union body. He was elected to the Congress of People's Deputies and assumed the post of Vice President in December 1990.

is required for it to adopt a policy. Council policies are then supposed to be implemented by presidential decrees. The powers of the Council are, however, not clearly differentiated from those of the Soviet of Nationalities and the Presidium of the Supreme Soviet, in which the fifteen union-republics are also represented.

Figure 6–5 The Council of the Federation

Mikhail S. Gorbachev

Nikolai I. Dementai	Belorussian. Born in May, 1931. CPSU member since 1957. Chairman of the Belorussian SSR Supreme Soviet.
Boris N. Yeltsin	Russian. Born on February 1, 1931. CPSU member since 1961. Chairman of the RSFSR Supreme Soviet.
Anatolii Gorbunov	Latvian. Born on February 10, 1942. President of the Supreme Council of the Latvian Republic.
Givi G. Gumbaridze	Georgian. Born in 1945. CPSU member since 1972. First Secretary of the Georgian Communist Party Central Committee. Chairman of the Presidium of the Georgian SSR Supreme Soviet.
Vladimir A. Ivashko	Ukrainian. Born on October 28, 1932. CPSU member since 1960. First Secretary of the Ukrainian Communist Party Central Committee. Chairman of the Ukrainian SSR Supreme Soviet.
Islam A. Karimov	Uzbek. Born on January 30, 1938. CPSU member since 1964. First Secretary of the Uzbek Communist Party Central Committee. President of the Uzbek SSR.
Vytautas Landsbergis	Lithuanian. Born on October 18, 1932. President of the Supreme Council of the Lithuanian Republic.
Kakhar M. Makhkamov	Tadzhik. Born on April 16, 1932. CPSU member since 1957. First Secretary of the Tadzhik Communist Party Central Committee. Chairman of the Tadzhik SSR Supreme Soviet.

| Absamat Masaliev | Kirgiz. Born on April 10, 1933. CPSU member since 1960. First Secretary of the Kirgiz Communist Party Central Committee. Chairman of the Kirgiz SSR Supreme Soviet. |

| Ayaz N. Mutalibov | Azeri. Born on May 12, 1938. CPSU member since 1963. First Secretary of the Azerbaidzhan Communist Party Central Committee. President of the Azerbaidzhan Democratic Republic. |

| Nursultan A. Nazarbaev | Kazakh. Born in 1940. CPSU member since 1962. First Secretary of the Kazakh Communist Party Central Committee. President of the Kazakh SSR. |

| Saparmurad A. Niyazov | Turkmen. Born on February 19, 1940. CPSU member since 1962. First Secretary of the Turkmen Communist Party Central Committee. Chairman of the Turkmen SSR Supreme Soviet. |

| Arnold Ruutel | Estonian. Born on May 10, 1928. President of the Supreme Council of the Estonian Republic. |

| Mircea I. Snegur | Moldavian. Born in 1940. CPSU member since 1964. Chairman of the Supreme Soviet of the Soviet Socialist Republic of Moldavia. |

| Grant M. Voskanyan | Armenian. Born on May 15, 1924. CPSU member since 1946. Chairman of the Armenian SSR Supreme Soviet. |

Members of the Council are all ex-officio, not appointed—thus, they may not necessarily support the President. It is unclear what procedures exist for accommodating differences—for example, those between Gorbachev and his reformist rival Boris Yeltsin, who was elected Chairman of the RSFSR Supreme Soviet in May 1990. It is likely that the makeup of the Council will result in interregional conflict and that it will not prove to be an effective institution.

Presidium of the Supreme Soviet. Because the new Supreme Soviet meets in two sessions that extend over the major portion of the year, the role of the Presidium of the Supreme Soviet is less prominent than that of its predecessor. There is less of a need for the Supreme Soviet to delegate responsibility to its Presidium. The Presidium currently is headed by Anatolii Lukyanov, and includes the chairmen of the Supreme Soviets of each of the fifteen union-republics. According to the USSR Constitution, the Presidium has the power to issue decrees that are legally binding, reorganize ministries and state committees, appoint and demote members of the Cabinet of Ministers, select chairmen for the standing committees of the Supreme Soviet, award state medals and prizes, receive foreign delegations, ratify treaties, and even declare war, all without the approval of the Supreme Soviet.

The pattern of Soviet state administration at the all-union level is repeated at the republic, regional, and local levels. Thus, in each of the fifteen republics there is a supreme soviet, which delegates some of authority to a presidium. Republic deputies are elected every five years. At the regional and local levels, the soviets perform legislative functions analogous to those of the USSR Supreme Soviet and the republic soviets. Elections are held for local and regional deputies every two and one-half years.

Cabinet of Ministers. For more than 70 years, the highest administrative institution in the USSR was the Council of Ministers. However, it was abolished in December 1990 and replaced by the Cabinet of Ministers. The Cabinet of Ministers includes some 80 members—heads of state ministries and chairmen of state committees. The large number of ministries in the USSR is explained by the state control and operation of the economy. Thus, in the Soviet Union, there are ministries for each sector of the economy (e.g., the coal industry, the chemical industry, and the automobile industry). More than half of the members of the Cabinet of Ministers occupy positions involving primarily economic responsibilities. This reflects the primary purpose and function of the body—to manage the massive Soviet economy.

With the introduction of *perestroika*, however, the need for central control and direction of the economy has diminished. The reorganization of the Cabinet of Ministers in late 1990 was intended to reflect the body's reduced responsibilities. The Cabinet of Ministers still plays a leading role in key areas—defense, security, foreign policy, finance, justice, ecology, energy, transportation and communications. Responsibility for economic management for other sectors has been, at least on paper, delegated to the republics. In practice, however, the central economic ministries have proven unwilling to give up their power over their respective sectors.

The Chairman of the Cabinet of Ministers is sometimes referred to as the Premier, Prime Minister, or head of government. The Premier, who is appointed by the President, is responsible for supervising the entire operation of the Soviet economy. Until recently, the office of Premier was one of the most powerful posts in the Soviet political system. Premiers were normally full members of the Politburo and wielded considerable authority on issues relating to the economy. In December 1990 the office of the Premier was downgraded to that of an aide to the President. The conservative Nikolai Ryzhkov, who rose through the powerful machine-building sector in the Urals to direct the Soviet economy from 1985 to 1990, became increasingly the target of frustrated liberals who wanted faster-paced reforms. He resigned and was replaced by Valentin Pavlov, the former Minister of Finance.

While Brezhnev and his successors Andropov and Chernenko all assumed the dual titles of General Secretary and President of the USSR, no party leader since Khrushchev has also held the title of Premier.

Executive and administrative functions of the republic governments are carried out by the republic councils of ministers. Union-republic ministries in every republic report both to the republic-level councils of ministers and to the USSR Cabinet of Ministers, through their respective ministries in Moscow.

Ministries and State Committees.   The Constitution of the USSR specifies two types of ministries in the Soviet governmental apparatus: all-union ministries and union-republic ministries. The former have no counterparts at the republic level, operating strictly on a centralized basis out of Moscow; the latter have counterparts in each of the fifteen republics. All-union ministries are generally devoted to industrial matters, while the union-republic ministries are concerned with the traditional jurisdiction of the executive branch of government (e.g., education, health, the interior).

In contrast to party secretaries, ministers tend to spend their careers within a single ministry or sector of the economy. Economic ministers normally have specialized educations and enter the Party's ranks through the factory, rather than through the Komsomol or universities. Unlike regional party secretaries, who may be rotated frequently from one position to another, ministers enjoy a long tenure in office, often fifteen or twenty years.[9] While cabinet members in the United States or other Western political systems may be shifted from agency to agency, Soviet ministers have exceedingly stable careers. For example, Gorbachev's ministerial appointments averaged seven years of experience in their respective ministries prior to being named ministers. Six of the ministers were appointed by Gorbachev in 1985, representing the critical sectors of the electronics industry, coal industry, transportation, construction, the medical industry, and aviation. Only two ministers predate Gorbachev. Nikolai Konarev has served as Minister of Railways since 1982 and Vladimir Chirskov has been Minister of Construction of Petroleum and Gas Complexes since 1984. The long tenure and career specialization of ministerial officials help them to acquire an impressive level of expertise. However, career stability in Soviet ministries also impedes the introduction of new blood and may reduce the likelihood of reform and innovation.

Directly under the ministers are *collegia*, small advisory bodies consisting of the minister and his or her chief deputies. These bodies are somewhat analogous to the ministerial cabinets prevalent in European political systems. The ministerial collegia were established at Lenin's urging, in order to broaden participation in administrative decision-making and as a check on the power of the minister. The collegium advises the minister on important policy matters but it has no independent authority to overrule ministerial decisions. In fact, Soviet state administration functions on the basis of "one-man management" (*edinonachalie*). In other words, state officials are held strictly accountable for their actions and the actions of their direct subordinates. This applies to the manager of a steel mill as well as to the Minister of the Steel Industry. Unlike the Communist Party, which stresses collective decision-making, Soviet state administration emphasizes clearly defined responsibilities resting with individual officials. *Edinonachalie* facilitates directing blame for inefficiency and maladministration, as well as identifying individual administrators who are especially adept and efficient.

Soviet ministries are exceedingly complex bureaucratic organizations, often employing one or two thousand staff personnel in their central and regional offices. To afford the necessary focus and expertise to manage economic matters efficiently, ministries are divided into administrations and departments. The chain of command extends directly from the minister to each state-owned factory, farm, and enterprise in the USSR.

Most administrative personnel are recruited directly from specialized technical institutes on the basis of a system of job placement called *rasprostranenie*. Other administrative officials enter at midcareer or by job transfer; they are hired on the basis of competitive application. There is no civil-service entrance examination in the USSR and no centralized professional training school. Job tenure is not guaranteed, although in practice few state employees are terminated.

The ministries are heavily involved with education and research. Ministries in charge of economic sectors normally have affiliated research institutes that are engaged in research and development, testing, and prototype production. Non-economic ministries also have research institutes. Thus, the Ministry of Justice has an institute that studies the problems of drafting Soviet legislation, and the Procuracy (public prosecutor's office) has an institute that studies the causes and prevention of crime. Most ministries also have subordinate institutes (*vuzy*) offering postgraduate specialized training for mid-level personnel of the ministry. Ministerial personnel undertake specialized training at these institutions as a routine part of their professional development. No tuition is charged, and in most cases the employee is excused from his or her normal responsibilities while at the *vuz*.

State committees in the Soviet Union differ from ministries in that their functions and responsibilities cut across various sectors and agencies. For example, the State Committee for Science and Technology has broad powers to set the agenda for research and development in every sector of the Soviet economy. Similarly, the State Committee for Prices sets prices on items produced in every economic ministry. State committees may be either union-republic or all-union in form; that is, they may have analogous committees at the republic, regional, and local levels, or they may function solely from a centralized office in Moscow. Two of the most important state committees are of the union-republic type: the People's Control Committee, and the Committee for State Security (KGB). Although these committees have republic and regional offices, those units have no independent authority and are strictly accountable to the center. Another very influential committee, the State Planning Committee (Gosplan), was abolished in December 1990 and its functions given to a new Ministry of Economics and Forecasting.

The dynamics of Soviet state administration result in two distinctive features. First, Soviet ministries have accumulated a tremendous amount of expertise that by far eclipses that of either the party apparatus or the newly created legislative bodies. Armed with this expertise, personnel, and material resources, ministries can become powerful advocates of policies affecting their economic sectors. Second, ministerial expertise, social cohesion, and personnel stability can foster the development of clear institutional interests. On appropriations issues, the agricultural interests and the consumer-goods-oriented Ministry of Light Industry frequently oppose a coalition consisting of the Ministries of Steel and Defense. Even within a single ministry, departmental interests are often visible. Thus, one department within the Ministry of the Automobile Industry may favor importation of technology from the West in order to improve production, while another department may push for increasing the educational standards and training of automobile assembly line workers.

During the last ten years of Brezhnev's reign, Soviet ministries increased their powers at the expense of both factory managers and central planners. Ministerial staffs swelled and the organizational structures of the ministries became increasingly complex. Gorbachev has tried to reduce the power of industrial ministries by granting greater decision-making authority to enterprise managers.

In some instances ministries have been consolidated into large "superministries" called bureaus or commissions. Currently there are five state commissions and four bureaus, each headed by a deputy chairman of the USSR Cabinet of Ministers. Gorbachev has also ordered a reduction in the staffs and budgets of the bloated government ministries. Since 1987, eighteen ministries or state committees have been abolished, and the staff of the Cabinet of Ministers has been reduced. A large number of ministers and other officials have been dismissed or forced into retirement.

The ministries and state committees are not sacrificing their power without a fight, however. High-ranking ministerial officials have expressed frustrations in the press, as well as in parliamentary debates, that their directives are now widely ignored at the factory level. The ability of these massive bureaucracies to delay the implementation of Gorbachev's economic reforms should not be underestimated. Despite all the recent power shifts and reorganizations, the ministries and state committees remain a conservative force opposing radical reform.

THE SOVIETS AND ELECTIONS IN THE USSR

For the first time in the seventy-two-year history of the USSR, relatively free competitive elections were held on March 26, 1989. The elections named 2250 deputies to the Congress of People's Deputies, 750 deputies from territorial districts, 750 from nationality areas, and 750 from social organizations, including the CPSU, Komsomol, trade unions, and the USSR Academy of Sciences. As we noted earlier, the nomination and election of the latter deputies has been criticized, since these social institutions often did not put forward multiple candidates for each post. In fact, in more than one-quarter of the nation's electoral districts, candidates ran unopposed. More fundamental objections were voiced that the electoral system guaranteed the representation of a large number of deputies from the CPSU and other party-dominated institutions, regardless of the popularity of these institutions with the general population. Consequently, the electoral laws have been amended, and for the next election to the Congress in 1994, deputies will be selected from territorial districts and nationality areas.

Candidates are nominated for ballots at grass-roots meetings in their factories or neighborhoods. Their nominations must then be approved by a district conference of electors. These sessions tend to be boisterous affairs at which disgruntled citizens vent their frustrations and anger at party-sponsored candidates, as we see from the following report.[10]

> Anna Saminskaya arrived Thursday afternoon at the voter's meeting in the Moscow House of Scholars, a wishful skeptic on the subject of Soviet politics.
>
> For more than ten hours, Mrs. Saminskaya, 37 years old, mother of six, teacher of the Russian language, joined with 622 other voters of Moscow Election District No. 1 in a riveting marathon of attempted democracy.
>
> And early Friday morning, after a narrow, guerilla victory of the local machine candidate, she walked the three blocks back to her apartment a born-again citizen.
>
> The meeting at the House of Scholars was the final hurdle for 12 candidates hoping to be on the district ballot when voters go to the polls March 26 to elect a new Congress of [People's] Deputies. The elections are the beginning stage of the first major revamping of the Soviet political system. For the first time, ordinary Soviet citizens are being invited into the process of selecting their legislators and, in many cases, have the opportunity to choose among several candidates.
>
> The district election meetings, which began this week in 1,500 precincts around the country, are a critical step in a new election procedure that many citizens view with suspicion.
>
> The hopefuls in District No. 1—among them a cosmonaut, a celebrity poet, a subway builder, a law professor, the head of the Novosti press agency and two economists—had been nominated by workplaces in the district and approved by voters in a first round of neighborhood pre-election meetings last month.
>
> For Mrs. Saminskaya and her friends, the suspicion was focused on one candidate, Anatoly Ivanovich Kiselev, director of the top-secret Khrunichev Machine Tool Factory and the clear favorite of the local party establishment.
>
> If, as she feared, the fix was in, it was in for Mr. Kiselev, a beefy, self-confident man with slicked-back hair, a pin-striped business suit, an entourage of functionaries and a powerful resumé.
>
> "It is no accident," said Mr. Kiselev's campaign leaflets, posted in the lobby alongside a television set that played a video of the apartments and Roman baths he had built for his factory workers, "that Anatoly Ivanovich Kiselev was chosen as a delegate to the 25th, 26th and 27th Congresses of the Communist Party of the Soviet Union and to the 19th All-Union Party Conference."
>
> Nor was it an accident that Mr. Kiselev arrived Thursday with a substantial head start, the largest block of committed voters in the hall.
>
> A twist in the election law that the other candidates said they had been unaware of allows a candidate to bring a block of supporters proportionate to the number of workplaces that nominated him.

Mr. Kiselev, who besides being the director of the machine tool plant is the chairman of the local council of factory directors, had garnered nominations from 18 plants, giving him 108 votes at the outset. Most of the other candidates had sought only one nomination, and arrived with six supporters apiece.

To fill out the hall, uncommitted electors were chosen at workplaces that had not nominated their own candidate—a likely hidden source of support for Mr. Kiselev—and at neighborhood meetings.

Mrs. Saminskaya said the neighborhood gathering that picked her as an elector was called on short notice and scheduled early last Friday evening, before most residents had gotten home from work. The participants, she said, were mostly pensioners mustered by local Communist Party organizers.

"They picked me because I'm the mother of six children," Mrs. Saminskaya explained, sitting at her kitchen table the night before the election meeting. "No one bothered to ask whom I would support. No one seemed to care."

Mrs. Saminskaya decided that her candidate was Gavriil K. Popov, a witty and audacious economist who formerly taught at Moscow State University and is now the editor-in-chief of the journal "Voprosy Ekonomiki" [and was elected mayor of Moscow in 1990].

Electors at a district meeting are allowed to vote for as many of the candidates as they want, so she also decided to throw her support behind three others known as independent thinkers and advocates of radical change: Aleksei M. Yemelyanov, who is head of the economics department at Moscow State University, Valerii M. Savitsky, a law professor, and the poet Yevgeny Yevtushenko.

The main thing, she decided, was to stop Mr. Kiselev. Once on the ballot, she said, his organization in the factories and the party would make him unstoppable.

As the candidates explained their platforms and answered questions from the hall Thursday night, the voters of District No. 1 faced a stark choice between the old politics of the Communist pork barrel and the new politics of change.

Mrs. Saminskaya's candidates stressed civil liberties, political pluralism and economic freedom.

Mr. Yevtushenko, describing the current Soviet legislature as "a puppet theater," called for the election of independent leaders, who would be reluctant to "send tanks to Czechoslovakia or Afghanistan."

Mr. Savitsky said perhaps a multi-party political system would not be such a dangerous thing.

Mr. Popov called for a volunteer, professional army and said the death penalty should be abolished "in a country where we have had to rehabilitate millions of people posthumously."

Throwing down the gauntlet to Mr. Kiselev, he urged voters not to send to their new congress a representative of "the military-industrial complex."

But after answering questions from the audience, Mr. Popov surprised the crowd by suddenly announcing his withdrawal from the race. The economist explained that he had also been nominated to run in the city of Voronezh, where he would be the only challenger to a member of the ruling Politburo, Vitalii I. Vorotnikov.

Mr. Kiselev, on the other hand, offered himself as a man who gets things done.

He contended that his plant makes no military equipment—only "peaceful space technology," auto parts and other consumer goods—and he promised he would be the first to vote for cuts in the military budget.

But Mr. Kiselev's strongest qualifications were also his major handicap.

Having achieved his lofty position under a system now largely discredited, he had trouble persuading voters that he would now be a champion of change, although he joined other candidates in enthusiastic attacks on the bureaucracy and in calling for greater restraints on the police and K.G.B.

Moreover, some voters said they were offended by what they considered Mr. Kiselev's steamroller tactics.

"It's a mafia, plain and simple," Mrs. Saminskaya said, during a break. "Everybody can see it."

If one man turned the tide Thursday night, it may have been a 74-year-old pensioner named Vladimir N. Lovin. It was more than six hours into the meeting, and the weary majority was ready to close off debate and distribute the ballots. An uproar ensued, with dozens of voters eager to have their first taste of real political combat.

Mr. Lovin stepped up to the microphone and silenced the crowd with a burst of righteous indignation: "We've waited 70 years for this and now they want us to shut up!"

The debate went on and it soon became clear that Mr. Kiselev's forces were not the only ones with a strategy. Mrs. Saminskaya and her allies began a well-planned series of short, passionate speeches promoting the lawyer, the economist, and the poet and attacking the factory director, who sat glowering on the stage.

"We should have as few deputies as possible from the military-industrial complex, whose budget is a secret to this day," one speaker declared.

"The legislature is not a factory," snorted another man.

When a local doctor took the stage to charge that Mr. Kiselev had reneged on a promise to provide transportation for a nearby hospital, the factory director looked as if his shirt collar had suddenly shrunk.

Mrs. Saminskaya was the 22nd speaker. Nervous but determined, she made her pitch as the representative of the district's mothers, and was warmly applauded.

Most of the voters were still in the hall at 1:20 A.M., when the vote counting committee emerged to read the result of the secret ballot. Mr. Savitsky, the lawyer, and Mr. Yemelyanov, the economist, won support from more than half the voters and will now face the district's public on March 22. Mr. Yevtushenko, who was often considered a voice of independence in repressed times, was too flamboyant and emotional for many voters' tastes, and was defeated.

And then the surprise: 292 votes for Mr. Kiselev, 309 against. There was a murmur of disbelief, followed by a roar of applause.

"To me, it seems that after all, the people have strength," Mrs. Saminskaya said. "It means that something has changed."

And as she exchanged phone numbers with many of her newfound allies, out in the corridors, a woman was collecting campaign posters from the walls, for an exhibit at the Soviet historical museum.

Election day is declared a national holiday in order to minimize conflicts with work schedules. To make it easier for people to vote, polling stations are set up in virtually every housing complex, factory, neighborhood, and village. Polling stations are even set up in hospitals, on ships, on long-distance trains, and in train stations and airports, to enable travelers to vote. Absentee voting is allowed simply by obtaining a certificate, permitting a citizen to vote in another precinct.

Turnout on March 26, 1989, was heavy for the elections for the Congress of People's Deputies, with 89.8 percent of all eligible voters voting.[11] Candidates ran unopposed in only about 30 percent of all races. Most of the top-ranking party leaders ran unopposed for one of 100 "safe seats" alloted to the CPSU. However, approximately fifty senior regional party secretaries and local government officials were defeated. Almost half of the candidates put forward by the military failed to win election, and those that did win tended to be of lower rank. Five chiefs of republic KGB offices also were rejected. In contrast, candidates favoring progressive reforms tended to do well. Gavriil Popov maintained that the progressive bloc consists of 300 deputies.[12]

Apart from the election outcomes, the March 26 elections were notable for being the first exercise of electoral democracy in the history of the USSR. No doubt, reforms are still necessary in order to improve the electoral process. Nevertheless, Gorbachev has placed the Soviet Union on a course toward democratization and citizen participation that has fundamentally altered the nature of the political system.

INSTITUTIONAL PLURALISM AND DEMOCRATIZATION

Until 1989, elections were of little significance in the determination of policy in the USSR; rather, they were exercises in mobilizing citizens for symbolic purposes. Under previous policies all candidates were put forward by the Party and ran unopposed. Citizens could vote against a candidate and, in rare instances, candidates were defeated because they failed to garner 50 percent of the votes. Since the electoral process was designed more as a display of national unity and support for the CPSU than as a mechanism for citizens to influence policies, conflicts over policies manifested themselves in other ways.

The Soviet political system has long been viewed as being heavily bureaucratic. In 1961, Alfred Meyer argued that the bureaucratic model should form the basis of our understanding of Soviet society.[13] In another influential work, Carl Friedrich and Zbigniew Brzezinski identified *bureaucratization* as a defining trait of totalitarian autocracy in the USSR.[14] Much of the early focus on bureaucracy in the USSR lent support to the "organizational society" or "administered society" models. These models, which grew out of the totalitarian model, sustained the view that the state bureaucracy is merely the pawn of the leadership and is used to enhance the Party's domination over society. The bureaucracy in this approach was viewed as a uniform, homogeneous organization, devoid of significant powers or interests of its own.

Others viewed the bureaucratic nature of politics in the USSR as presenting the opportunity for multiple power centers to arise. Barrington Moore noted that the technocrats who staff the bureaucracies make decisions on technical and rational criteria; they value predictability and conformity to objective rules.[15] Brzezinski noted that the increasing role of bureaucrats in policy-making threatened to reduce the Soviet political system to "a regime of clerks."[16] Implicit in these notions is the view that the increasing bureaucratization of the Soviet political system since World War II placed a constraint on the power of the CPSU. There is widespread recognition today that the leadership is dependent upon the various bureaucracies in the USSR for information and advice in order to enact effective policies. The President has no independent means of verifying Soviet military projections of American submarine strength, for example, or the capital investment needed to irrigate Central

Asia. The various ministries in the USSR, as in other political systems, have a near monopoly on vital information, which gives them some leverage over the political decisionmakers.

Bureaucrats also exert their influence through the implementation of policies. Most policy pronouncements of the political leadership are rather vague, general promises and statements of intent; they strike a new tone, indicate a new direction, or set new priorities. It is up to the staffs of the various ministries and state committees to translate those directives into concrete actions. In defining and shaping policies, the bureaucrats often wield extensive discretionary powers.

Bureaucrats also have the power to resist new policy initiatives that they do not favor. Bureaucratic inertia, obstructionism, and redefinition of policies can and do deflect the aims of the top leadership. This negative capacity of state bureaucrats can be overcome if the political authorities choose to make an issue of it and are willing to devote the necessary resources to eliminating opposition. More often than not, however, bureaucratic resistance goes unchallenged by the central authorities.

In short, ministries and state committees in the USSR are active participants in Soviet politics. More than mere pawns of the Party or the President, they are self-interested institutions, able and willing to promote their own policies and perspectives. They function as institutional interest groups, representing not a single, uniform bureaucracy but a diverse array of cooperating and conflicting institutions. On occasion, the interests of one or more of these institutional groups coincide with the interests of certain segments of the leadership; at other times, they are at odds. This dynamic and multifaceted conception of the Soviet political system has been variously referred to as "institutional pluralism,"[17] "bureaucratic pluralism,"[18] "centralized pluralism,"[19] and "participatory bureaucracy."[20]

These models derive from the interest-group approach to politics, which was first applied to the study of Soviet politics in the 1960s.[21] Unlike the Kremlinologists, who focus solely on factional conflict at the pinnacle of the Soviet system, the interest-group approach looks at conflict among bureaucratic or occupation groups. Thus, Soviet leaders are assumed to have their own constituencies and organizational bases for support (party apparatus, agriculture, military, secret police, and so forth). Since Stalin's time, power has become deconcentrated among these diverse interests, and policy-making has necessitated the balancing and coalescing of these interests. In the period after Stalin, as Jeremy Azrael has observed, there was a "reemergence of politics" in the Soviet system.[22] Conflict and consensus-building replaced the forced unanimity of the Stalin years. Social groups became more assertive and responsive to popular demands. Jerry Hough states that Soviet politics since 1953 has revolved around "conflict among a complex set of crosscutting and shifting alliances of persons with divergent interests."[23] Darrell Hammer notes, "Policy is the outcome of an ongoing political conflict."[24] No longer is political conflict regarded as the "mere personal struggle for power, largely divorced from questions of policy or ideology, or from the interests of social groups."[25] Nor is conflict limited to the highest ranks of the party apparatus.

Where and in what form do conflicts become manifest? While some authors have attempted to examine Soviet pluralism in terms of issue-oriented groups, the majority of the literature examines policy conflicts that find expression in bureaucracies, institutions, or occupations.[26] There are several reasons for the preponderance of this approach. First, until *glasnost'* changed the complexion of Soviet politics, strictures on free and open discussion of issues in the Soviet Union tended to reduce the formation of issue-oriented factions and restrict communication and discussion to intra-institutional channels. Second, in Soviet society there is a fusion of institutional and individual interests not found in the West. Third, in the Soviet system, where factionalism within the CPSU was officially outlawed until 1990, policy positions had to be articulated through legitimate organizational channels. Substantive issues of public policy have long divided the Soviet leadership—between "hawks" and "doves"; between those favoring centralization of economic decision-making and those favoring more autonomy for factory managers; between advocates of "law and order" and advocates of rehabilitation of criminals; between proponents of hard-line literary and artistic policies and proponents of a more liberal stance. But such divisions usually coincide with an occupational or bureaucratic group.

Thus, conflicts in the Soviet political system have tended to find expression in the bureaucratic struggle for influence. As Paul Cocks has stated, in the 1970s there was a "devolution of authority" to crucial bureaucratic subsystems—the military, factory managers, regional party secretaries, agricultural interests, and jurists.[27] Instead of the monolithic and autocratic system of the Stalin years, there is an oligarchy of conflicting interests, each represented by a powerful bureaucracy. Most policies are the outcome of "compromises and adjustments among these diverse bureaucratic groups and their interests in society."[28] Increasingly, individual party leaders must reach out to these bureaucracies for support and expertise.

Western notions of interest groups and the ways in which they influence the public-policy process had, until recently, only limited application to the Soviet case. In the West, interest groups are predominantly associational or voluntary; that is, citizens having particular, clearly identifiable demands to articulate form collective organizations to lobby on their behalf. In the Soviet Union, policy conflicts tend to form along institutional lines, rather than among voluntary lobby organizations. In a society that professes the belief that the CPSU and its policies reflect the will and best interests of *all* sectors of Soviet society, associational interest groups that pursue only their own limited interests were not accorded legitimacy in the political process.

The institutional basis for pluralism in the Soviet Union is reinforced by the fusion of individual interests with those of the various institutions within which they exist. The relative welfare of Soviet citizens is closely associated with the power and prestige of the institutions in which they are employed. Not only do people derive their livelihood from their jobs; they also derive a long list of fringe benefits, concessions, perquisites, and connections. For instance, most factories, state farms, institutes, enterprises, and educational institutions provide housing, child-care centers, and polyclinics for their employees. The quality of these services varies with the prestige of the institution. The Soviet military, for example, maintains its own department stores, selling items usually unavailable to the general public. It also has a fund to help military officers build summer cottages or take vacations at the most exclusive resorts. Given the relative equality of Soviet incomes, these preferential policies take on added significance. Workers have been known to transfer from one factory to another in order to take advantage of better housing, better polyclinics, or better day-care centers.

Bureaucratic officials, thus, have become influential, semiautonomous participants in the policy-making and implementing process. They identify with the professional standards of their occupations and the programs they administer, and they strive to represent their clientele in response to broader societal forces. Most bureaucratic groups have special organs through which to voice their institutional interests. For example, the viewpoint of factory managers is expressed in the newspaper Sotsialisticheskaya industriya (Socialist Industry), the military expresses its demands in the newspaper Krasnaya zvezda (Red Star), and the literary elite voices its concerns in Novy Mir (New World) and Literaturnaya gazeta (Literary Gazette).

Equally significant are the ways in which bureaucratic officials refine, alter, and reshape policies during the implementation phase, in order to make them coincide more closely with their own perceptions and preferences. In the late 1970s, when industrial ministries were informed that production targets would be lowered and bonuses raised for enterprises manufacturing improved-quality, innovative goods, many factories made minor revisions and improvements in their products; the ministries approved these revisions as "innovations" just so that the factories might receive the special benefits. Nor is bureaucratic opposition manifested only on economic matters. When Khrushchev proposed the extension of secondary education from ten to eleven years, he did so in order that all youth would have to engage in at least one year of "practical" work on a farm or in a factory. When the plan was implemented, however, on-the-job training became voluntary, and the university-bound sons and daughters of the intelligentsia never had to work. In the mid-1980s, Gorbachev's antialcohol campaign ran into extensive opposition from local officials, who adopted pro forma measures instead of vigorously pursuing the new policy direction.

From Stalin's time to the present, politics in the USSR has involved making compromises and adjustments among diverse bureaucratic groups and their interests in society. In most cases the final arbiters of these conflicts have been party officials. However, today the Soviet political system is in the midst of transition. In addition to this well-established system of behind-the-scenes bureaucratic conflict and compromise, policy differences now are openly manifested in public discussions, the media, and parliamentary debate. Most importantly, the newly created legislative and executive bodies are challenging the traditional role of the CPSU as the sole mediator of conflicting interests and the architect of political compromise. As the Party loses support in the society and becomes increasingly fragmented, the power and influence of the Supreme Soviet and the Presidency are bound to increase.

Notes

1. Constitution of the USSR (1977), Article 72.

2. Michael Florinsky, ed., *Encyclopedia of Russia and the Soviet Union* (New York: McGraw-Hill, 1961), 391.

3. Another 75 deputies from the Committee of Soviet Women and 75 from the All-Union Council of War and Labor veterans also ran unopposed. See Viktor Yasmann, "Quotas of Seats in Congress of People's Deputies for Public and Professional Organizations," *Radio Liberty Report on the USSR* 1, no. 4 (29 January 1989): 10.

4. *Izvestiya,* 6 May 1989, p. 3.

5. Constitution of the USSR (1977), Article 110.

6. *New York Times,* 28 June 1989, p. 1.

7. Ibid., p. 6.

8. Ibid.

9. Gordon B. Smith, "Gorbachev and the Council of Ministers: Leadership Consolidation and Its Policy Implications," *Soviet Union/Union Sovietique* 14, no. 3 (1987): 343–363.

10. *New York Times,* 12 February 1989, pp. 1, 12.

11. *Izvestiya,* 5 April 1989, p. 1.

12. Dawn Mann and Julia Wishnevsky, "Composition of Congress of People's Deputies," *Radio Liberty Report on the USSR* 1, no. 18 (1989) 5.

13. Alfred G. Meyer, "USSR Incorporated," *Slavic Review* 20 (October 1961): 370.

14. Carl J. Friedrich and Zbigniew K. Brzezinski, *Totalitarian Dictatorship and Autocracy,* 2d ed. (New York: Praeger, 1965), 205–218.

15. Barrington Moore, Jr., *Political Power and Social Theory* (Cambridge: Harvard University Press, 1958), 19–20.

16. Zbigniew Brzezinski, "Victory of the Clerks," *The New Republic* (14 November 1964): 15, 18.

17. Jerry Hough, *The Soviet Prefects* (Cambridge: Harvard University Press, 1969), 27–29.

18. Darrell P. Hammer, *USSR: The Politics of Oligarchy* (Hinsdale, IL: Dryden Press, 1974), 223–256.

19. H. Gordon Skilling, "Interest Groups and Communist Politics," in H. Gordon Skilling and Franklyn Griffiths, eds., *Interest Groups in Soviet Politics* (Princeton: Princeton University Press, 1971), 17.

20. Robert V. Daniels, "Soviet Politics Since Khrushchev," in John W. Strong, ed., *The Soviet Union under Brezhnev and Kosygin* (New York: Van Nostrand Reinhold, 1971), 22–23.

21. For example, see Skilling and Griffiths, *Interest Groups in Soviet Politics,* 3–18.

22. Jeremy Azrael, "Decision-Making in the USSR," in Richard Cornell, ed., *The Soviet Political System* (Englewood Cliffs, NJ: Prentice-Hall, 1970), 214.

23. Jerry Hough, "The Soviet System: Petrification or Pluralism?," *Problems of Communism* 21 (1972): 28.

24. Hammer, *USSR: The Politics of Oligarchy,* 286.

25. Skilling, "Interest Groups and Communist Politics," 9.

· 26. One case study of issue-oriented interest groups is Joel Schwartz and William Keech, "Group Influence and the Policy Process in the Soviet Union," *APSR* 62 (1968): 840–851. Examples of bureaucratic conflicts over policies appear in Hammer, *USSR: The Politics of Oligarchy;* Hough, *The Soviet Prefects;* and Daniels, "Soviet Politics Since Khrushchev."

27. Paul Cocks, "The Policy Process and Bureaucratic Politics," in Paul Cocks et al., eds., *The Dynamics of Soviet Politics* (Cambridge: Harvard University Press, 1976), 158.

28. Sidney Ploss, "Interest Groups," in Allen Kassof, ed., *Prospects for Soviet Society* (New York: Praeger, 1968), 95.

Selected Bibliography

Brzezinski, Zbigniew. *Dilemmas of Change in Soviet Politics*. New York: Columbia University Press, 1969.

Brzezinski, Zbigniew, and Samuel P. Huntington. *Political Power: USA/USSR*. New York: Viking Press, 1963.

Cocks, Paul. "Rethinking the Organizational Weapon: The Soviet System in a Systems Age." *World Politics* 32 (January 1980).

——. "The Policy Process and Bureaucratic Politics." In Paul Cocks et al., eds. *The Dynamics of Soviet Politics*. Cambridge: Harvard University Press, 1976, 156–178.

Downs, Anthony. *Inside Bureaucracy*. Boston: Little, Brown, 1967.

Friedgut, Theodore. *Political Participation in the USSR*. Princeton: Princeton University Press, 1979.

Hammer, Darrell P. *USSR: The Politics of Oligarchy*. Hinsdale, IL: Dryden Press, 1974.

Hough, Jerry. *The Soviet Prefects*. Cambridge: Harvard University Press, 1969.

Hough, Jerry, and Merle Fainsod. *How the Soviet Union Is Governed*. Cambridge: Harvard University Press, 1979.

Little, D. Richard. "Legislative Authority in the Soviet Political System." *Slavic Review* 30 (March 1971): 57–73.

——. "Soviet Parliamentary Committees after Khrushchev: Obstacles and Opportunities." *Soviet Studies* 24 (July 1972): 41–60.

Mote, Max E. *Soviet Local and Republic Elections*. Stanford: The Hoover Institution, 1965.

Ryavec, Karl W. "The Soviet Ministerial Elite: 1964–1979." Occasional Papers Series, no. 6, Program in Soviet and East European Studies, University of Massachusetts at Amherst, 1981.

Skilling, H. Gordon, and Franklyn Griffiths, eds. *Interest Groups in Soviet Politics*. Princeton: Princeton University Press, 1971.

Smith, Gordon B. *Public Policy and Administration in the Soviet Union*. New York: Praeger, 1980.

Urban, Michael. *The Ideology of Administration: American and Soviet Cases*. Albany, NY: SUNY Press, 1982.

Vanneman, Peter. *The Supreme Soviet*. Durham, NC: Duke University Press, 1977.

Zaslavsky, Victor, and Robert J. Brym. "The Functions of Elections in the USSR." *Soviet Studies* 30 (1978): 362–371.

7

Nationality Politics: The Threat of Fragmentation

Western analysis of the Soviet political system frequently tends to focus on national-level policies, events, and institutions. However, as Gorbachev's reforms have unfolded, republic, regional, and local interests have asserted a greater and greater claim on decision-making power. The future of the USSR as an "integral, federal, multinational state" is very much in doubt.[1] As we noted in Chapter 1, the USSR is made up of more than one hundred diverse ethnic groups, each speaking its own language and enjoying its unique cultural heritage. *Glasnost'* opened the door to public expression of long-suppressed national and ethnic frustrations. The result was a firestorm of ethnic and regional protest against the "center"—against Russia and the government's long-standing policies of Russification. Social, economic, educational, and environmental issues have taken on a decidedly national or ethnic nature. In short, the USSR today is suffering from a crisis of federalism that challenges the very fundamentals of its political system.

SOVIET FEDERALISM

Today, there are some 126 officially recognized nationalities in the USSR. They are usually categorized in terms of language groups.

The Slavs. The dominant nationality groups in the USSR, accounting for some 70 percent of the total population, are Slavic nationalities (Russians, Ukrainians, and Belorussians). For the most part, they live in the European part of the USSR (west of the Urals) and are Orthodox. According to the latest census, taken in 1989, Russians constitute slightly more than one-half (50.8 percent) of the total population. The proportion of the population that is Russian has steadily declined since World War II. The territory that is assigned to the Russians, the Russian Soviet Federated Socialist Republic (RSFSR), stretches from the Baltic to the Pacific and encompasses 76 percent of the total area of the USSR. More than one hundred other nationality groups reside within the republic as well.[2]

Because of modernization and population migration over the decades, Russians now reside in significant numbers in every republic of the USSR. Only in Lithuania and the Caucasus do they constitute less than 10 percent of the population.[3] Russians outside of the RSFSR tend to live in large urban centers. Thus, more than two-thirds of all Russians living in Central Asia reside in urban areas.[4] In Alma-Ata, the capital of Kazakhstan, over 70 percent of the population is Russian and only 12 percent Kazakh.[5]

Ukrainians constitute the second-largest nationality group in the USSR. The Ukraine, a rich agricultural region in the southwestern portion of the Soviet Union, gave rise to an ancient culture that subsequently formed the basis for Russian society. In the tenth century, Kiev, the capital of the Ukraine, dominated Moscow and other Russian principalities; through its influence, Orthodoxy was introduced into Russia. Later occupations and annexations of the Ukraine by Poland and Austria-Hungary introduced Catholicism. Partly because of its history of domination by neighboring powers, a fierce sense of national pride exists in the Ukraine. For many, this translates into the desire for autonomy and national independence.

Belorussians, the third major Slavic nationality in the USSR, occupy the western region of the country bordering on Poland. Belorussians today are thoroughly integrated into Soviet society; marriages between Belorussians and other Slavic groups are quite common. As a result of their assimilation and weakly defined national identity, the independence movement in Belorussia is not nearly as strong as in most other republics.

Western Nationality Groups.   On the Western fringes of the USSR reside four major non-Slavic, Western nationalities, who were incorporated into the country as a result of World War II. Three of these nationalities are often referred to collectively as the Baltic republics, although the religious, cultural, and linguistic heritages of the Latvians, Lithuanians, and Estonians are quite distinct. The Estonians are closely related to the Finns and are predominantly Lutheran. The Estonian language is part of the Finno-Ugric family of languages that also includes Finnish, Magyar (Hungarian), and Mongolian. In medieval times, the capital of the Estonian Republic, Tallinn, was a member of the Hanseatic League. Thus, the Estonians have always been more oriented toward Scandinavian and Germanic culture than to that of the Slavic regions to the east.

The Latvian and Lithuanian languages belong to the Baltic group of Indo-European languages. Latvia is predominantly Lutheran, while Lithuania is overwhelmingly Catholic. Immigration has adversely affected Latvia, but is less of a problem in Lithuania, the least urbanized of the three republics, because Slavic immigrants prefer to resettle in urban areas.

The fourth Western nationality group, the Moldavians, occupy a small region of Romania that was annexed into the USSR during the Soviet military occupation in 1940. Of the various nationalities in the Soviet Union, it is the most artificial; the Moldavians are linguistically, culturally, and historically indistinguishable from Romanians, and the Moldavian republic was created solely to justify Soviet annexation of the region.

The Caucasian People.   The Caucasus region comprises the Georgian, Armenian, and Azerbaidzhan republics. Their cultures have origins in prehistory. Armenia, which borders on Turkey, once had an empire that stretched from the Mediterranean to the Caucasus. The national symbol of Armenia, Mount Ararat (thought to be the site of the landing of Noah's ark), is located in what is now Turkey, although it is visible from the Armenian capital,

Yerevan. The Armenian Apostolic Church embodies Armenian nationalism and attracts a large and powerful following among Armenians both inside and outside the USSR. The Georgian Orthodox church, while less of a nationalistic rallying symbol, has its own patriarch and is independent of the Russian Orthodox church in Moscow.

The Armenians have demonstrated a high propensity for assimilation and upward mobility in Soviet society; together with the neighboring Georgians, they enjoy the highest levels of education in the USSR. Unlike the Georgians, however, one-third of the Armenians have migrated to other areas of the country; they also have the highest rate of intermarriage of any of the fifteen major nationalities.[6]

The third Caucasian group, the Azerbaidzhanis, are Islamic, and their language is Turkic. The capital of the Azerbaidzhan SSR is Baku, a city whose industry centers around the oil fields of the Caspian Basin.

Central Asian Nationalities.   Soviet Central Asia is comprised of five republics—the Turkmen, Kirgiz, Uzbek, Kazakh, and Tadzhik republics. With the exception of the Tadzhik, these nationality groups speak Turkic languages. (Tadzhik is derived from Persian.) All of the Central Asian nationalities are Muslim, and some of the most cherished mosques in the Islamic world are located in the ancient cities of Samarkand and Bukhara. The Central Asian peoples exhibit very high birthrates and retain their own family and cultural traditions. Consequently, they are the least assimilated into Soviet society. Many Central Asians in urban areas speak Russian, work in technical and professional jobs, and have adopted a modern, Russian standard of living; in their homes, however, native dietary and religious practices, as well as traditional family relations, persist.

Other Territorial Nationality Groups.   The remaining territorially based nationality groups in the USSR are extremely diverse. They include the Buriats and Kalmyks, whose languages and cultures are Mongolian and whose religious practices are either Buddhist or Shamanist; the Yakuts, a seminomadic people living in the far north of Siberia; the Chukchi, who are similar to the American Eskimos; the Turkic-speaking Tatars, who are clustered in the Tatar Autonomous Republic 500 miles east of Moscow; the Komi, who live off their reindeer herds like the Lapps of Scandinavia; and the Karelians, Finns who occupy a region taken over by the Soviets during the "Winter War" of 1939–1940. The ethnic groups below the level of the fifteen major nationalities are accorded varying levels of regional representation and autonomy, generally in accordance with their size and level of development. These ethnic groups range in size from several million to just one or two hundred.

Nonterritorial Nationality Groups.   A persistent problem in the USSR is how to cope with nationality groups that are not concentrated in a single region. Groups such as the Germans, Poles, and Jews reside throughout the European portion of the USSR. Granting these groups the right of autonomy and self-determination is thus impossible. In rural areas in which Poles and Germans are sufficiently populous, Soviet authorities allow a few schools to operate using those languages; newspapers and books appear in both German and Polish in these regions. The majority of the 1.8 million Jews in the USSR live in large urban centers in the European portion of the country. Linguistically, the Jews have been fully assimilated into Russian society for more than 150 years. The demand for Hebrew or Yiddish schools and publications today is extremely limited. In order to grant some degree of autonomy and self- determination to the Jews, Stalin created the Jewish Autonomous Region in a desolate area on the Chinese border, some 4000 miles from Moscow. In Birobidzhan, the capital of the region, there are some Yiddish schools and a thriving Yiddish theater, but few European Jews have been enticed to settle in the area. Rather than seeking the right to a separate cultural identity, Soviet Jews have clashed with the regime over educational quotas and job restrictions that have barred Jews from becoming further integrated into the society. For some Jews, however, the systematic discrimination has renewed a sense of Jewish consciousness.

Soviet nationality policy is frequently torn between the dual goals of promoting economic growth for the country as a whole and fostering greater economic equality among the diverse nationality groups in the USSR. At times, the regime has allocated resources to favor the least developed regions; at other times, it has invested resources strictly on the basis of economic efficiency. In the realm of social policy, however, the regime remains committed to eliminating class and ethnic divisions and continues to support national self-determination.

National self-determination and autonomy today apply primarily to language rights. Article 36 of the Constitution states: "Citizens of the USSR of different races and nationalities have equal rights. Exercise of these rights is ensured by a policy of all-round development and drawing together of the nations and nationalities of the USSR, by educating citizens in the spirit of Soviet patriotism and socialist internationalism, and by the possibility of using their native language and the languages of other peoples of the USSR."[7] In the various republics, nationality regions, and territories, newspapers, books, and cultural performances use indigenous languages. Primary and secondary schools provide instruction in native languages as well as in Russian. Courses at the universities, however, with the exception of those in the Ukraine, Georgia, and the Baltic republics, are taught in Russian, and fluency in Russian is necessary for upward mobility in most career fields. While governmental bodies at all levels function bilingually (in Russian and in the indigenous language), the official language of the CPSU, the security organs, and the military is exclusively Russian.

Evidence of the persistence of linguistic diversity in the Soviet Union is impressive. Almost 94 percent of all Soviet citizens use their native language as their primary language.[8] At the same time, more than three-fourths of the non-Russian population speaks Russian fluently.[9] Experts disagree as to the long-term prospects for bilingualism in the USSR. The French scholar Hélène Carrère d'Encausse considers the adoption of Russian a temporary phase in a larger movement toward the eventual elimination of other ethnic identities.[10] The British linguist E. G. Lewis, on the other hand, sees bilingualism as a stable and enduring feature of Soviet society.[11]

The official policy of the regime does not envisage the elimination of national languages, but it does emphasize bilingualism and word-borrowing among all of the languages in the Soviet Union. During the latter years of the Brezhnev period, however, there was a renewed emphasis on promoting the use of Russian in non-Russian areas. Conferences in Baku in 1981 and Riga in 1982 called for greater use of the Russian language in schools and for more publications in Russian. Since 1976, authorities in some areas have been restricting the circulation of non-Russian newspapers and magazines.[12]

Soviet authorities distinguish between the "drawing together" (*sblizhenie*) of nationalities and the "merger" (*sliianie*) of nationalities. The former implies the retention of national identities but the narrowing of social and economic differences among ethnic groups and the prevention of outbursts of national sentiment.[13] Merger refers to the elimination of all national differences and the assimilation of all nationalities into a uniform culture. Khrushchev resurrected the notion of the merging of nationalities in the 1961 Party Program; subsequent leaders, however, have adopted the much more cautious "drawing together" approach. Brezhnev once candidly observed, "Nationality relations, even in a society of mature socialism, are a reality that is contantly developing and raising new problems and tasks."[14]

Soviet nationality policies have also tended to heighten regional competition for resources. Since the 1930s, tremendous amounts of resources have been poured into Central Asia and other less-developed regions of the USSR. In part, these investments have been dictated by national economic priorities; they also have been motivated by the desire to create a uniform standard of living throughout the country, and in response to a vigorous lobbying effort by Central Asian leaders. In recent years, however, investment capital has become increasingly scarce and the competition for resources more acute. In the Baltic republics, Leningrad, Moscow, Kiev, and other well-developed areas of the USSR, local officials argue (with ample justification) that they have not been receiving their fair share of the state budget, but instead have been forced to pay (with reduced allocations) for development projects in Central Asia and Siberia.

Preferential treatment has also stirred some controversy within the ranks of the CPSU. Numerous articles by party officials have appeared stressing the importance of a nondiscriminatory cadre policy.[15] Being Uzbek, in and of itself, should not be a ticket to easy admission into the Party, they argue. The authors of such articles are invariably Slavic, and one suspects from their plaintive tone that there is an undercurrent of resentment against the Party's efforts to recruit non-Slavic elites into party posts.

The potential emergence of Russian nationalism in the 1970s was indicated by the leadership's frequent references to the concept of a *Soviet* people (*Sovetskii narod*). With developed socialism, it is believed, narrow ethnic and national identities will diminish and be replaced by a single, uniform, *Soviet* culture based on a common territory, a single ideology, a single political party, a common goal, a single, planned economy, harmonious relations among all classes, and proletarian internationalism.

Efforts to foster such an all-encompassing Soviet nationality, however, have often amounted simply to Russification. In 1978, drafts of the new constitutions for the union republics were circulated for public discussion and criticism. Minority nationalities quickly pointed out that the new versions of the republic constitutions dropped the guarantees that the official language of each republic would be the language of the indigenous people. After several months of heated discussion, these provisions were reinserted in the constitutions. An official announcement proclaimed that it was not the intent of the party leadership to undermine the languages of the national republics; rather, it had simply been assumed that the official language of each republic would be that of the native population.[16]

In the Ukraine, strong dissident and nationalistic sentiments have existed for centuries. Under the tsars as well as today, many Ukrainians have longed for national independence and sovereignty. Soviet authorities have dealt harshly with Ukrainian nationalism, reducing the extent of Ukrainian language usage in schools and universities in the republic and allowing many monuments to Ukrainian culture to be neglected or destroyed. In an effort to undermine Ukrainian nationalism, Stalin outlawed the Ukrainian Uniate church (eastern rite Catholics) and forced hundreds of thousands of people from the Western Ukraine to resettle in Russia, replacing them with an equal number of Russians.[17] The Ukraine also suffered staggering losses during Stalin's collectivization campaigns; the resulting terror-famine claimed as many as five million lives.[18] The region, which accounted for approximately one-third of the country's industrial output, was also devastated during World War II.

Under Khrushchev and Brezhnev there were widespread arrests of Ukrainian writers and historians who were attempting to preserve the Ukrainian cultural heritage. A crackdown on Ukrainian dissidents in 1972 succeeded in terminating publication of the *Ukrainian Herald*, the Ukrainian counterpart of the dissident publication *The Chronicle of Current Events*.

Repression, however, was often counterproductive, as in the case of the apparent murder in 1979 of a popular Ukrainian poet and folksinger, Volodymyr Ivasyuk. The twenty-five-year-old balladeer was asked to compose an oratorio marking the fortieth anniversary of the "reunification" of the Ukraine under Soviet rule after the defeat of Hitler. Ivasyuk refused, and was found a few days later hanging from a tree; the authorities claimed it was a suicide. More than 10,000 people attended Ivasyuk's funeral. Two of the prominent organizers of the funeral and members of the Ukrainian Helsinki Watch Group—Petro Sichko and his son Vasyl—were arrested after the funeral, convicted of "anti-Soviet slander," and sentenced to three years in a labor camp.[19]

In Central Asia and other regions of the USSR, economic development has worked against the emergence of nationalistic resentments and dissent. What dissent does exist in Central Asia usually centers around the persecution of religious groups, and leaders who refuse to abide by Soviet law and instead strictly follow the dictates of the Koran.

The repressive acts of Soviet authorities, whether in restricting the activities of the Catholic church in Lithuania or in silencing nationalistic sentiments in the Ukraine, often generate even more dissent. Two of the most ardent dissident nationality groups in the USSR are the Crimean Tatars and the Volga Germans. These groups were accused of collaboration with the Germans during World War II and were forcibly deported en masse to a desolate region in Central Asia. More than 200,000 Crimean Tatars (mostly women and children) were transported some 2000 miles in closed trucks and cattle cars with little food or water. Almost half the people died during the journey.[20] Despite the fact that they were officially exonerated in 1967, they have not been allowed to relocate to their native region in Crimea.

While the plight of Soviet Jews and the Crimean Tatars is well-known in the West, they are relatively isolated cases. The major points of friction today between the Soviet government and non-Russian ethnic groups are not, for the most part, over the right to emigrate, but over demands for more regional autonomy, curbs on Slavic migrations, use of native language, and claims on investment funds.[21]

GLASNOST' AND THE RISE OF NATIONALISM

Ironically, the recent explosion of nationalism in the USSR is in large part the product of Gorbachev's own reforms. Long-suppressed antagonisms over Russification could be openly expressed without fear of official reprisals. In addition, the greater freedom to communicate and the effort to reconstruct an accurate account of Soviet history for the first time enabled non-Russians to learn about their native history and cultures.

It was not immediately clear that the greater freedoms permitted under *glasnost'* would extend to airing national grievances. The first overt expression of ethnic discontent since Gorbachev's rise to power came in Kazakhstan in December 1986. D. A. Kunaev, Brezhnev's long-time first party secretary, was charged with corruption and replaced with Gennadii Kolbin, a Russian. Although Russians constitute 41 percent of the population of the republic compared to only 36 percent for Kazakhs, it had been long-standing practice to appoint a Kazakh as head of the party. The announcement of Kolbin's appointment sparked widespread riots in the republic's capital, Alma-Ata. According to Soviet sources, approximately 3000 people participated in the riots, setting fire to automobiles and smashing store windows.[22] It was not clear, however, that the manifestations of ethnic unrest in Kazakhstan established a precedent for other nationality groups.

Just such a precedent-setting event occurred in the summer of 1987 when a group of some 700 Crimean Tatars staged an unauthorized demonstration near Red Square. Although the protesters were carefully watched by plainclothes police and security officials, their demonstration was not disbanded; in fact, it received prominent coverage on the Soviet evening television news program *Vremya*. The message was clear: ethnic demands could be openly expressed without fear of harassment or imprisonment. It did not take long for a rising chorus of ethnic demands to develop into major crises that threaten to derail Gorbachev's attempts at social, political, and economic reform.

CRISIS POINTS

Rising national consciousness has resulted in a variety of clashes between ethnic groups and the center. As of early 1991, every republic with the exception of Tadzhikistan had passed legislation either seceding from the USSR or demanding a greater degree of autonomy from Moscow. In other areas, violent clashes have been precipitated not by demands for greater autonomy, but by long-standing interethnic hatred. Below we examine some of the major nationality crises confronting Gorbachev's regime.

The Baltics.   The three Baltic republics, Estonia, Latvia, and Lithuania, were forcibly incorporated into the USSR in 1940, as a result of the Molotov-Ribbentrop Pact. From 1920 until 1939 each was an independent country with democratic, parliamentary forms of government and a relatively healthy market economy. The annexation of the three countries into the USSR in 1940 was followed by the execution or deportation of approximately one million people.

The Baltic republics enjoy the highest standard of living of any region of the USSR. Consequently, there has been a steady in-migration of Russians and other Slavs. Russification is a major source of nationality dissent, especially in those areas where the influx of Russian immigrants and the low birthrate of the indigenous population combine to raise fears of the loss of national identity. These conditions exist particularly in the Baltic states. In Lithuania, a movement formed fusing Lithuanian nationalism and Catholicism, much as occurred in Poland with Solidarity. Protests against Russification in Estonia and Latvia center primarily around the designation of languages for schools. As more Russians move into these republics, there is a greater demand for Russian-language schools. When local officials have attempted to change a school's language from Estonian or Latvian to Russian, however, a storm of protest has often ensued.[23]

Intensive lobbying by the Baltic peoples preceded the Nineteenth Party Conference in June and July 1988, which was to take up questions of nationality policy and devolution of central authority. In addition to the immigration issue and the publication of the secret protocols, the movement for greater independence was also given impetus by growing awareness in all three republics of the extent of ecological damage resulting from almost fifty years of economic policies set in Moscow. For instance, massive deposits of shale oil, phosphorite, and limestone in Estonia had been so rapidly exploited that the Baltic was seriously polluted, and bathers had to be warned not to swim in it. Groundwater in Estonia is also suspected of being contaminated. In Lithuania, environmental concerns have focused on the Ignalina nuclear power station, which is identical in its design to the Chernobyl reactor.

At the Nineteenth Party Conference, Vaino Valjas, Estonian Party Secretary, charged that more than 90 percent of the economy was controlled by ministries in Moscow. He was echoed by the Latvian Party Secretary, Boris Pugo, who advocated "genuine sovereignty" and economic self-financing for each of the union-republics. The Lithuanian Party Secretary, Ringuadas Songaila, denounced administrative dictates from Moscow that were responsible for creating the deplorable political, economic, social, and ecological state of the republic. Although these sentiments were openly voiced at the Conference, the final document to emerge from the gathering only spoke in general terms about the need to transfer greater powers to lower levels of government.

In August 1988, the publication of the secret protocols of the Nazi-Soviet pact legitimized the claims of the three Baltic peoples that they had been illegally annexed into the USSR, and led to the creation of popular-front organizations in each republic. Massive demonstrations were held in all three republics on the anniversary of the signing of the Pact.

It was largely in response to their lack of success in bringing about a meaningful devolution of power at the Party Conference that popular-front organizations sprang up in each of the republics. The founding congresses for the three movements were convened in October 1988. Although their platforms and demands vary somewhat, they all advocate language rights, restriction on immigration, concern over environmental pollution, and greater sovereignty in legal and economic matters. In addition, the three republics reverted to using their pre–World War II flags. In Lithuania the Roman Catholic cathedral, which had been used as an art gallery, was returned to use as a place of worship, while in Latvia, the Great Cathedral, which had been used as a concert hall, was returned to the Lutheran church.

Some of the demands were particular to the republic. For instance, the Estonian movement demanded the resignation of the First Secretary of the Estonian Communist Party, Karl Vayno, a Brezhnev-generation hard-liner. The Estonian parliament also voted to put the republic in the same time zone as Finland, rather than staying on "Moscow time."

In October 1988, the Congress of People's Deputies published several draft revisions to the USSR Constitution. Some of the proposed changes would have further centralized authority, and they thus sparked widespread public protests in the Baltic republics. On November 16 the Estonian parliament sought to establish its own independence by adopting an amendment to the republic constitution that gave the republic the power to overrule legislative acts of central governmental bodies in Moscow. Four days later, the Presidium of the USSR Supreme Soviet ruled that the action of the Estonian parliament was unconstitutional. However, in an effort to mollify the restive republics, their representation was increased in the Council of Nationalities from seven to eleven seats for each republic. In addition, they were granted ex officio membership on the influential Constitutional Supervision Committee.

For their part, the Baltic republics adopted measures that exacerbated tensions with Moscow. In Lithuania, the parliament established a new law on Lithuanian citizenship and began issuing new Lithuanian passports to native Lithuanians, but not to people of other ethnic groups, including Russians and Jews. In Estonia, the republic parliament passed legislation that limited the right to vote to citizens who had lived in the same voting district for a minimum of two years, or who had lived in the republic for at least five years. In order to run for elected office, a person had to have resided in Estonia for at least ten years. These changes angered the largely blue-collar Russian workers in the republics, who banded together to form their own front organizations, such as the "Interfront" in Latvia. The Presidium of the USSR Supreme Soviet declared the Estonian legislation unconstitutional because it violated the principle of equal electoral rights.

The national leadership, as well as numerous speakers in the Supreme Soviet and the Congress of People's Deputies, expressed anger at the actions of the Baltic popular front organizations and republic officials. In August 1989, warnings were issued against "extremist elements." But the governments in each republic, reflecting public opinion, were moving closer and closer to secession. On August 23, the fiftieth anniversary of the signing of the Nazi-Soviet Pact, some two million persons formed a human chain spanning the three republics to symbolize their solidarity and to protest against the forced incorporation of the three independent countries into the USSR. The three popular-front organizations forged a Baltic Assembly to present Moscow with a united effort.

Faced with rapidly declining popularity and legitimacy, the communist parties of the three Baltic republics were forced to support popular demands for increased autonomy or risk being voted out of office in the upcoming local elections. In the Latvian elections, pro-independence candidates captured 120 of the 170 seats.[24] Members of the Latvian Popular Front were just three seats short of having a two-thirds majority in the Supreme Soviet. Under the influence of this pro-reform majority, Latvia was the first republic to legalize opposition parties.

In the February 1990 elections in Lithuania, members of the Lithuanian popular-front organization, Sajudis, and other pro-independence candidates took more than two-thirds of the seats in the Lithuanian Supreme Soviet. Vytautas Landsbergis was elected president of the republic on January 15, defeating the Communist Party chief, Algirdas Brazauskas. In Estonia, the Popular Front and other groups advocating independence captured 78 of 105 seats in the parliament, while the pro-Moscow International Movement claimed only 27.[25]

The most dramatic and direct challenge to federal authority occurred in Lithuania. On March 11, 1990, the Lithuanian Supreme Soviet voted to secede from the USSR. Unlike the other republics, which approached secession cautiously, the Lithuanians proceeded to enact laws directly contrary to national legislation. Republic border guards and security forces were created, conscription into the Red Army was halted, and Lithuanians serving in the Soviet army were encouraged to desert.

Gorbachev's response was to declare the Lithuanian actions "null and void." Military forces were sent into the region to intimidate the newly elected government and quell mass popular support for its policies. Finally, the Government resorted to an embargo, cutting off all energy supplies, food, and shipments of other goods to the breakaway republic. No doubt, Gorbachev's concern was that if he permitted Lithuania to secede, it would establish a dangerous precedent for the two other Baltic states, as well as possibly for Moldavia, Georgia, and Azerbaidzhan. For their part, the Lithuanians appeared to place their hopes in Western diplomatic recognition to protect them from Soviet reprisals. However, no major Western nation extended diplomatic recognition to Landsbergis' government.

Lithuanian–Moscow relations were at an impasse. Gorbachev, while maintaining in principle the right of any republic to secede, refused to negotiate with the Lithuanians until they revoked their "illegal" act of secession. Gorbachev wished to have the Legislative Proposals Committee of the Supreme Soviet work out a new Treaty of the Union, which would not only spell out the division of powers between all-union and republic institutions, but also set out a process to govern secession. The Lithuanians preferred to secede first and negotiate the terms of that secession later. Landsbergis maintained that the only way in which the republic could ensure that Gorbachev would agree to negotiations was to force him to the negotiating table by seceding. The embargo was eventually lifted on July 2, 1990 after the Lithuanian parliament voted to declare a moratorium on its declaration of independence. Relations between Lithuania and Moscow, however, remained at an impasse.

Estonia and Latvia pursued a different course. Rather than seceding, the Estonian parliament passed a decree on March 30, 1990, which declared that since the takeover of the republic in 1940 was illegal, the republic should be governed by its previous constitution, not by Soviet laws. A transitional period was established for independence from Moscow. The Communist Party of Estonia also severed its ties to the CPSU.

On May 4, 1990, the Latvian Supreme Soviet adopted a declaration of independence, much like the one passed in Estonia. It recognized the legitimacy of the pre–World War II constitution and called for a transition period for negotiations with Moscow over the terms and timetable for establishing full independence. President Anatolii Gorbunis and Prime Minister Ivars Godmanis tried diligently to avoid provoking the kind of confrontation that had resulted in the embargo of Lithuania.

In Latvia, however, the cause of republic independence was severely hampered by a large population of Russians. Latvians constitute only slightly more than one-half of the population of the republic and only one-third of the population in the capital city, Riga. The non-native, largely Russian, blue-collar population became increasingly vocal in opposing secession and formed an organization, Latvian Interfront, to articulate its demands. Interfront sponsored numerous rallies and marches throughout 1990 and early 1991, which attracted hundreds of thousands of members of the Russian-speaking minority in the republic. Similar movements, albeit smaller, exist in the other two republics, with Unity (*Edinstvo*) in Lithuania, and the International Movement (*Interdvizhenie*) in Estonia. The existence of vocal antisecessionist movements in the Baltics could provide justification for Moscow to use force, if necessary, to stem the tide of secession.

Moldavia.   The situation in the republic of Moldavia bears a striking similarity to the case of the three Baltic republics. Like Lithuania, Latvia, and Estonia, Moldavia was incorporated into the USSR in 1940. Prior to the war, the region had been part of Romania. As in the Baltics, annexation was followed by massive deportations, forced Russification, and an in-migration of large numbers of Russians, Ukrainians, and other non-Moldavians. The Moldavians, who speak a dialect of Romanian, were also forced to adopt the Cyrillic alphabet, an extraordinarily unpopular policy.

Sparked by Gorbachev's reforms, especially the greater freedom afforded by *glasnost'*, the Moldavians began in mid-1988 to express ethnic demands. Initially their concerns focused on environmental issues and the return to the Latin alphabet. These demands soon broadened, however, into open criticism of the leadership of Semen Grossu, one of the last of Brezhnev's republic party secretaries, who continued to rule over the republic in an authoritarian fashion.

The Moldavian Popular Front was established in January 1989 and immediately began to promote a broad reform agenda that included a return to the Latin alphabet, recognition of Moldavian as the official language of the republic, restrictions on immigration into the republic of non-Moldavians, restoration of the pre—World War II flag, recognition of the Moldavian Orthodox church, resignation of Grossu and other Brezhnevite leaders, and full sovereignty for the republic. The popular front was successful in obtaining the resignation of Grossu in November 1989, but most of its other demands continue unrealized.

As in the Baltic republics, the non-Moldavian ethnic groups formed a movement called Unity (*Edinstvo*), which has organized public demonstrations against secession since mid-1989.

Nagorno-Karabakh.   In a mountainous region of Western Azerbaidzhan is the territory of Nagorno-Karabakh. The region was ceded to the Azerbaidzhan republic in 1921 even though approximately 95 percent of the population were Armenian Christians.[26] The Armenians both in the region of Nagorno-Karabakh and in Armenia proper were unable to reverse Stalin's decision. For the next six decades, the Armenians in Nagorno-Karabakh were harrassed, ignored, and discriminated against by the majority Azeris, who are Moslem.

Long-standing interethnic grievances bubbled to the surface in 1988 as *glasnost'* permitted freer expression of opinions. According to the 1979 census, Armenians constituted 75.9 percent of the population of Nagorno-Karabakh, while Azeris accounted for only 22.9 percent.[27] An appeal from the Armenian population in early 1988 that the region be returned to the Armenian republic was rejected by Azerbaidzhani party and state officials and by central party authorities. Demonstrations followed in the regional capital, Stepanakert, and in Armenia.

Violence broke out in late February 1988 in the city of Sumgait in Nagorno-Karabakh when Azerbaidzhanis rampaged through Armenian neighborhoods, burning houses and killing residents as they fled. More than 30 people were killed and 197 injured.[28] The episode prompted central authorities to call for the resignation of the party leaders in both republics as well as in Nagorno-Karabakh. In addition, relief assistance was provided to improve housing, health care, and education in the region, which had been neglected for many years by the Azerbaidzhan republic leaders.

Despite assurances from Gorbachev that a "just solution" would be found, nothing had changed by the summer of 1988. On June 15, the Armenian Supreme Soviet voted unanimously for a resolution calling for the return of Nagorno-Karabakh to Armenia. Two days later, the Azerbaidzhan Supreme Soviet unanimously rejected Armenian claims to the region. On July 18, the Presidium of the USSR Supreme Soviet refused to cede the region to

Armenia, but did call for greater recognition of the rights of ethnic Armenians in Azerbaidzhan. Violence again broke out in November, claiming 30 lives and precipitating the migration of some 200,000 Armenians to Armenia and approximately 130,000 Azeris fleeing Armenia for Azerbaidzhan.[29]

Sporadic violence and demonstrations continued throughout 1989. In November the Azerbaidzhani Popular Front called for a strike to demonstrate resistance to any change in the status of Nagorno-Karabakh. All rail links to Armenia through Azerbaidzhan were cut, depriving Armenia of a vital supply route. As the situation deteriorated to civil war, Azeris launched violent attacks on the 200,000 Armenians still residing in the Azerbaidzhan capital, Baku. In order to stop the carnage, Soviet military forces were sent in on January 19, 1990. More than 150 people were killed and more than 500 injured.[30] Although the use of military force stabilized the situation, it offered no hope for a lasting settlement of the dispute. The Azerbaidzhan Popular Front continues to exist and there are periodic outbreaks of shooting, mob violence, and looting of police arms stockpiles.

Georgia.   The third republic in the Caucasus region, Georgia, has also proven to be a hot spot for Soviet authorities. In 1988 and 1989 a popular movement was founded in Georgia, calling for independence and incorporation of the Abkhaz region into the republic. Abkhazia, a portion of western Georgia on the shores of the Black Sea, had been pushing for the restoration of the union-republic status that it enjoyed from 1921 to 1931.

In the early spring of 1989, massive pro-independence demonstrations in the Georgian capital, Tbilisi, attracted some 15,000 protesters.[31] Demonstrators also denounced efforts by the people of Abkhazia to secede from Georgia. Authorities in Moscow as well as the central media denounced the organizers of the demonstrations as "extremist elements."[32] Despite opposition from Moscow, the Georgian popular front garnered significant support among state and party officials throughout Georgia.

By April 1989 the demonstrations in Tbilisi swelled to more than 100,000.[33] The demands again focused on Georgian independence and the full integration of Abkhazia into the country. Factories and shops were closed due to strikes, and tensions were rising. On the evening of April 9, interior ministry special troops were sent in to quell the demonstration. Twenty-three protesters were killed, most overcome by massive amounts of tear gas, but some also died from injuries suffered when the security forces beat protesters with shovels.

A state of emergency was declared, a curfew imposed, and tanks patrolled the streets. Hunger strikers took up residence in tents in front of the republic's state and party headquarters. Strikes disrupted industrial production. Meanwhile, resistance movements and parties sprang up, including the Party of National Independence, the National Democratic Party, and the Georgian Popular Front.

Foreign Minister Eduard Shevardnadze, himself a Georgian, flew to Tbilisi to meet with popular front leaders and to appeal for calm. A plenum of the Georgian Communist Party Central Committee was convened and the first secretary, Dzumber Patiashvili, resigned and was replaced by the former head of the Georgian KGB, Givi Gumbaridze. Two commissions were also created to investigate the April 9 massacre, one established by the Georgian Supreme Soviet and another by the USSR Congress of People's Deputies.

Violence also broke out in Abkhazia in July as a result of street protests and demonstrations calling for independence for the region or incorporation into the Russian republic. More than twenty people were killed in ethnic clashes, and military forces had to be called in to restore order.[34]

Following the violence of April 9 in Tbilisi, the direction of the Georgian popular movement turned from public demonstrations to political action and organizing. The Georgian Supreme Soviet formally legalized the formation of opposition parties, ending the Georgian Communist Party's monopoly on power. Parties and movements sprang up overnight representing a wide array of ideological, ethnic, and regional interests. In order to enable the newly formed parties to have a reasonable chance to succeed in regional and local elections, the elections were postponed from spring to autumn.

More than 100 parties or coalitions participated in the elections held on October 28.[35] A clear majority favored a coalition of seven pro-independence parties, referred to as the Round Table/Free Georgia coalition, headed by the well-known Georgian dissident Aviad Gamsakhurdia. The Round Table coalition won 54 percent of the vote, enabling it to claim 114 seats in the 250-member parliament. The Georgian Communist Party captured only 29 percent of the vote for a total of sixty seats. Four independent candidates and three deputies from other parties also won seats in the republic supreme soviet.[36] The manifesto of the Round Table coalition advocates the restoration of an independent and sovereign Georgian state by peaceful means and, if necessary, mass civil disobedience. The most likely points of conflict with Moscow will come as the Round Table attempts to assert its right to pass laws conflicting with all-union laws, or as it seeks to nullify legislation coming from the center.

In the republic itself, the Round Table is actively opposed by a still-more-radical faction, the Coordinating Center, led by Gia Chanturia. This group maintains that Soviet annexation of Georgia was illegal and therefore rejects cooperation with what it considers to be an illegal political system, including participation in the Supreme Soviet elections. Just two days prior to the elections, Chanturia was wounded in an assassination attempt. As in the Baltics, the transition to a pluralistic, multiparty democracy has proven to be difficult for the Georgians. The lack of democratic traditions, intolerance of other ethnic groups, deep-seated distrust of Moscow, and a propensity to settle old scores by resorting to violence do not bode well for the future of an independent and democratic Georgia.

Ferghana.   In 1989 in the Ferghana valley of Uzbekistan several hundred people were killed in rioting between Meskhetians and the native Uzbeks. The Meskhetians, a Turkish people, had been forcibly relocated to Central Asia from Georgia in 1944 by Stalin's order. Although the rights of the Meskhetians were restored in 1968, few of them returned to their native region.

The Meskhetians lived in very poor-quality housing and felt that they were being discriminated against. In June 1989, the party secretary in

Ferghana was shot and wounded when he attempted to address a demonstration of angry Uzbeks who wanted the Meskhetians evicted from the republic. Gangs of Uzbek youths went on a rampage through Meskhetian villages, destroying more than 400 houses, cars, and stores.[37] During the summer of 1989, some 11,000 Meskhetians fled their homes and either sought refuge in camps protected by the military or flocked to Moscow and other Russian cities, where they camped out in railroad stations and other public buildings.[38] More than 9000 members of the Ministry of Internal Affairs' special forces had to be called in to restore order. Efforts are currently under way to resettle some 16,000 Meskhetians in other parts of the USSR.[39] New factories are planned to provide jobs, and better housing is slated for those who choose to remain in Uzbekistan, but these measures alone will probably not erase ethnic hatreds.

THE RUSSIAN REACTION

The demands for independence of the diverse ethnic groups that make up the USSR have been met with responses ranging from anger to indifference among the Russians. It is widely felt that many of the non-Russian areas have been the recipients of development assistance, resources, and special benefits that have come at the expense of the Russian republic. While the Russian republic contributes more than its fair share to the national budget, living standards lag behind those in several other republics. Even where the case for Russian largess cannot be made, as in the Baltic republics, the Russians feel that they deserve credit for liberating these areas from Nazi occupation. Whereas a significant percentage of white-collar intellectuals in Moscow and Leningrad may recognize and support the rights of the Baltic peoples to secede from the USSR, attitudes are much less accommodating among blue-collar workers and farmers. Attitudes toward the largely Muslim populations of Central Asia and Azerbaidzhan manifest elements of the burden of empire.

The rise of ethnic nationalism in the Soviet Union among the myriad of non-Russian peoples has sharpened awareness of Russian ethnicity, history, and culture. In its most exaggerated form, Russian nationalism supports chauvinistic and anti-Semitic movements such as Pamyat. Politically, Russian nationalism has become a powerful mobilizing force behind organizations such as Soyuz (Union), which advocates maintaining the unity of the USSR. Soyuz represents an alliance between Russian populists and the conservatives in the Communist Party *apparat*, the group that was until early 1990 headed by Ligachev. Closely affiliated with Soiuz is the conservative United Front of Russian Workers, a blue-collar movement founded in the Urals industrial center Sverdlovsk in September 1989. This group opposes Gorbachev's liberal economic reforms, democratization, and especially the rising pressures of ethnic minorities. Vocal spokesmen, such as Ligachev and Nina Andreeva, argue that such reforms have introduced nothing but chaos and threaten to result in anarchy.

Alexander Solzhenitsyn, although in exile in the United States, was invited to publish an article in *Komsomolskaya Pravda* in 1990 in which he advocated the demise of the USSR and the birth of a new Slavic nation consisting of Russia, the Ukraine, and Belorussia. The idea was met with some support, although Gorbachev denounced the plan as unworkable.[40] Solzhenitsyn's idea had appeal for those among the Russophile intelligentsia who long for traditional Russian values. For example, the writers Valentin Rasputin and Fedor Abramov glorify Russian peasant culture, while decrying the impact of industrialization and urbanization on Russian society.

A small faction of monarchists have organized under the rubric of the Russian Orthodox Constitutional Monarchist Party, founded in May 1990. They call for, among other things, continued Russian dominance over the multiethnic empire.

In their less chauvinistic forms, Russian nationalism and pride have led to an active movement to restore full representation to the Russian republic. A separate Communist Party of the RSFSR was created in June 1990, and a series of new republic ministries were created. No longer would the interests of the Russian republic have to be represented by the CPSU and by all-union ministries.

Pro-reform organizations from the RSFSR came together to form the Bloc of Democratic Russia in early 1990. The coalition, which includes more than fifty pro-democracy organizations, called for the abolition of Article 6 of the Constitution, free and open elections, and expansion of *glasnost'* into legally protected freedom of speech. Democratic Russia achieved impressive results in the March 4, 1990 local and regional elections. Bloc candidates captured a majority of seats in the city soviets in Moscow, Leningrad, and several other cities, ousting Communist Party candidates and forcing a disentangling of the party and state bureaucracies that had become merged during the past seventy-three years of Soviet rule.

The most dramatic statement of Russian republic interests, as distinct from those of the nation as a whole, was the election of Boris Yeltsin to the presidency of the Russian republic in May 1990. Yeltsin, widely admired for his more radical approach to reform, was able to give meaning to the Russian parliament, which has not hesitated to pass laws at odds with national legislation. The newly formed Russian parliament even took the bold step of declaring its sovereignty and voted to reduce its 1991 contribution to the central USSR treasury from 142.4 billion rubles to 23.4 billion rubles, a reduction of 83 percent.[41] Ivan Silaev, the new prime minister of the Russian republic, has supervised the reorganization of ministries, making them independent from those at the all-union level.

Thus, the rise of ethnic nationalism presents the Soviet leadership today with a crisis of unprecedented proportions. The very existence of the Soviet Union as a federal state is in doubt. The centrifugal forces of ethnic nationalism, exacerbated by the rapid decline of the Soviet economy and the systematic weakening of the authority of central political institutions, is threatening the breakup of the USSR. Gorbachev's reaction to this situation has been vacillating and uncertain. In visits to the Baltic republics in mid-1989 he acknowledged their right under Article 72 of the Constitution to secede from the USSR, but he pleaded with them to hold off taking precipitous actions until the Government had a chance to draft a law defining a procedure for secession. Efforts to draft such a law began in 1989 but soon bogged down over the sheer complexity of the task. The draft called for a referendum to ensure that the population of the republic wished to secede. Just what portion of the electorate had to approve secession was very much disputed. Some pro-center spokespersons maintained that two referenda would be required, one in the republic and one in the USSR as a whole to establish whether the citizens of the USSR would condone the secessionist move.

A law on the mechanics of secession was finally adopted by the USSR Supreme Soviet in April 1990, but it established so many conditions on republics wishing to leave the union that it was widely regarded as a law on non-secession.

Given the complexities of disentangling a portion of the country that had been fully integrated politically, economically, and socially, the law on secession established a two-year minimum waiting period. Questions of resettlement of Russians and others wishing to keep their Soviet citizenship, reimbursement to the USSR for capital investments in the breakaway republic, military base rights, and border security provoked heated debate and drove a wedge further between Moscow and the republics.

As the economy worsened in 1990, ethnic demands escalated. Several other republics and regions followed the example of the Baltic republics and pressed for sovereignty over their own affairs, precipitating a "war of laws." On June 12, 1990 the Russian parliament adopted a declaration on sovereignty which included a provision that republic laws would take precedence over all-union legislation. Similar actions were taken by virtually every republic and autonomous republic. Even relatively small regions, including the Crimea, the Donbas, the Western Ukraine, and the cities of Moscow and Leningrad, pushed for greater independence from the center. Ethnic groups who have not heretofore been granted self-determination, such as the Poles in Lithuania and the Gagauz in Moldavia, also began to demand their own autonomous territories. *Nov. 1990: New Union Treaty Unveiled*

Gorbachev attempted to placate the rising ethnic demands in late 1990 by granting the Council of the Federation a greater role in policy-making. In November 1990, he also unveiled his proposed new Union Treaty that was intended to redefine the relations between the various republics, autonomous republics, national districts and the center. However, the draft law was widely criticized for failing to give republics control over their economic and natural resources, for maintaining the primacy of federal laws over republic laws, and for declaring Russian the official state language. Furthermore, the treaty failed to make reference to the right of secession and to establish a procedure by which republics could exercise such a right.

The Union Treaty was drafted at a time when Gorbachev was coming under extreme pressure from the conservatives, especially the armed forces, the KGB, and the CPSU apparatus. The draft Union Treaty reflected that conservatism and was wholly unacceptable to most nationality groups. The three Baltic republics and the Georgian republic refused to consult on or even discuss the treaty.

The failure of the draft of the Union Treaty to address demands for a confederation and devolution of power to the republics may have accelerated the movement toward secession in several republics. In February 1991, the Moldavian Supreme Soviet voted to reject the Union Treaty and, instead, endorsed a confederation of sovereign states. A referendum was held in Georgia in March 1991 to register public support for secession. More than 98 percent of the voters favored independence for Georgia.[42] Ten days later the Georgian parliament unanimously approved a declaration of independence. Armenia has also put itself on the path toward secession with a plebicite supporting independence in September 1991.

In an attempt too rally support for the preservation of the Union, Gorbachev proposed a national referendum held on March 17, 1991. Voters were asked to answer "yes" or "no" to the question: "Do you consider it necessary to preserve the Union of Soviet Socialist Republics as a renewed federation of equal sovereign republics, in which the rights and freedoms of an individual of any nationality will be fully guaranteed?" Six of the republics—Latvia, Lithuania, Estonia, Georgia, Armenia and Moldavia—refused to participate in the referendum. In the Russian republic, President Boris Yeltsin urged voters to consider the referendum a vote of no confidence in Gorbachev's leadership.

On the surface, the referendum was a victory for Gorbachev. In the Ukraine 70 percent voted "yes." In Belorussia 83 percent supported the Union, while in Central Asia more than 90 percent voted "yes." However, support for the referendum was surprisingly weak in Moscow and Leningrad where only 50 percent of the voters answered "yes," while negative results were recorded in Kiev and Sverdlovsk, Yeltsin's hometown.[43]

The situation was nearing an impasse in the spring of 1991. The leaders of the six most independence-minded republics—Latvia, Lithuania, Estonia, Georgia, Armenia, and Moldavia—met to coordinate their secession efforts and to pledge mutual assistance in case of political, economic or military pressure from Moscow. In a surprise move that was tantamount to acknowledging the *de facto* secession of these six republics, Gorbachev announced his intention of signing the Union Treaty with the nine remaining republics. In a major concession, he granted these republics control over their own economic resources and even approved the establishment of a separate security police and television network in the Russian republic. Yeltsin praised Gorbachev's flexibility in meeting the republic's demands and pledged support for collaborative efforts to resolve the miners' strike and other pressing problems.

Events of 1990 and 1991 tend to confirm that the only workable option available to Gorbachev for resolving the nationality problem in the USSR is the adoption of a very loose confederation, under which most power will reside with the republics. Attempts to reassert central control by force will only worsen tensions with the republics and strengthen their resolve to oppose attempts at Russification. The political and economic costs of continued interethnic unrest will, in time, force the government into meaningful power sharing. There remain, however, two major unanswered questions. Will the military, the KGB, the CPSU apparatus, and the central ministries permit Gorbachev to negotiate a new forumla of power-sharing? Will the restive ethnic groups settle for anything less than full independence and sovereignty, even if the cost of refusal to cooperate with Moscow is to be crushed by Soviet tanks? Currently Gorbachev appears caught between these two untenable positions. Room for maneuver and compromise is small to nonexistent, and his own vacillation and delaying have not helped the chances for the peaceful resolution of the conflicts.

The recent cooperative approach by Boris Yeltsin and the nine republics is a positive sign that a middle course can work. Now Gorbachev must convince the conservatives that this formula is both feasible and wise. Most disturbing of all, however, the success of Gorbachev's nationality strategy of cooperation may rest on the fate of the economy. As one Soviet observer commented: "When the pie is large, all the people are happy. But when the pie is small, everyone fights for his own piece."[44]

POLITICS AT THE GRASS ROOTS

For the average Soviet citizen the machinations of the political institutions at the national and even the republic levels can seem remote and often irrelevant. It is at the regional and local levels that Soviet citizens most frequently come into direct contact with their political system. Regional and local governments are responsible for a wide range of services that directly affect citizens: the provision of housing, health care, and education; the supervision of industrial production; the operation of stores, commercial enterprises, and cultural and recreational facilities; the monitoring of environmental pollution; and the provision of police and other essential services.

At the local level, the crosscutting regional and institutional interests come to bear on policies, and it is here that the powers and overlapping jurisdictions of the Party and the State must be worked out. In short, local politics in the USSR represents a microcosm of the larger Soviet political system. Our analysis of local and regional politics in the USSR begins with an examination of the dramatic changes that are shaping Soviet cities.

Despite its agrarian roots, Soviet society is increasingly becoming urbanized. In 1926, prior to Stalin's introduction of collectivization, 86.7 percent of the Soviet population lived in towns and villages of fewer than 15,000 people.[45] However, collectivization, the rising demand for industrial workers, and wartime dislocations all tended to accelerate the pace of urban growth. By 1977, only 38.1 percent of the population lived in towns of fewer than 15,000.[46] Since 1926, more than 1000 new cities have been founded, and the pace of urbanization continues unabated.[47] Thus, within a span of fewer than fifty years, the USSR was transformed from a predominantly rural country into a largely urban one. Somewhat surprisingly, the rate of urbanization today is fastest east of the Urals—in Siberia and the Far East, rather than in European Russia. The rapid development of massive new oil, gas, coal, timber, and other projects linked to the resource wealth of this region has contributed to a growth boom in many Soviet frontier towns.

While the fastest-growing regions of the Soviet Union are to the east, the bulk of the urban population still resides in the European portion of the country. Together, the Russian republic (RSFSR) and the Ukrainian republic account for 68 percent of all Soviet cities and 78 percent of the urban population.[48] These two republics contain fifteen of the nineteen cities currently having populations of more than one million.[49]

The rapid growth of the Soviet urban population is explained by immigration from rural areas—approximately three million new urban residents every year—as well as by a greater-than-average natural population increase. (Recent immigrants to the cities tend to be young married couples starting families.)[50] Thus, most adults living in Soviet cities today were born in rural areas, which helps to explain the persistence of rural attitudes and behavior among some urban residents. For instance, city people often prefer folk remedies, medicinal herbs, or mustard plasters to modern drugs. One sees Muscovites wearing garlic cloves around their necks to ward off colds, a carryover from rural customs. A startling reminder of the agrarian roots of Soviet urbanites is that the most common murder weapon in the USSR today is the ax.[51]

Although he or she may live in a huge city, the average Russian is never far from the soil—it is the connection to his or her roots in the countryside. City dwellers may rent a small plot of land (up to one-quarter acre) outside the city for a garden. These plots are an important source of vegetables and fruit, which are otherwise scarce in the summer and nonexistent in the winter in Soviet stores. Soviet citizens often construct tiny toolsheds on their garden plots to double as sleeping quarters on weekend outings.

To cope with the crowded, bleak urban existence, Soviet citizens often seek refuge in the country. On Friday nights, train stations are crowded with urbanites leaving for the weekend. In autumn, they flock to the woods to hunt for mushrooms, a national pastime. In winter, people of all ages—teenagers, pensioners, middle-aged men and women—don cross-country skis and glide along paths between rows of birch and spruce trees. In summer, urbanites crowd the banks of the Moscow River or the beaches on the Gulf of Finland, or they simply stroll amid the fields and hike through the forests to escape the heat and humanity of the city.

As might be expected, service, trade, and professional occupations in the USSR have been increasing much more rapidly than have blue-collar jobs, and the percentage of the population engaged in agriculture has declined steadily since 1926. Yet, despite the migration of workers from the countryside, Soviet cities still experience serious labor shortages, especially in the service and trade sectors. These shortages further hamper the ability of city governments to meet the needs of their rapidly expanding populations.

In order to moderate the demands on Soviet cities, a system of registration (*propiska*) has been instituted in Moscow, Leningrad, Kiev, and several other large cities. A citizen wishing to move to one of these cities must first obtain a *propiska* (registration document) from an employer. Employers are under pressure to hire from the local population and extend *propiski* to workers from other regions only if they are uniquely qualified for vacant positions. As one might expect, however, such a system is open to widespread abuses through favoritism and nepotism, or what the Soviets call *blat* (connections). Because of the extensive circumvention of the *propiska* restrictions, many cities exceed their planned size. For instance, the plan for Moscow called for a population of no more than 7.5 million by 1990, which was less than its population in the early 1980s.[52] Soviet authorities acknowledge the ineffectiveness of the *propiska* system as a means of limiting city growth, but they are powerless to stem the tide of urban migration. Many citizens bypass the residence restrictions by living in nearby villages and commuting to the cities to work. Others marry Muscovites or Leningraders simply to obtain the right to reside in one of those cities; still others live in the cities illegally with friends or relatives. Employers, especially in the service sector, may overlook the failure of job applicants to obtain a *propiska* and may even provide them with housing.

The rapid pace of urbanization in the USSR has resulted in the expansion of the activities of local party and state bodies. As the next section indicates, the powers of local governments to set policies affecting the distribution of social services are especially significant and potentially conflictual.

ECONOMIC FUNCTIONS OF THE LOCAL SOVIETS

Local and regional soviets are charged with a wide array of economic functions, including the allocation of funds, the distribution of goods and services, the control of expenditures by state administrative and social organizations, and the supervision of production in their jurisdictions. Over the past several decades, there has been a steady increase in the budgets of local governments in the USSR. For example, in 1950, local and republic agencies accounted for only 23 percent of the USSR's total expenditures. By 1984, local and republic budgets had increased to 48 percent of total expenditures.[53]

Although relatively few in number, city soviets account for almost one-half of all local spending.[54] Given the heavy demands on social services, housing, and transportation in large cities, it is not surprising that cities occupy a prominent place in local government expenditure in the USSR. Nationwide, cities account for almost two-thirds of all local expenditures on housing, industry, and other economic services.[55] Such factors as population, economic base, location, and level of administrative subordination, however, account for dramatic disparities among cities. For example, although Sverdlovsk and Minsk are roughly the same size in terms of population, Sverdlovsk is subordinate to regional party and state control, while Minsk, the capital of the Belorussian republic, is subordinated to republic-level organs. Moscow enjoys a special status, reporting directly to the all-union party and state organs and thus bypassing the Russian republic level of administration.

Article 147 of the 1977 Constitution states that local soviets have the authority to ensure "the comprehensive economic and social development of their territory."[56] In practice, however, local soviets are an integral and subordinate link in a highly centralized administrative chain that extends from the leading party and state organs and ministries down to the level of factories and enterprises. Most resources for Soviet cities are allocated through a comprehensive and centralized system of economic planning. The budgets for local governments in the USSR are determined at the center, leaving little room for adjustment or alteration by local authorities. Nevertheless, local officials can influence spending in subtle but important ways. Local soviets have three principal sources of revenue: (1) funds allocated through the state budget, (2) state subsidies earmarked for specific projects, and (3) incentives and other funds of branch ministries with enterprises in the area.

The centrally planned budgets for regional and local soviets in the USSR are broken down into specific items, severely restricting the ability of local party and state officials to shift resources from one sector to another. In the short run, the primary method for generating discretionary funds from the state budget is to undertake cost-saving measures. In the long run, local governments can influence future budgets by lobbying the central planning and construction agencies and informing them of local needs that may be raised to a higher-priority status over an extended period of time. The reality for most local and regional soviets in the USSR, however, is that they must secure funds for special projects from sources other than the state budget. The ability of local soviets to do this depends greatly on the cooperation and clout of local party officials.

The third source of local revenue, from factories and enterprises, is not inconsequential. In 1979, economic enterprises in the Soviet Union earmarked more than 50 million rubles for subsidizing projects of local soviets.[57] In the Lithuanian city of Kaunas, for example, contributions from factories and local enterprises constituted 12.5 percent of all local outlays for public works projects in the city: lighting, road repair, and landscaping.[58] Soviet sources indicate that enterprises in Bratsk spend five times the city's total budget for capital construction and services.[59]

The distribution functions of local soviets are among the most important and potentially conflict-ridden responsibilities of local governmental and party organs. Cities are responsible for providing a wide array of services: housing, health care, schools, cultural facilities, parks, entertainment enterprises, restaurants, stores, public transportation, utilities, sewage treatment, and garbage-collection services. The city of Moscow, for example, directly provides more than six hundred types of services.[60]

Given the wide scope of social services provided by local governments, they naturally constitute a significant portion of the total income (or benefits) of the average Soviet citizen. As much as 15 to 20 percent of the average industrial worker's aggregate family income is derived from educational, medical, and other services provided free of charge by local governmental agencies, or from housing and consumer services, which are heavily subsidized.[61] Soviet studies have shown that inadequate provision of these social services is the primary reason workers voluntarily terminate employment. For instance, more than 28 percent of all Soviet citizens moving out of the Ukraine in 1979 indicated dissatisfaction with social amenities as a major factor in their decision to move.[62]

Because most social services are provided either free or for a minimal charge, access to goods and services, rather than cost, becomes the critical factor. While many inner cities in the United States have suffered out-migration and decay, the inner cores of cities in the Soviet Union enjoy advantages over the peripheral areas. In the center of a Soviet city, stores tend to be better stocked than stores in outlying areas, public transportation is better and more accessible, there are more nursery schools and kindergartens, housing tends to be older but roomier, and the quality of construction is superior to the prefabricated apartment blocs that dominate suburban areas. In addition, parks and cultural amenities are more accessible in the heart of the city than in outlying areas.

Local governments in the USSR are responsible for verifying compliance with national policies. The past two decades have witnessed a broadening of these powers of local soviets to encompass enforcement of housing codes, fire regulations, and especially pollution control. The process of urbanization has also fostered increased attention to problems of zoning, urban development, building design, traffic control, industrial siting, and land-use policy.

Despite the extensive responsibilities of local administrative agencies, there is a critical need for regionally based planning in Soviet cities, instead of sectoral planning. Ministries and local governments frequently fail to coordinate their activities, resulting in waste, inefficiency, and bureaucratic squabbling. For instance, the Ministry of Steel may plan to expand production facilities at a given factory and increase the work force substantially. Such a decision may be made independently of local government officials, who are responsible for providing housing, transportation, health care, education, child care, water, electricity, sewage treatment, and other services to the new employees. Similarly, central ministries may reallocate resources originally designated for one region to another region considered to be of higher priority. The local party secretary in the adversely affected region has little recourse but to appeal to the Central Committee Secretariat or the Politburo; meanwhile, the resulting underfulfillment of the plan in the region may undermine the secretary's political position. In this manner, ministerial officials can exercise a large degree of influence over regional party officials.

GRASS-ROOTS PARTICIPATION IN THE USSR

With the introduction of Gorbachev's reforms, especially *glasnost'* and democratization, citizens have many more opportunities to become involved politically. The elections of regional and local soviets in 1990 were the first such contested elections in the seventy-three-year history of the USSR. As a result, the elected deputies, and the soviets as a whole, now enjoy a degree of legitimacy and credibility that no other official institution—including the Party—can claim. From the Nineteenth Party Conference in mid-1988 until early 1991, Gorbachev frequently spoke about the desirability of enhancing the scope and responsibilities of regional and local soviets.

Glasnost' also enabled average Soviet citizens to organize on a wide array of issues. Environmental pollution became a major rallying cause for hundreds of citizens' groups.

One such example of citizen mobilization occurred in the Brateevo neighborhood on the outskirts of Moscow. Brateevo is a cheerless housing project, consisting mostly of identical twenty-story apartment buildings housing some 60,000 residents.[63] The neighborhood is surrounded by a heavy industrial zone, with scores of factories that fill the air with choking smoke and caustic chemicals. In the 1970s, the Moscow health department declared the region "unfit for human habitation"; nevertheless, the housing units were constructed.

In 1988, the Moscow soviet proposed the expansion of the industrial park. Twenty-one additional industrial enterprises were slated for development. A teacher from Brateevo, Nina Shchedrina, was alarmed at the prospect of further pollution in the air around the neighborhood. She and some other concerned neighbors met with local officials, but found them unresponsive to their concerns. At that point, Shchedrina began to organize citizens in an effort to oust local officials who were not sympathetic to Brateevo's plight. They used bullhorns to announce a rally and organizational meeting at which the "Brateevo self-governing committee" was established. They advocated the development of a greenbelt on the site of the proposed industrial zone and called for a referendum to show public support for their plan. In the referendum, 99.9 percent of registered voters in Brateevo voted. The greenbelt idea won overwhelmingly, but the referendum was nonbinding.

The local soviet, none of whose members lived in the Brateevo neighborhood, met to decide the issue in early 1989. They were under pressure from the Moscow soviet and central ministries to permit industrial expansion in the region. Nevertheless, they voted to limit the number of new enterprises to be built, killing plans for several factories that would have added substantially to the region's already serious pollution problems. In addition, the local soviet allocated two million rubles to Brateevo for landscaping, developing parks, and planting trees.

The Brateevo case was not a clear-cut victory for citizens' action. Nevertheless, the "self-governing committee" became a model for citizens' participation in many other communities throughout the USSR. Most important, the experience left the citizens of the Brateevo neighborhood with a new sense of political efficacy. According to Sergei Druganov, one of the organizers, "People are beginning to comprehend that things depend on every individual. . . . In a sense, I am beginning to change from a citizen into a politician. We understand that we have to fight, to stand up for our rights."[64]

REGIONAL DEVELOPMENT

Within the USSR, vast economic, cultural, and demographic differences among regions present Soviet planners with many serious challenges. Regional differences also spark frequent disputes over the allocation of investment funds and the provision of housing and other social services. The Soviet Union is a classic example of uneven economic development. While Moscow is a bustling, modern city with intricate and efficient mass transportation and communications systems and a wide range of merchandise in the stores, not far outside the city, conditions are much more primitive. Just 100 miles to the northeast of Moscow is Vladimir, an *oblast'* capital with a population in excess of 250,000. In downtown Vladimir, women use wooden shoulder yokes to carry buckets of water from a public well. There are few paved streets in the city, and the store shelves are mostly bare. In the winter, women saw holes in the ice of a small river to wash clothes in the freezing water.

The disparities between standards of living in the city and in the country-side are even more evident east of the Urals in Siberia, Central Asia, and the Far East. The republic capitals of Tashkent and Alma-Ata boast skyscrapers and modern apartment blocs with all the amenities, but just a few miles beyond the city limits people live much as they have for centuries. Urbanization, more than any other factor, accounts for these differences in levels of economic development. The greater the population, the better and more accessible the education, health care, consumer goods, housing, and other services.

Recognizing the vast differences among various portions of the USSR, planners have divided the country into eighteen economic regions in order to promote coordination among economic enterprises within the regions and to facilitate long-range planning. During the period from 1971 to 1985, the Far East, East Siberia, and West Siberia regions were especially targeted for intensive development. Wage and material incentive policies were introduced to attract and retain labor in these regions. Workers may receive from 1.2 to 2.0 times their regular salaries for working in the hostile climates and underdeveloped regions in the north.[65] Some industries are able to offer larger bonuses than others, however, so that various occupations in the same city receive different levels of remuneration. The construction industry has been a major proponent of differential wage policies, being one of the chief beneficiaries of the policy. For example, the Baikal-Amur Mainline project, a vast project begun in the late 1970s to build a rail line from the mineral-rich region north of Lake Baikal to the Pacific, offered wage bonuses of 1.7 percent, even to its office employees.[66]

Young Russian males commonly take contract work in the mineral-rich regions north of Lake Baikal for one or two years in order to amass some money before getting married. However, such a practice results in high rates of labor turnover. Thus, in the far northern city of Norilsk, 19,000 new workers were recruited in 1969, but 18,500 workers left during the same year.[67] The consistent complaint of those leaving the development zones is inadequacy of consumer goods, medical facilities, housing, child care, and other services.

In Soviet Central Asia, the opposite problem exists: there is an excess of available labor. The 1979 census showed that Central Asians number more than 40 million, and they are increasing at a phenomenal rate—more than four times the national average. It is estimated that by the year 2000, Central Asians will outnumber Russians in the USSR.[68]

Culturally and economically, Central Asians are among the most underdeveloped and least urbanized groups in the USSR. A high proportion of the native population works in traditional occupations such as farming and animal herding. The percentage of Central Asian students admitted to universities and other institutions of higher education is among the lowest of any ethnic group in the USSR. Policies designed to encourage Central Asians to migrate to areas experiencing labor shortages have proven to be ineffective; cultural, familial, linguistic, and religious ties tend to keep Central Asians in their native regions.

During the early 1970s, the Soviet leadership appeared to favor attempts to equalize the standard of living across the entire USSR. Such a policy soon encountered resistance. Party and state officials in the Ukraine, the Baltic republics, Moscow, and Leningrad did not want their budgets cut to assist the development of lagging areas such as Central Asia and Siberia. Regional economic disparities, demographic trends, and population migration patterns thus raise thorny political problems for regional party officials as well as for the top leadership in the USSR.

MODELS OF SOVIET LOCAL POLITICS

The involvement of local and regional party and state officials, enterprise directors, scientists, academics, and the public in policy debates has important ramifications for our understanding of the nature of the entire Soviet political system. Clearly, the Soviet political system is no longer totalitarian. Soviet leaders do not simply dictate policies, expecting local officials, enterprises, and workers to obey dutifully. Politics and political conflict exist in the Soviet Union, and policy is the outcome of an ongoing struggle of competing pluralistic interests.

Regional secretaries still play a vital role in policy implementation, coordinating regional planning, interpreting central policy guidelines within the context of local conditions, resolving conflicts among enterprises and agencies, bargaining with state officials for regional appropriations, and bearing ultimate responsibility for the success or failure of policies within the region.[69] As the chief political figures in each region, they have been likened to the political bosses who dominated some American cities during the late 1800s and early 1900s.[70] The regional secretary, like the political boss, is usually the most powerful political figure in the area and thus can break through bureaucratic red tape to support a priority project. In lobbying central authorities for increased allocations for the region and in making appointments to influential posts, the party secretary also resembles a political boss.

Regional party secretaries also perform important coordinating and mediating functions; they act as political brokers. In Soviet society, as elsewhere, politics involves making compromises and adjustments among diverse bureaucratic groups and the interests they represent. Major officials of most of the powerful regional bureaucracies and organizations are represented on local party committees, and these are the arenas in which institutional conflicts are often expressed.

The broker model may understate the role and authority of the regional party secretary, whose power derives not only from brokering competing interests and claims on resources, but also from direct contacts with the highest political organs in the USSR. Regional secretaries constitute the single largest group in the CPSU Central Committee. In addition to mediating conflicting interests, they often have their own programs and policy agendas to promote. Regional secretaries are often in a position to use their contacts with top-level policymakers to promote certain programs or terminate others.

On many occasions, regional party secretaries also act as agents for change, applying political pressure to encourage reluctant administrative officials to innovate or to adopt new procedures. The heavily bureaucratized nature of the Soviet system and its centrally planned economy create enormous obstacles to innovation. Local administrators and factory managers see few rewards and many risks in innovation. In the absence of economic incentives that would stimulate innovation, the Party relies on political pressure from central party organs and local party officials to promote change.[71]

Recently, the rise of grass-roots popular movements, national front organizations, and duly elected republic, regional, and local soviets have challenged the preeminent role of the party secretaries. The consequences of these developments are immense for the future of the Soviet political system. Whereas policy differences among competing bureaucratic interests were once hammered out largely behind the closed doors of the Party's offices, today policies are often openly debated in the press, in neighborhood meetings, and in city and regional council sessions. While the party *apparat* may not welcome this challenge to their role, it is unlikely that they can reverse the trend toward greater participation of diverse regional and local groups and institutions in the policy process.

Notes

1. Constitution of the USSR (1977), Article 70.

2. Based on 1979 census data cited in Peter Zwick, "Soviet Nationality Policy: Social, Economic, and Political Aspects," in Gordon B. Smith, ed., *Public Policy and Administration in the Soviet Union* (New York: Praeger, 1980), 153.

3. Ibid.

4. Robert A. Lewis et al., *Nationality and Population Change in Russian and the USSR* (New York: Praeger, 1976), 147.

5. Zev Katz et al., eds., *Handbook of Major Soviet Nationalities* (New York: The Free Press, 1975), 11.

6 1979 census data from Peter Zwick, "Soviet Nationality Policy," 153.

7. Constitution of the USSR (1977), Article 36.

8. Peter Rutland, "The Nationality Problem and the Soviet State," in Neil Harding, ed., *The State in Socialist Society* (London: Macmillan, 1984), 164.

9. Ibid.

10. Hélène Carrère d'Encausse, *The Decline of an Empire* (New York: Newsweek Books, 1979), 192–193.

11. E. G. Lewis, *Multilingualism in the Soviet Union* (Elmsford, NY: Mouton Publishers, 1972).

12. See Ann Sheehy, "Call for More Education and Publication in Russian in Non-Russian Republics," *Radio Liberty Research Bulletin* 121 (17 April 1985): 2. On a recent campaign for Russian-language use in Estonia, see *Sovetskaya Estonya*, 26 February 1985.

13. This definition comes from Peter Zwick, "Soviet Nationality Policy," 144.

14. L. I. Brezhnev, *Pravda*, 22 December 1972, p. 3.

15. For example, see A. F. Dashdamirov, *Pravda*, 7 August 1981, p. 2.

16. The most widely publicized protests over the new republic constitutions occurred in Georgia, where on April 14, 1978, several thousand people took to the streets of Tbilisi to voice their opposition. The next day, the authorities backed down and reestablished Georgian as the official language of the republic.

17. Bohdan Nahaylo and Victor Swoboda, *Soviet Disunion* (New York: The Free Pess, 1989), 97.

18. Robert Conquest, *Harvest of Sorrow: Soviet Collectivization and the Terror-Famine* (New York: Oxford University Press, 1986), 303.

19. This case was reported in Joshua Rubenstein, "Dissent," in James Cracraft, ed., *The Soviet Union Today* (Chicago: Bulletin of the Atomic Scientists, 1983), 73–74.

20. Rudolf L. Tokes, *Dissent in the USSR* (Baltimore: The Johns Hopkins University Press, 1975), 82.

21. Mary McAuley, "Nationalism and the Soviet Multiethnic State," in Neil Harding, *The State in Socialist Society*, (Albany: SUNY Press, 1984) 180.

22. *Pravda*, 16 December 1986, p. 2.

23. Local education officials in Tallinn reported this to the author in November 1978.

24. Dzintra Bungs, "Supreme Soviet Elections in Latvia," *Radio Liberty Report on the USSR* 2, no. 13 (30 March 1990) 27.

25. Riina Kionka, "Elections to Estonian Supreme Soviet," *Radio Liberty Report on the USSR* 2, no. 14 (April 6, 1990) 23.

26. Cited in David Lane, *Soviet Society under Perestroika* (Boston: Unwin and Hyman, 1990), p. 190.

27. Stephen White, *Gorbachev in Power* (Cambridge: Cambridge University Press, 1990), 134.

28. *Sovetskaya Rossiya*, 22 March 1988, p. 4.

29. *Pravda*, 27 April 1989, p. 6; and *Pravda*, 2 June 1989, p. 2.

30. Vera Tolz, "The USSR This Week," *Radio Liberty Report on the USSR* 2, no. 7 (16 February 1990) 27.

31. *Guardian*, 27 February 1989, p. 8.

32. *Pravda*, 3 January 1989, p. 8.

33. *Pravda*, 4 June 1989, p. 6.

34. Vera Tolz, "The USSR This Week," *Radio Liberty Report on the USSR* 1, no. 34 (25 August 1989) 35.

35. Elizabeth Fuller, "Georgian Alternative Election Results Anounced," *Radio Liberty Report on the USSR* 2, no. 43 (26 October 1990): 22.

36. Elizabeth Fuller, "Round Table Coalition Wins Resounding Victory in Georgian Supreme Soviet Elections," *Radio Liberty Report on the USSR* 2, no. 46 (16 November 1990): 13.

37. *Pravda*, 7 June 1989, p. 8.

38. *Pravda*, 10 June 1989, p. 8.

39. *Pravda*, 24 June 1989, p. 6.

40. John Dunlop, "Russian Reactions to Solzhenitsyn's Brochure," *Radio Liberty Report on the USSR* 2, no. 50 (14 December 1990) 3–4.

41. Bruce Nelan, "A Slippery Slope," *Time* 137, no 1, 7 January, 1991, 60–62.

42. Elizabeth Fuller, "Georgia Declares Independence," *Radio Liberty Report on the USSR* 3, no. 16 (April 19, 1991) 11.

43. *Izvestiya*, 21 March 1991, p. 3.

44. From a conversation with the author, May 13, 1991.

45. Robert A. Lewis and Richard H. Rowland, *Population Redistribution in the USSR* (New York: Praeger, 1979), 166.

46. Ibid.

47. Timothy J. Colton, "The Political Economy of Soviet New Towns," in Steven A. Grant, ed. *Soviet Housing and Urban Design* (Washington: U.S. Department of Housing and Urban Development, September 1980), 54.

48. Carol W. Lewis and Stephen Sternheimer, *Soviet Urban Management* (New York: Praeger, 1979), 15–16.

49. Ibid.

50. Viktor Perevedentsev, "Novichok v gorode," *Molodoi kommunist* 7 (1971): 91–96.

51. Leslie Gelb, "What We Really Know About Russia," *New York Times Magazine*, 28 October 1984, p. 78.

52. M. Ia. Vydro, *Naselenie Moskvy* (Moscow: Statistika, 1976), 15.

53. Donna Bahry, *Outside Moscow* (New York: Columbia University Press, 1987), 1.

54. Carol W. Lewis, "The Economic Functions of Local Soviets," in Everett M. Jacobs, ed., *Soviet Local Politics and Government* (London: George Allen & Unwin, 1983), 50.

55. Ibid.

56. Constitution of the USSR (1977), Article 147.

57. A. Miasnikov, "Khozyain dolzhen byt' odin," *Ekonomika i organizatsiya promyshlennogo proizvodstva* 4 (1977): 126.

58. Ibid.

59. Ibid.

60. Lewis, "Economic Functions of Local Soviets," 61.

61. Ibid., 55.

62. A. Kocherga, "Problemy territorialnogo-planirovanya narodnogo blagosostoianya," *Planovoe khozyaistvo* 2 (1979): 92–99.

63. This case is taken from a PBS program, "Inside Gorbachev's USSR," Part I, "The Taste of Democracy," 30 April 1990.

64. Ibid.

65. See John Sallnow, "Soviet Wage Incentives and Regional Development Policies" (Paper presented to the Annual Convention of the American Association for the Advancement of Slavic Studies, Kansas City, 21–25 October 1983).

66. Ibid.

67. Andrew R. Bond, "Labor Retention, Social Planning, and Population Policy: The Example of the City of Norilsk" (Paper presented to the Annual Convention of the American Association for the Advancement of Slavic Studies, Kansas City, 21–25 October 1983).

68. Murray Feshbach and Stephen Rapaway, "Soviet Population and Manpower Trends and Policies," in *Soviet Economy in a New Perspective* (Washington, DC: U.S. Congress, Joint Economic Committee, 1976), 148.

69. For example, see Philip Stewart, *Political Power in the Soviet Union: A Study of Decision-Making in Stalingrad* (Indianapolis: Bobbs-Merrill, 1968); and Joel Moses, *Regional Party Leadership and Policy-Making in the USSR* (New York: Praeger, 1974).

70. The boss and broker roles of regional party secretaries are described in detail in Lewis and Sternheimer, *Soviet Urban Management*.

71. For example, see Gordon B. Smith, "Organizational and Legal Problems in the Implementation of New Technology in the USSR," in Gordon B. Smith et al., eds, *The Scientific-Technical Revolution and Soviet and East European Law* (Oxford and New York: Pergamon Press, 1981), 240–271.

Selected Bibliography

Allworth, Edward. *Ethnic Russia: The Dilemma of Dominance*. New York: Pergamon, 1980.

Azrael, Jeremy. *Soviet Nationality Policies and Practices*. New York: Praeger, 1978.

Bahry, Donna. *Outside Moscow: Power, Politics, and Budgetary Policy in the Soviet Republics*. New York: Columbia University Press, 1987.

Bennigsen, Alexandre, and Marie Broxup. *The Islamic Threat to the Soviet State*. London: Croom Helm, 1983.

Carrère d'Encausse, Hélène. *The Decline of an Empire*. New York: Newsweek Books, 1979.

Freedman, Robert O., ed. *Soviet Jewry in the Decisive Decade, 1971–1980*. Durham, NC: Duke University Press, 1984.

Friedgut, Theodore H. *Political Participation in the USSR*. Princeton: Princeton University Press, 1979.

Hahn, Jeffrey W. *Soviet Grassroots: Citizen Participation in Local Soviet Government*. Princeton: Princeton University Press, 1988.

Hough, Jerry F. *The Soviet Prefects: The Local Party Organs in Industrial Decision-Making*. Cambridge: Harvard University Press, 1969.

Jacobs, Everett M., ed. *Soviet Local Politics and Government*. Boston: Allen & Unwin, 1983.

Karklins, Rasma. *Ethnic Relations in the USSR*. Boston: Allen & Unwin, 1986.

Katz, Zev, et al., eds. *Handbook of Major Soviet Nationalities*. New York: The Free Press, 1975.

Krawchenko, Bohdan. *Social Change and National Consciousness in Twentieth Century Ukraine*. New York: St. Martin's Press, 1985.

Lewis, Carol W., and Stephen Sternheimer. *Soviet Urban Management*. New York: Praeger, 1979.

Lewis, Robert A., et al., *Nationality and Population Change in Russia and the USSR*. New York: Praeger, 1976.

Lubin, Nancy. *Labor and Nationality in Soviet Central Asia*. New York: St. Martin's Press, 1984.

Nahaylo, Bohdan, and Victor Swoboda. *Soviet Disunion: A History of the Nationalities Problem in the USSR*. New York: The Free Press, 1989.

Ross, Cameron. *Local Government in the Soviet Union*. New York: St. Martin's Press, 1987.

Suny, Ronald Grigor. *The Making of the Georgian Nation*. Bloomington: Indiana University Press, 1988.

Zwick, Peter. *National Communism*. Boulder: Westview, 1982.

8

Glasnost':
The Intelligentsia
and the Politics of Culture

The transformation of the Soviet political system in recent years can be credited in large measure to the policy of *glasnost'*. For seven decades Soviet citizens could not speak or write candidly without fear of reprisals. Censorship was all-pervasive. Topics that could not be discussed by journalists, contained on a list five pages long, included economic problems, shortages, lines, price increases, and salaries; inequities and special benefits (especially those received by party and state officials); crime statistics and other adverse social indicators; foreign policy involvements of the USSR (such as the invasion of Afghanistan, arms sales, and international aid); details of the private lives of Soviet leaders and their families and advance word about their traveling schedules; the activities of dissidents, religious believers, and other unofficial groups; national or ethnic demonstrations or expressions; statistics or reports on illnesses such as cholera; the activities of the KGB and the Soviet military; accidents and natural disasters; and censorship (acknowledging the existence of censorship was itself taboo).[1]

The fear of frank and open discussion not only had a chilling effect on Soviet citizens, it also resulted in poorly conceived policies. How can a society address chronic problems of the environment if it denies that pollution exists? How can leaders make reasonable and effective policies if they are insulated from the truth?

Gorbachev's policy of *glasnost'*—permitting a much wider range of acceptable public discussion of problems and issues—began as a trickle, but in the span of less than five years has revolutionized the Soviet system. In this chapter we analyze the motives behind Gorbachev's policy of *glasnost'* and the role of the media and intelligentsia in the reform process.

WHY *GLASNOST'*?

What accounts for the explosion of information in the Soviet Union in recent years? Why did Gorbachev break with a seventy-year tradition of tight party and state control over all forms of expression? There are several factors that help to explain this bold innovation.

We noted in Chapter 3 that the stagnation of Soviet society during the eighteen-year reign of Brezhnev mandated fundamental reforms in virtually every arena of Soviet life. The Brezhnev leadership had carried out a policy of tight censorship and directed harsh punishment against dissidents and others who offered even mildly critical remarks on social problems. It even banned Western rock music on the grounds that it would "corrupt Soviet youth." By the 1980s it was recognized that pervasive censorship itself was contributing to the malaise of Soviet society. Social problems could hardly be addressed in an effective manner when their existence was denied by the leadership. Moreover, the cult of Brezhnev and the grandiose claims of the ideology no longer measured up to the reality of Soviet life, resulting in widespread cynicism, disaffection, and corruption.

Mikhail Gorbachev represents a new generation of leader in the USSR. A product of the Khrushchev "thaw" of the 1950s, Gorbachev was raised in a Soviet Union whose superpower status was never in question. Whereas previous Soviet leaders did not dare permit frank discussion or open criticism for fear that it would destabilize the system, Gorbachev is the first leader to argue that frank and open criticism can strengthen the system, rather than undermine it. Within weeks of assuming the General Secretaryship in March 1985, Gorbachev declared: "Timely and frank release of information is evidence of trust in people, respect for their intelligence and feelings, and their ability to assess events."[2]

The first big test of Gorbachev's *glasnost'* policy was the accident at the Chernobyl nuclear reactor in the Ukraine in April 1986. Initially, the leadership maintained tight secrecy on news coverage of the disaster and even denied that there was a problem. In the weeks following the accident, however, press reports, television coverage, and news conferences gradually reconstructed the events surrounding the accident. While the Soviet handling of the Chernobyl episode represented a departure from previous practice, it clearly fell short of what some Western observers had expected.

Gorbachev has also fostered *glasnost'*, especially in literature and the arts, to win support among the influential intelligentsia. The intelligentsia have traditionally been viewed as an important political constituency for reform. Under the influence of *glasnost'*, long-suppressed novels, plays, films and other works were made available to the public. The intelligentsia were the prime beneficiaries of *glasnost'* in the arts and enthusiastically supported Gorbachev's policy. By 1989, however, the novelty of the new cultural policy had waned and frustrations had arisen over the slow pace of political and economic reform. Nevertheless, *glasnost'* was vital in winning support for Gorbachev during a crucial phase in his struggle to overcome conservative opponents such as Yegor Ligachev.

Gorbachev also utilized *glasnost'* to unleash Soviet public opinion in support of his economic and political reforms and to undermine his opponents. *Glasnost'* enabled citizens to speak out against corrupt and incompetent party and state officials, making it easier for Gorbachev to replace them with his own appointees.

Since market forces have not yet emerged to induce factory managers and economic planners to meet the needs of Soviet consumers, Gorbachev has encouraged the use of public opinion to make factory managers more respon-sive to consumer preferences. A Moscow television show called "Critical View" illustrates the point. Every week the "guest" on this popular talk show is a factory manager or a government official. The studio audience and view-ers across the country are invited to direct comments and questions to the official. The author watched one broadcast where the "guest" was the direc-tor of a refrigerator factory in Moscow.[3] The host introduced the factory manager, citing all the accolades and awards won by his factory. The studio audience was then invited to put the director "on the hot seat." They did not hesitate to cooperate. A woman stood and shouted, "Our refrigerator, made at your factory, broke down just a few months after we bought it and no spare parts are available. Yet your factory earns bonuses and prizes for its produc-tion. What are you going to do to improve the quality of service for your products?" The audience applauded vigorously. The factory director squirmed as he attempted to mollify the angry woman. After several such hostile questions from the audience, the host began to take equally hostile telephone calls from across the USSR. By the end of the program, the factory manager was perspiring heavily and acknowledging the failure of his factory to meet the needs of consumers.

Gorbachev has also manipulated *glasnost'* to bolster his own image and power. He has encouraged criticism of the Stalinist and Brezhnevite past to legitimize his own reform programs. In so doing, he has prompted the whole-sale reexamination of Soviet history. In a November 1987 speech marking the seventieth anniversary of the Revolution, Gorbachev praised the moderate so-cialist Nikolai Bukharin while denouncing Stalin by name. He concluded: "The guilt of Stalin and his immediate entourage before the Party and the people for the wholesale repressive measures and acts of lawlessness is enormous and unforgivable."[4] He established a commission to generate proposals for rehabili-tating Stalin's victims and for erecting a monument to their memory.

The anti-Stalin campaign continued unabated through mid-1988. The popular investigatory television program "Vzglyad" (Viewpoint) interviewed a former executioner in one of Stalin's labor camps. He described in graphic detail how he shot thousands of inmates. *Ogonek*, perhaps the most daring magazine published in the USSR, printed many stories exposing the excesses of the Stalin period—the violence, the disregard for law, the special privileges of the elite, and the unchecked power of the secret police and the Army.

Predictably, the anti-Stalin campaign prompted a counterattack by the conservatives. During Gorbachev's prolonged vacation following the June 1987 Central Committee plenum, Ligachev signaled a crackdown. On Sep-tember 1, a ban was imposed on street demonstrations in Moscow and the Minister of Internal Affairs denounced the demagogy and nihilism of many pro-reform writers and artists. After a critical article appeared in *Ogonek* about human rights abuses in the Army, Minister of Defense Dmitri Yazov went on national television to denounce "yellow journalism." The long-dormant censorship agency, Glavlit, began to reassert controls. Several arti-cles slated for publication in newspapers and magazines were suppressed and others were severely edited.

The conservative backlash culminated in the publication of a letter by a

Leningrad chemistry teacher, Nina Andreeva, in the conservative newspaper *Sovetskaya Rossiya*, on March 13, 1988. The letter, entitled "I Cannot Betray My Principles," although presumably authored by Andreeva, was a thinly disguised broadside on Gorbachev's reforms reflecting the stance of Yegor Ligachev, Gorbachev's conservative opponent on the Politburo. Andreeva criticized reformers for threatening the underlying concepts of socialism. She reprimanded the press for the one-sided negative treatment of Stalin, claiming that it detracted from an appreciation of the "unprecedented feats" achieved under his leadership. She directed extensive criticism against popular literary and artistic figures such as playwright Mikhail Shatrov (*The Brest Peace* and *Onward and Onward*), "whose essence was to sling mud at our past and present."[5]

Andreeva's letter was published while Gorbachev was visiting in Yugoslavia. Upon his return, he began to orchestrate a counteroffensive. He called together the editors of the most prominent newspapers and magazines to sharpen their attacks on Brezhnev and Stalin and redouble their efforts in support of *perestroika* and *glasnost'*. At this session, Gorbachev reportedly referred to Ligachev as "an impediment to reform."[6] On April 5, *Pravda* published a stinging editorial, attacking Andreeva's letter. The editorial noted that during the Brezhnev period of stagnation, "authoritarian methods, unthinking execution of orders, bureaucratism, the absence of control, corruption, extortion, and petit bourgeois degeneration flourished." It went on to note that these characteristics represent deviations from the principles of socialism and accused Andreeva of "whitewashing the past."[7] Similar attacks on Andreeva and Ligachev appeared in several publications and on radio and television programs, and Ligachev was reportedly reprimanded at a meeting of the Politburo.[8]

While Ligachev's career continued to wane after this episode, the voices of conservatism were not silenced. In the summer of 1989, Andreeva published another article, this time in *Molodaya gvardiya* in which she developed more fully her criticisms of *perestroika* and *glasnost'*. Conservative publications, such as *Moskovskaya pravda, Sovetskaya Rossiya,* and the Party's ideological journal, *Kommunist*, joined in the debate. Conservative forces argued that Gorbachev's reforms would further erode communist ideals, undermine social solidarity and society's commitment to equality, redistribute political power from the working masses to the intelligentsia, and engender ethnic and economic chaos.

The debate surrounding the Andreeva letter illustrates the wide divergence that emerged in the Soviet media in the span of only three years—from 1986 to 1989. We turn now to a survey of how *glasnost'* has influenced the media and the arts in the USSR.

GLASNOST' AND THE MEDIA

Today in the Soviet Union, more than 18,000 newspapers are published, with a combined circulation of more than 200 million.[9] They range from *Trud* (Labor), the newspaper of the labor unions, with a circulation of 18.7 million, to mimeographed leaflets of tiny splinter parties and movements, such as *Doverie* (Trust) and *Svobodnoe slovo* (The Free Word).[10] The main party newspaper, *Pravda* (Truth), boasted a circulation of 10.7 million in 1988, although readership has been falling in recent years as Soviet citizens turn to more provocative and daring publications.[11] *Izvestiya* (News) is the official organ of the State and claims a circulation of between 8 and 9 million.[12] *Komsomolskaya pravda* (Komsomol Truth), with a circulation of more than 10 million, is the organ of the communist youth organization.[13] It focuses especially on the concerns of Soviet youth. However, with the advent of *glasnost'* and the precipitous decline in Komsomol membership among young people, the newspaper has taken an aggressively pro-reform stance in an attempt to win back its following. *Krasnaya zvezda* (Red Star) represents the views of the Soviet armed forces and is noted for its hawkish stances on foreign policy issues.

Argumenty i fakty (Arguments and Facts), a weekly, has evolved from an obscure tabloid with a circulation of only 10,000 to a major publication selling more than 31 million copies every week.[14] It publishes short, factual pieces, but nevertheless has a strongly pro-reform orientation. It built this reputation primarily by publishing provocative interviews and public opinion polls tackling previously forbidden themes.

In 1989, the editor of *Argumenty i fakty*, Vladislav Starkov, published the results of a popularity survey in which Gorbachev came in behind several of his critics, including Yeltsin, the now-deceased human rights activist Andrei Sakharov, and Gavriil Popov, mayor of Moscow. The poll reportedly outraged Gorbachev and Starkov was called to Communist Party headquarters and told to resign. He refused to comply, however, noting that the Party had no authority to make such a request. *Argumenty i fakty* is not a party-controlled newspaper; rather it is the official publication of the *Znanie* (Knowledge) Society, which disseminates political and scientific information to the masses. Starkov weathered the controversy and *Argumenty i fakty* remains today an ardent voice in favor of *glasnost'* and reform.

Another strongly reformist newspaper is *Moscow News*. Begun in 1930 as an English-language newspaper, *Moscow News* now appears in several languages, including Russian, and sells out immediately when it appears on kiosk shelves Wednesday mornings. Under the lead of editor Yegor Yakovlev, *Moscow News* has explored many controversial issues ranging from the incarceration of dissidents in psychiatric hospitals to obstacles to *perestroika*. Perhaps because it is circulated widely among foreign audiences, *Moscow News* has come in for close scrutiny from Gorbachev and his media watchdog, Vadim Medvedev. In November 1989, the newspaper threw a lavish party celebrating its fifty-ninth birthday. When Yakovlev was asked why he did not wait one year until *Moscow News* was sixty years old, he replied, "Because we may not be here then."[15]

In addition to these central newspapers, there are more than 7000 regional and local papers, most of which are organs of party, state, or trade union organizations in their respective areas.[16] Thus, *Pravda Vostoka* (Truth of the East), published in Tashkent, is the party newspaper for Uzbekistan. Evening papers, such as *Vechernyaya Moskva* (Evening Moscow), carry a wider range of entertainment and political commentary than many of the morning newspapers. Regional newspapers and translations of the major central newspapers are published in some fifty-five languages.[17]

Despite the diversity of the Soviet press, the format of most Soviet newspapers is remarkably standardized. *Pravda* serves as the prime model for most other publications. The front page is devoted to reports of production achievements, an "agitational" editorial, and occasional announcements of government or party decrees and resolutions. Once a month, there is a brief article entitled "In the Politburo of the CPSU," which mentions some of the major agenda items brought up in the previous Politburo session. The remaining five pages of *Pravda* cover party affairs, editorial commentaries, correspondence, foreign news, sports reports, and the weather. Noticeably absent are advertisements, comics, horoscopes, and advice columns.

Soviet newspapers attract a large and diverse audience. A study conducted in Leningrad found that 75 percent of those polled read at least one newspaper every day, and that official communications by party and state bodies attract the largest audience.[18] Soviet newspapers are not generally sold by subscription, but are purchased at sidewalk kiosks. *Pravda* costs a mere 5 kopeks—one-fifth cent. The latest editions of the major newspapers are also pasted up on bulletin boards near bus stops and in public buildings.

One important function of Soviet newspapers is to receive and publish letters from Soviet citizens. Letters to the editor relate to a wide variety of subjects: suggestions, petty grievances, complaints about housing conditions, consumer complaints, and criticisms of mismanagement by low-level officials. Soviet authorities report that between 60 and 70 million letters are received every year; *Pravda* alone receives more than half a million.[19] Although only a small portion of the letters can actually be printed, all letters are supposed to be answered. Many are referred to local party, state, industrial, legal, and other officials for action. There are many instances reported every year in which corrupt officials are dismissed following probes into citizens' complaints sent to newspapers.

Soviet newspapers have their own reporters, but they also rely heavily on the two major news agencies, TASS and Novosti. In reality, Novosti is a propaganda agency with close ties to the KGB; it is primarily responsible for supervising the activities of foreign correspondents in the USSR. TASS, with its gigantic network of reporters and foreign correspondents, is the major news source for Soviet newspapers.

As in other aspects of Soviet society, the better connections one has, the more information one receives. The regular TASS service, known as "Blue" or "Green" TASS, is highly censored and sanitized for public consumption. "White" or "Service" TASS is a special, classified news and information service provided to selected ministers, military officers, party secretaries, and other high-ranking officials. "White" TASS contains accurate information on Soviet domestic affairs, including statistics on crime, economic problems, accidents, and epidemics that even now do not always appear in open sources.[20] "White" TASS also carries detailed international coverage from TASS correspondents as well as reprints of editorial commentary from foreign media. At the pinnacle of this news hierarchy is the highly classified "Red"

TASS, which is distributed only to chief editors of the major newspapers and to the highest state and party leaders.

More than five thousand journals and magazines are published in forty-five languages of the USSR and twenty-three foreign languages, covering a wide array of specialized and regional audiences.[21] One of the most widely read magazines in the USSR today is *Ogonek*, a weekly devoted to covering lively and controversial political issues. Founded in 1907, *Ogonek* began as a popular family magazine. It was banned in 1918, accused of having monarchical sympathies, but during the more liberal policies of NEP *Ogonek* was permitted to resume publication. During the Stalin era, the magazine became one of the worst of the Stalinist rags, and people bought it only for its crossword puzzles. During the Brezhnev years, the magazine was headed by Anatolii Sofronov, a party hack and sycophant. The current editor, Vitalii Korotich, reports that when he took over the editorial post he found on his predecessor's desk a list of the birth dates of every member of the Politburo. Among Sofronov's self-serving practices was printing the portraits of high-ranking party officials in honor of their birthdays.[22]

Korotich assumed the helm in the summer of 1986 and in only four and one-half years *Ogonek's* circulation swelled from 260,000 to more than 4,600,000.[23] Korotich attributes the magazine's success to its aggressive style of investigatory journalism. It exposed corruption within the upper echelons of the CPSU, unmasked the war in Afghanistan as a bloody and futile endeavor, uncovered widespread hazing and abuse of army recruits, and ridiculed Georgii Markov, a political hack and the head of the Writer's Union, who ordered a museum devoted to himself to be opened in his native village. The magazine was the first to publish excerpts of Rybakov's *Children of the Arbat* and works by Boris Pasternak, Vladimir Nabokov, and Nikolai Gumilov, a poet who was executed in 1921 as a counterrevolutionary. An interview with the widow of Nikolai Bukharin, an early Bolshevik and victim of one of Stalin's notorious show trials, led to Bukharin's rehabilitation.

Ogonek's reportage has angered officials sufficiently that they have sought to bring it back under party control. In October 1989, Korotich and the editors of *Moscow News* and *Argumenty i fakty* were summoned to a meeting with Gorbachev. The President told them he thought that they were pushing *glasnost'* too far and accused them of publishing "irresponsible" and "negative" articles, which only eroded public support for his reforms.[24] On another occasion, Korotich was summoned to a meeting with Vadim Medvedev, the Central Committee secretary specializing in ideological matters. Korotich recalls that Medvedev charged: "People reading *Ogonek* will stop believing in socialism." To which Korotich replied, "People who visit your supermarkets have already stopped believing in socialism."[25]

After the abolition of Article 6 of the Constitution in March 1990 and the passage of the new Law on the Press, the ability of party and governmental bodies to control newspapers and magazines directly was severely reduced. *Ogonek* and several other pro-reform publications became independent and self-financing. When party officials continued to send Korotich directives attempting to influence the magazine's content, he simply sent them back unopened.

Indirect methods of applying pressure still exist, however. The leadership can restrict *Ogonek's* circulation by limiting its supply of newsprint. Salaries are still set by the state, and *Ogonek's* reporters earn approximately one-third of the salaries commanded by reporters for *Pravda*.[26] Nevertheless, bold and daring editors fight back. When officials announced a planned cutback in the magazine's newsprint allocation, Korotich threatened to print an exposé on Soviet sales of newsprint abroad at a time when the leadership was bemoaning a critical shortage of newsprint for popular pro-reform newspapers and magazines. The ploy worked and *Ogonek's* paper allocation was restored.

Today the biggest challenges to magazines such as *Ogonek* are not threats of political intrusions, but the forces of self-financing, competition, falling profits, uncertain circulation, inadequate facilities and equipment, and understaffing.

Among the wide array of journals in the USSR today, *Novy mir* (New World), the literary monthly that gained fame during the Khrushchev "thaw," also has a reputation for pushing the boundaries of what can be printed. *Novy mir* has maintained strong reader interest by serializing all of the major works of Aleksandr Solzhenitsyn. On the right end of the political spectrum are *Nash sovremennik* (Our Contemporary) and *Molodaya gvardiya* (Young Guard), publications that stress patriotism and Russian nationalism.

There are more than 300 radio stations in the USSR broadcasting in seventy languages.[27] All radio stations rely heavily on the eight main national networks for their programs. These networks provide news and political commentary, education programs, and cultural performances, as well as programs for special audiences (children, youth, women, peasants, and so forth).

Western news reports are available from foreign broadcasts such as those of Voice of America, the BBC, and Radio Liberty. In late 1988 the jamming of Russian-language broadcasts of Radio Liberty and other Western stations ceased. Western rock music programs are especially popular with Soviet young people, who frequently tape them on their portable recorders. People in the Baltic republics and other northern regions can receive radio and television broadcasts from Finland and Sweden, while citizens in the Far East can pick up Japanese radio and television shows. As of 1991, Soviet citizens can also obtain CNN by cable; however, the demand has been heavy and there is a long waiting list to subscribe to the new service.

The television audience in the USSR has grown rapidly since 1960, when only 8 percent of all families owned a television set.[28] Today, there are some 85 million television sets in the USSR (more than the number of households), and television broadcasts reach approximately 98 percent of the population.[29] There are four main channels covering a wide variety of news, economic and political reporting, educational programs, cultural performances, sporting events, and documentary films. The major evening news program, "Vremya" (Time), attracts a large audience, despite its bland format.

Under the influence of *glasnost'*, Soviet television has changed dramatically. Lively and provocative programs, such as "Vzglyad" (Viewpoint), "Shestsot sekund" (600 Seconds), and "Dvenadtsatyi etazh" (Twelfth Floor), offer biting exposés in a format much like that of "60 Minutes." On the eve of Gorbachev's 1987 speech denouncing Stalin, Moscow television screened a documentary film called *Risk-1*, about the use of terror and summary executions during the Stalin period. According to some reports, the film was shown only after Gorbachev had personally screened it at his private dacha.[30] A sequel, *Risk-2*, won the Cannes Film Festival award for best documentary of 1988.

Even Soviet entertainment programming shows the effects of *glasnost'*. Prior to 1986, prime time was devoted largely to sporting events, political commentary, and reruns of movies about World War II. Now one channel includes an extended program of rock music videos patterned after MTV. Documentaries are still popular, but their subject matter tends much more toward the frank investigation of current problems ranging from AIDS to violence associated with soccer matches.

Because of their centralized nature, the broadcast media are much more vulnerable to government crackdowns. "Vzglyad," which used to be on the air live late Friday night for two hours, was taken off the air in 1990 and only reinstated because of vigorous lobbying by several reform politicians, including Boris Yeltsin. However, the program is no longer permitted to broadcast live. All the material must now be approved in advance. Even the major news program, "Vremya," appears to have lost its independent voice. As of early 1991, it began to take a strongly pro-centrist stance in its coverage of events in Lithuania. It also openly campaigned in support of Gorbachev's March 1991 referendum on national unity. Korotich, the editor of *Ogonek*, observed, "TV is part of the conservative establishment. TV is going in the wrong direction."[31]

GLASNOST' AND THE ARTS

Until the advent of *glasnost'*, the Party maintained tight controls over literature and the arts. The arts were seen as serving a political as well as an aesthetic purpose. Lenin decreed: "Art belongs to the people. It must penetrate with its deepest roots into the very midst of the toiling masses. It must be intelligible to these masses and moved by them. It must unite the feeling, thought, and will of these masses and elevate them. It must awaken in them artists and develop them."[32]

The primary organization responsible for policing culture in the USSR is the Ministry of Culture. When it was created in 1953, the Ministry of Culture was responsible for formulating and implementing cultural policies in all artistic fields. Today, however, it deals primarily with literature, music, dance, and theater. Separate state committees now supervise radio and television (Gostelradio), cinema (Goskino), and publishing (Goskomizdat).

In addition to supervising the arts and cultural fields, the Ministry of Culture is responsible for maintaining museums, libraries, parks, clubs, and "palaces of culture," and for the training of personnel for these establishments. In Soviet jargon, the latter function is known as "cultural-enlightenment" work and consumes a major portion of the Ministry's time and attention. Of some seventy educational institutions in the arts (art academies, conservatories, and so forth) in the USSR, fifty fall under the administrative aegis of the Ministry of Culture.[33]

Subordinate to the USSR Ministry of Culture are ministries in each of the fifteen republics, which have particular responsibility for managing culture in their respective regions. The interaction of the central ministry and the fifteen subordinate republic ministries is complex and fraught with conflict and confusion.

Policies and decisions made at the republic and local levels are subject to approval by the central ministry in Moscow, although with the rise of independence movements in virtually every republic, this system of centralized control is rapidly breaking down. Normally, local cultural departments are responsible for supervising museums, theaters, and other artistic and cultural institutions in their cities or regions. There are exceptions, however, especially for very prominent institutions. For example, the Kirov Ballet in Leningrad reports directly to the USSR Ministry of Culture, rather than to the culture department of the Leningrad city soviet.

All creative arts and literary organizations at the republic level are encouraged to reflect the nationality composition of their respective republics. Thus, newspapers, books, magazines, and journals are published in each of the fifteen major languages of the Soviet Union. The effort to make the arts accessible even to smaller ethnic groups is impressive. Scholarly journals in the USSR appear in forty-five languages, while books are published in sixty-eight languages, theatrical performances are presented in forty-seven languages, and radio broadcasts in seventy languages.[34] Theaters, ballet companies, and orchestras have been established in virtually every major city and town in the USSR. The quality and level of professional training varies widely, but many of the regional companies have won acclaim at home and abroad. Dance, dramatic, and musical troupes also tour remote areas that cannot support residential performing arts companies.

Although they are technically public organizations and not a formal part of the state machinery, the unions for members of the various artistic professions have traditionally played an integral role in the management of Soviet culture. There are separate unions for artists, dancers, musicians and composers, architects, and actors (including both cinema and drama). The unions receive ample support from the State in the form of offices, health resorts, and vacation facilities, as well as direct financial support.

The Ministry of Culture has considerable influence over the professional unions. For example, the Ministry has the right to "assist" unions in planning and to present proposals for consideration by their members. Until 1986, all top-level officials within the various unions occupied *nomenklatura* positions, which made them vulnerable to "proposals" coming from the Ministry and from the Party's Culture Department. However, most of the unions now freely elect the governing boards of their unions.

In addition to organizing artistic performances and sponsoring symposia and other professional activities, the unions provide a variety of services for their members. The unions manage pension programs and administer social insurance and welfare programs for the creative intelligentsia. Unions also operate exclusive resorts, health spas, clubs, restaurants, retirement homes, and summer cottages for their members, as well as special stores through which members can purchase everything from rare books to automobiles.

The Soviet government places great emphasis on making the arts accessible to all citizens, rather than keeping them the exclusive preserve of the intelligentsia. Concerts and theater and ballet performances are usually scheduled to begin in the early evening in order to attract workers coming home from their jobs. It is not unusual to see office workers, military officers, and even manual laborers attending performances still wearing their work clothes or uniforms.

Accessibility of the arts is also assured by holding down the cost of admission. Tickets to concerts by the Leningrad or Moscow Philharmonic Orchestras usually range in price from approximately 25 cents to one dollar. Ballet and opera tickets cost slightly more, especially at the prestigious Bolshoi or Kirov theatres, but even the most expensive ballet ticket costs less than ten dollars. Many cultural events are open to the public free of charge.

One consequence of low ticket prices in the USSR is that most performing arts companies operate at a loss and are dependent upon the Ministry of Culture for subsidies (*dotatsiya*). Subsidies are one of the most influential means by which the Ministry of Culture shapes the artistic policies of performing arts companies. Indirect subsidies are also received in the form of rent-free buildings, equipment, and even routine maintenance costs borne by the central ministry. By threatening to withhold subsidies, the Ministry can wield decisive power over most artistic groups. Ironically, however, the most avant-garde and controversial companies, such as the Taganka Theatre, play to packed houses and are the least dependent upon the Ministry's subsidies.

Censorship in literature and the arts was drastically reduced in 1986, as a central feature of Gorbachev's campaign of *glasnost'*. Now the principal responsibility for what is published rests with the editorial board of the individual publication or publishing house. Party cultural officers still attempt to communicate the CPSU's concerns about certain topics or individual works of art, but they can no longer force a publishing house to reject a manuscript or for a theatre to cancel a production.

As with the Khrushchev thaw in the arts in the 1950s, the cultural reforms of *glasnost'* preceded substantial political and economic reforms. The more open policy toward the arts under Gorbachev was signaled in 1986 with the forced retirement of the Minister of Culture Peter Demichev. He was replaced by Vasilii Zakharov, 52, a former associate of Yeltsin. The Brezhnevite chairman of the Union of Writers, Georgii Markov, was replaced by Vladimir Karpov, editor-in-chief of the liberal literary journal *Novy mir*. Karpov had once been jailed for criticizing Stalin. His successor at *Novy mir* is Sergei Zalygin, a leader in the "village prose" movement and noted for his eloquent criticisms of Stalin.

Perhaps the boldest challenge to the Brezhnevite cultural establishment came in the film industry, where 41-year-old Elem Klimov and other young "radicals" unseated a party-approved slate to head the Union of Film Workers at the Union's congress in May 1986. Klimov's films had been censored many times in the past and he vowed to change the system whereby budgets for films were awarded on the basis of political connections and seniority, rather than artistic merit. Klimov effectively reduced the power of Goskino (State Committee on Film) to intrude into the decisions of individual studios.

But the shake-up of of the film industry also facilitated the transition to full financial independence as of January 1, 1989. Thereafter, all studios had to cover their own production costs, exposing them to financial uncertainties they had never before encountered.

The period 1986 through 1989 witnessed many startling film releases. Documentaries such as *Risk-2* and *More Light* tried to explain how Stalin could have come to power and ruled through such autocratic methods. Alexander Proshkin's *The Cold Summer of '53* describes the release of prisoners from one of Stalin's forced labor camps.

More contemporary themes are the subject of other films, such as Valerii Ogorodnikov's *The Burglar*, which tells the story of a young boy who steals a musical instrument for his brother who wants to play in a rock band. In 1988, Vasilii Pichul's film, *Little Vera*, which deals with the dreariness of working-class life in a small town, shocked Soviet viewers by incorporating some love scenes in which the star appears nude. Another recent film by Yurii Podnieks, *Is It Easy to Be Young?*, explores how teenagers turn to violence and vandalism to relieve their boredom. Documentaries have investigated formerly taboo subjects such as the consequences of the Chernobyl disaster, the physical and psychological damage done by abusive training programs for Soviet gymnasts, the inhumane conditions in Soviet prisons, and adjustment problems of soldiers returning from Afghanistan.

In the words of one young Soviet documentary director: "We are the advance troops of *glasnost'* and *perestroika*. Gorbachev ordered the nation to march, and the filmmakers marched. Now we look around and see that we have left everybody else far behind. Of course, we will be the first to lose our heads if the struggle goes badly."[35]

GLASNOST' AND THE INTELLIGENTSIA

Throughout Russian history, members of the creative intelligentsia have been deeply involved in political affairs. The eighteenth-century poet Gavrila Derzhavin served as Minister of Justice under Alexander I. The most famous Russian poet, Alexander Pushkin, despite being occasionally exiled, came under the personal patronage of Nicholas I and was named a "Gentleman of the Chamber." The nineteenth-century playwright Alexander Griboedov was dispatched as the Russian ambassador to Teheran, where he was later beheaded by an angry mob. Moreover, the many writers who criticized the tsarist regime and were banished or imprisoned, such as Alexander Radishchev, Mikhail Lermontov, and Fyodor Dostoyevsky, helped bring about gradual social and political reforms. So too in the USSR today, the creative intelligentsia plays an important role in shaping policies both as supporters and as critics of the regime. Gorbachev has made a concerted effort to play to the intelligentsia, to cultivate them as a power base and to win their support for *perestroika*. His Presidential Council, which advised him on major policy issues until it was disbanded in November 1990, included two prominent writers, Chingis Aitmatov and Valentin Rasputin, as well as three scholars: the economist

Stanislav Shatalin, foreign policy expert Evgenii Primakov, and Yurii Osipian, a physicist and Vice President of the USSR Academy of Sciences.

The ability of an individual or group to influence policies in the Soviet Union depends on four factors: the status or prestige of the individual (or group); whether the individual (or group) seeking to influence policies is acting autonomously or as a representative of a recognized organization; the level of administration that the individual (or group) is seeking to influence; and the degree of political conflict and division within the political leadership.[36]

The higher the status of the individual or group, the greater the ability to influence policy. Thus, writers and filmmakers generally enjoy greater influence than ballet dancers or librarians, and nuclear physicists more than foreign-language teachers.

Many members of the creative intelligentsia have been named to prominent positions that bring them into close and frequent contact with high-ranking party and state officials. The Congress of People's Deputies, elected in March 1989, includes several members of the intelligentsia, including the noted poet Evgenii Evtushenko, dissidents Andrei Sakharov and Roy Medvedev; Vitalii Korotich and Yurii Chernichenko of *Ogonek*; and scholars Oleg Bogomolev, Evgenii Primakov, and Anatolii Sobchak. Beneath the level of national politics, directors of major orchestras, museums, theatres, libraries and institutes are powerful figures in local decision-making because they speak on behalf of highly respected institutions or groups.

The intelligentsia appear to have the greatest impact at the local level. Here, contacts with party and state officials are more likely to be informal, personal, and direct; attempts to influence the Politburo or the Minister of Culture, on the other hand, are usually indirect and formal.[37]

The intelligentsia also has direct links to top decision-making bodies through numerous artistic and literary bureaucratic organizations, including the Ministry of Culture, the professional unions (such as the writers' union), the Academy of Art, the Academy of Sciences, the State Committee on Radio and Television, and the State Committee on Cinematography. These institutions all have governing boards or "scientific councils" that assist and advise their respective directors on policy matters. For example, the "scientific council" of the Ministry of Culture includes several writers, artists, composers, playwrights, and directors. Occasionally, the council undertakes research projects and writes reports that influence the course of the Ministry's policies.

Soviet political leaders have, in the past, cultivated close personal ties to many members of the creative intelligentsia. During the Civil War, the Russian writer Maxim Gorky used his personal ties to Lenin to intercede on behalf of many starving members of the intelligentsia. In the late 1960s, the KGB arrested Andrei Voznesensky after a reading of his protest poems at a Moscow concert hall. Within hours, however, Voznesensky was released after the personal intervention of Politburo member A. N. Shelepin.[38]

The more divided the political leadership, the greater the opportunity for interest groups to influence policies.[39] The recent fragmentation of the Soviet political system into factions favoring rapid reform versus those favoring a more moderate pace of reform has created more opportunities for the intelligentsia to voice their views.

The immense popularity of some Soviet writers, poets, ballet dancers, and actors gives them a powerful political voice and at the same time shields them from blatant repression by the authorities. The poets and balladeers Bulat Okudzhava, Evgenii Evtushenko, and Vladimir Vysotsky have attracted huge and enthusiastic followings bordering on cults. Vysotsky was hailed as the "true bard of the people." Unfortunately, like many of his fellow citizens, Vysotsky died of alcoholism at an early age. On the day of his funeral, some 30,000 people crowded into Taganka Square in Moscow in front of the theater where he had so often performed.[40] Vysotsky's verse spoke of the trials of daily life in the Soviet Union. His friend, the Russian poet Bella Akhmadulina, wrote, "Their love of him is a sign of a profound weariness in our people of all the official gloss, a profound hunger to be told about things as they are."[41]

The dispersal of political authority among a variety of institutions, most notably the election of the Congress of People's Deputies and the Supreme Soviet, as well as elections of republic and local soviets, has created more opportunities for members of the intelligentsia to run for office and influence policy-making. Given their high visibility and status in Soviet society, it should not be surprising that many members of the intelligentsia were catapulted into elected offices in 1989 and 1990.

Traditionally, the creative intelligentsia has influenced the course of both tsarist and Soviet policies through criticism and dissent. Acting as the conscience of society, the Soviet intelligentsia has become a potent political force, calling for official adherence to Soviet laws, recognition of human rights, and the relaxation of censorship. Members of the intelligentsia have also on occasion used their prestige to speak out against environmental pollution and to denounce the invasion of Afghanistan. Whereas during the Brezhnev regime members of the intelligentsia generally tried to influence policies from outside the party and government, frequently as dissidents, today they are operating on the inside. For some, this change has forced them into an unaccustomed role. Before, they were the conscience of Soviet society and prided themselves on taking strong, uncompromising moral stands against the leadership on issues. Today they are part of the leadership and find themselves having to adjust to making legislative compromises. Before, the more the regime tried to silence them the more their voices were heard. Today, their voices are often lost in a cacaphony of political debate representing all points on the political spectrum and a variety of ethnic, regional, institutional, and issue-oriented interest groups.

THE BACKLASH

By late 1989, the momentum behind *glasnost'* had begun to wane. The Minister of Internal Affairs, Vadim Bakatin, generally a supporter of Gorbachev's reforms, lamented, "There is complete chaos in the press. People say whatever they feel like saying."[42] He went on to accuse the press of creating a national "psychosis" about rising crime rates and charged that "certain forces" were using the greater freedom of the press to advance their own ambitions.

The draft Law on the Press, published in December 1989, while significantly broadening press freedom, contains some provisions that are troubling to journalists. The law abolishes censorship except for reasons of "state security," but it requires all publications to be registered, which some critics argue could be used to shut down dissident publishers.[43] Furthermore, opinions espousing changes to the existing political and social system are expressly prohibited.[44]

Moreover, the State maintains the potential to exert indirect pressure on newspapers and journals by controlling allocations of paper and printing equipment. Tight centralized controls have also been maintained on the broadcast media. During 1990, as secessionist pressures ran high and local and republic governments sought to wrest control of their respective institutions, the central authorities refused to permit local or republic control of radio or television for fear that they would be used to "fan the flames of nationalist unrest." It is not a coincidence that the Gorbachev leadership resorted to violence in recapturing a communications center in Vilnius in early 1991.

There are also clear political motives for Gorbachev's recent crackdown on *glasnost'*. The intelligentsia, the prime beneficiaries of his policy of openness, have not proven to be grateful to him for introducing *glasnost'*, nor have they provided a solid power base on which he can rely for support. Instead, the intelligentsia has tended to fragment its political influence among several individuals and positions. The largest segment, which favors a faster transition to a pluralist democracy and a market economy, has thrown its support to Gorbachev's chief liberal opponents Yeltsin, Popov, and Sobchak.

While *glasnost'* remains very popular with the intelligentsia, it has not developed much support among rank-and-file Soviet workers. Their concerns, growing in urgency and political potential from 1989 onward, have focused on price increases, food shortages, unemployment, the alarming increase in crime, and the breakdown of public order, especially in non-Russian areas. The police, the military, the KGB, and the party apparatus—the four bastions of conservatism in the USSR today—have used public fears and uncertainties to justify a tightening of the reins. Korotich of *Ogonek* observes: "It's a really dangerous moment. Our hard-liners are pushing strongly ahead. I feel they are trying to show that democracy and anarchy are synonymous. Shevardnadze clearly resigned because he felt powerless [in the face of these forces], and I feel powerless too."[45]

Notes

1. See Hedrick Smith, *The Russians* (New York: Ballantine Books, 1976), 474–475.

2. *Pravda*, 27 March 1985, p. 1.

3. Two other similar programs are "Candid Talk" and "Facts and Commentary."

4. *Izvestiya*, 3 November 1987, p. 1.

5. *Sovetskaia Rossiya*, 13 March 1988. For an English translation of the Andreeva letter, see David Lane, *Soviet Society under Perestroika* (Boston: Unwin Hyman, 1990), 108–117.

6. Reported in Robert Kaiser, "How Gorbachev Outfoxed his Rivals," *Washington Post*, 12 June 1988, p. 1.

7. *Pravda*, 5 April 1988, p. 1.

8. Reported in Dev Murarka, "The Foes of Perestroika Sound Off," *The Nation*, 23 May 1988, p. 715.

9. *The Cambridge Encyclopedia of Russia and the Soviet Union* (Cambridge: Cambridge University Press, 1982), 407.

10. Lane, *Soviet Society under Perestroika*, 278.

11. In 1989, readership may have fallen as low as 5.5 million. *New York Times*, 23 October 1989, p. 4.

12. Ibid.

13. Ibid.

14. John Newhouse, "Chronicling the Chaos," *The New Yorker*, 31 December 1990, p. 39.

15. Ibid., p. 407.

16. *Cambridge Encyclopedia*, p. 406.

17. John L. Scherer, ed., *USSR Facts and Figures Annual*, vol. 9 (Gulf Breeze, FL: Academic International Press, 1985), 311.

18. *Cambridge Encyclopedia*, 407.

19. Ibid.

20. Smith, *The Russians*, 474–475.

21. Scherer, *USSR Facts and Figures Annual*, 311.

22. Newhouse, "Chronicling the Chaos," p. 49.

23. Ibid., p. 38.

24. Ibid., p. 39.

25. Ibid.

26. Ibid., p. 72.

27. Scherer, *USSR Facts and Figures Annual*, 311.

28. *Cambridge Encyclopedia*, 408.

29. Ibid.

30. Newhouse, "Chronicling the Chaos," p. 58.

31. Ibid., p. 64.

32. V. I. Lenin cited in Edward J. Brown, *Proletarian Episode in Russian Literature, 1928–1932* (New York: Columbia University Press, 1953), 178–179.

33. Darrell P. Hammer, "Inside the Ministry of Culture: Cultural Policy in the Soviet Union," in Gordon B. Smith, ed., *Public Policy and Administration in the Soviet Union* (New York: Praeger, 1980), p. 63.

34. Scherer, *USSR Facts and Figures Annual*, 311.

35. James Lardner, "A Moment We Had to Grasp," *The New Yorker*, 26 September 1988, p. 81.

36. L. G. Churchward, *The Soviet Intelligentsia* (London: Routledge and Kegan Paul, 1973), 111.

37. Ibid.

38. Ibid., 122–123.

39. Ibid.; and Thane Gustafson, *Reform in Soviet Politics* (Cambridge: Cambridge University Press, 1981), pp. 143–144.

40. David K. Shipler, *Russia: Broken Idols, Solemn Dreams* (New York: Times Books, 1983), 388.

41. Ibid.

42. *New York Times*, 23 October 1989, p. 4.
43. *New York Times*, 27 September 1989, p. 8.
44. Ibid.
45. Newhouse, "Chronicling the Chaos," p. 72.

Selected Bibliography

Brown, Deming. *Soviet Russian Literature since Stalin*. Cambridge: Cambridge University Press, 1978.

Brown, Edward J. *Russian Literature since the Revolution*. rev. ed. Cambridge: Cambridge University Press, 1982.

Churchward, L. G. *The Soviet Intelligentsia*. London: Routledge and Kegan Paul, 1973.

Cohen, Lewis H. *The Cultural-Political Tradition and Development of the Soviet Cinema, 1917–1972*. New York: Arno Press, 1974.

Cohen, Stephen F. and Katrina vanden Heuvel, eds. *Voices of Glasnost*. New York: W. W. Norton, 1989.

Gleason, Abbott, Peter Kenez, and Richard Stites, eds. *Bolshevik Culture: Experiment and Order in the Russian Reovlution*. Bloomington: Indiana University Press, 1985.

Hammer, Darrell P. "Inside the Ministry of Culture: Cultural Policy in the Soviet Union." In Gordon B. Smith, ed. *Public Policy and Administration in the Soviet Union*. New York: Praeger, 1980, 53–78.

Kagarlitsky, Boris. *The Thinking Red: Intellectuals and the Soviet State from 1917 to the Present*. London: Verso Press, 1988.

Mickiewicz, Ellen P. *Media and the Russian Public*. New York: Prager, 1981.

Mickiewicz, Ellen P. *Split Signals: Television and Politics in the Soviet Union*. Oxford: Oxford University Press, 1988.

Schwartz, Boris. *Music and Musical Life in Soviet Russia, 1917–1970*. New York: W. W. Norton, 1973.

Shlapentokh, Vladimir. *Soviet Ideologies in the Period of Glasnost*. New York: Praeger, 1988.

Solzhenitsyn, Aleksandr. *The Oak and the Calf: Sketches of a Literary Life in the Soviet Union*. New York: Harper & Row, 1980.

Tarasulo, Isaac J., ed. *Gorbachev and Glasnost: Viewpoints from the Soviet Press*. Wilmington, Delaware: SR Books, 1989.

9

The Legal System:
Toward a Civil Society

The law and lawyers have been in on the forefront of Gorbachev's reform effort, just as they were in the 1950s under Khrushchev. It is no doubt significant that Gorbachev was a student at Moscow University law school during the midst of the earlier reform movement. Today he is calling for the peaceful and gradual transformation of the Soviet economic, political, and legal systems, and he repeatedly turns to laws and legislation in order to bring about these changes. Speaking to the Nineteenth Party Conference in June 1988, Gorbachev called for the development of a legal system in which "the supremacy of law is ensured in fact."[1]

According to Soviet jurists, in order for the rule of law to exist in the USSR, the following principles must be observed:

- The role of law in Soviet society must be enhanced. All activities must take place within the strict framework of the law. Law must assume its own force, rather than serving merely as a tool of the political leadership.
- State and party officials and bodies must be made subordinate to the law. Judicial officials and law enforcement agencies must be made wholly independent of party and state agencies.
- A meaningful system of constitutional law must be developed. In order to protect constitutionally endowed rights, a constitutional court must be established with full enforcement powers, including the power to annul legislation and administrative acts that are deemed unconstitutional.
- Laws must be fairly and uniformly enforced. Selective enforcement and professional discretion exist in all legal systems; however, the grounds for selectivity should not be based on political expedience.[2]

Under the leadership of Mikhail Gorbachev, who is himself a lawyer, substantial progress has been made in realizing these goals. In order to appreciate fully the magnitude of the recent reforms in Soviet law, however, we must first examine the origins of the Soviet legal system, exploring both the legacy of pre-Revolutionary law and the influence of Marxism-Leninism on Soviet concepts of justice.

ORIGINS OF SOVIET LAW

Historically, Russian law belongs to the larger family of civil-law systems that are ultimately derived from the rules, principles, and practices elaborated in the ancient Roman Forum. Anglo-American students of Soviet law, who are accustomed to the common-law systems derived from England, are at a disadvantage in understanding Soviet law and legal procedure, while European scholars find the fundamentals of the Soviet legal system quite familiar. Thus, examining any given aspect of Soviet law involves determining whether it is a common characteristic of all civil-law systems or uniquely Soviet. Furthermore, only if no parallel exists in imperial Russian law does this aspect represent a unique trait of socialist law, rather than part of the Russian legal heritage acquired by the Soviets in 1917.

Historians have noted that civil law encouraged autocracy, while common law promoted democracy. The common-law principle was enshrined in the maxim *"Rex no debet esse sub homine sed sub Deo et Lege"* ("The king should not be under any man, but under God and the Law"), while the principle of civil law was *"Quod principi placuit legis habet vigorem"* ("The will of the sovereign has the force of law"). Generally, civil legal systems grant greater authority to state officials than do common-law systems.

Civil law and common law also differ markedly in the origins of laws. In common-law systems, judges make law by establishing precedent decisions. Laws thus change organically, growing as a result of piecemeal judicial decisions. In civil-law systems, all laws are the official enactments of executive or legislative bodies. These laws are gathered into codes and periodically updated and standardized. Greater importance is attached to official documents and reports in civil-law systems, and administrative officials are given broader discretionary powers.

Soviet law also displays many unique characteristics that derive from the existence of a socialist economy in the USSR and reflect the official ideology of Marxism-Leninism. Lenin accepted the Marxist conception of law and the State as instruments of coercion in the hands of the ruling class, the bourgeoisie. He envisaged the eventual transition to a communist society in which coercive instruments of the State and law would no longer be necessary and would, indeed, wither away. The situation Lenin confronted in the lawless and chaotic days following the overthrow of the Provisional Government in November 1917, however, called for a legal system to provide law and order. He wrote:

> There is no doubt that we live in a sea of illegality and that local influences are one of the greatest, if not the greatest obstacle to the establishment of legality and culture. . . . It is clear that in light of these conditions we have the firmest guarantee . . . that the Party create a small, centralized collegium capable of countering local influences, local and any bureaucratism and establishing an actual, uniform conception of legality in the entire republic and the entire federation.[3]

Yet the writings of Marx and Engels provided only scant guidelines for Lenin to follow in constructing a socialist state. Marx was first and foremost a social critic, not an architect of the new economic and political order. In the area of legal administration, Marx offered even fewer prescriptions. He merely stated that all crime is the result of social and economic contradictions; when those differences are eliminated under socialism, crime will vanish. The only concrete precedents for the administration of justice available to Lenin were the informal, popularly elected revolutionary tribunals established during the Paris Commune (March 28–May 28, 1871) and the 1905 Revolution in Russia.

In 1917, revolutionary tribunals sprang up throughout Russia, spontaneously or under the supervision of the Bolsheviks. To promote participation of the masses in the judicial process, judges and lay assessors (lay judges) were elected by the people for many tribunals. In some instances, accused persons were brought before public gatherings, at which comrades would serve as social accusers or defenders. Guided by a revolutionary sense of justice, the tribunals cracked down on economic crimes. Members of the aristocratic and middle classes were often convicted on flimsy evidence. Crime increased dramatically. One account states that the numbers of robberies and murders in Moscow in 1918 were ten to fifteen times higher than in 1913.[4]

In the face of the deteriorating situation, the Bolsheviks grappled with the problem of coercion and law. Some favored an end to state coercion. For instance, one tribunal official proclaimed, "The socialist criminal code must not know punishment as a means of influence on the criminal."[5] Others were reluctant to abandon punishment altogether. Lenin opted for strict state coercion to stamp out vestiges of bourgeois society. In the political pamphlet *State and Revolution,* he had outlined the fundamental principles of revolutionary justice: smash the old state machine and set up new revolutionary tribunals; make these tribunals simple, informal, and open to mass participation; subordinate law to revolutionary goals and the Party (for all law has a class character; if it does not serve the Bolsheviks' purposes, it will be serving the purposes of counterrevolutionary elements); and use merciless force toward the eventual goal of reaching a society in which there will be no need for coercion. He concluded, "to curb increases in crime, hooliganism, bribery, speculation, and outrages of all kinds . . . we need time and we need an iron hand."[6]

Thus, in the early days of the Soviet regime, there coexisted two countervailing trends in Soviet law: the Marxist, utopian trend, which stressed both the withering away of the State and the creation of popular, informal tribunals to administer revolutionary justice, and the dictatorial trend, which advocated the use of law and legal institutions to suppress all opposition.[7]

The dictatorial trend in Soviet legal policy reached its zenith during the Stalin era. The authoritarian tone of legal policy was voiced by Andrei Vyshinsky, Stalin's Procurator-General and chief prosecutor in the great purge trials of the 1930s. Vyshinsky defined law as a set of rules laid down by the State and guaranteed by the State's monopoly of force.[8] In the wake of Stalin's dictatorial legal policies, utopianism all but vanished. Vyshinsky, speaking before a group of public prosecutors in 1936, stated that "the old twaddle about the mobilization of socially active workers . . . must be set aside; something new is needed at the present time."[9]

Much of the legal administration of the Stalin years was carried on outside of established judicial institutions. Special boards of the Ministry of Internal Affairs were set up to facilitate campaigns against anti-Soviet elements and to silence potential opponents. The boards were given extraordinary powers and were not required to follow established judicial procedure. They had the authority to imprison or exile for a term of up to five years anyone considered to be "socially dangerous." Proceedings of the boards were not public, the accused had no right to counsel, and there was no appeal of verdicts. The boards consigned hundreds of thousands of Soviet citizens to "corrective labor camps." Some Western analysts estimate the prison labor force by 1941 at 3.5 million workers.[10] Thus, the security police apparatus was the single largest employer in the Soviet Union and wielded not only political but tremendous economic power.

The secret police combed the streets at night in their infamous "black marias" (black sedans), stopping at apartments to pick up people whom "informers" had reported. Rumors or a careless comment by a child at school were sufficient to result in imprisonment or death for a parent. Many Soviet citizens recall the years when they had suitcases packed with warm clothing waiting by the door in case they should be awakened by the secret police in the night and taken away.

Change was imminent after Stalin's death in 1953. Stalin's successors moved quickly to destroy the police state and to rebuild party and state organs, including legal institutions. The Party reestablished control over the secret police. Lavrenti Beria, Stalin's head of the Ministry of Internal Affairs, was arrested for crimes against the State and executed.

Having endured constant and pervasive fear for more than two decades, the Soviet people were ready for a respite from dictatorial coercion. Seizing upon the issue of de-Stalinization in order to solidify his position in the struggle for power, Nikita Khrushchev introduced far-reaching legal reforms. Following his lead, Soviet jurists began to attack the coercive use of law to bolster the monopoly on state power and urged changes in Soviet criminal and civil legislation. The special boards of the Ministry of Internal Affairs were abolished. All criminal cases, including political crimes, had to be prosecuted in the people's courts with regular judicial procedure, and the secret police could no longer make arrests without the authorization of a judge or procurator. The Procuracy,* which had suffered under Stalin's regime, was strengthened.

A new trend in Soviet law began to take shape during the de-Stalinization of the late 1950s. This new trend, represented by the catchwords "socialist legality," stressed the need for protecting the procedural and substantive rights of citizens in relation to the State and for all laws to be strictly and uniformly enforced. An editorial in the Party's theoretical journal, *Kommunist,* attacked the traditional Soviet interpretation of legality and stressed the need for a concept of legality designed to protect the rights and interests of citizens.[11] A study published by the USSR Academy of Sciences argued that citizens' rights are even binding on state authorities. It concluded: "That the

---

* The organization representing public prosecutors.

organs of state power be bound by law is an indispensable condition for the existence of legality and the subjective rights of citizens in relations with state authorities. For an organ of power to be bound by law means that it must fully observe the requirements contained in legal standards and unswervingly fulfill all obligations imposed on it by the law in the citizens' interests."[12]

Other Soviet jurists argued that cases involving citizens' personal and property rights should be examined by the courts, rather than by administrative agencies. They further demanded that state officials bear material and criminal responsibility for such violations.[13] Unlike either the utopian or dictatorial concepts of law, socialist legality began to resemble the Western concept of "rule of law."

Socialist legality coexisted with the dictatorial and utopian trends throughout Khrushchev's tenure. It was eclipsed somewhat, however, by a resurgence of legal utopianism in the early 1960s. Khrushchev, a poorly educated, blustery man from a small farming and mining village in the Ukraine, never fully mastered the controls of the complex bureaucracies that dominate the Soviet system. Distrusting bureaucracies and bureaucrats, he turned to the people for support. In order to stem crime, he urged housing units, factories, and shops to resuscitate comrades' courts and other informal tribunals. By the end of 1963, approximately 197,000 comrades' courts were disposing of more than four million cases per year.[14] Khrushchev also encouraged the formation of "antiparasite courts"—informal tribunals in housing districts and factories that brought pressure to bear on those who refused to work and others deemed to be social "parasites." Voluntary citizens' brigades (*druzhiny*) patrolled the streets to maintain law and order. As if to symbolize the decentralization of legal administration, Khrushchev abolished the All-Union Ministry of Justice, leaving only the fifteen republic ministries.

The legal establishment in general and the Procuracy in particular chafed under Khrushchev's policies. Cases were routinely channeled to comrades' courts for disposition, circumventing the established judicial institutions. Reports of comrades' tribunals meting out prejudicial, arbitrary justice and meddling in nonjudicial matters were common.

With Khrushchev's ouster in 1964, however, the legal profession took steps to bring "popular justice" under control. Jurists attacked the utopian notion of public participation in the administration of justice. A campaign was undertaken to professionalize legal administration and increase the legal competence of judicial personnel. "Socialist legality" again became the principal slogan of the legal apparatus. The return to socialist legality was consonant with the general trend under Brezhnev and his successors of allowing more input from specialists in formulating policy. Legal policies today are carried out primarily through established bureaucratic channels, not through informal, social institutions such as the comrades' courts, although these bodies continue to exist.

Beginning in the early 1960s and extending into the Brezhnev era, there was also a resurgence of the dictatorial trend in law. The powers of the police were expanded, new legislation severely restricted public demonstrations, and capital punishment was reintroduced for a wide variety of offenses, resulting in a rapid increase in the number of executions.

Due to increasing economic pressures and the generally more conserva-tive bureaucratic leadership style of the Brezhnev regime, the emphasis of socialist legality shifted from protecting the interests of individual citizens to protecting the economic interests of the State. The Twenty-Fifth Party Con-gress in 1976 stressed the need for legal regulation of economic activity to increase production, to strengthen the economic system, and to counter fraud, theft of socialist property, and the padding of accounts and plan-fulfillment reports. R. A. Rudenko, the late Procurator-General, noted that the Procuracy had been ordered to strengthen its supervision of legality in all economic organizations.[15] The 1979 Statute on the Procuracy also incorpo-rated several new provisions relating to economic violations. For example, Article 3 stated that "the fight against violations concerning the protection of socialist property" is one of the fundamental responsibilities of procurators.[16] Furthermore, the laws protecting socialist property and the punishments for economic crimes were substantially strengthened in the January 1983 revision of the Criminal Code of the RSFSR.

During the fifteen-month rule of Yuri Andropov, legal measures were used to enhance work discipline. Police rounded up idle workers in movie theaters, bathhouses, and stores and demanded to see their work documents. They sometimes called employers to verify that the apprehended workers were not supposed to be on the job. Under Andropov's leadership, new laws were enacted that raised the penalties for absenteeism, tardiness, drunkenness on the job, managerial incompetence, and theft of state property by workers. The campaign for improving labor discipline culminated in the enactment of the Law on Labor Collectives. The new legislation enlisted the support of the labor collectives in the fight for better work discipline by awarding bonuses on the basis of collective, rather than individual, performance. The work discipline and anticorruption campaigns begun by Andropov faltered under his successor, Konstantin Chernenko, but were renewed with increasing vigor by Mikhail Gorbachev during his first two years in power. These measures were consistent with past legal practice—namely the use of law to enforce control over the people to insure the interests of the State. By 1988, however, Gorbachev was advocating a fundamental restructuring of the political and legal basis of the system. We turn now to explore this remarkable transition toward what Soviet scholars call a "civil society."

GORBACHEV AND LEGAL REFORM

The process of reforming the Soviet legal system has evolved in a manner markedly similar to the course of Gorbachev's general reform program. That is, legal reform has proceeded through a number of stages. The first stage reflected the new openness of Soviet society; it was followed by the enactment of legislation on economic reform policies and expanded citizens' participa-tion in political life; most recently, reform has begun to address the core issues of the development of a legitimate, law-governed society. We examine each phase of legal reform in turn.

Legal Glasnost'.   As with *glasnost'* generally, *glasnost'* in the realm of law has moved unevenly through various stages, and has dealt with issues ranging from attacking the privileged status of the political elite, to reexamining Soviet legal history, criticizing the performance of judicial and law enforcement agencies, and addressing crime and other social problems in a candid fashion.

A common theme of the anti-corruption campaign of 1985 and 1986 was the need for all officials to abide by the law, and the need to punish those who abuse their position for private gain or to obtain privileged treatment. Charges of official corruption were published in national and local newspapers throughout the USSR, and resulted in the firing, or forced resignation, of as many as half the regional and local party first secretaries.

Legal *glasnost'* also entails the reexamination of Soviet legal history, in particular the abuses of the Stalin and Brezhnev regimes. In his speech on the eve of the seventieth anniversary of the Revolution, Gorbachev acknowledged that legal abuses during the Stalin era resulted in "many thousands of victims." He added: "The guilt of Stalin and his immediate entourage before the Party and the people for the wholesale repressive measures and acts is enormous and unforgivable."[17] In May 1988, a televised documentary film showed scenes from the purge trials and included personal testimony from some of the survivors of Stalin's infamous Gulag.

Criticism of the Brezhnev era concentrated on the abuse of power for personal gain by Brezhnev, his family, and other members of the political elite. The most notorious case to come to light involved Yuri Churbanov, the son-in-law of the late Leonid Brezhnev, who pleaded guilty to abusing his office as USSR Deputy Minister of Internal Affairs. Churbanov and eight of his colleagues were convicted in December 1988 of accepting bribes worth 415,000 rubles. He was sentenced to twelve years' imprisonment.[18]

The attack on official corruption, begun in 1985, was soon expanded to official meddling in the activities of the courts, the police, and other judicial agencies. In his address to the Twenty-Seventh Party Congress, Gorbachev stressed the need to safeguard the principles of judicial independence and equality of citizens before the law.

Exposés of "telephone justice" were published, illustrating the degree to which party and government officials intruded into the activities of the courts. For example, in a 1988 survey of 120 judges, 60 reported that within the past year they had been approached by a party or governmental official with a suggestion as to how to decide a particular case.[19] Soviet sources indicate that party officials intervene in 10 to 12 percent of all cases.[20]

In an interview with the Austrian communist newspaper *Volksstimme* soon after the Twenty-Seventh Party Congress, RSFSR Minister of Justice Aleksandr Sukharev called for insuring the equality before the criminal courts of members of the CPSU and citizens who are not members of the Party.[21] This was just the first salvo in a campaign by jurists to lessen party influence in the determination of cases, and to prevent preferential treatment of party members in criminal cases.

In 1986, the Procurator-General charged that certain local party officials consider themselves "above the law."[22] He urged local prosecutors to "stay within the strict framework of the law" in their efforts to combat crime.[23] He added: "Law guarantees inviolability of the individual and of citizens' homes, and a comprehensive, full, and objective investigation" of crime.

In a widely read article in *Literaturnaya gazeta* in May 1986, Arkadii Vaksberg criticized judicial irregularities and the failure of many judicial officers to observe proper legal procedures.[24] Citing numerous accounts of judicial misconduct, Vaksberg concluded that there are too many Soviet lawyers making "legal mistakes" for the irregularities to be regarded as merely "atypical."[25]

In the past six years, numerous exposés have appeared in nationally circulated newspapers and magazines concerning interference in criminal investigations by local party and government officials, fabrication of evidence, erroneous application of the death penalty, and other miscarriages of justice and due process violations.[26] The most notorious case was the Vitebsk Affair, in which a man was wrongly accused, and sentenced to death, for the rape and murder of several dozen women over a fifteen-year period. Fortunately, another man being held on other charges confessed to the murders before the death sentence was carried out. A follow-up investigation found that prosecutors and investigators were under considerable pressure from local party officials to solve the case, and had used "illegal methods" to obtain evidence and testimony. According to an editorial commentary in *Literaturnaya gazeta,* the case was not unusual.[27]

In mid-1986, local and regional party officials mounted a counteroffensive against *glasnost'*, especially as it related to criticism of their performance. Scattered attempts were made to intimidate the press or suppress critical reports.[28]

One of the most significant areas in which *glasnost'* has influenced Soviet legality has been in the reporting of crime and crime statistics. Criminal activity that was routinely hushed up by the authorities is now being reported. Reports of organized crime have been particularly prominent.[29] Racketeering, embezzling, and protection schemes, frequently involving party and Komsomol members, have also been exposed.[30]

In his first year or two in office, Gorbachev did not set out to reform the Soviet legal system in a systematic way. Rather, his policy of *glasnost'* was employed principally to increase the accountability of party, state, and economic officials, and to root out the corruption that had become so pervasive during "the period of stagnation."

Legal Perestroika.   Having created an atmosphere in which legal violations could be openly discussed and criticized, Gorbachev proceeded to utilize legal measures to realize his economic reform objectives. The thrust of Gorbachev's reform initiatives from 1985 until the Nineteenth Party Conference in 1988 centered on reconstructing the Soviet economy in order to stimulate economic performance, improve the technological level of production, increase efficiency in utilization of resources, and reinstitute work discipline. Not surprisingly, then, the largest portion of new legislation introduced during this period came in the area of economic law.

On February 8, 1987, *Pravda* published a new draft Law on the State Enterprise.[31] The law called for the election of enterprise directors, and also made enterprises self-financed. Prices remained centrally set, however. The law also provided for unprofitable enterprises to be declared insolvent and closed. The Law on the State Enterprise, thus, incorporated many of Gorbachev's early economic reform goals, giving them formal legal structure.

One of the most persistent problems in the Soviet economy has been underutilization of labor reserves. With projections for a serious decline in the growth rate of the Soviet labor force by the year 2000, the Gorbachev administration moved quickly to attempt to rationalize the assignment of workers within the economy. On September 12, 1985, *Pravda* published a joint decree of the USSR Council of Ministers and the Central Council of Trade Unions on "work place attestation."[32] The aim of the decree was to curb labor hoarding by Soviet enterprises. The decree also encouraged enterprises to scrap obsolete equipment.

New legislation was also introduced in 1985 and 1986 to step up supervision and punishment of economic crimes, including poor work discipline, substandard production, theft of state property, and intoxication in the workplace. On July 1, 1986, a decree of the Presidium of the USSR Supreme Soviet went into force that increased the financial liability of workers for damages caused by them to the enterprise in which they work.[33]

In 1986 the Gorbachev leadership also launched a vigorous campaign against black market activities and organized crime. On May 23, 1986, the Presidium of the Supreme Soviet adopted a decree "On Intensifying the Struggle against Derivation of Non-Labor Incomes."[34] The decree increased penalties for the unauthorized use of state-owned vehicles, machinery, or equipment. The maximum fine was raised from 30 rubles to 100 rubles, and to 200 rubles for officials. Article 156 of the RSFSR Administrative Code was stiffened with regard to the illegal use or expropriation of state property, tools, and equipment, and failure to report income derived from handicrafts or "after-hours labor."[35] A new clause was added to Article 157 of the Administrative Code, applicable to persons engaged in a prohibited trade (e.g., black-marketeers). The decree also increased criminal liability for taking bribes.

In 1987 and 1988 several other new enactments redefined ownership and property rights in the USSR. The Law on Joint Ventures, for the first time since the Revolution, enabled foreign corporations to own capital assets in the Soviet Union. In June 1988, the Supreme Soviet passed the Law on Co-operatives with the intent of stimulating private economic activity.

Two decrees relating to agriculture were published in the Soviet press on September 25, 1987.[36] The first decree related to the *podriad* (contract) system of assignment and remuneration, and called for placing all farms and food enterprises on full self-financing by 1988–1989. The second degree sought to stimulate production on private plots and to incorporate this production into the general economy. Both decrees were consistent with Gorbachev's stated desire to expand the realm of private initiative in the food and consumer goods sectors.

The most significant piece of new legislation to appear to date in the field of agriculture is the new draft Model *Kolkhoz* Statute, which was announced on January 10, 1988.[37] The draft statute called for greater farm autonomy, transition to self-financing by 1988–1989, and self-management. Under the provisions of the statute, members of *kolkhozes* have been granted a greater degree of participation in the affairs of the collective, including the right to select chairmen and set their salaries. Private plots of *kolkhoz* members are no longer limited in size, nor is the number of livestock that members may keep. The new statute is clearly an attempt to bring collective farm law into conformance with the Law on the State Enterprise by granting farm workers the same participatory rights enjoyed by industrial workers.[38]

Legal Democratization. From mid-1988 until early 1990, the pace of economic reforms slowed, and emphasis in Gorbachev's activities shifted to the political arena. While Gorbachev championed competitive elections, and succeeded in establishing a more powerful presidency, economic problems continued to fester. In large part, the economic crisis confronting the Soviet Union by early 1990 was a product of the reform policies themselves. Gorbachev's economic reforms succeeded, in large measure, in dismantling the centrally planned economy, yet the reforms have been sufficiently limited and compromised that a market system has been unable to fill the void.

While the past six years have witnessed a flurry of new legislation to implement Gorbachev's ambitious economic *perestroika,* changes in the legal system itself have been much more modest. "Legal democratization" entails a radical overhauling of the Soviet legal system, with a goal of creating a socialist *rechtstaat.** The most dramatic changes to date have occurred with the recent legal amendments and new legislation relating to competitive elections, and the elimination of Article 6 from the Constitution, which fundamentally altered the nature of the Soviet political system. By contrast, the laws defining the Soviet legal system have remained largely unchanged. Some new legislation has been introduced to enhance the independence of the courts, to strengthen the role of defense attorneys, and to expand citizens' redress against officials. Although these developments are encouraging, they do not amount to a fundamental restructuring of the Soviet legal system.

In December 1988, constitutional amendments were enacted creating a Constitutional Supervision Committee.[39] The Constitutional Supervision Committee is composed of twenty-three specialists in politics and law, who are selected by the Congress of People's Deputies to serve ten-year terms.[40] The Committee may consider an issue only when it is requested to do so by a governmental body, or on its own initiative, but not by petition of individual citizens. If the Committee finds that the Constitution has been violated by a statutory act adopted by the Congress of People's Deputies, or by a provision of a constitution of a union republic, that finding does not suspend the act. However, such an determination mandates that the dispute be brought before the next session of the Congress of People's Deputies, and if it disagrees with the Committee's finding by a two-thirds vote, then the act remains in force. Otherwise, it is revoked. All other statutory acts that the Committee finds to be in conflict with the USSR Constitution are suspended, and either referred to their originating body for revision, or brought before the Congress of People's Deputies for consideration. While the Constitutional Supervision

---

* *Rechtstaat* is a society governed by the rule of law.

Committee falls short of a fully functioning constitutional court, it does make some effort to translate constitutional provisions into legally protected rights.

Several measures have been introduced in recent years to minimize party and government interference with the courts. In 1988, Article 155 of the Constitution was amended to strengthen the language pertaining to judicial independence.[41] The Law on the Status of Judges, passed in 1989, makes it a criminal offense, punishable by up to three years' incarceration, to exert pressure in any form on a judge or people's assessor "with the intent of impeding a complete, full and objective handling of a particular case, or of securing an unlawful court decision."[42] (The law does not apply to attempts to influence police, investigators, procurators, or advocates, however.)

The procedure for selecting judges has also been altered in an attempt to insulate judges from political pressures in their respective regions. Judicial terms have been increased from five to ten years, and judges are now selected by the soviet at the next higher level of government. The nomination of judges has been removed from the province of the Party and vested in judicial selection panels comprised of judges chosen for a five-year term by judges at the regional level.[43]

Another mechanism for establishing the independence of the court is to expand the powers and number of people's assessors (lay judges). Considerable debate has been aired in legal journals during the past three years on whether to expand the number of people's assessors or adopt the jury system. In November 1989 the Supreme Soviet established a jury system for the most serious criminal cases—those for which the penalty is death or incarceration for more than ten years.[44] People's assessors are retained for less serious cases.

Some promising changes have also been introduced or discussed in relation to criminal law and procedure. Over the past several years there has been a trend toward the decriminalization of minor offenses, and an increasing willingness of procurators to halt criminal investigations before trial. In 1988 criminal prosecutions fell by approximately 30 percent.[45] The draft Fundamental Principles of Criminal Law, circulated in 1988, called for the decriminalization of several minor crimes and victimless offenses.

Sentencing and corrections practices are also being reexamined. There is a growing awareness among social workers, juvenile affairs officers, the courts, police, and prosecutors that incarceration in a correctional institution may further corrupt, rather than rehabilitate, some kinds of offenders.

Progress to date in developing a state governed by the rule of law has been impressive when viewed against Russian and Soviet legal traditions. The numerous legislative acts designed to bolster the independence of the courts, coupled with the establishment of an independent organization to represent defense attorneys, indicates progress toward achieving the requisites of a *rechtstaat* cited earlier. It is still too early, however, to assess whether these changes will, in fact, insure judicial independence and equality before the law. For such concepts to take root, they must become institutionalized and inculcated into the legal culture of a society.

A disturbing countervailing trend is also apparent today. In late 1990, the President was granted wide-ranging emergency powers, including the power to declare martial law in cases of civil emergencies, and the power to ban disturbances of the public order, including strikes, demonstrations, publications, movements, and organizations that pursue "militant and anticonstitutional goals." The President can also impose "temporary presidential rule" over particular regions or republics, suspending the authority of their governments, revoking their legislation, and dissolving their parliaments. In May 1990 the Supreme Soviet passed a law which imposes criminal penalties of up to six years in prison for publicly insulting the President. The future development of a civil society in the USSR will depend on these harsh measures' being used only rarely and in extreme situations.

Perhaps the area in which the least progress has been made in Gorbachev's "legal democratization" is in elevating the rights of the individual vis-à-vis those of the State. Commenting in an *Izvestiya* roundtable discussion on the role of the individual in a reformed legal system, Valerii Savitsky of the Institute of State and Law noted that the Soviet Union still had not developed a system in which individual rights take precedence.

SOVIET LEGAL INSTITUTIONS

That the concepts of social justice and the rule of law are prominent today in the USSR reflects the increasing role of jurists in the policy-making process. Legal policy in the Soviet Union is formulated by numerous agencies, bureaucracies, and groups, each representing particular interests. Generally, the interests that come into play in the formulation of legal policy in the Soviet Union coincide with the various occupations and specialties within the legal profession. Thus, the police and other organs of social control are generally proponents of a tough "law and order" stance, while defense lawyers and criminologists tend to favor a less rigid policy. The occupational differences within the Soviet legal profession are accentuated by the existence of large bureaucracies that enjoy a degree of independence from the CPSU and that have identifiable institutional interests on policy questions. They create a sense of common professional identity, frequently enhanced by a shared set of values developed in uniform, specialized training. These bureaucratic groups also maintain some form of access to public opinion, through which their interests can be voiced.[46] For example, the views of Soviet prosecutors are expressed in the Procuracy's journal, *Sotsialisticheskaya zakonnost'* (Socialist Legality), while the interests of judges are presented in the journal of the RSFSR Ministry of Justice, *Sovetskaya yustitsiya* (Soviet Justice).

The development of a strong identification of occupational interests is fostered by a high degree of career stability among Soviet jurists. For example, 30 percent of all prosecutors have worked for the Procuracy for three to ten years, and 50 percent have worked for more than ten years.[47] More than half of all advocates have at least ten years of experience in the *advokatura*, while more than 75 percent of all judges have been working in that capacity for five years or more.[48]

Finally, the bureaucracies representing the occupational interests of Soviet jurists provide each group with an "official presence" in the policy-making process. Some, such as the Procuracy and the Ministry of Internal

Affairs, have representatives in the Central Committee, the Security Council, the Supreme Soviet, or other influential policy-making bodies. The bureaucracies involved in legal policy implementation also include among their numbers many party members, who communicate information relevant to policy-making up through the Party's ranks.

Jurists have also been in the forefront of the reform movement. Several jurists have been elected to the Congress of People's Deputies and currently serve in the Supreme Soviet. Prominent among the reform-oriented jurists is Anatoli Sobchak, the former Leningrad University law professor and now the mayor of Leningrad. While reformist jurists, such as Sobchak, have developed their own personal appeal and following, they lack the institutional or bureaucratic power base that would infuse their political ideas with real authority and power. We now examine the principal bureaucratic groups that are involved in legal policy-making and implementation, noting their general stance on legal reform in the USSR.

The Procuracy.   By far the most powerful institution in the Soviet administration of justice is the Procuracy, the hierarchical organization representing all public prosecutors, from the city or village level up to the Procurator-General of the USSR. The Procuracy's central position in the administration of justice derives from its wide range of functions pertaining to criminal and administrative matters. The procurator is involved at every stage in the criminal process. The arrest of a suspect and the search for evidence require the procurator's written authorization. In Soviet criminal procedure, the prosecution of cases proceeds through two stages: preliminary investigation, and trial. The procurator participates in both stages. In most cases, investigators are procuratorial officials. Also falling within the realm of procuratorial action are the review or appeal of criminal and civil cases, the supervision of prisons, prisoner complaints, parole, and the release of prisoners; the supervision of actions of the police and secret police; the supervision of juvenile commissions; and the supervision of the legal operation of all government bodies, enterprises, officials, and social organizations. This latter function, the supervision of administrative and economic officials and bodies, resembles that of the Swedish ombudsman.[49]

The Procuracy employs approximately 15,000 lawyers, or almost 12 percent of the legal profession.[50] Supervised by the Procuracy are another 18,000 investigators, comprising over 14 percent of the legal profession.[51] The power of the Procuracy does not derive soley from its size or extensive functions in the legal system. Procurators also enjoy the greatest prestige of any legal occupation. N. S. Aleksandrov, former Dean of the Juridical Faculty of Leningrad University, reported that most law students want to become procurators.[52] Traditionally, the top law students in each graduating class go to work for the Procuracy, while less-distinguished graduates become jurisconsults, advocates, or judges—in that order. In addition to having a procuratorial journal, the Procuracy can express its institutional interests through the Procurator-General, the only practicing jurist represented in the CPSU Central Committee.

The Procuracy was the target of extensive public criticism in 1986 and 1987. Charges were made of fabrication of evidence, erroneous application of the death penalty, and other miscarriages of justice by procuratorial officials. In June 1987 the CPSU Central Committee criticized the Procuracy for failing to stem large-scale theft, bribery, falsification of plan reports and other deceptive practices within the Procuracy. The Procuracy was granted broader powers to issue binding directives, to suspend unlawful acts, and to enforce economic legislation.

Following on the heels of the restructuring of the Procuracy was a shake-up in its higher echelons. In February 1988, the Procurator-General A. Rekunkov was replaced by A. Ya. Sukharev, Minister of Justice of the Russian Republic. The fact that Gorbachev brought in an outsider indicates his intention of redirecting the Procuracy in support of economic *perestroika* and the protection of citizens' rights.

Advokatura. The Advokatura, or Soviet bar, is comprised of defense attorneys. Advocates are organized into "colleges" of about 150 lawyers each. These colleges maintain consultation bureaus in virtually every town and city throughout the Soviet Union. Each bureau has a staff of approximately twenty advocates.[53] Here Soviet citizens may seek legal advice on a vast array of questions: divorce, custody, inheritance, property rights, housing disputes, product liability complaints, labor conflicts, and so forth. The colleges also provide legal defense for people accused of criminal offenses. The Soviet Constitution, ratified in 1977, provides that a defendant is guaranteed the right to legal counsel and that legal assistance will be provided free of charge if the defendant cannot afford a lawyer.[54] As of September 1988, lawyers acquired the right to set their own legal fees. Prior to this change, fees were so low that advocates were forced to demand under-the-table payments, "gifts," and other "favors" in exchange for their services.

There are approximately 27,000 advocates in the Soviet Union.[55] Until February 1989 they were not represented by any professional organization. The creation of the Union of Advocates, however, for the first time gave defense attorneys a strong institutional basis for pressing their demands for legal reform. In particular, Soviet advocates want greater access rights to their clients early in criminal proceedings, as are provided by the Miranda ruling in the United States. Advocates also criticize the prosecutorial bias that results in defendants being found guilty in 99.7% of all case.[56] Finally, Soviet lawyers have called for the institution of the jury system. Their lobbying efforts have proven successful; in November 1989 the Supreme Soviet established a jury system for the most serious criminal offenses—those for which the penalty is death or incarceration for more than 10 years.[57] Thus, the Advokatura has become the most active and vocal supporter of legal reform.

The Judiciary. Any Soviet citizen who is at least twenty-five years old and possesses electoral rights can be nominated to the position of judge for a term of ten years. No prior legal experience or education is necessary. In practice, however, more than 95 percent of all judges have a higher legal education.[58]

Given the crucial role of the judge in the Soviet legal system, it is not surprising that until recently, the Party carefully screened all candidates for election to the bench. Virtually all Soviet judges above the local level were party members, and all judges fell under the Party's power of appointment, or *nomenklatura.*[59] Since 1989, the Party's influence over judges has been greatly reduced.

As in other civil-law systems, Soviet judges play an active part in judicial proceedings. They are the first to call for evidence, question witnesses, and cross-examine—before either the prosecution or the defense. Their function is not only to determine innocence or guilt, but also to educate the accused and all present in the courtroom. Soviet judges are an important instrument of socialization. When pronouncing sentence, judges often berate the accused for failing to uphold socialist values, for being drunk in public, or for setting a bad example for children.

In the court of first instance, one judge presides with the assistance of two people's assessors. People's assessors are ordinary citizens, elected at general meetings of factories, offices, collective farms, or residential blocs for a term of two years. Their function resembles that of a jury in a common-law system. They do not decide mere guilt or innocence, however, but are full, participating members of the bench with the right to call and question witnesses, examine evidence, and set punishment. All judicial decisions are voted on in closed chambers, so it is not known what impact people's assessors have on the courts' decisions. It is assumed that the judge's prestige and legal education are deciding factors in the resolution of cases. At the appellate level and above, where the questions under review are procedural or involve technical points of law, cases are decided by panels of professional judges. While people's assessors have little input into the policy process, Soviet judges are well-organized and are represented by the USSR Ministry of Justice and the fifteen public ministries.

The Police (Militia). The Soviet militia, or police, are charged with a wide array of duties: detecting crime, apprehending criminals, supervising the internal passport system, maintaining public order, combating public intoxication, supervising parolees, managing prisons and labor colonies, and controlling traffic. Since 1956, local police departments have been subject to dual subordination; consequently, they must report both to the executive committees of their respective local soviets and to their superior officers within the Ministry of Internal Affairs (MVD).

Local police departments are organized into several sections: Regular Police; Criminal Investigations; Theft of Socialist Property; Passports, Visas and Registrations (OVIR); Motor Vehicles; Preliminary Investigations and Prosecutions; and Recruitment and Training.

Early in the Gorbachev period, the militia played an active role in clamping down on corruption and violations of work discipline. More recently the police have been called upon to quell ethnic violence and ensure public safety in the face of an increasingly restive populace.

The KGB. The KGB is a massive organization, performing functions that, in the United States, fall within the purview of the Central Intelligence Agency, the FBI, the National Security Agency, and a number of other federal and state agencies. Western intelligence services estimate that the KGB employs over 90,000 staff officers and another 400,000 clerical staff, building guards, border guards, and special troops. The number of informants officially working in other organizations but cooperating with the KGB is probably several hundred thousand.[60] There are reported to be more than 250,000

KGB operatives working abroad.[61] In 1983, the FBI was said to be watching the activities of 450 Soviet spies operating in the United States under diplomatic cover.[62] However, the exact personnel strength of the KGB is impossible to determine from available information.

The KGB is headed by the chairman, who is an ex officio member of the Cabinet of Ministers. The Chairman of the KGB is assisted in his duties by a collegium, consisting of the chiefs of each of the agency's many directorates.

As a result of its size and complexity, the KGB is divided into several directorates, each with its own distinct responsibilities:

The First Chief Directorate is responsible for foreign operations, including clandestine activities abroad, and the theft or purchase of Western scientific, technical, and military-related hardware. The First Chief Directorate is also responsible for counterintelligence—that is, penetrating and neutralizing the activities of foreign security and intelligence services.

The Second Chief Directorate is generally responsible for monitoring the activities of Soviet citizens and foreigners within the Soviet Union.

The Third Directorate, one of the largest and most important units in the KGB, is usually referred to as the Armed Forces Directorate. It oversees the activities of military units through a network of agents in every echelon of the armed forces, down to the company level. KGB officers are responsible for the education and ideological training of the forces, and they also keep the Party informed about the reliability and loyalty of the troops.

The KGB has neither a Fourth nor a Sixth Directorate. There is no known reason for these omissions.

The Fifth Chief Directorate, created in 1969 to uncover and stamp out political dissent in the country, specialized in surveillance and infiltration of various ethnic, political, and religious groups in the USSR. The directorate was reorganized in 1989 and renamed the Administration for the Protection of the Constitutional Order, but it is unclear how this has affected the operations of this unit.[63]

The Seventh Directorate, or Surveillance Directorate, employs more than 3500 men and women whose sole occupation is to follow particular individuals in the USSR.

All foreign scholars in the USSR experience the attention of the Seventh Directorate at one time or another. During a stay as a research scholar at the Leningrad University Juridical Faculty, the author was followed periodically. Soon after arriving in Leningrad, he was befriended by an American family working in the United States consulate. On weekends, they often invited him to go cross-country skiing with them outside the city. The arrangements were usually confirmed by telephone, which was bugged both in the author's dormitory and in the consulate. The Americans usually were accompanied on these ski outings by a dull grey sedan carrying one or two KGB agents. Uncertain as to the Americans' true plans, the KGB "tails" would wear business suits and overcoats, but would also bring along skis. The image of KGB agents huffing and puffing on their skis to keep pace with the Americans was more comical than sinister. After one especially arduous afternoon of skiing, the author and his friends bought some beer at a nearby kiosk and left two bottles in a snowbank for their lagging companions.

Although there is rarely face-to-face contact, a rapport sometimes develops between the KGB tails and their assignments. Western diplomats have reported that KGB agents following them have assisted them in changing flat tires or making emergency auto repairs. In a few cases, KGB surveillance has even prevented Westerners from being mugged or having their automobiles stolen.

The Eighth Directorate, or Communications Directorate, specializes in intelligence-gathering by "national technical means": satellites, "fishing trawlers" monitoring United States naval operations, and sophisticated devices placed on top of Soviet embassies and consulates in most Western capitals. The Ninth Directorate, or Kremlin Guards, comprises a body of elite troops that function as bodyguards for prominent Soviet officials. The Kremlin Guards are the only individuals in the Soviet military allowed to carry loaded weapons in the presence of political leaders.

In addition to these directorates, the KGB maintains four unnumbered directorates. The Border Guards Chief Directorate patrols Soviet borders to prevent not only the unauthorized entry of foreign agents into the Soviet Union but also, more importantly, the unauthorized exit of Soviet citizens. The Technical Operations Directorate is responsible for researching, designing, and manufacturing the various gadgets used in spying. The Personnel Directorate recruits and trains KGB employees, while the Administration Directorate handles travel arrangements, the management of property, resorts, and apartments, and other routine functions.

Recruits to the KGB tend to be well-educated, white-collar professionals, often from families in which a parent is already working in the agency. Midcareer entry into the KGB from other organizations is rare.[64] Thus, the KGB has become a closed bureaucracy of specialists. The one exception remains at the highest ranks of the agency, where the political appointment of party officials is considered necessary to ensure control by the CPSU over the security police.

Employment in the KGB has obvious advantages, including good pay, travel opportunities, and numerous other perquisites. For example, the starting salaries of law-school graudates entering the KGB are two to three times higher than those of their classmates working in other legal agencies.[65] KGB employees also have access to special stores, where there is an abundance of goods unavailable to the general public. The agency also maintains social clubs and resorts that feature the finest foods and most luxurious accommodations in the USSR.

Under the influence of *glasnost'*, the KGB has come under unprecedented criticism and public scrutiny. In January 1987, the head of the KGB acknowledged his agency's unlawful persecution of a journalist who had exposed safety violations in Ukrainian coal mines. A Leningrad reporter turned the tables on the KGB by following one of its agents for a day and then reporting on his activities in a popular Leningrad newspaper. The activities of the KGB have also been the target of critical debates in the Supreme Soviet.

As the KGB struggled to repair its image and adjust to the more open political environment, in early 1990 it was rocked with a scandal of unprecedented proportions. A KGB Major-General, Oleg Kalugin, head of KGB counterintelligence in the 1970s, wrote an article in *Argumenty i fakty* exposing the extent of KGB infiltration of groups such as the Russian Orthodox church.[66] Kalugin argued that the KGB existed as an unchecked "state within a state" and warned of the agency's plans to undermine *perestroika*. Kalugin was stripped of his rank and criminal charges were brought against him, but his popularity among average citizens carried him to office in the local elections of 1990.

Other Jurists.   Among the remaining legal specialties, two deserve special note—jurisconsults and legal scholars. Jurisconsults are legal advisors who act as counsel to governmental agencies and departments, enterprises, factories, and state farms. Approximately 29,000 jurisconsults work in the Soviet economy. Although they constitute the single largest segment of the Soviet legal profession, they are not organized into a centralized bureaucracy and do not display any professional cohesion. Rather, jurisconsults tend to identify their own personal and career interests with the interests of the institutions in which they work, so much so that they are periodically criticized and sometimes prosecuted for covering up illegalities in the agencies and enterprises with which they are affiliated.[67]

Legal scholars in the Soviet Union number approximately 3500. For the most part, they are affiliated with universities or juridical institutes that train jurists. Some juridical scholars are also affiliated with the Ministry of Justice, the Procuracy's Institute for the Study of the Causes and Prevention of Crime, the Institute for the Improvement of Soviet Legislation, or the Institute of State and Law of the Academy of Sciences.

Although legal scholars do not have a distinct organization to represent their interests, they enjoy a high level of group awareness. This is partly the result of the frequent interaction among members of the scholarly community through symposia, conferences, and numerous legal journals and periodicals. The opinions of Soviet jurists are respected and sought after by policymakers, especially in drafting new legislation.

LAW AND THE CONSTITUTION OF THE USSR

The present Constitution of the USSR is the fourth such document to be ratified since the October Revolution of 1917. The first constitution of the Russian Soviet Federated Socialist Republic was enacted in 1918 in order to consolidate the victories of the Bolsheviks. The document stressed the revolutionary nature of the society, specified the rights of the "toilers and exploited peoples," placed all power in the soviets, abolished private ownership of the land, and established the fulfillment of socialism as the immediate goal of the society.

The incorporation of new territories into the republic during and after the Civil War led to the formal adoption of a federation in 1922 and, thus, to the need for a new constitution. That document, ratified in 1924, differed from its predecessor primarily in specifying and differentiating the powers of federal bodies and the powers of the constituent republics.

The "Stalin Constitution," ratified in 1936, redefined the USSR as "a socialist state of workers and peasants" and enshrined the CPSU as "vanguard." It reaffirmed socialist ownership of the means of production and created the Supreme Soviet (consisting of two houses) to replace the Congress of Soviets.

During Khrushchev's de-Stalinization drive, Soviet jurists began to urge the ratification of a new constitution that would reflect the achievements of the USSR and also would further extend the notion of citizens' rights. A drafting commission was established in 1962, but the new constitution was not ratified until 1977, in honor of the sixtieth anniversary of the Bolshevik Revolution. The 1977 Constitution does not differ radically from its predecessors; in fact, the preamble stresses the continuity of Soviet law. The document defines the USSR as a "socialist state of all the people" and formally recognizes the CPSU as "the leading and guiding force in Soviet society."[68]

A flurry of constitutional amendments have been incorporated in recent years, reflecting the changes instituted by the Gorbachev leadership. Most notable was the abolition of Article 6, which guaranteed the CPSU a monopoly role in the political process. Other changes recognized the newly established governmental bodies and positions—the Congress of People's Deputies, the Supreme Soviet, the Constitutional Supervision Committee, and the Presidency. More changes are also likely to appear in those sections of the constitution defining the powers of the union-republics and other ethnic regions, as well as Article 72, granting union-republics the right of secession.

The Constitution of the USSR plays a fundamentally different role in the Soviet legal system than, for instance, the United States Constitution does in the American system. The Soviet Constitution embodies the highest statement of the goals and principles of the Soviet system of government. It defines the powers of various state bodies, including the soviets at all levels, the Cabinet of Ministers, the courts, the Procuracy, and other state bodies. Unlike the United States Constitution, however, the Constitution in the USSR is not a binding legal document in the sense that its articles are cited in court determinations. Constitutional provisions in the Soviet Union have legal force only when they are implemented in one of the codes of law of the various republics. Many constitutional provisions remain unrealized, due to the absence of implementing legislation. For example, Article 58 states: "Actions of officials that contravene the law or exceed their powers, and infringe the rights of citizens, may be appealed in a court in the manner prescribed by law."[69] However, no code of administrative law was adopted to implement the provisions of this "guarantee" for more than ten years. Finally in 1987 the Supreme Soviet enacted the Law on Appeals, which expanded citizens' rights to seek judicial review of grievances against government agencies and officials.

CRIME IN THE USSR

According to Marx, crime is the manifestation of class antagonisms. With the abolition of classes under socialism, all crime should vanish. While crime has not vanished entirely in the USSR today, certain types of criminal activity are much less prevalent than in Western societies. Comparing crime rates is, however, difficult because until recent years crime statistics in the

Soviet Union were considered "state secrets." Nevertheless, there appear to be far fewer robberies, murders, and other violent crimes in Soviet cities than in the United States. Strict gun control, the threat of harsh punishment, the omnipresent police, and the low incidence of drug abuse largely account for this. There is also less monetary incentive for violent crime in the USSR than in the West. Until the recent devaluation of the ruble and price hikes, Soviet citizens had ample amounts of money; consequently, there is less motivation to commit robbery. The theft of desirable consumer goods is quite common, however, because they are in great demand and difficult to obtain legally.

Soviet sources indicate that between 80 and 85 percent of all violent crimes are committed under the influence of alcohol, and most of these crimes involve family members, close friends, or neighbors.[70] Committing a crime under the influence of alcohol is not a mitigating factor, according to Soviet law, but an aggravating factor. Alcohol abuse, which is widespread in the USSR, is listed as the primary cause of almost three-fourths of all divorces.[71] Overcrowded housing conditions combined with alcohol abuse often results in domestic violence.

Anonymous street crime is much less frequent in the Soviet Union than in other societies, although increasingly there are reports in the Soviet press of youth gangs attacking total strangers on the street "simply for something to do."[72] Juveniles account for approximately 12 percent of all murders, 22 percent of all robberies, 59 percent of all burglaries, and 49 percent of all rapes.[73] The portrait of the juvenile offender in the USSR does not differ greatly from that in other societies: the offender is usually male, lives in a city, comes from a broken home, and undertakes delinquent acts while under the influence of alcohol and as a member of a group. School dropouts are twenty-four times more likely to engage in criminal activity than are juveniles who remain in school. Similarly, youths who come from homes in which violence is common are nine to ten times more likely to become juvenile offenders.[74] A Soviet sociological study of juvenile offenders found that three-quarters were introduced to alcohol in the home—almost half before the age of thirteen.[75] As a rite of passage around the age of twelve or thirteen, a boy is expected to split a bottle of vodka with his father to celebrate becoming a man.

As Soviet society becomes increasingly urban, the traditional family structure is breaking down. Grandparents, who were traditionally responsible for child-rearing and supervision, are now often left in the countryside. In urban areas today, fewer than 15 percent of all families have a grandparent living in the home.[76] Approximately 80 percent of all women work, often leaving school-aged children to fend for themselves after school. (Russian men are notorious for failing to assume any household tasks, including child care.) Furthermore, the high incidence of divorce—surpassing 50 percent in some cities—results in large numbers of juveniles without fathers in the home, as women almost always get custody in divorce cases. Pioneer and Komsomol organizations try to fill the void by sponsoring afterschool activities, but these programs do not seem to appeal to crime-prone youth.

While violent crime is not as common as in many Western societies, economic crime is widespread. With the average salary of a Russian only 270 rubles per month, many workers consider it their "right" to steal from their employer. The best-quality merchandise is routinely saved under the counter for family and friends in exchange for "gifts" ranging from vodka to money. Automobile assembly-line workers supplement their incomes by stealing spare parts and selling them on the black market. (There are few spare-parts stores in the USSR, and thus headlights, taillights, antifreeze, and windshield wipers are in great demand.) As meat shortages became more prevalent in the early 1980s, some Soviet engineers and technicians reportedly left their posts in research and design bureaus and took menial jobs in cafeterias, restaurants, and other food establishments. The reason? In the research and design bureaus, there is nothing worth stealing, whereas in the food industry, one can always take home a shank of ham in a lunch pail.

The leadership has repeatedly launched campaigns against the theft of state property, but the campaigns only curtail the activity temporarily, they do not stamp it out altogether. Persons who are tried, found guilty, and given criminal penalties tend to be high-ranking party or state officials engaged in grand-scale theft of state property. In most cases, an employee apprehended for petty theft—stealing yarn from a textile factory or meat from a butcher shop—would receive a warning from a comrades' court, a small fine, or, at most, dismissal. With widespread public acceptance of petty theft, mild penalties, and the small chance of detection, there is little likelihood that the theft of state property will end soon.

PUNISHMENT AND REHABILITATION OF OFFENDERS

Marxist-Leninist ideology is perhaps more evident in sentencing and corrections than anywhere else in the Soviet legal system. Soviet ideology stresses state property over private property, and this is reflected in criminal law. The maximum sentence for the theft of personal property is two years; the maximum sentence for the theft of state property is three years.[77] Negligent destruction of private property may be punished by deprivation of freedom for a term of up to one year, while the term extends to three years for the negligent destruction of state property.[78]

Some activities that are normal in other societies are illegal and strictly punished in the USSR for ideological reasons. According to Marxist-Leninist doctrine, charging interest, speculation, and profiteering are all means of obtaining "unearned income" and are, therefore, exploitative. Speculation is defined as "buying up and reselling goods for the purpose of making a profit" and can result in a prison term of two years, confiscation of property, and a fine of 30 rubles.[79] The penalty for speculation on a grand scale is two to seven years. With all the talk of creating a market economy and stimulating entrepreneurial activity, it is curious that such legal provisions have not been revised.

Article 154-1 of the Criminal Code of the RSFSR illustrates one of the more Kafkasque aspects of the Soviet planned economy. In the USSR, the price of bread is artificially kept low in order to make it affordable for the average citizen. The price of feed for chickens and livestock, by contrast, is quite high. Consequently, many Soviet citizens buy bread to feed their animals on their private land plots. Article 154-1 was introduced in 1963 specifically to stop this practice. A fine is levied for the first offense, but for subsequent offenses the penalty may include up to one year of deprivation of freedom.

The maximum sentence for a first-time offender in the USSR is fifteen years, but for most crimes the sentence is no more than seven years. Soviet jurists are highly critical of Western legal systems that routinely mete out life sentences. One prominent jurist exclaimed, "How can you say that you have a system of *corrections* in the United States when you lock up prisoners for life?" By Soviet logic, fifteen years should be adequate time to rehabilitate a criminal.

Soviet law allows for the parole or conditional release of prisoners who have served as little as one-half of their sentences. Parole with compulsory work assignments can also be awarded after serving just one-third of the sentence. In addition, periodic amnesties are granted, usually commemorating a political holiday. In 1970, for instance, the sentences for most inmates were reduced in honor of the hundredth anniversary of Lenin's birth. In 1979, a selective amnesty was announced for many categories of female and juvenile inmates in honor of the International Year of the Child. Presumably, amnesties are intended to underscore socialist values. By releasing a prisoner early in honor of Lenin's birth or some other patriotic event, it is hoped that the former inmate will be more supportive of the Soviet system and the values it seeks to uphold.

The death penalty, by shooting, is applied in the USSR in cases of treason, espionage, terrorist acts, sabotage, and intentional homicide committed under aggravating circumstances (e.g., murder for profit, murder to cover up a previous crime, murder of a pregnant woman, or especially brutal murder). Capital punishment has also occasionally been employed to punish state or party officials in extreme cases of theft of state property. Party and state officials are expected to be model Soviet citizens. If they abuse their positions of public trust for their own profit, they are severely punished. For instance, in 1985, the head bookkeeper of a construction firm in the Ukraine was accused of forming a criminal conspiracy with a number of stores in Kiev to steal state property. Over a period of years, the group systematically embezzled more than 327,000 rubles (almost $225,000). The Kiev *oblast'* criminal court sentenced the bookkeeper to death. His accomplices were sentenced to long terms in labor colonies.[80] Press accounts in 1987 of the erroneous application of the death penalty, however, brought an end to executions for economic crimes.[81] The criminal code is currently being revised, and it is likely that the range of capital offenses will be reduced.

The ideological emphasis on the value of labor is reflected in corrections and the punishment of criminals. Few prisons exist in the Soviet Union, and they are only for hardened criminals who are too dangerous to be supervised at the normal labor colonies. The majority of inmates in the USSR serve their sentences in labor camps that are stratified in terms of degree of security, difficulty of work, quantity and quality of food, and privileges. For example, one Soviet source indicates that in a strict-regime camp (maximum security), inmates are expected to work in difficult jobs (frequently involving outdoor work such as construction, lumbering, mining, and so on). At a medium-security facility, the work is usually indoors, and the ration consists of bread, salt, and water with one hot meal every other day.[82] Inmates may be transferred from one regime facility to another as a reward for good behavior. Infringement of the rules of the labor colony can also prolong the sentence of an inmate or even result in a transfer to a stricter-regime facility. Thus, there is every incentive for the inmate to cooperate with the camp authorities. The Soviet correctional system has an astonishingly high success rate. Only 25 to 33 percent of all inmates repeat offenses, compared to more than 70 percent in the United States.[83]

THE EDUCATIONAL ROLE OF SOVIET LAW

As in other societies, law in the USSR both guides and punishes. Whether it is emphasizing the rehabilitation of offenders or communicating a "moral lesson" by imposing harsh penalties on officials guilty of abusing their positions for private gain, the Soviet legal system is designed to play an educational role. Law is a teacher; it conveys and enforces societal values and channels behavior into acceptable norms and patterns. As Harold Berman notes, a paternalistic strain marks Soviet law and practice:

> The subject of law, legal man, is treated less as an independent possessor of rights and duties, who knows what he wants, than as a dependent member of the collective group, a youth, whom the law must not only protect against the consequences of his own ignorance, but also must guide and train and discipline. . . . It is apparent that the Soviet emphasis on the educational role of law presupposes a new conception of man. The Soviet citizen is considered to be a member of a growing, unfinished, still immature society, which is moving toward a new and higher phase of development. As a subject of law, or a litigant in court, he is like a child or youth to be trained, guided, disciplined, protected. The judge plays the part of a parent or guardian; indeed, the whole legal system is parental."[84]

Paternalism is not a recent development in Soviet law. In 1917, D. I. Kurskii, Lenin's Commissar of Justice, remarked, "It does not matter that many points in our decrees will never be carried out; their task is to teach the masses how to take practical steps."[85] Soviet law, apart from governing the interactions of citizens and the relation of their rights and duties, is concerned with the development of citizens' moral well-being and their law-consciousness.

The dual purpose of Soviet law—to punish and to educate—surfaces in various concrete legal policies. In 1957, for example, Khrushchev initiated "antiparasite" laws aimed at those profiting from the fringe economy: prostitution, begging, vagrancy, private speculation, and other sources of "unearned income." Any able-bodied adult who was found leading an "antisocial, parasitic way of life" could be brought before a general meeting of townspeople and banished. Proceedings were neither trials nor the actions of a court; as such, they were condemned by many jurists as inconsistent with the concepts of "rule of law" and socialist legality. Proponents argued, however, that the parasite laws and their method of enforcement pointed toward realization of the utopian Marxist notion of the withering away of the institutions of the State.

Antiparasite legislation was introduced in nine republics, none of them major republics. With the exception of Latvia, parasite laws were not enacted in any of the European republics of the USSR, where Western traditions of law are more ingrained. While jurists appear to have been unable to alter the draft parasite laws, their objections were heeded in the major republics.

The parasite laws have become eclipsed by another significant legal development in the late 1950s—the codification of fundamental principles of criminal law and criminal procedure. A trend toward the "juridization" of law swept Soviet jurisprudence, enhancing the role of established legal institutions and the legal profession. Hereafter, the concern with fringe elements in Soviet society became relegated to the general area of criminal law. On May 4, 1961, the RSFSR enacted a decree on parasitism that subsequently served as a model for similar legislation in most of the other republics. The decree gave jurisdiction over parasite cases to the criminal courts, bypassing the comrades' courts, which could give only light sentences. Also spurned in the legislation were the public meetings of residential units. For cases of parasitism, the new legislation specified punishments of two to five years of exile with compulsory labor.

In the first six months after the enactment of the decree, there were at least 600 convictions.[86] Of those convicted in 1961, more than half received sentences of four or five years.[87] Despite this harsh policy, there apparently was considerable selectivity in enforcement and prosecution, even during a time of increasingly strident public campaigns against parasites. In the first half of 1961, approximately 96 percent of all parasites were given warnings only; they were never prosecuted, because they heeded the warnings and found proper work.[88]

The case of the antiparasite legislation illustrates several aspects of the Soviet legal system. The antiparasite laws were originally initiated to punish antisocial behavior and to socialize Soviet citizens by enlisting their assistance in combating parasitism and hooliganism. In time, however, the professional legal establishment exerted its influence and incorporated the antiparasite laws into regular judicial procedure. Since Khrushchev, such juridization has been a hallmark of socialist legality.

The case of the antiparasite laws also illustrates the use of law in the USSR as a means of social engineering—that is, as a means of ordering human relations to further the values of Soviet society. This practice is not unique to the Khrushchev era. Gorbachev's much-publicized antialcohol campaign mobilized the legal establishment in order to discourage alcohol consumption. Prosecution for public intoxication increased dramatically, and those convicted received harsher penalties.

Nowhere is the educational role of law more evident than in the ordinary courtroom, where the real-life problems of Soviet citizens come into contact with the Soviet legal system. This chapter closes with an account of a typical criminal case—one of many that the author witnessed in the Kalinin *raion* criminal court in Leningrad.

A bell rang, and everyone was asked to stand while the judge and two people's assessors took their places at the bench. They wore no robes; instead, the judge (a woman in her fifties) wore a blue polyester suit with a patriotic label pin. The two people's assessors, one a thin-faced, haggard-looking man in his fifties and the other a rotund man in his late forties, wore drab, dark grey suits, but no ties. Behind the bar was a large seal of the Russian republic. In one corner of the courtroom, there was a bust of Lenin with a small pot of flowers in front of it. The accused man, with an armed guard at his side, sat at a table with his defense advocate. At another table sat the prosecutor and an investigator, both wearing military-style uniforms. The audience was made up of an odd assortment of approximately twenty-five persons. Several *babushki* wearing brightly flowered kerchiefs and heavy black-flannel coats (even though it was quite warm in the chamber) sat talking quietly among themselves. They appeared to know one another and were most likely regular attendants. In the first row of the spectators gallery sat the defendant's wife, a gaunt woman in her mid-forties. She fidgeted in her seat and coughed occasionally. Beside her, another *babushka* (probably her mother) patted her on the shoulder. A bored-looking man sat near the rear door, reading a newspaper and eating a piece of sausage. He wore a red armband, indicating that he was the doorman charged with maintaining decorum in the chamber.

The judge called the court into session, announcing that this case involved one Boris Mikhailovich Petrov, who had been arrested and charged with assault with a deadly weapon, malicious hooliganism, and public intoxication. Petrov was asked to stand. His shaved head and three-or four-day growth of whiskers gave him a ghostly look. He wore a heavy workingman's coat, made of quilted flannel. Petrov appeared to be in his late fifties, but Russian men generally look older than their age. In fact, he told the judge that he was forty-eight years old and was born in Voronezh into the family of a "peasant" (i.e., collective farmer). His parents were killed during the Great Patriotic War, after which he was sent to Leningrad to live with an aunt. He was married and had two children, a girl of seventeen and a boy of thirteen. Petrov stooped over the defense table, his fingers nervously tracing circles on the table as he talked. After Petrov sat down, the judge began to read from the report of the preliminary investigation.

On a Thursday evening two months previously, Petrov had been riding home on the No. 17 tram. According to many witnesses, he was obviously intoxicated. One of the other passengers on the tram, a *babushka* named Olga Nikolaeva Barashkova, began to chide Petrov for his unsightly appearance and disgraceful behavior. Petrov responded crudely, which brought grumblings of censure from several other passengers. According to the report, Petrov then pulled a hunting knife from under his coat, staggered to his feet, and brandished the knife over his head, shouting at Barashkova, "I'll make cutlets out of you!" He was quickly restrained by the female tram operator and several male passengers, and he was arrested at the next stop.

The judge called on Barashkova, who stepped into the witness box. She gave her age, occupation, and address. She recounted the story, pointing out the accused in response to a question from the bench. The judge asked if she thought that Petrov had actually intended to "make cutlets" out of her. She responded: "Yes, I feared for my life." The people's assessors had no additional questions, and the prosecutor declined to ask any further questions. The defense advocate then stood and asked Barashkova whether the tram had been moving at the time of the "assault." She said that it had. This was later corroborated by the testimony of the tram driver. The defense attorney asked Barashkova how far away from her Petrov had been when he threatened her. She estimated it had been three or four meters.

"Did he ever actually point the knife at you?"

"No, he was waving it wildly over his head." She was dismissed.

Petrov took the stand. In response to questions from the judge, he said that he had been arrested twice previously, once as a juvenile for hooliganism, for which he was sentenced to two years in a juvenile facility, and once for assault, the result of a drunken brawl on the street. The latter offense resulted in a three-year prison term. He had been out of prison less than one year. As for the tram incident, Petrov said that he recalled almost nothing. He remembered being chastised by some *babushki,* but that was all.

The prosecutor stood and asked Petrov about the knife. Yes, it was his, a gift from his uncle who had used it on hunting and fishing trips. The prosecutor then began to ask about Petrov's criminal record and his history of alcoholism. Petrov admitted that several times he had been suspended from work and fined for absenteeism and for showing up for work drunk. (This was substantiated by his work records, which were submitted in evidence.)

After Petrov stepped down, the tram driver, several witnesses, and Petrov's supervisor were called in to testify. Only one of the witnesses offered an alternative version of the story. A teenage girl who had been on the tram said that she thought Petrov was so inebriated that he could not possibly have posed a threat to Barashkova or anyone else. This elicited several remarks from the audience. One *babushka* exclaimed, "But what about the knife?" Another joined in, "He's a rascal. Just look at him!" The judge warned them to be quiet and rapped the gavel. The doorman looked up from his paper, unperturbed. Asked by the judge whether Petrov had "lunged" at Barashkova with the knife, the witness replied, "The tram lurched, and he was staggering, trying to keep his balance." The audience again offered various opinions on the testimony. This time, the judge banged her gavel fiercely and warned the women to keep their opinions to themselves. If there was another "outburst," she said, she would have them removed from the court.

Finally, after all the witnesses had testified and been cross-examined, the prosecution and defense attorneys made their closing statements. The prosecutor noted Petrov's long history of "violence" and his chronic alcoholism. He indicated that Petrov was a serious recidivist and called for the maximum sentence—seven years in a strict-regime labor colony. The defense advocate contended that the *babushka* Barashkova was certainly correct that Petrov's public drunkenness was disgraceful, and that his rude remarks and carrying of a dangerous weapon were inexcusable. He asked the court, however, to lower the charge to public intoxication and hooliganism—a crime punishable by one to two years' imprisonment. The defense advocate noted that it was not reasonable for Barashkova to have considered herself in imminent danger of her life. Petrov had been very drunk and hardly able to stand. He had not pointed the knife at Barashkova, and he had been a safe distance away from her.

The judge and two people's assessors retired to their chamber behind the bench. The audience talked quietly among themselves. Petrov sat dejectedly at the defense table, the armed guard still at his side. After approximately thirty minutes, the judge and people's assessors reemerged. Everyone stood. Petrov was asked to face the bench, and the judge announced that he was found guilty of assault and malicious hooliganism. In anger, she shook her finger at him and called him a disgrace to Soviet society. "You have two children, and yet you are ignoring your responsibility to them and your long-suffering wife. Twice before you have run afoul of the law and been 'rehabilitated' in correctional institutions. Yet, your behavior indicates that you have not changed your ways." She sentenced him to the maximum of seven years in a strict-regime labor colony for repeat offenders. Petrov was immediately led away in handcuffs. His wife sobbed quietly and was comforted by the old women at her side. The *babushki* in attendance chatted contentedly among themselves and waited for the next case, while the doorman put the newspaper down and went into the corridor to smoke a cigarette.

Notes

1. *Izvestiya*, 29 June 1988, p. 1

2. For example, see Vladimir Kudryavtsev, "Toward a Socialist Rule-of-Law State," in A. G. Aganbegyan, ed. *Perestroika* (New York: Charles Scribner & Sons, 1988), pp. 109–125.

3. V. I. Lenin, "O dvoinom podchinenii i zakonost," reprinted in *Sovetskaya prokuratura: sbornik vazhneishikh dokumentov* (Moscow: Yuridicheskaya literatura, 1972), 100–102.

4. Peter Juviler, *Revolutionary Law and Order* (New York: Free Press, 1976), 18–19.

5. Ibid.

6. V. I. Lenin, *Polnoe sobranie sochinenii*, 4th ed., vol. 36 (Moscow: Politizdat, 1958–1965), 195.

7. See Darrell P. Hammer, "Bureaucracy and the Rule of Law in Soviet Society," in Clifford M. Foust and Warren Lerner, eds., *The Soviet World in Flux: Six Essays* (Atlanta: Southern Regional Education Board, 1966), 87–100.

8. Zigurds Zile, *Ideas and Forces in Soviet Legal History* (Madison, WI: College Printing, 1967), 250–256.

9. Andrei Vyshinsky, "Raise Higher the Banner of Socialist Legality," *Sotsialisticheskaya zakonnost'* 11 (1936).

10. Naum Jasny, "Labor and Output in Soviet Concentration Camps," *Journal of Political Economy* 59 (October 1951): 405.

11. "Ukreplenie sotsialistichesoi zakonnosti i yuridicheskaya nauka," *Kommunist* 11 (November 1956); 20.

12. S. Kechekyan, *Pravootnosheniya v sotsialistichesoi obshchestve* (Moscow: Yuridicheskaya literatura, 1958), 68.

13. For example, see *Izvestiya*, 19 December 1961, p. 2.

14. V. Kazin, "Sud tovarishchei," *Pravda,* 13 November 1963, p. 4.

15. R. A. Rudenko, "Leninskie idei sotsialisticheskoi zakonosti, printsipy organizatsii i deiatel'nosti sovetskoi prokuratury," in *Sovetskaya prokuratura* (Moscow: Yuridicheskaya literatura, 1977), 25–26.

16. Statute on the Procuracy of the USSR (1979), Article 3.

17. *Izvestiya,* 3 November 1987, p. 1.

18. *Pravda,* 31 December 1988, p. 3.

19. John Quigley, "Law Reform and the Soviet Courts," *Columbia Journal of Transnational Law* 28, no. 1 (1990): 66.

20. George P. Fletcher, "In Gorbachev's Courts," *New York Review of Books* 36, no. 8 (18 May 1989): 13.

21. *Volksstimme,* 5 March 1986, p. 12.

22. *Pravda,* 18 January 1986, p. 1.

23. *Izvestiya,* 22 January 1986, p. 1.

24. *Literaturnaya gazeta,* no. 19 (1986): 12.

25. Ibid.

26. *Sovetskaya Belorussiya,* 3 June 1987; *Sovetskaya Belorussiya,* 5 October 1986, p. 3; and *Sovetskaya Rossiya,* 14 June 1987.

27. See *Literaturnaya gazeta,* no. 52 (1986): 13.

28. Cited in *Pravda,* 14 June 1986, p. 1.

29. Ibid.; *Pravda,* 28 January 1987 p. 1; and Dmitrii Likhanov, "Klan: Ocherk-preduprezhdenie," *Strana i mir,* no. 4 (40) (July–August 1987): 45–53.

30. Likhanov, ibid.

31. *Pravda,* 8 February 1987, pp. 1–2.

32. *Pravda,* 12 September 1985, p. 1.

33. *Vedomosti Verkhovnogo Soveta SSSR,* no. 22 (1986): 367–368.

34. *Vedomosti Verkhovnogo Soveta SSSR,* no. 22 (1986): 369–373; and *Pravda,* 28 May 1986, p. 2.

35. Ibid.

36. *Pravda,* 25 September 1987, p. 1.

37. See Karl-Eugen Waedekin, "The New Kolkhoz Statute: A Codification of Restructuring on the Farm," *Radio Liberty Research Bulletin* (28 January 1988) 32, no. 5 (28 January 1988), 1–4.

38. M. Mozyr' and F. Rayanov, *Sel'skaya zhizn',* 14 January 1988, p. 1.

39. *Vedomosti Verkhovnogo Soveta SSSR* (no. 49), item 727, translated in *Comparative Text of the 1977 USSR Constitution with Draft and Final Amendments, Review of Socialist Law,* vol. 15, no. 75 (1989).

40. Constitution of the USSR, Article 125, as amended by 1988 Constitutional Amendments.

41. Ibid., Article 155.

42. *Law on Responsibility for Disrespect to a Court,* reprinted in *Izvestiya,* 16 November 1989, p. 1.

43. *Law on the Status of Judges,* reprinted in *Izvestiya,* 12 August 1989, p. 1.

44. *1989 Fundamental Principles on Court Structure,* reprinted in *Izvestiya,* 16 November 1989, p. 1.

45. Eugene Huskey, "Between Citizen and State: The Soviet Bar under Gorbachev," *Columbia Journal of Transnational Law* 28, no. 1 (1990): 111.

46. For a definition of bureaucratic groups, see Darrell P. Hammer, *USSR: The Politics of Oligarchy* (Hinsdale, IL: Dryden Press, 1974), 224–225.

47. M. P. Malyarov, ed., *Organizatsiya roboty raionnoi (gorodskoi) prokuratury* (Moscow: Yuridicheskaya literatura, 1974), 44.

48. These approximate figures are calculated from statistics cited in I. I. Martinovich,

Advokatura v BSSR (Minsk: 1973); and "Narodnogo doveriya—dostoiny," *Leningradskaya pravda* 13 (April 1976): 1.

49. See Walter Gellhorn, *Ombudsman and Others* (Cambridge: Harvard University Press, 1966).

50. Gordon B. Smith, *The Soviet Procuracy and the Supervision of Administration* (Leiden, The Netherlands: Sijtoff & Noordhoff, 1978), p. 23.

51. Ibid.

52. Consultation with N. S. Aleksandrov, Dean of the Juridical Faculty, Leningrad State University, November 6, 1975.

53. For a discussion of the *advokatura*, see Zigurds Zile, "Soviet Advokatura: Its Situation and Prospects," in Donald Barry, George Ginsburgs, and Peter Maggs, eds., *Soviet Law after Stalin,* vol. 3 (Leiden, The Netherlands: Sijtoff, 1979).

54. Ibid.

55. Robert Rand, "Legal Reform within Soviet Courtrooms," Paper presented at the Kennan Institute for Advanced Russian Studies, Washington, D.C., 27 March 1989.

56. Interview with A. Sukharev, Procurator-General of the USSR, *Moscow News,* no. 23, 11–18 June 1989, p. 13.

57. *Izvestiya,* 16 November 1989, p. 1.

58. M. A. Kopylovskaya, *Nauchno-prakticheskii kommentarii k osnovam zakonodatel'stva o sudoustroistve soyuza SSR, soyuiznikh avtonommnikkh respublik* (Moscow: Yuridicheskaya literatura, 1961), 67.

59. T. H. Rigby, *Communist Party Membership in the USSR, 1917–1967* (Princeton: Princeton University Press, 1968), 425.

60. John Barron, *KGB Today: The Hidden Hand* (New York: Holt, Rinehart & Winston, 1983), 41. *The Economist* claims that the total number of KGB officers, agents, and informants may be as high as 1.5 million. See *The Economist,* 27 November 1982, pp. 105–106.

61. Barron, *KGB Today,* 41.

62. *Washington Post,* 21 June 1983, p. 1.

63. See Alexander Rahr, "New Evidence of the KGB's Political Complexion Published," *Radio Liberty Report on the USSR* 3, no. 3 (18 January 1991): 2.

64. Amy W. Knight, "The CPSU and Cadres Policy in the State Security Organs," Paper presented to the annual convention of the American Association for the Advancement of Slavic Studies, New York, 1–3 November 1984, p. 31.

65. Consultation with students in the Juridical Faculty, Leningrad State University, 3 February 1976.

66. *Argumenty i fakty,* no. 26 (1990): 6–7.

67. V. G. Rozenfeld, *Prokurorskii nadzor za soblyudeniem zakonnosti dolzhnostnykh lits predpriyatii* (Voronezh: Voronezh University, 1973), 49–51.

68. The new CPSU Program drops the reference to the "state of all the people." CPSU Program, *Pravda,* 7 March 1986, p. 1.

69. Constitution of the USSR (1977), Article 58.

70. David Shipler, *Russia: Broken Idols, Solemn Dreams* (London: Macdonald, 1983), 237.

71. *Molodoi kommunist,* no. 9 (September 1975): 102.

72. See comments by S. Gusev, First Vice-Chairman of the USSR Supreme Court, *Izvestiya,* 19 April 1984, p. 2.

73. These figures were compiled by Il'ya Zemstov in "Problems of Soviet Youth," *Radio Liberty Research Paper,* no. 125 (March 1975): 10.

74. *Sotsialogicheskie issledovaniya,* no. 3 (1977).

75. Ibid.

76. Shipler, *Russia: Broken Idols, Solemn Dreams,* 237.

77. Criminal Code of the RSFSR, Articles 89 and 144.

78. Ibid., Articles 99 and 150.

79. Ibid., Article 154.

80. *Selskaya zhizn'*, 24 March 1985, p. 4.

81. For example, see *Moscow News*, nos. 16, 25, 41 and 50, 1987; *Nedelya*, nos. 42 and 51, 1987; and *Ogonek*, nos. 33 and 49, 1987.

82. M. S. Studenikina, *Zakonodatel'stvo ob administrativnoi otvetstvennosti kodifikatsiya* (Candidate dissertation, All-Union Scientific Research Institute on Soviet Legislation, Moscow, 1968), 250–251.

83. Valery Chalidze, *Criminal Russia: Crime in the Soviet Union* (New York: Random House, 1977), p. 203.

84. Harold J. Berman, *Justice in the USSR* (Cambridge: Harvard University Press, 1966), 283–284.

85. D. I. Kurskii, cited in Eugene Kamenka, "The Soviet View of Law," in Richard Cornell, ed., *The Soviet Political System* (Englewood Cliffs, NJ: Prentice-Hall, 1970), 315.

86. Leon Lipson, "Hosts and Pests: the Fight Against Parasites," *Problems of Communism* no. 9 (March–April 1965): 78–79.

87. Ibid., 80.

88. Ibid., 78–79.

Selected Bibliography

Barry, Donald, William Butler, and George Ginsburgs, eds. *Contemporary Soviet Law*. The Hague, the Netherlands: Martinus Nijhoff, 1974.

Barry, Donald, George Ginsburgs, and Peter Maggs, eds. *Soviet Law after Stalin*. Leiden, the Netherlands: Sijtoff, 1977–1979.

Berman, Harold J. *Justice in the USSR*. Cambridge: Harvard University Press, 1966.

Chalidze, Valery. *Criminal Russia: Crime in the Soviet Union*. New York: Random House, 1977.

Columbia Journal of Transnational Law, "Legal Reform in the Soviet Union" 28, no. 1 (1990), 1–328.

Conquest, Robert, ed. *Justice and the Legal System in the USSR*. New York: Praeger, 1968.

Feifer, George. *Justice in Moscow*. New York: Simon and Schuster, 1964.

Feldbrugge, F. J. M., et al., eds. *Encyclopedia of Soviet Law*. 2d rev. ed. Dordrecht, the Netherlands: Martinus Nijhoff, 1985.

Feldbrugge, F. J. M. and William B. Simons, eds. *Perspectives on Soviet Law for the 1980s*. The Hague: Martinus Nijhoff, 1982.

Grzybowski, K. *Soviet Legal Institutions*. Ann Arbor: University of Michigan Press, 1962.

Hazard, John N. *Managing Change in the USSR: The Politico-Legal Role of the Soviet Jurist*. New York: Columbia University Press, 1983.

Hazard, John N., Isaac Shapiro, and Peter Maggs, *The Soviet Legal System*. Dobbs Ferry, New York: Oceana, 1969.

Ioffe, Olimpiad S. *Soviet Law and Soviet Reality*. Dordrecht, the Netherlands: Martinus Nijhoff, 1985.

Juviler, Peter. *Revolutionary Law and Order*. New York: Free Press, 1976.

Knight, Amy W. *The KGB: Police and Politics in the Soviet Union*. Boston: Unwin Hyman, 1988.

Kucherov, Samuel. *The Organs of Soviet Administration of Justice: Their History and Operation*. Leiden, the Netherlands: E. J. Brill, 1970.

Sharlet, Robert. *The New Soviet Constitution of 1977: Analysis and Text*. Brunswick, Ohio: King's Cross, 1978.

Shelley, Louise I. *Lawyers in Soviet Work Life*. New Brunswick, New Jersey: Rutgers University Press, 1984.

Simis, Konstantin. *USSR, The Corrupt Society*. New York: Simon and Schuster, 1982.

Smith, Gordon B. *The Soviet Procuracy and the Supervision of Administration*. Leiden, the Netherlands: Sijtoff and Noordhoff, 1978.

Solomon, Peter H. *Soviet Criminologists and Criminal Policy*. New York: Columbia University Press, 1978.

10

Perestroika: Reforming the Economy

The driving force behind Gorbachev's reforms is the precipitous decline in Soviet economic performance in recent decades. GNP growth rates declined steadily from 9.9 percent in 1958 to −1.0 percent in 1989. In 1990 the economy declined by 3 to 10 percent, depending on whose figures you believe.[1] Why have the reforms that Gorbachev championed only worsened economic conditions? Is the recent economic performance a relatively short-term phase that will stimulate future growth? What are the prospects of developing a market economic system in the USSR? Is Gorbachev, in fact, committed to bringing about market-oriented reforms? These are important questions that we will address later in this chapter, but first we need to examine the economic system as it existed prior to the introduction of *perestroika.*

THE SOCIALIST ECONOMIC SYSTEM

The Soviet Union represents the first major experiment in devising a centrally planned socialist economy. The development of a Marxist economy, however, did not occur immediately after the Bolsheviks seized power in 1917. In fact, prior to the Revolution, few if any socialists had seriously considered how to organize and plan an economy; they were too preoccupied with overthrowing the existing capitalist system. Some elements of the new Marxist economic order were predictable, however. State ownership of the means of production would replace private ownership, and the State would dictate allocations of investment capital and labor resources, as well as set prices. Centralized state planning was not a fundamental tenet of Marx and came to be a prominent feature of the Soviet economy only in 1928.

The appallingly difficult problems confronting Lenin and his colleagues in the early days after the Revolution forced the new leadership to improvise. The land, large factories, and housing were declared public property. The agricultural production of the peasants was requisitioned, and resources were allocated by the central authorities. Because of the conditions of civil war and the widespread resistance among the peasants, however, attempts to institute centralized planning or collectivized agriculture were abandoned.

Under the New Economic Policy (NEP), from 1921 to 1928, peasants were allowed to farm as they wished and sell their produce on a relatively free market. Small-scale private enterprise was legalized, while large-scale industry, banking, and foreign trade remained in the hands of the State. State enterprises produced in response to consumer demand, not in response to centrally issued directives.

The relatively relaxed atmosphere of NEP gave way to a more ambitious system of centralized planning under Stalin, with the introduction of the First Five-Year Plan in 1928. Stalin set the USSR on a course of rapid industrial development with greater investment in heavy industries than could be achieved in a market economy. His goal was accomplished, but not without exacting a high price in political coercion, neglect of the consumer goods and agricultural sectors, and a depression in urban and rural living standards. Collectivization of agriculture squeezed capital out of the agrarian sector to finance rapid industrialization. The industrial sector grew at an unprecedented rate. By the end of the Stalin era the USSR outproduced the United States in steel, oil, cement, and textiles.

In the 1950s, however, the Soviet economy began to slow down. In part, this was the result of natural maturation: the larger the total GNP of a country, the more difficult it is to sustain large percentage increases. In addition, it was becoming increasingly apparent by the mid-1950s that Soviet economic resources were not inexhaustible. The leadership began to confront serious shortages in investment capital, labor, and arable land. The rate of growth of the national income fell from 9.9 percent in 1958 to 3.9 percent in 1959, 5.0 percent in 1960, 6.5 percent in 1961, and 2.2 percent in 1962.[2] Not only did the overall economic growth rate decrease, but worker productivity also declined, from 5 percent in 1958 to 3.3 percent in 1962.

There were many indications that the problems confronting the Soviet economy in the 1950s and 1960s were more than simply the "aging" of a rapidly growing economy. The capital-output ratio (an index that measures how many inputs are required to produce a given amount of outputs) increased steadily. Furthermore, the Soviet economy in the 1960s exhibited very low and declining rates of consumption as an ever-larger portion of the productive resources were devoted to producers' goods and defense, rather than to consumer items. In 1962, the Soviet national income was approximately half that of the United States, yet per capita consumption was only one-quarter that of the United States.[3] The problems in the Soviet economy were clearly systemic.

Attempts to reform the Stalinist economic system under Khrushchev, as we saw in Chapter 3, proved controversial and ultimately unsuccessful. The proposals of Evsei Liberman to stimulate market forces by judging factory performance in terms of profitability threatened to create unemployment, disrupt established supply channels between producers and consumers, and shift allocations from defense and heavy industry to consumer goods. Not the least objection to Liberman's reforms was that they would undercut the powers of industrial ministries by giving more decision-making power to factory managers.

Brezhnev came into office promising stability and conservatism. Few reform initiatives were undertaken. Meanwhile, the Soviet economy experienced further retardation in growth, and the leadership responded with a new round of reforms and organizational reshufflings. Détente with the West and expanded contacts between economic officials in the USSR and Western corporations heightened Soviet awareness of the advantages of large, diversified production units. Thus, in 1973, Soviet economic officials began to consolidate factories and enterprises into production associations, patterned after Western multinational corporations. The aggregation of several steel mills into one association, for instance, was intended to eliminate redundant administrative posts; facilitate procurement, repairs, and coordination among plants; and allow enterprises to pool their resources in order to create research and design bureaus.

Since their introduction in 1973, production associations have grown to encompass almost half of all factories and enterprises in the USSR, representing a drive toward greater concentration of industrial production. By 1979, enterprises employing more than a thousand workers accounted for more than 70 percent of all industrial output, employed almost three-quarters of the industrial labor force, and used more than 80 percent of all capital funds.[4] The average number of employees in a Soviet enterprise is 565, compared to 48 in the United States. In metal-working enterprises, the contrast is even more dramatic—2608 employees in the USSR, compared to 74 in the United States.[5] The creation of the production associations reflects this Soviet preference for large-scale production complexes—what some Western scholars have dubbed "gigantomania."

The massive scale of the Soviet industrial system created under Stalin is responsible both for many impressive achievements and for many of the USSR's present economic difficulties. In the relatively short span of thirty years, Stalin transformed the USSR from a backward, weak, primarily agricultural nation into an industrial and military superpower. Under his system of centralized planning, all resources were harnessed in the drive to modernize the economy. By the 1970s, however, the Soviet economy had developed to the point where the myriad of economic activities were too complex to be coordinated by a central plan. Nevertheless, planning remained a fundamental feature of the Soviet economy.

In the late 1970s, Brezhnev introduced measures to improve agricultural production, reduce waste, and alleviate the gap between the standards of living of urban and rural workers, in an effort to stem the out-migration of youth from the countryside. The hallmark of Brezhnev's proposals was the "agro-industrial complex." Drawing on his earlier experience in Moldavia, Brezhnev advocated relocating light industry, especially food-processing industries, in agricultural regions. Thus, canning plants were built near vegetable farms, processing plants for sugar beets were located close to the fields, and so forth. The complexes also merged collective and state farms into still-larger units in an effort to enhance efficiency and productivity. So far, the agro-industrial complexes have been limited to meat, dairy, fruit, vegetable, and wine production.

By the time of Brezhnev's death in 1982, the Soviet national income was roughly half that of the United States. Nevertheless, total Soviet industrial output was over 80 percent of that in the United States.[6] The Soviet Union

outproduced the United States in steel, oil, cement, and textiles. Despite repeated efforts to shift resources into agriculture, consumer goods, and service
industries, heavy industrial production remained the highest-priority sector of
the Soviet economy. More than 70 percent of Soviet industrial output consisted of producers' goods.[7] In other words, most Soviet industrial enterprises
produced goods for other industrial enterprises, not for public consumption.

PLANNING IN THE USSR

It is difficult for the Westerner to grasp the extent of Soviet centralized
planning. Until recently, the State, not individual factory managers, entrepreneurs, or corporate officials, decided what and how much should be produced, and in what assortment of sizes, qualities, and colors. The State determined what portion of output should be devoted to consumption and what
portion to investment, and the State allocated consumption and investment
funds to every district, city, region, and republic of the USSR. The State also
fixed the prices on more than nine million types of raw materials, finished
goods, and services.

As one might imagine, the apparatus required to carry out these tasks is
enormous and often cumbersome. Yet the centrally planned nature of the
Soviet system also gives the leadership powerful and direct means to affect
policy. If the planners wish to stimulate employment in the far north or
Siberia, for example, they institute pay incentives and increase factory personnel budgets in the region. If they decide to develop the country's natural gas
and oil reserves rather than invest in nuclear power and coal, investment
capital funds are allocated accordingly. If the leadership wishes to curb alcohol consumption, as Gorbachev advocated, breweries and distilleries find
their work forces and purchasing budgets slashed, wholesalers are told to cut
back on deliveries to stores, and liquor stores are ordered to reduce their
hours and raise prices. In contrast, when Western governments wish to alter
economic or social conditions, they usually must rely on such indirect methods as increasing or decreasing the money supply, altering taxes, or manipulating government spending.

Since the initiation of planning by Stalin in 1928, overall growth targets
for each sector of the Soviet economy have been specified in five-year plans.
The Five-Year Plan (currently the Thirteenth Five-Year Plan, 1991–1995)
contains detailed production targets for each branch of the economy (chemicals, petroleum, steel, agriculture, and so forth). Plan projections are typically
stated in terms of the percentage increase over production levels of the previous five-year period. For example, the Twelfth Five-Year Plan called for a 30
to 32 percent increase in chemical production, a 20 to 23 percent increase in
public consumption, and a 14 to 16 percent increase in agricultural output
over the five-year period.[8] These aggregate projections are then broken down
into annual plans, which are in turn disaggregated into quarterly and monthly
plan quotas. Five-year and annual plans are also broken down for each
republic, territory, region, city, district, and enterprise (factory, state farm, or
collective) in the USSR. For instance, the Red Proletariat Machine-Tool Plant

in Moscow receives numerous directives from the Ministry of Economics and Forecasting (formerly Gosplan)* and the Ministry of General Machine-Building specifying quotas not only for production but also for sales, investment, wages and labor, profits, incentives, technical innovation, and productivity. These directives are obligatory for management; failure to fulfill the plan targets may result in demotions or financial penalties. During Stalin's reign, failure to fulfill plan targets was a criminal offense punishable by imprisonment or death.

The Soviet planning system employs "taut planning"—in other words, the target level of production is set intentionally high, given the amount of labor and resources allocated. The rationale behind taut planning is that workers will have to make efficient and maximum use of resources in order to fulfill their production quotas.

Bonuses and rewards for overfulfilling the plan range from salary bonuses to preferential access to vacation facilities, increased investment funds, and political favor. Bonuses constitute an important portion of a worker's income—as much as one-third of total earnings.[9]

The plan is devised through a complicated interaction of officials in numerous bureaucracies, including the Ministry of Economics and Forecasting (MEP), the State Committee on Prices, the State Bank, the Ministry of Finance, the State Committee on Material and Technical Supplies (Gossnab), and approximately forty-eight ministries that oversee the various branches of the Soviet economy (e.g., Ministry of the Electronics Industry, Ministry of the Chemical Industry, and Ministry of Ferrous Metallurgy). These ministries then disaggregate the plan targets into individual plans for each enterprise and association. On the basis of these general targets, enterprises outline their own production and input requirements in allocation requests called *zayavki;* these are passed on to the respective ministries, which aggregate them and finally communicate them to MEP. Enterprises normally overestimate their personnel and other input needs; when added together, the total resources requested usually exceed the total available resources in the economy. Consequently, the plan typically goes through several rounds of adjustment, lowering production quotas as well as appropriations until a balanced plan is achieved.

The construction of the plan is a highly politicized process. Ministries lobby on behalf of their industries' needs and development programs; republic and regional state and party officials push proposals benefiting their respective areas; domestic and foreign trade organizations request more for their sectors to satisfy customers. All these decisions have important economic and political implications. For instance, the decision to export more gas may require additional investment in drilling and pipe-laying, more foreign currency for buying pipe from the West, and less gas for domestic consumption. In addition, such a decision would likely benefit gas-producing regions while siphoning resources from coal-producing areas.

MEP is responsible for balancing these competing demands by reducing

---

*The State Planning Commission (Gosplan) was abolished in late 1990 and its planning functions were assigned to the newly formed Ministry of Economics and Forecasting (MEP).

requests to practical levels, but it does not make these important distributive decisions independently. Through the Cabinet of Ministers, the political leaders communicate to MEP the priorities they wish to pursue. Such priorities may relate either to particular sectors (e.g., gas versus coal and nuclear energy) or particular regions (e.g., Siberia versus European Russia).

It should be emphasized that the targets set forth in the Five-Year Plan are by no means unchangeable. In fact, they are usually altered once, twice, or even several times during the course of the plan period. In contrast, however, annual plans are binding and seldom altered. The process of formulating the annual plan requires almost twelve months, while the Five-Year Plan usually requires two years to complete.[10]

While the division of ministerial jurisdictions over various sectors of the Soviet economy appears on the surface to be quite rational, there is a great deal of overlap, which complicates planning considerably. Enterprises producing farm machinery are likely to be subordinated to any number of ministries, including the Ministry of Defense Industries. Refrigerators are manufactured in factories operated by the Ministry of the Radio Industry, and television sets are produced by some defense plants. This diversity of production comes about when a factory has excess production capacity or personnel and uses those resources to manufacture an unrelated product. Redundancy and overlapping production can also result when enterprises are continually frustrated in obtaining necessary components, equipment, or other items. For instance, A. I. Shokin, former Minister of the Electronics Industry, noted that when his ministry could not get adequate measuring and testing equipment from outside suppliers, they began to manufacture the necessary equipment themselves.[11] Factories under the jurisdiction of the Ministry of the Electronics Industry are now producing equipment that would normally fall under the purview of the machine tool, chemical, nonferrous metallurgy, instrument-building, and radio-technical industries.

The performance of enterprises in the USSR is judged across a wide array of indicators. Currently, twelve measures of performance are used:

1. total output
2. assortment
3. proportion of high-quality or export-quality output
4. labor productivity
5. profit, profitability
6. capital construction
7. introduction of new technology
8. investment
9. material incentive fund
10. improvements in technical qualifications of workers
11. sociocultural activities
12. fulfillment of delivery schedules

All of these indicators are not weighted equally by central planners, however. A factory that introduces new techniques, raises the level of worker qualifications and labor productivity, but suffers a decline in total output will be reprimanded; a factory that fails to modernize and improve product quality or worker qualifications but overfulfills its production plan is likely to be rewarded with bonuses, even if its products are of poor quality and are not purchased by consumers.

Even when focusing solely on the most important indicator—gross output—Soviet planners have continually encountered difficulties in measuring performance in such a way that desirable results are achieved. Soviet economists sometimes illustrate the "success indicator" problem by referring to the case of a fictitious factory—the May Day Nail Factory. If the output of the May Day Nail Factory is specified in the plan in terms of the number of nails produced, this will encourage factory managers to produce small tacks. On the other hand, if output is specified in terms of the gross weight of nails produced, it is more advantageous for the factory to produce railroad spikes. The Soviet satirical journal *Krokodil* ("Crocodile") poked fun at this sort of behavior in a cartoon depicting a plant manager congratulating the workers in a nail factory for overfulfilling their plan, as a single, huge nail rolls off the assembly line. Such absurdities, unfortunately, do exist in reality. During the 1930s and 1940s, furniture in the USSR was among the heaviest in the world. Some bed frames were constructed from lead. The reason—the performance of furniture factories was judged by total weight of furniture produced. When this indicator was changed under Khrushchev, furniture suddenly appeared in the stores made of lightweight plywood.

The combination of illogical plan incentives and pressure to fulfill plan quotas on time results in other distortions as well. On one visit to Leningrad, the author noticed row after row of concrete slabs on the outskirts of town. When he asked a woman in the neighborhood what the slabs were for, she explained that the central planners measure the performance of housing construction firms by the number of housing starts (i.e., the number of foundations laid). A housing construction firm that had fallen behind in its production had laid the foundations, even though they would never have apartments built upon them. Russians call this phenomenon of pushing to fulfill plan production quotas at all costs "storming." One Soviet source indicates that 35 percent of all housing starts occur in the last quarter of the plan year, and 70 percent of those are in the last week of December—hardly an ideal time for pouring concrete.[12]

Pressures to fulfill plan targets result in a variety of other distortions. One of the most enduring features of the Soviet economy is hoarding. Supply channels in the USSR are not well established, and factories continually confront shortages of inputs. If an automobile plant has not received a shipment of sheet steel, it has little recourse but to cut back production. If the factory falls short of its production target because of the nondelivery of steel, the workers are penalized nonetheless. Consequently, factories stockpile large quantities of raw materials, spare parts, and other goods to cover this contingency.

Spare parts are generally not available for automobiles, trucks, and tractors in the USSR, because the output of automobile factories is measured in terms of the number of automobiles produced, not the number of parts produced. State farms and factories are forced to "cannibalize" their tractors and other machinery for spare parts. If a state farm manager calls to inquire whether a neighboring state farm has a spare carburetor for a tractor, the manager is likely to respond: "Yes, but I can't give it to you. What if one of *our* tractors breaks down and needs a carburetor?"

The lack of spare parts has given rise to a thriving black market, often supplied with goods stolen by production workers. There is such a demand for windshield wipers that citizens do not dare to leave them attached to their cars for fear they will be stolen. Most drivers keep their wipers in the glove compartment. When it begins to rain, all traffic stops for a few seconds while drivers jump out and hurriedly reattach their wipers.

The hoarding of resources also applies to labor. As noted earlier, the most important indicator of economic performance is total output. The profitability and labor productivity indices, which would be affected adversely by employing excess numbers of workers, are only secondary in importance. Consequently, most factories, stores, and state farms hire more workers than necessary, in case extra workers are required at the end of the plan period for "storming" to fulfill the plan. In addition, it has been reported that on any given day as much as 20 percent of the labor force shows up at work drunk or fails to show up at all; thus, excess labor is needed just to ensure a full complement of workers.[13] The underutilization of workers, however, seriously erodes the efficiency of the economy, especially in the service sector. For example, a pancake (*bliny*) shop on Nevsky Prospekt, the main street of Leningrad, employs seven people (two cooks, three waitresses, and two dishwashers), even though it has a seating capacity for only six customers.

Plan pressures combined with shortages of components have also caused some factory managers to produce incomplete products or falsify their plan fulfillment reports. During the final days of the plan period, production will continue in an automobile assembly plant even if it means that the "finished" automobiles have no headlights, taillights, or windshield wipers because the plant has run out of the necessary parts (often due to pilfering by the workers). When the cars arrive to be sold, the officials will report that the parts were stolen while the cars were being shipped. Having waited up to ten years to buy a car, it is unlikely that customers will refuse to accept the automobiles; they will simply try to acquire the missing parts on the black market.

Soviet economists admit that their planning efforts are often insufficient. Ultimately, however, the level of acceptable economic performance is a political issue. Although a shoe factory that overfulfills its production quota may be rewarded even when the products are of low quality, it runs the risk of being singled out for chastisement by political officials. It is the uncertainty of political reprisals as much as plan directives that keeps industrial managers in line. In some areas, such as stimulating enterprises to adopt new technologies, political pressures can be more effective than the economic incentives built into the plan.[14]

Plan violations can be very serious and can even entail criminal prosecution. Several years ago, for instance, violations by a manufacturer of surgical sterilization machines resulted in criminal action. The factory ran out of critical electrical coils that were necessary for proper functioning of the machines, but the pressures to fulfill the production quota were so great that the factory produced and delivered a shipment of incomplete sterilization machines anyway. After several hospital patients died of massive post-operative infections, an investigation uncovered the cause. The factory manager, the chief engineer, and the quality control chief were all convicted of gross negligence and were executed.[15]

Planning in the USSR extends into virtually every facet of life. Lawyers have a plan for the number of clients they must serve; hospitals are evaluated on the number of patients they treat, and artists by the number of paintings they produce. At the end of every Five-Year Plan, the faculty of the Leningrad University law school meets to "review faculty performance in light of the plan." One by one, each faculty member rises and reads a memo detailing his or her accomplishments during the past five years—the number of books and articles published, public lectures presented, and so on. After each recitation, the faculty votes on whether or not the individual has fulfilled the plan. On most occasions, faculty members receive unanimously favorable evaluations.

The incorporation of the plan mentality into the Soviet mind-set is evident even on some solemn occasions. At the conclusion of burial services, it is often proclaimed, "Rest in peace, comrade. Your plan has been fulfilled!"

WORK LIFE IN THE USSR

The Bolshevik Revolution of 1917 was ostensibly carried out on behalf of the workers and peasants in order to create the first workers' state. Lenin and his colleagues conceived of themselves as the champions of the working man and woman. The Revolution was intended to free the workers' creative energies so they could work for their own benefit, rather than for the benefit of a ruling class. Even today the image of "the worker" is at the center of political propaganda. Banners on buildings, tram cars, and construction cranes proclaim "Glory to Labor!" or "Our Labor Is for the Motherland!" Yet, for all the lofty rhetoric, the reality of work life in the Soviet Union is that most workers are employed in menial, dreary, and low-paying jobs.

The normal workweek in the Soviet Union averages 42 hours; Soviet employees work a five-day week except for the last week of the month, when they must also work on Saturday—colloquially referred to as "black Saturday." Overtime work is common, and many workers are coerced into working overtime toward the end of a plan period, although it is officially not mandatory. In April each year, workers are expected to devote an additional Saturday of uncompensated work in honor of Lenin's birthday (April 22). The practice of "Lenin Saturday" extends even to university students, who are mobilized by their Komsomol organizations into brigades and assigned to rake lawns in parks, pick up litter, and spruce up public places.

Salaries and wage rates of Soviet workers are set by central authorities according to the difficulty, degree of danger, and technical qualifications of the job. In addition, an elaborate job classification system sets salaries depending on seniority, past performance on the job, and range of responsibilities. Thus, taxi drivers are ranked first class, second class, third class, and so on, and pay levels vary accordingly.

The average salary nationwide is approximately 270 rubles per month, or about $10. Although this is very low, one must also consider the benefits that Soviet citizens receive free or at minimal cost. Health and dental care are provided free of charge, and rent and utilities are heavily subsidized. Whereas rent accounts for more than one-quarter of the average wage earner's monthly salary in Washington, D.C., rent constitutes only about one-sixteenth of a worker's monthly salary in Moscow.[16] Public transportation, cultural activities, and basic foodstuffs are subsidized in order to make them affordable for average citizens. The subway costs 15 kopeks (1 cent), a ticket to hear the Moscow Philharmonic may be purchased for only 50 cents, and a loaf of bread costs a half cent.

Salaries in the Soviet Union reflect, in part, the Marxist notion of rewarding manual labor more than white-collar labor. For instance, a coal miner is paid more than a teacher or doctor because of the dangerous and difficult nature of the work. Income differentials exist in the USSR, but they are not nearly as dramatic as in the West. The ratio of Soviet workers in the bottom 10 percent of wage earners to the highest 10 percent has declined to approximately 3:1, compared to roughly 4.5:1 in the United States.[17] The relative equality of incomes in the USSR is evident in Table 10–1, which presents some average salaries for various types of workers and officials.

Table 10-1. Average Monthly Income of Soviet Workers (in rubles)

Marshal of the USSR	2000
General Secretary of the CPSU	900
First Secretary, Union of Composers	800
Director, scientific-research institute	700
First Secretary of a Union-Republic	600
Major General	600
Colonel	500
Well-known ballet dancer	500
Director, large industrial enterprise	450–500
Professor	325–525
Attorney	250
Editor, *Union-Republic* newspaper	240
Coal miner	210
Doctor	183
Chairman, collective farm	180
Steel worker	145
Taxi driver	140
Secondary school teacher	140
Collective farmer	122
Forklift operator	110
Clerical worker	90
Janitorial worker	70

Sources: Mervyn Matthews, *Privilege in the Soviet Union* (London: George Allen & Unwin, 1978), 23, 26 and 27, and Murray Yanowitch, *Social and Economic Inequality in the Soviet Union* (New York: M. E. Sharpe, 1977), 30, 32, 34, 35, and 39.

Bonuses and salary increments are offered to encourage workers to seek employment in priority sectors or in far-off regions. The chief driller on an oil rig north of the Arctic Circle, for example, receives 1200 rubles per month— five times the national average.[18] He works a four-day shift, is off one day, and then works four more days. Young men are often attracted to these high-paying jobs in order to amass some savings prior to getting married.

Salary figures, however, mask the substantial inequalities that exist in access to special perquisites and benefits. For example, high-ranking party and military officials are provided with spacious apartments, summer houses in the country, limousines with chauffeurs, maids, cooks, gardeners, and extensive entertainment allowances.

Public officials, top military officers, well-known scientists and artists, and foreign diplomats in the USSR are granted access to special stores that carry export-quality merchandise not normally found in stores. The author was in one of the "diplomatic stores" on a bitterly cold February day shopping for a few "luxury" goods—tomatoes and cucumbers—when a limousine pulled up to the front door and an important-looking woman got out. The woman approached the salesclerk and asked for fresh strawberries. The clerk hurriedly motioned her into the back room. In a short time, she emerged carrying a small package. When the author boldly approached the same salesclerk and asked for fresh strawberries, he was told: "Young man, you must be crazy. We don't have strawberries at this time of year!"

How well one lives in the USSR depends a great deal on who one is and who one's friends are. Russians call this *blat*—connections. Nevertheless, compared to top corporate executives or political officials in the West, prominent figures in the Soviet Union enjoy a rather modest standard of living. At the other end of the income scale, the policy of relative equality of incomes and provision of extensive social welfare benefits has virtually eliminated poverty in the USSR.

WOMEN AND WORK

Women play a major role in the Soviet labor force, constituting more than 51 percent of all workers.[19] Approximately 85 percent of women under the age of 55 work outside the home.[20] Women are heavily represented in clerical, sales, and catering professions, as well as in teaching and health care. Women account for 68 percent of all doctors (*vracha*), 71 percent of all teachers, and 33 percent of all engineers.[21]

In addition, women are heavily represented in the construction trades, light industry (e.g., textiles), and in menial jobs. Most bricklayers, carpenters, painters, crane operators, and plasterers in the USSR are women. In the winter, it is common to see a brigade of women shoveling snow into a dumptruck while the male driver sits in the heated cab reading a book. In the spring, armies of women use crowbars to chip away at the thick layers of ice and packed snow that have accumulated on the sidewalks and streets during the winter.

One senses that it is the strength of its women that has enabled the Soviet

Union to survive. During World War II, women operated lathes and forged steel while the men were at the front. Women in Russia have traditionally been responsible for planting and harvesting the crops, even when this requires long hours of swinging a scythe or baling hay and shocking wheat by hand. While the women worked the fields, the men were responsible for the livestock and machinery. In agricultural areas, this division of labor is still evident today.

Although they occupy a major role in the work force, relatively few women rise to supervisory positions. Fewer than 2 percent of collective farm managers, 9 percent of enterprise directors, 12 percent of construction supervisors, and 28 percent of school principals are women.[22] Women invariably receive lower salaries than their male counterparts; the average Soviet woman earns about 65 percent as much as the average male worker.[23] Women pensioners often find that they have to take low-paying jobs such as museum guards, coatroom attendants, or janitors in order to supplement their pensions.

Although women's rights are loudly proclaimed by the government, most Soviet women in fact find themselves in inferior jobs and saddled with second jobs at home. The average Soviet apartment lacks modern conveniences such as the dishwashers, washing machines, and clothes dryers that have greatly simplified the tedious work of housewives elsewhere. Shopping for a single meal can easily consume hours of standing in lines at the bakery, the dairy, the meat market, and the vegetable store. Russian husbands are notorious for refusing to assist in household or child-rearing chores, preferring instead to drink with their buddies. The Soviet press has in recent years encouraged more men to assume their fair share of household duties, but change comes slowly.

This combination of circumstances has left many Soviet women bitter and cynical. March 8, International Women's Day, was originated by radical leftist women during the Paris Commune, but in the USSR today it bears a closer resemblance to Mother's Day in the United States. Moscow Radio plays an endless barrage of syrupy songs with such lyrics as, "Oh, our women, how sweet they are!" The songs are interrupted by occasional political statements reminding Soviet women that they have more rights than women anywhere else on earth and by reminders to husbands to buy their wives flowers and chocolates (two commodities that never seem to be in short supply). Attending a reception in honor of International Women's Day at Leningrad University law school, the author extended salutations to one of the female faculty members. She scoffed in reply, "International Women's Day, indeed! That is when all the men invite their drinking buddies over for dinner and the woman has to cook and clean up afterwards!"

THE CONSUMER ECONOMY

The predominant characteristic of the Soviet economy is the ever-present shortage of decent-quality consumer goods. With little incentive to produce desirable goods, manufacturers simply produce in order to fulfill plan targets.

Similarly, stores and shops have no incentive to assist shoppers; long lines and surly clerks make shopping even for simple, everyday items an ordeal.

Lines have become a national institution in the USSR. Most stores are organized so that customers must stand in three lines just to buy one item. They must stand in one line to place their orders, in another line to pay the cashier, and in a third line to pick up their merchandise. Enterprising Soviet shoppers have developed an elaborate etiquette for standing in line. When someone joins the line behind you, you turn to that person and say, "I'm in front of you," and your place in line is thus reserved. You are then free to establish a place in another line by following the same procedure. The object of the exercise is to time your spots in line so that you place your order before you pay for it and that you pay before you pick up your order. In a large Kiev department store with numerous departments and cashier booths, the author once managed to hold places in nine lines simultaneously.

Lines perform both an economic and a social function. Because prices are centrally determined, there is no need to shop around. A bottle of milk costs the same in a store in the dairy region of Lithuania as it does in Tashkent, in the south, or in Murmansk, above the Arctic Circle. Most items have the price stamped on them indelibly to prevent stores from overcharging. Prices are artificially set and bear little relation to demand or cost of production. Thus, the cost of meat does not determine who buys steak and who buys hamburger; rather, allocations are determined primarily by availability. Buying steak in the meat market is a combination of luck, timing, and patience.

Because prices are fixed, there has been no inflation in the USSR until recently. Yet hidden inflation exists and can be measured in longer lines and poorer quality. Western journalists have noted over the past several years that the quality of bread is deteriorating while the size of the loaves is getting smaller. Russian bread that once was golden brown and very tasty is now tasteless and often has a slightly grey color—the result of adding sawdust to make the flour go further.

While standing in line, Soviet citizens gossip, chat, and share their woes or offer helpful hints as to where to find garlic or toilet paper. Soviet stores are filled with the constant hum of conversation among the shoppers in line. The author never had occasion to consider the social function of standing in line until he returned to the United States after a long stay in the USSR. He was accompanying a newly arrived Soviet émigré family to a large supermarket to show them how to shop *po-Amerikanskii* (American-style). In the produce section, the family was wide-eyed at the sight of mountains of apples, oranges, bananas, and pears. They had never seen a pineapple, and the author had to explain how to cook artichokes. In the canned-goods section, they were impressed by the variety and colorful packaging. They looked a bit bewildered, however, by the rows of frozen dinners, pizzas, and juice containers; with the exception of small bricks of ice cream, frozen foods do not exist in Soviet stores. In the meat section, the author noticed that the wife was frowning. Glancing over an assortment of neatly wrapped cuts of beef and pork, she asked, "Why is everything packaged?" The author cited the convenience and sanitary advantages, to which she replied, "But we have been in this store 20 minutes and haven't said a word to anyone. Maybe you Americans wrap your meat so you won't have to talk with the butcher." There is some truth in her observation; it illustrates the extent to which shopping in the Soviet Union represents an important way in which Soviets interact. Shopping provides immediate, interpersonal contact with fellow citizens; it gives a feeling of belonging.

The Soviet economy functions strictly on a cash basis. Checking accounts and credit cards do not exist for Soviet shoppers. As a consequence, consumers carry wads of rubles, in case they should happen to be in the produce store when strawberries go on sale or in the department store when a shipment of Italian shoes arrives. Many of the most desirable items never reach the store shelves; they are sold from the backs of delivery trucks. The author was once on a street in downtown Leningrad when a truck pulled up outside a department store. A line immediately began to form at the back of the truck, even before anyone knew what was inside. Word was passed back through the line, "We're in luck! It's toilet paper! Ten rolls maximum." The author bought the maximum and passed them out as presents to his friends back in the dormitory. Over the course of the year, his friends repaid the favor when they were lucky enough to find imported oranges in January or when they received a package of home-canned tomatoes from an aunt on a collective farm.

"Deficit items" also are sold *na levo*, or "on the left"—that is, illegally through an extensive "second economy." Sales clerks save the Italian shoes in the back room or under the counter for friends and relatives. The butcher in the local meat market told the author that he knew how much Americans love steak, so he would save the best cuts for the author. With a wink, the butcher told the author not to stand in line, but to come directly to him. As is customary, the author repaid the butcher occasionally with a bottle of Scotch.

The scarcity of some food items has sparked a thriving unofficial distribution network, as Uzbeks, Georgians, and others from the warmer regions of the south bring produce to Moscow or other cities to be sold at an attractive profit in the farmers' markets (*rynki*). With their profits, these enterprising people purchase rugs, pots and pans, clothing, and other goods that are not available in their home regions. Because Soviet airline tickets are quite cheap (and regulations governing carry-on baggage are quite lax), many of these people fly to the big cities carrying huge net bags filled with tomatoes, cucumbers, oranges, and even live chickens.

The farmers' markets are the only places in the Soviet economy where market forces appear to work relatively unimpeded. Each collective farmer is entitled to a private plot of land of up to 1.5 acres. The produce from these plots may be sold at the farmers' markets for whatever price the seller wishes to charge. Consequently, one can find fresh vegetables at the market virtually any time of the year, although the prices may be four or more times higher than the same item at a state store. The difference is that the state stores are virtually barren much of the year.

The private plots play no small role in Soviet agriculture, contributing approximately 25 percent of total production.[24] They account for 30 percent of all milk, 31 percent of all eggs, 32 percent of all vegetables, 41 percent of all fruit, and 63 percent of all potatoes produced in the USSR.[25] While some see this as proof of the superiority of the free market, it is also true that collective farmers routinely shirk their duties on the collective farmland and devote their time to tending their private plots. Fertilizer, seed, and pesticides are often stolen from the collective's storehouses and used on private plots. The collective's harvest may suffer as a result, but the lower earnings of the *kolkhozniki* are more than compensated for by increased earnings from the produce from their private plots.

The extensive "second economy" in the USSR consists of a wide variety of illegal or quasi-legal economic activities operating beyond the realm of state regulations and directives. By far the most prevalent form of illegal economic activity is theft of state property. Given the low salary levels of most workers and the chronic shortages of numerous items, workers often feel they are justified in stealing from their employers. Collective farmers steal seed and tools; automobile assembly-line workers steal spare parts; waiters and cooks in restaurants steal food; physicians steal medicine; taxi drivers steal gasoline and use state-owned cars as unofficial "gypsy" taxis. Theft of state property is becoming so prevalent that some engineers and technicians are reportedly leaving their posts in research and design bureaus to work in restaurants, where they will have the opportunity to steal food.[26]

While theft of state property entails a high cost to the State, it fuels an enormous black market in agricultural products, spare parts, food, medicine, gasoline, and other commodities. This illegal network unquestionably is more efficient than the state bureaucracy would be at distributing such items.

Grey market activities—that is, economic transactions that are technically legal but outside the structure of the official Soviet economy—are especially common in the service sector. Doctors, lawyers, dentists, mechanics, repair people, dressmakers, and hairdressers provide services on the side, often on state time and using state-owned tools, equipment, and materials. Similarly, the service trades are notorious in the Soviet Union for requiring bribes or "gifts" in order to provide good service. Gorbachev has tried to incorporate these activities in the legal economy by permitting a limited degree of private enterprise.

Officials can use the power of their positions to acquire special favors. Whether it is the director of a construction trust who has his workers build him a summer cottage, or the director of a collective farm who gets first pick of the collective's garden plot, officials and influential people are the recipients of many benefits of the grey market. A Soviet economist who emigrated to the West developed a typology of colored markets in the "second economy," as shown in Table 10–2.

PERESTROIKA

When Gorbachev came to power in March 1985 he did not immediately begin the radical restructuring of the economy with the goal of establishing a market-oriented system. Rather, he sought to make relatively minor adjustments that would enable the economic system to function more efficiently. In a speech on February 20, 1985, a few weeks prior to assuming the post of General Secretary, he blamed the Soviet economic slowdown on the failure of

Table 10-2. Colored Markets in the USSR

Nature of Market	Commodity	Source	Method of Sale	Example
White (legal)	Legal	Legal	Legal	Sale of food in a state store or farmers' market
Grey (semi-legal)	Legal	Legal	Semi-legal	Selling Italian shoes "under the counter"
	Legal	Semi-legal	Legal	Providing dental treatment on the side, using state-owned equipment and supplies
	Legal	Semi-legal	Semi-legal	Purchase of blue jeans from a foreign tourist
Black (illegal)	Legal	Legal	Illegal	Speculation—selling vodka for more than the mandated price
	Legal	Semi-legal	Semi-legal	Selling blue jeans purchased from foreign tourist
	Legal	Illegal	Illegal	Sale of stolen auto parts
	Illegal	Illegal	Illegal	Prostitution; narcotics

Source: This table is a revised version of a typology of colored markets developed by A. Katsenelinboigen in "Coloured Markets in the Soviet Union," *Soviet Studies* 29, no. 1 (1977): 63.

economic officials to undertake necessary changes.[27] He advocated granting greater decision-making authority to factory, state farm, and collective farm managers, which would free central planners and ministerial officials to concentrate on larger problems, such as investment priorities, regional development, living standards, and foreign economic policy.

Gorbachev advocated consolidating the more than sixty industrial ministries and state committees into five to seven "superministries," thus reducing the fragmentation of the economy that impedes the development of advanced technology and undermines coordination among sectors. In his first year in office, he succeeded in creating three such "superministries"—in agriculture, machine building, and energy.[28]

Gorbachev also proposed scaling back on the extensive increases in agricultural investment that had characterized previous five-year plans. He favored a moderate reduction in agricultural investment, a stable rate of investment in energy and raw materials, and dramatic increases in investments in high-technology engineering industries. The latter were slated to rise by 80 to 100 percent during the Twelfth Five-Year Plan (1986–1990).[29] Gorbachev proposed increases in investments in the computer, electronics, chemicals, and other "new technologies" sectors, but he also expected those resources to result in even larger increases in production. A major thrust of the increased investment was targeted toward reequipping existing factories and enterprises and introducing automated production techniques to increase quality and efficiency.

Gorbachev's reformist orientation was also confirmed by his support for the reform-oriented Institute of Economics and Organization of Industrial Production of the Siberian division of the USSR Academy of Sciences. Abel Aganbegyan, the former director of the Institute and a widely recognized advocate of fundamental economic reforms, was brought from Novosibirsk to Moscow to be Gorbachev's chief economic advisor. Many proposals for reforming the economy were openly discussed after Gorbachev took office. These proposals included greater self-financing of R&D and capital expansion projects; reduction in the number of output indicators; placing greater emphasis on labor productivity, profitability, and contract fulfillment; and greater stability in plan inputs and targets. In agriculture, Aganbegyan noted that a land rent was being considered to stimulate agricultural units to use land more efficiently.[30]

In order to actually undertake fundamental economic reforms, however, Gorbachev would have to overcome the opposition of the status-quo-oriented interests. The ministries and mid-level economic administrators in industrial associations represent the single most consistent obstacle to the introduction of economic reforms in the USSR. They are the most conservative segments in the economy and are also the groups criticized by Aganbegyan and Gorbachev.[31] Past reforms, such as those introduced in 1973 and 1979 and the "economic experiments" launched in five ministries in 1984, encountered foot-dragging and outright opposition; ministers refused to delegate power to enterprise managers and fought to preserve their powers to shift inputs and adjust enterprise production plans in order to ensure overall plan fulfillment by the ministry. Gorbachev's ability to overcome this opposition depended on his success in expanding his authority and extending his power through patronage.

During his first year in office, Gorbachev kept on a moderate course of economic reform. In his public statements, Gorbachev assiduously avoided using the word "reform," preferring instead the phrase "improving the economic mechanism." Aganbegyan's positions also seemed to become more moderate and compromising after he came to Moscow. He too avoided using "reform" and instead talked of a "major structural rebuilding" of the economy.[32] Gorbachev's appointments of industrial ministers during this time also reflected his recognition that efficient, high-technology production was possible within the existing organization and incentive structures of the Soviet economy.

Following the Twenty-Seventh Party Congress in February 1986, Gorbachev launched a more radical and vigorous series of economic reforms. Below, we examine each component of *perestroika* in greater detail. As we will see, the reforms introduced under the banner of *perestroika* attempt to address chronic problems that have persisted in the Soviet economy since Stalin's time. On the other hand, the reforms have some negative consequences that may undermine their implementation.

Decentralization of Economic Decision-Making.   As we have seen, centralized planning of the economy was extended under Stalin to every factory and farm in the USSR. As the economy grew in size and complexity, the ability of central planners to allocate resources and direct enterprises efficiently was severely diminished. Rather than deciding for themselves when to plant crops, apply fertilizer, or harvest crops, farm managers waited for directives to filter down from the ministry in Moscow. Factory managers were instructed what to produce, in what assortment, how many workers to employ, what price to charge for their products, and where they should be sold. This system of micromanagement by distant officials resulted in countless fiascos. For example, a state farm manager once confided to the author that a shipment of fertilizer for his farm arrived too late to be applied to the fields prior to planting. Fearful that state agricultural inspectors would discover the fertilizer had not been applied, in violation of an order from the central ministry, he had the fertilizer burned.

Gorbachev recognized the inefficiency of such minute central planning and in 1987 moved to grant factory managers and farm directors more discretion in making production decisions. Enterprises now determine what they produce, how many people to employ, and to whom they will sell their products. While this is good news for factory managers and farm directors who display initiative and have chafed under the restrictions imposed on them from the center, for others it asks them to take risks and make decisions which they are unaccustomed to doing.

Numerous Soviet commentators have noted that factory managers lack the training to assess market trends and consumer demand.[33] Nikolai Shmelev, one of Gorbachev's economic advisors, noted that these new responsibilities have tended to confuse factory management and that it will take some time for them to develop the necessary skills and psychological disposition to be willing to assume risks as Western managers do.[34]

Self-Financing.   Beginning in 1987 and gradually phased in by 1989, Soviet enterprises went onto a system of self-financing. Under self-financing, Soviet enterprises are expected to generate sufficient income to cover their operating costs and personnel expenses. In other words, Soviet factories and farms are expected to be profitable, and if they are not they may be closed down. While self-financing addresses the need to revamp or close inefficient and unproductive factories, it is not without its problems. Factory managers were initially uncertain how to proceed without ministerial subsidies. Capital investment funds necessary to modernize plants and equipment now have to be generated from enterprise earnings. However, it is unclear how many enterprises are going to be able to generate the necessary funds to accomplish this task.

Another consequence of self-financing is that factories have sought to minimize operating costs. Soviet factories that had previously employed as much as 20 percent more workers than they needed have laid off excess labor force to reduce operating costs. Those laid off tend to be the least-productive workers—alchoholics, older workers, unskilled laborers, and young women.[35] Already hundreds of obsolete factories have been shut down and workers have had to find new jobs. Soviet sources estimate that by the year 2000 some 16 million workers will have been forced to change their work.[36]

While there are ample jobs for workers in the USSR, the majority of new jobs are in the service sector, where the average wage is 30 percent below that in manufacturing.[37] The loss of job security coupled with the threatened reduction of earnings is indeed troubling to Soviet workers.

Quality Control Program.   During the Brezhnev years, work discipline declined dramatically. Workers showed little concern for the quality of the goods they produced. Thefts of spare parts from factories often resulted in products being turned out that were incomplete or inoperative.

Recognizing this problem, in 1987 Gorbachev proposed the creation of a quality control inspection agency, similar to the system used in defense industries. Today quality control inspectors must certify that all items produced in their factories meet quality norms. If the products fail to measure up to standards, they will not count toward the production quota of the factory.

According to a TASS report, the stricter quality control regime resulted in 900 factories' failing to meet their production quotas in January 1987 alone.[38] In the Gorky region as many as one-third of all industrial enterprises failed to meet their planned quotas and as a consequence their workers did not receive bonuses.[39] Bonuses have traditionally accounted for a significant portion of a worker's income—as much as one-third of total earnings.

As Gorbachev moved to stricter accountability and efforts to tie earnings to performance, the net result for many workers has been a loss in income. For example, the Soviet press reported on a strike of bus drivers in Chekhov.[40] The drivers were protesting the introduction of a performance-linked pay plan. The drivers noted that it was unfair to hold them accountable for keeping to a set schedule when their buses were in poor repair and they had no funds for keeping them in working condition. They estimated that the new pay scheme had resulted in an average reduction in their monthly wage of more than 10 rubles.

Price Reforms.   Prices in the USSR have long been set with little regard for actual cost of production. Consumer goods, food items, and rents, among other goods and services, have been heavily subsidized by setting prices artificially low. For example, the price of a loaf of bread—16 kopeks or approximately one half cent—is so low that youngsters, unable to buy soccer balls in the stores, can be seen playing soccer with loaves of bread.

Western estimates indicate that these subsidies on food alone cost the Soviet economy some 130 billion rubles per year and account for some 30 percent of the state budget.[41] Furthermore, subsidies have risen relative to the general economy—a twenty-fold increase in the past 25 years. Subsidized prices are the primary cause of the rapidly increasing budget deficit in the USSR. By 1989 the Soviet economy was running a deficit of some 100 billion rubles ($17 billion), which represents approximately 10 percent of the total output of the Soviet economy.[42] Another cause of the budget deficit in the USSR is the precipitous drop in government earnings from alchohol sales due to Gorbachev's anti-alchohol campaign. Alchohol sales fell by 37 percent in 1986, representing a loss to the state of some 16 billion rubles.[43]

Even without an official and systematic change in prices, the inflation rate is estimated to be between 8 and 10 percent per year.[44] Incomes are rising at a steady rate, but there is little for the Soviet worker to purchase. Jan Vanous of PlanEcon estimates that 73 percent of additional income is saved.[45] Bank account savings in the USSR average more than $1700 per person—an amount approximately equal to one-half year's salary. Soviet citizens are hoarding money in expectation of higher prices.

Privatization.   In January 1987 the USSR Supreme Soviet introduced a law that expanded the range of private economic activity. In an effort to draw a wide range of black market activities into the legal economy, the law permitted people to establish privately owned and operated businesses. The majority of "cooperatives" are in the service sector—beauty parlors, tailors, cafés and restaurants, and shoe repair shops. However, private cooperatives have also expanded to include a wide range of activities such as farming and small-scale manufacturing, as well as white-collar areas such as software programming, management consulting, and medical and dental services.

The laws governing private cooperatives initially were quite restrictive, limiting the cooperatives to no more than ten employees. They are taxed at very high rates, and the bureaucratic obstacles that must be overcome in setting up such a cooperative have discouraged many potential entrepreneurs.

Private cooperatives have also encountered popular resistance. *Moscow News* cited the case of a privately owned pig farm outside of Moscow that was opposed by neighbors because of their concerns that it would smell.[46] After several attempts to shut down the cooperative, it was finally burned to the ground. *Moscow News* commented that apparently it wasn't the smell of the pigs that bothered the people, but the smell of capitalism. Many Soviet citizens fear that private cooperatives will result in gross income differentiation—some people will become very wealthy, while average workers will fall behind. Others complain that cooperatives charge inflated prices and siphon off resources—especially food—from state-run stores where prices are much less. To some extent these complaints are valid. For example, on the main commercial street in Moscow, Tverskaya Street (formerly Gorky Street), a private café offers a meal for approximately eight times the price of the same meal in a state-run restaurant. The difference is that state-run restaurants are crowded and dirty, the employees are surly, and they rarely have even one-quarter of the items listed on the menu. Some government-operated restaurants complain that for weeks at a time they have not had meat, eggs, or cheese to serve, while the private cooperatives that can afford to pay high prices for scarce produce appear to have ample supplies. For many Soviet citizens, however, especially those on fixed incomes, cooperatives are a luxury they cannot afford.

Privatization of agriculture has existed on some level since 1917. As we noted earlier, private land plots accounted for a sizable portion of poultry, dairy products, and fruits and vegetables in the USSR. Gorbachev broadened the concept of the private land plots. He initiated legislation that permits farmers to lease land from the State for a period of up to ninety years, and to farm privately, selling their produce to the State or on the private farmers' markets.

Private farming, however, has not proven to be very popular with Soviet farmers. They fear that they will be the lowest-priority recipients of seed grain, fertilizer, herbicides, livestock feed, gasoline, and other essentials. Few farmers have the capital to purchase their own tractors or harvesters, and no one is certain how they would manage to transport their crops or livestock to market, since the trucking and rail systems are still state-controlled.

Fundamental doubts, uncertainties, and unaccustomed risks prompt many farmers to decline the opportunity to farm privately. "Some of these younger men may have the head for it," observed one old Russian peasant; "As for me, I don't have the proper training to make all those decisions." Another adds, "What if we have a bad harvest? How am I supposed to get by? As it is now, the State guarantees my salary regardless."[47]

REDEFINING THE SOCIAL CONTRACT

Collectively, Gorbachev's economic reforms have substantially changed the work environment for the Soviet labor force. During the Brezhnev years, workers liked to recite the saying, "I pretend to work, and they pretend to pay me." Gorbachev's reforms have altered the equation. Workers can no longer be idle on the job, or steal from their factories, or show up for work late and leave early. They now have to be concerned that their products meet quality standards or they may lose their bonuses. For the first time ever, they are confronted with the prospect of unemployment. Factory managers and private entrepreneurs have to learn to assume risks in making production decisions. Consumers are having to adjust to shortages and steep price increases on goods.

Perestroika has succeeded in destroying the centrally planned and directed economy constructed under Stalin. However, a market system has not yet evolved to replace the old system. Soviet experience shows that the transition from a centrally planned to a quasi-market system is a difficult process. It is natural that such a transformation, at least in the short run, will produce a great deal of dislocation and chaos.

Compounding Gorbachev's problem is the fact that his economic reforms have created rapidly inflated and unrealistic expectations in both East and West. In May 1988, a telephone poll of Muscovites found that 73 percent strongly supported *perestroika;* 23 percent supported it with reservations.[48] Forty percent of the respondents expected their standard of living to improve in the next five years. By October 1989, just one and one-half years later, 90 percent of respondents to a public opinion poll considered the nation's economic situation bad or critical and a majority attributed the worsening situation to Gorbachev's reforms.[49]

The widening gap between popular expectations and dismal economic performance translates into public frustration, skepticism, and the erosion of political support for Gorbachev's economic reforms. Yet Gorbachev needs mass popular support if he is to overcome the conservative and entrenched bureaucratic interests that are opposing the restructuring of the economy. The future of *perestroika* is very much in doubt.

Notes

1. For example, see John Tedstrom, "Economic Slide Continues," *Radio Liberty Research Bulletin* 12, no. 37: 10.

2. For Soviet national income data, see *Narodnoe khozyaistvo v SSSR, 1974* (Moscow: Statistika, 1975), 5.

3. Ibid.

4. Andrew Freris, *The Soviet Industrial Enterprise: Theory and Practice* (London: Croom Helm, 1984), 8.

5. Alec Nove, *The Soviet Economic System* (Boston: Allen and Unwin, 1977), 84.

6. *Narodnoe khozyaistvo, 1922–1982* (Moscow: Statistika, 1982), 91–92.

7. Alec Nove, *The Soviet Economic System*, 84.

8. *Izvestiya*, 9 November 1985, pp. 1–6.

9. See Paul R. Gregory and Robert C. Stuart, *Soviet Economic Structure and Performance* (New York: Harper & Row, 1974), 199.

10. See Freris, *Soviet Industrial Enterprise*, 13.

11. *Pravda*, 27 May 1984, p. 2.

12. V. Kim and L. Ivanov, "Nadzor za ispoleneniem zakonov ob otetstennosti za nedobrokachestvennoe stroitel'stvo," *Sotsialisticheskaya zakonnost'* (May 1975): 35–38.

13. Fydor Turovsky, "Society Without a Present," in Leonard Schapiro and Joseph Godson, eds., *The Soviet Worker from Lenin to Andropov*, 2d ed. (London: Macmillan, 1984), 197.

14. See Gordon B. Smith, "Organizational and Legal Problems in the Implementation of Technology in the USSR," in Gordon B. Smith, Peter Maggs, and George Ginsburgs, eds., *Soviet and East European Law and the Scientific-Technical Revolution* (New York: Pergamon Press, 1981), 240–271.

15. Cited in M. S. Studenikina, "Zakonodatel'stvo ob administrativnoi otvetstennosti kodifikatsii" (Moscow: Candidate dissertation, VNIISZ, 1968), p. 145–146.

16. Keith Bush, "Retail Prices in Moscow and Four Western Cities in March 1982," *Radio Liberty Research Supplement* (4 June 1982).

17. J. G. Chapman, "Recent Trends in the Soviet Industrial Wage Structure," in A. Kahan and Blair Ruble, *Industrial Labor in the USSR* (New York: Pergamon Press, 1979), 175.

18. Murray Seeger, "Eyewitness to Failure," in Schapiro and Godson, *The Soviet Worker*, 94.

19. Gail Warshofsky Lapidus, *Women in Soviet Society* (Berkeley: University of California Press, 1978), 55.

20. Yu. B. Ryurikov, "Family Matters? No, Matters of State!" *Ekonomika i organizatsiya promyshlennovo proizvodstva*, no.10 (October 1982): 149–170.

21. *Zhenshchiny v SSSR* (Moscow: Politizdat, 1983), 12–13.

22. Alastair McAuley, *Women's Work and Wages in the Soviet Union* (London: George Allen & Unwin, 1981), 87–89.

23. Ibid., 21.

24. *Istoriya SSSR*, no. 5 (September-October 1984): 120–126.

25. Ibid.

26. George Feifer, "Russian Disorders: The Sick Man of Europe," *Harper's* (February 1981): 48.

27. *Pravda*, 21 February 1985, p. 2.

28. In the case of agriculture, all of the former agriculturally related ministries were abolished and placed under the direction of the State Committee for the Agro-Industrial Complex. In the other two sectors, however, the ministries were retained, but were subordinated to an "umbrella" coordinating body within the presidium of the USSR Council of Ministers.

29. Speech by Mikhail Gorbachev on Moscow Television, June 11, 1985.

30. Cited in Elizabeth Teague, "Aganbegyan Outlines Gorbachev's Economic Policy," *Radio Liberty Research Bulletin 29,* no. 42 (9 October 1985), p. 5.

31. For example, see "The Novosibirsk Report," *Survey* (Spring 1984): 88–108; and Abel Aganbegyan, "Na novom etape ekonomicheskogo stroitel'stva," *EKO,* no. 8 (1985): 3–24.

32. Aganbegyan, "Na novom etape ekonomicheskogo stroitel'stva"; and Abel Aganbegyan, "Strategiya uskoreniya sotsial'no-ekonomicheskogo razvitiya," *Problemy mira i sotsializma,* no. 9 (1985): 13–18.

33. For example, see Aaron Trehub, "The Importance of Psychological Restructuring," *Radio Liberty Research Bulletin,* 32, no. 43 (26 October 1988).

34. John Tedstrom, "Soviet Economist Sounds the Alarm over Perestroika," *Radio Liberty Research Bulletin,* 32, no. 20 (11 May 1988): 4.

35. See discussion of "structural unemployment" in D. J. Peterson, "Unemployment in the USSR," *Radio Liberty Report on the USSR* 1, no. 34 (25 August 1989): 5–10.

36. Aaron Trehub, "Joint Party-Government Resolution on Employment," *Radio Liberty Research Bulletin,* 32, no. 6 (10 February 1988), 2.

37. Ibid.

38. *New York Times,* 24 March 1987, p. 8.

39. Ibid.

40. *Moscow News,* 20 September 1987, p. 9.

41. *New York Times,* 25 May 1990, p. A6.

42. Marie Lavigne, "Financing the Transition in the USSR," Public Policy Paper no. 2, New York: Institute for East-West Security Studies, 1990, p. 29.

43. *New York Times,* 24 May 1987, p. 8.

44. *New York Times,* 13 May 1990, p. 12.

45. Ibid.

46. *Moscow News,* 24 July 1988, pp. 8–9.

47. From "Inside Gorbachev's Russia: Part III: Perestroika." Public Broadcasting Corporation, 1990.

48. *New York Times,* 13 May 1990, p. 12.

49. Ibid.

Selected Bibliography

Aganbegyan, Abel. *Inside Prestroika: The Future of the Soviet Economy.* New York: Perennial Library,1989.

Aganbegyan, Abel and Timor Timofeyev, *The New Stage of Perestroika.* New York: Institute for East-West Security Studies, 1988.

Bergson, Abram, and Herbert S. Levine, eds. *The Soviet Economy Toward the Year 2000.* London: George Allen & Unwin, 1983.

Bornstein, Morris, ed. *The Soviet Economy: Continuity and Change.* Boulder, CO: Westview Press, 1981.

Campbell, Robert W. *Soviet-Type Economies: Performance and Evolution.* New York: Houghton Mifflin, 1974.

Colton, Timothy. *Dilemma of Reform in the USSR.* New York: Council on Foreign Relations, 1985.

Freris, Andrew. *The Soviet Industrial Enterprise: Theory and Practice.* London: Croom Helm, 1984.

Hewett, Ed A. *Reforming the Soviet Economy: Equality versus Efficiency.* Washington: Brookings Institution Press, 1988.

Kahan, A., and Blair A. Ruble, eds. *Industrial Labor in the USSR*. New York: Pergamon Press, 1979.

Lane, David. *Soviet Economy and Society*. Oxford: Basil Blackwell, 1985.

Lane, David, and Felicity O'Dell. *The Soviet Industrial Worker*. Oxford: Martin Robertson, 1978.

Lapidus, Gail Warshofsky. *Women in Soviet Society*. Berkeley: University of California Press, 1978.

Lavigne, Marie. "Financing the Transition in the USSR: The Shatalin Plan and the Soviet Economy." Public Policy Paper no. 2, New York: Institute for East-West Security Studies, 1990.

McAuley, Alastair. *Women's Work and Wages in the Soviet Union*. London: George Allen & Unwin, 1981.

Matthews, Mervyn. *Privilege in the Soviet Union*. London: George Allen & Unwin, 1978.

Moskoff, William. *Labor and Leisure in the Soviet Union*. London: Macmillan, 1984.

Nove, Alec. *The Soviet Economic System*. 3d ed. Boston: Unwin Hyman, 1986.

Ruble, Blair A. *Soviet Trade Unions*. Cambridge: Cambridge University Press, 1981.

Schapiro, Leonard, and Joseph Godson, eds. *The Soviet Worker from Lenin to Andropov*. London: Macmillan, 1984.

U.S. Congress, Joint Economic Committee. *Soviet Economy in the 1980s: Problems and Prospects*. Washington, DC: U.S. Government Printing Office, 1982.

Yanowitch, Murray. *Social and Economic Inequality in the Soviet Union*. New York: M. E. Sharpe, 1977.

11

Social Policy and Problems

In the twentieth century, advanced industrialized nations increasingly have sought to guarantee to all citizens certain minimum living standards. The Soviet Union is no exception; in fact, in several respects it epitomizes the social welfare state. The 1936 Constitution guaranteed Soviet citizens the right to a job, health care, education, maintenance in old age, and leisure. The 1977 Constitution added to these fundamental human rights the right to housing and access to cultural achievements. The rapid decline of the economy in recent years, however, has hit the social welfare area especially hard. To what extent has the Soviet system translated the formal pronouncement of these social and economic rights into reality, and how has the commitment to social equality changed under *perestroika?* This chapter seeks to answer these questions by analyzing Soviet policies and performance in three areas of social policy: housing, health care, and social security.

HOUSING IN THE SOVIET UNION

Bolshevik housing practices initially reflected the experimental family policies of Madame Kollontai, who advocated the radical transformation of the family, with familial ties subordinated to those of the collective or commune. Kollontai envisaged house-communes, rather than the traditional single-family houses or apartments.

Communal housing was indeed prevalent during the 1920s, but it was more the result of economic necessity than a reflection of revolutionary ideology. The day after the Bolshevik seizure of power, Lenin issued a decree confiscating all large urban houses and townhomes from the aristocracy and the middle class. These were used to house workers and peasants whose homes had been destroyed by the ravages of World War I and the Revolution. The Civil War destroyed even more housing. From 1918 to 1921, the housing stock in Petrograd (currently Leningrad) declined by 17 percent, while in Moscow it declined by 30 percent.[1] Famine in the countryside prompted a massive exodus from rural areas to the cities, worsening an already overcrowded situation. Urban homes and apartments initially intended for one family had to accommodate several families per room—all sharing a single bath and kitchen. Workers in the newly established industrial areas were forced to live in hurriedly constructed barracks.

The fledgling Soviet regime proved incapable of managing the existing housing supply, much less making repairs or building new residential units.

During the New Economic Policy (NEP), housing was, in effect, denational-ized in an effort to stimulate residents to take responsibility for the repair and upkeep of their own units. In 1922, individuals were given the right to con-struct houses, and land was provided free of charge. By 1926, two-thirds of all new housing was privately built.[2]

The moderate policies of NEP ended abruptly in 1928, when Stalin redirected the emphasis to industrialization. Private leases were terminated, and building supplies were absorbed by Stalin's ambitious development proj-ects. During the First Five-Year Plan (1928—1932), private construction of housing fell from 40 percent of total housing construction to less than 1 percent.[3] Collectivization further drove peasants from the countryside to the city, adding to the strain on the existing housing supply.

Under Stalin, the social welfare goals of the USSR were inevitably subor-dinated to the realities of rapid industrialization, collectivization, and social modernization. In order to finance his program of rapid industrial develop-ment, Stalin asked Soviet citizens to make "serious sacrifices" and imposed a "regime of the strictest economy."[4] Investments in housing, health care, and other social programs fell sharply, while massive amounts of capital were funneled into industrial production. As a proportion of total investment in the economy, housing fell from 17 percent in the 1920s, to 9 percent during the First Five-Year Plan, to 8 percent by 1939.[5] Plans for housing construction routinely went unfulfilled—by as much as 50 percent.[6] The economic strin-gency of Stalin's policies forced hard choices among various competing social policies. Stalin favored education and health care because they had a more immediate impact on worker productivity. Consequently, greater efforts were made in those spheres, while housing languished.

Under Stalin, the gap widened between the quality of housing provided to the political elite, high-ranking military officers and the intelligentsia and that provided to average workers and peasants. Thus, members of the elite strata were insulated from the generally poor living conditions that prevailed in the country.

While private housing construction tapered off under Stalin, industrial enterprises were encouraged to construct housing for their employees, espe-cially in the new towns springing up around the country. By the beginning of World War II, factory housing represented 20 percent of all residential units.[7]

The war devastated the housing supply in the USSR. More than 1710 cities and towns were destroyed, including more than 6 million dwellings—one-quarter of the total housing in the USSR.[8] More than 25 million people were displaced and without housing after the war.[9] Millions more lived in severely damaged or substandard accommodations. The bulk of capital and resources, however, was earmarked for reconstructing the Soviet Union's demolished industrial base, rather than its housing. Private construction was again encouraged in order to alleviate the situation, but the impoverished citizens could not afford to build their own houses, and supplies were scarce or nonexistent.

At the time of Stalin's death in 1953, the living conditions of the average Soviet family were actually worse than they had been in 1926.[10] Western experts estimate that Soviet housing in the mid-1950s was roughly comparable to that of tenement dwellers in the United States in the 1890s.[11] John Gunther describes the deplorable condition of Soviet housing:

> Every citizen is supposed to have nine square meters of floor space, but most do not have even half of this . . . people are crowded three, four, five or even more to a room, with disastrous social consequences. Young people cannot marry, because they can find no place to live. Scarcely any Soviet family is without a covey of in-laws living on the premises, and it is rare for any family to have its own private bath and kitchen . . . sometimes a single doorway leads to a nest of stalls where a dozen people live. . . . One reason why the streets are so thronged at night, even in the winter . . . is that homes are so unbelievably crowded, squalid, and uncomfortable.[12]

Under the populist leader Nikita Khrushchev, housing and other social policies were finally given high priority. A resolution of the CPSU Central Committee and the USSR Council of Ministers in 1957 acknowledged that housing conditions in the Soviet Union were intolerable for the vast majority of the population and promised to rectify the situation. The decree reorganized the housing construction industry, shifting production to favor prefabricated units. Thanks to the new thrust, housing construction during the late 1950s for the first time exceeded planned levels; approximately 2 million units were being built per year, more than in any other country. Investment in housing during the Sixth Five-Year Plan (1956–1960) reached a high of 23.2 percent of total capital investment.[13]

Between 1956 and 1970, 34.2 million housing units were built in the USSR.[14] These units were occupied by 126.5 million citizens, more than one-half of the entire population of the Soviet Union. This represents a stunning achievement and a major commitment by the Khrushchev and Brezhnev regimes to improve living conditions for average citizens.

During the building boom under Khrushchev and Brezhnev, large numbers of single-family apartments (otdel'nye kvartiry) were constructed, with the goal of entirely eliminating communal apartments. Quality of construction, square footage, attractiveness, and access to social services and public transportation were sacrificed to meet this primary objective. "Khrushchev houses," as they came to be called, were uniform, prefabricated, grey concrete apartment buildings, usually five to seven stories tall (with no elevators). These apartment buildings were situated on the fringes of the major cities, where land was readily available. The units normally consisted of two-room apartments—living room and one bedroom, with a small entrance hall, bath, and kitchen. The average size of the apartments was 45 square meters, less than the minimum sanitary norm established by the housing authorities.[15] Most apartments housed at least four people, often as many as six or seven. Shoddy construction gave rise to numerous complaints, but with pent-up demand for housing still unsatisfied, the authorities continued to focus on new construction rather than on repairing existing housing.

Planners organized "Khrushchev houses" into microdistricts (mikroraiony) in which several apartment buildings formed a cluster. In the middle of the cluster, buildings to accommodate stores, libraries, polyclinics, schools, kindergartens, and community centers were planned. However, in the rush to satisfy the demand for housing, these amenities were accorded low priority. Most of the new neighborhoods also lacked playgrounds, parks, and access to public transportation. Nevertheless, they were an improvement over the overcrowded communal flats in the center-city areas, and there were long waiting lists of people requesting the new units.

Khrushchev attempted to centralize the management of housing through the local soviets, thus stripping industrial enterprises of housing they had built at Stalin's urging. In the 1950s, the State managed almost half of all housing; in rural areas, the majority of housing remained privately owned, and most new construction was undertaken by individuals or collective farms.

Under Brezhnev, housing construction advanced considerably. The typical apartment buildings constructed during the 1970s were nine to fourteen stories tall (with elevators), containing slightly larger two-room apartments. Each apartment building might house as many as seven hundred families. Given this phenomenal population density, concerted efforts were made to improve the quality of social services and public transportation in the newly established microdistricts.

Overcrowding in housing units gives rise to serious social consequences. Soviet youth complain of a lack of privacy. It is virtually impossible for a single young adult to locate a private apartment or even a room in a communal flat. Most young people do not leave their parents' homes until they are married. Once a young couple is married and their names are placed on the waiting list for housing, it may still be another eight to ten years before they actually receive a separate apartment.

Because bars and other drinking establishments are few in the USSR, most alcohol is consumed at home. Cramped living conditions combined with alcohol abuse frequently give rise to domestic violence. Most murders and other violent crimes are committed under the influence of alcohol, in the home, and among people who are related or close friends. Alcohol abuse is reported to be the most common cause of divorce. Not surprisingly, the divorce rates in urban areas are rising rapidly, exceeding one out of every three marriages.[16]

The crowded housing conditions often preclude more than two generations' living in the same apartment. Young couples who are attracted to the cities tend to leave their parents behind in the countryside. Without the assistance of the grandmother (*babushka*), who was traditionally responsible for child care, cooking, and cleaning, these tasks fall to the mothers, who are also employed full-time in other jobs in most cases. In addition, the lack of supervision of children in after-school hours has resulted in increased incidence of juvenile delinquency.

The housing boom under Brezhnev barely kept pace with the urban population growth caused by out-migration from rural areas. In order to restrict the growth of urban centers, a registration (*propiska*) system has been enforced in Moscow, Leningrad, Kiev, and several other cities. Persons wishing to move to one of the "closed" cities must first acquire a *propiska*, usually from an employer. The registration system has had only marginal success, however, in stemming the flow of people to urban areas. Individuals find various ways to circumvent the system and obtain the necessary documentation for a *propiska*. Some even arrange fictitious marriages with Muscovites or Leningraders in order to obtain authorization to live in those cities.

The influx of people has kept demand for housing high despite the government's efforts to build more housing. Many urban residents still live in substandard accommodations. One-quarter of all urban families, most of them newly married couples, live in communal apartments and must share a kitchen and bath with others.[17] Shoddy workmanship continues to characterize housing construction; the Soviet press frequently prints letters to the editor complaining about newly constructed buildings in which the plumbing is faulty or even nonexistent. In 1971, a total of 23 percent of all urban housing lacked running water, 18 percent lacked central heat, 35 percent had no bath or shower, and 27 percent had no toilet facilities.[18]

Housing space has risen gradually from 4.7 square meters per capita in 1950 to 10.6 square meters per capita today.[19] Yet some 38 million people still live in apartments with less than 5 square meters per person.[20] Eight million families live in dormitories or communal apartments, and five million citizens live in housing units that are judged "in disastrous condition" by housing officials.[21] The sanitary norm is currently met in only five of the fifteen republics.

Investment in housing has declined steadily since the mid-1950s, as Table 11–1 shows. Declining rates of growth of national income coupled with ever-increasing demands for investment capital in the military and industrial sectors have resulted in drastically reduced investments in housing and other social services.

The average age of the housing stock is growing rapidly, making upkeep a serious problem in Soviet housing today. The "Khrushchev apartments" built in the 1950s were in a serious state of decay soon after they were built; today more than thirty years old, they may soon be uninhabitable if major renovations are not undertaken.

Repairs and upkeep are complicated by the low rents on housing in the

Table 11-1. Investments in Housing as a Percentage of Total Capital Investment

Sixth Five-Year Plan (1956–1960)	23.2
Seventh Five-Year Plan (1961–1965)	18.3
Eighth Five-Year Plan (1966–1970)	17.0
Ninth Five-Year Plan (1971–1975)	14.7
Tenth Five-Year Plan (1976–1980)	13.6
Eleventh Five-Year Plan (1981–1985)	13.3
Twelfth Five-Year Plan (1986–1990)	12*

*Estimate.
Sources: Henry W. Morton, "What Have Soviet Leaders Done about the Housing Crisis?" in Henry W. Morton and Rudolf L. Tokes, eds., *Soviet Politics and Society in the 1970s* (New York: The Free Press, 1974), 168; *Narodnoe khozyaistvo v SSSR v 1983* (Moscow: Finansy i statistika, 1984); and "Stoiteli v startovom godu pyatiletki," *Ekonomika stroitel'stva*, no. 1 (1986): 3–11.

USSR. Rent is calculated on the basis of square footage; in Moscow, rents average only 7 rubles (less than one dollar) per month. Utilities are likewise subsidized and average 10 to 15 rubles per month.[22] With rents so low, money for repairs and upkeep must come from state housing budgets, but officials are reluctant to divert money for repairs when there is still pent-up demand for new housing.

Much of the money for housing is distributed to high-priority industrial sectors or regions to stimulate labor productivity and to attract workers. In 1980, for example, Soviet planners announced a three-year plan for accelerating housing construction in the oil and gas region of Tiumen *oblast'*. More than 1.5 million square meters of new housing were built, tripling the level of housing construction in the region.[23] The apartments built there were also larger than the national norm, averaging 10 square meters per capita.[24]

The quality of housing of a factory or institution is directly related to its prestige. Thus, the apartments owned by the Academy of Sciences for its researchers are among the most desirable in Moscow. Similarly, award-winning factories and production associations boast attractive and relatively spacious apartments for many of their workers, while low-priority enterprises and state farms receive fewer housing funds and provide apartments of much poorer quality to their employees.

Factories and enterprises also maintain furnished dormitory-style hostels for young single workers. Approximately 3.5 million young people reside in these institutions.[25] The hostels are managed by "commandants" and have a curfew; nevertheless, they are often dirty and noisy. Life in the worker hostels was depicted in a popular Soviet movie, *Moscow Does Not Believe in Tears*. In the movie, several young women, attracted by the glamour of city life, leave their villages and move to Moscow. There they discover that life in a worker hostel and dreary jobs in a factory are all they can expect. Some return home disillusioned; others manage, by luck, wheeling and dealing, or marriage, to escape the hostel.

Local soviets and enterprises manage 78 percent of all urban housing while 22 percent remains privately owned. In rural areas, however, 85 percent of the housing is privately owned.[26]

Local soviets administer their housing stock through housing commissions in each *raion* of a city. The commissions screen applicants and place those eligible on a waiting list. Single young people and persons already occupying housing that meets minimum standards are not eligible to apply for accommodations. Once placed on the waiting list, citizens can expect to wait as long as ten years to secure new lodging. In the USSR today there are an estimated 14 million people on waiting lists for new apartments. One-sixth of these have waited more than ten years.[27] In Moscow alone, there are one and a quarter million people on waiting lists for housing.[28]

Certain categories of citizens are entitled to extra space, priority on the waiting list, or other special consideration. These include people suffering from certain diseases, the handicapped, and families with many children. The largest group of persons exempted from the normal housing regulations and waiting period, however, are party and state officials, high-ranking military officers, scientists, writers, and artists. In some of the newer apartment blocs, the top floors have higher-than-average ceilings, large windows, and ample floor space and are reserved for artists' studios.

Citizens who do not wish to wait several years to obtain cramped and poorly constructed apartments can pool their resources to form a building society and hire a construction firm to put up an apartment building for them. Residents in such "condominiums" own their units and may sell them at a price established by the local housing commission, thus preventing speculation. This option is expensive and available only to relatively wealthy citizens in urban areas. Cooperative housing currently accounts for only 6 percent of all new construction.[29]

Given the intense demand for urban housing and the cumbersome system for assigning apartments, it is perhaps inevitable that many housing transactions occur "on the left" in the "second economy." In Leningrad, the author became acquainted with a young couple who lived in a communal apartment off Herzen Street. One night over dinner, the conversation turned to a familiar subject—housing. The couple had been on the waiting list for an apartment for more than two years. The author asked them what would happen if they did not like the apartment offered to them when their name came up on the housing list. What if it were located on the opposite side of the city from where they worked, or on the top floor of a seven-story walk-up? They both looked at him in astonishment. After waiting so long, it was inconceivable to them that anyone would turn down an offer for any apartment. The husband responded, "If our new apartment does not suit us, we will simply exchange it on the black market."

In an old section of Leningrad not far from the Kirov Ballet Theatre, the street fills every Sunday with people wishing to exchange apartments. Carrying placards advertising their apartments, they mill around chatting, occasionally gathering to overhear a transaction being conducted. A typical placard reads: "Will exchange two-room apartment in Kalinin *raion* for two-room apartment in Lenin *raion*."

Some of the placards tell of personal or family joys or troubles. A pregnant woman has a sign pinned to her wool coat: "Will exchange two-room Stalin apartment for three-room apartment." "Stalin apartments," built during the 1930s and 1940s, are in great demand. In contrast to the prefabricated "Khrushchev apartments," they have large rooms, high ceilings, and good-quality construction, and are located close to the city center. A woman carrying a sign reading "Will exchange two-room apartment for two single apartments" is most likely getting a divorce. The demand for housing is so great that frequently couples who get divorced have to remain together for a long time before they can locate separate housing.

Housing exchanges can become dehumanizing affairs. For instance, the Soviet press reported the case of an elderly woman who was dying of cancer. Her son switched apartments with her, moving her from her spacious two-room "Stalin apartment" in the center of the city to his cramped and noisy "Khrushchev apartment" on the outskirts of town. The "exchange" had to be finalized with the local housing authorities prior to the woman's death, or her apartment would have reverted to the housing commission for reassignment to someone on the waiting list.[30]

Some enterprising "speculators" acquire one-room apartments and build partitions in them, creating small two-room apartments. They then attempt to trade these apartments on the black market for legitimate two-room apartments, and so forth. Mikhail Bulgakov, the satirist, describes just such an "entrepreneur" in his novel *The Master and Margarita.*

> One man in this town was given a three-room flat on the Zemlyanoi Rampart and he had turned it into four rooms by dividing one of the rooms in half with a partition. Then he exchanged it for two separate flats in different parts of Moscow, one with three rooms and the other with two. . . . He then exchanged the three-room one for two separate two-roomers, and thus became the owner of six rooms altogether, though admittedly scattered all over Moscow. He was about to pull off his last and most brilliant coup by offering six rooms in various districts of Moscow in exchange for one five-room flat on the Zemlyanoi Rampart when his activities were suddenly and inexplicably curtailed. He may have a room somewhere now, but not, I can assure you, in Moscow.[31]

Bulgakov's hapless real estate tycoon notwithstanding, the authorities in the USSR today generally allow the black market to operate without intervention. Black marketeers run afoul of housing officials only when they speculate in housing to earn a profit.

Under Gorbachev, few initiatives have been undertaken to resolve the housing crisis. A decree of the USSR Council of Ministers in December 1988 allowed citizens to purchase their apartments from the State. In the first six months, however, only 19,000 apartments were sold to their occupants.[32] Residents were reportedly reluctant to assume responsibility for repairs and up-keep, utilities and financing.

Restrictions have been eased on private new construction, and this is a rapidly growing area. Almost one-fifth of all new residential units built in 1989 were privately owned.[33] Such developments, however, have not begun to satisfy pent-up demand for adequate housing. In some areas, popular frustrations over long waiting periods and fears of favoritism in housing allocations have resulted in rioting. The current five-year plan calls for the construction of 14 million new housing units by 1994. This is slated to increase to 15–16 million in 1995–1999.[34] Such optimistic projections, however, clearly cannot be realized if the economy continues in its current rate of decline.

HEALTH CARE IN THE SOVIET UNION

The goals of the Soviet health system from its inception in 1918 have been the provision of comprehensive medical care by a unified state health service free of charge to all citizens. Initially, Soviet medicine was founded on the ideological notion that disease was a product of capitalism and that clinical intervention would eventually wither away under socialism, to be replaced by preventive medicine and public health education. The Commissariat of Health was established in 1918 to oversee health policies, but the Bolsheviks decided that health services should be run by local soviets in order to increase "the broad participation of the masses" in implementing health services.

The health of the Soviet population after the Revolution was a serious problem. The prerevolutionary health-care system collapsed during the turmoil of World War I and the revolutions of 1917. The Civil War brought further famine and disease. Epidemics ravaged the country. Between 1916 and 1924, an estimated 10 million people died in epidemics—primarily typhus, typhoid, smallpox, and relapsing fever.[35] Addressing the second Congress of Medical Workers in 1920, Lenin declared, "Either the lice will defeat Socialism, or Socialism will defeat the lice!"[36]

It was neither socialism nor the efforts of the newly established public health system that defeated the lice, however, but the improved living standards resulting from NEP. Medical schools resumed instruction in the return to normalcy of the NEP period, and the number of doctors tripled between 1917 and 1928. The combination of these factors helped to eradicate most epidemics in urban areas by the end of the 1920s. Health services in rural areas, however, remained in a primitive state. Medical care was provided by "feldshers"—traveling medical paraprofessionals. Low living standards and the poor quality of transportation, housing, and educational facilities discouraged most doctors from working in the countryside.

Predictably, the emphasis within the health-care system changed dramatically under Stalin. Stalin rejected several elements of Bolshevik health policy: the ideological assumption that illness resulted from capitalism, the preference for mass participation in health-care policy-making, the decentralized system for delivering health services, and the stress on preventive medicine. Instead, Stalin ordered that the quality of health services within industrial enterprises be upgraded. The number of medical personnel within factories quadrupled during the first six months of 1932.[37] As more and more women were added to the industrial work force, special efforts were made to improve health services to them and to their children. In addition, greater emphasis was placed on sanitation in rapidly growing urban areas.

Soviet authorities made it clear, however, that the principal goal of industrial medicine was to ensure a healthy labor force, which was necessary to achieve Stalin's ambitious economic aims. One of the primary functions of industrial medical personnel, therefore, was to detect fraudulent requests for sick leave.

The proletarianization of the Soviet health-care profession during the 1930s lowered the status of doctors relative to other occupations (especially engineers), and the pay and the quality of training of doctors declined precipitously. Medical education was removed from the universities and relegated to special institutes in 1929. As the status of doctors dropped relative to engineers, so too did the availability of drugs and instruments. Because most males were employed in the industrial labor force, women were actively recruited into the health professions during the 1930s. By 1934 three-quarters of all doctors were women.[38]

Administratively, the health services became more centralized during Stalin's reign. The Ministry of Health was charged with making and administering health policy, while the operations of polyclinics and the public health service were subordinated to local hospitals.

The health-service sector received a large share of the funds earmarked for social services throughout the Stalin and Khrushchev periods, and the results are reflected in various health statistics. Prior to the Revolution, the life expectancy of women was only 33 years; by the time of Khrushchev's ouster in 1964, it was 75.6 years.[39] In 1913, more than one out of every four babies died before the age of one. By 1971, infant mortality in the USSR had fallen to 2 percent.[40] In 1964, the mortality rate for the Soviet population was less than that in the United States and many other developed nations of the West, leading Khrushchev to boast that the USSR "long ago left the capitalist countries behind" in the provision of health services.[41]

The achievements of Soviet health care are impressive. Indeed, during the 1950s and 1960s, health care was one field in which Western experts acknowledged Soviet successes and even suggested that Western societies could learn from the Soviet example in providing inexpensive, high-quality health services to the entire population.

The Soviet health-care delivery system has remained essentially unchanged since Stalin's time. Primary health care is provided through polyclinics located in microdistricts and industrial enterprises. Polyclinics provide initial treatment for common, minor ailments—colds, flu, sprains, and so on. They are staffed with general practitioners (*vracha*) and nurses and have basic equipment for routine treatments and laboratory tests. Citizens may choose to receive medical treatment either at the polyclinic in their microdistrict or at the polyclinic attached to their place of employment. All medical care in the USSR, including treatment at a polyclinic, is provided free of charge. There is, however, a minimal charge for drugs.

Polyclinics refer patients with more serious illnesses and those requiring more specialized treatment to the general hospital located in each town and city. (In Moscow and other large cities, there are general hospitals in various parts of the city.) Hospitals provide a wide range of services—both inpatient and outpatient. Hospitalization rates in the Soviet Union are high. In contrast to trends in other developed countries, the average length of hospital stays has increased in recent years and is double that of the United States.[42] Two factors account for this phenomenon: housing conditions are so overcrowded that people prefer to recuperate in the hospital; and in rural areas, where polyclinics are poorly staffed and equipped, it is more difficult for patients to receive qualified care outside of the hospitals. In Moscow and Leningrad, groups of physicians have taken advantage of the new Law on Cooperatives to open private medical and dental clinics. Patients pay premium prices for health care at these clinics, but the quality of care they receive is substantially better than in the state-run clinics.

In addition to the general hospitals, specialized hospitals exist for a variety of diseases and conditions. The most common specialized health facilities are maternity hospitals. Other specialized facilities exist for the treatment of cancer, tuberculosis, mental illness, and kidney disease, and for geriatrics. Admission to one of these facilities is on a referral basis.

Several years ago, the author was accompanying a group of American officials on a tour of a specialized cancer-treatment hospital being built on the outskirts of Moscow. It was truly an impressive complex. One building for pediatric patients had already been completed, and a high-rise tower for adult patients was under construction. In a corridor of the tower building, the group came across two women busily plastering the walls. One of the American physicians asked whether there was asbestos in the plaster. One of the women, splattered with the grey plaster, replied, "*Konezhno*" ("of course"). The American then asked whether she was aware that asbestos was a proven cause of lung cancer. She was not. She simply shrugged and went back to her job.

The number of hospitals and physicians has continued to grow since the 1960s, although at a slower rate. The number of hospital beds per 10,000 of population has increased from 80 in 1960 to more than 128 today. At the same time, the number of physicians per 10,000 of population has increased from 20 in 1960 to more than 40 today, roughly twice as many doctors per capita as in the United States.[43] There are fewer auxiliary medical personnel in the USSR than in the United States, however, and many Soviet doctors perform duties that in the United States are the responsibility of nurses, laboratory technicians, physical therapists, and other medical professionals.

The vast majority of physicians in the USSR are general practitioners (*vracha*), who are responsible for providing primary health care through the polyclinics and general hospitals. All students in medical school are expected to specialize in one of three fields: general clinical medicine, obstetrics-gynecology-pediatrics, or public health medicine. The level of training within these specializations is, however, generally considered inferior to that of physicians in the United States. Approximately 70 percent of all general practitioners are women.[44] By Western standards, Soviet general practitioners are very poorly paid; their average salary is only 183 rubles per month ($7), far less than that of the average industrial worker.[45]

Medical-school training consists of a seven-year program that includes one year of internship. Doctors who wish to pursue more intensive specializations usually do so after several years of general practice. Specialist doctors constitute a relatively small percentage of all physicians in the USSR, and the vast majority of them are men. Women account for only 20 percent of medical-school professors, 40 percent of all tertiary-care physicians, and 50 percent of all hospital administrators.[46] Some medical schools have recently instituted separate entrance examinations for men and women, and others have imposed quotas to ensure that 50 percent of all admissions are men.[47]

Medical-school training is free, and most students also receive a living allowance to cover food and housing expenses. After graduating, however, they are obliged to fulfill a three-year assignment, usually in a rural area.[48] Regional disparities have plagued the delivery of health services in the Soviet Union since 1917. The quality of health care provided in rural areas still lags far behind that in the cities.

In the countryside, the number of doctors per capita is approximately one-half that of urban areas, despite the fact that doctors in rural areas receive 15 percent incentive bonuses. It was recently reported that twenty-five rural hospitals in Soviet Georgia did not have even one trained physician.[49] In Krasnoyarsk *krai* polyclinics that were designed to handle 260 patients per day are seeing more than 1300.[50]

In 1977, in an effort to encourage more physicians to stay in rural areas, new policies were introduced allowing rural physicians three times the salary of their urban counterparts after ten years of service, a free apartment, priority in purchasing an automobile, and the right to buy food directly from state farms in the vicinity. Nevertheless, few doctors appear to be taking advantage of this opportunity.

Even in the cities, the quality of health-care services varies dramatically from polyclinic to polyclinic. Polyclinics associated with large, industrial complexes and prestigious institutions tend to be well-staffed and well-equipped, while polyclinics in small, marginal factories suffer from persistent problems in staffing and supply.

Hospitals also vary in terms of quality. In Leningrad, for instance, foreigners are usually treated at Hospital No. 1, which caters to influential politicians and members of the intellectual elite. The surgical ward of Hospital No. 1 is equipped with the latest American, Swiss, and German equipment, surgical instruments, and pharmaceuticals. In contrast, other hospitals can be dirty, overcrowded, ill-equipped, and understaffed.

Under Brezhnev, Soviet health care deteriorated markedly. In the 1970s, the defense and industrial sectors of the economy absorbed a steadily increasing portion of the state budget, placing a strain on health services. The percentage of the state budget earmarked for health care fell from 6.5 percent in 1965 to 5.2 percent in 1975, and to 5.0 percent in 1980.[51]

The impact of reduced funding for health care was apparent in rising infant mortality and decreasing life expectancy. Infant mortality, which had decreased steadily since 1917, almost doubled between 1971 and 1980. (See Table 11-2.) At the same time, adult life expectancy for men decreased from 67.0 years in 1964 to 61.9 years in 1980; for women it fell from 75.6 years in 1964 to 73.5 years in 1980.[52] Soviet authorities were sufficiently embarrassed by these trends that, from 1976 until 1988, they refused to release statistics on infant mortality and life expectancy. Since 1989 concerted efforts have diminished infant mortality.

Table 11–2. Infant Mortality in the Soviet Union (deaths per 1000 live births)

1950	60.0
1971	22.9
1974	28.0
1976	31.1
1980	39–40 (est)
1989	22.2 *

* Western sources estimate that this figure must be increased by approximately 15 percent (or 25.5 per 1000 live births) in order to make it comparable to Western statistics.
Sources: Christopher Davis and Murray Feshbach, Rising Infant Mortality in the USSR in the 1970s, U.S. Bureau of the Census, Series P-95, no. 74 (Washington DC: U.S. Government Printing Office, September 1980); D. J. Peterson, "Goskomstat Report on Social Conditions," Radio Liberty Report on the USSR 2, no. 6 (9 February 1990): 5.

The causes of the alarming deterioration of the health of Soviet citizens are several. In addition to declining allocations for health care, other important contributing factors include alcohol abuse, environmental pollution, and the high incidence of abortion.

The level of alcohol consumption in the USSR is among the highest in the world. Unlike France, where there are high levels of wine consumption, or Germany, which favors beer, the preferred alcoholic beverage in the Soviet Union is vodka, drunk straight from the bottle. The USSR ranks first in the world in the consumption of distilled spirits. Furthermore, alcohol consumption is growing at an alarming rate. From 1940 through 1980, the Soviet population increased by 36 percent, while alcohol consumption rose by more than 800 percent.[53] A report by the USSR Ministry of Internal Affairs estimates that 37 percent of all male workers abuse alcohol.[54] Alcohol consumption is highly differentiated by region, with the worst problem centered in the Slavic and Baltic regions; wine consumption is highest in Moldavia, Armenia, and Georgia.

Especially troublesome is the recent increase in alcoholism among women and teenagers. Alcohol abuse is currently growing more rapidly among women than among men and is being blamed for increasing incidence of birth defects (including brain damage), miscarriages, and premature births.[55]

Public health officials as well as the press and local party organs have launched repeated campaigns to educate Soviet citizens about the dangers of alcohol abuse—without noticeable effect. Sales of alcohol have been curtailed and prices have been increased to discourage consumption. Demand for alcohol, however, appears to be inelastic. In other words, when the price of vodka is increased, it simply means that alcohol consumes a larger share of the average family's budget, threatening to reduce money spent on food, clothing, and entertainment.

People who are apprehended for public intoxication or drunk driving are taken to sobering-up stations (*vytreziteli*). They are fined, and their names are reported to their employers. In 1979, 16 to 18 million people, or 12 to 15 percent of the adult population, were processed through the stations.[56]

Most drinking is done at home or outdoors, because of the limited number of bars and pubs. It is not unusual on a winter evening to see clusters of middle-aged men in heavily padded wool coats standing on the street sharing a bottle of vodka "three ways." Workers refer to this as a form of "primitive communism." By splitting a bottle among three people, it is relatively affordable, and the amount of alcohol, while sufficient to get a person quite drunk, is not normally enough to kill one.

Government efforts to curb alcohol abuse, such as Gorbachev's ban on alcohol sales and production in 1986, often unwittingly encourage even more dangerous practices, such as the consumption of home-brewed alcohol (*samogon*) or alcohol surrogates. An estimated 1.7 billion liters of 80-proof *samogon* are produced every year in the USSR.[57] Vladimir Treml notes that in 1978 there were 51,000 deaths in the Soviet Union due to alcohol poisoning—or 19.5 deaths per 100,000 of population (compared to 400 instances in the United States or 0.18 per 100,000).[58]

As the price of alcohol has been increased to discourage consumption, Russians have begun to consume large quantities of alcohol surrogates, such as lotions, medical alcohol, shellac, varnish, and brake and deicing fluids. Treml estimates that 1,200 people died in 1976 from drinking ethylene glycol (antifreeze), cleaning fluids, and solvents.[59] Another 5000 died from ingesting vinegar concentrate, considered to be a good (although sometimes permanent) remedy for hangover.[60]

With the exception of alcoholism, the biggest health risks in the USSR are related to diet and lack of exercise. The leading cause of death in the USSR is heart disease, followed by cancer and alcohol-related illnesses. The typical Russian diet is heavily laden with starch and dairy products, while fresh fruits and vegetables are difficult to come by most of the year. Furthermore, few Soviet citizens exercise on a regular basis after leaving secondary school. A Soviet medical official recently estimated that more than 40 percent of all Soviet men are overweight.[61] Compounding the risks of heart disease are alcohol abuse and the relatively widespread use of cigarettes by Soviet males. As with alcohol consumption, smoking is increasingly common among young women.

Also affecting the health of the female population is the widespread practice of abortion. Lenin and his chief advisor on family and women's issues, Madame Kollontai, considered abortion to be the legal right of every Soviet woman. Abortion was officially decriminalized in 1920, and since that time, abortion has been the most widely practiced form of birth control in the Soviet Union.[62] Other forms of birth control suffer from the same problems that beset other consumer goods—poor quality, lack of consideration of consumers' preferences, and sporadic availability. Soviet birth-control pills, although effective, have a variety of unpleasant side effects, such as hair loss, cramps, and nausea. Yet, Soviet pharmaceutical companies appear reluctant to produce a better pill. In addition, shortages are chronic, so one can never count on being able to obtain birth-control pills on a regular basis. The same problems plague other forms of birth control. In contrast, abortions are readily available, and are cheap or free depending on one's income level. On the average, a typical Soviet woman has six abortions during her child-bearing years.[63] In urban areas, the abortion rate may be even higher. Abortions entail obvious health risks to women and reduce the chances of subsequently delivering a healthy baby; thus, they may be a primary factor in the increase of infant mortality.

Environmental pollution also affects infant mortality rates in the USSR. In the push to industrialize and match its adversaries in the arms race, the USSR has accorded scant attention to environmental concerns. Soviet researchers report increasing numbers of "birth abnormalities" and respiratory conditions linked to air and water pollution and increasing exposure to radiation.[64]

Dental care is another problem area in the Soviet health-care system. While recent émigrés have generally given Soviet health care high marks, the same is not true for Soviet dentistry. Examinations conducted by Soviet dental researchers found that 70 to 90 percent of all Soviet citizens are in need of dental work.[65] The USSR has roughly one-half the number of dentists per capita as has the United States.[66] Because dental care is not essential to the productivity of the labor force, it was not accorded a high priority under Stalin and his successors. While routine fillings (using silver or gold) are performed, more complicated procedures, such as root canals or orthodontia, are not widely available. Dentists treat an abscessed tooth by extracting the tooth and replacing it with a gold or stainless-steel model.

The Soviet health-care system is not immune to the workings of the "second economy." Most doctors and dentists perform private practice "on the left" and may be paid in antiques, rare books, vodka, meat, or even live chickens. It is widely known that when a woman goes in for an abortion, she must "tip" the doctor in order to receive a double dose of anesthetic so that she will not experience any pain. With the normally prescribed dosage, the procedure is painful, but not excruciating.

Perhaps the two most underdeveloped areas of the Soviet health-care system are the production of medical supplies and pharmaceuticals, and medical transport. There are chronic shortages of sophisticated medical equipment and instruments, such as kidney dialysis machines and intensive-care monitoring devices. Modern, effective drugs are often unavailable or extremely difficult to obtain. Even such relatively basic supplies and drugs as X-ray film, thermometers, disposable syringes, surgical gloves, insulin, and novocaine are often unavailable. In Moscow, it may take as long as nine months to receive a pair of glasses, and much longer in more remote areas.[67] Medical transport is also primitive. Ambulance service is slow and only available in large metropolitan areas.

In recent years, some effort has been devoted to reverse-engineering* of Western drugs. On one trip to the USSR, the author noticed customs officials at the Leningrad airport collecting samples of all prescription drugs brought in by foreigners. When the author asked a customs officer why he was taking the samples, he responded that they were aware of "serious drug problems in the West" and wanted to be certain that no illegal drugs were being smuggled into the USSR. It is more likely, however, that the drugs were being collected in an effort to copy Western pharmaceuticals.

Soviet authorities have also instituted educational campaigns to impress upon citizens the need for regular checkups. Regular physical examinations were not common until recently and are still not universal. Consequently, many illnesses often reach an advanced stage before citizens seek treatment.

Despite the impressive achievements of the Soviet health-care system and the extensive efforts of the government to improve the quality of citizens' health, many problems persist and some may actually be increasing. Some of these problems can be resolved by increasing appropriations, training more health-care professionals, and enforcing stiffer environmental and occupational safety regulations. However, many of the problems, such as alcoholism, smoking, and abortion, are more difficult to tackle because they reflect ingrained habits, values, and behavior. Educational efforts may help, but they are unlikely to eradicate the problems entirely.

---

*Reverse engineering, or copying Western technology, is widely practiced not only in the pharmaceutical industry, but in many sectors.

The social costs associated with the deteriorating state of health in the USSR commanded the attention of the Gorbachev leadership. Under the influence of *glasnost'*, there was a flood of information about the dire state of health in the USSR. Responding to the crisis, the Gorbachev leadership began by tackling the most pressing problems—infant mortality and the shortage of medicine and medical supplies. Efforts to improve maternal and infant care were already showing results by 1989. Infant mortality fell by some 10 percent from 1988 levels, to 22.2 deaths per 1000 live births, which represents a major turnaround for Soviet health care.[68] The medical equipment industry recorded a 7 percent increase in production in 1989, the best performance of any engineering sector in the USSR.[69]

Despite the additional efforts, however, problems persisted. Soviet pharmaceutical production meets only 40 percent of the needs of the Soviet population. Imports account for another 35 percent, leaving a shortfall of 25 percent.[70] While the country needs an estimated 3 billion disposable syringes a year, it produces only 200 million per year—less than 7 percent of the number required.[71]

The chronic shortage of disposable syringes has inadvertently created another health-care crisis—the spread of the AIDS virus. In 1989 there were 428 reported cases of persons infected with HIV, 23 active cases of AIDS and 14 AIDS-related deaths.[72] It is thought that the majority of people with the AIDS virus in the USSR became infected through contaminated needles used by doctors and nurses in hospitals and polyclinics.[73]

The Gorbachev leadership has encouraged foreign pharmaceutical and medical supply companies to establish joint ventures in the USSR to help relieve critical shortages. Several such joint ventures have been established, but many more will be required to fill the void.

Meanwhile, efforts to step up pharmaceutical production are running into stiff opposition from environmentalists and local officials. Environmental protests have halted production at the Azot plant in Kemerovo. Construction of new pharmaceutical plants in Arkhangelsk, Kursk, Saratov, Novosibirsk, and in the Mari Autonomous Republic, Latvia, and Uzbekistan has also been halted. Of the 36 proposed new pharmaceutical projects slated for the 1986–1990 planning period, 21 were seriously delayed or abandoned because local officials, concerned over potential pollution, refused to allocate the necessary land.[74] In testimony before the committee on the Protection of Public Health of the USSR Supreme Soviet, the Minister of the Pharmaceutical Industry, Valerii Bykov, lamented, "Green extremism will not let the pharmaceutical industry take a breath."[75]

On February 6, 1990 a special commission was formed by the USSR Council of Ministers to look into the shortage of medicines, which was rapidly becoming a national crisis. Citing the urgent need for medicine, the commission ordered all pharmaceutical factories to resume production immediately, even if they fail to comply with environmental regulations.

As was the case with housing, the ability of the USSR to cope with its medical care crisis depends ultimately on the fate of the economy. For that reason, the future of Soviet health care is not bright.

SOCIAL SECURITY IN THE SOVIET UNION

A third principal element in the social welfare state is the provision of assistance to the elderly, the unemployed and those injured on the job. Social insurance benefits and relief for the poor under the tsarist regime were the responsibility of local authorities through the *zemstva* (county councils). The resources of the *zemstva* were, however, clearly inadequate for the task. The dislocations created by World War I, compounded by famine in the country-side, drove millions of peasants to the cities, where most were unemployed and lived in squalor.

In his address to the sixth conference of the Russian Social Democratic Party in Prague in 1912, Lenin outlined a plan for a socialist system of social security. Such a system should, he declared, provide the following:

1. assistance in all cases of incapacity—including old age, accidents, illness, and death of the breadwinner—as well as maternity and birth benefits;
2. comprehensive coverage to all wage earners and their families;
3. compensation equal to full earnings, with total costs to be borne by employers and the state.[76]

Furthermore, Lenin stipulated that social security should be uniform throughout the country and should be administered by local soviets with the widespread participation of workers in the management of the system. Excluded from coverage under Lenin's social security plan were peasants—the vast majority of Russian society—and self-employed artisans.

Less than a month after the Bolshevik seizure of power in 1917, two laws on social insurance guaranteed comprehensive unemployment, sickness, and maternity benefits as well as death grants to all Soviet wage earners. Initially, the social insurance programs were administered by local trade unions.

In an effort to gain the support of the peasantry during the Civil War, Lenin expanded social security coverage to the entire population and broadened coverage to include all major risks—unemployment, sickness, maternity, disability, old age, and loss of the breadwinner. The scheme was to be financed mainly from employers' contributions supplemented with earnings derived from confiscated private property. In practice, however, Soviet industry was unable to pay for such extensive social security programs. The economic chaos wrought by the Civil War forced the government to assume the burden of supporting social security programs through general revenues. Despite the government's intervention, most eligible recipients failed to receive their benefits; top priority was given to providing relief for families of those who died fighting with the Reds during the Civil War. As the government assumed financial responsibility for social security programs, it also assumed administrative control. Administration of social security programs was gradually transferred from local trade unions to offices of the local soviets.

With the conclusion of the Civil War in 1921, the social security system was scaled down to make it more financially feasible. Peasants and self-employed persons were no longer eligible to receive benefits and, instead, were encouraged to join self-financed mutual aid societies. As the economic conditions of the country improved under NEP and more and more workers returned to their jobs, the coverage of social security programs broadened. By 1928, it encompassed some 11 million workers.[77]

Stalin's drive to industrialize the economy resulted in important modifications in Lenin's original conception of social security. Gone was the stress on egalitarianism. Instead, social benefits were structured to favor shock workers (Stakhanovites) and laborers with long and exemplary work records. In other words, social security benefits were considered a reward bestowed on the best workers and denied to shirkers.

In 1930, unemployment benefits were abolished, and sick leave required a medical certificate. In 1938, maternity leave was reduced from sixteen weeks to nine weeks. Furthermore, length of uninterrupted employment became an important factor in determining eligibility for most social benefits. Stalin introduced these changes in order to reinforce work discipline and cut down on unemployment and high labor turnover.

When some social service departments of local soviets failed to institute all of Stalin's directives, he ordered the administration of social security programs transferred to the trade unions, which were placed under the strict hierarchical control of central party and trade union officials. Despite this restructuring of the social security system, the growth of the industrial labor force under Stalin resulted in more and more people being covered. The number of persons eligible to receive social security benefits increased from 10 million in 1928 to over 30 million in 1940.[78]

Changes in social security in the USSR followed Stalin's death in 1953. Revamping social programs became one of Khrushchev's high-priority items. In a series of legislative changes, social security coverage was extended to most workers and their dependents (collective-farm workers were, however, still excluded). The level of pensions doubled, while disability and survivor allowances increased substantially. Furthermore, efforts were made to eliminate inequalities in benefits. These expansions of social security coverage under Khrushchev were financed by government funds supplemented with employers' contributions. Between 1964 and 1970, most social security provisions were extended to collective farmers in order to eliminate inequities, stimulate agricultural production, and stem the migration of rural workers to the cities.

No major reforms of social security have been introduced since 1970, although some policies have been altered. Length of employment has been removed as a condition for sick leave and maternity benefits, and a family allowance program has been introduced to reduce the effects of poverty.

Today all civilian state employees (that is, all employees except persons in the armed forces or private cooperatives) are entitled to an old-age pension on reaching 60 years of age (55 years for women), provided they have worked at least 25 years (20 years for women). Lower retirement ages are granted to coal miners and certain other types of workers engaged in dangerous and difficult jobs. Since 1967, collective farmers have been entitled to pensions at the same ages and at the same rates as corresponding state employees.

The pension rate is determined by a person's income during the last twelve months of employment. Those workers earning the minimum wage of 70 rubles per month receive pensions of 45 rubles per month. For persons with higher incomes, the pension rate is 50 percent of salary, to a maximum of 120 rubles per month.[79] In contrast to recipients of social security in the United States, pensioners in the Soviet Union do not lose their benefits if they earn additional income. Thus, as many as one-third of all pensioners continue to work to supplement their pensions.[80] There is no mandatory retirement age in the USSR; in fact, with a declining birthrate and a slowing rate of growth in the labor force, pensioners are encouraged to continue in their jobs. They play a major role in the service sector. Many elderly citizens work as museum guards, hotel and coatroom attendants, or even as public service workers, raking leaves in parks.

Social welfare benefits are also awarded to dependent children, grandchildren, parents, and surviving spouses upon the death of state employees. The amount of the "survivors' pension" varies with the number of dependents and the income of the deceased.

Disability pensions are paid to persons who, because of industrial accidents, occupational diseases, or other incapacity, are unable to continue to work. Benefits vary depending on the degree of incapacity, and they are higher if the disability was work-related. In 1970, the disability benefits of collective farmers were brought into line with those of state employees.

Sickness benefits in the USSR cover the entire period of illness. Benefit levels are tied to salary, type of employment, and cause of illness, and may range as high as 90 percent of a worker's normal earnings.[81] In addition, mothers can receive up to seven days of paid leave to care for sick children at home. These provisions were also extended to collective farmers in 1970.

In the last two decades, the birthrate in the USSR has fallen, raising concerns among officials about the impact on future labor resource needs. Child allowances have been instituted to encourage larger families. Mothers are paid a one-time allowance of 50 rubles on the birth of their first child. Upon the birth of their second and third children, the grant is 100 rubles plus an allowance of 4 rubles per month until the child is five years old.[82] Benefits increase up to the tenth child. The Soviet government has also introduced the "Hero Mother Medal," which is awarded to a woman upon the birth of her tenth child.

Surveys of Moscow working women reveal that the majority would like to have two children; only 3 percent favored having just one child.[83] Crowded living conditions and the fact that more than 80 percent of all women work outside the home create strong disincentives to having large families. Approximately 60 percent of all families in the USSR are composed of two or three persons.[84]

A notable exception to small family size, however, are the Central Asian ethnic minorities, who have a birthrate four times the national average. A survey of young Uzbek women conducted by a team of Soviet sociologists found that more than half hoped to have six or more children, and almost one-third wanted more than ten children.[85] It is estimated that Russians will constitute less than half of the population by the year 2000, while the Muslims of Central Asia will represent one out of every three Soviet citizens.

Finally, family allowances have been instituted to assist low-income families. Families below the poverty line of 50 rubles per person per month receive 12 rubles per month for each child under eight years of age. Approximately 37 percent of all children now qualify for relief.[86]

Taken together, total social welfare benefits in the USSR account for approximately 18 percent of personal income. Including medical, educational, housing, and other social services, Soviet social welfare programs constitute as much as 30 percent of the total annual income of the average family.[87]

The welfare system is financed from payroll taxes and budgetary revenues, which are, in turn, derived from indirect taxes and profit taxes. It is difficult to assess precisely how progressive or regressive Soviet social welfare programs and the taxation system are. Some evidence suggests that because many of the benefits are tied to a person's income, high wage earners tend to receive more benefits than low wage earners. In addition, the taxation scheme that supports the Soviet social welfare system appears to place a relatively heavier burden on those with lower incomes. Regardless of whether the combined effects of social welfare programs and taxation are neutral or regressive, it is clear that the Soviet social welfare system does not radically pursue Lenin's original goals of income redistribution and egalitarianism.[88]

The biggest changes in Soviet social security in recent years are the increased demand for existing social security benefits and the emerging needs for new kinds of programs, which have occurred as a result of demographic changes. As in many other industrialized societies, the Soviet population is aging. On the eve of World War II, approximately 9 percent of the population were of retirement age; today, some 15.5 percent are of retirement age and the percentage continues to grow.[89] The "greying" of the population has resulted in a serious reduction in the rate of growth of the Soviet labor force and has increased the amount of social security funds being paid out in pensions.

Total expenditures on social welfare programs in the USSR increased at a rate of 6 to 7 percent per year through the 1970s and early 1980s. However, with the economic disruption brought about by Gorbachev's economic reforms, expenditures on pensions and assistance programs have not kept pace. (See Table 11–3.) Pensions account for the largest share by far of these expenditures. As a result of the increased number of pensioners in the Soviet Union, social security expenditures have increased from approximately 8 percent of the national income in 1970 to more than 10 percent today.[90]

In comparison, other social programs have not been keeping pace with pensions. In particular, the increased incidence of divorce and the absence of provisions for either alimony or child support have created a drastic need for increased public support for divorced women with children.

As noted earlier, the official poverty level in the USSR is 50 rubles per person per month. Western estimates based on Soviet statistics indicate that in the mid-1960s as much as one-third of the working class was below the poverty line.[91] While poverty remains a real problem in the USSR, it must also be recognized that a poverty level of 50 rubles per month is relatively high when compared to the average industrial wage, and when compared to poverty levels in other industrialized countries.

Table 11-3. Social Welfare Expenditures in the USSR, 1940–1983 (in billions of rubles)

Year	Pensions	Assistance	Other	Total
1940	0.3	0.5	0.1	0.9
1960	7.1	2.6	0.2	9.9
1970	16.2	6.1	0.5	22.8
1975	24.4	9.2	1.0	34.6
1980	33.3	11.0	1.3	45.6
1981	35.4	11.3	1.6	48.3
1982	37.8	11.9	1.6	51.3
1983	40.0	13.2	1.9	55.1
1988	43.6	25.5	0.7	69.8

Sources: Narodnoe khozyaistvo v SSSR v 1983 (Moscow: Finansy i statistika, 1984), 408; Gosudarstvennyi Byudzhet SSSR 1989 (Moscow: Finansy i statistika, 1989), p. 16.

A large portion of the Soviet population below the poverty level falls into one of two groups: single-parent families and pensioners. The government has sought to reduce the burden on these two groups by increasing family allowances and day-care services for working single mothers and by encouraging pensioners to continue working. Those who are either unwilling or unable to work, however, will continue to fall below the minimum level of income deemed necessary for subsistence by Soviet authorities and will have to rely on private support from relatives.

On the whole, the Soviet social welfare system today meets the provisions established by Lenin in 1912. It provides comprehensive assistance to all workers in most cases of incapacity, illness, accident, or death of the breadwinner. The system falls short of Lenin's ideal, however, over the principles that workers should be compensated for 100 percent of their salaries, that citizens should be actively engaged in making and implementing policies, and that the system should reduce inequalities in the standard of living among various social classes and groups. In these respects, the Soviet welfare system does not differ markedly from those of many West European countries; as in social welfare programs in the West, the two groups most likely to fall through the safety net are single women with children and the elderly.

This chapter began by asking whether the Soviet social welfare system has translated social and economic rights into reality. Having assessed Soviet performance in housing, health care, and social security, the answer must be a qualified yes. Given the abysmal level of public services prior to the Revolution, Soviet achievements in the past seventy years have been truly remarkable.

Despite these achievements, however, problems persist. In several cases, these problems are growing faster than the regime's ability to solve them. Many of the problems, including increased divorce, alcoholism, abortion, rural migration, declining birthrates, and the aging of the Soviet population, are social or demographic phenomena that cannot be resolved simply by increasing budgetary allocations. Other social problems, such as housing shortages, inadequate medical facilities, and persistent poverty, are more amenable to resolution through expanded welfare programs and increased expenditures. The Soviet economy, however, has entered a stage of dramatically reduced growth rates, necessitating stringent controls on government spending.

At the same time, increased industrialization and improved living standards have led to the growth of special interests. Soviet society is no longer divided simply into workers, peasants, and the intelligentsia, but into numerous regional, occupational, ethnic, and bureaucratic subgroups. Under conditions of economic stringency, competition between the demands of the industrial, defense, agricultural, and social service sectors has grown more intense.

Further complicating the dilemma confronting the leadership is the fact that the progress achieved in raising the living standards of Soviet citizens may not be enough to keep up with public expectations. To a considerable degree, the legitimacy of the Soviet system rests on its ability to deliver a better life to its citizens. During his first two years in office, Gorbachev was fond of admonishing citizens, "If you want to live better, you will have to work harder." Hard work alone will not resolve these problems, however. Gorbachev's economic reforms have unleashed rapid inflationary pressures that have hit people on fixed incomes especially hard. The decision in February 1991 to take all 50- and 100-ruble notes out of circulation wiped out a lifetime of savings for millions of pensioners. The government has promised to raise pensions, but it is unlikely that they will keep pace with inflation.

In Lenin's original conception, social programs were designed not only to address chronic problems, but also to build mass support for the Bolshevik regime. The social contract upon which Soviet citizens came to rely ensured them a job, free and accessible (if not very high-quality) health care, adequate housing, and security in old age. Today that social contract is being severely threatened by the precipitous decline in the economy and rising public demands for higher-quality services. Even with all the recent emphasis on private enterprise and decentralization of authority, it is clear that citizens still turn to the State for support. Thus, the crisis confronting social policy in the USSR today is rapidly becoming a crisis of plummeting popularity for Gorbachev and waning credibility for the system he heads.

Notes

1. Alexander Block, "Soviet Housing—I," *Soviet Studies* 3, no. 1 (July, 1951): 12.

2. Alexander Block, "Soviet Houslng—II," *Soviet Studies* 3, no. 3 (January, 1952): 248–249.

3. T. Sosnovy, "Housing in the Workers' State," *Problems of Communism* 5, no. 6 (1956): 52–55.

4. J. V. Stalin, *Works*, vol. 13 (Moscow: Foreign Languages Publishing House, 1955), 178.

5. Sosnovy, "Housing In the Workers' State," 57.

6. Ibid., 66.

7. Block, "Sovlet Housing—I," 7.

8. M. S. Parkins, *City Planning in Soviet Russia* (Chicago: University of Chicago Press, 1953), 56.

9. Ibid.

10. Henry W. Morton, "What Have Soviet Leaders Done about the Housing Crisis?" in Henry W. Morton and Rudolf L. Tokes, eds., *Soviet Politics and Society in the 1970s* (New York: The Free Press, 1974), 170.

11. Gertrude E. Schroeder, "Consumption in the USSR: A Survey," *Studies on the Soviet Union* 10 (1970): 16.

12. John Gunther, *Inside Russia Today* (New York: Harpers, 1958), pp. 47–48.

13. Morton, "What Have Soviet Leaders Done?," 168.

14. Ibid., 164.

15. Hedrick Smith, *The Russians* (New York: Ballantine, 1976), 98.

16. David K. Shipler, *Russia: Broken Idols, Solemn Dreams* (New York: Times Books, 1983), 91.

17. Smith, *The Russians*, 98.

18. Ibid.

19. Gertrude E. Schroeder, "Consumption," in Abram Bergson and Herbert S. Levine, eds., *The Soviet Economy: Toward the Year 2000* (London: George Allen & Unwin, 1983), 313; cited in N. J. Peterson, "Goskomstat Report on Social Conditions in 1989," *Radio Liberty Report on the USSR* 2, no. 6 (9 February 1990): 4.

20. Margot Jacobs, "Soviet Housing Woes Continue," *Radio Liberty Report on the USSR* 2, no. 13 (30 March 1990): 8.

21. Ibid.

22. Calculated from figures in *The Cambridge Encyclopedia of Russia and the Soviet Union* (Cambridge: Cambridge University Press, 1982), 348.

23. *Sotsialisticheskaya industriya*, 17 April 1980, cited in Leslie Dienes, "Regional Economic Development," in Bergson and Levine, *The Soviet Economy*, 250.

24. Ibid.

25. Basile Kerblay, *Modern Soviet Society* (New York: Pantheon Books, 1983), 63.

26. *The Cambridge Encyclopedia*, 348.

27. Jacobs, "Soviet Housing Woes Continue," 8.

28. Cited in *Moscow News*, 11–18 March 1990, nos. 8–9, p. 19.

29. Carol Nechemias, "Welfare in the Soviet Union: Health Housing, and Personal Consumption," in Gordon B. Smith, ed., *Public Policy and Administration in the Soviet Union* (New York: Praeger, 1980), 189.

30. A similar case forms the basis for Iuri Trifonov's short story "The Exchange."

31. Mikhail Bulgakov, *The Master and Margarita* (London: Fontana, 1983), 265–266.

32. Jacobs, "Soviet Housing Woes Continue," 9.

33. Peterson, "Goskomstat Report on Social Conditions in 1989," 4.

34. Jacobs, "Soviet Housing Woes Continue," 9.

35. Mark G. Field, *Soviet Socialized Medicine* (New York: The Free Press, 1967), 52.

36. V. I. Lenin, *Sochineniya*, vol. 30 (Moscow: Politicheskaya literatura, 1950), 375–376.

37. G. Hyde, *The Soviet Health Service* (London: Lawrence & Wishart, 1974), 99.

38. Vicente Navarro, *Social Security and Medicine in the USSR* (Lexington, MA: Lexington Books, 1977), 48.

39. Murray Feshbach and Stephen Rapawy, "Soviet Manpower Trends and Policies," U.S. Congress, Joint Economic Committee, *The Soviet Economy in a New Perspective* (Washington, DC: U.S. Government Printing Office, 1976).

40. Christopher Davis and Murray Feshbach, *Rising Infant Mortality in the USSR in the 1970s*, U.S. Bureau of the Census, Series P-95, no. 74 (Washington, DC: U.S. Government Printing Office, September 1980).

41. N. S. Khrushchev, "Report to the Central Committee of the CPSU at the 22nd Congress," in *Materialy XXIII S'ezda KPSS* (Moscow: Gospolitizdat, 1961), 73.

42. Murray Feshbach, "Issues in Soviet Health Problems," in U.S. Congress, Joint Economic Committee, *Soviet Economy in the 1980s: Problems and Prospects* (Washington, DC: U.S. Government Printing Office, 1982), 216.

43. *Narodnoe khozyaistvo SSSR v 1983* (Moscow: Finansy i statistika, 1984), 446.

44. *Cambridge Encyclopedia*, 394.

45. Christopher Davis, "The Economics of the Soviet Health System," U.S. Congress, Joint Economic Committee, *Soviet Economy in the 1980s*, 244.

46. Navarro, *Social Security and Medicine*, 76.

47. *Zarya Vostoka*, 15 July 1984, p. 1.

48. During their three-year obligation, Soviet doctors earn a regular salary.

49. Feshbach, "Issues in Soviet Health Problems," 209.

50. *Sovetskaya Rossiya*, 30 September 1981, p. 1.

51. Davis, "Economics of the Soviet Health System," 250.

52. Feshbach, "Issues in Soviet Health Problems," 205.

53. David E. Powell, "A Troubled Society," in James Cracrak, ed., *The Soviet Union Today* (Chicago: Bulletin of the Atomic Scientists, 1983), 326.

54. Ibid.

55. B. Levin and M. Levin, *Literaturnaya gazeta*, 20 December 1978, p. 12.

56. Cited in Vladimir G. Treml, "Alcohol Abuse and Quality of Life in the USSR," in Helmut Sonnenfeldt, ed., *Soviet Politics in the 1980s* (Boulder, CO: Westview Press, 1985), 59.

57. Vladimir G. Treml, "Death from Alcohol Poisoning in the USSR," *Wall Street Journal*, 10 November 1981, p. 13.

58. Treml, "Alcohol Abuse," 57.

59. Treml, "Death from Alcohol Poisoning."

60. Ibid.

61. Reported by John Kenneth Galbraith in "Reflections: A Visit to Russia," *The New Yorker*, 3 September 1984, p. 59.

62. Abortion was outlawed from 1936 to 1955.

63. Davis and Feshbach, *Rising Infant Mortality*, pp. 16–17.

64. For example, see M. S. Bednyy, *Mediko-demiograficheskoe izuchenie narodonaseleniya* (Moscow: Statistika, 1979), 128.

65. *Pravda*, 14 February 1974, p. 3.

66. Ibid.

67. Feshbach, "Issues in Soviet Health Problems," 209.

68. D. F. Peterson, "Goskomstat Report on Social Conditions in 1989," 5.

69. Ibid.

70. Ibid.

71. Ibid.

72. Ibid.

73. See *New York Times*, 12 February 1989, p. 12 for an account of how 27 babies were infected in a maternity hospital in the city of Elista.

74. D.F. Peterson, "Medicines, Newspapers and Protecting the Environment," *Radio Liberty Report on the USSR* 2, no. 12 (23 March 1990): 11.

75. Ibid.

76. V. I. Lenin, *Polnoe sobranie sochineniya*, vol. 17 (Moscow: Foreign Languages Publishing House, 1963), 476.

77. Cited in Vic George and Nick Manning, *Socialism, Social Welfare and the Soviet Union* (London: Routledge and Kegan Paul, 1980), 38.

78. Ibid., 41.

79. *Cambridge Encyclopedia*, 397.

80. Ibid.

81. Ibid.

82. Ibid.

83. *Problemy ekonomiki* 24 (November 1981): 180–181.

84. *Vestnik statistiki*, no. 11 (1981): 60.

85. V. A. Belova et al., *Skol'ko detei budet v sovetskoi sem'e: Sbornik statei* (Moscow: Statistika, 1977), p. 123.

86. *The Cambridge Encyclopedia*, 380.

87. Ibid., 398.

88. This assessment is reached by George and Manning in *Socialism, Social Welfare and the Soviet Union*, 60.

89. Stephen Sternheimer, "The Graying of the Soviet Union: Labor and Welfare Issues for the Post-Brezhnev Era," *Problems of Communism* (September–October, 1982): 81–82.

90. Calculated from Soviet statistics in *Narodnoe khozyaistvo v SSSR v 1983* (Moscow: Finansy i statistika, 1984), 407, 410.

91. Mervyn Matthews, *Class and Society in Soviet Politics* (London: Allen Lane, 1972), 88.

Selected Bibliography

Andrusz, Gregory D. *Housing and Urban Development in the USSR*. London: Macmillan, 1984.

Brine, Jenny, Maureen Perrie, and Andrew Sutton. *Home, School and Leisure in the Soviet Union*. Boston: Allen & Unwin, 1980.

Davis, Christopher, and Murray Feshbach. *Rising Infant Mortality in the USSR in the 1970s*. Washington, DC: U.S. Bureau of the Census, 1980.

Dimaio, A. J. *Soviet Urban Housing*. New York: Praeger, 1974.

Field, Mark G., ed. *Social Consequences of Modernization in Communist Societies*. Baltimore: The Johns Hopkins University Press, 1976.

Field, Mark G. *Soviet Socialized Medicine*. New York: The Free Press, 1967.

George, Vic, and Nick Manning. *Socialism, Social Welfare and the Soviet Union*. London: Routledge & Kegan Paul, 1980.

Hyde, G. *The Soviet Health Service*. London: Lawrence & Wishart, 1974.

Kaser, Michael. *Health Care in the Soviet Union and Eastern Europe*. London: Croom Helm, 1976.

Kerblay, Basile. *Modern Soviet Society*. New York: Pantheon Books, 1983.

Kornarova, D. P. *Social Security in the USSR*. Moscow: Progress, 1971.

Lane, David. *Soviet Economy and Society*. London: Basil Blackwell, 1985.

Lane, David. *Soviet Society under Perestroika*. Boston: Unwin Hyman, 1990.

Lisitsin, Y. *Health Protection in the USSR*. Moscow: Progress, 1972.

Littlejohn, Gary. *A Sociology of the Soviet Union*. London: Macmillan, 1984.

Madison, Bernice Q. *Social Welfare in the Soviet Union*. Stanford: Stanford University Press, 1968.

Matthews, Mervyn. *Class and Society in Soviet Russia*. London: Allen Lane, 1972.

McAuley, Alastair. *Economic Welfare in the Soviet Union*. London: George Allen & Unwin, 1979.

Millar, James R., ed. *Politics, Work, and Daily Life in the USSR*. Cambridge: Cambridge University Press, 1987.

Navarro, Vicente. *Social Security and Medicine in the USSR*. Lexington, MA: Lexington Books, 1977.

Osborn, Robert J. *Soviet Social Policies: Welfare, Equality, and Community*. Homewood, IL: Dorsey Press, 1970.

Rimlinger, G. V. *Welfare Policy and Industrialization in Europe, America, and Russia*. Boston: Wiley & Sons, 1971.

Ryan, T. M. *The Organization of Soviet Medical Care*. London: Basil Blackwell, 1978.

Smith, Gordon B., ed. *Public Policy and Administration in the Soviet Union*. New York: Praeger, 1980.

Zhukov, K., and V. Fyodorov. *Housing Construction in the Soviet Union*. Moscow: Progress, 1974.

12

Science, Technology, and Education

From its founding, the Soviet regime has manifested an ambivalent attitude toward science and scientists. On the one hand, science has been accorded a prominent role in Soviet ideology. Marx noted that the progression to socialist society depended on the general condition of science and technology and their application to production.[1] Lenin echoed this stress on science and technology by urging Bolsheviks "to take all science, technology, knowledge" because communism could not be built without them.[2] Lenin frequently referred to a "technical revolution," which would change the nature of the society. Throughout the Bolshevik period, science and technology were seen as the great transformers of society. The Bolsheviks expected the development of a "new," revolutionary science, free of ties to bourgeois society, to unleash the creative powers of science on behalf of all social classes. A clear illustration of Lenin's views on the revolutionizing effect of technology was the GOELRO (electrification) plan. For Lenin, electrification was not simply a technical problem, but a socioeconomic one with profound political and social implications.

On the other hand, however, scientists have often been at odds with official policies in the USSR, and a few have become outspoken critics of the Soviet system. Lenin and his successors found that creative, scientific minds cannot be channeled exclusively toward technical and scientific problems; scientists who are capable of envisioning revolutionary scientific discoveries are also capable of analyzing and criticizing social and political issues as well.

At the same time, the expertise of the Soviet scientific and technical community has proven invaluable to policymakers. Resolving the complex issues that confront the leadership demands minds and talents of the highest quality. Yet the policymakers are sometimes not pleased with the advice they receive from the experts. Thus, while Soviet scientists are indispensable to the Soviet regime, they also pose many challenges for the leadership. The study of the role of science and scientists in Soviet society illustrates the policy-formulation process in a dynamic and vitally important field.

THE DEVELOPMENT OF SOVIET SCIENCE

As in so many other fields, the Bolsheviks inherited a scientific establishment that had been created under the imperial government. Prior to the revolution, Russian science was closely tied to the State; all universities and research institutes, as well as the Imperial Russian Academy of Sciences, fell under the direct supervision of the government. Scientists were members of a privileged elite. Although they occupied a broad range of the political spectrum, from ultraconservatives to radicals, the largest group supported the Constitutional Democrats (Kadets). During the Civil War, professors and academics were considered enemies of the Bolshevik regime, and many were arrested and died during the Red Terror. Nikolai Koltsov, the famous biologist, was condemned to death, but he was spared because of Bolshevik writer Maxim Gorky's personal appeal to Lenin.

The repression of scientists during the early years of the Soviet regime resulted in the emigration of a large number of distinguished scientists, including Igor Sikorsky, the prominent aircraft designer; V. Korenchevsky, a biologist and noted specialist on gerontology; G. B. Kistyakovsky, a chemist who would later serve as science advisor to President Eisenhower; Pitirim Sorokin, a sociologist; and Wasily Leontiev, who would later receive the Nobel Prize in economics. Recognizing the damage caused by this "brain drain," Lenin introduced a resolution at the Eighth Party Congress in 1919 that signaled a more moderate stance toward science: "The problem of industrial and economic development demands the immediate and widespread use of experts in science and technology whom we have inherited from capitalism, in spite of the fact that they inevitably are impregnated with bourgeois ideas and customs."[3]

Meanwhile, the foundations were being laid for training a new generation of "revolutionary" scientists and technical experts, who would eventually replace the scientists held over from the tsarist period. Despite the precarious status of Soviet science during the Civil War period, many new research institutes were established, often housed in large estates confiscated from wealthy industrialists and former members of the aristocracy.

The end of the Civil War, the introduction of the New Economic Policy (NEP) in 1921, and the liberalized political climate combined to create favorable conditions for the development of science. International scholarly cooperation and exchanges of scientific literature were resumed. Financial support for new research institutes and laboratories was increased, and ideological strictures were eased in the natural and physical sciences. The humanities and social sciences, however, continued under strict ideological controls enforced by Bolshevik political activists, few of whom had any scientific training.

Science policy during NEP was directed by *Glavnauka*, a special department of the People's Commissariat of Education. *Glavnauka* was responsible for allocating government research contracts as well as for authorizing foreign travel for scientists. Under the leadership of A. V. Lunacharsky, chief of *Glavnauka*, Soviet science flourished. The number of scientific papers, conferences, and journals increased rapidly. Major advances were made in the fields of genetics, biochemistry, physiology, biology, physics, chemistry, mathematics, geology, and geophysics.

Like virtually every other sphere of Soviet life, however, science changed dramatically in 1928 with Stalin's introduction of forced industrialization, centralized state planning, and collectivization of agriculture. In March 1928, a major purge of scientists, engineers, and technical personnel began with the arrest, trial, and execution of eleven persons accused of sabotaging coal mines. Émigré Soviet scientist Zhores Medvedev argues that the campaign directed against scientific experts was part of Stalin's plan to replace the older generation of scientists with a new generation of "red" experts.[4] Supposed anti-Soviet organizations were "exposed," and with them many prominent scientists and numerous professors in universities and technical colleges. The arbitrary and groundless arrests of scientists often encouraged their opponents and enemies to declare whole branches of science or theoretical approaches "bourgeois" or "reactionary." For instance, in 1929, when the noted biologist and founder of the Russian school of genetics, S. S. Chetverikov, was arrested and exiled to a remote region of the Urals, the whole field of genetics also came under attack. Koltsov, A. Serebrovsky, and many other geneticists were subsequently arrested and replaced by a younger generation of poorly trained but ideologically "pure" specialists. Largely because of the elimination of a whole generation of geneticists, T. D. Lysenko was able to rise to prominence, advocating the dubious theory (later proved erroneous) of the inheritance of acquired characteristics. Lysenko and other members of the new breed of scientists offered false hopes to Stalin that by subordinating pure science to practice (*praktikat*), science would dramatically and immediately enhance industrial and agricultural performance.

In 1929, the Leningrad Party Committee organized a special commission to investigate the USSR Academy of Sciences, whose headquarters were still located in the city. The commission found the Academy to be a "center for counterrevolutionary work against Soviet power."[5] Hundreds of academicians and staff members were either arrested or dismissed. Prior to 1928, the Academy had managed to remain apolitical, but with new elections scheduled, great pressure was brought on the Academy to elect party members as academicians. Political controls over the Academy further increased in 1934, when the Academy was moved to Moscow and merged with the Communist Academy, a party-controlled body that had attempted unsuccessfully to duplicate the functions of the Academy.

The need for scientific and technical expertise grew under Stalin's industrialization program, and the repression of scientists eased somewhat after 1932. A few scientists were released from prison, while others were allowed to continue their research in prison. The easing of pressure on scientists was, however, only temporary. Stalin's Great Terror of 1936–1938 wiped out many thousands of scientists and other academics, decimating every branch of science and learning. While the economy continued to function, all new research and development came to an abrupt end. International scientific and technical ties were severed. Technological development, even in such important fields as aircraft design, were halted with the arrest, imprisonment, and execution of leading experts. What little research and development was performed during the war years occurred within the confines of Stalin's Gulag prison system. Medvedev describes the absurdities of prison research centers.

The chief engineers of these centers, although prisoners, headed large teams of experts, some of whom were not prisoners themselves. After the long working day, the free employees would return home to their families while their superiors were taken back to their prison cells.[6]

The prison research network is credited with designing a series of new tanks, aircraft, artillery, and locomotives as well as laying the groundwork for the early Soviet missiles. Scientists and academicians in fields with no potential military applications were sent to work in mines or to harvest timber in Siberia. S. P. Korolev, who would later design the first sputniks and the Soviet Union's first intercontinental missiles, spent the war years working in the notorious mines of Kolyma, north of the Arctic Circle. By the time the war ended and he was released, he was close to death from fatigue and malnutrition.

The war demonstrated to Stalin the inferiority of Soviet technology, and from 1946 on all branches of military-oriented technology received highest state priority. Allocations for science increased dramatically, and the powers of the Academy were extended. The salaries of scientists were doubled or even tripled. New institutes and research centers sprang up, and the scientific community suddenly became a privileged elite.

Especially prominent in the post–World War II emphasis on scientific advancement was the program to develop an atomic bomb. The program, headed by Igor Kurchatov, drew on the finest available talent, including several captured German physicists. One of the Germans was later awarded the title "Hero of Socialist Labor" and appointed head of a nuclear research team in East Germany, but soon escaped to West Germany.[7] Lavrenti Beria, Stalin's infamous chief of secret police, was responsible for mobilizing prison labor to increase uranium production. Beria also utilized the resources of the prison-camp system in the years following the war to construct masssive science and space complexes.[8]

The development of Soviet atomic capability also benefited other branches of science. The sudden availability of isotopes spurred new advances in chemistry, biochemistry, physiology, and medicine. These fields, however, did not receive the high priority accorded to the Soviet atomic project.

In lower-priority branches of Soviet science, political intrusions were frequent. Stalin considered himself an authority in many scientific fields, including biology, evolution, linguistics, philosophy, and the social sciences, and he did not hesitate to impose his theories. Furthermore, he extended his own authoritarian style of leadership to each branch of science. Scientific leaders in each research field were charged not only with administering their respective research projects, but also with developing the "correct" theoretical line to be followed by all researchers. In the natural sciences, all research had to be based on the principles of dialectical materialism as expounded in Stalin's political tract on the subject. From the late 1940s until Khrushchev's ouster in 1964, Lysenko, the scientific leader in the fields of biology and agricultural sciences, exerted dictatorial powers over research, and a number of his pseudoscientific theories became official dogma. Under Lysenko, genetics research stopped for almost twenty years, doing irreparable damage to the field in the Soviet Union.

A new wave of purges of Soviet scientists was planned in conjunction with the "Doctors' Plot" but was cut short by Stalin's death in March 1953. The more relaxed political climate introduced by Khrushchev spurred scientific and technological development. At the Twentieth Party Congress in 1956, the First Secretary shocked the delegates with a stinging denunciation of Stalin's crimes, including the arrest and imprisonment of thousands of the Soviet Union's leading scientists. Many scientists were "rehabilitated" during Khrushchev's de-Stalinization campaign. For others, however, the rehabilitation came too late—they had already been executed or had died in the camps.

Reflecting the new, more open attitude toward science, international scientific communication and cooperation resumed after twenty years of isolation imposed by Stalin. Expanded contacts with the American and European scientific communities, however, further illustrated the scientific and technological gap that existed between the USSR and the West. Khrushchev initiated a program of actively assimilating foreign technology in an effort to narrow the gap. Technical and agricultural attachés were assigned to Soviet embassies abroad, scientific exchanges were initiated, Western scientific journals were made available to Soviet scientists, and specialists were allowed to attend international conferences and symposia abroad.

Khrushchev's emphasis on duplicating Western scientific and technological achievements, while well-intentioned, further widened the technological gap in some cases. Medvedev notes that while Soviet scientists were busy trying to copy imported instruments and equipment, Western scientists were introducing many innovations, resulting in equipment that was several generations ahead of the Soviet efforts.[9]

The Soviet thrust in scientific and technical fields under Khrushchev was impressive nevertheless. In 1957, the Soviets shocked the world with the first successful launching of an unmanned satellite, Sputnik I. During the Khrushchev years, the number of research workers almost tripled, while the number of research institutes doubled.[10] The proliferation of institutes under the jurisdiction of the USSR Academy of Sciences burdened its budget and managerial resources to the point that in 1961, about half of the institutes were shifted from the Academy to various industrial ministries, where they were to conduct applied research to enhance the performance of their respective industrial sectors. Thus, the Institute of Fisheries was transferred to the Ministry of Fisheries, and the Institute of Oil was placed under the aegis of the Ministry of the Petroleum Industry. Institutes remaining under the jurisdiction of the Academy tended to focus on pure or basic research rather than applied research.

Khrushchev also promoted the decentralization of the Soviet scientific establishment. Under Stalin, the concentration of scientific research centers in Moscow had reached high levels. For instance, 70 to 80 percent of all biologists lived in that city.[11] Khrushchev considered this concentration unhealthy and even dangerous, so he ordered the construction of several gigantic science centers far from Moscow. The best-known example is Akademgorodok (Academy Town), near Novosibirsk in Central Siberia. The new planned community was the site of the prestigious Siberian Division of the Academy of Sciences, and several noted scientists were encouraged to establish research institutes there. In order to attract scientists and technical personnel to the region, Khrushchev authorized salary bonuses of 50 to 100 percent.[12]

The Khrushchev era was also marked by extensive discussions of the dynamic role of science and technology in altering Soviet society and ushering in communism. In the mid-1950s, books and articles began to appear discussing the "scientific-technical revolution" (STR) that was sweeping the modern world and would radically transform social and economic relations. The Program of the Twenty-Second Party Congress in 1961 stated, "Humanity is entering a period of scientific and technical revolution connected with the mastering of nuclear power, the conquest of space, the development of chemistry, the automation of production, and other achievements of science and technology."[13] This official recognition by the Party stimulated even more research on the STR.

Specialists during this period were sensitive to the political and cultural ramifications of the scientific-technical revolution. A leading Czechoslovakian scholar referred to the STR as "a cultural revolution of unprecedented proportions."[14] Inherent in this revolution were changes affecting not only industrial production, but also the full range of people-machine relations, interpersonal relations, and the relationship of people to their environment. During the late 1960s, a team of Soviet and Czech specialists working on the STR noted that it involved a "fundamental transformation of science and technology . . . leading to the application of science as a direct productive force" in the economy.[15]

During the 1960s and early 1970s, there was a veritable flood of monographs, texts, research symposia, and newspaper articles devoted to the scientific-technical revolution. Discussions of the STR were not limited to economists, engineers, scientists, and others most directly affected by it; instead virtually no discipline was left untouched. Legal scholars, urban planners, sociologists, health-care specialists, artists, and writers all speculated on the impact of the STR on their respective fields.

As research on the scientific-technical revolution gained momentum, however, it became apparent that expectations of its accomplishments were outpacing actual societal change. A conservative backlash occurred under Brezhnev, and the early optimism that had permeated discussions of the STR became clouded with cautionary statements. In 1968, a major philosophical journal warned against "illusions" about the omnipotence of science and technology in effecting change.[16] Other authors chose to downgrade the ambitious scope of the STR and instead began referring to "scientific and technical progress."[17]

The history of Soviet science is replete with examples of scientific fads and trends (like the STR or cybernetics) that begin with the imaginative work of Soviet scientists but soon expand to dominate all scientific discussions. As a fad takes hold, it becomes the subject of an intensive campaign and is thus transformed into an element of the official ideology. Inevitably, scientific fads fail to live up to expectations, and they eventually generate conservative reactions and are superseded by other trends or fads.

In the late 1960s and early 1970s, the emerging policy of détente under Brezhnev greatly facilitated international scientific contacts and cooperation.

Because of these increased contacts, Soviet science gradually shifted from the duplication of Western achievements to cooperation with the West and integration into worldwide developments in scientific and technical progress.

The Brezhnev leadership recognized that the numerous and embarrassing failures of Khrushchev's policies had occurred in large part because of a failure to consult with scientific experts or to heed their advice. Consequently, the Brezhnev regime began to incorporate technical specialists in policy-making to a degree never before seen in the USSR.

Throughout the 1960s, the Soviet scientific community also became increasingly vocal on political matters, using their privileged status and scholarly credibility to support various political causes. In 1966, a group of twenty-five prominent scientists, literary experts, and artists sent a strongly worded letter to the CPSU Central Committee protesting Stalin's rehabilitation. Scientists also protested the trial of the prominent Soviet writers Andrei Sinyavsky and Yuri Daniel and the harassment of Aleksandr Solzhenitsyn. But the event that crystallized opposition within the scientific community more than any other was the 1968 Soviet invasion of Czechoslovakia. Hundreds of Soviet scientists signed letters or attended meetings protesting the suppression of the liberal reforms that had occurred during the "Prague Spring."

The Brezhnev regime responded to this rising criticism with a crackdown on dissident scientists. Scientists who signed petitions or spoke out publicly were often called in by party authorities and asked to retract their statements. Those who refused were expelled from the Party, stripped of security clearances (making them ineligible to work in most institutes that conducted classified research), and blacklisted by government censors. Some dissident scientists were even dismissed, arrested, and convicted of anti-Soviet agitation. Academician Andrei Sakharov, father of the hydrogen bomb in the USSR, lost his security clearance and was not allowed to enter his institute in Moscow.

The Brezhnev regime's crackdown on intellectual dissent also resulted in a policy of abolishing the separate, privileged status of the Soviet scientific community. The isolated, scholarly towns were "proletarianized" by relocating industries and by transferring thousands of working-class families there to alter their social composition. Akademgorodok was incorporated into Novosibirsk, losing its autonomy and even its name.

At the same time, the Brezhnev leadership began to criticize the overconcentration of Jews in the scientific and academic professions. Measures were taken to restrict the admission of Jews to colleges and universities and the hiring of Jews. The number of Jews entering universities declined from 112,000 in 1968 to 105,800 in 1970, 88,500 in 1972, and an estimated 50,000 in 1980.[18] Jewish scientists and researchers were dismissed from their institutes, and quotas on hiring were instituted in some cities.[19] These harsh and restrictive measures prompted a sudden outpouring of demands by Jewish intellectuals to emigrate from the USSR, creating another thorny political issue to complicate Brezhnev's foreign-policy objectives and catalyzing even greater dissent within the scientific and scholarly community.

The stagnation of the Soviet economy during the latter Brezhnev years also took its toll on Soviet science. The rate of annual increase in the number of scientists dropped from the phenomenal figure of 7.8 percent in the period from 1963 to 1968, to 6.1 percent from 1968 to 1973, and to 3.2 percent from 1973 to 1978.[20] The average annual increase in budget allocations for scientific and technological research fell from 15 percent in the 1950s and early 1960s to 8 percent in the mid-1960s, to a low of 1.7 percent in 1976.[21] Despite the reduced growth rates, however, more than 1.3 million scientists are employed in research institutes in the USSR, almost 60 percent more than in the United States.[22]

SCIENTISTS AND POLICY-MAKING

As we have seen, the role of scientists and other specialists in the policy-making process has waxed and waned in the years from 1917 to the present. Despite these fluctuations, however, there has been a general increase over the long run in scientists' influence over policymakers. This trend was especially evident during the Brezhnev period.

Academicians first became involved in advising the Soviet government in the early 1930s, when Stalin began to emphasize tying research to the industrial needs of the country. The range of issues on which scientists could express opinions was limited to technical matters, however, and policy-making retained its highly centralized character. Khrushchev's failure to allow specialists to become involved in policy-making and his disregard for their advice when it was offered accounts for many of his disastrous policies.

Brezhnev heeded the advice of specialists much more extensively than had previous Soviet leaders. Whether it was agronomists advising the leadership on the potential of the non–black-earth zone, criminologists advising on policies to counteract juvenile delinquency, or environmental scientists describing the potential detrimental impact of the diversion of Siberian rivers, specialist involvement in the policy-making process became institutionalized under Brezhnev. With their growing influence, various Soviet research institutes have developed reputations for supporting certain positions on issues, and inter-institute rivalries are common, especially in attempting to influence the political leadership. While one's title or position within a given research institute is important, the biggest determinant of an individual scientist's degree of influence on policy questions appears to be his or her reputation and personal connections to the ruling elite.

In addition to being more involved in policy-making in recent years, scientists have also been given a freer hand in setting their own research agendas and managing research institutes. There is a fine line between party coordination of scientific research activities and *podmena*—party interference in questions of pure research. The political intrusions into the realm of science that characterized the Stalin and Khrushchev eras have been largely absent under Brezhnev and his successors. Speaking to a congress marking the two hundred and fiftieth anniversary of the Academy of Sciences, Brezhnev said: "We have no intention of dictating to you the details of your research subjects, nor how to go about it—that is a matter for the scientists themselves."[23]

In contrast to earlier periods, there is relatively little pressure on young scientists to join the Party. Yet the presidents of the Academy since 1961 have all been party members. In addition, scientific personnel are expected to attend periodic meetings and political lectures organized by the party committee in each research institute.

Under Brezhnev, the role and functions of academic councils (*uchenye sovety*) in scientific institutes were expanded. These councils, which consist of the institute director, academicians and corresponding members of the Academy, and other leading specialists, advise institute directors on administrative as well as scientific matters. Since 1972, the academic councils have met jointly with local party bureaus to discuss budgetary allocations, planning, and fulfillment of research programs.

The Party's primary mechanism for influencing research and development (R&D) policies is the party committee (*partkom*) within each scientific research institute. Chairmen of *partkomy* act as liaisons between institute directors and local party officials. They report to their superiors on plan fulfillment, labor discipline, and worker morale within their research institutes. In addition, they can use party connections and influence to acquire additional personnel, larger budgets, and better equipment. Party committees also participate in many administrative and managerial decisions, including the selection and assignment of projects, the awarding of promotions and raises, and the distribution of bonuses and social funds.

Innovations in the USSR are greatly facilitated when research institutes find powerful patrons in the higher party apparatus or obtain contracts from powerful ministries. When a minister or a member of the Central Committee throws his or her support behind an R&D project, bureaucratic obstacles are more easily overcome and rival institutes are less able to attack the project. Similarly, much of the innovative research in the Soviet Union is performed under contract. There is intense competition among research institutes over contracts, especially for defense projects, because of the defense sector's political clout, abundance of funds, and general openness to innovative ideas.

THE MANAGEMENT OF SCIENCE IN THE USSR

Scientific and technological research in the USSR is carried out through three main administrative structures: the Academy of Sciences of the USSR, the industrial ministries and their affiliated research institutes, and universities and technical colleges. The latter are relatively minor and are engaged primarily in graduate-level training rather than in conducting major research projects.

Traditionally, the power and prestige of the Academy of Sciences has far surpassed that of the other research organizations. The Academy comprises approximately 260 "academicians," or full members, and approximately 480 "corresponding members."[24] It convenes twice a year in a General Assembly to discuss major trends and problems of science policy in the USSR. In addition, the General Assembly elects new members by secret ballot and resolves organizational matters. The policy-making and administrative functions of the Academy are delegated to a presidium, chaired by the President of the Academy.

The Academy is divided into four branches: (1) physics, engineering, and mathematics; (2) chemistry and biology; (3) geosciences; and (4) social sciences. The Academy directly supervises more than three hundred of the most prestigious research institutes.

Each of the republics of the USSR has its own academy of science, which reports to the USSR Academy of Sciences in Moscow. Research institutes that are subordinate to the republic academies tend to focus on scientific or technical problems relevant to their regions. Thus, the Azerbaidzhan Academy of Sciences is noted for its work in petrochemicals, while the Armenian Academy operates an observatory high in the mountains and is noted for its research in astrophysics.

In addition, the USSR Academy of Sciences maintains branches throughout the Soviet Union. The three largest of these are the Siberian Division in Novosibirsk (formerly Akademgorodok), the Far Eastern Center in Khabarovsk, and the Urals Center in Sverdlovsk. In aggregate, the Academy system, including institutes subordinated to the republic academies and regional branches, contains approximately 1500 research institutes and employs more than 49,000 scientists and 150,000 staff.[25]

In recent years, research institutes affiliated with industrial ministries have grown in numbers and importance. Many of these institutes were originally under the authority of the Academy; they were transferred to the jurisdiction of industrial ministries in 1961 in an effort to separate institutes engaged in applied research from those conducting fundamental research. This division of institutes, which is responsible for some of the present problems of Soviet science, created the need for a new organization, parallel to the Academy, to coordinate the activities of institutes engaged in applied research. Such an institution, the State Committee for Science and Technology, was created in 1965. The State Committee, which reports directly to the Cabinet of Ministers, is responsible for formulating and directing science policy, assisting the Ministry of Economics and Forecasting and the Academy in allocating funds for research, identifying high-priority research projects, coordinating R&D efforts, and supervising the acquisition of technology from the West. Although the State Committee can influence scientific and technological work in important ways, it does not directly supervise the operations of the industrial institutes. Those institutes frequently concentrate on the narrow interests of their ministries or industrial sectors, placing more emphasis on short-term production goals than on the long-term innovation favored by the State Committee.

Brezhnev and his successors emphasized the need for improving economic performance through technological innovation. Soviet political leaders have become more and more insistent that research projects have practical payoffs. As a result, the State Committee has grown in power and prestige and can now occasionally challenge the dominance of the Academy of Sciences. The trend toward applied research has also strengthened the position of some of the industrial institutes. Their status and their level of financial support now equal that of many of the Academy institutes.

During the early 1980s, the Academy came under considerable pressure to devote greater attention to the potential industrial applications of its research. In his speeches, A. P. Aleksandrov, President of the Academy from 1960 to 1986, stressed the need for rapid advances in the fields of energy, computer technology, genetic engineering, and agriculture—all of which have direct industrial or agricultural applications.[26] In what has been interpreted as a jab at the role of the State Committee in encouraging technology imports from the West, Aleksandrov also warned about the dangers of relying too heavily on imported technology. He reported that 70 percent of the technical apparatuses, measuring devices, and instruments used in Soviet laboratories are of foreign origin.[27]

In June 1985, the Central Committee sponsored a special conference to discuss how the assimilation of science and technology into the economy might be improved. One of the central points made by many speakers at the conference was the need to shift the emphasis toward indigenous development of science and technology, rather than relying on foreign sources.[28]

At the level of the enterprise or production association, R&D has been enhanced since the early 1970s by the creation of science–production associations (*nauchno-proizvodstvennie ob'edineniya-NPO*). NPOs were formed by amalgamating different research institutes, design bureaus, and production units under the leadership of a single research institute. By creating larger R&D units, it was hoped that redundancy would be reduced, bureaucratic staff would be cut back, coordination and cooperation would be facilitated, and the research-production cycle would be shortened. The reform has been credited with substantial improvements. For example, at Pozitron, a leading microelectronics firm in Leningrad, the introduction of an NPO shortened the average lead-time for a R&D project from 4 years to 1.7 years.[29] NPOs play a prominent role in electronics, chemical engineering, and instrument-building, and in the radio and communications industries to a lesser extent.

The adoption of the NPO system in other sectors and branches has been hampered, however, by bureaucratic interests that wish to preserve the status quo. Some industrial ministries opposed the divestiture of their research institutes because these institutes provided a source of revenue through their contract research activities. Many enterprises and small design bureaus also opposed amalgamation into NPOs, fearing the loss of their independent status.

PROBLEMS AND PROSPECTS FOR SOVIET SCIENCE

With all the resources that are devoted to science and technology in the USSR, one might wonder why Soviet scientists do not perform better than they do. By most measures—numbers of Nobel prizes, major scientific or technical breakthroughs, citations by fellow scientists, and sheer volume of scientific publication—American scientists in most fields far surpass their Soviet counterparts.[30] The reason for this relatively lower level of Soviet scientific achievement stems not from political intrusions into science, but from the organization and management of science in the Soviet Union.

This chapter has already alluded to some of the problems in Soviet science. For instance, there is a relatively sharp distinction among Soviet research institutes between fundamental research and applied research. Scientists working in research institutes of the Academy of Sciences frequently disregard potential industrial applications of their research. Similarly, research institutes attached to industrial branches frequently focus on narrow, applied problems, such as how to eliminate production bottlenecks in existing technologies or processes, rather than pursuing more revolutionary and innovative research. Not only are fundamental and applied research separated organizationally, but there are few financial incentives for fundamental scientists to be concerned with applications, and for applied scientists to keep abreast of developments in basic theoretical research.

Organizational fragmentation also hampers scientific achievement by reducing coordination among research institutes. A research institute within the Ministry of the Electronics Industry, for example, will find it virtually impossible to acquire the assistance of specialists from institutes affiliated with other ministries. The development of an electrical component may be delayed by years or even scrapped altogether because the Ministry of the Chemical Industry does not produce the necessary polymers or other elements, or the Ministry of Instrument-Making and Control Systems does not manufacture a specialized measuring device.

Furthermore, scientific discoveries and breakthroughs in one field often are not reported to other branches of science for which they may have important consequences. In part, this is because the majority of R&D projects are conducted under security classifications, but it is also because of an inadequate system for publicizing research findings within the scientific community. One study found that it took Soviet enterprises one to two years longer to introduce new processes that were first developed in other branches or ministries than to adopt those that were developed in-house.[31] It simply takes enterprises longer to learn about innovations that occur outside their respective ministerial chains of command.

In order to facilitate the dissemination of technical information within the research community, the All-Union Institute of Interbranch Information (VIMI) was created. The Institute acts as a clearinghouse for information received from industrial ministries concerning their innovations. VIMI sends copies of this information to other ministries and research institutes that may find it useful. The system, however, has proved overly cumbersome and bureaucratic.

Scientific progress is also retarded in the USSR by inadequate equipment, instruments, and supplies. A survey of 300 Soviet institutes found that 85 percent had no photocopiers; thus, designs and technical drawings had to be reproduced by hand.[32] Partly as a result of chronic shortages of equipment, Soviet scientists excel in the theoretical, or "blackboard," sciences, including theoretical condensed-matter physics, theoretical astrophysics, theoretical seismology, mathematical psychology, elementary particle theory, and plasma physics. These fields do not require extensive laboratory equipment or elaborate computer technology. However, in the experimental sciences (e.g., astronomy, interferometry, experimental physics, computer science, the social sciences, and all fields of engineering) where equipment needs are vital, the Soviets lag considerably behind their American and European counterparts. Even when Soviet scientists make a crucial breakthrough, they are often unable to maintain their lead because of the inadequate infrastructure. For example, although Soviet scientists are credited with founding the field of low-temperature physics, their leadership in the field has declined, in part, because of a lack of high-vacuum components and other ancillary technologies.[33]

Despite the impressive achievements of Soviet science in some fields, the technological level of the Soviet economy is far from uniform. Traditional values, a poorly trained labor force, and primitive operating conditions frequently render advanced technology useless or seriously impair its efficiency. Several years ago, for example, the Soviets imported a multimillion-dollar American computer system and installed it in a research institute. The system was plagued by breakdowns, however, because the room in which the computer was installed was not climate controlled. In addition, the Soviets decided to use their own paper in the printer. The paper was of poor quality, and when the humidity in the room increased, the paper swelled and jammed the printer.[34] The transmission of computerized information by telephone is commonplace in the United States, but in the Soviet Union the telephone lines are so inefficient (partly because of the KGB's tapping of the lines) that computers often malfunction or send erroneous information.

Some advanced technology in the USSR exists primarily as "decorative technology," or window dressing. On a visit to the Soviet Union, the author stayed at the Cosmos Hotel in Moscow, which was built for the 1980 Olympics. He was impressed to see that the attendant on each floor had a computer terminal on her desk. When the author asked one attendant what she used the terminal for, she replied that it was empty and she kept her purse in it.

Finally, Soviet performance in engineering and other technical fields has been hampered by the practice of following the lead of Americans, Japanese, and Europeans. In computer technology, genetic engineering, as well as military technologies, the Soviets appear to be engaged primarily in copying Western developments rather than in pursuing their own innovations.[35] By choosing to follow the technological lead of the West, the USSR assures the West a critical lead-time advantage.

The economic stringencies confronting the Gorbachev regime will probably further retard the rate of growth of Soviet science and technology in the years ahead. Yet the Soviet system is still capable of mobilizing massive resources in a few specially targeted areas. Major efforts are currently under way in the fields of computer engineering and microelectronics, lasers and charged particle beam technology, and genetic engineering. The Soviet regime is discussing the possibility of creating a new ministry devoted solely to genetic engineering. The obvious driving factor in each of these cases is the fear of falling behind American efforts in such critical, militarily related technological fields.

The future will likely see the continuation of the struggle for dominance between the Academy of Sciences and the State Committee for Science and

Technology. Because of the latter's responsibility for technology imports, its influence seems to increase during periods of détente and expanded trade with the West and to diminish with heightened East–West tensions.

Gorbachev has made it clear that he intends to harness the potential of science and technology in order to improve economic performance through technical innovation. The emphasis on applied research will undoubtedly continue for the foreseeable future. While the focus on applied research may help invigorate the faltering Soviet economy in the short run, the long-term consequences for fundamental, basic research are troubling to many in the Academy of Sciences and to Western observers of Soviet science. The Soviet Union is not alone in shifting its emphasis from fundamental to applied research, especially in the light of the ever-increasing share of research funds supporting the development of new weapons systems. A similar trend has occurred in the United States in the past decade. It is too early to determine the long-term effects of this trend on scientific and technological development in either the East or the West.

PERESTROIKA AND SCIENCE

Gorbachev's policy of glasnost', which was designed in part to appeal to the intelligentsia, had a special resonance with the scientific community. Not only did they favor the easing of general restrictions on what could be said and published, but they also saw in glasnost' the possibility of freeing scientific research from the cumbersome bureaucratic and political controls.[36]

The freer atmosphere afforded by glasnost' and perestroika is not uniform, however. For instance, Soviet scientists now find it easier to acquire scientific journals from the West or obtain permission to attend international conferences. Yet restrictions still exist on access to scientific and technical information within the USSR. Research topics that were once forbidden, such as nuclear safety and the ethics of biotechnology, are encouraged. In the basic sciences, however, approval of research topics and publication of results are still controlled by a relatively closed and conservative group of senior scientists.[37]

In September 1987 the CPSU Central Committee and the USSR Council of Ministers issued a joint decree that transferred all scientific research institutions to a system of self-financing and cost-accounting.[38] The new funding procedures meant that one-quarter of the research undertaken by the Academy had to be financed through contracts with ministries, enterprises, and other "outside" sources. While external contract funding is possible and even desirable in the applied sciences, the new policy was a serious setback for basic research. Academician Lev Tanson projected that self-financing will reduce fundamental research in the Academy to 40 to 45 percent of its total research effort.[39] At the Nineteenth Party Conference in mid-1988, the President of the USSR Academy of Sciences, Gurii Marchuk, complained that basic science in the USSR is poorly funded—2 billion rubles per year compared to $15 billion per year in the United States.[40]

The portion of funding provided directly by the Academy is no longer allocated in block grants to institutes, but is earmarked for specific priority research projects and programs. The result has been countless power struggles within and among research institutes, often with the money going to projects of politically influential but oftentimes conservative senior scholars.

Many disgruntled younger and middle-aged scientists have taken advantage of relaxed travel and emigration policies and gone to the West for temporary or permanent employment. In 1989 alone, 246 Academy scientists left the USSR for assignments outside the country.[41] Academician Vladimir Zuev characterized the crisis in Soviet science as follows: "The old generation is seeking money, the middle generation is rushing to the West, while the younger generation is rushing to cooperatives."[42]

By mid-1989 there were some 300 privately operated scientific cooperatives engaged in a wide range of contract research, consulting, and production.[43] There is a rapidly growing market for scientific and technical expertise outside of traditional channels. Enterprising young scientists find that in private cooperatives they can make much more money and avoid the bureaucratic and political obstacles that characterize Academy research institutes.

The growing politicization of the scientific community has also prompted calls for democratizing the strictly hierarchical and conservative USSR Academy of Sciences. In the past, the presidium of the Academy has had a very low turnover rate, and directors of academy institutes had a "lock" on their positions. In March 1987, Marchuk instituted a strict retirement policy that forced scientists to resign administrative posts at age 65. By October 1988, 17 institute directors, 29 deputy directors, and 250 laboratory chiefs had been replaced and five new vice-presidents were brought into the presidium.[44]

The October 1987 General Assembly of the Academy approved the involvement of institute scientists in the selection of institute directors and the election of academic councils (*uchenye sovety*) which allocate research funds, laboratory space, equipment, and personnel. By March 1990, 195 institute directors were elected or appointed on a competitive basis.[45] Nevertheless, this represents less than 8 percent of Academy-affiliated institutes.

When the "old guard" in the Academy attempted to control nominations for seats in the new Congress of People's Deputies in early 1989, it touched off a heated debate. Many scientists, researchers, and even a few senior academicians revolted, demanding the selection of Academy representatives by secret competitive ballot. As a result, several reform-minded "outsiders" were elected, including Andrei Sakharov, Roal'd Sagdeev, economist Nikolai Shmelev, and philosopher Yuri Karyakin.

Nor is Soviet science immune to the regional and nationality disputes that are threatening the very survival of the USSR as a federal state. For example, at the March 1990 meeting of the Ukrainian Academy of Sciences General Assembly, there was a heated debate over the impact of Ukrainian independence on the development of science in the republic. The President of the Ukrainian Academy, academician Boris Paton, presented a proposal to transform the Ukrainian Academy into an independent, autonomous organization.

In the Russian republic a separate Russian Academy of Sciences was established in January 1990. Although assurances were made that the Russian Academy did not intend to supplant, or compete with, the USSR Academy, the evolution of this new scientific establishment will likely reflect the increasingly strained political and economic relations between the RFSFR and the USSR. For example, with the encouragement of Boris Yeltsin, President of the Russian republic, the Russian Academy has moved to establish direct bilateral ties with the academies in the other republics, in defiance of central authorities.[46]

The problems confronting the Soviet scientific community—the impact of the economic decline, resulting in shortages and austerity; the bureaucratic uncertainty engendered by *perestroika;* regional and republic demands for greater independence from central authorities; and the ongoing struggle between those who want *perestroika* to proceed more rapidly and those who fear the loss of their status and influence—are the same problems that confront the USSR in general. Likewise, the resolution of these issues will depend on the fortunes of *perestroika, glasnost',* and democratization. Science in the USSR today remains fundamentally subordinated to politics.

EDUCATION IN THE USSR

One of the early goals of the Soviet regime was the provision of universal education to all citizens. At the time of the Revolution, approximately 70 percent of the population was illiterate.[47] Education was provided through a modest but steadily growing educational system. Primary schools operated by the central government, local authorities, and the Church enrolled approximately one-half of the children between the ages of eight and eleven.[48] A significantly smaller percentage of Russian youth—primarily the sons of the aristocracy and the emerging middle class—went on to secondary school, which was provided through a variety of public and private gymnasia, military schools, technicums, and teachers' colleges.

After the 1917 Revolution, Marxist-Leninist doctrine not only radically altered the content of the school curriculum, but also dictated the form and style of instruction. Individual achievement was denounced as a bourgeois concept. Instead, communist education stressed collective activities and values. The school and class were seen as a cohesive whole. In addition, Leninist principles of education emphasized the unity of theory and practice. Consequently, efforts were made to include "polytechnical" practice in the educational experience. Students were organized into brigades and set to work on "productivity activities bearing a class, proletarian character."[49] In other words, students were made to work in factories or on farms.

A decree of September 1931, however, refocused education on the abstract sciences, language, history, and geography. Manual labor gradually disappeared from the curriculum. Under Stalin, the Soviet educational system was centralized. Pupils no longer had a hand in managing school affairs; instead, the role of school director was enforced. Standardized curricula, textbooks, attendance policies, and examinations were dictated by central authorities.

Soviet education today still bears Stalin's imprint; the structure of the school system has changed little since the 1930s. Soviet schoolchildren enter the general secondary school system at the age of six. Approximately 50 to 55 percent of the students entering first grade have attended nursery schools or kindergartens, but neither is mandatory.[50] Students in general secondary education are expected to complete an eleven-year course of study and receive the equivalent of a high-school diploma at the age of seventeen or eighteen. There are, however, various tracks by which students may complete the last two years of their general secondary education. After nine years in the general secondary school, students may:

- enroll for two additional years of general secondary education, preparing them for the intensely competitive examination to enter universities and other institutions of higher education (about 60 percent of the pupils take this option).
- enroll for three to four years at a specialized secondary school (technicum), which provides general education along with technical training for a middle-level job.
- enroll for two to four years at a vocational–technical school offering practical training preliminary to entering the labor force.
- enter the labor force and complete their education in evening or correspondence courses.

As many as half the students who go to work after the ninth grade fail to complete their secondary education, however.[51] The dropout rate is highest in rural and non-Russian areas, and special efforts are being made to improve education coverage in those regions.

The 1984 Education Reform extended general secondary education from ten years to eleven years. The reforms were to be phased in gradually between 1984 and 1990. In the final two years of secondary school, vocational education is required, even for students bound for universities. Those students who do not pursue higher education are required to take an additional year of vocational training.[52]

The level of educational achievement in Soviet secondary schools is quite impressive. A nationwide standardized curriculum places a heavy emphasis on mathematics, the natural sciences, and language. By the time Soviet students have completed eleven years of pre-university schooling, they have taken six years of a foreign language, two years of algebra, two years of geometry, one year of trigonometry, one year of calculus, one year of physics, one year of chemistry, and one year of biology. The humanities and social science courses tend to be ideological in orientation. Thus, upper-level Russian history courses are dominated by the history of the CPSU. Approximately 10 percent of class time is devoted to such political subjects.[53]

With *glasnost'*, however, the nature of courses in history and social sciences has changed remarkably. In 1987, final examinations in history were abolished because it was recognized that so much of the material in textbooks was inaccurate or wholly fabricated. A government commission was established to write new, accurate history textbooks, dealing frankly with issues such as the purges, the Nazi–Soviet Pact, and the ouster of Khrushchev. Moreover, obligatory courses in Marxism-Leninism, scientific atheism, and the history of the CPSU have been dropped from most curricula.

Pupils in secondary schools also take required courses in physical education, art (mandatory through the sixth grade), music (mandatory through the seventh grade), and on-the-job training. All tenth- and eleventh-graders are required to take two hours of military training per week. For boys, this consists of basic drill and target practice, while for girls it stresses civil defense and first aid.

The school year is long—approximately 235 days, compared to an average of 178 days in the United States. Students attend school six days a week, from September 1 to early June. Extracurricular activities are scheduled after school hours. Discipline in Soviet schools is strict. Students wear uniforms, and the class is designed to form a cohesive unit. All students in a given first-grade class will remain together throughout their secondary-school years, although the teachers rotate from year to year and from subject to subject. (In the first three grades, however, one teacher teaches all subjects to the same class all year.)

Optional courses and programs from the eighth grade onward allow students to develop their skills in computer science, natural science, physics, mathematics, foreign languages, the humanities, and the arts. Beginning in the second grade, students can also apply to attend special schools (*spetsshkoly*) for foreign languages. In the *spetsshkoly*, courses in history and social studies are conducted in a foreign language (English, German, French, Spanish, or several other languages), while Russian literature, mathematics, and science courses are taught in Russian. As early as the first grade, pupils with exceptional aptitude in sports or the arts are recruited for special schools. A few special schools have recently been created for students who are especially gifted in science, mathematics, and computer programming. The system of scientific competitions, called Olympiads, has also promoted the achievements of students in mathematics, physics, and other scientific disciplines.

As a result of the tracking options available after the eighth grade and the special schools and programs for gifted and talented pupils, Soviet education has lost much of its early egalitarian character. A highly stratified system exists today that tends to favor children from urban, ethnically Russian, white-collar families.

The Soviet Constitution guarantees citizens the right to receive instruction in their native languages. With more than one hundred ethnic groups in the USSR, however, multilingual education poses a real challenge. In practice, schools currently offer instruction in approximately sixty languages.[54] Schools using languages other than Russian are, for the most part, located in the union-republics, territories, autonomous republics, and regions dominated by non-Russian ethnic groups, while Russian-language schools exist throughout the USSR. In native-language schools, Russian is taught as a mandatory second language.

Russian is the language of instruction in the universities and other institutions of higher education located in the Russian republic. In recent years, universities in the non-Russian republics have opted to resume using the native language of the republic. The predominance of the Russian language in institutions of higher learning puts non-Russians at a distinct disadvantage.

Consequently, many non-Russian parents wishing to enhance their child's chances of being accepted at a university opt to send the child to Russian schools rather than native-language schools.

The language of instruction in general secondary schools has been a contentious political issue in recent years, especially in the Baltic republics. The large influx of Russians and other Slavic peoples and the declining birth-rate among the indigenous Latvians, Lithuanians, and Estonians have resulted in a shift in the composition of the population in the three republics. In order to meet the resulting increased demand for Russian-language schools, some school officials have attempted to change the language of instruction from the indigenous language to Russian. Such attempts have provoked storms of protest from the ethnic minorities.

Technical Secondary Education.   The technical education system in the USSR is very large, encompassing more than 4000 schools and 9 million students—almost half of all secondary-school pupils.[55] In the late 1970s, there was a resurgence of "polytechnization," much as it existed under Khrushchev in the mid-1950s. In 1977, the Minister of Education suggested that all secondary schools must prepare pupils for work directly in the factory or on the state farms.[56] The head of the Academy of the National Economy, M. Rutkevich, projected: "In the near future the implementation of universal secondary education is to be combined with the implementation of universal vocational education."[57] The educational reforms enacted in 1984 require vocational education in the ninth and tenth grades for all students.

Technical education in the Soviet Union is free, and more than three-quarters of the students in technicums receive stipends and dormitory accommodations at a nominal charge.[58] Upon graduation, technicum students must accept the positions assigned to them by the placement officers in their schools. After the mandatory minimum of two years, however, they are free to move to other jobs.

Technical education in the USSR extends to a much broader range of disciplines and fields than in the United States or many other Western nations. Thus, engineering, nursing, medical technology, journalism, agricultural sciences, business, accounting, law enforcement, library science, dietetics, home economics, and military science all fall within the scope of technical secondary education, as opposed to general secondary or higher education.

Higher Education in the USSR.   Institutions of higher education (*vysshie uchebnye zavedeniya-VUZy*) in the USSR are of two types—universities and institutes. Universities, which are generally more prestigious than institutes, number about sixty-five, while there are more than 800 institutes awarding degrees equivalent to the American bachelor's degree.[59]

Universities are organized into colleges and departments and offer programs in the social sciences and humanities, natural sciences, mathematics, and law. Most university degree programs are five years in duration, and the curriculum is much more narrowly focused than in undergraduate programs in the West. Soviet university students normally are required to take one foreign language, and physical education. All other courses are concentrated in the student's major field. As a result, Soviet university graduates normally have much more intensive training in their fields of specialization than do their American counterparts, but their overall education lacks the breadth of the Western liberal-arts education.

Advanced degree programs in the Soviet Union are organized differently from those in the United States. The initial postgraduate degree is the *Kandidat Nauk* (Candidate of Sciences), which is conferred upon completion of three years of graduate-level coursework, three comprehensive examinations, and a dissertation. Many observers equate the *Kandidat* degree with the Ph.D. in the United States. The highest degree in the USSR, the *Doktor Nauk* (Doctor of Sciences), resembles the doctorate in European academic systems and is awarded to established scholars well advanced in their careers.

Admission to universities is by competitive written and oral examinations that are given twice a year. Both examinations concentrate on the applicant's intended field of specialization. Applications must be filed to specific programs in specific universities, and a student cannot apply to more than one program at a time. The level of competition varies considerably from program to program and from university to university. Perhaps the most difficult programs to enter are those in English or other Western languages at the two most prestigious universities, Moscow State University and Leningrad State University. The number of entrants into each program is set by central authorities in the State Committee of Public Education in light of projections of the economy's future needs for persons with various specialties. Thus, the entering class in English literature at Leningrad State University is usually limited to fewer than thirty-five, while many more students are accepted in physics or mathematics. In some of the most popular fields, there may be as many as two hundred applicants for each seat in the entering class. Consequently, many students are forced to apply to less prestigious universities or less competitive programs. It is not unusual to hear Soviet university students say that they wanted to major in literature or philosophy but the competition was so intense that they applied instead to the program in physics or Chinese language. Once a student has been admitted, he or she cannot switch programs.

Although merit is the primary criterion for admission to the universities, the State Committee of Public Education also sets quotas for each nationality group and for the social composition of the student population at institutions of higher education. This amounts to a kind of Soviet affirmative action policy, designed to grant better access to education for non-Russian minorities and for children from working-class and peasant families. Quotas for various nationality groups, however, as well as the introduction of the oral examination, have resulted in discrimination against Jewish students, who have traditionally been very successful in attaining admission to the universities.[60]

Periodically, the Soviet press prints letters charging favoritism in university admissions for the sons and daughters of influential families. Children of the political elite and the intelligentsia frequently receive better-quality secondary educations, often through the *spetshkoly*, which attract the best teachers, materials, and equipment. As a group, students from urban, white-collar families with well-educated parents demonstrate a higher level of achievement and more frequently aspire to complete their university educations, while students from rural, working-class backgrounds whose parents are not well-educated may decide not to pursue advanced training.[61]

Political pull undoubtedly plays a part in gaining admission to some particularly prestigious universities and institutions. For instance, admission to the Moscow Institute for International Relations, which trains future diplomats, requires the recommendation of a *raion* party secretary plus considerable influence even at the Central Committee level. It is not uncommon to find "diplomatic families" in which several generations have all followed the same educational and career course. The military academies display similar tendencies in admissions and family ties.

University education is free, and students receive stipends to help them meet their living expenses. The amount of the stipend varies depending on the student's year, program, and level of performance.

In contrast to higher education in the United States, which is centered around the university, advanced training in many professional and technical fields in the USSR is provided only through specialized institutes. Medicine, education, engineering, agriculture, architecture, international relations, nursing, pharmacy, journalism, library science, management science, and military science are taught exclusively in special professional institutes and academies. Advanced training in the arts (music, theater, ballet, and the visual arts) is provided through conservatories and art academies. Professional and technical institutes are supervised both by the State Committee of Public Education and the relevant ministry for that field. Thus, the conservatories report to the Ministry of Culture, while the Azerbaidzhan Oil and Chemistry Institute reports to the Ministry of Petroleum Refining and the Petrochemical Industry.

The curriculum of the professional schools and technical institutes varies in length from five to six years, depending on the program. As in the universities, all students are required to take at least one foreign language and physical education. In contrast to university programs, which tend to stress theoretical approaches, professional and technical institutes emphasize practical, applied training. Some professional and technical institutes, although not all, offer advanced degrees—the *Kandidat Nauk* and the *Doktor Nauk*.

Graduates of the universities as well as the technical and professional institutes are placed into jobs by an appointment commission attached to each VUZ. The Ministry of Economics and Forecasting and the various industrial ministries develop a list of job vacancies and communicate the list downward through the State Committee of Public Education to the appointment commission in each institute. The commission then interviews each graduate and typically proposes one or more positions on the list. The most desirable positions tend to be offered to the students with the highest records of academic achievement. The commission may consider any request a student makes, and family, health, or other factors may be taken into account. Fulfillment of the placement plan is, however, of utmost importance; students are obliged to accept their assigned positions whether or not they find them satisfactory.[62]

The separation of husband and wife is not always sufficient reason to be released from a job assignment. A Soviet graduate student lamented to the author that he was obliged to return to his teaching job in a secondary school in Kemerovo in Central Siberia upon completion of his *kandidat* degree, despite the fact that his wife was being assigned to a teaching post in Murmansk, near the Finnish border, some 2000 miles away.[63]

Inevitably, many graduates find themselves assigned to jobs they do not want or in locations they do not like. A survey of university graduates in Gorky demonstrates the discrepancies that exist between desired placements and actual appointments. (See Table 12–1.)

Mandatory appointments are for a term of two years, after which time graduates are free to seek other employment. Many students, however, are able to circumvent the system of job placement. Students can approach prospective employers and ask them to make personal requests for their services. Children of the elite are more likely to know people in influential positions and are also better able to bring pressure to bear on employers to make such requests.

Despite its imperfections, the Soviet system of job placement ensures all graduates a job. At the same time, it provides a steady flow of trained workers to remote regions that might not otherwise attract doctors, lawyers, dentists, engineers, teachers, and others whose skills are needed by the local population.

Turnover among young graduates sent to remote regions is high, however. The disparities in living standards in the USSR are so vast that many people are willing to accept positions beneath their levels of training as long as the jobs are located in Moscow or Leningrad.

An often-aired criticism of the Soviet education system at all levels is that it is overly structured and stresses rote learning rather than creative, inquisitive thinking. A group of American educators visiting a "model" Soviet kindergarten were struck by the uniformity of the children's paintings that were on display. All the trees were green and round, all the houses were brown with red roofs, and there was a fox next to the tree in most of the paintings. The children had obviously been told not only what to paint, but how to paint it. When an American teacher asked whether Soviet kindergartners use finger paints, the answer was, "No, it is too unstructured for them."[64] In secondary schools, children stand beside their desks, face the teacher at the front of the classroom, and recite from their texts. Rote learning exists even at the univer-

Table 12-1. Placement of University Students (in percent)

Assignment	History Graduates		Biology Graduates	
	Desired	Received	Desired	Received
Teacher (secondary)	18.0	65.6	0.0	25.0
Production	2.6	10.3	5.0	37.0
Research	18.0	5.8	67.7	5.7
University teaching	40.0	2.3	33.0	4.3
Other	21.4	16.0	0.0	28.0
Total	100.0	100.0	105.7*	100.0

*Discrepancy not explained.
Source: Mervyn Matthews, "Soviet Students—Some Sociological Perspectives," *Soviet Studies* 27 (January 1975): 107.

sity level. In classes the author attended at Leningrad University law school, teachers read directly from the textbooks, rather than lecture, while students took verbatim notes. The only available copies of the textbooks were on reserve in the law school library. Besides being deadly boring, such teaching methods discourage analytical inquiry. Furthermore, Soviet textbooks often fail to note that some questions in various disciplines are open to controversy and dispute within the Soviet scholarly community. Students tend to acquire a simplistic, one-dimensional view of their fields. Leaders in the scientific community have expressed concern that the regimentation of education in the USSR is stamping out creativity, and thus jeopardizing future scientific and technological progress.

The shortage of textbooks also illustrates the woeful inadequacy of educational materials in the USSR. With photocopying virtually nonexistent, there is a heavy demand for carbon paper, but this is a "deficit" item only rarely found in stationery stores. Typewriters are similarly hard to find. While planners in Moscow talk glowingly about the computerized classroom of the future, local school officials complain about shortages of such basic supplies as chalk.[65] University professors and research scientists charge that inadequate laboratory equipment and limited access to computers are seriously eroding the quality of the training that the next generation of scientists and engineers is receiving.

Shortages of equipment and supplies are due, in part, to the steady decline in educational funding over the past fifteen years. In 1964 education accounted for 6.7 percent of the national budget, but in 1982 it accounted for only 4.2 percent.[66]

EDUCATION AND *PERESTROIKA*

One might expect that *glasnost'* and *perestroika* would have been enthusiastically welcomed by educators in the USSR. However, many of the same divisions and factions we saw within the scientific community also characterize the educational establishment.

In the forefront of educational *perestroika* are the "teacher-innovators," led by Shalina Amonashvili. The pro-reform faction is a comparatively small but active group which favors abolishing authoritarian principles in education and giving teachers greater freedom and flexibility in the choice of methods and textbooks. Opposed to these ideas are large numbers of conservative teachers and school administrators who favor retention of policies favoring uniform teaching methods and strict classroom discipline.

Pro-reform educators sought in 1989 to democratize the USSR Academy of Pedagogical Sciences by asking that the "stagnant" body be dissolved and new members elected.[67] However, the Academy voted to fill only those seats that had become vacant. Only nineteen innovation-minded academicians and twelve corresponding members were elected to the Academy.[68]

Perhaps the strongest voice for educational *perestroika* has been the reorganized USSR State Committee of Public Education. Under the direction of Gennadii Yagodin, the State Committee has since 1987 sought to democratize school management by encouraging the creation of school councils, involving both students and parents. It has also awarded grants to schools to develop pioneering curricula and reward innovative teaching techniques.

The demands for regional and republic autonomy have also affected education. At the December 1988 All-Union Congress of Educational Workers, Lithuanian delegates submitted proposals calling for granting republics the right to make educational policy, including decisions on the length of schooling, course content, curriculum, and management of schools. The Lithuanian proposals were endorsed by representatives from several other republics, including Estonia, Latvia, Georgia, and Armenia. The proposals elicited heated debate at the Congress and were referred to the newly elected All-Union Education Council. The Council ultimately accepted in principle the Lithuanian proposals for granting greater responsibility to republic ministries of education. Upon their return to Vilnius after the Congress, the Lithuanian delegates were greeted by large enthusiastic crowds at the railroad station.[69] However, when the outcome of the Council's actions were published in the leading education journal, all references to increasing the powers of republic officials had been deleted.

The case of the Lithuanian proposals illustrates the difficulties in carrying out reform in the USSR. Education is one area in which granting greater autonomy to republics should be relatively painless, yet it has not been possible to overcome the resistance to change that remains in the center.

The problems confronting the Gorbachev leadership in the areas of science, technology, and education have crucial implications for the regime and for the future of *perestroika*. On the one hand, Gorbachev and other prominent officials recognize the necessity of reforms in these areas to rejuvenate the economy and stimulate greater efficiency. On the other hand, there is a reluctance to release the controls. Reforms inevitably redistribute resources, threaten vested interests, and challenge conservative bureaucrats. As we have seen in other areas, these conservative forces have succeeded in blunting the influence of *perestroika* in Soviet science, technology, and education.

Notes

1. Karl Marx, *Capital*, vol. 1 (New York: Modern Library, 1906), 475–476.

2. V. I. Lenin, *Collected Works*, vol. 23 (Moscow: Foreign Language Publishing House, 1960), 70.

3. See *Communist Party of the USSR in Statements and Decrees of Congresses, Conferences, and Plenums of the Central Committee*, vol. 2 (Moscow; Politizdat, 1970), 52.

4. Zhores A. Medvedev, *Soviet Science* (New York: W. W. Norton, 1978), 23–24.

5. Loren R. Graham, *The Soviet Academy of Sciences and the Communist Party, 1927–1932* (Princeton: Princeton University Press, 1967), p. 120.

6. Medvedev, *Soviet Science*, 35–36.

7. Ibid., 46–47.

8. Ibid., 57.

9. Ibid., 67.

10. *Narodnoe khozyaistvo SSSR v 1974* (Moscow: Statistika, 1975), p. 194.

11. Medvedev, *Soviet Science*, 73–74.

12. Ibid., 76.

13. *Programma kommunisticheskoi partii sovetkogo soyuza* (Moscow: Pravda, 1961), 27.

14. Radovan Richta et al., *Civilization at the Crossroads: Social and Human Implications of the Scientific and Technical Revolution* (White Plains, NY: International Arts and Sciences Press, 1969), p. 22.

15. *Chelovek—nauka-tekhnika* (Moscow: Politizdat, 1973), 352.

16. See Robert F. Miller, "The Scientific-Technical Revolution and the Soviet Administrative Debate," in Paul Cocks et al., *The Dynamics of Soviet Politics* (Cambridge: Harvard University Press, 1976), 150.

17. Ibid.

18. William Korey, "Jewish Emigration and Soviet Policy Models," *Survey* (Winter 1976): 128–129; and U.S. Congress, House of Representatives, Committee on Foreign Affairs, Subcommittee on Human Rights and International Organizations, testimony of Theodore R. Mann, Chairman, National Conference on Soviet Jewry (Washington, DC: U.S. Government Printing Office, June 23 and 28, 1983), 40.

19. According to numerous accounts of Soviet émigrés, the Leningrad Party Secretary ordered that the percentage of Jews in scientific research institutes be reduced to less than 1 percent, roughly the percentage that Jews constitute in the general population. For example, see Henry Firdman, *Development of Microelectronics in the USSR* (Washington, DC: Delphic Associates Monograph Series, 1985).

20. Louvan E. Nolting, *Sources of Financing the Stages of Research, Development and Innovation Cycle in the USSR*, Foreign Economics Report, no. 3 (Washington, DC: U.S. Department of Commerce, 1973).

21. Ibid.

22. Louvan E. Nolting and Murray Feshbach, "R&D Employment in the USSR," *Science* (1 February 1980): 493–503.

23. *Pravda*, 8 October 1975, p. 2.

24. In addition, there are approximately seventy honorary foreign members. Cited in *The Cambridge Encyclopedia of Russia and the Soviet Union* (Cambridge: Cambridge University Press, 1982), 259.

25. *Narodnoe khozyaistvo SSSR, 1922–1982* (Moscow: Statistika, 1982), 125.

26. For example, see A. P. Aleksandrov, "Vstupitel'noe slovo," *Vestnik akademii nauk*, no. 4 (1983): 8.

27. Cited in U.S. Congress, Senate Committee on Foreign Relations, *The Premises of East–West Commercial Relations* (Washington, D.C.: U.S. Government Printing Office, 1982), 104.

28. See *Pravda*, 12 June 1985, p. 1.

29. V. I. Kushlin, *Uskorenie vedreniya nauchnykh dostizhenii v proizvodstvo* (Moscow: Ekonomika, 1976), 123.

30. Thane Gustafson, "Why Doesn't Soviet Science Do Better Than It Does?," in Linda L. Lubrano and Susan Gross Solomon, eds., *The Social Context of Soviet Science* (Boulder, CO: Westview Press, 1980), 33.

31. John A. Martens and John P. Young, "Soviet Implementation of Domestic Inventions: First Results," in U.S. Congress, Joint Economic Committee, *Soviet Economy in a Time of Change* (Washington, DC: U.S. Government Printing Office, 1979), 499.

32. *Pravda*, 3 January 1975, p. 3.

33. Gustafson, "Why Doesn't Soviet Science Do Better?," 33.

34. This account was related to the author by a representative of Control Data Corporation in 1981.

35. This argument is made by David Holloway in "Innovation in the Defense Sector," in Ronald Amann and Julian Cooper, eds., *Industrial Innovation in the Soviet Union* (New Haven: Yale University Press, 1982), 350.

36. Much of the material in this section was drawn from Linda L. Lubrano, "New Initiatives and Old Bureaucats: The Future Challenges the Past in Academic Science," *Technology and Society*, Vol. 13, no. 1/2 (1991), 91–108.

37. For example, see *Literaturnaya gazeta*, 8 March 1989, p. 12.

38. A majority of research institutes and design bureaus were converted to the new system in 1988 and all Academy institutes were required to do so in 1989.

39. L. V. Tauson, "Vinovata li Akademiya?" *Vestnik Akademiya nauk SSSR*, no. 9 (1989): 33.

40. Michael Tsypkin, "Turmoil in Soviet Science," *Radio Liberty Report on the USSR* 1, no. 29 (21 July 1989): 19.

41. *Pravda*, 21 March 1990, p.2.

42. *Pravda*, 23 March 1990, p.2.

43. *Poisk*, no. 7, 1989, pp. 1–2.

44. Lubrano, "New Initiatives and Old Bureaucrats," p. 99.

45. *Pravda*, 21 March 1990, p.2.

46. Lubrano, "New Initiatives and Old Bureaucrats," p. 103.

47. Basile Kerblay, *Modern Soviet Society* (New York: Pantheon Books, 1983), 147.

48. Mervyn Matthews, *Education in the Soviet Union* (London: George Allen & Unwin, 1982), 2.

49. Ibid., 5.

50. Kerblay, *Modern Soviet Society*, 152.

51. Matthews, *Education in the Soviet Union*, 159.

52. "Basic Guidelines for Reform in the General Education and Vocational Schools," *Pravda*, 10 April 1984, pp. 3–4.

53. Matthews, *Education in the Soviet Union*, 47–48.

54. Vadim Medish, *The Soviet Union* (Englewood Cliffs, NJ: Prentice-Hall, 1981), 205.

55. *Narodnoe khozyaistvo SSSR, 1922–1982*, pp. 499–500.

56. M. A. Prokof'ev, "Novyi uchebnyi god," *Narodnoe obrazovanie*, no. 9 (1977): 10–11.

57. *Sovetskaya Rossiya*, 21 September 1983, pp. 1–2.

58. Medish, *The Soviet Union*, 209.

59. Harley D. Balzer, "Education, Science, and Technology," in James Cracraft, ed., *The Soviet Union Today* (Chicago: Bulletin of the Atomic Scientists, 1983), 238.

60. For a discussion of inequalities in university admissions, see Murray Yanowitch, *Social and Economic Inequality in the Soviet Union* (New York: M. E. Sharpe, 1977), 58–99. Concerning discrimination against Jews in education, see Robert O. Freedman, ed., *Soviet Jewry in the Decisive Decade, 1971-1980* (Durham, NC: Duke University Press, 1984).

61. Yanowitch, *Social and Economic Inequality*, 60.

62. Matthews, *Education in the Soviet Union*, 170.

63. The student told the author about this case while he was at Leningrad State University in 1975–1976.

64. Comment made by a teacher to a group of visiting Americans, November 1978. For official criticism of rote learning, see *Literaturnaya gazeta*, 22 February 1984, p. 11.

65. Balzer, "Education, Science, and Technology," 237.

66. *Sotsialisticheskaya industriya*, cited in *Christian Science Monitor*, 18 February 1988, p. 6.

67. See Sergei Voronitsyn, "After the Unsuccessful Teaching Revolution," *Radio Liberty Report on the USSR* 1, no. 12 (24 March 1989): 8–10.

68. *Pravda*, 3 February 1989.

69. Kestutis Girnius, "Dispute over Education Between Lithuania and Moscow," *Radio Liberty Report on the USSR* 1, no. 6 (10 February 1989): p. 15.

Selected Bibliography

Afanas'ev, V. G. *The Scientific and Technical Revolution—Its Impact on Management and Education.* Moscow: Progress, 1975.

Amann, Ronald, and Julian Cooper, eds. *Industrial Innovation in the Soviet Union.* New Haven: Yale University Press, 1982.

Berliner, Joseph S. *The Innovation Decision in Soviet Industry.* Cambridge, MA: MIT Press, 1976.

Churchward, L. G. *The Soviet Intelligentsia.* London: Routledge & Kegan Paul, 1973.

Fleron, Frederic J., ed. *Technology and Communist Culture.* New York: Praeger, 1977.

Graham, Loren R. *Science and Philosophy in the Soviet Union.* New York: Knopf, 1972.

Grant, Nigel. *Soviet Education.* 4th ed. London: Penguin Books, 1979.

Gvishiani, D. M., ed. *The Scientific Intelligentsia in the USSR.* Moscow: Progress, 1976.

Hoffmann, Erik P., and Robbin F. Laird. *The Politics of Economic Modernization in the Soviet Union.* Ithaca: Cornell University Press, 1982.

Hoffmann, Erik P., and Robbin F. Laird. *Technocratic Socialism: The Soviet Union in the Advanced Industrial Era.* Durham, NC: Duke University Press, 1985.

Hutchings, Raymond. *Soviet Science, Technology, Design.* London: Oxford University Press, 1976.

Jacoby, Susan. *Inside Soviet Schools.* New York: Hill & Wang, 1974.

Kassel, Simon, and Cathleen Campbell. *The Soviet Academy of Sciences and Technological Development.* Santa Monica, CA: Rand Corporation, 1980.

Kneen, Peter. *Soviet Scientists and the State.* London: Macmillan Press, 1984.

Kuzin, N. P. *Education in the USSR.* Moscow: Progress, 1972.

Lampert, Nicholas. *The Technical Intelligentsia and the Soviet State.* New York: Holmes & Meier, 1979.

Lubrano, Linda, and Susan Gross Solomon, eds. *The Social Context of Soviet Science.* Boulder, CO: Westview Press, 1980.

Matthews, Mervyn. *Education in the Soviet Union.* London: George Allen & Unwin, 1982.

Medvedev, Zhores. *Soviet Science.* New York: W. W. Norton, 1978.

Parrott, Bruce. *Politics and Technology in the Soviet Union.* Cambridge, MA: MIT Press, 1983.

Remnek, Richard B., ed. *Social Scientists and Policy-Making in the USSR.* New York: Praeger, 1977.

Thomas, John R., and Ursula Kruse-Vaucienne, eds. *Soviet Science and Technology.* Washington, DC: National Science Foundation, 1977.

Zajda, J. I. *Education in the USSR.* New York: Pergamon, 1980.

13

"New Thinking" in Foreign Policy

The crisis confronting the Soviet Union when Gorbachev took power in March 1985 was manifested not only in mounting domestic problems resulting from the previous two decades of political and economic stagnation, but also in a rapidly deteriorating international position. The Soviet Union was still embroiled in a costly and bloody war in Afghanistan, and after almost four and one-half years, there was still no indication that victory was near. Hostility toward the United States was greater than at any time since the height of the Cold War. The relatively brief period of détente of the early 1970s soon gave way to mutual suspicion and distrust over such issues as Jewish emigration, human rights violations, trade disputes and technology embargoes, the failure of the United States Senate to ratify the SALT II agreement, Soviet support for national liberation movements in Africa and Central America, the deployments of the SS-20 missiles and the subsequent deployments of Pershing and cruise missiles in Western Europe, the declaration of martial law in Poland, and the initiation by President Reagan of the Strategic Defense Initiative, popularly known as the "Star Wars" program.

The Soviet Union's relations with its immediate neighbors were not much better than its relations with the United States. The Eastern European economies were proving to be a drain on the country's resources, especially its resources of oil and gas, thus denying the Soviets hard currency that they could have earned through the export of those commodities to the West. Politically, the Eastern European societies were stagnating under the weight of Brezhnevite leaders who were unable or unwilling to undertake serious reforms. The major exception was Poland, where an immensely popular national movement, Solidarity, commanded substantially more authority than the Polish Communist Party leadership of General Wojciech Jaruzelski.

Soviet–Chinese relations were also proving to be thorny. CIA estimates indicated that as much as twenty-five percent of Soviet defense spending was for deployments along the 4000-mile border with China. The Chinese raised three conditions for the normalization of relations: reduction of Soviet troop concentrations along the Chinese borders, termination of support for Vietnam's occupation of Cambodia, and withdrawal from Afghanistan. Thus, the situation the USSR faced in 1985 led one wag to observe: "The Soviet Union is the only country today that is surrounded by hostile *communist* countries."

The disarray in Soviet foreign policy alone might have been sufficient to convince the post-Brezhnev leadership of the need for serious restructuring. However, immediately after assuming office in March 1985, Gorbachev also took note of the connection between Soviet foreign policy and the country's domestic political and economic situation. Since coming to office, he has articulated a foreign policy that has not only restructured Soviet goals and objectives in the world, but promises to usher in a new world order based on interdependence, nonintervention, and cooperation among nations. In this chapter, we assess Gorbachev's "new thinking" in foreign policy, analyzing the extent to which it has, in fact, transformed Soviet foreign policy. We begin by defining terms: What does Gorbachev mean by "new thinking" in foreign policy? What are his goals and objectives for Soviet foreign policy?

WHAT IS "NEW THINKING"?

The outlines of Gorbachev's new approach to Soviet foreign policy began to emerge at the Twenty-Seventh Party Congress in 1986. In his opening remarks to the Congress, Gorbachev declared:

> A turning point has arisen not only in internal but also in external affairs. The changes in the development of the contemporary world are so profound and significant that they require a rethinking and comprehensive analysis of all its factors. The situation of nuclear confrontation calls for new approaches, methods, and forms of relations between different social systems, states, and regions.[1]

In the Congress address, as well as in subsequent speeches, most notably before the United Nations General Assembly on December 7, 1988, Gorbachev fleshed out the fundamental principles of "new thinking" (*novoe myshleniye*). Those principles can be summarized as follows:

Interdependence of Nations.   Gorbachev recognized "the growing tendency towards interdependence of the states of the world community."[2] Given this interdependence, it would be erroneous and dangerous for the Soviet Union to continue to view the world as divided into opposing social systems. The theme of interdependence has direct relevance for the Soviet view of deterrence in the nuclear age. According to Anatolii Dobrynin, long-time Soviet ambassador to the United States and former head of the CPSU Central Committee's International Department, "interdependence of survival" has acquired "cardinal significance" in light of the nuclear arms race and the proliferation of nuclear weapons.[3] This theme was foreshadowed in a 1984 article entitled "The Logic of Political Thinking in the Nuclear Era" by Georgii Shakhnazarov in the philosophical journal *Voprosy filosofii*.[4] Shakhnazarov, a reform-minded ideologist and close associate of Gorbachev today, noted that a "formal interdependence" of security has arisen in the nuclear age and that security can only be collective. Foreign Minister Eduard Shevardnadze picked up this theme in 1988 when he proclaimed, "The struggle between two opposing systems is no longer a determining tendency of the present era."[5]

The idea of interdependence among states with differing social systems and the revision of the traditional Marxist-Leninist notion of international class struggle were criticized in Yegor Ligachev's attack on "new thinking" in mid-1988. In an August 1988 address, he maintained that Soviet foreign policy should continue to be based on the "class character of international relations" and decried the "slow-down" in the national liberation struggle in the Third World.[6] Gorbachev mounted a counterattack on Ligachev at the September 1988 emergency plenum of the Central Committee. Ligachev was replaced as head of the ideology commission by Vadim Medvedev, a strong supporter of "new thinking." Meanwhile, Ligachev was given responsibility for agriculture, a traditionally problem-plagued area of the economy. Not only did this remove Ligachev from foreign policy considerations, but it set him up for later dismissal for failure to introduce effective reforms in agriculture. In his first address as ideology chief, Medvedev vigorously rejected Ligachev's notions of class struggle in foreign relations.[7]

Cooperation in Resolving Global Problems. Gorbachev also emphasized that humanity now faces a number of global problems that can only be resolved by "cooperation on a world-wide scale."[8] Chief among these problems are pollution, the depletion of natural resources, and the proliferation of nuclear weapons. Speaking to members of the British parliament, Gorbachev observed that we all live "in a vulnerable, rather fragile but interconnected world."[9] In his address to the U.N. General Assembly in December 1988, he pledged Soviet cooperation and support for the U.N. as the most appropriate body to address the issues confronting the global community.[10] The willingness of the Soviet Union to work through the United Nations was a clear departure from past practice. Traditionally, the Soviet Union has tended to pursue direct bilateral solutions to problems, rather than granting multinational institutions the authority to resolve or mediate disputes.

Equal Security. The new party program, approved at the Twenty-Seventh Party Congress in 1986, stated that nuclear deterrence must be replaced by nuclear disarmament. In Gorbachev's words, "War (at least world war) has ceased to be the continuation of state policy by other means."[11] Thus, the emphasis in Soviet policy is on the right of nations to enjoy equal security. Gorbachev declared, "The USSR does not want anything it would deny others. However, the Soviet Union will never agree to an abridged status or discrimination."[12] He also noted that this stable mutual security could not be based solely on nuclear parity; rather, ensuring national security is becoming increasingly a political and diplomatic task. In his address to the United Nations, Gorbachev floated the concept of a comprehensive system of international security built upon the renunciation of war, the destruction of nuclear and chemical weapons, and the reduction of conventional forces. According to his formulation, nations would only be permitted to retain "reasonable sufficiency" of forces to ensure their own defense and territorial integrity.

Noninterference in Foreign States. While not altogether shedding its rhetorical support for the cause of socialism, the Soviet leadership no longer adovcates exporting violent revolution. Even among socialist countries, the leadership now acknowledges problems. "In a number of countries of socialist orientation, the situation remains unstable, fraught with the possibility of regression."[13] But policymakers maintain that the further development of socialism must proceed at its own pace, dictated by local conditions and not subject to direction by the USSR. The most dramatic illustration of this new principle of permitting socialist societies to determine their own fate came in the events in Eastern Europe in 1989 and 1990, which we will examine in detail later in this chapter. Gorbachev also used the principle of noninterference in the internal affairs of foreign states as a justification for withdrawing Soviet military forces from Afghanistan and for his refusal to commit Soviet military forces to the Persian Gulf war.

Support for the New International Economic Order.   In his address to the Twenty-Seventh Party Congress, Gorbachev noted that international security was integrally linked to a country's domestic security.[14] The rapid decline in Soviet economic performance mandated concerted efforts to eliminate the economic isolation of the USSR from the rest of the global economy. Thus, Gorbachev has advocated reduction of trade barriers, renunciation of embargoes and other forms of economic coercion, the transfer of resources from the arms race to mutual US-Soviet development cooperation in the Third World, and relief of debt burdens on developing states.

To this end, the Soviet Union has mounted a largely successful campaign to become a member of the International Monetary Fund (IMF), the World Bank, and GATT (General Agreement on Tarrifs and Trade). Following the Malta Summit in December 1989, the USSR was invited to become an observer in GATT. It is anticipated that the Soviet Union will become a full, participating member of these organizations within the near future.

Human Rights.   A fundamental principle of "new thinking" is the promotion of human rights both at home and abroad. In his address to the U.N. General Assembly, Gorbachev stressed the need for greater international cooperation to defend personal, political and social rights "while respecting the law of each country."[15] He convened an international human rights conference in Moscow in February 1987. Andrei Sakharov, who had been released from house arrest in Gorky only three months earlier at Gorbachev's insistence, attended the gathering and praised the release from labor camps of many Soviet dissidents. Likewise, Gorbachev used the celebration of the millenium of Christianity in Russia to ease restrictions on churches and religious practice in the USSR. Restrictions on foreign travel and emigration were eased and resulted in a mass exodus. By 1989, Jews were leaving the Soviet Union at a rate of 100,000 every year.[16] Large numbers of Germans and Armenians also took advantage of the relaxed emigration policy to leave the country. In order to regain membership in the World Psychiatric Association, in late 1989 Soviet authorities invited a team of observers to inspect Soviet psychiatric facilities. It is generally recognized that the widespread abuse of psychiatric "treatment" of political dissidents has stopped and the USSR has been granted membership in the world body again.

These measures, all centering on previously divisive human rights issues, have been undertaken to establish a greater degree of trust between the USSR and other members of the community of nations. A new section was created within the USSR Ministry of Foreign Affairs and charged with monitoring human rights issues. Chief of the human rights section, Yuri Reshetov, observed, "Humanitarian problems are as important as political and economic exchanges" in building trust among nations.[17]

"NEW THINKING" AND THE FORMATION
OF SOVIET FOREIGN POLICY

Just as "new thinking" has resulted in the systematic and fundamental reconsideration of Soviet foreign policy goals and objectives, it has also prompted a restructuring of those institutions and bodies charged with making and implementing Soviet foreign policy. Below we examine the principal institutions and organizations that participate in the formulation and implementation of Soviet foreign policy.

The Politburo. Historically, responsibility for making the most fundamental decisions and policies affecting the USSR, including foreign policy, rested with the Communist Party Politburo. As we noted in Chapter 5, the Politburo has until recently normally included the General Secretary, the Ministers of Defense and Foreign Affairs, the Chairman of the KGB, and the Party Secretary specializing in international affairs. However, in December 1990, the composition of the Politburo was radically altered. Its members now include a relatively undistinguished group of professional party *apparatchiki*, none of whom have foreign policy expertise. We have argued earlier in this book that Gorbachev's policies of *perestroika* have resulted in a shift of power and authority from party institutions to those of the state apparatus. Nowhere is this more evident than in the area of foreign policy formulation.

International Policy Commission. The Central Committee's International Policy Commission, headed by Gennadi Yanaev, is responsible for formulating CPSU policies relating to international relations. The Commission is not supposed to intrude into the implementation of Soviet foreign policy, which is the responsibility of the Ministry of Foreign Affairs. Yanaev, the former Chairman of the All-Union Central Committee of Trade Unions, had no prior foreign policy experience, in contrast to his distinguished predecessor, Aleksandr Yakovlev. Yakovlev served for ten years as Soviet ambassador to Canada and then as director of the leading foreign policy "think tank," the Institute of World Economy and International Relations (IMEMO), prior to assuming the chairmanship of the 22-member International Policy Commission. Yakovlev proved to be a highly popular spokesman for radical reform, and his replacement reflects Gorbachev's conservative shift following the Twenty-Eighth Party Congress.

The President. The executive Presidency of the USSR was created in March 1990 and invested with major responsibilities for making and directing policies affecting domestic political and economic affairs, as well as Soviet foreign policy. According to the USSR Constitution, the President is elected to a five-year term and may be reelected once. Although Gorbachev was elected to the Presidency by the Congress of People's Deputies, he has pledged that in March 1995, the people will directly elect the President.

In the realm of foreign policy, the President has far-reaching powers. He appoints the Premier and the Ministers of Defense and Foreign Affairs, and the head of the KGB. He is empowered to negotiate and sign treaties on behalf of the USSR. He may issue decrees, including orders to commit military forces at home and abroad. In this sense, his powers approximate those of the Commander in Chief in the United States. He names ambassadors and other top foreign policy personnel. He may also introduce legislation in the Supreme Soviet or the Congress of People's Deputies pertaining to foreign policy matters.

Much of the authority of the current Presidency derives from the personal appeal and charisma of Mikhail Gorbachev. Although in the past few years Gorbachev's popularity with Soviet citizens has fallen to dangerously low levels, he is still widely praised and admired in the rest of the world. *Time* magazine selected Gorbachev as "the man of the decade" in 1990 and he was the recipient of the Nobel Peace Prize that same year. From an institutional perspective, however, the Presidency has not existed long enough to command automatic authority and popular support. Other societies have experienced difficulties routinizing charismatic authority after the passing of a revolutionary leader (e.g., Mao and Lenin). In time, however, the Presidency will most likely acquire a power and authority independent of the person who occupies the position.

Security Council.   Until December 1990, the primary institution advising Gorbachev on foreign policy matters was the Presidential Council, a group of seventeen influential officials appointed by Gorbachev. In November, however, the Presidential Council was abolished and Gorbachev proposed transferring primary power to the Council of the Federation, made up of the presidents of the fifteen union-republics. However, the Council of the Federation lacks the necessary expertise to advise the President on foreign policy issues. Consequently, a new Security Council was formed. Little is known about the Security Council. Its membership includes Gorbachev and his Vice-President, Gennadi Yanaev; Premier Valentin Pavlov; Foreign Minister Bessmertnykh; Defense Minister Yazov; Chairman of the KGB Vladimir Kryuchkov; Minister of Internal Affairs Boris Pugo; the former Minister of Internal Affairs, Vadim Bakatin; Director of IMEMO and noted diplomat Evgenii Primakov; and Gorbachev's personal assistant, Valerii Boldin.[18] The Security Council appears to replace the former Presidential Council. Its composition suggests that it will take primary responsibility for advising Gorbachev on matters of foreign policy and internal maintenance of law and order.

Supreme Soviet.   The restructuring of the legislative branch, most importantly of the Supreme Soviet, in 1989 for the first time gave that body meaningful powers in the realm of foreign affairs. Not only does the Supreme Soviet, like its larger parent body, the Congress of People's Deputies, provide a forum in which major foreign policy issues can be openly debated; the Supreme Soviet also has two permanent joint committees with primary responsibility for international relations. The Joint Committee for Defense and State Security supervises government policy on the armed forces, defense industries, and the security police. The Joint Committee for International Affairs monitors Soviet foreign policy generally and has under its jurisdiction subcommittees focusing on Foreign Economic, Scientific, Technical and Trade Relations; Foreign Policy and Legal Questions; and Humanitarian and Cultural Relations. The Joint Committee for International Affairs has held hearings into a wide range of foreign policy questions and also confirms all of Gorbachev's ambassadorial and high-level appointments within the Ministry of Foreign Affairs.

Both Supreme Soviet committees suffer from a lack of tradition and institutional support. The sudden restructuring of the Supreme Soviet in 1989 caught the Soviet government unprepared. No parliament building was readily available, much less offices, libraries, and staffs to assist Soviet legislators in performing their functions as elected representatives of the people. Deputies to the Supreme Soviet live and work out of cramped hotel rooms in downtown Moscow. Under such circumstances, it is clear that these committees have a long way to go before they can function as do the Senate Foreign Relations Committee and the House Committee on Foreign Affairs in the United States Congress.

Ministry of Foreign Affairs. The Ministry of Foreign Affairs has primary responsibility for implementing Soviet foreign policy. The Ministry is divided into territorial and functional sections, much like those of the State Department in the United States. There are regional sections for Europe, North America, Asia, the Middle East and North Africa, the Pacific and Southeast Asia, Sub-Saharan Africa, and Latin America. Functional sections focus on Political, Economic, Cultural, Counselor, and Administrative Affairs.

Just four months after assuming the General Secretaryship, Gorbachev named Eduard Shevardnadze to replace Andrei Gromyko, who had served as Minister of Foreign Affairs for some 26 years. Gromyko's hard-line approach to the West had earned him the nickname "Mr. Nyet," and his views were increasingly out of step with those of Gorbachev. During Gromyko's long tenure as Minister of Foreign Affairs, the Ministry had become more and more powerful and independent of the top political leadership. The appointment of Shevardnadze, the former First Secretary of the Georgian Communist Party, was designed to bring the Ministry of Foreign Affairs under tighter central control. Although Shevardnadze had no prior foreign policy experience, he managed to shake up the top echelons of the Ministry, forcing the replacement of both first deputy ministers and naming four new deputy ministers to head up units dealing with arms control; humanitarian issues; information; and the Pacific region. In his first year in office, Gorbachev appointed more than forty new ambassadors, including the ambassadors to the United States, Britain, China, Japan, France, and Germany.[19]

Shevardnadze proved to be an adept diplomat and is credited with a major reevaluation of Soviet foreign policy. He successfully negotiated the withdrawal of the American Pershing and cruise missiles from Western Europe. He also presided over the disintegration of Soviet control of Eastern Europe. In May 1989, as communist party leaders throughout Eastern Europe were being threatened by rapidly growing popular resistance movements, Shevardnadze announced that he could not imagine circumstances under which Soviet forces could be used to intervene in a Warsaw Pact country.[20]

His stance on events in Eastern Europe resulted in Shevardnadze being publicly criticized by conservative members in the Congress of People's Deputies. In a debate over Gorbachev's election to the new Presidency, Army General Al'bert Makashov charged, "The realities of the world today are such that continuing unilateral disarmament would be an act of stupidity, or a crime."[21] At the Twenty-Eighth Party Congress in mid-1990 he renewed his criticism of Shervardnadze's policies in Eastern Europe: "In these troubled times when, because of the so-called victories of our diplomacy, the Soviet army is being driven without a fight out of countries that our fathers liberated from fascism—it is important for the Party and people to look after our soldiers."[22] He went on to ask why NATO had been allowed to strengthen itself while the Warsaw Pact had ceased to exist. Major General Ivan Mikulin, commander of the Southern Group of Forces, laid the blame "for the loss of Eastern Europe" on Gorbachev's "new thinking."[23] He predicted that the Vienna talks on conventional arms control would lead to unilateral Soviet disarmament. Admiral Genadii Khvatov, commander of the Pacific Fleet, joined in the criticism: "We have no allies in the West. We have no allies in the East. Consequently, we are back where we were in 1939."[24]

Shevardnadze responded to the criticism in a long interview in *Pravda* on June 23, 1990. He defended the decision to withdraw Soviet forces from Eastern Europe, noting that history had taught the limited utility of strong-arm methods.[25] However, dissatisfaction with Shevardnadze's policies erupted at the Twenty-Eighth Party Congress. Criticisms of Shevardnadze continued through the fall of 1990. Lieutenant Colonel Viktor Alksnis, a people's deputy from Latvia and chairman of the conservative "Soyuz" faction, berated the Minister of Foreign Affairs before the Supreme Soviet. In response to these attacks and frustrated over Gorbachev's steady shift to the right to placate the conservatives, Shevardnadze resigned in December 1990. In a fiery speech to the Congress of People's Deputies he denounced Gorbachev's consolidation of emergency presidential powers, warning that the Soviet Union was facing the potential creation of an authoritarian dictatorship.

Shevardnadze's successor was the former Soviet ambassador to the United States, Aleksandr Bessmertnykh. Bessmertnykh, unlike Shevardnadze, has had a long career in the diplomatic service. He was part of Shevardnadze's team of top advisors, and his appointment appears to have been intended to signal continuity in Soviet foreign policy. *Komsomolskaya pravda* had speculated that Gorbachev would appoint a hard-liner such as Aleksandr Dzasokhov, chairman of the Supreme Soviet Committee on Foreign Affairs and expert on the Third World, in order to placate conservatives.[26] Primakov's name was also reportedly floated, but American officials reacted negatively.[27] The appointment of Bessmertnykh appears to have been designed to reassure Washington after violent clashes in Lithuania, in which Soviet forces silenced pro-independence protesters.[28]

The KGB.   The activities of the KGB were described in detail in Chapter 9. It is noteworthy that the public criticism of KGB activities in the early years of *glasnost'* focused on operations within the USSR and not on the KGB's activities abroad. The Chairman of the Committee on State Security, Vladimir Kryuchkov, rose through the ranks of the KGB's foreign intelligence gathering and analysis division. Gorbachev's appointment of Kryuchkov was thought at the time to reflect his preference that the KGB limit its domestic surveillance activities and focus its energies on foreign intelligence gathering and analysis.

In 1990, however, as economic chaos and outbreaks of organized crime became worse, the KGB's domestic role again became important. Kryuchkov was increasingly outspoken on the disorder confronting the USSR at home and the loss of respect abroad. In several speeches before the Supreme Soviet and the Congress of People's Deputies, Kryuchkov went to some lengths to distance himself from Shevardnadze. At the December 1990 session of the Congress of People's Deputies, he charged that "destructive political forces" allied with foreign intelligence services were plotting economic sabotage against the USSR.[29]

The Armed Forces and the Ministry of Defense. The highest-level policy and planning organ for the Soviet military is the Defense Council of the USSR, about which little is known. In fact, its existence was not confirmed until 1976, when Brezhnev was identified as Chairman of the Council. In addition to the General Secretary of the CPSU, who serves as its Chairman, the Defense Council is thought to consist of the Minister of Defense, the "second secretary" of the Central Committee Secretariat, the secretary specializing in foreign policy and defense matters, the Premier of the USSR, and probably the Chief of the General Staff. Other military and civilian officials may be called upon to attend meetings, depending on the subjects to be discussed. Among these are the Minister of Foreign Affairs, the Chairman of the KGB, the Minister of Internal Affairs, and the commanders of the various forces and theatres of the Soviet armed forces. The fact that the Defense Council includes a number of party officials and other noncareer military officers underscores its role as a policy-making and advisory body, one in which Soviet leaders can benefit from the considerable expertise of the professional military without giving them official and extensive representation in other state and party bodies. The Defense Council seems to focus on overseeing military policies and making recommendations to the President. An especially important aspect of the council's work is designing programs for the development of new weapons systems.

Subordinate to the Defense Council is the Military-Industrial Commission, which includes representatives of the various defense-related industries, the Ministry of Economics and Forecasting, the Ministry of Defense, and the Party. The commission supervises the procurement of armaments and materiel, ensuring that sufficient resources are available to meet production targets and coordinating delivery schedules to meet the needs of the military.

Another influential military body is the Main Military Council within the Ministry of Defense. This body, which is chaired by the Minister of Defense, is responsible for the overall command and control of the armed forces in peacetime. Its functions include resolving interservice disputes, allocating funds and personnel, and determining how best to implement decisions of the Politburo and the Defense Council. Members of the Main Military Council include the head of the Main Political Administration, the commanders of the five services, other branch chiefs, deputy ministers, chiefs of the General Staff, and, until March 1991, the Commander-in-Chief of the Warsaw Pact Forces. In time of war, the Main Military Council would be replaced by the *Stavka*, or Headquarters of the Supreme High Command.

Also within the Ministry of Defense is the General Staff of the Armed Forces. Modeled on its imperial Russian predecessor, this body is responsible for strategic planning to coordinate the activities of the five services.

Figure 13-1. Organization of the Soviet Armed Forces

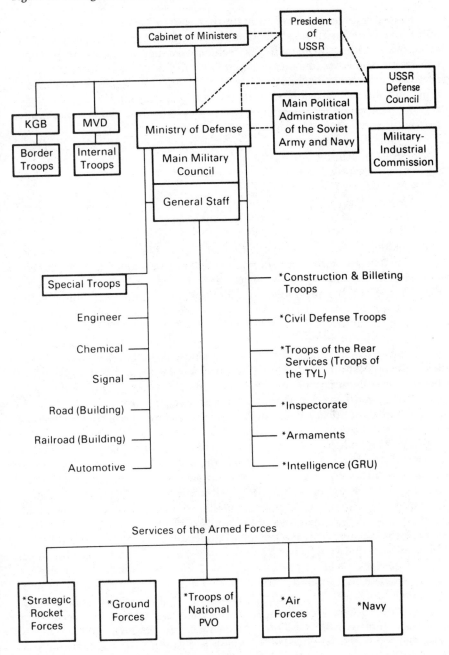

*Each headed by a Deputy Minister of Defense.

Source: Based on material from Harriet Fast Scott and William F. Scott, *The Armed Forces of the USSR*, 2d rev. ed. (Boulder: Westview Press, 1984), 143.

Subordinate to the General Staff are several directorates, including the influential Main Intelligence Administration (GRU). The GRU gathers intelligence information on enemy forces, technological developments, and combat conditions, and estimates enemy capabilities. Although its functions are much narrower than those of the KGB, there is a degree of overlap in their operations; this has, on occasion, resulted in interagency disputes.

The following are the military services or branches of the Soviet armed forces:

- Strategic Rocket Forces
- Ground Forces
- Air Defense Forces
- Air Forces
- Navy

Soviet publications always list the five services in this order, which roughly approximates their relative prestige and influence, although the navy has been gaining influence in recent years. There has also been some speculation in the West that, given the prominent role of the United States Air Force in the Persian Gulf war, Soviet military planners will accord the air force higher priority in the future.

Also subordinate to the General Staff is the Main Political Administration, whose structure has changed little since its reorganization in 1958. Below the highest officers of the MPA, the chief (*nachal'nik*) and his deputies, there exists a hierarchy of full-time political officers that parallels the command structure of the armed forces. At each level, a single political officer is in charge of all political work. The MPA currently employs more than 40,000 political officers.[30] In addition, the MPA supervises the activities of some 62,000 primary party organizations within military units.[31] Party membership is especially common among the officer corps. It is estimated that 40 percent of all party members in the military are officers in staff organizations.[32] In contrast, the Komsomol organizations within the armed forces are primarily for rank-and-file soldiers and noncommissioned officers. Eighty percent of all enlisted personnel are members of the Komsomol.[33]

For the Westerner, it is difficult to understand the degree of public, as well as official, praise that is heaped upon the Soviet armed forces. The huge military parades on November 7 and May 1 and the public celebrations on Armed Forces Day can all be rationalized as the result of a well-orchestrated effort of party workers to mobilize support for the military. But much of the adulation of the armed forces appears to be voluntary and spontaneous. Next to the Kremlin wall in Moscow is a memorial to the Soviet war dead. A perpetual flame burns, guarded by young Komsomols. It is the custom for brides to lay their bouquets at the memorial. One can hardly imagine a bride in the United States or elsewhere going straight from her wedding to a war memorial.

People in the United States are not accustomed to seeing large numbers of military men in uniform on the streets. Yet in the USSR, military personnel constitute a large and visible portion of the population, especially in cities such as Leningrad. Members of the armed forces wear their uniforms proudly and are seldom seen in public in civilian attire. Veterans of World War II, which the Soviets still refer to as the Great Patriotic War, are encouraged to wear their medals.

The CIA estimates that the Soviet military consumes from 15 to 17 percent of the gross national product, and this unquestionably results in a lower standard of living for the average citizen. Soviet critics charge that the CIA's estimates are low. Oleg Bogomolev, director of the reform-minded Institute of International Economics and Political Studies, estimated Soviet defense spending in 1990 at 20 to 25 percent of the GNP.[34] It is likely that with the rapid decline in the Soviet GNP in the past two years, the portion devoted to the armed forces has grown even larger. Public acceptance of defense spending has waned substantially in recent years. Prior to *glasnost*,' Soviet citizens would seldom question defense spending, even privately. However, surveys conducted in 1991 found that 56 percent of all respondents favored lowering defense spending and only 5.5 percent favored an increase in spending on new weapons systems.[35]

Children are taught respect for the armed forces from an early age. In elementary schools and Pioneer organizations, children march and practice military drills using toy rifles. Mandatory military training for both boys and girls begins in the ninth grade. In addition, boys are required to attend summer camp, where they learn to fire weapons using live ammunition.

All males are eligible for the military draft as of age eighteen, and almost all are conscripted. The normal term of service is two years, followed by reserve duty until the age of fifty. (Women are not subject to the draft and only a relative small number of women serve in non-combat positions.) Universal service in the Soviet military results in a very large standing army— almost four million in 1990. Military service is considered important, not only to provide the armed forces with the necessary personnel, but also to instill in the citizen a sense of responsibility for the defense of the USSR.

Service in the Soviet armed forces is also intended to assimilate non-Russian ethnic minorities into Soviet society. The command language throughout the armed forces is Russian; military units are not supposed to be configured on the basis of ethnicity or native language. All non-Russians are supposed to have had a minimum of six years of Russian-language training in school before entering the army. Nevertheless, experience in Afghanistan demonstrated the inability of Central Asian troops to understand their Russian officers. *De facto* segregation of some ethnic groups (especially Central Asians) has occurred simply in order to facilitate communication and control.

A sizable portion of the military conscripts in the Soviet Union work in construction battalions, building housing, digging ditches, and constructing highways. In 1980, Soviet soldiers were employed in the construction of the Olympic Village in Moscow, and more recently they were put to work on sections of the Baikal-Amur Railroad in Siberia. In the autumn, army units are often mobilized to assist in the harvest. The majority of Central Asian inductees are assigned to these "pick-and-shovel brigades," where language problems are less troublesome.

Long-term personnel prospects for the Soviet armed forces are not bright. It is estimated that non-Russians will constitute almost three-quarters of the draft-age population by the year 2000.[36] In contrast, the officer corps of the Soviet armed forces is dominated by Russians—at least 80 percent.[37]

Future officers receive their military education in one of the 140 higher military schools, most of which supply four or five years of training which results in a commission as lieutenant. In addition, sixteen higher military academies have been created in the various branches and divisions of the armed forces. In recent years, it appears that the majority of persons entering the officer-training programs are Russian, Ukrainian, or Belorussian; well-educated; and from white-collar families, often military families. Some Western experts have even characterized the higher officer pool as a "new class" that discourages penetration by "outsiders."[38]

Given the high esteem in which the Soviet armed forces are held, and the sizable percentage of the budget they consume, it should be no surprise that the members of the military are relatively well compensated. The salaries of top-level officers are among the highest in the Soviet Union, while middle- and lower-level officers live more modestly, but nonetheless comfortably. An especially significant component of income for officers is access to military department stores, clubs, resorts, hospitals, and housing, which provide a much better quality of goods and services than is generally available to civilians. Soviet military officials justify these perquisites as appropriate rewards for enduring the difficulties and dangers of military service, and as necessary to entice talented young people into seeking military careers.

Soviet involvement in Afghanistan and the use of military forces to quell public disturbances in Tbilisi, Central Asia, and the Baltic republics have tarnished the image of the armed forces somewhat in the eyes of Soviet citizens. In a 1990 survey, 79 percent of all respondents said they were either "dissatisfied" or "totally dissatisfied" with the state of affairs in the Soviet armed forces.[39] Forty-three percent of those responding considered the views of military representatives in the Congress of People's Deputies and the Party Congress to be "conservative and backward." According to defectors, morale among Soviet forces is very low. Drug and alcohol abuse appear to be widespread, as does harassment of new recruits.

Even more surprising are recent calls for reforms in the Soviet military coming from within the armed forces. In 1990, Major Vladimir Lopatin, a 30-year-old political officer from the northern city of Vologda, spearheaded the drafting of a military reform plan. The plan calls for significant cuts in military personnel and for a gradual transition to an all-professional army. Of 194 political officers in the Turkestan Military District surveyed, more than one-third favored an all-volunteer army, while almost half favored a mixture of draft and voluntary service.[40] More than 80 percent of those responding indicated that with the abolition of Article 6 of the Constitution, no parties should be allowed to have representatives or cells in the armed forces. Only 13.9 percent argued that Communist Party structures should be allowed to continue to operate within the armed forces.[41]

Gorbachev's approach to reforms within the military has been fairly circumspect. In August 1990, on the eve of the Supreme Soviet's fall session, Gorbachev addressed military officers in Odessa on his conception of military reform. He noted that the reduced foreign threat permitted a reassessment of the need for the traditional five separate services within the Soviet military.[42] On the more controversial issues of defense spending, volunteer service, and continued deployments of Soviet forces abroad (e.g., in Mongolia and in Eastern Europe), he noted arguments on various sides without committing himself to any.

The Soviet armed forces have not been immune to the struggle for change that has manifested itself in other areas of Soviet society in recent years. Support for Lopatin's radical reform proposals appears to rest primarily with younger, junior-grade officers. The senior officers, who managed to hold on to power throughout Gorbachev's early anticorruption campaigns and waves of forced retirements, are now reasserting their power. They represent a powerful constituency and one that Gorbachev cannot afford to disregard, not only on the question of reforming the armed forces, but on the full range of issues and problems confronting Soviet society today. No action demonstrates Gorbachev's recent reliance on the military more than his granting them police powers to maintain order at home.

"NEW THINKING" IN ACTION:
THREE CASES

One can best evaluate the impact of Gorbachev's policy of "new thinking" in foreign policy by examining specific cases. Below we analyze Soviet behavior in three pivotal episodes: the negotiations with the Reagan administration leading up to the conclusion of an Intermediate-Range Nuclear Forces (INF) agreement in 1987; the collapse of communist regimes in Eastern Europe; and the Iraqi invasion of Kuwait. These cases should indicate whether Gorbachev's policy of "new thinking" has resulted in significant changes in Soviet international behavior, or whether "new thinking" is primarily empty rhetoric.

The INF Agreement.   In the mid-1970s, when détente began to unravel, the Soviet leadership moved to replace its aging single-warhead SS-4 and SS-5 missiles in Eastern Europe and along the Chinese border with a new triple-warhead intermediate-range missile, the SS-20. At the time, neither NATO nor China possessed countervailing intermediate-range nuclear forces with which to threaten the Soviet Union. By 1977, the USSR had deployed 378 SS-20s in Europe and another 150 in Asia.[43] The Reagan administration pursued a vigorous policy designed to match or eliminate the Soviet Union's advantage in theatre nuclear weapons. President Reagan followed a "dual-track" policy—negotiating with the USSR on dismantling INF installations, and at the same time developing and deploying American INF missiles, the Pershing IIs and the ground-launched cruise missiles (GLCMs), to counter the Soviet threat in case the negotiations failed.

The INF talks proved difficult, as Western threats to deploy the Pershings and GLCMs encountered intransigence on the Soviet side. Soviet responsiveness at the negotiating table was hampered by leadership turnover in the Kremlin. During the two and one-half year period from November 1982 to

March 1985, there were four different General Secretaries in the USSR. In addition, the Soviet leaders may have been overly confident that they could persuade the European countries to veto the American deployments as they had during the neutron bomb controversy in the mid-1970s. For whatever reason, the Soviet leadership put its energy into mobilizing European public opinion against deployment of the "Euromissiles," rather than into negotiating an agreement. The campaign failed, however, and in November 1983 the United States began deployments. In response to this development, Soviet negotiators walked out of the arms talks in Geneva and U.S.–Soviet relations entered a phase of deep chill.

Gorbachev's succession to power in March 1985 signaled a potential for more constructive relations between the two superpowers. Gorbachev renewed calls for negotiating a reduction in intermediate-range weapons in Europe, although he wanted to include in the equation British and French nuclear forces that were not included under U.S. or NATO command. The Reagan administration responded that these forces were independent of the United States and, therefore, could not be lumped together in an INF agreement. By late 1986, the U.S. deployment of INF weapons totaled 316.[44] Another point of dispute was how to count those SS-20s that were deployed in Asia. The American side argued that since the SS-20 is a mobile missile, Asian-based systems had to be included since they could be moved into the European theatre after the signing of an arms agreement.

Negotiations proceeded for more than two years, resulting in major concessions on both sides. At a conference in Stockholm in September 1986, both sides agreed to give each other advance warning of troop maneuvers and to permit on-site inspection. The latter concession was a sharp departure from past Soviet practice. The next month at the Reykjavik summit, Gorbachev presented a sweeping proposal that would have cut strategic forces on both sides by 50 percent in a matter of a few years, and by the end of the century would have eliminated the total nuclear arsenals of both superpowers. As part of this proposal, Gorbachev agreed to exclude the French and British missiles from INF limits. In return, Gorbachev wanted Reagan to agree to limiting the SDI program to laboratory research—testing and deployment would be outlawed. President Reagan balked at Gorbachev's demand and both parties walked away from the summit discouraged about the prospects of future arms control agreements.

In February 1987, Gorbachev again raised hopes for an INF agreement, when he embraced the "zero option" plan and went on to advocate the elimination of short-range nuclear forces. By the autumn of 1987, both sides had managed to overcome the last remaining stumbling block—verification.

Agreement on the INF treaty was reached at the third summit between Gorbachev and Reagan, in Washington in December 1987. For the first time, a U.S.–Soviet arms agreement eliminated a whole class of nuclear weapons. Although these weapons represented a relatively small portion of the nuclear aresenals on both sides, the fact that the superpowers could overcome their mutual distrust signaled a new era in Soviet–American relations. Both sides pledged to build on the INF agreement by renewing efforts to limit or reduce conventional weapons in Europe and renew their commitment to the ABM treaty. Gorbachev hailed the treaty as a "major event in world politics" and a "victory for new thinking." [45] The INF agreement also bolstered his popularity at home.

The INF Treaty was officially signed at the May–June 1988 Reagan-Gorbachev summit in Moscow. The joint communiqué of the signing session proclaimed that the treaty was "an important step in the process of putting U.S.–Soviet relations on a more productive and sustainable basis."[46] The leaders built on the success of the INF negotiations to explore other issues, including human rights, regional conflicts, conventional force reductions in Europe, and limitations on strategic weapons.

The signing of the INF treaty was more than just a successful arms control negotiation; it represented a fundamental shift in the policies of both the United States and the Soviet Union. Following the conclusion of the INF Treaty, the superpowers were actively engaged in a broad range of negotiations and other forms of cooperation. Gone were the days of one leader denouncing the other side as an "evil empire." In large measure, the new atmosphere in U.S.–Soviet relations was the result of Gorbachev's "new thinking"—the willingness to make concessions and to be flexible in order to achieve larger goals, such as reducing tensions, building trust, and expanding international cooperation.

The Collapse of Communist Regimes in Eastern Europe.   From the time of their incorporation into the Soviet sphere during World War II until late 1989, the Soviet Union maintained rigid controls over the countries of Eastern Europe. When independence movements threatened to destabilize Soviet control, as in Hungary in 1956 and Czechoslovakia in 1968, tanks were used to put down the uprisings. More subtle but even more effective controls were imposed by integrating these countries politically, economically, and militarily into a bloc in which the Soviet Union was clearly the major partner. Soviet domination over Eastern Europe was justified under the "Brezhnev Doctrine," a policy decreeing it the collective obligation of all members of the "Socialist Commonwealth" to guarantee and defend socialism in each member state.

Gorbachev's approach to Eastern Europe was dramatically different from that of his predecessors. He saw Eastern Europe, as well as the USSR, in a larger context of a united Europe—a "common European home." This phrase, first uttered by Gorbachev during a visit to Paris in 1985, became a frequent theme in his speeches thereafter. He also frequently invoked Charles de Gaulle's vision of a "Europe extending from the Atlantic to the Urals." At the Twenty-Seventh Party Congress in 1986, he called for an "end to the division of Europe."

Gorbachev's desire to reunite Eastern and Western Europe was, in part, a response to plans by the European Community to become integrated economically by 1992. Gorbachev's fear was that an integrated and inward-looking Western Europe would further isolate the USSR and Eastern Europe. In order to keep an open door to Western Europe, Gorbachev initiated a series of moves that had critical implications for both the Soviet Union and Eastern Europe.

In 1986 and 1987 Gorbachev traveled throughout Eastern Europe preaching the gospel of *perestroika, glasnost'*, and democratization to skeptical party leaders. While the East European leaders (most notably Erich Honecker in East Germany and Gustav Husak in Czechoslovakia) were hesitant to follow Gorbachev's advice, the message was enthusiastically received by huge crowds chanting "Gorby! Gorby!" Not long after Gorbachev's visit, Husak was replaced by a more reform-minded party secretary, Milos Jakes. Gorbachev welcomed the change and reasserted his support for diversity within the socialist movement.

Reform movements were also introducing monumental changes in Hungary and Poland. First, the Hungarian Communist Party voted in May 1988 to replace long-time First Secretary Janos Kadar with Karoly Grosz. The next year, the Hungarian government announced its intention to hold multiparty, democratic elections. In Poland, the Polish Socialist Workers' Party lost to a slate of Solidarity candidates in the June 1988 elections, necessitating the eventual creation of a coalition government.

Glasnost' also played a part in weakening the Eastern European regimes. Exposés of the Czech invasion of 1968 were aired on Soviet television in 1988 to mark the twentieth anniversary of that event. They challenged the legitimacy of the Party's dominance of Czechoslovakia in the face of mass popular resistance.

On July 6, 1989, Gorbachev addressed the Council of Europe in Strasbourg. He pledged his support for the principles of "new thinking": noninterference in the internal affairs of other states; recognition of human rights; multinational cooperation in resolving common European problems; and the rejection of the use of force against friend or foe:

> The philosophy behind the concept of a common European home excludes the likelihood of an armed clash and the very possibility of the use or threat of force, above all military force, by one alliance against another, within alliances, or anywhere else.[47]

Gorbachev's Strasbourg speech had ramifications far beyond Western Europe. It was the clearest statement yet that the Brezhnev Doctrine no longer applied; that Soviet forces would not be used to put down reform movements in Eastern Europe. It was, therefore, appropriate that Gorbachev left Strasbourg and went immediately to Bucharest to attend the last major meeting of the Warsaw Pact countries. The communiqué from the summit acknowledged the right of member countries to make policies "without outside interference."[48] In a television interview after the conference, Gorbachev openly speculated that the Warsaw Pact alliance would change: "Probably this alliance will be transformed first of all from a military and political one to a political and military one. And then probably we shall come near to solving the last problem and achieve the goal that we have all been talking about . . . . The time when there is need for this will pass."[49] The leader of the Hungarian delegation to the conference declared, "The period of enforcing the so-called Brezhnev Doctrine is over once and for all."[50]

The Soviet leadership acknowledged the profound sociopolitical changes that were rapidly transforming Eastern Europe—official corruption; popular demoralization; loss of large numbers of members from the communist parties of the region; difficulties in winning support among the intelligentsia, youth, and progressive segments of the working class; difficulties in transforming ruling parties into competitive parliamentary parties.[51] Responding to these conditions, the Soviet leadership ceased using party channels to coordinate Soviet policy to the region; Soviet policy was carried out exclusively through official governmental channels.

During the fall of 1989 the Soviet leadership watched as former communist party regimes were toppled in Czechoslovakia, Hungary, Bulgaria, and Romania. However, nothing symbolized the change in Soviet policy more clearly than Gorbachev's support for German reunification. As the Berlin Wall, which had long symbolized Soviet domination over Eastern Europe, fell, Gorbachev proclaimed that a new world order had arrived.

Why did the Gorbachev government permit events to unfold in Eastern Europe as they did? First, in the past three decades Eastern Europe had come to be a drain on Soviet economic and military resources. The Soviet Union supplied oil, gas, and other raw materials to the East Europeans at below market prices, while it paid inflated prices for East European manufactured and consumer goods. Second, the use of force to stop the tide of social and political change in the region, even if it had been possible, would have been too expensive in real economic terms, and also damaging to Soviet efforts to improve relations with Western Europe and the United States. Third, Gorbachev could not champion *perestroika* and democratization at home but suppress the same policies abroad. Fourth, Soviet commentators, including former Foreign Minister Eduard Shevardnadze, noted that an independent and economically vibrant Eastern Europe could be a bigger asset to the Soviet Union than a docile but backward ally. It was, perhaps, not accidental that during his visit to Finland in October 1989, during the height of these changes in Eastern Europe, Gorbachev repeatedly stressed how beneficial Soviet–Finnish relations had been for each side. However, the last and most compelling reason the Soviets did not respond vigorously to stop the course of change in Eastern Europe is that they miscalculated the extent of public disaffection in the region, and by the time they understood the magnitude of the problem, events were beyond their control. The draft platform of the CPSU Twenty-Eighth Party Congress in July 1990 acknowledged that the transformation of Eastern Europe was "a painful and crisis-like process."[52] It concluded: "The changes in Eastern Europe are not going to upset our friendly relations with the people. The CPSU is of the opinion that the reforms commencing there and the continuing *perestroika* here in the USSR will provide a natural and more stable basis for voluntary contacts of mutual benefit."[53]

Despite efforts to put the best face on a bad situation, the transformation of Eastern Europe and the demise of the Warsaw Pact is widely perceived in the USSR as a loss, and it has been used to mobilize conservative opponents of "new thinking." As we noted earlier, Foreign Minister Shevardnadze became the focal point for this conservative criticism, and his resignation left a void that continues to be felt. A political commentator in *Izvestiya* concluded that Shevardnadze resigned not because of the conservative criticism, but because no one rose to defend him against his critics. "Why didn't anyone mount the rostrum to share the responsiblity and defend Shevardnadze? If you think about it, the answer is readily apparent: The President needs the Army's support more than ever before, and he doesn't want to see its patience exhausted. International support is easier to secure than domestic support."[54]

The Persian Gulf War.   In the Middle East, the Soviet Union has traditionally aligned itself with radical Arab governments such as Syria, Libya, and South Yemen. Gorbachev's policy of "new thinking," however, forced a reassessment of that stance even before Iraq's invasion of Kuwait in August 1990. Gorbachev initiated dialogue with Israel that resulted in the normalization of relations; he condemned hostage-taking in Lebanon; he favored a negotiated settlement of the Iran–Iraq war; and he opened trade relations with conservative states in the region—Saudi Arabia, Oman, Qatar, and the United Arab Emirates. The basic goal in Gorbachev's "new thinking" in the Gulf was to maintain security and stability in the region.

The Iraqi invasion of Kuwait catapulted the Soviet Union into a leading role in international efforts to resolve the crisis. The Soviets have had long and productive relations with Iraq. Likewise, the Soviet Union has diplomatic ties with Kuwait, the one Gulf state with which it has such ties. Over the past decade both Iraq and Kuwait have purchased large amounts of military hardware from the USSR. However, there were no Soviet military advisors in Kuwait as there were in Iraq; instead, training was provided by Egyptians and Syrians. Thus, the Soviet Union was in an ideal position to mediate the conflict.

While somewhat more guarded and moderate in its criticisms of Iraq than Western states, the Soviet government supported all of the U.N. Security Council resolutions relating to the conflict, including those imposing economic sanctions, enforced by a naval blockade; establishing the January 15 deadline for an Iraqi pullout; approving the use of "all necessary means" to liberate Kuwait; and holding Iraq accountable for damage to Kuwaiti and foreign assets.

Initially, Soviet support for the Security Council resolutions was justified in terms of abstract principles of nonaggression and sovereignty, rather than national interest.[55] Before departing for the Middle East on his first round of discussions with Saddam Hussein in August 1990, Primakov told *Literaturnaya gazeta* that the Gulf crisis presented the superpowers with a "unique laboratory for testing our efforts to create a new world order after the end of the Cold War."[56]

While upholding the principles of "new thinking," the Soviet leadership was careful not to alienate Iraq. For example, after Shevardnadze announced Soviet support for the imposition of sanctions, he remarked, "It was no easy matter for me to make a decision on sanctions: the friendliest of relations existed between our countries. As old friends we call on him [Saddam Hussein] to think again."[57]

By the fall of 1990, Gorbachev's (and Shevardnadze's) stance on the Gulf crisis was raising problems at home. Members of the conservative "Soyuz" faction in the USSR Supreme Soviet demanded that the body be consulted before the Soviet ambassador cast votes on any further U.N. Security Council resolutions, despite the fact that no prior parliamentary approval is required under the USSR Constitution. Appearing before the Supreme Soviet in October, Shevardnadze promised to consult with them prior to voting on a resolution to use force to free Kuwait.[58] However, the pledge was not honored, and in response, angry deputies called for a special session in January 1991 to discuss the Soviet stance in the Gulf crisis.

Even among top foreign policy advisors there was a split between the "Westernizers," who advocated cooperation with the Western-led alliance against Iraq, and the "Arabists," who argued that the USSR should maintain its close economic, political, and military ties with Iraq. Primakov, a graduate of the Moscow Institute of Oriental Studies and a specialist on the region, appears to fall in the latter camp, while Shevardnadze clearly belongs to the former group. A similar split occurred within the Ministry of Foreign Affairs, pitting the Middle East experts against Shevardnadze's top tier of advisors, who wanted to preserve good relations with the West.

The resignation of Shevardnadze on December 20, 1990 benefited Primakov's position and can be seen as one reason for the softening of Soviet support for the Western alliance and diplomatic initiatives just prior to the onset of the fighting. Primakov repeatedly stressed the need to give Hussein a chance to save face, and also favored guarantees that an Iraqi pullout would be linked to discussion of the Palestinian question.[59]

Even before the initiation of conflict, rifts were apparent between the United States and the Soviet Union. A commentator for *Sovetskaya Rossiya* observed: "The American presence in the Persian Gulf region is now many times in excess of the reasonable limits of sufficiency for combat operations aimed at liberating Kuwait. . . . One has to conclude that the objective is not to liberate Kuwait, but to overthrow Saddam Hussein's regime, something that can be accomplished only through total war against the Iraqi people."[60]

Once fighting broke out, the Soviet Union repeatedly urged the United States and other Western allies to limit the damage to Iraq. On February 11, 1991 Gorbachev reaffirmed his government's support for the U.N. Security Council resolutions, but he asserted that Western military operations were exceeding the U.N. mandate in attempting to destroy Iraq's military and economic infrastructure.[61] He urged Hussein to agree to a pullout and at the same time indicated Soviet willingness to broaden negotiations to the entire region, including the Palestinian problem. Such a position was clearly unacceptable to the United States.

Thus, Soviet behavior in the Persian Gulf war communicates mixed signals. On the one hand, it illustrates the power of "new thinking," especially the concepts of the inadmissibility of the use of force and the right of nations to sovereignty. The principle of multilateral action to resolve regional conflicts under the auspices of the United Nations was also firmly upheld. On the other hand, Soviet behavior during the crisis aroused harsh criticism of Shevardnadze and Gorbachev. With Shevardnadze gone, the future of "new thinking" rests with Bessmertnykh and Gorbachev, and neither appears to be very secure.

TOWARD A NEW WORLD ORDER

What can we conclude about the prospects of "new thinking"from these three cases? Has it ushered in a new world order, as some Soviet commentators have claimed? There is no question that the USSR is behaving in ways that few would have predicted ten years ago. Soviet concessions in order to arrive at an INF agreement, unilateral troop demobilizations from Afghanistan and Eastern Europe, acceptance of on-site inspection, cooperation with Security Council resolutions in a regional conflict, relaxation of travel and emigration restrictions, and refusal to use force to maintain communist regimes in Eastern Europe all point in a radically new direction.

Underlying these decisions and actions is a shift in Soviet policy formulation from stressing national interest, as it is traditionally understood, to stressing abstract principles that we noted at the outset of this chapter. Gorbachev has presented his policy of "new thinking" in moral terms. The sovereignty of states, noninterference in the internal affairs of other states, multilateral cooperation in solving global problems, equal security, and defending human rights are considered to be moral imperatives. Nevertheless, they run counter to the ingrained way of thinking of powerful constituencies in the Soviet Union. In recent months, these conservative forces have successfully mounted an attack on other elements of Gorbachev's reform program and they have also succeeded in forcing Shevardnadze's resignation. Whether Gorbachev can sustain his vision of a new world order depends more than ever on his success in placating his domestic critics. We explore Gorbachev's prospects for surviving this conservative onslaught in our concluding chapter.

Notes

1. TASS report, 25 February 1986.
2. Ibid. See also *Pravda*, 13 March 1986, p. 1.
3. *Kommunist*, no. 9 (1986): 24–25.
4. G. Kh. Shakhnazarov, "Logika politicheskogo myshleniya v yadernuyu eru," *Voprosy filosofii* no. 5 (1984): 63–74.
5. Report of the Minister of Foreign Affairs to a conference on 25 July 1988, cited in W. Raymond Duncan and Carolyn McGiffert Ekedahl, *Moscow and the Third World under Gorbachev* (Boulder, CO: Westview Press, 1990), 53
6. *Pravda*, 5 August 1988, p. 1.
7. *Pravda*, 5 October 1988, p. 1.
8. Quoted in M. S. Gorbachev, *Izbrannye rechi i stat'i*, vol. 2 (Moscow: Politizdat, 1987–1989), 109–116.
9. Ibid.
10. *New York Times*, 8 October 1988, p. 1.
11. *Pravda*, 10 July 1987, p. 4.
12. *Kommunist*, 9 June 1986, p. 10.
13. *Izvestiya*, 11 July 1987, p. 1.
14. *Pravda*, 26 February 1986, p. 1.
15. *New York Times*, 8 December 1988, p. 1.
16. *Pravda*, 22 July 1990, p. 2. During the first seven months of 1990 emigration increased

to 233,680, more than half of these were on so-called "Israeli visas." *Izvestiya*, 29 August 1990, p. 2.

17. *New York Times*, 6 January 1989, p. A-13

18. Boldin's nomination was not confirmed by the Supreme Soviet in March 1991, but his name was to be resubmitted. Associated Press report, *The State*, 8 March 1991, 6A.

19. See Alexander Rahr, "Winds of Change Hit Foreign Ministry," *Radio Liberty Research Bulletin* 30, no. 30 (23 July 1986), p. 2.

20. *Izvestiya*, 3 June 1989, p. 8.

21. *Izvestiya*, 16 March 1990, p. 6.

22. *Sovetskaya Rossiya*, 21 June 1990, pp. 3–4.

23. Cited in Stephen Foye, "Defense Issues at the Party Congress," *Radio Liberty Report on the USSR* 2, no. 30 (27 july 1990): 2.

24. Ibid.

25. *Pravda* 26 June 1990, p. 3.

26. *Komsomolskaya pravda,* 25 December 1990, p. 1. 27. Associated Press report, 21 December 1990, cited in Suzanne Crow, "Change of Command at Foreign Ministry," *Radio Liberty Report on the USSR* 3, no. 4 (25 January 1991): 20.

27. Associated Press report, 21 December 1990, cited in Suzanne Crow, "Change of Command at Foreign Ministry," *Radio Liberty Report on the USSR* 3, no. 4 (25 January 1991): 20.

28. This argument was suggested in Ibid., 20–21.

29. *Izvestiya*, 24 December 1990, pp. 2–8.

30. Timothy J. Colton, *Commissars, Commanders, and Civilian Authority: The Structure of Soviet Military Politics* (Cambridge, MA: Harvard University Press, 1979), 15.

31. Ibid., 17. This figure is for 1945.

32. Ibid., 18.

33. Ibid., 21.

34. Cited in *Izvestiya*, 23 November 1990, p. 2.

35. Survey data cited in *New Outlook*, 2, no. 1 (Winter 1990/91): 56–57.

36. D. R. Jones, ed., *Soviet Armed Forces Review Annual*, vol. 2 (Gulf Breeze, FL: Academic International Press, 1978), 39.

37. S. E. Wimbush and Alex Alexiev, *The Ethnic Factor in the Soviet Armed Forces* (Santa Monica: Rand Corporation, 2787/1, March 1982), 22.

38. Michael Voslensky, *Nomenklatura* (New York: Doubleday, 1984), 107–109.

39. *New Outlook*, 56–57.

40. Ibid., 58.

41. Ibid., 59.

42. *Krasnaya zvezda*, 19 August 1990, pp. 1–2.

43. Peter Zwick, *Soviet Foreign Relations* (Englewood Cliffs, NJ: Prentice Hall, 1990), 256.

44. Ibid., 257.

45. *Vizit General'nogo sekretariya TsK KPSS M.A. Gorbacheva v Soedinennye Shtaty Ameriki 7–10 dekabrya 1987 goda. Dokumenty i materialy* (Moscow: Politizdat, 1987), 164–169.

46. Ibid., 141–153.

47. *Pravda*, 7 July 1989, p. 1.

48. Vladimir V. Kusin, "Gorbachev's Evolving Attitude toward Eastern Europe," *Radio Liberty Report on the USSR* 1, no. 31 (4 August 1989): 9.

49. Ibid.

50. Ibid.

51. L. Shevtsova, "The Communist Parties of Eastern Europe," *Moscow News*, no. 4 (1990), p. 8.

52. *Pravda*, 13 February 1990, p. 1.

53. Ibid.

54. *Izvestiya,* 2 January 1991, p. 7.

55. Some commentators stressed the need to pursue a national interest approach, but they were a minority at first. See Suzanne Crow, "The Gulf Conflict and Debate over Soviet National Interests," *Radio Liberty Report on the USSR* 3, no. 6 (8 February 1991): 15–17.

56. *The Washington Post,* 4 October 1990, p. 1.

57. TASS, 26 September 1990.

58. *New York Times,* 16 October 1990, p. 1.

59. Suzanne Crow, "Primakov and the Soviet Peace Initiative," *Radio Liberty Report on the USSR* 3, no. 9 (1 March 1991): 14–17.

60. *Sovetskaya Rossiya,* 11 January 1991, p. 5.

61. *Izvestiya,* 11 February 1991, 1.

Selected Bibliography

Adomeit, Hannes. *Soviet Risk-Taking and Crisis Behavior.* Boston: Allen & Unwin, 1982.

Bialer, Seweryn. *The Domestic Context of Soviet Foreign Policy,* 2nd ed., Boulder: Westview Press, 1988.

Dawisha, Karen. *Eastern Europe, Gorbachev and Reform.* 2nd ed., Cambridge: Cambridge University Press, 1990.

Duncan, W. Raymond and Carolyn McGiffert Ekedahl. *Moscow and the Third World under Gorbachev.* Boulder: Westview Press, 1990.

Garthoff, Raymond L. *Detente and Confrontation: American-Soviet Relations from Nixon to Reagan.* Washington: Brookings Institution Press, 1985.

Garthoff, Raymond L. *Deterrence and the Revolution in Soviet Military Doctrine.* Washington: Brookings Institution Press, 1990.

Gati, Charles. *The Bloc that Failed.* Bloomington: Indiana University Press, 1990.

George, Alexander L., ed. *Managing U.S.-Soviet Rivalry.* Boulder: Westview Press, 1983.

George, Alexander L., Philip J. Farlye and Alexander Dallin, eds. U.S.-Soviet Security Cooperation. New York: Oxford University Press, 1988.

Geron, Leonard. *Soviet Foreign Economic Policy under Perestroika.* New York: Council on Foreign Relations, 1990.

Laird, Robbin F. and Susan Clark, eds. *The USSR and the Western Alliance.* Boston: Unwin Hyman, 1990.

Laird, Robbin F. and Dale R. Herspring. *The Soviet Union and Strategic Arms.* Boulder: Westview Press, 1984.

Light, Margot. *The Soviet Theory of International Relations.* New York: St. Martin's Press, 1988.

McCain, Morris. *Understanding Arms Control: The Options.* New York: W. W. Norton, 1989.

Nogee, Joseph L. and Robert H. Donaldson. *Soviet Foreign Policy Since World War II.* New York: Pergamon Press, 1988.

Parrott, Bruce. *Trade, Technology, and Soviet-American Relations.* Bloomington: Indiana University Press, 1985.

Roskin, Michael G. *The Rebirth of East Europe.* Englewood Cliffs, N.J.: Prentice-Hall, 1991.

Stoll, Richard J. *U.S. National Security Policy and the Soviet Union.* Columbia: University of South Carolina Press, 1990.

White, Stephen, John Cardner, George Schopflin, and Tony Saich. *Communist and Postcommunist Political Systems,* 3rd ed. New York: St. Martin's Press, 1990.

Woodby, Sylvia. *Gorbachev and the Decline of Ideology in Soviet Foreign Policy.* Boulder: Westview Press, 1989.

Zwick, Peter. *Soviet Foreign Relations.* Englewood Cliffs, N.J.: Prentice-Hall, 1990.

14

Whither the Soviet Union?

> The horses fly like a whirlwind . . . and the troika dashes away. . . . Russia, art thou also flying onwards like a spirited troika that nothing can overtake? What is the meaning of this terrifying onrush? Russia, whither flyest thou?
>
> Nikolai Gogol, *Dead Souls*

> We have met the enemy, and he is us.
>
> Pogo

Reform has never come easily to Russia. Forceful and farsighted leaders such as Ivan the Terrible, Peter the Great, Lenin, and Stalin introduced wrenching reforms in order to modernize and transform what was seen as an inefficient, weak, and backward society. The result was not peaceful evolution, but upheaval and disorder. Reform in Russia and the Soviet Union has always been a chaotic process of fits and starts, of progressive changes followed by backlash and repression. Yet, what Gorbachev is attempting is a peaceful restructuring of society. While his reforms have enjoyed some success, they have also sharpened the debate between proponents of even more liberal reform, and conservatives who fear the destabilizing consequences of those reforms. As it has so frequently in the past, the Soviet Union today is a society struggling with change.

Gorbachev's reforms have succeeded in demolishing the old Stalinist system, breaking down long-established political, social, and economic relations. *Perestroika* has redefined relations between factories and enterprises and their respective ministries in Moscow. Many factories now openly disregard directives from the center and are establishing their own network of suppliers and customers. Democratization has eroded support for the CPSU and other institutions of power. Millions have left the ranks of the Party over the course of the past two years. Power has shifted to elected governmental bodies and the executive presidency, leaving the Politburo a pale shadow of its former self. *Glasnost'* expanded the boundaries of free expression and in the process unleashed public opinion to challenge officials and policies.

The collapse of the Stalinist system, however, has resulted in a power vacuum. Factories and enterprises are largely devoid of talents and resources to act independently. Newly created political institutions lack staff and resources to enable them to operate effectively. Most important, they lack a tradition of legitimacy and power that would invest them with enduring authority. The public is unaccustomed to the greater freedoms and responsibilities afforded by democratization and *glasnost'*. Intolerance, whether for those with differing political views or for those of differing ethnic origins, is openly expressed. New political, social, and economic relations will take time to develop. But they will have to develop in the midst of a crisis—a crisis precipitated by the very reforms that Gorbachev has championed. A new social contract must be negotiated between Soviet citizens and the State, but this is difficult to do in times of economic hardship and breakdown of the trust that holds societies together. In the words of Aleksandr Yakovlev, a close Gorbachev confidant, "We are trying to sail a ship and simultaneously rebuild it. We don't have a spare ship to step into for a moment and sail."[1]

The breakdown of trust is manifesting itself in localism and regionalism (often expressed in terms of nationalism). Local economic and government officials want to restrict the assets of their respective regions for the use of their own constituents. When confronted with food shortages in 1990 and early 1991, many Soviet cities issued special coupons to local residents enabling them to buy goods denied to "outsiders." A major political controversy erupted between the Ukraine and the Russian republic when the Ukrainian leadership prohibited the shipment of meat outside its own borders. The Russian republic government responded by banning oil and gas deliveries to the Ukraine. The conflict was eventually resolved through negotiations between the leaders of both republics, but the episode illustrates the "Balkanization" of politics in the USSR today. When shortages and hardships occur, there is a natural tendency for people to want to preserve their own resources and use them for those with whom they identify. People in the USSR today have a firmer sense of identity with their immediate neighbors, with people in their own region, with people of the same nationality, than they do with people in a far-flung corner of the USSR. The persistence of local and regional identities in the Soviet Union should not surprise us. According to many historians of the United States, it was not until well after the Civil War that American citizens developed as much identity with and attachment for the United States as a whole, as they had for their home states.[2]

Localism is a deep-seated characteristic of the Russian people, dating back to their centuries-long existence in villages. We noted in Chapter 7 that the USSR is an increasingly urbanized society. Yet the vast majority of its urban residents are first generation city-dwellers, and many of their attitudes and patterns of behavior still reflect village society.

Some observers have asked why in Western Europe the 1990s appear to mark dramatic progress toward increased integration, whereas in Eastern Europe and the Soviet Union we see fragmentation and disintegration. The process of integration has been a long one for Western Europe. Centuries-long hostilities, suspicions, and jealousies have had to be overcome. Crucial in this regard is the attainment of a relatively uniform, high standard of living among the dominant Western European states. In contrast, in the Soviet Union there are glaring discrepancies in the standards of living across regions and between urban and rural areas. Even the wealthiest regions rank below the poorest countries of Western Europe.

Given the economic chaos in the USSR today, it is inevitable that interethnic and interregional rivalries should surface. However, the same process that has fostered disintegration between regions and ethnic groups has reinforced intraregional and ethnic loyalties. At the regional and local levels, people identify more with governing bodies and have a greater sense of political efficacy. Local leaders also appear to have greater support among their constituents, a critical factor in weathering hard economic times. Only as citizens begin to realize that their parochial interests are best served by forging new linkages beyond their immediate region can the process of reintegration occur. Trust must be rebuilt from the ground up.

The strain on the Gorbachev government of trying to preserve the union is all too apparent. It is unlikely that the three Baltic states will accept anything less than full sovereignty and independence. Georgia, Armenia, and Moldavia are also likely to push hard to secede from the USSR. Currently, Gorbachev is politically weak and cannot afford to capitulate to secessionist demands. To do so would almost certainly result in active resistance from within the armed forces and the security police. However, the costs of maintaining these republics within the USSR against their wishes could well outweigh the benefits. A president in a stronger political position might well accede to secessionist demands in these areas.

"Balkanization" also describes the effect of Gorbachev's reform program on the Soviet political system. In the past three years, lines have been sharply drawn between liberal reformers and conservatives. The middle of the political spectrum has vanished. Ironically, it was the middle of the political spectrum on which Gorbachev traditionally relied. By his very nature, Gorbachev is a moderate. He has built his career on reaching compromises between the extremes of reform and reaction. However, the chaos and confusion in the USSR today have polarized the situation, forcing people to more extreme positions. The old political adage that the middle of the road is the safest position, except during a revolution, appears to be valid in the Soviet case.

For his first two or three years in office, Gorbachev successfully steered a course between the conservatives, led by Ligachev, and the radical reformers such as Yeltsin. In fact, the existence of these polar extremes seemed to legitimize his centrist stance. However, as the economic crisis worsened and political fighting intensified with elections and the emergence of competing centers of power, it was increasingly difficult for Gorbachev to steer a middle course. By the time of the Twenty-Eighth Party Congress in the summer of 1990, Soviet citizens were tired of Gorbachev's compromises and vacillations. They wanted decisive leadership.

THE LIBERALS

The liberal, pro-reform constituencies are themselves heavily fragmented, having thrown their support to Yeltsin, Gavriil Popov and his deputy Sergei Stankevich in Moscow, and Anatoli Sobchak in Leningrad. In non-Russian areas, the liberal reform agenda has also been complicated by ethnic demands and loyalties. Many Soviets feel that the only man who could have acted as a moral compass and unifier of the liberals was Andrei Sakharov, who died on the eve of the crucial December 1989 session of the Congress of People's Deputies. Sakharov, a distinguished scientist and scholar, suffered as a dissident throughout the Brezhnev years. He alone commanded the respect and authority to lead the nation through the perilous transition to democracy and a market economy. While Yeltsin, Popov, Stankevich and Sobchak are widely respected, they are seen as politicians. Sakharov, on the other hand, was seen as a combination of saint and martyr.

The liberal position has also been hampered by waning public support for reform even among the intelligentsia. *Glasnost'* only seemed to buy Gorbachev the support of the intelligentsia until 1988 or 1989. Like the nineteenth-century radical socialists, the liberal intelligentsia today tends to approach reform in an uncompromising way. Gorbachev, the politician, has had to confront the realities and constraints placed on him by opposing factions and interests, and has made compromises. The liberals condemn these compromises as "selling out." Consequently, they have tended to support the most radical, the most uncompromising spokesman for the radical cause, Boris Yeltsin.

The liberal reforming intelligentsia, while representing a significant percentage of the population, does not have impressive institutional bases of power. They do not control any of the major bureaucratic power centers that have dominated the Soviet political scene since Stalin's time. Pockets of pro-reform sentiment can be found virtually everywhere and in every institution in the USSR, even in the KGB and the military. However, most of the positions of power in the crucial bureaucracies are still dominated by men in their sixties. Support for liberal reforms appears to be strongest among the well-educated, white-collar, urban population, especially those between the ages of 30 and 50. These people have the greatest investment in society. Many state that they were frustrated by the stagnation of the Brezhnev years and now welcome the opportunity to become more actively involved in making their lives and the lives of their children better.

THE CONSERVATIVES

The conservative bastions of power—the armed forces, the KGB, the police, the party apparatus, and the economic ministries—were initially thrown off balance by Gorbachev's reforms. *Glasnost'* put the KGB, the police, and the armed forces on the defensive. The anticorruption campaigns disrupted the party apparatus and opened the door for a wholesale turnover among regional and local party secretaries under Gorbachev. *Perestroika* granted Soviet factories and enterprises a much greater degree of control over their own affairs, thus undermining the directives of central ministries and Gosplan. Members of these powerful conservative institutions had grown complacent during the Brezhnev years of stagnation. They were accustomed to ruling by *diktat*, rather than by persuasion. From their subordinates they commanded loyalty and in return they provided special perquisites and favors. The idea of representing a broad constituency whose interests they served was beyond their comprehension. Power trickled down; it did not bubble up from below. Democratization and the process of electing representatives to the Congress of People's Deputies, the Supreme Soviet, and republic, regional and local soviets forced conservative party and state representatives to make fundamental adjustments. At first, military and police representatives in the Supreme Soviet and the Congress of People's Deputies were unaccustomed to the game of parliamentary politics, and sat in stunned silence while deputies attacked them for the invasion of Afghanistan or the misallocation of resources. However, in 1990 the conservative groups began to rebound. Younger, more daring and articulate members of the armed forces and the KGB took the podium of the Supreme Soviet and the Congress of People's Deputies to defend the interests of their institutions and to attack Gorbachev and the reformers. Others used the new channels afforded by *glasnost'* to publish commentaries expounding their conservative criticisms and expressing their fears of the impending disintegration of the USSR.

Unlike the liberal reformers, the conservatives have a great deal of institutional support to back up their preferences. The collective bureaucratic power of the armed forces, the KGB, the police, and the CPSU is daunting. They employ millions of people and control vast resources ranging from publishing houses, office buildings, and motor pools, to resort facilities, luxury housing complexes and special stores. They have not hesitated to use these resources to reward their friends and to punish their enemies.

Furthermore, these bureaucratic interests have been able to legitimize their conservative positions by playing on the frustrations and fears of average Soviet citizens. By 1988, rank-and-file workers and peasants had grown skeptical of Gorbachev's promised economic turnaround. The greater freedom to speak and read and travel does not mean much to citizens who must stand in line for hours on end to buy milk, eggs, or bread. For them, *perestroika* meant a lowering of their already marginal standard of living.

CAN REFORM SUCCEED?

What are the prospects for successful reform? Can Gorbachev survive? Despite all the difficulties confronting the Soviet Union in general and Gorbachev in particular, there are several positive signs. First, the leadership is gradually making difficult decisions that must be made to address the problems of the Soviet economy. They have introduced austerity measures; prices have been increased by 60 to 1000 percent in order to curb hoarding and bring the prices of goods more into line with the costs of production. In so doing, they have taken meaningful steps toward the restoration of a money economy. By 1990, the ruble had lost all value, both inside the country and abroad. Citizens had ample stockpiles of cash at home, but there was nothing in the stores on which to spend it. As the winter approached, people went on a buying frenzy, snatching up anything they could find in the food stores and stockpiling it at home. In early 1991 the Gorbachev regime pulled from circulation all large-denomination bills, effectively wiping out the savings of millions of Soviet citizens and severely limiting their ability to continue panic shopping. On April 2, 1991, steep price increases went into effect for virtually all products and services. As the money that has been out of circulation, stuffed in mattresses and cookie jars, is absorbed into the economy by higher prices, the ruble will gradually regain its purchasing power. The resumption of a money economy also creates an incentive for enterprises to increase production in order to enhance profits. The process of shoring up the ruble and restoring the money economy is the very direction that economic advisers Abel Aganbegyan and Stanislav Shatalin have long been advocating, but they caution that it may take two or three years to begin to show positive results.[3]

Second, the power of central authority appears to be holding its own against the centrifugal forces of fragmentation. Gorbachev was elected to serve as President until March 1995. Barring unforeseen circumstances, there is little reason to suspect that he will not do so. The chances of his reelection in 1995 do not currently appear to be great. His public approval rating has fallen to around 14 percent, while his chief rival, Boris Yeltsin, musters between 60 and 70 percent favorable ratings. However, in presidential systems, the chief executive serves a set term despite fluctuations in public opinion. Unlike a prime ministerial system, in which a vote of no confidence can force a change in leadership at any time, Gorbachev's tenure appears reasonably secure. Only a *coup d' etat* by the military, impeachment, resignation, or death could shorten his tenure. The first appears unlikely, especially in light of his recent move to the right. A coup would also establish an unfortunate precedent of subverting the Soviet Constitution. No one, including the military, is eager to return to the Stalinist system of rule by naked force. Gorbachev could be impeached, but in order for this to happen, he would have to be found guilty of violating the Constitution. Furthermore, impeachment requires a two-thirds vote of the Congress of People's Deputies, a body in which Gorbachev's support appears to remain high. Resignation also does not appear likely, given Gorbachev's demonstrated resolve and toughness. Death is inevitable, but at 60, Gorbachev appears to be vigorous and in good health.

By April 1991, Gorbachev had managed to convince nine of the fifteen republics to sign the Union Treaty. Collectively, these republics represent 98 percent of the land mass of the USSR, 92.7 percent of the population and the bulk of its industrial and natural resource wealth. By agreeing to turn over to the republics greater control of their respective economies, Gorbachev was able to win the crucial support of Boris Yeltsin, as well as that of other republic presidents. In addition, Gorbachev's more conciliatory stance brought the potentially crippling miners' strike to a peaceful conclusion after eight weeks. Even Eduard Shevardnadze, who had just four months earlier resigned as Foreign Minister to protest Gorbachev's accumulation of dictatorial powers, praised the President's cooperation with Yeltsin and urged Western governments to lend their support for *perestroika*. All these developments bode well for the future of Gorbachev's leadership and his ability to weather the crisis confronting the country.

Third, the stalemate that now exists between the reformers and the conservatives strengthens Gorbachev's hand. His newly won emergency powers enable him to suppress public unrest and maintain at least a modicum of order. This may prove to be enough to placate the law-and-order conservatives. Even a respected reform-minded lawyer, such as Sergei Alkseyev, a member of the Constitutional Supervision Commission, acknowledges the need for strong leadership in times of crisis: "We find ourselves in a position where there is a paralysis of power. Power has not been functioning. Parliamentary proceedings may block the decision-making process and bring policy-making to a deadlock . . . . This can lead to dictatorship . . . . We need strong power, without which our system will disintegrate."[4] Aleksandr Yakovlev concurs: "In the history of Russia, you have both Alexander the Liberator and Ivan the Terrible. In Russian history, in the Russian psyche, a strong man must be the head of government. Historically, psychologically, it may be explained by the constant invasions, by the peasant, rural psychology—what is a house without the head of the house? So it has some appeal, this idea of a strong man on top."[5] Nikolai Shmelev, an economist and proponent of radical reform, argues: "It is very important for a huge, multiethnic country like ours to have a supreme arbiter. What we need is the authority of political power that will make unpopular decisions. I am afraid it will be impossible to get past long-established dogma without massive presidential power, without the full weight of the presidency coming down on all this prejudice."[6]

Some Western commentators have argued that Gorbachev has effectively been deposed and that the real authority rests behind the scenes with senior military and party officials. Shevardnadze alluded to a *de facto* coup when, in an interview on American television, he acknowledged that some decisions are being made without Gorbachev's knowledge or approval, including the decision to use force against protesters in Vilnius, Lithuania.[7] No doubt the conservatives would like to think they have succeeded in coopting Gorbachev. However, they may find that they are being coopted by him. Gorbachev has been forced to make tactical compromises in the name of preserving the unity of the USSR and restoring law and order, but the general outlines of his policies remain in place. In April 1991, speaking before a military audience that had demanded he take "decisive actions" to silence Yeltsin, Gorbachev responded: "If 'decisiveness' is intended to mean a return to old methods, to suppression and violence, then I must tell you firmly, I will not resort to that. I am for pluralism of opinions, for political pluralism, for every party winning its authority by proving the attraction of its program's aims."[8]

Fourth, the conservatives have little to offer the people other than law and order. They have no real solutions to the country's difficult economic and social problems. In the span of two years, 1990 and 1991, the Soviet GNP fell by an estimated 20 percent.[9] Such a collapse is much more severe than that experienced in the United States during the Great Depression. The closest approximation to the transition confronting the Soviet economy today is that experienced in Poland in 1980–1981. The magnitude of the USSR's economic catastrophe will itself mandate further reforms. In this sense, Gorbachev's strategy has worked: the Stalinist command economy has been destroyed, and no one, not even the conservatives, believes it can be rebuilt; no one wants to return to command methods.

Fifth, the conservatives have proven to be just as uncompromising and naive as the radical reformers. They want a vibrant market-based economy, but without any pain—without unemployment, without cuts in social benefits, without price increases, without shortages, and most of all, without civil unrest. They are willing to live with greater freedom of expression, as long as people do not criticize the military or the CPSU. They are willing to grant republics and regional and local governments the right to self-determination, as long as it does not weaken central authority. They seem to deny that these positions are contradictory and that politics, by its very nature, involves making compromises and difficult choices.

Finally, from a longer-range sociological and demographic perspective, there is reason to be optimistic. Soviet society of the 1990s is a far cry from Soviet society under Stalin. The population is much better educated and more urbanized—two of the prime prerequisites for political participation in any society. The experience of *glasnost'*, more than six years old now, has given people a sense of involvement and empowerment which, even in the face of setbacks, cannot be totally suppressed. New, popularly elected institutions exist that can act as a check on governmental and party authority. True, they are not yet powerful enough to veto executive actions, but they are evolving and in time may develop greater institutional legitimacy and authority.

It is also a positive sign that all sides (with the exception of some of the smaller ethnic groups) appear to recognize what the permissible limits are. When Gorbachev issued a presidential ban on public demonstrations in Moscow in advance of the April 2, 1991 price increases, reformers defied his order. More than 100,000 protesters took to the streets of Moscow to demonstrate their support for Yeltsin and for *glasnost'*. But the organizers of the protest were careful to avoid a potentially violent clash with the police and moved the demonstration away from Red Square and the Kremlin. The police and the military in turn showed restraint against protesters by not attempting to disperse the crowds even though they were defying Gorbachev's order. It is remarkable that with all the recent demonstrations—"pro-Yeltsin, anti-Gorbachev" and "pro-Gorbachev, anti-Yeltsin"—demonstrations that have drawn as many as half a million protesters—not a single act of violence or vandalism has been recorded.

If this record can be sustained, public demonstrations may fulfill the public's need to express their frustrations over the inevitable economic hardships that lie ahead on the road to a market economy. Reform movements often develop a momentum of their own. Of course, the danger is that public expectations will rise faster than actual changes. Gorbachev's economic reform program was introduced, together with *glasnost'* and democratization, with the recognition that economic reform would generate painful adjustments and hardships on Soviet citizens. However, it was hoped that the freer expression of opinions afforded by *glasnost'* and democratization would channel public frustrations in ways that would not threaten the progress of the reform itself. Gorbachev has also tried to dampen public expectations. During his first two years in office, one of the frequently recurring themes of his speeches was the phrase, "If you want to live better, you will have to work harder."

Perhaps the biggest impediment to Gorbachev's reform comes not from the conservatives, but from deep-seated Russian cultural values. At the outset of this book we noted the ambivalence in Russian political culture toward change and reform. Russia's political culture is reasserting itself with a stress on order (*poriadok*) and a pathologic fear of anarchy, a tendency to look to the leader for direction and to hold him accountable for one's own failures and hardships. André Smirnov, a Soviet filmmaker, comments, "The masses expect change to come from the top. They do not understand that real democracy, or real changes in the economy, must come from below. They resist the idea that we must change ourselves."[10]

Gorbachev's talk of a market economy worries many Soviet citizens. Not only do they fear the uncertainty of the market and the prospects of unemployment; they also fear the loss of the equality that has deep roots in communist and pre-Revolutionary Russian peasant life. Nikolai Shmelev, the reform-minded economist, notes, "Apathy, indifference, pilfering and lack of respect for honest work have become rampant as has aggressive envy of those who earn a lot, even if they earn it honestly."[11] Anatoli Sobchak, the mayor of Leningrad, observed: "Our people cannot endure seeing someone else earn more than they do. Our people want equal distribution of money, whether that means wealth or poverty. They are so jealous of other people that they want others to be worse off, if need be, to keep things equal. We have a story: God comes to a lucky Russian peasant one day and offers him any wish in the world. The peasant is excited and starts dreaming his fantasies. 'Just remember,' God says, 'whatever you choose, I will do twice as much for your neighbor as I do for you.' The peasant is stumped because he cannot bear to think of his neighbor being so much better off than he is, no matter how well off he becomes. Finally, he gets an idea and tells God, 'Strike out one of my eyes and take out both eyes of my neighbor.' Changing that psychology is the hardest part of our economic reform," Sobchak concluded. "That psychology of intolerance toward others who make more money, no matter why, no matter whether they work harder, longer or better—that psychology is blocking economic reform."[12]

Vladimir Pozner, the noted Soviet television commentator, observed: "People are looking for some external transformation to take place under *perestroika,* but *perestroika* is first of all internal. *Perestroika* has to happen in the mind. For it to work, people's outlooks have to change, and that happens as society changes. It's a push–pull, gradual process. It cannot be decreed."[13]

For millions of well-educated Soviet citizens living in urban areas, the psychological transition has already been made. Young adults have taken to the streets to demand better schools for their children, better health care and pensions for their elderly parents. Thousands of entrepreneurs have taken advantage of the new laws allowing private enterprise and have opened their own businesses. Yet for the elderly, recent changes appear to mock the cherished values of Stalinist society—egalitarianism, patriotism, and defense of socialism against a hostile and crassly commercial capitalist world. For rank-and-file workers and peasants, the promises of *perestroika* have remained largely empty promises. For these groups, the transition to a democratic, pluralistic society and to a market economy will be slow and difficult.

The fate of Gorbachev's reforms, and the fate of his government, rest on the ongoing struggle between opposing forces. It is not simply a struggle between liberals and conservatives, urban and rural, or white-collar and blue-collar; it is a struggle between contradictory forces deeply woven into the fabric of Russian and Soviet political culture: between the aspirations of the people for democracy and their abiding fear of anarchy, between their dreams of a prosperous market economy and their traditions of envy and reluctance to take risks, between their desire for greater freedoms and their intolerance of those who are different. The Soviet Union is today, and will remain, a society struggling with itself, a society struggling with change.

Notes

1. Cited in David K. Shipler, "Between Dictatorship and Anarchy," *The New Yorker*, 25 June 1990, p. 54.
2. For example, see Paul C. Nagel, *One Nation Indivisible: The Union in American Thought 1776–1861* (Oxford: Oxford University Press, 1964) and Paul D. Escott, *After Secession: Jefferson Davis and the Failure of Confederate Nationalism* (Baton Rouge: Louisiana State University Press, 1978).
3. For a thorough discussion of Shatalin's plan for the stabilization of the Soviet economy, see Marie Lavigne, *Financing the Transition: The Shatalin Plan and the Soviet Economy* (New York: Institute for East–West Security Studies, 1990).
4. Shipler, "Between Dictatorship and Anarchy," p. 48.
5. Ibid., p. 54.
6. Ibid.
7. Interview with Eduard Shevardnadze, "Prime Time," ABC, 21 February 1991.
8. *The State*, 5 April 1991, p. 4A.
9. See Leonard Silk, "Soviet Crisis Worse, Economists Declare," *New York Times*, 15 March 1990, p. C-16; and Steven Greenhouse, "Soviet Economist Says Shift to Free Market Is Inevitable," *New York Times*, 18 February 1991, p. 21–22.
10. Quoted in Hedrick Smith, "The Russian Character," *New York Times Magazine*, 28 October 1990, p. 62.
11. Ibid., p. 60.
12. Ibid., p. 71.
13. Ibid., p. 60.

Selected Bibliography

Aganbegyan, Abel. *Inside Perestroika: The Future of the Soviet Economy*. New York: Perennial Library, 1989.

Cohen, Stephen F. and Katrina vanden Heuvel, eds. *Voices of Glasnost*. New York: W. W. Norton, 1989.

Colton, Timothy J. *The Dilemma of Reform in the Soviet Union*. rev. ed., New York: Council on Foreign Relations, 1986.

Daniels, Robert V. *Is Russia Reformable? Change and Resistance from Stalin to Gorbachev*. Boulder: Westview Press, 1988.

Doder, Dusko, and Louise Branson. *Gorbachev: Heretic in the Kremlin*. New York: Viking, 1990.

Kemme, David M. "Economic Transition in Eastern Europe and the Soviet Union: Issues and Strategies," Occasional Paper no. 20, New York: Institute for East-West Security Studies, 1991.

Lane, David. *Soviet Society under Perestroika*. Boston: Unwin Hyman, 1990.

Lavigne, Marie. "Financing the Transition in the USSR: The Shatalin Plan and the Soviet Economy," Public Policy Paper no. 2, New York: Institute for East-West Security Studies, 1990.

Mlynar, Zdenek. *Can Gorbachev Change the Soviet Union?* Boulder: Westview Press, 1990.

Sakwa, Richard. *Gorbachev and His Reforms, 1985–1990.* Englewood Cliffs, N.J.: Prentice-Hall, 1990.

White, Stephen. *Gorbachev in Power.* Cambridge: Cambridge University Press, 1990.

Yeltsin, Boris. *Against the Grain.* New York: Summit Books, 1990.

Zacek, Jane Shapiro, ed. *The Gorbachev Generation: Issues in Soviet Domestic Policy.* New York: Paragon House, 1989.

Afterword

Of all the momentous events of the six and one-half years since Mikhail Gorbachev assumed the leadership of the USSR, none has transformed the Soviet political system more radically than the attempted ouster of Gorbachev on August 19, 1991. Why did the coup fail? It failed because an aroused public was willing to risk injury and even death to defend the country's fledgling democratic institutions. It failed because of the daring and energetic leadership displayed by Boris Yeltsin, Eduard Shevardnadze, Aleskandr Yakovlev, Gavriil Popov, Anatolii Sobchak, and others, who were able to rally support both at home and abroad. Finally, it failed because the leaders of the coup were either unwilling or unable to use brutal force to quell public resistance, capture Yeltsin and the other leading opponents of the regime, and disband the Russian parliament. The refusal of several military units, including the KGB's specially trained antiterrorist "Alpha Group," to storm the Russian parliament building was a crucial blow to the co-conspirators. Resistance to the coup within the military raised the specter of internecine warfare between various units of the Soviet army.

Although Gorbachev survived the coup and was returned to office, he is a president with little power or following. Gorbachev's only hope to restore his power was to throw his support decisively to the cause of radical democratic reform. But he was slow to do so. Upon returning to Moscow, he did not go immediately to the Russian parliament to thank Yeltsin and his supporters for engineering his release. Rather, he spent the night in his luxurious Kremlin apartment.

During a press conference the next day, Gorbachev was asked whether, in light of the attempted ouster, he would now favor outlawing the CPSU. Gorbachev responded that he still had faith in the Communist Party. "I will struggle until the very end for the renewal of this party," he said. "I remain a committed socialist to the depths of my soul."

Gorbachev's appointments of officials to fill vacancies following the collapse of the coup also indicated that he was out of touch with the mood of the public. All three appointments were remarkably conservative. General Mikhail Moiseev, head of the General Staff, was promoted to Minister of Defense, while Lt. General Leonid Shebarshin, head of foreign intelligence gathering, assumed the chairmanship of the KGB. Deputy Interior Minister Lt. General Vasily Trushin was promoted to fill Boris Pugo's post as Minister of Internal Affairs. None of these men openly opposed the coup, and it was subsequently disclosed that some of them actually collaborated in it.

Gorbachev appeared before a nationally televised session of the Russian parliament on Friday, August 23. The restive deputies interrupted his speech to demand an explanation for his appointments of the previous day. He was also accused of being out of touch, of not seeing a threat to his leadership, and failing to give full credit to Russian President Yeltsin and the Russian parliament for defeating the coup. Yeltsin, sharing the podium with Gorbachev, presented him with the confidential minutes of a cabinet meeting held during the attempted takeover, which clearly indicated that every member of Gorbachev's government except one either supported the coup or refused to speak out against it. Reluctantly, Gorbachev conceded that his entire government must resign.

Gorbachev is not in a strong position to bargain with Yeltsin. In fact. in the days following the collapse of the coup, it appeared that Yeltsin was dictating policy to the President. The appointments of acting Ministers of Defense and Internal Affairs, and Chairman of the KGB were reversed after two days, and new, more prodemocratic officials were named to replace them. Numerous other officials, including foreign minister Aleksandr Bessmertnykh and Chairman of the USSR Supreme Soviet Anatolii Lukyanov, were fired for supporting the coup. The Communist Party's offices in downtown Moscow were sealed, and all activities of the Party were suspended. The heads of the state-controlled media were fired, and six party newspapers were closed down.

Crowds gathered in front of the headquarters of the KGB, demanding the removal of a huge statue of Felix Dzerzinsky, the founder of Lenin's secret police agency. Elsewhere in the USSR, the euphoria of victory over the former system of communist party rule prompted citizens to storm communist party headquarters and hastened moves in many republics to secede from the USSR.

It is ironic that the attempted coup succeeded in doing what neither Gorbachev and the moderates nor what Yeltsin and the radical reformers could do—namely, discredit the conservative forces that blocked the way to the development of a democratic and pluralistic society. Having broken the hold of the former conservative and corrupt power structure, the work of forging a new political system will present even more serious challenges.

The Soviet Union is facing crises on every front. The economy is in a shambles. An estimated one-third of the 1991 crop will not be harvested, but will rot in the fields because of a lack of tractors, gasoline, railcars, and storage facilities. The threat of famine in parts of the country this winter are very real. Even the most ambitious economic reform programs, as those offered by Stanislav Shatalin and Grigori Yavlinsky, do not anticipate economic recovery for at least two years.

The Union Treaty, which incorporated a carefully worked out arrangement for sharing power between nine of the republics and Moscow, will have to be renegotiated in an atmosphere of heightened ethnic demands. The Baltic republics of Moldavia, Georgia, and Armenia now appear to be proceeding quickly toward independence. The Ukraine and Belorussia have also indicated their desire to secede from the USSR. Working together, Gorbachev and Yeltsin must try to slow the process of fragmentation. What will emerge is likely to be a loose confederation of the three Slavic republics—Russia, the Ukraine, and Belorussia—in which most powers reside with the constituent republics. The five Moslem republics of Central Asia may opt to affiliate with such a Slavic union for reasons of economic self-interest, but the forces of ethnic nationalism are also strong in the region and may result in the formation of a huge Moslem state on Russia's southern border.

In this time of political, economic, and ethnic crisis it is important that the Soviet Union have leaders that the people trust and are willing to follow. It is likely that Yeltsin and the reformers will demand that new elections be scheduled for the President and the USSR Supreme Soviet. Gorbachev, whose popularity was low even before the attempted coup d'état, is likely to be faced with a difficult choice: either run for office and face the real potential for defeat at the hands of a reform candidate such as Shevardnadze, Yakovlev, or Sobchak, or step down altogether. Either prospect must be humiliating for Gorbachev, who started the very processes that now threaten his tenure as President. But events seem to have overwhelmed Gorbachev. The reform process has developed a momentum of its own that has left Gorbachev behind. For all his attempts to reform the Soviet political system, he is still the product of that system, and he cannot seem to navigate in the new political landscape before him.

Boris Yeltsin, who has emerged from the coup stronger than ever before, will probably prefer not to run for the USSR Presidency, recognizing that real power will, in the future, rest with the republics. While Yeltsin is the most popular figure today in the USSR, there are also concerns that he is an egotist and demagogue. His public bullying of Gorbachev before the Russian parliament has raised doubts in the minds of many observers. On the other hand, there are many other powerful and popular figures among the supporters of democracy in the USSR that can moderate Yeltsin.

More than at any time in the history of Russia, the future course of the country depends on the people. For the first time, they have stood up to tyranny and won. Now the challenge facing them is to forgo the natural urge to wage a bloody campaign against the former power structure, and instead to build democratic institutions that can provide leadership, and also provide a check on potential abuses of power. Another challenge is to not forsake concepts of rule of law, even while they search out enemies of the new regime. Yet another challenge is to learn tolerance for people of different ethnic and religious backgrounds and political persuasions. If they succeed in these challenges, they will have demonstrated that the struggle for change, the struggle with their own long history of tyranny and dogmatism, has been won.

Appendix A

The Constitution (Fundamental Law) of the USSR*

The Great October Socialist Revolution, made by the workers and peasants of Russia under the leadership of the Communist Party headed by Lenin, overthrew capitalist and landowner rule, broke the fetters of oppression, established the dictatorship of the proletariat, and created the Soviet state, a new type of state, the basic instrument for defending the gains of the revolution and for building socialism and communism. Humanity thereby began the epoch-making turn from capitalism to socialism.

After achieving victory in the Civil War and repulsing imperialist intervention, the Soviet government carried through far-reaching social and economic transformations and put an end once and for all to exploitation of man by man, antagonisms between classes, and strife between nationalities. The unification of the Soviet Republics in the Union of Soviet Socialist Republics multiplied the forces and opportunities of the peoples of the country in the building of socialism. Social ownership of the means of production and genuine democracy for the working masses were established. For the first time in the history of humanity a socialist society was created.

The strength of socialism was vividly demonstrated by the immortal feat of the Soviet people and their Armed Forces in achieving their historic victory in the Great Patriotic War. This victory consolidated the influence and international standing of the Soviet Union and created new opportunities for growth of the forces of socialism, national liberation, democracy, and peace throughout the world.

Continuing their creative endeavors, the working people of the Soviet Union have ensured rapid, comprehensive development of the country and steady improvement of the socialist system. They have consolidated the alliance of the working class, collective-farm peasantry, and people's intelligentsia and the friendship between the nations and nationalities of the USSR. The sociopolitical and ideological unity of Soviet society, in which the working class is the leading force, has been achieved. The aims of the dictatorship of the proletariat having been fulfilled, the Soviet state has become a state of the whole people.

In the USSR a developed socialist society has been built. At this stage, when socialism is developing on its own foundations, the creative forces of the new system and the advantages of the socialist way of life are becoming increasingly evident, and the working people are more and more widely enjoying the fruits of their great revolutionary gains.

It is a society in which powerful productive forces and a progressive science and culture have been created, in which the well-being of the people is constantly rising,

*This version of the Constitution reflects changes and amendments as of August 1, 1991.

348

and more and more favorable conditions are being provided for the all-round development of the individual.

It is a society of mature socialist social relations, in which, on the basis of the drawing together of all classes and social strata and the juridical and factual equality of all its nations and nationalities and their fraternal cooperation, a new historical community of people has been formed—the Soviet people.

It is a society of high organizational capacity, ideological commitment, and consciousness of the working people, who are patriots and internationalists.

It is a society in which the law of life is the concern of all for the good of each and concern of each for the good of all.

It is a society of true democracy, the political system of which ensures effective management of all public affairs, ever more active participation of the working people in running the state, and the combining of citizens' real rights and freedoms with their obligation and responsibility to society.

Developed socialist society is a logical, necessary stage on the road to communism.

The supreme goal of the Soviet state is the building of a classless communist society in which there will be public, communist self-government. The main aims of the people's socialist state are: to lay the material and technical foundation of communism, to perfect socialist social relations and transform them into communist relations, to mold the citizen of communist society, to raise the people's living and cultural standards, to safeguard the country's security, and to further the consolidation of peace and development of international cooperation.

The Soviet people, guided by the ideas of scientific communism and true to their revolutionary traditions, relying on the great social, economic, and political gains of socialism, striving for the further development of social democracy, taking into account the international position of the USSR as part of the world system of socialism, and conscious of their internationalist responsibility, preserving continuity of the ideas and principles of the first Soviet Constitution of 1918, the 1924 Constitution of the USSR and the 1936 Constitution of the USSR, hereby affirm the principles of the social structure and policy of the USSR, and define the rights, freedoms, and obligations of citizens, and the principles of the organization of the socialist state of the whole people, and its aims, and proclaim these in this Constitution.

I. PRINCIPLES OF THE SOCIAL STRUCTURE AND POLICY OF THE USSR

Chapter 1   The Political System

Article 1. The Union of Soviet Socialist Republics is a socialist state of the whole people, expressing the will and interests of the workers, peasants, and intelligentsia, the working people of all the nations and nationalities of the country.

Article 2. All power in the USSR belongs to the people.

The people exercise state power through Soviets of People's Deputies, which constitute the political foundation of the USSR.

All other state bodies are under the control of, and accountable to, the Soviets of People's Deputies.

Article 3. The Soviet state is organized and functions on the principle of democratic centralism, namely the election of all bodies of state authority from the lowest to the highest, their accountability to the people, and the obligation of lower bodies to observe the decisions of higher ones. Democratic centralism combines central leadership with local initiative and creative activity and with the responsibility of each state body and official for the work entrusted to them.

Article 4. The Soviet state and all its bodies function on the basis of socialist legality, ensure the maintenance of law and order, and safeguard the interests of society and the rights and freedoms of citizens.

State organizations, social organizations and officials shall observe the Constitution of the USSR and Soviet laws.

Article 5. Major matters of state shall be submitted to nationwide discussion and put to a popular vote (referendum).

Article 6. The Communist Party of the Soviet Union and other political parties, as well as trade unions, youth and other social organizations, and mass movements, participate in the formulation of the policy of the Soviet state and in the administration of state and social affairs through their representatives elected to the Soviets of People's Deputies and in other ways.

Article 7. All political parties, social organizations, and mass movements, in the exercise of the functions stipulated in their programs and statutes, operate within the framework of the Constitution and Soviet laws.

The formation and operation of parties, organizations, and movements having the aim of forcibly changing the Soviet constitutional system and the integrity of the socialist state, undermining its security, or kindling social, national, or religious strife are not permitted.

Article 8. Labor collectives take part in discussing and deciding state and public affairs, in planning production and social development, in training and placing personnel, and in discussing and deciding matters pertaining to the management of enterprises and institutions, the improvement of working and living conditions, and the use of funds allocated both for developing production and for social and cultural purposes and financial incentives.

Labor collectives promote socialist competition, the spread of progressive methods of work, and the strengthening of discipline, educate their members in the spirit of communist morality, and strive to enhance their political consciousness and raise their cultural level and skills and qualifications.

Article 9. The principal direction of the developing of the political system of Soviet society is the extension of socialist democracy, namely ever broader participation of citizens in managing the affairs of society and the state, continuous improvement of the machinery of state, heightening of the activity of public organizations, strengthening of the system of people's control, consolidation of the legal foundations of the functioning of the state and of public life, greater openness and publicity, and constant responsiveness to public opinion.

Chapter 2 The Economic System

Article 10. The foundation of the economic system of the USSR is socialist ownership of the means of production in the form of state property (belonging to all the people), and collective farm and cooperative property.

The state creates the conditions necessary for the development of diverse forms of ownership and ensures equal protection for them.

The land, its mineral resources, water resources, and the plant and animal world in their natural state are the inalienable property of the peoples inhabiting a given territory, are under the jurisdiction of the Soviets of People's Deputies, and are granted to citizens, enterprises, institutions, and organizations for their utilization.

Article 11. A USSR citizen's property is his personal property and is used to meet material and spiritual needs and carry out autonomous economic activity and other activity that is not banned by law.

Any property for consumption and production purposes acquired out of earned income and on other lawful grounds may be under the ownership of a citizen, with the exception of those forms of property whose acquisition by citizens for their ownership is not permitted.

In order to pursue peasant and personal subsidiary farming and for other purposes stipulated by law, citizens are entitled to hold land plots for their use in perpetuity.

he right of inheritance of a citizen's property is acknowledged and protected by law.

Article 12. Collective property is the property of leaseholding enterprises, collective enterprises, cooperatives, joint-stock companies, economic organizations, and other associations. Collective property is created through the transformation, by methods stipulated by law, of state property and through the voluntary amalgamation of the property of citizens and organizations.

Article 13. State property is all-union property, the property of union republics, and the property of autonomous republics, autonomous regions, autonomous districts, territories, and other administrative-territorial units (communal property).

Article 14. The source of the growth of social wealth and of the well-being of the people, and of each individual, is the labor, free from exploitation, of Soviet people.

The state exercises control over the measure of labor and of consumption in accordance with the principle of socialism: "From each according to his ability, to each according to his work." It fixes the rate of taxation on taxable income.

Socially useful work and its results determine a person's status in society. By combining material and moral incentives and encouraging innovation and a creative attitude to work, the State helps transform labor into the prime vital need of every Soviet citizen.

Article 15. The supreme goal of social production under socialism is the fullest possible satisfaction of the people's growing material, and cultural and intellectual requirements.

Relying on the creative initiative of the working people, socialist emulation, and scientific and technological progress, and by improving the forms and methods of economic management, the state ensures the growth of the productivity of labor, raising of the efficiency of production and of the quality of work, and dynamic, planned, proportionate development of the economy.

Article 16. The economy of the USSR is an integral economic complex comprising all the elements of social production, distribution, and exchange on its territory.

The economy is managed on the basis of state plans for economic and social development, with due account of sectoral and territorial principles, and by combining centralized direction with the managerial independence and initiative of enterprises, associations, and other organizations for which active use is made of management accounting, profit, cost, and other economic levers and incentives.

Article 17. In the USSR, the law permits individual labor in handicrafts, farming, the provision of services for the public, and other forms of activity based exclusively on the personal work of individual citizens and members of their families. The state makes regulations for such work to ensure that it serves the interests of society.

Article 18. In the interests of the present and future generations, the necessary steps are taken in the USSR to protect and make scientific, rational use of the land and its mineral and water resources, and plants and animals, to preserve the purity of the air and water, ensure reproduction of natural wealth, and improve the human environment.

Chapter 3 Social Development and Culture

Article 19. The social basis of the USSR is the unbreakable alliance of the workers, peasants, and intelligentsia.

The state helps enhance the social homogeneity of society, namely the elimination of class differences and of the essential distinctions between town and country and between mental and physical labor, and the comprehensive development and drawing together of all the nations and nationalities of the USSR.

Article 20. In accordance with the communist ideal—"The free development of each is the condition of the free development of all"—the state pursues the aim of giving citizens more and more real opportunities to apply their creative energies, abilities, and talents and to develop their personalities in every way.

Article 21. The state concerns itself with improving working conditions, safety and labor protection, and the scientific organization of work, and with reducing and ultimately eliminating all arduous physical labor through comprehensive mechanization and automation of production processes in all branches of the economy.

Article 22. A program is being consistently implemented in the USSR to convert agricultural work into a variety of industrial work, to extend the network of educational, cultural, and medical institutions, and of trade, public catering, service, and public utility facilities in rural localities, and transform hamlets and villages into well-planned and well-appointed settlements.

Article 23. The state pursues a consistent policy of raising people's pay levels and real incomes through increase in productivity.

In order to satisfy the needs of the Soviet people more fully, social consumption funds are created. The state, with the broad participation of public organizations and work collectives, ensures the growth and just distribution of these funds.

Article 24. In the USSR, state systems of health protection, social security, trade and public catering, communal services and amenities, and public utilities operate and are being extended.

The state encourages cooperatives and other public organizations to provide all types of services for the population. It encourages the development of mass physical culture and sport.

Article 25. In the USSR there is a uniform system of public education, which is being constantly improved, that provides general education and vocational training for citizens, serves the communist educational and intellectual and physical development of the youth, and trains them for work and social activity.

Article 26. In accordance with society's needs, the state provides for the planned development of science and the training of scientific personnel and organizes introduction of the results of research into the economy and other spheres of life.

Article 27. The state concerns itself with protecting, augmenting, and making extensive use of society's cultural wealth for the moral and aesthetic education of the Soviet people, for raising their cultural level.

In the USSR, development of the professional, amateur, and folk arts is encouraged in every way.

Chapter 4 Foreign Policy

Article 28. The USSR steadfastly pursues a Leninist policy of peace and stands for the strengthening of the security of nations and broad international cooperation.

The foreign policy of the USSR is aimed at ensuring international conditions favorable for building communism in the USSR, safeguarding the state interests of the Soviet Union, consolidating the positions of world socialism, supporting the struggle of peoples for national liberation and social progress, preventing wars of aggression, achieving universal and complete disarmament, and consistently implementing the principle of the peaceful coexistence of states with different social systems.

In the USSR, war propaganda is banned.

Article 29. The USSR's relations with other states are based on observance of the following principles: sovereign equality; mutual renunciation of the use or threat of force; inviolability of frontiers; territorial integrity of states; peaceful settlement of disputes; noninterference in internal affairs; respect for human rights and fundamental freedoms; the equal rights of peoples and their right to decide their own destiny; cooperation among states; and fulfillment in good faith of obligations arising from the generally recognized principles and rules of international law, and from the international treaties signed by the USSR.

Article 30. The USSR, as part of the world system of socialism and of the socialist community, promotes and strengthens friendship, cooperation, and comradely mutual assistance with other socialist countries on the basis of the principle of socialist internationalism, and takes an active part in socialist economic integration and the socialist international division of labor.

Chapter 5   Defense of the Socialist Motherland

Article 31. Defense of the Socialist Motherland is one of the most important functions of the state and is the concern of the whole people.

In order to defend the gains of socialism, the peaceful labor of the Soviet people, and the sovereignty and territorial integrity of the state, the USSR maintains Armed Forces and has instituted universal military service.

The duty of the Armed Forces of the USSR to the people is to provide reliable defense of the Socialist Motherland and to be in constant combat readiness, guaranteeing that any aggressor is instantly repulsed.

Article 32. The state ensures the security and defense capability of the country, and supplies the Armed Forces of the USSR with everything necessary for that purpose.

The duties of state bodies, public organizations, officials, and citizens in regard to safeguarding the country's security and strengthening its defense capacity are defined by the legislation of the USSR.

II. THE STATE AND THE INDIVIDUAL

Chapter 6   Citizenship of the USSR Equality of Citizens' Rights

Article 33. Uniform federal citizenship is established for the USSR. Every citizen of a Union Republic is a citizen of the USSR.

The grounds and procedures for acquiring or forfeiting Soviet citizenship are defined by the Law on Citizenship of the USSR.

When abroad, citizens of the USSR enjoy the protection and assistance of the Soviet state.

Article 34. Citizens of the USSR are equal before the law, without distinction of origin, social or property status, race or nationality, sex, education, language, attitude to religion, type and nature of occupation, domicile, or other status.

The equal rights of citizens of the USSR are guaranteed in all fields of economic, political, social, and cultural life. Privileges for separate categories of citizens are to be established only on the basis of the law. No one in the USSR may enjoy unlawful privileges.

Article 35. Women and men have equal rights in the USSR.

Exercise of these rights is ensured by according women equal access with men to education and vocational and professional training, equal opportunities for employment, remuneration, and promotion, and in social and political and cultural activity, and by special labor and health protection measures for women; by providing conditions enabling mothers to work; by legal protection and material and moral support for mothers and children, including paid leaves and other benefits for expectant mothers and mothers, and the gradual reduction of working time for mothers with small children.

Article 36. Citizens of the USSR of different races and nationalities have equal rights.

Exercise of these rights is ensured by a policy of all-round development and drawing together of all the nations and nationalities of the USSR, by educating citizens in the spirit of Soviet patriotism and socialist internationalism, and by the possibility to use their native language and the languages of other peoples of the USSR.

Direct or indirect limitation of the rights of citizens or establishment of direct or indirect privileges on grounds of race or nationality, and any advocacy of racial or national exclusiveness, hostility, or contempt are punishable by law.

Article 37. Citizens of other countries and stateless persons in the USSR are guaranteed the rights and freedoms provided by law, including the right to apply to a court and other state bodies for the protection of their personal, property, family, and other rights.

Citizens of other countries and stateless persons, when in the USSR, are obliged to respect the Constitution of the USSR and observe Soviet laws.

Article 38. The USSR grants the right of asylum to foreigners persecuted for defending the interests of the working people and the cause of peace, or for participation in the revolutionary and national-liberation movement, or for progressive social and political, scientific, or other creative activity.

Chapter 7 The Basic Rights, Freedoms, and Duties of Citizens of the USSR

Article 39. Citizens of the USSR enjoy in full the social, economic, political and personal rights and freedoms proclaimed and guaranteed by the Constitution of the USSR and by Soviet laws. The socialist system ensures enlargement of the rights and freedoms of citizens and continuous improvement of their living standards as social, economic, and cultural development programs are fulfilled.

Enjoyment by citizens of their rights and freedoms must not be to the detriment of the interests of society or the State or infringe the rights of other citizens.

Article 40. Citizens of the USSR have the right to work (that is, to guaranteed employment and pay in accordance with the quantity and quality of their work, although not below the state-established minimum), including the right to choose their trade or profession, type of job, and work in accordance with their inclinations, abilities, training, and education, taking into account the needs of society.

This right is ensured by the socialist economic system, steady growth of the productive forces, free vocational and professional training, improvement of skills, training in new trades or professions, and development of the systems of vocational guidance and job placement.

Article 41. Citizens of the USSR have the right to rest and leisure.

This rights is ensured by the establishment of a working week not exceeding forty-one hours for workers and other employees, a shorter working day in a number of trades and industries, and shorter hours for night work; by the provision of paid annual holidays, weekly days of rest, extension of the network of cultural, educational, and health-building institutions, and the development of a mass scale of sport, physical culture, camping and tourism; by the provision of neighborhood recreational facilities, and of other opportunities for rational use of free time.

The length of collective-farmers' working and leisure time is established by their collective farms.

Article 42. Citizens of the USSR have the right to health protection.

This right is ensured by free, qualified medical care provided by state health institutions; by extension of the network of therapeutic and health-building institutions; by the development and improvement of safety and hygiene in industry; by carrying out broad prophylactic measures; by measures to improve the environment; by special care for the health of youth, including prohibition of child labor, excluding the work done by children as part of the school curriculum; and by developing research to prevent and reduce the incidence of disease and ensure citizens a long and active life.

Article 43. Citizens of the USSR have the right to maintenance in old age, in sickness, and in the event of complete or partial disability or loss of the breadwinner.

This right is guaranteed by social insurance of workers and other employees and collective farmers; by allowances for temporary disability; by the provision by the State or by collective farms of retirement pensions, disability pensions, and pensions for loss of the breadwinner; by providing employment for the partially disabled; by care for the elderly and the disabled; and by other forms of social security.

Article 44. Citizens of the USSR have the right to housing.

This right is ensured by the development and upkeep of state and socially owned housing; by assistance for cooperative and individual housing construction; by fair distribution, under public control, of the housing that becomes available through fulfillment of the program of building well-appointed dwellings; and by low rents and low charges for utility services. Citizens of the USSR shall take good care of the housing allocated to them.

Article 45. Citizens of the USSR have the right to education.

This right is ensured by the free provision of all forms of education, by the institution of universal, compulsory secondary education, and the broad development of vocational, specialized secondary, and higher education, in which instruction is oriented toward practical activity and production; by the development of extramural, correspondence, and evening courses; by the provision of state scholarships and grants and privileges for students; by the free issue of school textbooks; by the opportunity to attend a school where teaching is in the native language; and by the provision of facilities for self-education.

Article 46. Citizens of the USSR have the right to enjoy cultural benefits.

This right is ensured by broad access to the cultural treasures of their own land and of the world that are preserved in state and other public collections; by the development and fair distribution of cultural and educational institutions throughout the country; by the development of television and radio broadcasting and the publishing of books, newspapers, and periodicals, and by the extension of the free library service; and by the expansion of cultural exchanges with other countries.

Article 47. Citizens of the USSR, in accordance with the aims of building communism, are guaranteed freedom of scientific, technical, and artistic work. This freedom is ensured by broadening scientific research, encouraging invention and innovation, and developing literature and the arts. The State provides the necessary material conditions for this and support for voluntary societies and unions of workers in the arts, organizes introduction of inventions and innovations in production and other spheres of activity.

The rights of authors, inventors, and innovators are protected by the State.

Article 48. Citizens of the USSR have the right to take part in the management and administration of state and public affairs and in the discussion and adoption of laws and measures of All-Union and local significance.

This right is ensured by the opportunity to vote and to be elected to Soviets of People's Deputies and other elective state bodies, and to take part in nationwide discussions and referendums, in people's control, in the work of state bodies, public organizations, and local community groups, and in meetings at places of work or residence.

Article 49. Every citizen of the USSR has the right to submit proposals to state bodies and public organizations for improving their activity, and to criticize shortcomings in their work.

Officials are obliged, within established time limits, to examine citizens' proposals and requests, to reply to them, and to take appropriate action.

Persecution for criticism is prohibited. Persons guilty of such persecution shall be called to account.

Article 50. In accordance with the interests of the people and in order to strengthen and develop the socialist system, citizens of the USSR are guaranteed freedom of speech, of the press, and of assembly, meetings, street processions, and demonstrations.

Exercise of these political freedoms is ensured by putting public buildings, streets, and squares at the disposal of the working people and their organizations, by broad dissemination of information; and by the opportunity to use the press, television, and radio.

Article 51. USSR citizens have the right to form political parties and social organizations and to participate in mass movements that promote the development of political activeness and independent activity and the satisfaction of their various interests.

Social organizations are guaranteed conditions for the successful performance of their statutory tasks.

Article 52. Citizens of the USSR are guaranteed freedom of conscience, that is, the right to profess or not to profess any religion, and to conduct religious worship or atheistic propaganda. Incitement of hostility or hatred on religious grounds is prohibited.

In the USSR, the church is separated from the State, and the school from the church.

Article 53. The family enjoys the protection of the state.

Marriage is based on the free consent of the woman and the man; the spouses are completely equal in their family relations.

The state helps the family by providing and developing a broad system of child care institutions, by organizing and improving communal services and public catering, by paying grants on the birth of a child, by providing children's allowances and benefits for large families, and other forms of family allowances and assistance.

Article 54. Citizens of the USSR are guaranteed inviolability of the person. No one may be arrested except by a court decision or on the warrant of a procurator.

Article 55. Citizens of the USSR are guaranteed inviolability of the home. No one may, without lawful grounds, enter a home against the will of those residing in it.

Article 56. The privacy of citizens, and of their correspondence, telephone conversations, and telegraphic communications is protected by law.

Article 57. Respect for the individual and protection of the rights and freedoms of citizens are the duty of all state bodies, public organizations, and officials.

Citizens of the USSR have the right to protection by the courts against encroachments on their honor and reputation, life and health, and personal freedom and property.

Article 58. Citizens of the USSR have the right to lodge a complaint against the actions of officials, state bodies, and public bodies. Complaints shall be examined according to the procedure and within the time limit established by law.

Actions by officials that contravene the law or exceed their powers and infringe the rights of citizens may be appealed against in a court in the manner prescribed by law.

Citizens of the USSR have the right to compensation for damage resulting from unlawful actions by state organizations and public organizations, or by officials in the performance of their duties.

Article 59. The exercise of rights and freedoms is inseparable from the performance by the citizens of their duties.

Citizens of the USSR are obliged to observe the Constitution of the USSR and Soviet laws, comply with the rules of the socialist community, and uphold the honor and dignity of Soviet citizenship.

Article 60. It is the duty of, and a matter of honor for, every able-bodied citizen of the USSR to work conscientiously in his chosen, socially useful occupation and strictly to observe labor discipline. Evasion of socially useful work is incompatible with the principles of socialist society.

Article 61. Citizens of the USSR are obliged to preserve and protect socialist property. It is the duty of a citizen of the USSR to combat misappropriation and squandering of state and socially owned property and to make thrifty use of the people's wealth.

Persons encroaching in any way on socialist property shall be punished according to the law.

Article 62. Citizens of the USSR are obliged to safeguard the interests of the Soviet state and to enhance its power and prestige.

Defense of the Socialist Motherland is the sacred duty of every citizen of the USSR.

Betrayal of the Motherland is the gravest of crimes against the people.

Article 63. Military service in the ranks of the Armed Forces of the USSR is an honorable duty of Soviet citizens.

Article 64. It is the duty of every citizen of the USSR to respect the national dignity of other citizens and to strengthen friendship of the nations and nationalities of the multinational Soviet state.

Article 65. A citizen of the USSR is obliged to respect the rights and lawful interests of other persons, to be uncompromising toward antisocial behavior, and to help maintain public order.

Article 66. Citizens of the USSR are obliged to concern themselves with the upbringing of children, to train them for socially useful work, and to raise them as worthy members of socialist society. Children are obliged to care for their parents and help them.

Article 67. Citizens of the USSR are obliged to protect nature and conserve its riches.

Article 68. Concern for the preservation of historical monuments and other cultural values is a duty and obligation of citizens of the USSR.

Article 69. It is the internationalist duty of citizens of the USSR to promote friendship and cooperation with peoples and other lands and help maintain and strengthen world peace.

III. THE NATIONAL-STATE STRUCTURE OF THE USSR

Chapter 8   The USSR—A Federal State

Article 70. The Union Soviet Socialist Republics is an integral, federal, multinational state formed on the principle of socialist federalism as a result of the free self-determination of nations and the voluntary association of equal Soviet Socialist Republics.

The USSR embodies the state unity of the Soviet people and draws all its nations and nationalities together for the purpose of jointly building communism.

Article 71. The Union of Soviet Socialist Republics unites:

- the Russian Soviet Federative Socialist Republic,
- the Ukrainian Soviet Socialist Republic,
- the Belorussian Soviet Socialist Republic,
- the Uzbek Soviet Socialist Republic,
- the Kazakh Soviet Socialist Republic,
- the Georgian Soviet Socialist Republic,
- the Azerbaidzhan Soviet Socialist Republic,
- the Lithuanian Soviet Socialist Republic,
- the Moldavian Soviet Socialist Republic,
- the Latvian Soviet Socialist Republic,
- the Kirghiz Soviet Socialist Republic,
- the Tajik Soviet Socialist Republic,
- the Armenian Soviet Socialist Republic,
- the Turkmen Soviet Socialist Republic, and
- the Estonian Soviet Socialist Republic.

Article 72. Each Union Republic shall retain the right freely to secede from the USSR.

Article 73. The jurisdiction of the Union of Soviet Socialist Republics, as represented by its highest bodies of state authority and administration, shall cover:

1. the admission of new republics to the USSR; endorsement of the formation of new autonomous republics and autonomous regions within Union Republics;
2. determination of the state boundaries of the USSR and approval of changes in the boundaries between Union Republics;
3. establishment of the general principles for the organization and functioning of republican and local bodies of state authority and administration;
4. the ensurance of uniformity of legislative norms throughout the USSR and establishment of the fundamentals of the legislation of the Union of Soviet Socialist Republics and Union Republics;
5. pursuance of a uniform social and economic policy; direction of the country's economy; determination of the main lines of scientific and technological progress and the general measures for rational exploitation and conservation of natural resources; the drafting and approval of state plans for the economic and social development of the USSR, and endorsement of reports on their fulfillment;
6. the drafting and approval of the consolidated Budget of the USSR and endorsement of the report on its execution; management of a single monetary and credit system; determination of the taxes and revenues forming the Budget of the USSR; and the formulation of prices and wages policy;
7. direction of the sectors of the economy and of enterprises and amalgamations under Union jurisdiction, and general direction of industries under Union-Republican jurisdiction;
8. issues of war and peace, defense of the sovereignty of the USSR and safe-

guarding of its frontiers and territory, and organization of defense, direction of the Armed Forces of the USSR;

9. state security;
10. representation of the USSR in international relations; the USSR's relations with other states and with international organizations; establishment of the general procedure for, and coordination of, the relations of Union Republics with other states and with international organizations; foreign trade and other forms of external economic activity on the basis of state monopoly;
11. control over observance of the Constitution of the USSR, and insurance of conformity of the Constitutions of Union Republics to the Constitution of the USSR;
12. and settlement of other matters of All-Union importance.

Article 74. The laws of the USSR shall have the same force in all Union Republics. In the event of a discrepancy between a Union Republic law and an All-Union law, the law of the USSR shall prevail.

Article 75. The territory of the Union of Soviet Socialist Republics is a single entity and comprises the territories of the Union Republics.

The sovereignty of the USSR extends throughout its territory.

Chapter 9   The Union Soviet Socialist Republic

Article 76. A Union Republic is a sovereign Soviet socialist state that has united with other Soviet Republics in the Union of Soviet Socialist Republics.

Outside the spheres listed in Article 73 of the Constitution of the USSR, a Union Republic exercises independent authority on its territory.

A Union Republic shall have its own Constitution conforming to the Constitution of the USSR with the specific features of the Republic being taken into account.

Article 77. A Union Republic participates in the resolution of questions coming under the jurisdiction of the USSR at the Congress of USSR People's Deputies, the USSR Supreme Soviet, the USSR Supreme Soviet Presidium, the Council of the Federation, the USSR Cabinet of Ministers, and other organs of the USSR.

A Union Republic shall ensure comprehensive economic and social development on its territory, facilitate exercise of the powers of the USSR on its territory, and implement the decisions of the highest bodies of state authority and administration of the USSR.

In matters that come within its jurisdiction, a Union Republic shall coordinate and control the activity of enterprises, institutions, and organizations subordinate to the Union.

Article 78. The territory of a Union Republic may not be altered without its consent. The boundaries between Union Republics may be altered by mutual agreement of the Republics concerned, subject to ratification by the Union of Soviet Socialist Republics.

Article 79. A Union Republic shall determine its division into territories, regions, areas, and districts and decide other matters relating to its administrative and territorial structure.

Article 80. A Union Republic has the right to enter into relations with other states, conclude treaties with them, exchange diplomatic and consular representatives, and take part in the work of international organizations.

Article 81. The sovereign rights of Union Republics shall be safeguarded by the USSR.

Chapter 10   The Autonomous Soviet Socialist Republic

Article 82. An Autonomous Republic is a constituent part of a Union Republic. In spheres not within the jurisdiction of the Union of Soviet Socialist Republics and the Union Republic, an Autonomous Republic shall deal independently with matters within its jurisdiction.

An Autonomous Republic shall have its own Constitution conforming to the Constitutions of the USSR and the Union Republic with the specific features of the Autonomous Republic being taken into account.

Article 83. An Autonomous Republic takes part in decision making through the highest bodies of state authority and administration of the USSR and of the Union Republic respectively, in matters that come within the jurisdiction of the USSR and the Union Republic.

An Autonomous Republic shall ensure comprehensive economic and social development on its territory, facilitate exercise of the powers of the USSR and the Union Republic on its territory, and implement decisions of the highest bodies of state authority and administration of the USSR and the Union Republic.

In matters within its jurisdiction, an Autonomous Republic shall coordinate and control the activity of enterprises, institutions, and organizations subordinate to the Union or the Union Republic.

Article 84. The territory of an Autonomous Republic may not be altered without its consent.

Article 85. The Russian Soviet Federative Socialist Republic includes the Bashkir, Buryat, Daghestan, Kabardin-Balkar, Kalmyk, Karelian, Komi, Mari, Mordovian, North Ossetian, Tatar, Tuva, Udmurt, Chechen-Ingush, Chuvash, and Yakut Autonomous Soviet Socialist Republics.

The Uzbek Soviet Socialist Republic includes the Kara-Kalpak Autonomous Soviet Socialist Republic.

The Georgian Soviet Socialist Republic includes the Abkhasian and Adzhar Autonomous Soviet Socialist Republics.

The Azerbaidzhan Soviet Socialist Republic includes the Nakhichevan Autonomous Soviet Socialist Republic.

Chapter 11   The Autonomous Region and Autonomous Area

Article 86. An Autonomous Region is a constituent part of a Union Republic or Territory. The Law on an Autonomous Region, upon submission by the Soviet of People's Deputies of the Autonomous Region concerned, shall be adopted by the Supreme Soviet of the Union Republic.

Article 87. The Russian Soviet Federative Socialist Republic includes the Adygei, Gorno-Altai, Jewish, Karachai-Circassian, and Khakass Autonomous Regions.

The Georgian Soviet Socialist Republic includes the South Ossetian Autonomous Region.

The Azerbaidzhan Soviet Socialist Republic includes the Nagorno-Karabakh Autonomous Region.

The Tajik Soviet Socialist Republic includes the Gorno-Badakhshan Autonomous Region.

Article 88. An Autonomous Area is a constituent part of a Territory or Region. The Law of an Autonomous Area shall be adopted by the Supreme Soviet of the Union Republic concerned.

IV. SOVIETS OF PEOPLE'S DEPUTIES AND ELECTORAL PROCEDURE

Chapter 12   The System of Soviets of People's Deputies and the Principles of their Work

Article 89. The Soviets of People's Deputies—Congress of USSR People's Deputies and USSR Supreme Soviet, Congresses of People's Deputies and Supreme Soviets of union and autonomous republics, and Soviets of People's Deputies of autonomous oblasts and of krais, oblasts, and other administrative-territorial units—shall constitute a single system of bodies of state authority.

Article 90. The term of office of soviets of people's deputies is 5 years.

Elections of people's deputies are to be set no later than 4 months prior to the expiry of the term of office of the corresponding organs of state power.

Elections of USSR people's deputies shall be called not later than 4 months before the term of the Congress of USSR People's Deputies expires.

The timing and procedure for calling elections of people's deputies of union and autonomous republics and to local soviets of people's deputies shall be determined by the laws of union and autonomous republics.

Article 91. The most important questions of unionwide, republican, and local significance are resolved at sessions of the congresses of people's deputies and sessions of supreme soviets and local soviets of people's deputies or are put to referendums by them.

Union Republic and autonomous republic Supreme Soviets are elected directly by the voters, or, in those republics in which provision is made for the creation of congresses, by the Congress of People's Deputies.

Soviets of People's Deputies shall form committees and permanent commissions and shall create executive and administrative organs and other organs accountable to them.

Officials elected or appointed by Soviets of People's Deputies, with the exception of judges, cannot hold office for more than two consecutive terms.

Any official can be released from his post early if he fails to perform his official duties properly.

Article 92. The Soviets of People's Deputies form organs of people's control, combining state control with social control by working people at enterprises, institutions, and organizations.

People's control bodies shall check on the fulfillment of state plans and assignments, combat breaches of state discipline, localistic tendencies, narrow departmental attitudes, mismanagement, extravagance and waste, red tape and bureaucracy, and help improve the working of the state machinery.

Article 93. The Soviets of People's Deputies, directly and through the organs they set up, lead all sections of state, economic, and sociocultural building, adopt decisions, ensure their execution, and exercise control over the implementation of decisions.

Article 94. The activity of the Soviets of People's Deputies is based on collective, free, and businesslike discussion and resolution of questions, glasnost, regular accountability and executive and management organs and other organs created by the soviets to them and to the population, and the wide involvement of citizens in participation in their work.

The Soviets of People's Deputies and the organs set up by them take account of public opinion, submit the most important questions of national and local significance for discussion by citizens, and systematically inform citizens about their work and the decisions adopted.

Chapter 13   The Electoral System

Article 95. Elections of People's Deputies are conducted for single-seat or multiple-seat election districts on the basis of universal, equal and direct suffrage and by secret ballot.

Some Union Republic and autonomous republic People's Deputies, if so stipulated by the republic constitutions, can be elected from public organizations.

Article 96. Elections of People's Deputies from electoral districts shall be universal—USSR citizens who have reached the age of 18 shall have the right to vote.

USSR citizens who have reached the age of 21 can be elected USSR people's deputies.

A citizen of the USSR may not be a deputy of more than two Soviets of People's Deputies simultaneously.

Persons belonging to the USSR Cabinet of Ministers, the Councils of Ministers of union and autonomous republics, and local soviet executive committees, with the exception of the chairmen of these organs, leaders of divisions, departments, and administrations of local soviet executive committees, and judges may not be deputies of the soviet to which they are appointed or elected.

Citizens who are mentally ill or have been adjudged incompetent by a court and persons kept in places for deprivation of freedom under a court sentence do not participate in elections. Persons who are remanded in custody according to procedures laid down by criminal procedure legislation do not participate in elections.

Any direct or indirect restriction of the voting rights of USSR citizens is impermissible and punishable by law.

Article 97. Elections of People's Deputies from electoral districts are equal: A voter for each electoral district has one vote; voters participate in elections on an equal basis.

Article 98. Elections of People's Deputies from electoral districts are direct: People's Deputies are elected by citizens directly.

Article 99. Voting at elections of People's Deputies is secret: Monitoring of the voters' exercise of franchise is not permitted.

Article 100. The right to nominate candidates for People's Deputy from electoral districts is vested with labor collectives, public organizations, collectives of secondary specialized and higher education establishments, voters' meetings at places of residence, and servicemen's meetings in military units. Organs and organizations with the right to nominate candidates for People's Deputy from public organizations are determined by the laws of the USSR and of union and autonomous republics respectively.

The number of candidates for People's Deputy is unrestricted. Any participant in an election campaign meeting may propose anyone's nomination, including his or her own, for discussion.

Any number of candidates can be included in the election ballots.

Candidates for People's Deputy participate in the election campaign on an equal basis.

With a view to ensuring equal conditions for every candidate for People's Deputy, the expenditure associated with the preparation and holding of elections for People's Deputies shall be met by the corresponding electoral commission from a single fund created at the state's expense and from voluntary contributions by enterprises, public organizations, and citizens.

Article 101. Preparations for elections of People's Deputies are carried out openly and in an atmosphere of glasnost.

The holding of elections shall be conducted by electoral commissions consisting of representatives elected by meetings (conferences) of labor collectives, public organizations, collectives of secondary specialized and higher education establishments, voters' meetings at places of residence, and meetings in military units.

USSR citizens, labor collectives, public organizations, collectives of secondary specialized and higher education establishments, and members of the armed forces in military units shall be guaranteed an opportunity for free and comprehensive discussion of the political, professional, and personal qualities of candidates for People's Deputy, as well as the right to campaign for or against a candidate at meetings, in the press, and on television and radio.

The procedure for holding elections of People's Deputies is defined by laws of the USSR and of union and autonomous republics.

Article 102. Voters and social organizations give mandates to their deputies.

The appropriate Soviets of People's Deputies examine the mandates, take them into account when formulating economic and social development plans and drawing up the budget, and also in preparing decisions on other questions, organize the fulfillment of mandates, and inform citizens about their implementation.

Chapter 14   People's Deputies

Article 103. Deputies are the plenipotentiary representatives of the people in the Soviets of People's Deputies.

In the soviets, deputies deal with matters relating to state, economic, and social and cultural development, organize implementation of the decisions of the soviets, and exercise control over the work of state bodies, enterprises, institutions, and organizations.

Deputies shall be guided in their activities by the interests of the state, and shall take into account the requests of the electoral district's population and the expressed interests of the social organization which has elected them, and strive to implement the mandates of the voters and the social organization.

Article 104. Deputies exercise their powers without, as a rule, discontinuing their regular employment or duties.

During sessions of congresses of People's Deputies and sessions of Supreme Soviets or local Soviets of People's Deputies, and also for the exercise of deputy powers in other instances envisaged by the law, deputies are released from carrying out their regular employment or duties and are reimbursed for expenses occasioned by their activities as deputies from funds provided in the relevant state or local budget.

Article 105. Deputies have the right to address inquiries to the appropriate state organs and officials, which are obligated to respond to them at a Congress of People's Deputies or a session of the Supreme Soviet or local Soviet of People's Deputies.

Deputies have the right to approach any state or public body, enterprise, institution, or organization on matters arising from their work as Deputies and to take part in considering the questions raised by them. The heads of the state of public bodies, enterprises, institutions, or organizations concerned are obliged to receive Deputies without delay and to consider their proposals within the time limit established by law.

Article 106. Deputies shall be ensured conditions for the unhampered and effective exercise of their rights and duties.

The immunity of deputies, and other guarantees of their activity as deputies, are defined in the Law on the Status of Deputies and other legislative acts of the USSR and of Union and Autonomous Republics.

Article 107. Deputies are obligated to report on their own work and the work of a Congress of People's Deputies or a Supreme Soviet or local Soviet of People's Deputies to the voters, the collectives and social organizations which nominated them to be candidate deputies, or to the social organization which elected them.

Deputies who fail to justify the confidence of their constituents or the social organization may be recalled at any time in the legally established manner by a decision of the majority of voters or the social organization which elected them.

V. HIGHER BODIES OF STATE AUTHORITY AND ADMINISTRATION OF THE USSR

Chapter 15

The USSR Congress of People's Deputies and the USSR Supreme Soviet.
Article 108. The highest body of state authority in the USSR is the USSR Congress of People's Deputies.

The USSR Congress of People's Deputies is empowered to adopt for its examination and decide any question within the jurisdiction of the USSR.

The following are within the exclusive jurisdiction of the USSR Congress of People's Deputies:

1. the adoption and amendment of the USSR Constitution;
2. the adoption of decisions on questions of the national-state structure within the jurisdiction of the USSR;
3. the definition of the USSR state borders; the ratification of changes in the borders between union republics;
4. the definition of the basic guidelines of USSR domestic and foreign policy;
5. the ratification of long-term state plans and highly important all-union programs for the economic and social development of the USSR;
6. the election of the USSR Supreme Soviet and the chairman of the USSR Supreme Soviet;
7. the ratification of the chairman of the USSR Supreme Court, the USSR Prosecutor-General, and the Chairman of the USSR Higher Court of Arbitration;
8. the election of the USSR Constitutional Supervision Committee on the submission at the chairman of the USSR Supreme Soviet;
9. the repeal of acts adopted by the USSR Supreme Soviet;
10. the adoption of decisions on holding nation-wide polls (referendums).

The Congress of USSR People's Deputies adopts USSR laws and resolutions, upon a vote, by a majority of the total number of USSR People's Deputies.

Article 109. The USSR Congress of People's Deputies consists of 2,250 deputies who are elected as follows:

750 deputies from territorial electoral districts with an equal number of voters;

750 deputies from national-territorial electoral districts in accordance with the following norms: 32 deputies from each union republic, 11 deputies from each autonomous republic, 5 deputies from each autonomous region, and 1 deputy from each autonomous district;

750 deputies from all-union social organizations in accordance with the norms laid down by the USSR Law on Elections of People's Deputies.

Article 110. The USSR Congress of People's Deputies is convened for its first session no later than 2 months following the elections.

On the representation of the credentials commission elected by it, the USSR Congress of People's Deputies adopts a decision to recognize the powers of the deputies, and—in the event of a violation of election legislation—to recognize the invalidity of individual deputies' election.

The USSR Congress of People's Deputies is convened by the USSR Supreme Soviet.

Regular sessions of the Congress of USSR People's Deputies are held at least once a year. Extraordinary sessions are convened on the initiative of the USSR Supreme Soviet on the proposal of one of its chambers, the President of the USSR, or at least one-fifth of the USSR People's Deputies, or on the initiative of a union republic in the persons of its highest body of state authority.

The first session of the Congress of USSR People's Deputies following elections is conducted by the chairman of the Central Electoral Commission for elections of USSR People's Deputies, and thereafter by the chairman of the USSR Supreme Soviet.

Article 111. The USSR Supreme Soviet is the permanently operating legislative and monitoring organ of state power of the USSR.

The USSR Supreme Soviet is elected by secret vote from among the USSR People's Deputies by the USSR Congress of People's Deputies and is accountable to the latter.

The USSR Supreme Soviet consists of two chambers: the Soviet of the Union and the Soviet of Nationalities, which are numerically equal. The chambers of the USSR Supreme Soviet possess equal rights.

The chambers are elected at the USSR Congress of People's Deputies by a general vote by the deputies. The Soviet of the Union is elected from among the USSR People's Deputies from the territorial electoral districts and the USSR People's Deputies from social organizations taking into account the number of voters in the union republic or region. The Soviet of Nationalities is elected from among the USSR People's Deputies from the national-territorial electoral districts and the USSR People's Deputies from the social organizations in accordance with the following norms: 11 deputies from each union republic, 4 deputies from each autonomous republic, 2 deputies from each autonomous region, and 1 deputy from each autonomous district.

The Congress of USSR People's Deputies annually replaces up to one-fifth of the composition of the Soviet of the Union and Soviet of Nationalities.

Each chamber of the USSR Supreme Soviet elects a chairman and two deputy chairmen. The chairmen of the Soviet of the Union and Soviet of Nationalities preside at the sessions of their corresponding chambers and are in charge of their internal proceedings.

Joint sessions of the chambers are chaired by the chairman of the USSR Supreme Soviet or the chairmen of the Soviet of the Union and the Soviet of Nationalities in turn.

Article 112. The USSR Supreme Soviet is convened annually by the chairman of the USSR Supreme Soviet for regular—spring and fall—sessions lasting, as a rule, three to four months each.

Extraordinary sessions are convened by the chairman of the USSR Supreme Soviet on his own initiative or at the proposal of the President of the USSR, a union republic in the person of its highest body of state authority, or at least one-third of the deputies of one of the chambers of the USSR Supreme Soviet.

USSR Supreme Soviet sessions take the form of separate and joint sessions of the chambers and of sessions of the chambers' permanent commissions and the USSR Supreme Soviet committees held between sessions. A session is opened and closed at separate or joint sessions of the chambers.

Upon the expiry of the term of powers of the USSR Congress of People's Deputies, the USSR Supreme Soviet retains its powers right until the formation of a new composition of the USSR Supreme Soviet by the newly elected USSR Congress of People's Deputies.

Article 113. The USSR Supreme Soviet:

1. schedules elections of USSR People's Deputies and ratifies the composition of the Central Electoral Commission on Elections of USSR People's Deputies;
2. on representations from the President of the USSR, forms and abolishes USSR ministries and other central agencies of USSR state administration;
3. on representations from the President of the USSR, confirms the Prime Minister, gives its approval at a session to candidates for members of the USSR Cabinet of Ministers and members of the USSR Security Council or rejects them, and gives its approval for relieving the indicated persons of their duties;
4. lects the USSR Supreme Court and the USSR Higher Court of Arbitration, appoints the USSR Prosecutor-General, confirms the collegium of the USSR Prosecutor's Office, and appoints the Chairman of the USSR Control Chamber;
5. regularly hears reports by organs constituted or elected by it and by officials appointed or elected by it;
6. ensures the uniformity of legislative regulations throughout the territory of the USSR and lays the foundations for legislation by the USSR and the union republics;
7. carries out, within the limits of the competence of the USSR, legislative regulation of the procedure for the exercise of citizens' constitutional rights, freedoms, and duties, ownership relations, and organization of management of the national economy and sociocultural building, and budget and financial system, labor remuneration and pricing, taxation, environmental conservation and the utilization of natural resources, and other relations;
8. interprets USSR laws;
9. lays down general principles of the organization and activity of republic and local organs of state power and administration; determines the foundations of the legal status of social organizations;
10. submits for ratification by the USSR Congress of People's Deputies draft long-term state plans and the most important all-union programs for the USSR's economic and social development; ratifies the state plans for the USSR's economic and social development and the USSR state budget; monitors progress in the implementation of the plan and budget; ratifies reports on their performance; introduces amendments to the plan and budget whenever necessary;
11. ratifies and renounces the USSR's international treaties;
12. oversees the granting of state loans and economic and other assistance to foreign states, and also the conclusion of agreements on state loans and credits obtained from foreign sources;
13. determines the main measures in the sphere of defense and the safeguarding of state security; imposes martial law or a state of emergency countrywide; declares war in the event of the need to fulfill international treaty commitments on mutual defense against aggression;
14. adopts decisions on the utilization of USSR Armed Forces contingents in the event of the need to fulfill international treaty commitments on maintaining peace and security;
15. establishes military ranks, diplomatic ranks, and other special ranks;
16. institutes USSR orders and medals; confers honorary titles of the USSR;
17. promulgates all-union acts of amnesty;
18. has the right to annul acts of the USSR Cabinet of Ministers if they do not conform to the USSR Constitution and USSR laws;
19. repeals resolutions and orders by union republic councils of ministers if they are inconsistent with the USSR Constitution and USSR laws;

20. during the period between Congress of USSR People's Deputies, adopts decisions on conducting nationwide votes (USSR referendums);
21. decides other issues falling within the jurisdiction of the USSR, apart from issues which fall within the exclusive jurisdiction of the USSR Congress of People's Deputies.

The USSR Supreme Soviet adopts USSR laws and resolutions.

Laws and resolutions adopted by the USSR Supreme Soviet cannot be contrary to laws and other acts adopted by the USSR Congress of People's deputies.

Article 114. The right of legislative initiative at the Congress of USSR People's Deputies and the USSR Supreme Soviet belongs to USSR People's Deputies, the Soviet of the Union, the Soviet of Nationalities, the Chairman of the USSR Supreme Soviet, standing commissions of the chambers and committees of the USSR Supreme Soviet, the President of the USSR, the Council of the Federation, the USSR Constitutional Supervision Committee, union and autonomous republics in the person of their highest organs of state power, autonomous regions, autonomous districts, the USSR Supreme Court, the USSR Prosecutor-General, and the USSR Higher Court of Arbitration.

The right of legislative initiative also belongs to social organizations in the person of their all-union organs, and to the USSR Academy of Sciences.

Article 115. Draft laws submitted for examination by the USSR Supreme Soviet are discussed by its chambers at separate or joint sessions.

A USSR law is deemed adopted if a majority of chamber members votes for it in each chamber of the USSR Supreme Soviet.

Draft laws and other important issues may be submitted for nationwide discussion following a decision by the USSR Supreme Soviet adopted either on its own initiative or on a proposal by a union republic.

Article 116. Each chamber of the USSR Supreme Soviet is empowered to examine any questions falling within the jurisdiction of the USSR Supreme Soviet.

The Soviet of the Union primarily examines questions of socioeconomic development and state building of general importance for the entire country; of the rights, freedoms, and duties of USSR citizens; of USSR foreign policy; of the USSR's defense and state security.

The Soviet of Nationalities primarily examines questions of ensuring national equality and the interests of nations, nationalities, and ethnic groups in combination with the general interests and needs of the Soviet multinational state; of improvements to USSR legislation regulating interethnic relations.

Each chamber adopts resolutions on questions within its competence.

Any resolution adopted by one of the chambers, if necessary, is referred to the other chamber and, when approved by it, acquires the force of a USSR Supreme Soviet resolution.

Article 117. In the event of disagreement between the Soviet of the Union and the Soviet of Nationalities, the question is handed over for resolution to a conciliation commission formed by the chambers on a parity basis, after which it is again examined by the Soviet of the Union and the Soviet of Nationalities at a joint session.

Article 118. A USSR Supreme Soviet Presidium headed by the Chairman of the USSR Supreme Soviet is set up to organize the work of the USSR Supreme Soviet. The USSR Supreme Soviet Presidium includes: the chairmen of the Soviet of the Union and the Soviet of Nationalities, their deputies, the chairmen of the standing commissions of the chambers and committees of the USSR Supreme Soviet, and other USSR People's Deputies—one from each union republic, and also two representatives from autonomous republics and one from autonomous regions and autonomous districts.

The USSR Supreme Soviet Presidium prepares Congress sessions and USSR Supreme Soviet sessions, coordinates the activity of the standing commissions of the chambers and committees of the USSR Supreme Soviet, and organizes nationwide discussions of USSR draft laws and other most important questions of state life.

The USSR Supreme Soviet Presidium ensures publication, in the languages of the union republics, of the texts of USSR laws and other acts adopted by the Congress of USSR People's Deputies, the USSR Supreme Soviet, its chambers, and the President of the USSR. Decisions of the Presidium of the USSR Supreme Soviet are drawn up in the form of resolutions.

Article 119. The Chairman of the USSR Supreme Soviet is elected by the Congress of USSR People's Deputies from among the USSR People's Deputies by secret ballot for a term of five years and for not more than two successive terms. They may be recalled by the Congress of USSR People's Deputies at any time by secret ballot.

The Chairman of the USSR Supreme Soviet is accountable to the Congress of USSR People's Deputies and the USSR Supreme Soviet.

The Chairman of the USSR Supreme Soviet issues resolutions on the convocation of USSR Supreme Soviet sessions and instructions on other matters.

Article 120. The Soviet of the Union and Soviet of Nationalities elect from among the members of the USSR Supreme Soviet and other People's Deputies of the USSR standing commissions of the chambers to carry out the drafting of laws and preliminary examination and preparation of matters falling within the jurisdiction of the USSR Supreme Soviet, and also to promote the implementation of USSR laws and other decisions adopted by the USSR Congress of People's Deputies and the USSR Supreme Soviet and to monitor the activity of state organs and organizations.

For the same purposes, the chambers of the USSR Supreme Soviet may set up USSR Supreme Soviet committees on a basis of parity.

The USSR Supreme Soviet and each of its chambers, when they deem it necessary, set up investigating auditing, or other commissions on any matter.

Up to one-fifth of the composition of the standing commissions of the chambers and the committees of the USSR Supreme Soviet is annually replaced.

Article 121. Laws and other decisions of the USSR Congress of People's Deputies and the USSR Supreme Soviet and resolutions of its chambers are adopted, as a rule, after preliminary discussion of the drafts by the appropriate standing commissions of the chambers or committees of the USSR Supreme Soviet.

The appointment and election of officials to the USSR Cabinet of Ministers, the USSR Supreme Court, the USSR Higher Court of Arbitration and the collegium of the USSR Prosecutor's Office, as well as to the Chairman of the USSR Control Chamber, are to be accompanied by conclusions from the relevant standing committees of the chambers of the USSR Supreme Soviet or its joint committees.

All state and social organs, organizations, and officials must fulfill the requirements of the commissions of the chambers, commissions, and committees of the USSR Supreme Soviet and provide them with the necessary materials and documents.

The recommendations of commissions and committees are subject to compulsory examination by state and social organs, institutions, and organizations. The results of the examination and the measures adopted must be reported to the commissions and committees within the time laid down by them.

Article 122. A USSR People's Deputy has the right to submit a question at sessions of the Congress of USSR People's Deputies and sessions of the USSR Supreme Soviet to the USSR Cabinet of Ministers and leaders of other organs formed or elected by the Congress of USSR People's Deputies and the USSR Supreme Soviet, and to the President of the USSR at sessions of the Congress of USSR People's Deputies. An organ or official to whom a question is submitted is obliged to give an oral or written answer at the Congress sitting in question or the USSR Supreme Soviet session in question within no more than three days.

Article 123. USSR People's Deputies are entitled to be relieved of the performance of their regular employment or duties for the period necessary to implement their activity as deputies in the Congress of USSR People's Deputies, the USSR Supreme Soviet, its chambers, commissions, and committees and also among the population.

A USSR People's Deputy cannot be subjected to criminal proceedings, be arrested, or incur judically imposed administrative penalties without the consent of the USSR Supreme Soviet or, in the period between its sessions, without the consent of the USSR Supreme Soviet Presidium.

Article 124. The USSR Constitutional Supervision Committee is elected by the Congress of USSR People's Deputies from the ranks of specialists in the field of politics and law and consists of a chairman, deputy chairman, and 25 members including one for each union republic.

The term of the authority of persons elected to the USSR Constitutional Supervision Committee is 10 years.

Persons elected to the USSR Constitutional Supervision Committee may not simultaneously be members of bodies whose acts are reviewable by the Committee.

In the performance of their duties, persons elected to the USSR Constitutional Supervision Committee are independent and subordinate only to the USSR Constitution.

The USSR Constitutional Supervision Committee:

1. at the behest of the Congress of USSR People's Deputies submits to it findings concerning the correspondence to the USSR Constitution of draft laws of the USSR and other instruments submitted for examination by the Congress;
2. at the proposals of no less than one-fifth of USSR People's Deputies, the President of the USSR, and the supreme organs of state power in the union republics, the Constitutional Supervision Committee submits findings to the Congress of USSR People's Deputies regarding the correspondence between USSR laws and other acts adopted by the Congress and the USSR Constitution. On the instructions of the Congress of USSR People's Deputies or at the proposal of the USSR Supreme Soviet, submits findings regarding the correspondence between decrees of the President of the USSR and the USSR Constitution and USSR laws;
3. On the instructions of the Congress of USSR People's Deputies or at the proposal of the USSR Supreme Soviet, the President of the USSR, the chairman of the USSR Supreme Soviet, or the supreme organs of state power in the union republics submit findings to the Congress of USSR People's Deputies or the USSR Supreme Soviet regarding the correspondence between union republic constitutions and the USSR Constitution and between union republic laws and USSR laws;
4. On the instructions of the Congress of USSR People's Deputies or at the proposal of no less than one-fifth of the members of the USSR Supreme Soviet, the President of the USSR or the supreme organs of state power in the union republics submit findings to the USSR Supreme Soviet or the President of the USSR regarding the correspondence between acts adopted by the USSR Supreme Soviet and its chambers and draft acts submitted for consideration by these organs and the USSR Constitution and USSR laws adopted by the Congress of USSR People's Deputies, and also the correspondence between resolutions and instructions adopted by the USSR Cabinet of Ministers and USSR laws adopted by the USSR Supreme Soviet; on the correspondence between

USSR and union republic international treaty and other obligations and the USSR Constitution and USSR laws;

5. On the instructions of the Congress of USSR People's Deputies or at the proposal of the USSR Supreme Soviet, its chambers, the President of the USSR, the Chairman of the USSR Supreme Soviet, the chambers' standing commissions, USSR Supreme Soviet committees, the USSR Cabinet of Ministers, the supreme organs of state power in the union republics, the USSR Control Chamber, the USSR Supreme Court, the USSR Prosecutor-General, the USSR Higher Court of Arbitration, all-union organs of public organizations, or the USSR Academy of Sciences submit findings regarding the correspondence between normative legal acts adopted by other state organs and public organizations to which supervision by the prosecutor's office does not apply under the USSR Constitution and the USSR Constitution and USSR laws.

Article 125. The Congress of USSR People's Deputies and the USSR Supreme Soviet monitor all the state organs accountable to them.

The USSR Supreme Soviet directs the activity of the USSR Control Chamber and periodically hears reports from it on the results of its monitoring of receipts and expenditures of Union budget monies and the use of All-Union property.

The organization of and procedures for the activity of the USSR Control Chamber are determined by USSR law.

Article 126. The procedure of work of the USSR Congress of People's Deputies, the USSR Supreme Soviet, and their organs is determined by the regulations of the USSR Congress of People's Deputies and the USSR Supreme Soviet and by other USSR laws promulgated on the basis of the USSR Constitution.

Chapter 15(1)   The President of the USSR

Article 127. The head of the Soviet state—the Union of Soviet Socialist Republics—is the President of the USSR.

Article 127(1). Any citizen of the USSR no younger than 35 and no older than 65 years can be elected President of the USSR. The same person can be President of the USSR for no more than two terms.

The President of the USSR is elected by USSR citizens on the basis of universal, equal, and direct suffrage by secret ballot for a 5-year term. The number of candidates for the post of President of the USSR is not limited. Elections for the President of the USSR are considered valid if at least 50 percent of voters participated in them.

The candidate who has received over half the votes of voters taking part in the election in the USSR as a whole and in the majority of union republics is deemed to be elected.

The procedure for elections of the President of the USSR is defined by USSR law.

The President of the USSR cannot be a People's Deputy.

The person who is President of the USSR can receive wages for that post alone.

Article 127(2). Upon inauguration, the President of the USSR swears an oath at a session of the Congress of USSR People's Deputies.

Article 127(3). The President of the USSR:

1. is the guarantor of observance of Soviet citizens' rights and freedoms and of the USSR Constitution and laws;
2. takes the necessary measures to protect the sovereignty of the USSR and union republics and the country's security and territorial integrity and to implement the principles of the national-state structure of the USSR;

3. represents the Union of Soviet Socialist Republics inside the country and in international relations;

4. heads the system of bodies of state administration and ensures their interaction with the USSR's supreme bodies of state power;

5. submits to the Congress of USSR People's Deputies annual reports on the state of the country; briefs the USSR Supreme Soviet on the most important questions of the USSR's domestic and foreign policy;

6. taking into consideration the opinion of the Council of the Federation and with the concurrence of the USSR Supreme Soviet, forms the USSR Cabinet of Ministers, makes changes in its membership, and presents a candidate for the post of Prime Minister to the USSR Supreme Soviet; with the concurrence of the USSR Supreme Soviet, relieves the Prime Minister and members of the USSR Cabinet of Ministers of their duties;

7. submits to the USSR Supreme Soviet candidates for the posts of chairman of the USSR Supreme Court, USSR Prosecutor-General, and Chairman of the USSR Higher Court of Arbitration, and then submits these officials to the Congress of USSR People's Deputies for confirmation; makes representations to the USSR Supreme Soviet and the Congress of USSR People's Deputies regarding releasing the aforementioned officials, with the exception of the Chairman of the USSR Supreme Court, from their duties;

8. signs USSR laws; is entitled within a period of no more than two weeks to refer a law along with his objections back to the USSR Supreme Soviet for repeat discussion and voting. If the USSR Supreme Soviet confirms its earlier decision by a two-thirds majority in each chamber, the President of the USSR signs the law;

9. has the right to annul resolutions and orders of the USSR Cabinet of Ministers, acts of USSR ministries and other agencies subordinate to him; has the right, on questions falling within USSR jurisdiction, to suspend resolutions and orders of republic Councils of Ministers if they violate the USSR Constitution and USSR laws;

10. heads the USSR Security Council, which is entrusted with the task of working out recommendations on the implementation of All-Union policies in the field of the country's defense, on maintaining the reliable state, economic and ecological security of the country, on overcoming the consequences of natural disasters and other emergency situations, and on ensuring stability and law and order in society. The members of the USSR Security Council are appointed by the President of the USSR, taking into account the opinion of the Council of the Federation and with the concurrence of the USSR Supreme Soviet;

11. coordinates the activity of state organs to ensure the defense of the country; is the supreme commander in chief of the USSR armed forces, appoints and replaces the supreme command of the USSR armed forces, and confers the highest military ranks; appoints the judges of military tribunals;

12. holds talks and signs the USSR's international treaties; accepts the credentials and letters of recall of diplomatic representatives of foreign states accredited to it; appoints and recalls the USSR's diplomatic representatives in foreign states and in international organizations; confers the highest diplomatic ranks and other special titles;

13. awards USSR orders and medals and confers USSR honorary titles;

14. decides questions of admittance to USSR citizenship, withdrawal from it, and the deprivation of Soviet citizenship and the granting of asylum; grants pardons;

15. declares general or partial mobilization; declares a state of war in the event of a military attack on the USSR and immediately refers this question for examination to the USSR Supreme Soviet; declares martial law in particular localities in the interests of the defense of the USSR and the security of its citizens. The procedure for introducing martial law and the regime thereof are determined by the law;

16. in the interests of safeguarding the security of citizens of the USSR, gives warning of the declaration of a state of emergency in particular localities and, if necessary, introduces it at the request or with the consent of the supreme soviet presidium or supreme organ of state power of the corresponding union republic. In the absence of such consent, introduces the state of emergency and submits the adopted decision for ratification by the USSR Supreme Soviet without delay. The USSR Supreme Soviet resolution on this question must be adopted by a majority of at least two-thirds of the total number of its members.

    In the cases indicated in the first part of this point, can introduce temporary presidential rule while observing the sovereignty and territorial integrity of the union republic.

    The regime for a state of emergency, and also for presidential rule is laid down by the law;

17. in the event of disagreements between the USSR Supreme Soviet Soviet of the Union and Soviet of Nationalities that cannot be eliminated via the procedure envisaged by Article 117 of the USSR Constitution, the President of the USSR examines the contentious issue with a view to formulating an acceptable solution. If it is not possible to reach consensus and there is a real threat of disruption to the normal activity of the USSR's supreme organs of state power and management, the President can submit to the Congress of USSR People's Deputies a proposal regarding the election of a new USSR Supreme Soviet.

Article 127(4). The President of the USSR heads the Council of the Federation, which comprises the supreme state officials of the union republics. The supreme state officials of autonomous republics, autonomous regions, and autonomous districts are entitled to participate in sessions of the Council of the Federation.

The Council of the Federation: examines questions of compliance with the Union Treaty; elaborates measures to implement the Soviet state's nationalities policy; submits to the Soviet of Nationalities of the USSR Supreme Soviet recommendations on resolving disputes and settling conflicts in interethnic relations; and coordinates the union republics' activity and ensures their participation in resolving questions of unionwide significance within the competence of the president of the USSR.

Questions affecting the interests of peoples who do not have their own national state formation are examined in the Council of the Federation with the participation of representatives of these peoples.

The Vice-President of the USSR is elected on a representation by the candidate for President of the USSR and at the same time as the President. The Vice-President of the USSR performs certain functions of the President of the USSR on the latter's instructions and acts in place of the President in the event of his absence or inability to carry out his duties.

The Vice-President of the USSR may not be a People's Deputy.

Article 127(5). The president of the USSR, on the basis of and in execution of the USSR Constitution and USSR laws, issues decrees that are binding throughout the territory of the country.

Article 127(6). The president of the USSR has the right of inviolability and may only be replaced by the Congress of USSR People's Deputies in the event of his violating the USSR Constitution or USSR laws. This decision is made by the Congress of USSR People's Deputies on the initiative of the Congress itself or of the USSR Supreme Soviet by a majority of at least two-thirds of the total number of deputies, taking into account the findings of the USSR Constitutional Oversight Committee.

Article 127(7). If the President of the USSR is for any reason unable to continue to execute his duties until the election of a new president his powers are transferred to the Vice-President of the USSR, or if that is not possible, to the Chairman of the USSR Supreme Soviet. In this case the election of a new President of the USSR must take place within three months.

Chapter 15(2)   The Council of the Federation.

Article 127(8). The President of the USSR heads the Council of the Federation, which is made up of the Vice-President of the USSR and the Presidents (top state officials) of the republics. The top state officials of autonomous republics and autonomous regions have the right to participate in meetings of the Council of the Federation with the right to vote on questions affecting their interests.

On the basis of the guidelines for the USSR's domestic and foreign policy that are set by the Congress of USSR People's Deputies, the Council of the Federation exercises coordination of the activity of Union and republic supreme bodies of state administration, monitors observance of the Union Treaty, determines measures for implementation of the Soviet state's nationalities policy, ensures the republics' participation in the resolution of questions of All-Union significance, and makes recommendations regarding the resolution of disputes and the settlement of conflict situations in relations between nationalities.

Questions affecting the interests of peoples that do not have their own national-state formations are considered in the Council of the Federation with the participation of representatives of these peoples.

Article 127(9). A member of the Council of the Federation who is the highest state official of a republic, representing and defending the sovereignty and legitimate interests of that republic, participates in the resolution of all questions submitted for consideration by the Council of the Federation.

A member of the Council of the Federation ensures the implementation of decisions of the Council of the Federation in the appropriate republic; monitors the fulfillment of these decisions; receives all necessary information from Union agencies and officials; may protest decisions by Union bodies of state administration that violate the rights of a republic as established by law; on instructions from the President of the USSR, represents the USSR abroad and exercises other powers.

Article 127(10). Decisions of the Council of the Federation are adopted by a majority vote of at least two-thirds and are drawn up in the form of decrees of the President of the USSR.

The Chairman of the USSR Supreme Soviet may participate in meetings of the Council of the Federation.

Chapter 16   The USSR Cabinet of Ministers

Article 128. The USSR Cabinet of Ministers is the executive and administrative body of the USSR and is subordinate to the President of the USSR.

Article 129. The USSR Cabinet of Ministers consists of the Prime Minister, the Deputy Prime Ministers and the USSR ministers.

The structure of the USSR Cabinet of Ministers is determined by the USSR Supreme Soviet, on the basis of representations from the President of the USSR.

The heads of republic governments may participate in the work of the USSR Cabinet of Ministers with the right to vote.

Article 130. The USSR Cabinet of Ministers is responsible to the President of the USSR and the USSR Supreme Soviet.

A newly formed USSR Cabinet of Ministers submits a program of forthcoming activity for its term of office to the USSR Supreme Soviet for its consideration.

The USSR Cabinet of Ministers reports on its work to the USSR Supreme Soviet at least once a year.

The USSR Supreme Soviet may express a lack of confidence in the USSR Cabinet of Ministers, which entails the Cabinet's resignation. A resolution on this question must be adopted by a majority vote of at least two-thirds of the total number of members of the USSR Supreme Soviet.

Article 131. The USSR Cabinet of Ministers is empowered to resolve questions of state administration within the jurisdiction of the USSR, insofar as they do not, according to the USSR Constitution, come within the purview of the Congress of USSR People's Deputies, the USSR Supreme Soviet and the Council of the Federation.

Article 132. USSR Cabinet of Ministers ensures:

the implementation, in conjunction with the republics, of a unified financial, credit and monetary policy based on a common currency; the drafting and fulfillment of the Union budget; the implementation of All-Union economic programs; the creation of interrepublic development funds and funds for eliminating the consequences of natural disasters and catastrophes;

the administration, in conjunction with the republics, of the country's unified fuel-and-power and transportation systems; the administration of defense enterprises, space research, Union systems of communications and information, meteorology, geodesy, cartography, metrology and standardization; the implementation of a coordinated policy in the field of environmental protection, ecological safety and the use of natural resources;

the implementation, in conjunction with the republics, of All-Union programs dealing with food, health care, social security, employment for the population, care for mothers and children, culture and education, basic scientific research, and incentives for scientific and technical progress;

the taking of measures to safeguard the country's defense and state security;

the implementation of the USSR's foreign policy, the regulation of the USSR's foreign-economic activity, the coordination of the republics' foreign policy and foreign economic activity, and customs operations;

the implementation of measures, agreed upon with the republics, to ensure legality, the rights and liberties of citizens and the safeguarding of property and public order, and to provide for the struggle against crime.

Article 133. On the basis of and in fulfillment of USSR laws and other decisions of the Congress of USSR People's Deputies and the USSR Supreme Soviet and decrees of the President of the USSR, the USSR Cabinet of Ministers issues resolutions and orders and verifies their execution. The execution of resolutions and orders of the USSR Cabinet of Ministers is mandatory throughout the USSR.

Article 134. The USSR Cabinet of Ministers coordinates and directs the work of the USSR ministries and other agencies under its jurisdiction.

For the coordinated resolution of questions of state administration, collegiums are created in USSR ministries and other central bodies of state administration, and the heads of the corresponding republic bodies are ex-officio members of these collegiums.

Article 135. The jurisdiction of the USSR Cabinet of Ministers, the procedure for its activity, its relations with other state agencies, as well as the list of USSR ministries and other central bodies of state administration, are determined by a USSR law.

VI. BASIC PRINCIPLES OF THE STRUCTURE OF THE BODIES OF STATE POWER AND ADMINISTRATION IN UNION REPUBLICS

Chapter 17   Supreme Bodies of State Power and Administration in a Union Republic

Article 136. The supreme bodies of state power in union republics are the union-republic Supreme Soviets, and in union-republics where provision is made for the creation of congresses—the Congresses of People's Deputies;

Article 137. The powers, structures, and procedures governing the activity of the supreme organs of state authority in union-republics shall be determined by the constitutions and laws of the union-republics;

Article 138. The Supreme Soviet of a Union Republic shall form a Council of Ministers of the Union Republic, that is, the Government of that Republic, which shall be the highest executive and administrative body of state authority in the Republic.

Article 139. The Council of Ministers of a Union Republic issues decisions and ordinances on the basis of, and in pursuance of, the legislative acts of the USSR and of the Union Republic, and of acts of the President of the USSR and the USSR Cabinet of Ministers, and shall organize and verify their execution.

Article 140. The Council of Ministers of a Union Republic has the right to suspend the execution of decisions and resolutions of the Councils of Ministers of Autonomous Republics, to rescind the decisions and orders of the Executive Committees of Soviets of People's Deputies of Territories, Regions, and cities (that is, cities under Republic jurisdiction), and of Autonomous Regions, and in Union Republics not divided into regions, of the Executive Committees of district and corresponding city Soviets of People's Deputies.

Article 141. The Council of Ministers of a Union Republic shall coordinate and direct the work of the Union-Republican and Republican ministries and of state committees of the Union Republic and other bodies under its jurisdiction.

The Union-Republican ministries and state committees of a Union Republic shall direct the branches of administration entrusted to them, or exercise interbranch control, and shall be subordinate to both the Council of Ministers of the Union Republic and the corresponding Union-Republican ministry or state committee of the USSR.

Republican ministries and state committees shall direct the branches of administration entrusted to them, or exercise interbranch control, and shall be subordinate to the Council of Ministers of the Union Republic.

Chapter 18   Supreme Bodies of State Power and Administration in an Autonomous Republic

Article 142. The supreme bodies of state power in autonomous republics are the autonomous republic Supreme Soviets, and in autonomous republics where provision is made for the creation of congresses—the Congress of People's Deputies.

Article 143. The Supreme Soviet of an autonomous republic shall form the autonomous republic Council of Ministers—the autonomous republic's government—which is the highest executive and administrative organ of state power in the autonomous republic.

Chapter 19 Local Bodies of State Power and Administration

Article 144. The bodies of state power in autonomous rural regions, territories, districts, cities, boroughs, settlements, rural communities, and other administrative-territorial units, constituted in conformity with the laws of union and autonomous republics, shall be the corresponding Soviets of People's Deputies.

In accordance with republic legislation, in addition to local Soviets of People's Deputies, agencies of territorial public self-government, citizens' assemblies and other forms of direct democracy may operate within the system of local self-government.

Article 145. Local Soviets of People's Deputies shall deal with all matters of local significance in accordance with the interests of the whole state and of citizens residing in the area under their jurisdiction, implement decisions of higher bodies of state authority, guide the work of lower Soviets of People's Deputies, take part in the discussion of matters of Republican and All-Union significance, and submit their proposals concerning them.

Local Soviets of People's Deputies shall direct state, economic, social and cultural development within their territory; endorse plans for economic and social development and the local budget; exercise general guidance over state bodies, enterprises, institutions, and organizations subordinate to them; ensure observance of the laws, maintenance of law and order, and protection of citizens' rights; and help strengthen the country's defense capacity.

Article 146. Within their powers, local Soviets of People's Deputies shall ensure the comprehensive, all-round economic and social development of their areas; exercise control over the observance of legislation by enterprises, institutions, and organizations subordinate to higher authorities and located in their area; and coordinate and supervise their activity as regards land use, nature conservation, building, employment of manpower, production of consumer goods; and social, cultural, communal, and other services and amenities for the public.

Article 147. Local Soviets of People's Deputies shall decide matters within the powers accorded them by the legislation of the USSR and of the appropriate Union Republic and Autonomous Republic. Their decisions shall be binding on all enterprises, institutions, and organizations located in their areas and on officials and citizens.

Article 148. The executive and administrative agencies of the local Soviet of People's Deputies are the executive committees and other agencies that the soviets elect.

The executive and administrative agencies of the local Soviets reports at least once a year to the Soviets that elected them, and they also make reports at meetings of labor collectives and of citizens at their places of residence.

Article 149. The executive and administrative agencies of local Soviets of People's Deputies are obliged to fulfill the laws, decrees of the USSR President, and other acts of the USSR and republic supreme bodies of state power and administration that are adopted within the limits of their jurisdiction.

The executive and administrative agencies of the local Soviets are directly subordinate both to the Soviet that elected them and to higher executive and administrative bodies.

VII. JUSTICE AND PROCURATOR'S SUPERVISION

Chapter 20 The Courts

Article 150. In the USSR justice is administered only by the courts.

In the USSR there are the following courts: the Supreme Court of the USSR; the

Supreme Courts of Union Republics; the Supreme Courts of Autonomous Republics; Territorial, Regional, and city courts; courts of Autonomous Regions; courts of Autonomous Areas; district (city) people's courts; and military tribunals in the Armed Forces.

Article 151. All courts in the USSR are formed on the basis of the principle of the election of judges and people's assessors, with the exception of the judges of military tribunals.

People's judges of region (city) people's courts and the judges of territorial, regional, and city courts are elected by the relevant superior Soviets of People's Deputies.

Judges of the USSR Supreme Court, the supreme courts of the union and autonomous republics, and the courts of autonomous regions and autonomous districts are elected by, respective, the USSR Supreme Soviet, the supreme soviets of the union and autonomous republics, and the Soviets of People's Deputies of autonomous regions and autonomous districts.

The people's assessors of district (city) people's courts are elected at citizens' meetings at their places of residence or work by open ballot, and the people's assessors of superior courts are elected by the relevant Soviets of People's Deputies.

The judges of military tribunals are appointed by the President of the USSR, while people's assessors are elected in an open ballot by members of the armed forces.

Judges of all courts are elected for a term of 10 years. Lay assessors of all courts are elected for a term of 5 years.

Judges and peoples assessors may be recalled in accordance with the legally established procedure.

Article 152. The USSR Supreme Court is the supreme judicial organ in the USSR and oversees the judicial activity of USSR courts and of union republic courts within the parameters laid down by the law.

The USSR Supreme Court consists of a chairman, his deputies, members, and people's assessors. Chairmen of union republic supreme courts are ex officio members of the USSR Supreme Court.

The organization and procedure of work of the USSR Supreme Court are determined by the Law on the USSR Supreme Court.

Article 153. The hearings of civil and criminal cases in all courts is collegial; in courts of first instance, cases are heard with the participation of people's assessors. In the administration of justice, people's assessors have all the rights of a judge.

Article 154. Judges and people's assessors are independent and subject only to the law.

Conditions are provided for judges and people's assessors to effectively exercise their rights and duties without hindrance. Any interference in the activity of judges and people's assessors in the administration of justice is impermissible and entails legal liability.

The immunity of judges and people's assessors and other guarantees of their independence are laid down by the Law on the Status of Judges in the USSR and other USSR and union republic legislative acts.

Article 155. Justice is administered in the USSR on the principle of the equality of citizens before the law and the court.

Article 156. Proceedings in all courts shall be open to the public. Hearings *in camera* are only allowed in cases provided for by law, with observance of all the rules of judicial procedure.

Article 157. A defendant in a criminal action is guaranteed the right to defense.

Article 158. Judicial proceedings shall be conducted in the language of the Union Republic, Autonomous Republic, Autonomous Region, or Autonomous Area, or in the language spoken by the majority of the people in the locality. Persons participating in court proceedings who do not know the language in which they are being conducted shall be ensured the right to become fully acquainted with the materials in the case, the services of an interpreter during the proceedings, and the right to address the court in their own language.

Article 159. No one may be adjudged guilty of a crime and subjected to punishment as a criminal except by the sentence of a court and in conformity with the law.

Article 160. Colleges of advocates are available to give legal assistance to citizens and organizations. In cases provided for by legislation, citizens shall be given legal assistance free of charge.

The organization and procedure of the bar are determined by legislation of the USSR and Union Republics.

Article 161. Representatives of public organizations and of work collectives may take part in civil and criminal proceedings.

Article 162. The settlement of economic disputes in the USSR is carried out by the USSR Higher Court of Arbitration and by agencies created in the republics, in accordance with their laws, for the settlement of economic disputes.

Interference by any agencies, organizations or officials in the activity of judges regarding the settlement of disputes is not permitted.

The organization of and procedures for the activity of the USSR Higher Court of Arbitration are determined by a USSR law.

Chapter 21   The Procurator's Office

Article 163. Supervision over the precise and uniform execution of USSR laws by all ministries and other bodies of state administration, enterprises, institutions, organizations, local Soviets of People's Deputies, their executive and administrative agencies, political parties, public organizations and mass movements, officials and citizens is carried out by the USSR Prosecutor-General, the Union-Republic prosecutors and prosecutors subordinate to them.

Article 164. The USSR Prosecutor-General is responsible to the USSR Congress of People's Deputies and the USSR Supreme Soviet and is accountable to them.

Article 165. The republic prosecutors are appointed by the republics' supreme bodies of state power, with the concurrence of the USSR Prosecutor-General, and are subordinate to those bodies. In activity involving supervision over the execution of USSR laws, the republic prosecutors are also subordinate to the USSR Prosecutor-General.

Article 166. The term of office of the USSR Prosecutor-General is five years.

Article 167. The agencies of prosecutor's offices exercise their powers independently of all local agencies.

The organization of and procedures for the activity of prosecutor's offices are determined by USSR and Union-republic legislation.

VIII. THE EMBLEM, FLAG, ANTHEM, AND CAPITAL OF THE USSR

Article 168. The State Emblem of the Union of Soviet Socialist Republics is a hammer and sickle on a globe depicted in the rays of the sun and framed by ears of wheat, with the inscription "Workers of All Countries, Unite!" in the languages of the Union Republics. At the top of the Emblem is a five-pointed star.

Article 169. The State Flag of the Union of Soviet Socialist Republics is a rectangle of red cloth with a hammer and sickle depicted in gold in the upper corner next to the staff and with a five-point red star edged in gold above them. The ratio of the width of the flag to its length is 1 to 2.

Article 170. The USSR national anthem is approved by the USSR Supreme Soviet.

Article 171. The Capital of the Union of Soviet Socialist Republics is the city of Moscow.

IX. THE LEGAL FORCE OF THE CONSTITUTION OF THE USSR AND PROCEDURE FOR AMENDING THE CONSTITUTION

Article 172. The Constitution of the USSR shall have supreme legal force. All laws and other acts of state bodies shall be promulgated on the basis of and in conformity with it.

Article 173. The amendment of the USSR Constitution takes place by a decision of the USSR Congress of People's Deputies adopted by a majority of at least two-thirds of the total number of People's Deputies of the USSR.

Appendix B

Draft Treaty on the Union of Sovereign Republics*

The sovereign states that are parties to the treaty,

expressing the will of their peoples for the renewal of the Union;

recognizing the right of nations and peoples to self-determination;

proceeding from the declarations of state sovereignty proclaimed by the republics;

taking into account the closeness of their historical fates, striving to live in friendship and concord, and ensuring equal cooperation;

wishing to create conditions for the comprehensive development of every individual and the provision of reliable guarantees of his or her rights and liberties;

showing concern for the material well-being and spiritual development of the peoples, the mutual enrichment of national cultures, and the ensuring of general security;

drawing lessons from the past and taking into consideration the changes in the life of the country and throughout the world;

have decided to construct their relations in the USSR on new principles.

I. BASIC PRINCIPLES

First. Each republic that is a party to the treaty is a sovereign state.

The USSR is a sovereign federal democratic state formed as a result of the voluntary association of equal republics and exercising state power within the bounds of the powers it is endowed with by the parties to the treaty.

Second. The republics forming the Union retain the right to the independent resolution of all questions of their development, and they guarantee to all peoples living on their territories political rights and opportunities for social, economic and cultural development. The republics will resolutely oppose racism, chauvinism, nationalism and all attempts to limit the rights of peoples. The parties to the treaty will proceed from a combination of universal human and national values.

Third. The republics recognize the priority of human rights, in accordance with generally recognized norms of international law, as a highly important principle. All citizens are guaranteed the possibility of the study and use of their native language,

*Author's Note: This revised version of the Draft Treaty on the Union of Sovereign Republics was published in *Pravda* on 9 March 1991, pp. 1, 3. This document served as the basis for extensive discussions between nine of the republics and the all-union organs of state authority, namely President Gorbachev and the USSR Supreme Soviet. As of early August 1991, the final text of the Union Treaty had not been made public and, therefore, we were unable to include it in this text.

unhindered access to information, freedom of religion, and other political, social, economic and personal rights and liberties.

Fourth. The republics see the formation and development of a civil society as a highly important condition for freedom and well-being. They will strive to satisfy people's requirements on the basis of a free choice of the forms of ownership and the methods of economic management and implementation of the principles of social justice and safeguards.

Fifth. The republics forming the Union possess full state power and will independently determine their national-state and administrative-territorial structure and system of bodies of power and administration. They recognize democracy based on popular representation and direct expression of the peoples' will as a common fundamental principle, and they are striving to create a state based on the rule of law that will serve as a guarantee against any tendencies toward authoritarianism and highhandedness.

Sixth. The republics consider the preservation and development of national traditions and state support for education, science and culture to be one of their most important tasks. They will promote intensive exchanges and the mutual enrichment of the peoples of the country and the whole world with humanistic spiritual values.

Seventh. The parties to the treaty declare that the main goals of the Union in the international arena are lasting peace, the elimination of nuclear and other weapons of mass destruction, cooperation among states and the solidarity of peoples in solving mankind's global problems.

The republics are full-fledged members of the international community. They have a right to establish direct diplomatic, consular, trade and other ties with foreign states, to exchange authorized representatives with them, to conclude international treaties, and to participate directly in the activity of international organizations that does not infringe on the interests of the parties to this treaty or their common interests and does not violate the USSR's international commitments.

II. THE STRUCTURE OF THE UNION.

Art. 1. Membership in the USSR. The republics' membership in the USSR is voluntary. The republics that are parties to the treaty possess equal rights and have equal duties.

The republics that are parties to the treaty enter the Union directly or as part of other republics, which does not infringe on their rights or relieve them of their duties under the treaty.

Relations between republics one of which is part of another are regulated by treaties and agreements between them.

The USSR is open to entry into it by other sovereign states that recognize the treaty. Decisions on admitting new members to the Union are adopted with the consent of all parties to the treaty.

The republics that are parties to the treaty have the right to freely secede from the Union in accordance with procedures established by the parties to the treaty.

Art. 2. Citizenship. A citizen of a republic that is part of the USSR is at the same time a citizen of the USSR.

Citizens of the USSR have equal rights, freedoms and duties that are codified in the Constitution, laws and international treaties of the USSR.

Art. 3. Territory. The territory of the USSR consists of the territories of all the republics that are parties to the treaty.

The republics that are parts of the USSR recognize the boundaries between them that existed at the time the treaty was signed.

Boundaries between republics may be changed only by agreements between them.

Art. 4. Relations Between Republics. Relations between the republics are regulated by this treaty and by other treaties and agreements that are not at variance with it.

The republics that are parties to the treaty construct their relations within the Union on the basis of equality, respect for sovereignty, territorial integrity, noninterference in internal affairs, the resolution of disputes through peaceful means, cooperation, mutual assistance, and the conscientious fulfillment of commitments under the Union Treaty and interrepublic agreements.

The republics that are parties to the treaty pledge not to use force or the threat of force against one another, not to carry out any forcible actions, and not to infringe on the territorial integrity of other republics.

The republics pledge not to allow the stationing of armed formations of foreign states on their territory or the siting of foreign military bases there, and not to conclude agreements that are at variance with the goals of the Union or that are aimed against the interests of republics that are parts of the Union.

Art. 5. The Demarcation of Powers in the USSR. The parties to the treaty endow the USSR with the following powers:

- protecting the sovereignty and territorial integrity of the Union and of the republics that are parts of the Union;
- ensuring the state security of the USSR; fixing and guarding the USSR State Border; changing the USSR State Border, with the consent of the relevant republic;
- organizing defense and the leadership of the USSR Armed Forces and the USSR border, internal and railroad troops; declaring war and concluding peace;
- managing defense enterprises and organizations involved in the creation and production of arms and military equipment;
- implementing all-Union foreign policy; representing the USSR in relations with foreign states and international organizations; concluding international treaties of the USSR; coordinating the foreign-policy activity of the Union and the republics;
- implementing foreign-economic activity within the bounds of the powers of the USSR;
- confirming and fulfilling the Union budget;
- managing space research, all-Union communications and information systems, geodesy, cartography, metrology and standardization;
- monitoring observance of the USSR Constitution and laws; adopting legislation on questions falling under Union jurisdiction; establishing principles of legislation on questions agreed upon with the republics;
- coordinating activity to safeguard public order and combat crime.

The USSR exercises the following powers in conjunction with the republics:

- adopting the USSR Constitution, and making changes in and additions to it; ensuring the rights and liberties of citizens of the USSR;
- determining the USSR's foreign-policy course and monitoring its implementation through the system of the Union's supreme bodies of state power; protecting the rights and interests of citizens of the USSR and the republics in international relations; establishing the principles of foreign-economic activity; unified

customs operations; exercising the sovereign rights of the Union and the republics to the natural resources of the USSR's economic zone and continental shelf;

- determining the strategy of state security for the USSR and the republics that are parts of it; ensuring the state security of the members of the Union; establishing the conditions governing the USSR State Border and the USSR's waters and airspace;
- determining the military policy of the USSR; carrying out measures to organize and ensure the defense of the USSR; resolving questions associated with the stationing and activity of troops and military procedures for call-up to and the performance of military service; organizing the mobilization of the national economy;
- determining the strategy for the country's social and economic development, and creating conditions for the development of an all-Union market; conducting a uniform financial credit, monetary, tax and price policy based on a common currency; drawing up the Union budget and monitoring its fulfillment; using the USSR's gold reserves and its diamond and foreign-currency stocks; developing and carrying out all-Union programs; creating all-Union funds for regional development and for eliminating the consequences of natural disasters and catastrophes, as well as other funds agreed upon with the republics, and managing these funds; providing assistance to foreign states, and concluding agreements on international loans and credits; regulating the external and internal state debts;
- managing defense enterprises and organizations involved in the creation and production of civilian output;
- managing the country's unified fuel and power system and railroad, air, maritime and trunk-pipeline transportation;
- establishing principles for the use of natural resources and environmental protection, and conducting a coordinated ecological policy;
- establishing the principles of social policy, including questions of employment and migration, working conditions and job safety, social security and insurance, public education, public health, and protection of the family, mother and child; providing a guaranteed minimum subsistence level; promoting cultural development;
- ensuring the preservation of the primeval habitat for numerically small peoples, and providing the necessary conditions for their economic and cultural development;
- organizing and conducting basic scientific research and encouraging scientific and technical progress; determining policy and the basic principles of its implementation in the development of higher schools and in the training and certification of highly skilled research-and-teaching personnel.

The powers defined in this article may be changed only with the consent of all the republics that are parties to the Union Treaty.

Disputes over questions of exercising the USSR's powers or implementing rights and fulfilling duties in the field of the joint powers of the USSR and the republics are resolved through conciliatory procedures. When an accord is not reached, disputes are submitted to the USSR Constitutional Court for consideration.

Art. 6. The Republics' Participation in the Exercise of the Union's Powers. The republics participate in the exercise of the USSR's powers through the joint formation of Union bodies and the creation of other mechanisms and procedures for coordinating interests and actions.

Each republic may, by concluding an agreement with the USSR, additionally delegate to the latter the exercise of certain of the republic's powers, and the Union, with the consent of all the republics, may turn over the exercise of certain of its powers to one or several republics on their territory.

Art. 7. Property. The USSR and the republics ensure the unrestricted development and protection of all forms of property provided for by USSR and republic legislation, and promote the functioning of a single all-Union market.

The republics are the owners of the land, its mineral wealth and other natural resources on their territory, as well as of state property, with the exception of that part which, on the basis of treaties, is assigned to Union ownership for the exercise of the powers entrusted to the Union.

Union property is used and augmented exclusively in the common interests of the republics, including evening out the levels of their social and economic development.

The republics have the right to a share of the USSR's gold, diamond and foreign-currency stocks and participate in their utilization.

The use of land, its mineral wealth and other natural resources for implementing the Union's powers is carried out within the framework of legislation of the republics, which are to create the necessary conditions for the USSR's activity.

Art. 8. Taxes and Fees. The republics independently establish taxes and fees and determine their budgets.

Union taxes and fees are established for the exercise of the USSR's powers, in amounts determined by agreement with the republics; pro rata payments for all-Union programs are also established, with the amounts and destination of these payments regulated by an annual agreement between the Union and the republics, taking into account the indices of their social and economic development.

Art. 9. The USSR Constitution. The Union Treaty is the foundation of the USSR Constitution.

The USSR Constitution is adopted by a Congress of representatives of the states that are parties to the treaty.

The USSR Constitution must not be at variance with the Union Treaty.

Art. 10. Laws. USSR laws and republic Constitutions and laws must not be at variance with the provisions of the Union Treaty.

USSR laws on questions within USSR jurisdiction have supremacy and are binding on the territory of all republics.

On republic territory, republic laws have supremacy on all questions, with the exception of those falling within the Union's jurisdiction.

USSR laws on questions falling within the joint jurisdiction of the USSR and the republics take effect if the republic whose interests are affected by the given laws does not object.

A republic has the right to protest a USSR law if it violates the Union Treaty or is at variance with the republic's Constitution, or with republic laws adopted within the bounds of the republic's powers. The USSR has the right to protest republic laws if they violate the Union Treaty or are at variance with the USSR Constitution, or with USSR laws adopted within the bounds of the USSR's powers. In both cases, disputes are resolved through conciliatory procedures or turned over to the USSR Constitutional Court.

III. UNION BODIES.

Art. 11. The Formation of Union Bodies. Union Bodies of power and administration are formed on the basis of the representation of the republics and operate in strict accordance with the provisions of this treaty.

Art. 12. The USSR Supreme Soviet. The Union's legislative power is exercised by the USSR Supreme Soviet, which consists of two chambers:

The Council of the Republics—the upper chamber of the USSR Supreme Soviet—is formed from an equal number of representatives elected in the republics that have directly entered the Union.

The Council of the Union—the lower chamber of the USSR Supreme Soviet—is elected by the population of the entire country on the basis of election districts having equal numbers of voters.

All national-territorial formations are guaranteed representation in the USSR Supreme Soviet.

An Alternative Reading:

(The Union's legislative power is exercised by the USSR Supreme Soviet, which consists of two chambers:

The USSR Supreme Soviet's Council of the Republics is formed from an equal number of representatives elected in the republics that are parties to this treaty.

The USSR Supreme Soviet's Council of the Union is elected by the population of the entire country on the basis of election districts having equal numbers of voters.

All national-territorial formations are guaranteed representation in the USSR Supreme Soviet.)

Art. 13. The President of the USSR. The President of the USSR is the head of the Union state and wields supreme administrative and executive power.

The President of the USSR acts as the guarantor of observance of the Union Treaty and the Constitution and laws of the USSR; he is Commander in Chief of the USSR Armed Forces; he represents the Union in relations with foreign countries; and he monitors the fulfillment of the USSR's international commitments.

The President is elected by the citizens of the USSR on the basis of universal, equal and direct suffrage and by secret ballot for a term of five years, and may serve no more than two consecutive terms. A candidate who receives more than half of the votes of the voters taking part in the election, in the Union as a whole and in a majority of the republics, is considered elected.

Art. 14. The Vice-President of the USSR. The Vice-President of the USSR is elected together with the President of the USSR. The Vice-President of the USSR, when authorized by the President of the USSR, performs certain of the latter's functions, and he acts for the President of the USSR in the event of the President's absence or inability to perform his duties.

Art. 15. The Council of the Federation. The Council of the Federation is created under the leadership of the President of the USSR and consists of the Vice-President of the USSR and the Presidents (highest state officials) of the republics, for the purposes of considering basic questions of the Union's domestic and foreign policy and coordinating the republics' actions and relations between the Union and the republics.

Art. 16. The USSR Cabinet of Ministers. The USSR Cabinet of Ministers is formed by the President of the USSR, with the agreement of the USSR Supreme Soviet, and consists of the USSR Prime Minister, Deputy Prime Ministers and Ministers, and the heads of other USSR state agencies.

The republic's heads of government may participate in the work of the Cabinet of Ministers with the right to cast a vote.

The USSR Cabinet of Ministers operates in accordance with the Union's powers; it is subordinate to the President of the USSR and accountable to the USSR Supreme Soviet.

Art. 17. The USSR Constitutional Court. The USSR Constitutional Court examines questions of the conformity between USSR and republic legislative acts, decrees of the USSR President and the republic Presidents and normative acts of the Cabinet of

Ministers, on the one hand, and the Union Treaty and the USSR Constitution, on the other, and it also resolves disputes between the Union and republics and between republics regarding the constitutionality of their legislative acts.

Art. 18. Union Courts. The Union courts are the USSR Supreme Court, the USSR Higher Court of Arbitration, and the courts in the USSR Armed Forces.

The USSR Supreme Court and the USSR Higher Court of Arbitration exercise judicial power within the bounds of the Union's powers. The chairmen of the republics' supreme judicial and arbitration bodies are ex officio members of the USSR Supreme Court and the USSR Higher Court of Arbitration, respectively.

Art. 19. The USSR Prosecutor's Office. Supervision over the fulfillment of USSR legislative acts is exercised by the USSR Prosecutor General, the republic Prosecutors General (Prosecutors) and prosecutors subordinate to them.

The USSR Prosecutor General is appointed by the USSR Supreme Soviet and is accountable to it.

The republic Prosecutors General (Prosecutors) are appointed by the republics' supreme legislative bodies and are ex officio members of the collegium of the USSR Prosecutor's Office. In their activity to supervise the fulfillment of Union laws, they are accountable both to the republics' supreme legislative bodies and to the USSR Prosecutor General.

IV. CONCLUDING PROVISIONS.

Art. 20. The Official Language of the USSR. The parties to the treaty recognize Russian as the official language of the USSR.

Art. 21. The Capital of the USSR. The city of Moscow is the capital of the USSR.

Art. 22. The State Symbols of the USSR. The USSR has a state emblem, a state flag and a national anthem.

Art. 23. The Entry Into Effect of the Union Treaty. The Union Treaty is adopted by the republics' supreme bodies of state power and enters into effect as of the moment it is signed by authorized delegations of the republics. The Union Treaty is opened for signing by decision of the USSR Council of the Federation.

For the republics that sign the Union Treaty, the 1922 Treaty on the Formation of the USSR is considered null and void as of the same date.

Relations between the Union and republics that do not sign the Union Treaty are subject to regulation on the basis of existing USSR legislation and mutual commitments and agreements.

Art. 24. Changes in the Union Treaty. The Union Treaty or individual provisions thereof may be rescinded, changed or supplemented, on representations by the republics, only with the consent of all member-states of the USSR.

Art. 25. Appendices to the Treaty. This treaty has appendices in which the procedures, mechanism and timetable for implementing the treaty's articles are set forth.

The list of appendices and the timetable for preparing and signing them are agreed upon by the republics that are parties to the treaty in a protocol, which is a part of the treaty.

Index